HUMAN DEVELOPMENT 94/95

Twenty-Second Edition

Editor

Larry Fenson
San Diego State University

Larry Fenson is a professor of psychology at San Diego State University. He received his Ph.D. in child psychology from the Institute of Child Behavior and Development at the University of Iowa in 1968. Dr. Fenson is a member of the MacArthur Foundation Research Network on Infancy and Early Childhood. His research focuses on early conceptual development, and he has authored articles on infant attention, symbolic play, concept development, and language acquisition.

Editor

Judith Fenson
Children's Hospital, San Diego

Judith Fenson received a B.A. from Ohio University in 1963 and an M.A. from the University of New Mexico in 1965. She is the Language Data Coordinator at the Language Research Center at Children's Hospital. She has contributed to a variety of research projects in medicine, psychology, and linguistics, and has authored a variety of materials and study aids for students in psychology and child development.

Annual Editions
A Library of Information from the Public Press

Cover illustration by Mike Eagle

The Dushkin Publishing Group, Inc.
Sluice Dock, Guilford, Connecticut 06437

The Annual Editions Series

Annual Editions is a series of over 60 volumes designed to provide the reader with convenient, low-cost access to a wide range of current, carefully selected articles from some of the most important magazines, newspapers, and journals published today. Annual Editions are updated on an annual basis through a continuous monitoring of over 300 periodical sources. All Annual Editions have a number of features designed to make them particularly useful, including topic guides, annotated tables of contents, unit overviews, and indexes. For the teacher using Annual Editions in the classroom, an Instructor's Resource Guide with test questions is available for each volume.

VOLUMES AVAILABLE

Africa
Aging
American Foreign Policy
American Government
American History, Pre-Civil War
American History, Post-Civil War
Anthropology
Biology
Business Ethics
Canadian Politics
Child Growth and Development
China
Comparative Politics
Computers in Education
Computers in Business
Computers in Society
Criminal Justice
Drugs, Society, and Behavior
Dying, Death, and Bereavement
Early Childhood Education
Economics
Educating Exceptional Children
Education
Educational Psychology
Environment
Geography
Global Issues
Health
Human Development
Human Resources
Human Sexuality
India and South Asia
International Business
Japan and the Pacific Rim

Latin America
Life Management
Macroeconomics
Management
Marketing
Marriage and Family
Mass Media
Microeconomics
Middle East and the Islamic World
Money and Banking
Multicultural Education
Nutrition
Personal Growth and Behavior
Physical Anthropology
Psychology
Public Administration
Race and Ethnic Relations
Russia, Eurasia, and Central/Eastern
   Europe
Social Problems
Sociology
State and Local Government
Third World
Urban Society
Violence and Terrorism
Western Civilization,
   Pre-Reformation
Western Civilization,
   Post-Reformation
Western Europe
World History, Pre-Modern
World History, Modern
World Politics

Library of Congress Cataloging in Publication Data
Main entry under title: Annual Editions: Human development. 1994/95.
    1. Child study—Periodicals. 2. Socialization—Periodicals. 3. Old age—Periodicals.
I. Fenson, Larry, comp.; Fenson, Judith, comp. II. Title: Human development.
ISBN 1–56134–278–5   155'.05   72–91973
HQ768.A55

© 1994 by The Dushkin Publishing Group, Inc., Guilford, CT 06437

Twenty-Second Edition

Printed in the United States of America

Printed on Recycled Paper

Editors/ Advisory Board

Members of the Advisory Board are instrumental in the final selection of articles for each edition of Annual Editions. Their review of articles for content, level, currentness, and appropriateness provides critical direction to the editor and staff. We think you'll find their careful consideration well reflected in this volume.

EDITORS

Larry Fenson
San Diego State University

Judith Fenson
Children's Hospital, San Diego

ADVISORY BOARD

Judith E. Blakemore
Indiana University-Purdue University

Karen Duffy
State University College Geneseo

Bonnie Duguid-Siegal
University of Western Sydney

Mark Greenberg
University of Washington

Don Hamacheck
Michigan State University

Gregory F. Harper
SUNY College, Fredonia

Alice S. Honig
Syracuse University

Helen Lemay
SUNY, Stony Brook

Lynda G. MacCulloch
Acadia University

David S. McKell
Northern Arizona University

Carroll Mitchell
Cecil Community College

Martin Murphy
University of Akron

Harriett Ritchie
American River College

Gary M. Schumacher
Ohio University

William H. Strader
Fitchburg State College

Harold R. Strang
University of Virginia

Margaret Varma
Rutgers University

James R. Wallace
St. Lawrence University

Karen Zabrucky
Georgia State University

STAFF

Ian A. Nielsen, Publisher
Brenda S. Filley, Production Manager
Roberta Monaco, Editor
Addie Raucci, Administrative Editor
Cheryl Greenleaf, Permissions Editor
Diane Barker, Editorial Assistant
Lisa Holmes-Doebrick, Administrative Coordinator
Charles Vitelli, Designer
Shawn Callahan, Graphics
Steve Shumaker, Graphics
Lara M. Johnson, Graphics
Libra A. Cusack, Typesetting Supervisor
Juliana Arbo, Typesetter

To the Reader

In publishing ANNUAL EDITIONS we recognize the enormous role played by the magazines, newspapers, and journals of the *public press* in providing current, first-rate educational information in a broad spectrum of interest areas. Within the articles, the best scientists, practitioners, researchers, and commentators draw issues into new perspective as accepted theories and viewpoints are called into account by new events, recent discoveries change old facts, and fresh debate breaks out over important controversies.

Many of the articles resulting from this enormous editorial effort are appropriate for students, researchers, and professionals seeking accurate, current material to help bridge the gap between principles and theories and the real world. These articles, however, become more useful for study when those of lasting value are carefully *collected, organized, indexed,* and *reproduced* in a *low-cost format,* which provides easy and permanent access when the material is needed. That is the role played by *Annual Editions.* Under the direction of each volume's *Editor,* who is an expert in the subject area, and with the guidance of an *Advisory Board,* we seek each year to provide in each *ANNUAL EDITION* a current, well-balanced, carefully selected collection of the best of the public press for your study and enjoyment. We think you'll find this volume useful, and we hope you'll take a moment to let us know what you think.

Any history of the field of human development will reflect the contributions of the many individuals who helped craft the topical content of the discipline. For example, Binet launched the intelligence test movement, Freud focused attention on personality development, and Watson and Thorndike paved the way for the emergence of social learning theory. However, the philosophical principles that give definition to the field of human development have their direct ancestral roots in the evolutionary biology of Darwin, Wallace, and Spencer, and in the embryology of Preyer. Each of the two most influential developmental psychologists of the early twentieth century, James Mark Baldwin and G. Stanley Hall, was markedly influenced by questions about phylogeny (species adaptation) and ontogeny (individual adaptation). Baldwin's persuasive arguments challenged the assertion that changes in species precede changes in individual organisms. Instead, Baldwin argued, ontogeny not only precedes phylogeny but is the process that shapes phylogeny. Thus, as Robert Cairns points out, developmental psychology has always been concerned with the study of the forces that guide and direct development. Early theories stressed that development was the unfolding of already formed or predetermined characteristics. Many contemporary students of human development embrace the epigenetic principle that asserts that development is an emergent process of active, dynamic, reciprocal, and systemic change. This system perspective forces one to think about the historical, social, cultural, interpersonal, and intrapersonal forces that shape the developmental process.

The study of human development involves all fields of inquiry comprising the social, natural, and life sciences and professions. The need for depth and breadth of knowledge creates a paradox: While students are being advised to acquire a broad-based education, each discipline is becoming more highly specialized. One way to combat specialization is to integrate the theories and findings from a variety of disciplines with those of the parent discipline. This, in effect, is the approach of *Annual Editions: Human Development 94/95.* This anthology includes articles that discuss the problems, issues, theories, and research findings from many fields of study. In most instances, the articles were written specifically to communicate information about recent scientific findings or controversial issues to the general public. As a result, the articles tend to blend the history of a topic with the latest available information. In many instances, the reader is challenged to consider the personal and social implications of the topic. The articles included in this anthology were selected by the editors with valued advice and recommendations from an advisory board consisting of faculty from community colleges, small liberal arts colleges, and large universities. Evaluations obtained from students, instructors, and advisory board members influenced the decision to retain or replace specific articles. Throughout the year we screen many articles for accuracy, interest value, writing style, and recency of information. Readers can have input into the next edition by completing and returning the article rating form in the back of the book.

Annual Editions: Human Development 94/95 is organized into six major units. Unit 1 focuses on the origins of life, including genetic influences on development, and unit 2 focuses on development during infancy and early childhood. Unit 3 is divided into subsections addressing social, emotional, and cognitive development. Unit 4 addresses issues related to family, school, and cultural influences on development. Units 5 and 6 cover human development from adolescence to old age. In our experience, this organization provides great flexibility for those using the anthology with any standard textbook. The units can be assigned sequentially, or instructors can devise any number of arrangements of individual articles to fit their specific needs. In large lecture classes, this anthology seems to work best as assigned reading to supplement the basic text. In smaller sections, articles can stimulate instructor-student discussions. Regardless of the instructional style used, we hope that our excitement for the study and teaching of human development is evident and catching as you read the articles in this twenty-second edition of *Human Development.*

Larry Fenson

Larry Fenson

Judith Fenson

Judith Fenson
Editors

Contents

Unit 1

Genetic and Prenatal Influences on Development

Eleven selections discuss genetic influences on development, reproductive technology, and the effects of substance abuse on prenatal development.

The concepts in bold italics are developed in the article. For further expansion please refer to the Topic Guide and the Index.

Unit 2

Development During Infancy and Early Childhood

Six selections profile the impressive abilities of infants and young children, examine the ways in which children learn, and look at sex differences.

The concepts in bold italics are developed in the article. For further expansion please refer to the Topic Guide and the Index.

Unit 3

Development During Childhood

Eleven selections examine human development during childhood, paying specific attention to social and emotional development, cognitive and language development, and development problems.

The concepts in bold italics are developed in the article. For further expansion please refer to the Topic Guide and the Index.

Unit 4

Family, School, and Cultural Influences on Development

Fourteen selections discuss the impact of home, school, and culture on childrearing and child development. The topics include parenting styles, family structure, and cultural influences, as well as the role of education in social and cognitive development of the child.

The concepts in bold italics are developed in the article. For further expansion please refer to the Topic Guide and the Index.

The concepts in bold italics are developed in the article. For further expansion please refer to the Topic Guide and the Index.

Unit 5

Development During Adolescence and Early Adulthood

Seven selections explore a wide range of issues and topics concerning adolescence and early adulthood.

Unit 6

Development During Middle and Late Adulthood and Aging

Eight selections review a variety of biological and psychological aspects of aging, questioning the concept of set life stages.

The concepts in bold italics are developed in the article. For further expansion please refer to the Topic Guide and the Index.

Topic Guide

This topic guide suggests how the selections in this book relate to topics of traditional concern to students and professionals involved with the study of human development. It is useful for locating articles that relate to each other for reading and research. The guide is arranged alphabetically according to topic. Articles may, of course, treat topics that do not appear in the topic guide. In turn, entries in the topic guide do not necessarily constitute a comprehensive listing of all the contents of each selection.

TOPIC AREA	TREATED IN:	TOPIC AREA	TREATED IN:
Adolescence/ Adolescent Development	38. Alienation and the Four Worlds of Childhood 44. Much Riskier Passage 46. Teenagers and AIDS 49. Is There Love after Baby?	Drug Abuse	7. What Crack Does to Babies 27. Clipped Wings 44. Much Riskier Passage
Adult Development	50. New Middle Age 52. Myth of the Miserable Working Woman 53. Growing Old 54. Prime of Our Lives	Education/ Educators	38. Alienation and the Four Worlds of Childhood 40. Tracked to Fail 41. Creating Creative Minds 42. Learning from Asian Schools
Aggression/ Violence	19. TV Violence 20. Push for PG-Rated Playthings 35. Children of Violence	Emotional Development	17. Day Care Generation 18. The Good, the Bad, and the Difference 21. Your Loving Touch 31. Can Your Career Hurt Your Kids? 33. Lasting Effects of Child Maltreatment 35. Children of Violence 36. Children after Divorce 38. Alienation and the Four Worlds of Childhood 40. Tracked to Fail 44. Much Riskier Passage 52. Myth of the Miserable Working Woman
Aging	53. Growing Old 55. How Old Is Old?		
Attachment	21. Your Loving Touch 23. Miracle of Resiliency 31. Can Your Career Hurt Your Kids?		
Brain Organization/ Function	16. Sizing Up the Sexes 28. Of a Different Mind	Erikson's Theory	54. Prime of Our Lives
Child Abuse	23. Miracle of Resiliency 33. Lasting Effects of Child Maltreatment	Ethics	39. Culture, Race Too Often Ignored in Child Studies
Cognitive Development	12. New Perspective on Cognitive Development in Infancy 13. Amazing Minds of Infants 23. Miracle of Resiliency 24. Toddler Talk 31. Can Your Career Hurt Your Kids?	Family Development	17. Day Care Generation 21. Your Loving Touch 22. Places Everyone 31. Can Your Career Hurt Your Kids? 36. Children after Divorce 37. Kids Have a Lot to Cry About 38. Alienation and the Four Worlds of Childhood 48. Proceeding with Caution 49. Is There Love After Baby? 52. Myth of the Miserable Working Woman
Competence	12. New Perspective on Cognitive Development in Infancy 13. Amazing Minds of Infants 23. Miracle of Resiliency 35. Children of Violence		
Culture	19. TV Violence 20. Push for PG-Rated Playthings 39. Culture, Race Too Often Ignored 42. Learning from Asian Schools	Fertilization/ Infertility	4. Reproductive Revolution 6. Choosing a Perfect Child 8. Sperm Under Siege
Day Care	31. Can Your Career Hurt Your Kids? 49. Is There Love after Baby?	Genetics	1. Gene Dream 8. Sperm Under Siege 10. Nature or Nurture? 11. Eugenics Revisited
Depression/Despair	35. Children of Violence 36. Children after Divorce 40. Tracked to Fail	High Risk Infants	7. What Crack Does to Babies 9. War Babies 27. Clipped Wings
Developmental Disabilities	7. What Crack Does to Babies 23. Miracle of Resiliency 27. Clipped Wings 28. Of a Different Mind	Infant Development	12. New Perspective on Cognitive Development in Infancy 13. Amazing Minds of Infants 17. Day Care Generation 21. Your Loving Touch
Divorce	36. Children after Divorce	Kohlberg's Theory	18. The Good, the Bad, and the Difference

TOPIC AREA	TREATED IN:	TOPIC AREA	TREATED IN:
Language Development	13. Amazing Minds of Infants 24. Toddler Talk 26. Understanding Bilingual/Bicultural Young Children 28. Of a Different Mind	**Piaget's Theory**	12. New Perspective on Cognitive Development in Infancy
Learning	12. New Perspective on Cognitive Development in Infancy 13. Amazing Minds of Infants 14. Child's Theory of Mind 24. Toddler Talk	**Prenatal Development**	6. Choosing a Perfect Child 7. What Crack Does to Babies 8. Sperm Under Siege 9. War Babies 27. Clipped Wings
Love/Marriage	37. Kids Have a Lot to Cry About 49. Is There Love After Baby?	**Preschoolers**	36. Children after Divorce
Maternal Employment	17. Day Care Generation 31. Can Your Career Hurt Your Kids? 38. Alienation and the Four Worlds of Childhood 52. Myth of the Miserable Working Woman	**Psychoanalytic Theory**	38. Alienation and the Four Worlds of Childhood
		Self-Esteem/ Self-Control	23. Miracle of Resiliency 52. Myth of the Miserable Working Woman
Mid-Life Crisis	50. New Middle Age 54. Prime of Our Lives	**Sex Differences**	16. Sizing Up the Sexes
Parenting	17. Day Care Generation 18. The Good, the Bad, and the Difference 22. Places Everyone 23. Miracle of Resiliency 31. Can Your Career Hurt Your Kids? 37. Kids Have a Lot to Cry About 38. Alienation and the Four Worlds of Childhood	**Social Skills**	19. TV Violence 20. Push for PG-Rated Playthings 33. Lasting Effects of Child Maltreatment 48. Proceeding with Caution 54. Prime of Our Lives
		Stress	35. Children of Violence 36. Children after Divorce 38. Alienation and the Four Worlds of Childhood 40. Tracked to Fail 52. Myth of the Miserable Working Woman
Peers	38. Alienation and the Four Worlds of Childhood	**Teratogens**	7. What Crack Does to Babies 8. Sperm Under Siege 27. Clipped Wings
Personality Development	23. Miracle of Resiliency 54. Prime of Our Lives		

Genetic and Prenatal Influences on Development

Advances in our knowledge of human development are becoming increasingly linked to progress in the fields of genetics, biochemistry, and medicine. Among these frontiers of knowledge are the latest technological possibilities for human reproduction, reviewed in "Reproductive Revolution Is Jolting Old Views." No longer are menopause or infertility impediments to having a baby.

New knowledge has also introduced a host of problems that society will have to confront, including those generated by new ways of detecting anomalies prior to birth (see "Choosing a Perfect Child") and by improved methods for sustaining life in highly premature infants. Thirty years ago, prematurity generally referred to infants born a few weeks to 2 months prior to the expected date. Today, infants born well before the seventh month following conception are frequently brought to term with the assistance of biomedical technology. Unhappily, a substantial proportion of these babies suffer from a range of serious medical problems. Many of these babies are victims of substance abuse. "What Crack Does to Babies" provides an in-depth look at the damage done to the fetus when crack cocaine crosses the placental barrier.

Until recently, the mother's lifestyle has been considered solely responsible for the health of the unborn child. However, as dramatically described in "Sperm Under Seige," new findings suggest that the father's sperm may be affected by such factors as smoking, alcohol, drugs, and radiation, causing spontaneous abortions or birth defects.

Another long-term concern has centered on the effects of maternal malnutrition on the health of the growing fetus. The almost daily accounts of hunger in America have refocused attention on this issue. The article "War Babies" relates an absorbing tale of how researchers used public health records to assess the effects of varying degrees of maternal malnutrition in the besieged Netherlands during World War II.

The question of whether human behavior is more heavily influenced by genetics or by upbringing continues to be one of the central issues in developmental psychology. As documented in "Nature or Nurture? Old Chestnut, New Thoughts," an increasing number of scientists are now ready to assign more importance to heredity, after decades of strong resistance. Part of this new respect for genetics is attributable to the rapid advances now occurring in the science of genetics. "The Gene Dream" describes a colossal new government-backed project that has as its target no less than the mapping of the complete set of instructions for making a human being. This work promises to revolutionize the fields of medicine and biology and perhaps even psychology and sociology. Some scientists foresee the day when individuals can obtain a computer readout of their complete genetic makeup, along with a diagnosis, prognosis, and suggested treatment.

Biologists are succeeding in identifying genetic markers for a rapidly expanding list of disorders, such as muscular dystrophy and cystic fibrosis. Meanwhile, psychologists are assembling evidence that heredity plays an important role in many complex human traits, including intelligence, personality, and even mental disorders. These two strands of research have combined to generate renewed interest in and speculation about the potential of genetic manipulation as a weapon against a variety of social problems, including mental disorders and even criminality. "Eugenics Revisited" reviews the basis for these claims, and presents a balanced view of the probable future role of genetic manipulation.

Looking Ahead: Challenge Questions

Almost every human development textbook lists the steps that pregnant women should take to promote healthy fetal growth. What steps should prospective fathers take? What are some of the factors that account for the dramatic increase in the infertility rate today? What are some of the techniques that offer hope to these couples?

Consider your current beliefs about abortion, genetic engineering, and socialized medicine. How do you think these views would be challenged if you learned that your baby-to-be was expected to be profoundly retarded?

If manipulation of genetic material can prevent the appearance of physical dysfunctions, might not similar procedures be used to engineer intellectual abilities, personality traits, or socially desirable behaviors? What factors would constrain a society that actively and explicitly practiced eugenics?

Of the many child-related issues facing our society today (e.g., prenatal care, vaccination programs, sex education, child abuse), which ones would you give the greatest priority to, and why?

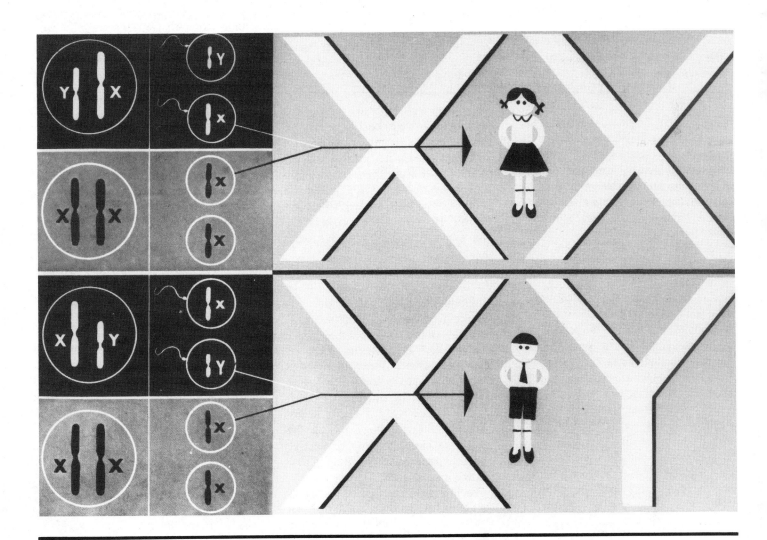

THE GENE DREAM

Scientists are mapping our complete genetic code, a venture that will revolutionize medicine—and ethics.

Natalie Angier

Natalie Angier, *a New York City– based science writer, is the author of* Natural Obsessions: The Search for the Oncogene.

At first glance, the Petersons* of Utah seem like a dream family, the kind you see only on television. They're devout, traditional and very, very loving. Bob Peterson works at a hospital near home to support the family while he finishes up a master's program in electrical engineering. Diane, who studied home economics at Brigham Young University, is a full-time wife and mother. And her time is certainly full: The Petersons have five sons and two daughters, ranging in age from two to 13. (As Mormons, the parents don't practice birth control.)

The children are towheaded, saucer-eyed and subject to infectious fits of laughter. During the summer months, the backyard pool is as cheerily deafening as the local Y. Says Diane, "Our kids really like just spending time together."

Yet for all the intimacy and joy, the Petersons' story is threaded with tragedy. One of the daughters has cerebral palsy, a nerve- and muscle-cell disorder. The malady isn't fatal, but the girl walks with great difficulty, and she's slightly retarded.

*Not their real name.

Three of the other children suffer from cystic fibrosis, a devastating genetic disease in which the lungs become clogged with mucus, the pancreas fails, malnutrition sets in, and breathing becomes ever more labored. Thus far, their children's symptoms have been relatively mild, but Bob and Diane know the awful truth: Although a person with cystic fibrosis may live to be 20 or even 30, the disease is inevitably fatal.

"Right now, the kids don't act sick," says Bob. "They go on thinking, 'I have a normal life.' " But, he admits softly, " We know it won't last forever. If they do get bad, then we won't have a choice. We'll have to put them in a hospital."

The Petersons realize their children's ailments aren't likely to be cured in the immediate future, but they're battling back the best way possible. Bob, Diane, and their seven children, as well as the three surviving grandparents, have all donated blood samples to biologist Ray White and his team at the University of Utah in Salt Lake City. Scientists are combing through the DNA in the blood, checking for the distinctive chemical patterns present only in cystic fibrosis patients.

Their work is part of a vast biomedical venture recently launched by the government to understand all the genes that either cause us harm or keep us healthy. It's medicine's grandest dream: By comprehending the genome—the complete set of genetic information that makes us who we are—in minute detail, scientists hope to answer the most enigmatic puzzles of human nature. The effort is so immense in its scale and goals that some have called it biology's equivalent of the Apollo moonshot, or the atom bomb's Manhattan project.

In fact, it's the most ambitious scientific project ever undertaken; it will cost a whopping $3 billion and take at least 15 years to complete. By the time researchers are through, they will have deciphered the complete genome. They'll have drawn up a detailed genetic "map," with the size, position and role of all 100,000 human genes clearly marked. And they'll have figured out each gene's particular sequence of chemical components, called nucleotides.

Though there are only four types of nucleotides, represented by the letters A, T, C and G, spelling out all the combinations that make up our total genetic heritage will fill the equivalent of one million pages of text. "What we'll have," says Dr. Leroy Hood, a biologist at the California Institute of Technology in Pasadena, "is a fabulous 500-volume 'encyclopedia' of how to construct a human being." Nobel laureate Walter Gilbert goes so far as to describe the human genome as "the Holy Grail of biology."

From *American Health*, March 1989, pp. 103-106, 108. © 1989 by American Health Partners and the author. Reprinted by permission.

HUMAN GENE MAPS

The latest maps for chromosomes one through six show the location of genes associated with hereditary disorders.

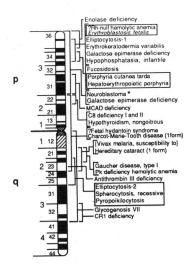

Enolase deficiency
[?Rh-null hemolytic anemia]
Erythroblastosis fetalis
Elliptocytosis-1
Erythrokeratodermia variabilis
Galactose epimerase deficiency
Hypophosphatasia, infantile
Fucosidosis
Porphyria cutanea tarda
Hepatoerythropoietic porphyria
Neuroblastoma *
Galactose epimerase deficiency
MCAD deficiency
C8 deficiency I and II
Hypothyroidism, nongoitrous
?Fetal hydantoin syndrome
Charcot-Marie-Tooth disease (1 form)
[Vivax malaria, susceptibility to]
Hereditary cataract (1 form)
Gaucher disease, type I
Pk deficiency hemolytic anemia
Antithrombin III deficiency
Elliptocytosis-2
Spherocytosis, recessive
Pyropoikilocytosis
Glycogenosis VII
CR1 deficiency

Factor V deficiency

1

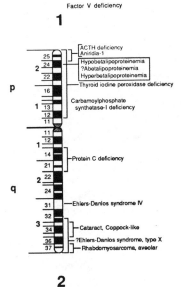

ACTH deficiency
Aniridia-1
Hypobetalipoproteinemia
?Abetalipoproteinemia
Hyperbetalipoproteinemia
Thyroid iodine peroxidase deficiency
Carbamoylphosphate
synthetase-I deficiency

Protein C deficiency

Ehlers-Danlos syndrome IV

Cataract, Coppock-like
?Ehlers-Danlos syndrome, type X
Rhabdomyosarcoma, aveolar

2

☐ Allelic disorders (due to different mutations in the same gene)
[ ] Nondisease
* Cancers
■ Malformation syndrome
{ } Specific infections with a single-gene basis for susceptibility
italics Maternofetal incompatibility

**Adapted from gene maps provided
by Dr. Victor A. McKusick**

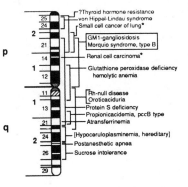

?Thyroid hormone resistance
von Hippel-Lindau syndrome
Small cell cancer of lung*
GM1-gangliosidosis
Morquio syndrome, type B
Renal cell carcinoma*
Glutathione peroxidase deficiency
hemolytic anemia
Rh-null disease
Oroticaciduria
Protein S deficiency
Propionicacidemia, pccB type
Atransferrinemia
[Hypoceruloplasminemia, hereditary]
Postanesthetic apnea
Sucrose intolerance

3

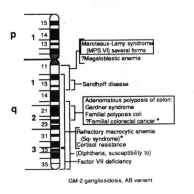

Huntington disease
PKU due to dihydropteridine
reductase deficiency
Juvenile periodontitis
[Dysalbuminemic hyperzincemia]
[Dysalbuminemic hyperthyroxinemia]
Analbuminemia
[Hereditary persistence of alpha-fetoprotein]
Dentinogenesis imperfecta-1
?Acute lymphocytic leukemia
Mucolipidosis II
Mucolipidosis III
C3b inactivator deficiency
Rieger syndrome *
Dysfibrinogenemia, alpha,
beta, gamma types
Sclerotylosis
Anterior segment mesenchymal dysgensis
Hepatocellular carcinoma *
Aspartylglucosaminuria

Pseudohypoaldosteronism

4

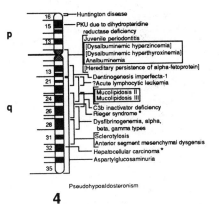

Maroteaux-Lamy syndrome
(MPS VI) several forms
?Megaloblastic anemia
Sandhoff disease
Adenomatous polyposis of colon:
Gardner syndrome
Familial polyposis coli
?Familial colorectal cancer *
Refractory macrocytic anemia
(5q- syndrome)*
Cortisol resistance
[Diphtheria, susceptibility to]
Factor VII deficiency

GM-2 gangliosidosis, AB variant

5

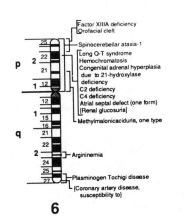

Factor XIIIA deficiency
Orofacial cleft
Spinocerebellar ataxia-1
Long Q-T syndrome
Hemochromatosis
Congenital adrenal hyperplasia
due to 21-hydroxylase
deficiency
C2 deficiency
C4 deficiency
Atrial septal defect (one form)
[Renal glucosuria]
Methylmalonicaciduria, one type
Argininemia
Plasminogen Tochigi disease
[Coronary artery disease,
susceptibility to]

6

Some scientists, however, think their colleagues are chasing a will-o'-the-wisp. Current genetic engineering techniques, say critics, are too embryonic to attempt anything as massive as sequencing the entire genome. Dr. Robert Weinberg of the Whitehead Institute in Cambridge, MA, calls the whole project "misguided" and doubts that scientists will gain major insights even if they can sequence it.

Still, researchers involved in the Human Genome Initiative insist the knowledge will revolutionize the fields of medicine, biology, health, psychology and sociology, and offer a bounty of applications. Using advanced recombinant DNA techniques, scientists will pluck out the genes that cause the 4,000 known hereditary diseases, including childhood brain cancer, familial colon cancer, manic depression, Huntington's disease—the neurological disorder that killed folk singer Woody Guthrie—and neurofibromatosis, or Elephant Man's disease. Beyond analyzing rare inherited disorders, researchers will glean fresh insights into the more common and complicated human plagues, such as heart disease, hypertension, Alzheimer's, schizophrenia, and lung and breast cancer. Those studies will enable scientists to develop new drugs to combat human disease.

But the Genome Initiative is not restricted to the study of sickness. As biologists decode the complete "text" of our genetic legacy, they'll be asking some profound questions: Are there genes for happiness, anger, the capacity to fall in love? Why are some people able to gorge themselves and still stay slim, while others have trouble losing weight no matter how hard they diet? What genetic advantages turn certain individuals into math prodigies, or Olympic athletes? "The information will be fundamental to us *forever*," says Hood, "because that's what we are."

The most imaginative scientists foresee a day when a physician will be able to send a patient's DNA to a lab for scanning to detect any genetic mutations that might jeopardize the patient's health. Nobel laureate Paul Berg, a biochemistry professor at Stanford, paints a scenario in which we'll each have a genome "credit card" with all our genetic liabilities listed on it. We'll go to a doctor and insert the card into a machine. Instantly reading the medical record, the computer will help the doctor to put together a diagnosis, prognosis and treatment course. Says Caltech's Hood, "It's going to be a brave new world."

Coping with that new world will demand some bravery of our own. Once our genetic heritage has been analyzed in painstaking detail, we'll have to make hard choices about who is entitled to that information, and how the knowledge should be used. This technology is proceeding at an incredible rate, and we have to be sure that it doesn't lead to discrimination in jobs, health insurance or even basic rights, says Dr. Jonathan Beckwith, a geneticist at Harvard Medical School. "We don't want a rerun of eugenics, where certain people were assumed to be genetically inferior, or born criminals."

For better or worse, politicians are convinced that the knowledge is worth seeking. This year, Congress has earmarked almost $50 million for genome studies and, if current trends continue, by 1992 the government should be spending about $200 million annually. Opponents worry the price tag could leave other worthy biomedical projects in the lurch.

Even at that level of funding, the genome project could be beyond the resources of any single country. That's why research teams from Europe, Asia, North America and New Zealand have joined to form the Human Genome Organization. Among other goals, the newly created consortium plans to distribute money for worthwhile projects worldwide. Meanwhile, the Paris-based Center for the Study of Human Polymorphism distributes cell samples to researchers and shares their findings through an international data bank.

In this country, Nobel laureate James Watson, the co-discoverer of the molecular structure of DNA, is in charge of human genome research at the National Institutes of Health. And Dr. Charles Cantor, a highly respected geneticist from New York's Columbia University, has accepted the top spot at the Department of Energy's Human Genome Center.

THE GENETIC HAYSTACK

The Genome Initiative is sure to af-
fect everybody. Doctors estimate that each of us carries an average of four to five severe genetic defects in our DNA. The majority of those mutations are silent: They don't affect you. However, if you were to marry someone who carries the same defect, you could have a child who inherits both bad genes and is stricken with the disease.

Most genetic flaws are so rare that your chances of encountering another silent carrier are slim—let alone marrying and conceiving a child with such a person. But some defects are widespread. For example, five out of 100 people harbor the mutant cystic fibrosis gene; seven out of 100 blacks carry the trait for sickle cell anemia. Bob and Diane Peterson are both cystic fibrosis carriers—but they didn't realize their predicament until they gave birth to afflicted children.

For all the improvements of the last 10 years, prenatal diagnosis techniques remain limited. Doctors can screen fetuses for evidence of about 220 genetic disorders, but most of the tests are so time-consuming and expensive they won't be done unless family history suggests the child may have a disease.

One reason it's difficult to screen for birth defects is that most genes are devilishly hard to find. The 50,000 to 100,000 genes packed into every cell of your body are arrayed on 23 pairs of tiny, sausage-shaped chromosomes, which means that each chromosome holds a higgledy-piggledy collection of up to 4,400 genes. Scientists cannot look under a microscope to see the individual genes for cystic fibrosis, Down's syndrome or any other birth defect; instead, they must do elaborate chemical operations to distinguish one human gene from another. So daunting is the task of identifying individual genes that scientists have determined the chromosomal "address" of only about 2% of all human genes. "It's like finding a needle in a haystack," says Utah's Ray White.

Scientists must first chop up the 23 pairs of human chromosomes into identifiable pieces of genetic material and then study each fragment separately. To make the cuts, they use restriction enzymes—chemicals that break the bonds between particular sequences of nucleotides, the chemical components of genes.

Normally, restriction enzymes snip genetic material at predictable points, as precisely as a good seamstress cuts a swatch of fabric. But scientists have found that the enzymes also cut some fragments at unexpected places, yielding snippets that are longer than normal. It turns out that these variations are inherited, and many have been linked to certain genetic abnormalities. The fragments even serve as reference points for map-making efforts. The DNA segments produced by this technique are nicknamed "riff-lips," for restriction fragment length polymorphisms (RFLPs).

In the past three years, DNA sleuths have used the technique to isolate the genes for Duchenne muscular dystrophy, one of the most common genetic diseases; a grizzly childhood eye cancer; and a hereditary white-blood-cell disease commonly called CGD. But the technique remains labor-intensive and in some ways old-fashioned. Armies of graduate students and postdoctoral fellows do the bulk of the work, using tedious, error-prone methods.

Scientists everywhere are racing to build superfast computers to sort through chromosome samples and analyze RFLP patterns. Until they're devised, researchers are learning to make do. At White's lab, for instance, researchers have jerry-rigged a device that automatically dispenses exceedingly small samples of DNA into rows of test tubes. "It can do in two days what used to take a researcher two weeks," says a technician.

THE HAPGOODS BECOME IMMORTAL

Despite all the technology, the genome project remains deeply human—even folksy. That's because the people donating their blood and genes are from ordinary families who happen to have something extraordinary to offer. They're families like the Petersons, whose DNA may contain clues to cystic fibrosis.

Or they're families like the Hapgoods, whose greatest claim to fame may be their ability to live long and multiply. Brenda and Sam Hapgood,* a Mormon couple in their early 50s, are plump and boisterous, and love to be surrounded by people. That may explain why, although they have five

---
* not their real name.

girls, four boys, three sons-in-law, two daughters-in-law and five grandchildren, they wouldn't mind having a few more kids around. Says Brenda, "I almost wish I hadn't stopped at nine!"

The Hapgoods are one of 40 Utah families helping White construct a so-called linkage map of human DNA. He's trying to find chemical markers in the genome that are "linked" with certain genes. The markers will serve as bright signposts, dividing the snarl of genes into identifiable neighborhoods—just as road signs allow a traveler to pin down his location. Finding those markers is a crucial first step toward identifying the genes themselves, and for providing researchers with a decent chart of the terrain.

That's where the Hapgoods come in. To detect those tiny patches in the DNA that stand out from the background of surrounding genetic material, White must be able to compare the genomes of many related people over several generations. Mormon families are large, and they don't tend to move around much, so it's easy for White to get blood samples from many generations of a given family.

"The researchers told us there are lots of big families around," says Brenda. "What made us special was that all the grandparents were still with us."

In 1984, Brenda, Sam, their parents and nine children all donated blood to White's researchers. Lab technicians then used a special process to keep the blood cells alive and dividing forever—ensuring an infinite supply of Hapgood DNA for study. "Our linkage families are becoming more and more important as we go to the next stage of mapping," says Mark Leppert, one of White's colleagues. "Hundreds of researchers from all over will be using the information from their DNA."

"We're going to go down in medical history!" Brenda says excitedly. "But you know what I'm really worried about?" one son-in-law teases her. "They might decide to clone you!"

Another reason the Hapgoods were chosen for the linkage study is because, in contrast to the Petersons, they didn't seem to have any major hereditary diseases. White wanted his general-purpose map to be a chart of normal human DNA. Ironically, however, two years after the Hapgoods first donated blood, one of the daughters gave birth to a son with a serious genetic defect known as Menkes' disease, a copper deficiency.

The child is two years old but looks like a deformed six-month-old. He has 100 or more seizures a day. Half his brain and most of his immune system have been destroyed. Cradled in his mother Carol's arms, he moans steadily and sadly. "This is as big as he'll get," says Carol. "He'll only live to be four at the very most."

Carol and Brenda hope that the genome project will someday bring relief for Menkes victims. "We originally volunteered for the study to help the scientists out, to help their research," says Brenda. "But now we see that it could be important for people like us."

THE BIG PAYOFF

"You don't need to have the whole project done before you start learning something," says Dr. Daniel Nathans, a Nobel laureate and professor of molecular biology and genetics at Johns Hopkins University in Baltimore. "There are things to be learned every step of the way." The first spin-offs are likely to be new tests for hereditary diseases. Within one to three years, biologists hope to have cheap and accurate probes to detect illnesses known to be caused by defects in a single gene, such as susceptibility to certain kinds of cancers.

Another inherited ailment that could quickly yield to genome research is manic depression, which is also thought to be caused by an error in any one of several genes. The psychiatric disorder afflicts 1% of the population—2.5 million people in the U.S. alone—yet it's often difficult to diagnose. With the gene isolated, experts will be better able to distinguish between the disease and other mood disorders, explains Dr. Helen Donis-Keller, a professor of genetics at Washington University in St. Louis.

Of even greater relevance to the public, the Genome Initiative will give investigators their first handle on widespread disorders such as cancer, high blood pressure and heart disease. Researchers are reasonably certain that multiple DNA mutations share much of the blame for these adult plagues, but as yet they don't know which genes are involved. Only when biologists have an itemized map of the genome will they be able to detect complex DNA patterns that signal trouble in many genes simultaneously.

As the quest proceeds, surprises are sure to follow. "There are probably hundreds or thousands of important hormones yet to be isolated," says Dr. David Kingsbury, a molecular biologist at George Washington University. Among them, he believes, are novel proteins that help nerve cells grow, or *stop* growing. Such hormones could be made into new cancer drugs that target tumors while leaving the rest of the body unscathed.

"I have an intuitive feeling that this is going to open up all sorts of things we couldn't have anticipated," says Donis-Keller. "Even mundane things like obesity and baldness—imagine the implications of having new therapies for them!"

The human genome also holds keys to personality and the emotions. Department of Energy gene chief Charles Cantor says it's estimated that half of our 100,000 genes are believed to be active only in brain cells, indicating that much of our DNA evolved to orchestrate the subtle dance of thought, feeling, memory and desire. "There are genes that are very important in determining our personality, how we think, how we act, what we feel," says Cantor. "I'd like to know how these genes work." Donis-Keller is also curious. "Is panic disorder inherited? Is autism?" she wonders. "These are controversial questions we can start to clarify."

Like the first Apollo rocket, the Human Genome Initiative has cleared the launch pad in a noisy flame of promise. Its crew is international, and so too will be the fruits of exploration. When the human genome is sequenced from tip to tail, the DNA of many people is likely to be represented—perhaps that of the Hapgoods and the Petersons, perhaps that of a Venezuelan peasant family. "It's going to be a genetic composite," predicts Yale professor of genetics Frank Ruddle. "The Indians will work on their genomes, the Russians on theirs, the Europeans on theirs. We'll pool the data and have one great patchwork quilt.

"I get a lot of pleasure out of thinking of this as a world project. No one single person will be immortalized by the research. But it will immortalize us all."

A New Genetic Code

The ABCs of DNA are changing radically. And that can bring tragedy.

SHARON BEGLEY

Puttering about the abbey garden 130 years ago, Gregor Mendel wasn't content to leave the birds and the bees to the birds and the bees. The Austrian monk carefully sprinkled pollen from a purple-flowered plant onto a white-flowered plant. He brushed pollen from a plant that grew wrinkled peas onto one that made smooth peas. He crossed whites with whites and purples with purples, smooth with smooth and wrinkled with wrinkled. Besides harvesting enough peas to turn the monks green and the abbey into allergen heaven, Mendel also discovered the rules of biological inheritance. His lessons were simple and, in their modern version, seemingly infallible. Babies inherit 23 chromosomes from each parent. Some genes (for blue eyes, say) are recessive and others (brown eyes) dominant; an offspring shows the recessive trait only if he inherits two copies of that gene and one of the dominant one. So went the rule book.

Well, even Newton had his Einstein, and now genetics revolutionaries are showing that Mendel's laws can be broken. Genes, it turns out, act so perversely they would have shocked the monk into a vow of perpetual silence. Mutant genes grow from one generation to the next like a sci-fi escapee, so that Grandma's tiny and innocuous mutation becomes Grandson's tragic birth defect. Genes costume themselves so that one inherited from Mom has a markedly different effect from the exact same gene inherited from Dad. "It's the sort of stuff that's just not supposed to happen," says geneticist and pediatrician Judith Hall of the University of British Columbia. "But it does."

The violations of Mendel's laws represent a true paradigm shift for genetics. They also have sobering clinical implications. Prenatal testing and genetic counseling both rely on Mendel's rules. Because Mendel wasn't 100 percent right, neither are they. Scientists don't know how often the rules fail "because we pick it up only when it leads to disease," says Hall. But the rules being violated are many:

■ **The Gertrude Stein rule.** A gene is a gene is a gene, says Mendelian genetics. But that was before researchers stumbled over "imprinted" genes a couple of years ago. It seems that some bits of DNA—genes strung along the chromosomes like beads on a string—can be marked, with the molecular equivalent of a pink or blue ribbon, as having come from a particular parent (diagram). For these genes, says Hall, "it makes a difference whether they are inherited from the mother or the father." (New molecular techniques can trace any gene in an individual to one or the other parent.) If the father's chromosome 15 is missing some DNA, for instance, his child will have the rare Prader-Willi syndrome, which is marked by mental retardation and growth abnormalities; if the mother is missing the same bit, the child will have Angelman syndrome, marked by more severe retardation, excess laughing and unusual movement. In other cases a paternal gene leaves the child healthy, but the identical maternal gene produces a birth defect. Psoriasis, diabetes and some forms of mental retardation all manifest themselves differently depending which parent they are inherited from. "It isn't nice and clean like it used to be," says Hall.

Even cancer may have a "parent of origin" effect. In some cases of a neck tumor called paraganglioma, patients inherited a bit of DNA on the chromosome 11 inherited from the father. Inheriting the identical bit from the mother doesn't cause tumors. Say a boy and girl, call them Dick and Jane, inherit the defective gene on chromosome 11 from their father; both develop the neck tumor. Jane passes the same gene she inherited from her father to her own children, but they don't develop the tumor: the gene came from a mother. But when Dick passes the DNA to his daughters, they do develop the tumor—the gene came from Dad. His daughters' children don't get the tumor.

How the sperm or egg gets tagged with these pink or blue bows remains a mystery. For eggs, at least, it happens when the child's mother is in the womb. That's when eggs form. A grandmother's exposure to chemicals, radiation or disease during her pregnancy, which affects her fetus's eggs, can affect her grandchildren's health.

■ **The stability rule.** Genes can mutate. But mutations are not supposed to grow like a loaf of bread with too much yeast. Yet consider Martha (not her real name), who has 50 copies of a particular snippet of DNA on her X chromosome (two X's make a girl a girl). Her daughter, Zoe, has 100 copies but is still healthy. Zoe's child has 1,000 copies—and is mentally retarded. Somehow, when the X was passing down through the generations, the dangerous bit grew like Topsy. In growing, it knocked out healthy genes; the more it grew the more healthy genes it toppled. "The same mutation, depending what gene it knocks out, can cause very different problems," says Dr. Haig Kazazian of Johns Hopkins medical school. "They could include manic depression, schizophrenia, coronary-artery disease and learning disabilities." So much for the conclusion of classical genetics that one mutation causes one specific defect.

■ **Federalism.** A cell supposedly has a strong central government. Its seat is the cell nucleus, and the laws are writ in the chromosomes within. But now geneticists find a rogue government in the hinterlands. The rebels are mitochondria, little bodies inside cells that generate energy to make muscles move, heart tissue contract, lungs expand. Each cell has hundreds of mitochondria. Each mitochondrion contains its own genes, which sometimes mutate. Mito-

 From *Newsweek*, November 2, 1992, pp. 77, 78.

chondria with mutant genes do not generate as much energy as normal mitochondria.

The trouble starts when the mutation hits a cell that is dividing to form, say, eggs. By chance, one egg may get the lion's share of mutant mitochondria. If it goes on to develop into a fetus, the child could grow up to have a disease of the heart, brain, muscle or other energy-guzzling organ. But that baby's sister, if born of an egg that happened to get very few mutant mitochondria, would be perfectly healthy. "Mendel's rules say that a single mutation should cause a single change and thus a single medical effect," says Douglas Wallace of Emory University. "But a mutation in mitochondria can have many different clinical effects, depending on what [percentage] of mutant mitochondria an individual inherits."

The effect also depends on what organs the mutants wind up in. When a fertilized egg divides and multiplies, the mutant mitochondria randomly go into one or another embryonic organ-to-be. If the nascent heart cells get a lot of mutants, for instance, the child will get heart disease. But if, in that child's brother, the mutants happen to go to the brain, the brother would have epilepsy. "Mitochondrial genetics defies everything you've ever learned about genetics," says Wallace. Among the diseases traced to mitochondrial mutations: adult-onset diabetes and blindness.

■ **Sexual equality.** According to the rules, children get their 23 pairs of chromosomes equally from Mom and Dad: one of each pair comes from Mom, the other from Dad. Now it turns out that both chromosomes of a pair

Mendel's Mistakes

The Sexual Equality Rule: Textbooks say each parent gives us one of each member of a pair of chromosomes. Turns out you can get two from mom and none from dad, and thus inherit a recessive disease like cystic fibrosis.

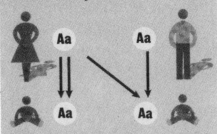

The Gertrude Stein Rule: A gene is a gene is a gene, goes dogma. But for some genes, which parent it came from makes a big difference. Inheriting the gene from father causes a rare disorder; inheriting the identical gene from mother doesn't.

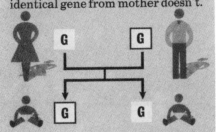

ROHR—NEWSWEEK

can come from the same parent (diagram). Eggs and sperm are supposed to have just half of a human's requisite DNA per cell; when they fuse, the fetus has the right allotment. But sometimes an egg, or a sperm, has all the needed DNA; when it meets its mate, the embryo has too much DNA. Usually such an embryo aborts. But sometimes it survives, by shedding the extra DNA. If it's the DNA from the sperm that gets jettisoned, then the fetus grows with a double dose of maternal DNA.

And that can make genetic counselors look no wiser than palm readers. Say a couple is tested for cystic fibrosis. Joe doesn't have the gene; Carol has one CF gene and one normal gene. Since the normal gene masks the CF gene, she doesn't have CF. (As Mendel found, someone can show a recessive trait only if she has two of the recessive genes.) The counselor tells the couple that their child cannot inherit CF. But say the child inherits both chromosomes from Carol and, by chance, two copies of her disease gene. There is no healthy gene from Joe to defeat the CF gene. The child will have cystic fibrosis. At least five babies who "couldn't" inherit CF have recently been born with it.

Exceptions to Mendel's rules, and the heartbreak they cause, are probably rare. But then it took scientists more than a century after Mendel harvested his bumper crop of genetic laws to see that people are more complicated than peas. So far this genetics revolution has hit the lab more than the doctor's or counselor's office; researchers say practitioners hardly know what to make of it all. They should figure it out quickly.

Clone Hype

Science: *A small step forward in biotechnology sets off a storm of protest. When it comes to human reproduction, nothing is simple.*

It is one of the most sought-after coups of 20th-century journalism, along with the identity of Deep Throat and Senator Packwood's diaries—the first story that can plausibly use "human" and "clone" in the same headline. Fifteen years ago a previously (and subsequently) obscure writer named David Rorvik created a brief sensation with a best-selling book about an anonymous millionaire who had himself cloned, a story that scientists universally denounced as a hoax. Last week, The New York Times, based on an apparent misunderstanding of a paper reporting a technical advance in embryology, touched off an echo of the same hysteria with a page-one story whose headline suggested that human embryos were being cloned in the laboratory. Within days medical ethicists were gravely measuring the slipperiness of the slope on which humanity now teetered, while demonstrators marched outside laboratories insisting that no one would ever clone *their* DNA. This was all to the bemusement of Dr. Jerry Hall and his colleagues at George Washington University, who had set out merely to find a more efficient technique for in vitro fertilization, and weren't sure they had achieved even that much.

Of course, Hall was not unprepared for controversy, because virtually any research in human reproduction is by definition controversial. "I've never seen anything like this gut, visceral fear of cloning," says Art Caplan, director of the Center for Biomedical Ethics at the University of Minnesota. "People are afraid of it because they don't know anything about it." Opposition comes partly from religious conservatives who believe that the creation of human life is too important to entrust to anyone but a husband and wife having sexual relations in the time-honored way. The Vatican newspaper L'Osservatore Romano responded to the news last week by urging the U.S. government to regulate scientists who "venture into a tunnel of madness."

But opposition comes also from some on the left, who over the last few years have transferred the onus of presumptively destroying the human race from nuclear physicists to molecular geneticists. Research into human DNA is viewed not as a potential boon to humanity but a sinister attempt by the government, universities and big business to control individuality at its very source. Cloning—holding out the promise, or threat, of producing unlimited numbers of genetically identical, perfect individuals—provokes an especially fierce reaction. Who would control the rights to perfect babies? Was it only a coincidence that this research came to light just as the Home Shopping Network emerged as the most powerful force in America's economy for the next century? "We are at the point of being able to mass-produce human beings," warned biotech gadfly Jeremy Rifkin, who said he plans to lead weekly anti-cloning demonstrations at laboratories and clinics all over the country. "That is no less important than the first time they split the atom."

What ifs: Against that apocalyptic background, the work by Hall and his colleagues appears somewhat less than atom shattering. "I'm surprised that people have not been able to separate the 'what if' from what we actually did," says Dr. Robert J. Stillman, director of GWU's in vitro fertilization program. What most people understand by "cloning" is what Rorvik's book purported to describe: copying the DNA from an existing organism (or, as in "Jurassic Park," a dead one) and producing new individuals with the identical genetic makeup. Numerous comic books have also described how a mad scientist could seek world domination by cloning a lock of Hitler's hair. Fortunately, no one knows how to do that yet, at least not with mammals. Very early in its development a mammal's cells specialize and thereafter can make only copies of themselves. A lock of Hitler's hair, even if scientists could extract its DNA, would only give rise to the world's most disgusting hairball. But Hall's work had nothing to do with this kind of cloning anyway.

The kind of cloning known to work in mammals starts with embryos at a very early stage of development, before the cells have begun to specialize. The embryo is separated into as many as eight individual cells. The cells' DNA is extracted and transferred to individual eggs; each egg grows into an embryo which can be implanted into the uterus of a surrogate mother, giving rise to eight identical offspring. That technique is actually in use now in cattle; a prized milch cow can have eight times as many offspring as she would by normal gestation. And that is what the Times erroneously reported Hall had done with human embryos. (The newspaper did not respond to numerous requests for comment last week.) But that's not what Hall's work was, either.

What Hall actually did, to stretch a point, was to show the possibility of making test-tube twins. He took a fertilized human egg, let it divide into a two-cell embryo, separated the cells and showed that they would continue to grow into two separate, identical embryos. Conceptually, this was no great breakthrough, since something akin to this presumably happens inside the body when a woman conceives identical twins. Technically, Hall's achievement lay in

 From *Newsweek*, November 8, 1993, pp. 60-62. © 1993 by Newsweek, Inc. All rights reserved. Reprinted by permission.

providing an artificial substitute for the zona pellucida, the membrane that surrounds the embryo. To split the two cells (which was done chemically, not with a knife), he had to dissolve the zona pellucida. His work showed that sodium alginate, a seaweed derivative, would serve as a substitute. It did not show whether these embryos could be successfully implanted into a woman and grow into babies—and that was for a very good reason. Since it would be unethical to experiment on viable embryos, Hall used abnormal ones—eggs accidentally fertilized by more than one sperm, which therefore had three sets of chromosomes rather than the normal two. Such embryos invariably die early in development anyway; all of Hall's died within six days or less.

Better odds: In any case, Hall's purpose was not to rule the world, bring back the dinosaurs or even, for that matter, create twins. His concern was to improve the chances of success with in vitro fertilization, the by-now common technique for fertilizing eggs outside the body, growing them on petri dishes and implanting the resulting embryos in the wombs of women who have had trouble conceiving. Overall, GWU has gotten its success rate up to 40 percent, but the figure is dependent on the number of eggs that can be extracted from the woman and fertilized; when only one egg is available, the chances of a successful pregnancy drop to about one in 10. The GWU technique, by providing multiple embryos from a single egg, could—if it works—substantially improve the odds for some infertile couples.

There are two views of this development. Stillman's naturally, is that the lab is helping couples fulfill "one of the most basic, fundamental Darwinian laws . . . preservation of the species." Rifkin's is that it is "opening the door to Brave New Worlds . . . of human eugenics," in which the random work of natural selection is superseded by a planned program of technologically assisted human breeding. It's a little hard to imagine plausible scenarios in which Hall's work could be put to unintended uses, but perhaps not impossible. Most of these involve creating duplicate embryos, implanting one and freezing the other for some future purpose. What if . . . a couple raised the first child and then decided later that they liked the way he turned out, so they thawed the other and had him, too—creating, in effect, identical twins of different ages? Or the first one develops a fatal illness which can be cured by a transplant from an identical twin—who would have to be sacrificed in the procedure? Or a wife implants the embryo her mother-in-law froze all those years ago, so her husband could have himself for a son? Or the boy grows seven feet tall and signs an NBA contract for $140 million—how much would his twin be worth to some childless couple looking for security for their old age?

Heredity: They'll Be the Same, But Different

Suppose the day comes when scientists can clone humans. The copies will be identical, but will the people be the same? Probably not.

For a century, scientists have been trying to figure out which factors play the most important role in the development of the human personality. Is it nature or nurture, heredity or environment? The best information so far has come from the study of identical twins reared apart. Like the embryo clones of the future, their genes are identical because they come from the same egg and sperm. The fertilized egg splits in half shortly after conception, forming two identical embryos. (Fraternal twins come from two separate eggs and sperms and are no closer genetically than ordinary siblings.)

Uncannily alike: Raised together, twins often are unusually close, sometimes developing their own private language. But even when they are reared apart, twins show amazing similarities as adults. Twins Jim Springer and Jim Lewis, separated at birth in 1939, were reunited 39 years later in a study of twins at the University of Minnesota. Both had married and divorced women named Linda, married second wives named Betty and named their oldest sons James Allan and James Alan. More coincidences: both drove the same model of blue Chevrolet, enjoyed woodworking, vacationed on the same Florida beach and had dogs named Toy.

Perhaps the superficial details of the Springers' parallel lives were just a coincidence, but scientists who study twins like them say they have discovered fundamental personality traits that are the same no matter how the twins were reared. In the Minnesota study, 350 pairs of identical twins reared apart were put through a battery of physical and psychological tests. The results showed that such characteristics as leadership ability, imagination, vulnerability to stress and alienation were largely inherited. On the other hand, the environment the child was raised in seemed to account for a whole host of other traits, including aggression, achievement, orderliness and social closeness.

Heredity may also play a role in determining sexual orientation. In a controversial 1991 study, researchers from Northwestern and Boston universities found that if one identical male twin is gay, the other is almost three times more likely to be gay than if the twins are fraternal. Earlier this year the same scientists released a study of 147 lesbians with similar results.

While these studies do reveal tantalizing clues about how personalities are born and bred, they're far from the whole story. Some identical twins turn out very different from their siblings. One twin in the Minnesota study, for example, grew up to be a stellar pianist even though she was adopted by a nonmusical family. Her sister, adopted by a piano teacher, never sits down at the keyboard. Genes may do the initial programming, but a lifetime of experiences, unique for each person, shape the soul.

'The Science of Scrambling an Egg'

Researchers wanted to see if splitting a human embryo would produce two new, viable embryos. To avoid ethics problems, they chose a defective, three-nuclei egg that could not survive for long.

Nuclei   **Zona**   **Embryo**   **Artificial zona**

An abnormally fertilized egg, containing two sperm and one egg nuclei, is culled from a set of eggs intended for in vitro fertilization.

The egg is allowed to grow into a two-cell embryo inside its own natural shell, called a zona pellucida.

Once the two cells are clearly developed, researchers use an enzyme to dissolve the protective zona.

A chemical solution divides the embryo into two distinct cells; each is capable of further growth.

Each cell is placed in an artificial zona, sheltering cell development.

The cells continue dividing though they die out within a week.

ROHR—NEWSWEEK

Sane forum: Well, we may never know, because at the moment GWU has no plans to take the research any further, and certainly not while Rifkin's troops are parading outside its gates. "We took one small step," Stillman says, "If the 'what if' is important, let's debate it in a sane, rational forum." Unfortunately, the forum in which it is likely to be debated is Congress, which Caplan, the bioethicist, thinks is not going to be much reassurance to people. "If our politicians can't make up a coherent policy for Haiti . . . how are we supposed to design our descendants?" Still, all agree that guidelines are needed, because without them, nothing is likely to get done. As a first step, the rules could stipulate that no one should be allowed to clone Hitler, carnivorous dinosaurs or himself. And then, if everyone is satisfied with the rules, scientists could get on with work that may save some lives or bring wanted life into the world. Rifkin is right in implying that if Madame Curie had been stopped from fooling around with radium, there might never have been atom bombs. On the other hand, there wouldn't be X-rays, either.

JERRY ADLER *with* MARY HAGER *in Washington and* KAREN SPRINGEN *in Chicago*

Reproductive Revolution Is Jolting Old Views

Gina Kolata

Suppose that Leonardo da Vinci were suddenly transported to the United States in 1994, says Dr. Arthur Caplan, an ethicist at the University of Minnesota. What would you show him that might surprise him?

Dr. Caplan has an answer. "I'd show him a reproductive clinic," he said. "I'd tell him, 'We make babies in this dish and give them to other women to give birth,' " And that, Dr. Caplan predicted, "would be more surprising than seeing an airplane or even the space shuttle."

It was only 15 years ago that the world's first baby was born through the use of in vitro fertilization, the method of combining sperm and egg outside the body and implanting the embryo in the uterus. That step ushered in a new era of reproductive technology that has moved so far, so fast that ethicists and many members of the public say they are shaken and often shocked by the changes being wrought.

Although its aims are laudable—helping infertile couples to have children—the new reproductive science is raising piercing challenges to longstanding concepts of parenthood, family and personal identity.

It is now possible for a woman to give birth to her own grandchild—and some women have. It is possible for women to have babies after menopause—and some have. There may soon be a way for a couple to have identical twins born years apart. It may also become feasible for a woman to have an ovary transplanted from an aborted fetus, making the fetus the biological mother of a child.

These events are frightening, Dr. Caplan said. "I never thought that technology would throw the American public into a kind of philosophical angst, but that's what's going on here," he said.

Dr. Mark Siegler, director of the clinical ethics program at the University of Chicago, said that it does not matter so much whether large numbers of people use the new technologies. Their very existence throws long-held values into deep confusion. They introduce, he said, "the idea that making babies can be seen as a technological rather than a biological process and that you can manipulate the most fundamental, ordinary human process—having children."

In the most recent stunning development, a scientist at Edinburgh University said last week that he was working on transplanting the ovaries of a fetus into infertile women, adding that he can do this already in mice. The scientist, Dr. Roger Gosden, said that a 10-week-old human female fetus has six million to eight million eggs. He estimated that it might take a year for a newly transplanted fetal ovary to grow and start producing mature eggs. Several ethicists pointed out that an ovary transplant could lead to a bizarre situation: women who donated their fetus's ovaries might become grandmothers without ever being mothers.

Dr. Gosden said he also expected to be able to help women undergoing chemotherapy, which can destroy the ovaries, by freezing strips of a patient's own ovary and then putting them back after the treatment was over. He has perfected this method in sheep, he said. In principle, both of these ovary transplant methods could also allow women to avoid menopause altogether, remaining potentially fertile until the end of their days.

A few months ago, researchers at George Washington University said they had cloned human embryos, splitting embryos into identical twins or triplets. The method could enable couples to have identical twins born years apart.

But ovary transplants and clones are in the future. Already here are other methods that were unimaginable just a short while ago. For example, doctors routinely freeze extra human embryos that are produced by in vitro fertilization, storing them indefinitely or until the couple asks for them again. Thousands of embryos rest in this frozen limbo in freezers around the nation.

THE MEANING OF 'MOTHER'

Using donated eggs, women can now have babies after menopause. And egg donors are enabling women to give birth to babies to whom they bear no genetic relationship.

Each new development gives rise to new questions of personal identity, experts say. For example, several ethicists said they were repelled by the idea of using eggs from a fetus to enable an infertile woman to become pregnant. They asked, for example, how a child would feel upon discovering its genetic mother was a dead fetus.

The cloning experiment elicited questions of what it says about the uniqueness of individuals if embryos can be split into identical twins or triplets. Just as copying a work of art devalues it, might copying humans devalue them?

Egg donors raise the question of what it means to be a biological mother. Is the mother the woman who donated her egg or is it the woman who carried the baby to term? At least one ethicist and lawyer, George Annas of Boston University, argues that the only logical answer is that both are the mother. This means, he added, that for the first time in history, children can have two mothers.

Pregnancy after menopause threatens the ancient concept of a human life cycle. Until now, there was a time when a woman's reproductive life came to an end. Now, she can be fertile indefinitely. "It makes the life course incoherent," Mr. Annas said.

The growing hordes of frozen embryos call into question the status of these microscopic cell clusters. Do they deserve some consideration as potential humans or is it acceptable to simply discard them if they go unclaimed? Are they potential brothers and sisters of children already born, or are these just spare cells, not much different from blood in blood banks?

"It really is a brave new world," said Jay Katz, a law professor at Yale University.

TROUBLED BY TECHNOLOGY

Yet, said Dr. Susan Sherwin, a professor of philosophy and women's studies at Dalhousie University in Nova Scotia, "the profound question is whether we treat these developments as profound or take them for granted." Although, she said, "our technologically oriented society is fairly good at adapting quickly," the new reproductive technologies give her pause.

For example, Dr. Sherwin said, the possibility of pregnancy after menopause means that there no longer is a point when an infertile couple must give up their quest for a child. If women can have ovarian transplants, will it be even less acceptable for them to grow old without fighting it through medical intervention?

"An enormous industry has grown up in recent years to postpone or prevent menopause through hormone replacement therapy; now reproductive life can also be prolonged," Dr. Sherwin said. She added, "There are questions of what we value in women."

Making babies can now be seen as a technological, not a biological, process.

Mr. Annas said he hopes that people in the next century will look back on these reproductive technologies and find them "as strange as can be." He added: "We have a couple of billion more people on this planet than we need. What are we doing trying to figure out new ways to let couples have more babies? On a societal level, we have to ask, 'What's driving this?' "

But others said they thought the new technologies are heralding a future so astonishing as to be almost unbelievable.

"We're starting to see hints of 21st century reproductive technology," Dr. Caplan said. "We're getting early sightings and we can start to talk about them."

DEATH AND BIRTH

Dr. Siegler predicted that the technologies would change views of the start of life just as profoundly as the developments in the past quarter century changed views of life's end.

A generation ago, Dr. Siegler said, "death was not optional," adding, "When people reached the natural end of their lives thorough a failure of their heart or liver or kidneys or lungs, they died." But then researchers discovered kidney dialysis, machines that could take over kidneys and allow people to live even when their kidneys had failed. And they developed respirators that allowed people to keep breathing when they no longer could draw a breath on their own. Those machines, Dr. Siegler said, "opened a new rang of options about life and death."

"By what process do people decide to use them?" he asked. "Who is in control? When do you start? When do you stop?"

As a consequence of these technologies, Dr. Siegler added, "the first 25 years of medical ethics has been devoted heavily to death and dying and informed consent."

The Human Mind
Touching the intangible

The human brain is the most complex object in the known universe. But out of that complexity emerges a stranger structure still—the human mind

ONLY connect. Forster's injunction is the crux of modern thinking on the mechanisms of the mind. As neurologists have taken the brain apart, they have been astonished at how bitty it is. Outwardly coherent behaviour, like talking and listening, is subcontracted all over the place. Nouns are stored here, adjectives there, syntax elsewhere. Verbs spelled with regular endings are learned using one sort of memory, those spelt with irregular endings are learnt by another; for memory, too, has been atomised into so many pieces that psychologists cannot agree on their number. And the senses, the brain's link with wider reality, do not simply imprint an image of the world upon it; they decompose that image, and shuttle the pieces around like the squares in a Chinese puzzle.

Yet that intangible organ, the conscious mind, seems oblivious to all this. The connections are perfect, the garment apparently seamless. The mental sewing-machine connects nerve cell to nerve cell, senses to memory, memory to language, and consciousness to them all. At every level, the mind is a connection machine.

To understand brains (the traditional task of neurologists), and therefore minds (which psychologists have laboured to do), first remember that they have evolved to do a specific job. Each is there to run a body, keep it out of trouble and see that it passes its genes on to the next generation. Abilities to do things irrelevant to these tasks are likely to get short shrift from natural selection. Computers, with which brains are often compared, can turn their circuits to almost anything—pop in a new program and your computerised accountant is transformed into a chess grandmaster. Brains are not like this. Flexibility, except in a few, limited areas, is not at a premium. Neural "programs" are wired in during development. Circuits which deal with vision cannot be switched over to hear-

ing or taste. And such changes as do occur—for instance, when a new word or face is learnt—take place by modifying the wiring.

The nerve cells, known as neurons, which make up this wiring are rather unusual affairs. Most living cells measure a few millionths of a metre across, but neurons have filamentous projections which often go on for centimetres and occasionally for metres. These projections—called axons if they transmit messages, and dendrites if

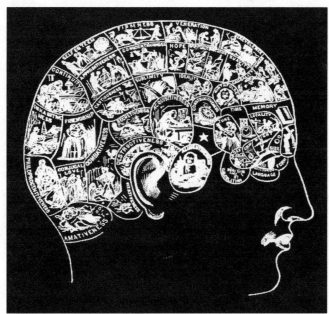

Right idea, wrong compartments

they receive them—enable neurons to talk to each other over long distances, to gather information, to pass it on, and to give and take orders.

The messages themselves are trains of electrical waves called action potentials. Unlike the current in a metal wire, which is caused by things (in this case electrons) moving along the wire, action potentials happen when electrically charged atoms (known as ions) of sodium and potassium move in and out of a filament. An action potential is like a bore in a river: the wave moves on even though the water merely

goes up and down.

Messages pass from neuron to neuron at junctions called synapses, where the tip of an axon touches the surface of a dendrite. Synapses act as the diodes of neurology, allowing the signal to go in only one direction. Action potentials cannot cross them; instead, a synapse passes the signal on via a chemical messenger known as a neurotransmitter. These neurotransmitters can leap the gap to the next cell, where special proteins are ready to greet them. Each sort of receptor protein fits hand-in-glove with a particular neurotransmitter (about 50 of which have been identified so far). If enough receptors are stimulated, one of two things may happen. The cell on the far side of the synapse may become excited and start firing pulses of its own, or it may be inhibited, damping down any pulse-firing that is already going on.

Neurons are thus devices that monitor the exciting and inhibiting signals arriving at their dendrites, weigh up the balance between them, and then decide whether or not to send out pulses of their own. This rather prosaic process is the basis for the activity of the brain. The magic lies in the way the neurons are wired together. But with around 100 billion neurons in a healthy human brain, and 60 trillion synapses, there is plenty of scope for sleight of hand.

Human conjurors have shown that the trick can work. Artificial neural networks, made by wiring lots of microprocessors together and programming them to behave like neurons, can do the same sorts of tricks as real ones. Give them senses, for example, and they can learn to recognise things. And the way they do so is instructive.

A common design for an artificial neural network is to arrange the "neurons" in a three-layered sandwich: an input layer connected to a sense organ such as a television camera; an output layer, which passes the result on to the human operator; and an intermediate, or "hidden" layer, connected to both. The network learns by changing the strengths (or "weights") of the connections between neurons in the three layers. With the correct pattern of weights, simple sensory data (such as handwritten numbers, or faces presented from different angles) can be distinguished and identified.

Real brains, of course, are much more

complicated. The main information-processing part of the brain, the cerebral cortex, has six layers of neurons, rather than three. It is, nevertheless, a layered structure. And the way an artificial network learns by varying the strength of the connections between its silicon neurons is, as will be seen later, reminiscent of the way neurologists think that learning happens in what their computing colleagues disparagingly refer to as "wetware".

Sense and sensibility

Look at the triangle below. Now look closely. There is no triangle. So why did you see it? This may sound a trivial question,

but it isn't. Imposing order on the world is not a two-stage process of first creating an image of outside events, and then interpreting it. The two things happen simultaneously as the sensory information is dismantled and re-assembled in ways which, given the coherence of the result, seem bizarre. Only occasionally, when a sensory illusion or a specific piece of damage to the brain produces some strange result, is it clear that sense and sensibility are inextricably linked.

Vision, the best-understood sense, illustrates the point. For visual information to be processed by the brain, it must first be converted into a form that neurons can deal with—action potentials. This is done by cells in the retina, the place where the image formed by the eye's lens ends up. Some retinal cells have catholic tastes, and respond to many wavelengths. Others are tuned in to specific parts of the spectrum. But each connects to a neuron, and via this to the optic nerves. These nerves carry the signals to the back of the brain, where they are processed.

The connections between the eyes and the primary visual cortex, as the receiving area is called, have been known about for decades. They are orderly. Adjacent parts of the retinal image seemed to end up next to each other. The primary visual cortex appeared, in effect, to be a map of the retina—the mind's eye. Whatever happened next—action, learning or thought—was assumed

to involve the whole image.

It all looked very neat. But it was wrong. The map is not passed around as a whole. It is broken up into different sorts of information—edges, movement, colour—which are then processed in different parts of the visual cortex. This can be seen by watching brains in action. Positron emission tomography (PET) enables researchers to watch people think. It uses a radioactive form of oxygen, mixed into the blood via a catheter in the wrist, to find out which parts of the brain are working hardest from moment to moment. Active areas need more oxygen, and the local blood supply increases to provide it. Positrons emitted by the oxygen annihilate nearby electrons—of which they are the anti-matter equivalent—producing detectable gamma rays.

PET, combined with studies of the electrical signals from single neurons in monkeys and the examination of people with localised brain damage, has revealed the true fate of the image. It does, indeed, pass first to the primary visual cortex (known to neurologists as V1). But this area is just a clearing-house. It contains two sorts of neuron. One sort, organised into columns which penetrate all six layers of the cortex, responds to colour. The other sort, between the columns, responds to form.

Area V1 is surrounded by area V2 (as medieval anatomists preferred Greek and Latin, so modern ones prefer letters and numbers). Here, instead of columns, there are stripes. Thin stripes respond to colour again, thick ones to motion. But the information in V1 and V2 is local: their cells get excited only about signals from their particular patch of the retina. From then on, the information is passed on to areas imaginatively named V3, V4 and V5. V3 and V4 both deal with shape, but V4 also deals with colour, while V3 is colourblind. V5 specialises in detecting motion. It is from these specialised areas, not from the more general-purpose image of V1, that visual information is passed on to the other areas of the brain that need it.

This parcelling-out of tasks explains some of the predicaments of people whose visual cortices have been damaged. Those who have lost V4 can no longer conceive of colour. Those with damage to V5 can see things only when they are stationary—the reverse of the case of Dr P, described in Oliver Sacks's book, "The Man Who Mistook His Wife For A Hat", who could not distinguish stationary objects, and was probably suffering from damage to area V2.

There is also a strange phenomenon called blindsight which, like the loss of the concept of colour in people with damaged V4, touches directly on the issue of consciousness. Lose area V1, and you will believe yourself blind. But you might not be. There are some direct connections from the retina to the other vision-processing areas.

People with V1 damage can often track the movement of objects through space, or tell you the colour of things they truly believe that they cannot see.

And the triangle? The illusion seems to be caused by a conflict between the cells of V1 and those of V2. V1 cells handle only smalls parts of the visual field. Some see bits of the design, some see space. V2 cells, which deal with larger areas, use the bites out of the circles and the ends of the arrows to infer a line, rather as rows of lights on an advertising hoarding are mentally connected into letters. The conflicting interpretations leave the viewer with the uncomfortable feeling of seeing a border where he knows that none exists. Neurology and a psychological test have combined to show specialisation in the brain.

Memory and learning

Another area where psychology and neurology have combined to demonstrate these specialisations is memory. On the face of it, memory seemed, like visual perception, to be a single entity. In fact, it is also highly compartmentalised, with different functions carried out in different parts of the brain.

The first evidence for this specialisation came from neuroanatomy. In the 1950s, surgeons found that, as a last resort, they could control severe epilepsy by destroying parts of the brain. One target for this surgery was the temporal lobe. Some patients suffered a strange form of amnesia after such surgery. They were able to recall things that had happened to them until a few weeks before the operation, and they were also able to remember the very recent past, a matter of a few minutes. But they could not form permanent memories any more—they could no longer learn. All these people had suffered damage to the hippocampus, a structure inside the temporal lobe. Since then, experiments done on monkeys have confirmed that the hippocampus and its neighbours in the limbic system are way-stations to the formation of permanent memories.

The actual information is stored in the cortex; but, for several weeks after it is first learnt, it is passed around via the hippocampus. If it is recalled and used, more direct connections develop in the cortex, and the hippocampus is gradually excluded. If not recalled, it may be forgotten. But if the hippocampal nexus is broken, it is always forgotten. Without a hippocampus, learning is impossible.

Or, rather, some sorts of learning are impossible. For, partly as a consequence of observations on patients with damaged hippocampuses, it has become clear that learning comes in two broad forms: the explicit, or "declarative", sort which remembers objects and events; and the implicit sort, which remembers how to do things.

Implicit learning is part of unconscious

behaviour, and is encapsulated in the phrase "practice makes perfect". It is the sort of incremental improvement which allows people to acquire skills almost incidentally and it does not require an intact hippocampus. One hippocampally damaged patient, for instance, learnt how to read mirror writing, an extraordinary feat for a man who could not remember the faces of his nurses.

Psychologists argue endlessly over how many types of implicit learning there are, and neurology has not yet come to their rescue. But another phenomenon exposed by hippocampal damage has been neatly dissected by psychology.

Patients with such damage are still able to hold the events of the very recent past in their heads, and to synthesise them with knowledge they already have. This enables them to do crosswords, for example. This short-term, or "working", memory is very amenable to psychological testing.

Such tests suggest that working memory has at least three subcomponents. They are known as the "central executive" (which controls attention), the "visuospatial sketchpad" (which manipulates visual information) and the "phonological loop" (which deals with speech). Teasing out these components was done by making people do more than one thing at a time and seeing how well they performed.

Broadly speaking, people can hold about seven pieces of information in their minds at once. But if some of that information is visual, and some linguistic, the total increases. And if an experimenter disrupts a verbal task, a parallel visual one is usually unaffected. The systems which deal with the data are independent of one another.

So how are memories actually stored? PET scanning shows that working memory is located in the pre-frontal cortex. When something is being "kept in mind", that is where it is. Working memories are retained by the continuous activity of particular neurons. These neurons stimulate themselves, either directly or via a loop involving others. When they stop firing, the memory is lost unless it has been passed on to the hippocampus for more permanent storage.

The process by which the hippocampus begins the laying down of permanent memories is different, and intriguingly like the one used to train artificial neural nets—the weights of the connections between nerve cells are altered. This process, called long-term potentiation (LTP), happens when a particular neurotransmitter called glutamate is released by the axon side of a synapse and picked up on the dendrite side by a particular sort of receptor, the N-methyl-D-aspartate (NMDA) receptor. The reaction between glutamate and NMDA stimulates two things. First, the production of proteins called kinases, which enhance the passage of action potentials by opening up passages

that pass ions through the cell membrane. Second, the manufacture in the dendrite of a messenger molecule (believed to be nitric oxide) which flows back to the axon and, in turn, stimulates more glutamate production, thus keeping the whole process going.

However, NMDA is receptive to glutamate only if enough action potentials are already passing along the dendrite it is in. This means that the strengthening of one synaptic connection depends on what is happening to generate action potentials at others. This is the key to neural networks, whether wet or dry, because it enables activity in one part of the net to affect another part indirectly. The pattern of input-signals acts in unison to produce a particular output.

LTP can preserve memories for hours or days. The final stage of the process, permanent storage, seems to involve the formation of new synapses in active areas, and the withering of those which remain unstimulated. Recent research suggests that this happens during sleep. In particular, it seems to happen during the type of sleep known as rapid eye movement (REM) sleep. During REM sleep, people dream, and one of the many explanations suggested for dreams is that they are like the film on a cutting-room floor—the bits left over when experiences that have been waiting in hippocampal limbo are edited into permanent memories. Now there is some evidence to back this up. It has been shown that disrupting REM sleep also disrupts the formation of long-term declarative memories.

Other recent work has shed some light on how memories become tinged with emotion. Fear, at least, seems to be injected by the hippocampus's limbic-system neighbour the amygdala. Drugs which block LTP (and therefore learning) if injected into the hippocampus merely block the learning of

fear if applied to the amygdala. Rats whose amygdalas have been treated in this way behave as if they do not know the meaning of fear. And it seems likely that at least some people who suffer from anxiety attacks have over-active amygdalas.

Speaking in tongues

Despite the claims made for chimpanzees, dolphins, sea-lions and even parrots, it is the use of language which distinguishes man from his fellow creatures. Language—which allows knowledge and ideas to be shared within a community and passed from generation to generation—is the basis of civilisation and of human dominion over the rest of nature. It is also bound up in consciousness; the "inner dialogue" that people often have with themselves is one example of conscious introspection.

Language, unlike memory and sensation, is not even-handed. It generally inhabits the left-hand side of the brain, a fact discovered over a century ago by studying people with localised brain-damage, and dramatically shown up in PET scans. The reason for this geographical imbalance is unclear, but it is associated with another uniquely human phenomenon: "handedness". Right-handed people almost always do their language-processing in their left cerebral hemispheres. Left-handers tend to favour the right hemisphere, although the distinction is not so clear. Indeed, there is evidence associating dyslexia with a failure of the asymmetry, an observation which helps explain why left-handers are more often dyslexic than right-handers.

Within whichever hemisphere commands the process, the component parts of language, like those of sensibility and memory, appear to be parcelled out over the cortex. Broca and Wernicke, two nineteenth-century neurologists who studied failures of

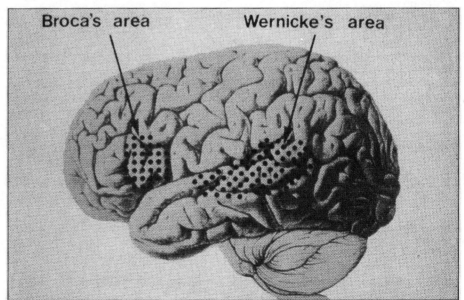

Getting closer

speech and comprehension, mapped areas of the brain where damage seemed to cause specific problems. PET shows up a broadly similar pattern. When words are heard, part of the temporal lobe lights up. Speaking provokes activity in the frontal lobe. There also seems to be a distinction between the handling of nouns (done in the temporal lobe) and verbs (where the frontal lobe seems to predominate).

The meaning of these distinctions is not clear. Some see a specific language function, separately evolved, which deals with all aspects of the phenomenon including the formation of abstract concepts. Others believe that speech developed merely because changes to the muscles of the mouth and throat (which came about when people began to walk upright) allowed it to. According to this view, speaking and listening are merely matters of training. The concepts are already there (which is why other animals can also be trained into language-like abilities); what has to be learnt is a way of attaching words to them, and this is done by the normal mechanisms of memory. Regular verbs, for instance, are learnt implicitly, but declarative memory kicks in for the irregular ones.

In any case, the concepts associated with words are also to be found in widely scattered parts of the brain, and not necessarily on its left-hand side. Colours, for instance, live in region v4 of the visual cortex. And some people with serious damage to the language-control areas can still swear like troopers. Other specific bits of damage can cause problems akin to losing colour-conception—an inability to remember the names of otherwise-familiar people, for instance. Though the connections are not so well understood as those in vision and learning (perhaps because they impinge on more mental functions), they are being thoroughly studied.

The elusive whole

Sensibility, working memory and language are all aspects of mind, but they are not the whole thing. What binds them together? What is the conscious mind? It is certainly not the be-all and end-all of complex behaviour. Anyone who has driven along a motorway and suddenly realised he cannot remember the past few miles will realise this. Nor does partial loss of faculty make a person mindless—although dementias which attack the pre-frontal cortex might.

Whatever the conscious mind is, though, it is no longer regarded by students of the brain as the proper province of philosophers and divines. The problem is under experimental attack.

Hypotheses of how the mind evolved are still vague and contradictory, but they fall into two groups. One interpretation is that consciousness is an epi-phenomenon—a side-effect of increased complexity in the brains of higher primates and particularly of people. Such side-effects, known as emergent properties, are just starting to be explored. Some theories of the origin of life see life itself as an emergent property. They think it suddenly "switched on" when a network of chemical reactions grew so big that each reaction was able to assist the progress of another. On this theory, brains, and particularly cerebral cortices, passed some threshold of size and complexity during their evolution which allowed the system to feed upon itself and generate the phenomenon now labelled consciousness.

Others believe that consciousness has evolved specifically. In their view consciousness is an evolutionary advantage which has dictated the brain's complexity rather than the other way round. One widely held theory is that consciousness is a way of dealing with the diplomatic niceties of group living. It is there mainly to answer the question, "what would I do if I were in the other person's shoes?" Armed with the answer, arrived at by conscious introspection, you can make a better guess at what the other person will actually do next, and modify your behaviour accordingly. Some evidence to support this idea comes from experiments on self-awareness. Among primates, at least, the ability to recognise oneself in a mirror is restricted to man and a few of the great apes. Even monkeys see the reflection as a stranger.

As to the question of mechanism, most neurologists agree that it is the continuity of the process—how the connections produce the stream of consciousness—that most needs to be explained. Occasionally this stream breaks down. Some people who suffer from schizophrenia report seeing the world in freeze-frame, a phenomenon which healthy people can also experience if they are very tired but are forced to concentrate on some task. Among schizophrenics, freeze-framing is associated with problems in the working memory, another piece of evidence that this structure has a key role in maintaining consciousness. But this does not explain how the information is co-ordinated.

One of the most promising lines of inquiry in the co-ordination problem is known as the 40 hertz binding frequency. Particular stimuli will set neurons all over a brain firing together at between 40 and 70 action potentials per second. Different stimuli excite different networks. This network of simultaneous firing serves to illuminate the fragmented information scattered around the brain. Change the input and, like a simple neural network switching from recognising one face to another, you change the output. Change fast enough and the result appears, like a cinema film, to be continuous. In nature, the change seems to come every tenth of a second.

Of course, there is no reason why such integration necessarily implies consciousness; but a refinement of the model looks promising. This is based on a hierarchy of the sort found in the visual system. Each level of the hierarchy is a "convergence zone", gathering information from lower levels and passing it on to a higher one if the processing task cannot be completed at that level. The system can oscillate because some axons from each level reach back into the lower ones, feeding information back to them. If the task is so difficult that it is necessary to recruit the central executive of the working memory, then it enters the stream of consciousness. Your executive normally has better things to do than drive your car, but if someone cuts you up, it connects.

Choosing a Perfect Child

Brave new technology is allowing us to look at tiny preembryonic 8-cell clusters and decide which ones are healthy enough to be allowed to develop into babies.

Ricki Lewis

Ricki Lewis is the author of Life, *a college biology text, and has just written a human genetics text. She is a genetic counselor and an adjunct assistant professor at SUNY Albany and Miami University, where she has taught human genetics and bioethics courses. She has published hundreds of articles for both laymen and scientists.*

Chloe O'Brien, who celebrates her first birthday this month, is a very wanted child, perhaps more so than most. When she was a mere ball of cells, smaller than the smallest speck of sand, a test determined that she would be free of the cystic fibrosis genes that each of her parents carries. Chloe-to-be, along with another ball of cells (a potential twin), was implanted into her mother's uterus. Only one of the two balls of cells, Chloe-to-be, survived the rigors of prenatal development, and Chloe today is a healthy little girl.

The O'Briens had already had a child who suffered from the stiflingly thick mucus clogging the lungs that is a hallmark of cystic fibrosis, the most common genetic disease among Caucasians. They wanted to spare their future children this fate—but they also wanted to avoid having to end a pregnancy that would yield an affected child.

"Previously, couples had to wait from 9 to 15 weeks [after

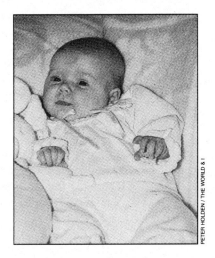

PETER HOLDEN / THE WORLD & I

conception] to find out if their developing baby was affected by a known genetic disease. Now, we can diagnose these inherited diseases within three days after an egg is fertilized in the laboratory, before it is transferred back to the woman," says Mark Hughes of the Baylor College of Medicine in Houston. Hughes, along with John Lesko, also of Baylor, and Alan Handyside, Robert Winston, and Juan Tarin, of Hammersmith Hospital in London, reported the preimplantation diagnosis of cystic fibrosis in September 1992 in the *New England Journal of Medicine*.

The preimplantation genetic diagnosis that confirmed Chloe to be free of the cystic fibrosis gene is built primarily on three existing technologies: in vitro fertil-

ization (IVF); gene amplification, a way to rapidly copy a single gene from a single cell; and gene probing, which detects the gene responsible for the disorder. The latter two interventions are performed on the 8-cell "preembryo."

Few couples have so far had their preembryos examined for genetic problems, and the high costs of the procedure will likely keep the numbers down. However, with the rapid progress being made by the Human Genome Project in identifying genes associated with specific genetic disorders, preembryos in the future may be scrutinized for a wider range of diseases, from rare inherited ailments to the more common heart disease and cancer.

Is a brave new world of mechanized reproduction upon us? To understand how we may someday pick and choose the traits of our children, we must understand the procedures that serve as a backdrop to preimplantation genetic diagnosis.

Prenatal diagnosis—the state of the art

A generation ago, pregnancy was shrouded in secrecy. A woman would discover her expectant state in the second or third month and announce it in the fourth month, when most risk of miscarriage was past. Today, pregnancy is marked by a series of medical tests providing prenatal peeks into the health of the child-to-be.

The most familiar prenatal test is amniocentesis, a procedure in which a needle is inserted into the amniotic sac cushioning a fetus and a small amount of fluid is withdrawn. The fluid contains a few fetal cells, whose nuclei contain the rod-shaped chromosomes, which consist of the genes. If examination reveals missing or extra chromosomes, the fetus is likely to develop into a baby with a serious syndrome.

Today, amniocentesis is a rite of passage for pregnant women over age 35, because at that age the chance of the fetus having a chromosomal problem about equals the risk of amniocentesis causing miscarriage (1 in 200). (The risk of abnormal fetal chromosomes increases with maternal age.)

The major limitation of amniocentesis is that it is performed in the 16th week of pregnancy. By then the fetus is quite well developed. If a chromosome abnormality is detected, the parents are faced with an agonizing choice: either terminate the pregnancy or prepare for the birth of a physically or mentally challenged child.

An alternative to amniocentesis is chorionic villus sampling (CVS), which also examines fetal chromosomes. This procedure can be performed earlier, usually between weeks 8 and 10. The fetus is far smaller and less well developed, about the size and weight of a paper clip, making the decision to end the pregnancy somewhat easier.

CVS was pioneered in China in the 1970s and became available in the United States only in the mid-1980s. Though the World Health Organization endorsed CVS in 1984, it also suggested

The biological basis of preimplantation genetic diagnosis is that all the cells of an individual have the same genes.

that ways be found to diagnose genetic disease earlier, perhaps before the preembryo implants in the uterus. This occurs on the 6th day after sperm meets egg.

The biological basis of preimplantation genetic diagnosis is that all the cells of an individual have the same genes no matter what the stage of development. In principle, the techniques used to examine the genetic material of cells obtained through amniocentesis or CVS should work for cells obtained at other stages of prenatal development, even at the preembryonic stage.

Screening genes

An individual gene in a preembryo's cell can be identified through a technique invented in 1985, the polymerase chain reaction (PCR).

In PCR an enzyme, DNA polymerase, that is essential to the multiplication of DNA in every cell in the body, selectively multiplies only the DNA from the gene of interest. If that gene is present in the original genetic sample being tested it will be rapidly mass-produced in a test tube. If the gene of interest is not present, then it won't be multiplied by the PCR.

If PCR of a single cell from the 8-cell preembryo results in many copies of the target DNA sequence, then the disease-causing gene is there—as happened to a few of Chloe's potential siblings who were not implanted. If the DNA is not amplified, then the sequence of interest is not there. When the cell from 8-cell Chloe-to-be failed its PCR test, it meant that the 7-cell preembryo could develop into a cystic fibrosis-free baby.

The first experiments using PCR to identify preembryos free of a genetic disease took place in 1989 and 1990 in Hammersmith Hospital. Handyside and his team screened preembryos from couples in which the mothers carried a variety of conditions, called X-linked conditions, that occur mostly in males. X-linked conditions are caused by genes on the X chromosome. Since females have two X chromosomes, and males have one X and one Y chromosome, a male preembryo with a Y chromosome and an X chromosome bearing a disease-causing gene would be destined to have the X-linked condition. By using PCR to amplify a DNA sequence unique to the Y chromosome, Handyside's team could choose a female preembryo that could not inherit the disease carried by the mother. The disorders avoided thanks to early attempts at preimplantation genetic diagnosis include adrenoleukodystrophy, a nervous system degeneration that is lethal in early childhood; Lesch-Nyhan syndrome, in which the profoundly retarded child mutilates himself; and other forms of mental retardation.

In August 1992 Jamie Grifo and colleagues at New York Hospital–Cornell Medical Center reported the first child born in the United States after successful blastomere biopsy and genetic testing to avoid X-linked hemophilia.

Candidates for preimplantation genetic diagnosis

Preimplantation genetic diagnosis is a promising option for couples who know that their children are at a high risk for inheriting a certain disease.

According to the laws of inheritance, parents who both carry the same disorder not on the X chromosome, but on one of the other 22 chromosomes, can conceive children who inherit either two normal genes, or two abnormal genes, or, like the parents, one normal and one abnormal gene. The probability of inheriting two of the same gene, either normal or abnormal, is 1 in 4. The probability of being a carrier like the parents with one normal and one abnormal gene is 1 in 2.

Chloe's parents, for example, each have one disease-causing copy of the cystic fibrosis gene, and one normal copy. Thus there

is a 1 in 4 chance that a child conceived by them will suffer with cystic fibrosis.

The mechanics of preimplantation diagnosis

A human preembryo can be obtained in two ways—it can be flushed out of the uterus after being conceived in the normal manner, in which case it is more than 8 cells, or it can be nurtured from an egg fertilized by a sperm in a laboratory dish, the technique of in vitro fertilization (IVF). The first IVF or "test tube baby," Louise Joy Brown, was born in England in 1978, and has since been followed by thousands of other such children.

IVF is now a fairly routine, if difficult and costly, procedure, with hundreds of facilities providing it in the United States alone, and hundreds of others elsewhere. For the IVF procedure, the woman is given pergonal, a drug that causes the ovary to ripen more than one egg at a

time. Eggs, which appear as small bulges in the ovarian lining, are harvested by inserting a laparoscope, a tiny, illuminated telescopelike device, through an incision made near the woman's navel.

The eggs are placed with sperm donated by the man into a laboratory dish, along with other chemicals that simulate the environment in the woman's body. If all goes well, sperm and egg meet and merge. Extra fertilized eggs are frozen and saved in case they are needed later.

On the third day after fertilization comes the blastomere biopsy. The 8-cell, or 8-blastomere, preembryo is immobilized with a holding pipette (a narrow glass tube). Then a single blastomere is removed from the preembryo by exposing the target cell to a stream of acid and gently prodding it with a second, smaller pipette.

The next step is to thoroughly clean the blastomere, because PCR, the gene amplification part

■ In blastomere biopsy, as shown left to right in the sequence below, the 8-cell preembryo is held by one pipette while another narrower one is used to capture a single blastomere, which is used for genetic testing; the remaining seven cells can continue to develop normally. (Magnification 330x)

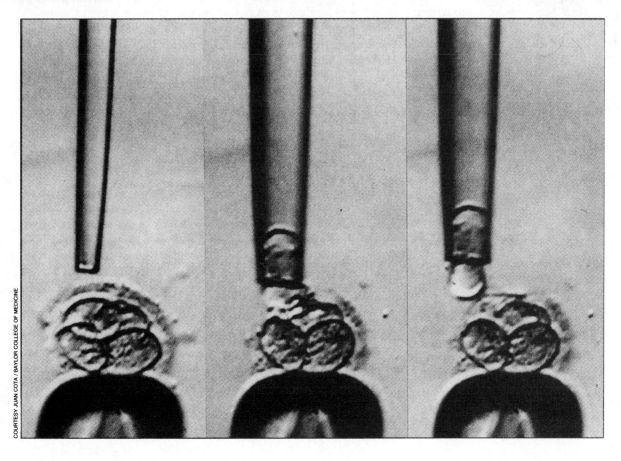

COURTESY JUAN COTA / BAYLOR COLLEGE OF MEDICINE

Genetic Disease Diagnosis Before Fertilization

The time when we can probe a prenatal human's genes is creeping ever earlier, from the 16-week peek permitted with amniocentesis, to the 8–10-week scrutiny of chorionic villus sampling, to preimplantation genetic diagnosis of an 8-celled, 2–3-day-old preembryo. Yet another technique on the horizon, called polar body removal, may reveal the genetic makeup of an egg before it is fertilized.

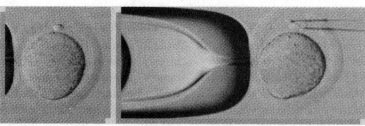

REPRINTED FROM *PREIMPLANTATION DIAGNOSIS OF GENETIC DISEASES*, EDITED BY Y. VERLINSKY AND A.M. KULIEV, COPYRIGHT © 1992, BY PERMISSION OF WILEY-LISS, A DIVISION OF JOHN WILEY AND SONS, INC.

■ *Left:* **Diagnosing a genetic disease before fertilization relies on the fact that each egg shares the mother's divided genetic material with a much smaller companion, called the polar body.** *Right:* **In polar body biopsy, as shown here, the egg is held by the large pipette while the polar body is captured by drawing it into the smaller pipette. (Magnification 188x)**

In the first step of a two-step cell division that produces an egg with 23 chromosomes, division of the 46-chromosome progenitor germ cell distributes 23 chromosomes to each of the two daughter cells. But one cell, destined to develop into the egg, receives the lion's share of nutrients and other cell components, while the other, called the first polar body, is deprived and scrawny by comparison. The egg and its first polar body are stuck together in the ovary.

If the woman is a carrier for a genetic disease, when the chromosomes are divvied up between the polar body and the egg, one normal gene goes to one, and the disease-causing gene to the other. So, if the polar body is examined and found to have the disease-causing gene, then it can be inferred that the corresponding egg does not. That egg can then be fertilized in the lab.

Polar body removal has been tested for more than three years at the Reproductive Genetics Institute of the Illinois Masonic Center in Chicago, yielding one pregnancy that spontaneously aborted due to incidental chromosomal abnormality. So far a dozen couples have undergone the procedure, for such conditions as cystic fibrosis, hemophilia A, and Duchenne muscular dystrophy, but none has delivered a child.

Researchers are not sure why PBR's track record has so far been so poor. Perhaps the intervention is harming the egg, or perhaps it is just allowing us to see previously unknown ways that development can go awry.

—*R.L.*

of the process, can give a false genetic diagnosis if even one stray sperm happens to be clinging to the blastomere. When the blastomere is clean, it is broken open by a series of temperature changes to expose and disentangle the DNA. The PCR evaluation is then used to determine if the disease-causing gene is present.

After the blastomere biopsy and PCR, one or two preembryos that have passed the genetic test are implanted into the woman. If pregnancy occurs, human chorionic gonadotropin (hCG), the "pregnancy hormone," appears in the woman's blood and urine by the 14th day. By the fourth week, an ultrasound exam will show a small, oval area in the uterus. This is the sac containing the embryo.

What we can do versus what we should do

At this time, the two biggest drawbacks to preimplantation genetic diagnosis are the low efficiency and high cost of IVF. In 1990, the American Fertility Society surveyed IVF clinics and found a 14 percent "take-home baby rate." However, Yury Verlinsky, director of the Reproductive Genetics Institute of the Illinois Masonic Medical Center in Chicago, and Anver Kuliev, director of the research/cell bank at the same facility, point out that the typical couple seeking IVF has fertility problems and tends to be older, whereas couples seeking IVF as a prelude to preimplantation genetic diagnosis would be younger and more fertile.

The cost is out of reach for many. "The average cost of IVF is $7,000-8,000," says James Douglas of the Trinity Medical Center in Carrollton, Texas. Blastomere biopsy plus PCR can add another $2,000—all for a procedure that may have to be repeated.

"Blastomere biopsy is being performed only at a few IVF centers that are associated with a major medical teaching facility."

Although physicians who perform IVF are excited about the value of preimplantation diagnosis for couples whose offspring are at high risk for genetic disease, they are nevertheless pessimistic about the technology's general utility. This is because once the procedure grows beyond its research stage, it will be prohibitively expensive. And even though there are expectations that automating some of the steps could bring the price down, these developments are on the far horizon.

Also, as Margaret Wallace, assistant professor in the genetics division at the University of Florida in Gainesville, points out, there is the problem of the "slippery slope"—who decides that a disorder is awful enough to intervene to prevent a birth? In 1990, she discovered the gene behind neurofibromatosis (NF1), another common inherited illness. NF1 presents a sticky problem—finding the responsible gene does not indicate how severely an individual may be affected. Manifestations of NF1 can range from a few brown spots on the body to thousands of tumors just beneath the skin.

So far, the diseases detected by preimplantation genetic diagnosis cause extreme suffering to very young children, and the goal is prevention. "But for preimplantation diagnosis of some less devastating disorders, some physicians and insurers might not think it is ethical" to choose against implanting a diagnosed preembryo, says Wallace.

Another factor that may stifle development of preimplantation genetic diagnosis is that treatments for some genetic disorders are being developed so rapidly that selecting out affected preembryos may become obsolete before the technology can be perfected. "Cystic fibrosis research is moving so quickly that some may say, who cares who is born with it? We can treat them," says Wallace.

For now, preimplantation genetic diagnosis remains highly experimental. "Blastomere biopsy is being performed only at a few IVF centers that are associated with a major medical teaching facility," says Douglas.

However, Verlinsky and Kuliev predict that, once the success stories accumulate and the price drops, preimplantation genetic diagnosis will be offered at a few fetal medicine centers, where teams of embryo experts, molecular biologists, geneticists, and obstetricians will perform genetic tests that will grow ever more numerous as the trek through the human genome nears completion.

Although clearly not yet suitable for the general public, preimplantation genetic diagnosis will allow certain couples to avoid what was once their genetic fate—passing on a disease. And so Chloe O'Brien is today what Louise Joy Brown was to the world 15 years ago—a medical pioneer, after whom many will follow.

WHAT CRACK DOES TO BABIES

JANICE HUTCHINSON

Janice Hutchinson is a pediatrician and former senior scientist for the American Medical Association. She is now the medical director of the Child and Youth Services Administration of the District of Columbia Department of Mental Health.

INQUIRING TEACHERS want to know: Who are these kids and how did they get this way? The question refers to the unprecedented numbers of children—estimates range as high as one-half to one million—who are entering the classroom having suffered inutero exposure to cocaine.

Crack, the cooked form of cocaine, became widely available in 1985; the children of the first crack addicts are now in school. Teachers have described them as a new breed, unlike other children with histories of drug exposure. They are often in constant motion, disorganized, and very sensitive to stimuli. Crawling, standing, and walking take longer to develop. They are irritable and hard to please. It is hard for them to make friends. They respond less to the environment. Internal stability is poor. Learning is more difficult. Smiling and eye contact are infrequent. They do not seem to know how to play with toys or with others. And nothing you do for them seems to matter or help.

If teachers are to meet the challenges that these children bring, they may find it helpful to understand the bio-neuro-physiological effects of cocaine on the developing fetus. Scientists are just beginning to understand these effects; research in the area is incomplete and at times conflicting. Thus what we know and what we can speculate about, some of which is summarized below, is just the tip of a rather unknown iceberg. There are surely many more effects—and more complicated avenues of effect—than those so far identified. Nonetheless, there are findings—mainly from research sponsored by the National Institutes of Health and the National Institute on Drug Abuse—that allow us to begin to make some sense of what is happening to the behaviors and learning styles of these children.

IMAGINE THAT a crack molecule has entered the body. It enters into the mucous membranes of the mouth. From there it enters the lungs, where it is absorbed into the bloodstream, and through which it then passes to the heart and, very quickly, to the brain. The immediate effect is an increase in breathing, blood pressure, and heart rate.

Upon arriving in the brain, crack acts at several sites along what is known as the brain's "pleasure pathway"—a collection of sites in the brain that seem in some ways to relate and affect each other. At one point on the pleasure pathway is the limbic system, which is the seat of strong emotional responses, including the very primitive urges to feed, flee, fight, and reproduce. At another point along the pathway is the motor cortex of the brain, which directs the body's movement. Between the limbic system and the motor cortex lies the nucleus accumbens. This is the "attraction center" of the brain; it is what pulls you toward pleasurable activity.

Indications are that crack acts on the fetus precisely the same way it acts on the mother.

The crack is very active here in the nucleus accumbens; a ripple effect then seems to carry the destruction around to other points along the pleasure pathway. With-

Reprinted with permission from *American Educator,* Spring 1991, pp. 31-32. *American Educator,* the quarterly journal of the American Federation of Teachers.

in the nucleus accumbens, as elsewhere in the brain, are numerous nerve cells; the space between each nerve cell ending is known as the synaptic space. Each of these nerve cells communicates with the others across the synaptic space by sending a variety of neurotransmitters back and forth.

One such neurotransmitter is dopamine. Under normal biological conditions, dopamine, like other neurotransmitters, is continually moving across the synaptic space. In a constantly recurring pattern, the dopamine leaves its home cell, crosses the synaptic space, and reaches receptors on the receiving cell, an action that sends an electrical signal through the receiver cell. The dopamine then disattaches from the receptor cell and returns to its cell of origin where it will be recycled.

But if crack has been ingested, this normal cycle will be disrupted. Crack, upon entering the brain and then the pleasure pathway, seems to settle into the synaptic space between the neurotransmitters. It then acts to prevent the dopamine from returning to its home cell. Unable to return home, the dopamine continues to stimulate the receiver cell until the crack has spent itself and dissipated. It is probably this constant stimulation of the receiver cell that causes the euphoric feeling associated with the first few minutes of cocaine ingestion. But the crack high lasts only a few minutes, after which the user will either replenish his intake or experience an often devastating "low." The constant resupply soon leads to a physical addiction, the breaking of which is accompanied by extremely painful withdrawal symptoms.

WHILE THE crack is acting on the mother's brain, what is happening to the fetus? The crack crosses the placental barrier and heads for the inutero brain. The exact effect of the crack on the fetus will depend on the age of the fetus, the dosage of the crack, and probably on other variables that we have not yet identified. But it seems likely that in general a number of things happen. First, the crack probably acts on the fetal nucleus accumbens in the same way that it acts on the user's, leading the fetus to become highly stimulated and, often, addicted. As it stimulates the nucleus accumbens, and surely in other ways as well, the crack damages fetal brain cells and thus causes neurological damage all along the pleasure pathway and in other nearby parts of the brain.

Damage to brain cells in the limbic system, the nucleus accumbens, and elsewhere along the pleasure pathway would likely impair or alter a wide range of the child's normal emotional responses, including, for example, the ability to respond to pleasurable experiences, to form emotional attachments, or to make certain kinds of judgments. Perhaps this explains in part why the crack baby is often unable to proceed through the normal phases of separation-individuation described by child psychiatrist Margaret Mahler; crack babies appear to experience much greater anxiety and difficulty in leaving their mothers when it is time for school.

In addition, the brain's motor cortex may be damaged, which might explain such effects as the slow development of crawling, standing, and walking. The brain location for speech is also nearby, and damage to it may

account for the speech impairments suffered by many crack babies. In turn, the speech impairment inhibits the child's ability to communicate, which may, in turn, account for some of the difficulty these children have in forming relationships.

Children who have been exposed to crack in their prenatal stage require an emotionally supportive and structured atmosphere.

In addition, crack, like nicotine, constricts the adult and fetal arteries, thus slowing the blood—and therefore the oxygen flow—to the fetus and around it. This condition of low oxygenation—known as hypoxia—can also produce brain damage, and it can bring on low birthweight. Low birthweight is, in turn, associated with a wide range of disabling symptoms, including intellectual disabilities.

Reading, mathematics, spelling, handwriting, and the arts are often difficult tasks for low-birthweight babies. Speech and language problems are prominent. Temperamental problems, such as low adaptability, low persistence, and arrhythmicity (for example, the failure to sleep and wake at normal, regular times) may be part of their behavioral style. They typically cry when separated from the mother, have trouble expressing themselves, speak only in short phrases, are very active, and clumsy. Findings to date suggest that temperament influences both behavior and cognition.

These low birthweight children tend to perform poorly on the Mullen Scale of Early Learning. This test, which consists of four scales, suggests the range of learning abilities that seem to be impaired in the children exposed inutero to crack. The Visual Receptive Organization (VRO) scale assesses visual discrimination, short-term memory, visual organization and sequencing, and visual spatial awareness, including position, size, shape, left/right, and detail. The Visual Expressive Organization (VEO) assesses bilateral and unilateral manipulation, writing, visual discrimination, and visual-motor plan and control. The language receptive organization (LRO) scale assesses auditory comprehension, short- and long-term auditory memory, integration of ideas and visual spatial cues, auditory sequencing, and verbal spatial concepts. The language expressive organization (LEO) scale assesses spontaneous and formal verbal ability, language formulation, auditory comprehension, and short- and long-term memory.

What all of this means ultimately is that these low-birthweight crack children experience the world around them in a very different way from other children. Adults, including teachers, are often unaware that these children see and hear their environment in a completely different manner from adults or even other children. What the teacher often does not realize is that this difficult-to-teach, hard-to manage child is processing information in an unusual way that the child does not determine. Hence, conflict and frustration can arise between teacher and student (and also at home between parent and child).

The combined effects of prenatal drug exposure with a home environment that provides little or no nurturance, understanding, or support for the child create a terrible challenge to teachers. But initial experimental programs suggest that these children can benefit greatly from placement in highly structured, highly tailored educational day care settings beginning in early infancy. In four Washington, D.C.-area therapeutic nurseries that provide such care, two-thirds of the children seem so far to have been successfully mainstreamed into first grade.

Among the characteristics that seem to make such programs successful are early identification of the infants and very low student-teacher ratios. The establishment of an emotionally supportive atmosphere and structure is necessary. Teaching must be intense and focal. Tasks should initially be simple and singular. Too many tasks or activities overstimulate these children, and they cannot respond. Teachers must also provide emotional support and form bonds with the children. Success also depends on aggressively approaching and engaging parents in the psychotherapeutic progress. Consultation with mental health professionals may assist teachers, parents, and students. Intellectually limited students may still require individual tutoring; some students will eventually require special education; and very emotionally disturbed students may require a mental health-based psychotherapy program.

But it does seem clear that with early, appropriate interventions many of these children can improve their behavior and academic performance. Like most childhood problems, the time to act is now; later is too late.

SPERM UNDER SIEGE

MORE THAN WE EVER GUESSED, HAVING A HEALTHY BABY MAY DEPEND ON DAD

Anne Merewood

IT DIDN'T MAKE SENSE. Kate Malone's* first pregnancy had gone so smoothly. Yet when she and her husband Paul* tried to have a second child, their efforts were plagued by disaster. For two years, Kate couldn't become pregnant. Then she suffered an ectopic pregnancy, in which the embryo began to grow in one of her fallopian tubes and had to be surgically removed. Her next pregnancy heralded more heartache—it ended in miscarriage at four months and tests revealed that the fetus was genetically abnormal. Within months, she became pregnant and miscarried yet again. By this point, some four years after their troubles began, the couple had adopted a son; baffled and demoralized by the string of apparent bad luck, they gave up trying to have another child. "We had been to the top doctors in the country and no one could find a reason for the infertility or the miscarriages," says Kate.

Soon, however, thanks to a newspaper article she read, Kate uncovered what she now considers the likely cause of the couple's reproductive woes. When it all started, Paul had just been hired by a manufacturing company that used a chemical called paradichlorobenzene, which derives from benzene, a known carcinogen. The article discussed the potential effects of exposure to chemicals, including benzene, on a man's sperm. Kate remembered hearing that two other men in Paul's small office were also suffering from inexplicable infertility. Both of their wives had gone through three miscarriages as well. Kate had always considered their similar misfortunes to be a tragic coincidence. Now she became convinced that the chemical (which has not yet been studied for its effects on reproduction) had blighted the three men's sperm.

Paul had found a new job in a chemical-free workplace, so the couple decided to try once more to have a baby. Kate conceived immediately—and last August gave birth to a healthy boy. The Malones are now arranging for the National Institute for Occupational Safety and Health (NIOSH), the

*These names have been changed.

federal agency that assesses work-related health hazards for the public, to inspect Paul's former job site. "Our aim isn't to sue the company, but to help people who are still there," says Kate.

The Malones' suspicions about sperm damage echo the concerns of an increasing number of researchers. These scientists are challenging the double standard that leads women to overhaul their lives before a pregnancy—avoiding stress, cigarettes and champagne—while men are left confident that their lifestyle has little bearing on their fertility or their future child's health. Growing evidence suggests that sperm is both more fragile and potentially more dangerous than previously thought. "There seems to have been both a scientific resistance, and a resistance based on cultural preconceptions, to accepting these new ideas," says Gladys Friedler, Ph.D, an associate professor of psychiatry and pharmacology at Boston University School of Medicine.

But as more and more research is completed, sperm may finally be stripped of its macho image. For example, in one startling review of data on nearly 15,000 newborns, scientists at the University of North Carolina in Chapel Hill concluded that a father's drinking and smoking habits, and even his age, can increase his child's risk of birth defects—ranging from cleft palates to *hydrocephalus,* an abnormal accumulation of spinal fluid in the brain. Other new and equally worrisome studies have linked higher-than-normal rates of stillbirth, premature delivery and low birthweight (which predisposes a baby to medical and developmental problems) to fathers who faced on-the-job exposure to certain chemicals. In fact, one study found that a baby was more likely to be harmed if the father rather than the mother worked in an unsafe environment in the months before conception.

The surprising news of sperm's delicate nature may shift the balance of responsibility for a newborn's wellbeing. The research may also have social and economic implications far beyond the concerns of couples planning a family. In recent years a growing number of companies have sought

From *Health*, April 1991, pp. 53-57, 76-77. © 1991 by Anne Merewood. Reprinted by permission.

to ban women of childbearing age from jobs that entail exposure to hazardous substances. The idea is to protect the women's future children from defects—and the companies themselves from lawsuits. Already, the "fetal protection policy" of one Milwaukee-based company has prompted female employees to file a sex discrimination suit that is now before the U.S. Supreme Court. Conversely, if the new research on sperm is borne out, men whose future plans include fatherhood may go to court to *insist* on protection from hazards. Faced with potential lawsuits from so many individuals, companies may be forced to ensure that workplaces are safe for *all* employees.

SPERM UND DRANG

At the center of all this controversy are the microscopic products of the male reproductive system. Sperm (officially, spermatozoa) are manufactured by *spermatagonia,* special cells in the testes that are constantly stimulated by the male hormone testosterone. Once formed, a sperm continues to mature as it travels for some 80 days through the *epididymis* (a microscopic network of tubes behind the testicle) to the "waiting area" around the prostate gland, where it is expelled in the next ejaculation.

A normal sperm contains 23 chromosomes—the threadlike strands that house DNA, the molecular foundation of genetic material. While a woman is born with all the eggs she will ever produce, a man creates millions of sperm every day from puberty onwards. This awesome productivity is also what makes sperm so fragile. If a single sperm's DNA is damaged, the result may be a mutation that distorts the genetic information it carries. "Because of the constant turnover of sperm, mutations caused by the environment can arise more frequently in men than in women," says David A. Savitz, Ph.D., an associate professor of epidemiology and chief researcher of the North Carolina review.

If a damaged sperm fertilizes the egg, the consequences can be devastating. "Such sperm can lead to spontaneous abortions, malformations, and functional or behavioral abnormalities," says Marvin Legator, Ph.D., director of environmental toxicology at the department of preventative medicine at the University of Texas in Galveston. And in some cases, sperm may be too badly harmed even to penetrate an egg, leading to mysterious infertility.

Though the findings on sperm's vulnerability are certainly dramatic, researchers emphasize that they are also preliminary. "We have only a very vague notion of how exposure might affect fetal development, and the whole area of research is at a very early stage of investigation," says Savitz. Indeed, questions still far outnumber answers. For starters, there is no hard evidence that a chemical damages an infant by adversely affecting the father's sperm. A man who comes in contact with dangerous substances might harm the baby by exposing his partner indirectly—for example, through contaminated clothing. Another theory holds that the harmful

pollutants may be carried in the seminal fluid that buoys sperm. But more researchers are becoming convinced that chemicals can inflict their silent damage directly on the sperm itself.

THE CHEMICAL CONNECTION

The most well-known—and most controversial—evidence that chemicals can harm sperm comes from research on U.S. veterans of the Vietnam war who were exposed to the herbicide Agent Orange (dioxin), used by the U.S. military to destroy foliage that hid enemy forces. A number of veterans believe the chemical is responsible for birth defects in their children. The latest study on the issue, published last year by the Harvard School of Public Health, found that Vietnam vets had almost twice the risk of other men of fathering infants with one or more major malformations. But a number of previous studies found conflicting results, and because so little is known about how paternal exposure could translate into birth defects, the veterans have been unsuccessful in their lawsuits against the government.

Scientific uncertainty also dogs investigations into other potentially hazardous chemicals and contaminants. "There seem to be windows of vulnerability for sperm: Certain chemicals may be harmful only at a certain period during sperm production," explains Donald Mattison, M.D., dean of the School of Public Health at the University of Pittsburgh. There isn't enough specific data to make definitive lists of "danger chemicals." Still, a quick scan of the research shows that particular substances often crop up as likely troublemakers. Chief among them: lead, benzene, paint solvents, vinyl chloride, carbon disulphide, the pesticide DBCP, anesthetic gases and radiation. Not surprisingly, occupations that involve contact with these substances also figure heavily in studies of sperm damage. For example, men employed in the paper, wood, chemical, drug and paint industries may have a greater chance of siring stillborn children. And increased leukemia rates have been detected among children whose fathers are medical workers, aircraft or auto mechanics, or who are exposed regularly to paint or radiation. In fact, a study of workers at Britain's Sellafield nuclear power plant in West Cambria found a sixfold leukemia risk among children whose fathers were exposed to the plant's highest radiation levels (about 9 percent of all employees).

Workers in "high-risk" industries should not panic, says Savitz. "The credibility of the studies is limited because we have no firm evidence that certain exposures cause certain birth defects." Yet it makes sense to be watchful for warning signs. For example, if pollution levels are high enough to cause skin irritations, thyroid trouble, or breathing problems, the reproductive system might also be at risk. Another danger signal is a clustered outbreak of male infertility or of a particular disease: It was local concern about high levels of childhood leukemia, for instance, that sparked the investigation at the Sellafield nuclear plant.

The rise in industrial "fetal protection policies" is

adding even more controversy to the issue of occupational hazards to sperm. In 1984, employees brought a class-action suit against Milwaukee-based Johnson Controls, the nation's largest manufacturer of car batteries, after the company restricted women "capable of bearing children" from holding jobs in factory areas where lead exceeded a specific level. The suit—which the Supreme Court is scheduled to rule on this spring—focuses on the obstacles the policy creates for women's career advancement. Johnson Controls defends its regulation by pointing to "overwhelming" evidence that a mother's exposure to lead can harm the fetus.

In effect, the company's rule may be a case of reverse discrimination against men. Males continue to work in areas banned to women despite growing evidence that lead may not be safe for sperm either. In several studies over the past 10 years, paternal exposure to lead (and radiation) has been connected to Wilms' tumor, a type of kidney cancer in children. In another recent study, University of Maryland toxicologist Ellen Silbergeld, Ph.D., exposed male rats to lead amounts equivalent to levels below the current occupational safety standards for humans. The rats were then mated with females who had not been exposed at all. Result: The offspring showed clear defects in brain development.

Johnson Controls claims that evidence linking fetal problems to a father's contact with lead is insufficient. But further research into chemicals' effects on sperm may eventually force companies to reduce pollution levels, since *both* sexes can hardly be banned from the factory floor. Says Mattison: "The workplace should be safe for everyone who wants to work there, men and women alike!"

FATHER TIME
Whatever his occupation, a man's age may play an unexpected role in his reproductive health. When researchers at the University of Calgary and the Alberta Children's Hospital in Canada examined sperm samples taken from 30 healthy men aged 20 to 52, they found that the older men had a higher percentage of sperm with structurally abnormal chromosomes. Specifically, only 2 to 3 percent of the sperm from men between ages 20 and 34 were genetically abnormal, while the figure jumped to 7 percent in men 35 to 44 and to almost 14 percent in those 45 and over. "The findings are logical," says Renée Martin, Ph.D., the professor of pediatrics who led the study. "The cells that create sperm are constantly dividing from puberty onwards, and every time they divide they are subject to error."

Such mistakes are more likely to result in miscarriages than in unhealthy babies. "When part of a chromosome is missing or broken, the embryo is more likely to abort as a miscarriage [than to carry to term]," Martin says. Yet her findings may help explain why Savitz's North Carolina study noted a doubled rate of birth defects like cleft palate and hydrocephalus in children whose fathers were over 35 at the time of conception, no matter what the mothers' age.

Currently, there are no tests available to pre-identify sperm likely to cause genetic defects. "Unfortunately there's nothing offered, because [the research] is all so new," says Martin. But tests such as amniocentesis, alpha fetoprotein (AFP) and chorionic villi sampling (CVS) can ferret out some fetal genetic defects that are linked to Mom *or* Dad. Amniocentesis, for example, is routinely recommended for all pregnant women over 35 because with age a woman increases her risk of producing a Down's syndrome baby, characterized by mental retardation and physical abnormalities.

With respect to Down's syndrome, Martin's study provided some good news for older men: It confirmed previous findings that a man's risk of fathering a child afflicted with the syndrome actually drops with age. Some popular textbooks still warn that men over 55 have a high chance of fathering Down's syndrome babies. "That information is outdated," Martin insists. "We now know that for certain."

THE SINS OF THE FATHERS?
For all the hidden dangers facing a man's reproductive system, the most common hazards may be the ones most under his control.

Smoking. Tobacco addicts take note: Smoke gets in your sperm. Cigarettes can reduce fertility by lowering sperm count—the number of individual sperm released in a single ejaculation. "More than half a pack a day can cause sperm density to drop by 20 percent," says Machelle Seibel, M.D., director of the Faulkner Centre for Reproductive Medicine in Boston. One Danish study found that for each pack of cigarettes a father tended to smoke daily (assuming the mother didn't smoke at all), his infant's birthweight fell 4.2 ounces below average. Savitz has found that male smokers double their chances of fathering infants with abnormalities like hydrocephalus, *Bell's palsy* (paralysis of the facial nerve), and mouth cysts. In Savitz's most recent study, children whose fathers smoked around the time of conception were 20 percent more likely to develop brain cancer, lymphoma and leukemia than were children whose fathers did not smoke (the results still held regardless of whether the mother had a tobacco habit).

This is scary news—and not particularly helpful: Savitz's studies didn't record how frequently the fathers lit up, and no research at all suggests why the links appeared. Researchers can't even say for sure that defective sperm was to blame. The babies may instead have been victims of passive smoking—affected by Dad's tobacco while in the womb or shortly after birth.

Drinking. Mothers-to-be are routinely cautioned against sipping any alcohol while pregnant. Now studies suggest that the father's drinking habits just before conception may also pose a danger. So far, research hasn't discovered why alcohol has an adverse effect on sperm, but it does suggest that further investigation is needed. For starters, one study of laboratory rats linked heavy alcohol use with infertility because the liquor lowered testosterone levels. Another study, from the University of Washington in Seattle, discovered that newborn babies whose fathers drank at least two glasses of wine or two bottles of beer per day weighed an average of 3 ounces less than babies whose fathers were only occasional sippers—even when all other factors were considered.

Illicit Drugs. Many experts believe that a man's frequent use of substances such as marijuana and cocaine may also result in an unhealthy fetus, but studies that could document such findings have yet to be conducted. However, preliminary research has linked marijuana to infertility. And recent tests at the Yale Infertility Clinic found that long-term cocaine use led to both very low sperm counts and a greater number of sperm with motion problems.

WHAT A DAD CAN DO

The best news about sperm troubles is that many of the risk factors can be easily prevented. Because the body overhauls sperm supplies every 90 days, it only takes a season to get a fresh start on creating a healthy baby. Most experts advise that men wait for three months after quitting smoking, cutting out drug use or abstaining from alcohol before trying to sire a child.

Men who fear they are exposed to work chemicals that may compromise the health of future children can contact NIOSH. (Write to the Division of Standards Development and Technology Transfer, Technical Information Branch, 4676 Columbia Parkway, Mailstop C-19, Cincinnati, OH 45226. Or call [800] 356-4674.) NIOSH keeps files on hazardous chemicals and their effects, and can arrange for a local inspection of the workplace. Because it is primarily a research institution, NIOSH is most useful for investigating chemicals that haven't been studied previously for sperm effects (which is why

the Malones approached NIOSH with their concerns about paradichlorobenzene). For better-known pollutants, it's best to ask the federal Occupational Safety and Health Administration (OSHA) to inspect the job site (OSHA has regional offices in most U.S. cities).

There is also advice for men who are concerned over exposure to radiation during medical treatment. Direct radiation to the area around the testes can spur infertility by halting sperm production for more than three years. According to a recent study, it can also triple the number of abnormal sperm the testes produce. Men who know they will be exposed to testicular radiation for medical reasons should consider "banking" sperm before the treatment, for later use in artificial insemination. Most hospitals use lead shields during radiation therapy, but for routine X-rays, even dental X-rays, protection might not be offered automatically. If it's not offered, patients should be sure to request it. "The risks are really, really low, but to be absolutely safe, patients—male or female—should *always* ask for a lead apron to protect their reproductive organs," stresses Martin.

Though the study of sperm health is still in its infancy, it is already clear that a man's reproductive system needs to be treated with respect and caution. Women do not carry the full responsibility for bearing a healthy infant. "The focus should be on both parents—not on 'blaming' either the mother or the father, but on accepting that each plays a role," says Friedler.

Mattison agrees: "Until recently, when a woman had a miscarriage, she would be told it was because she had a 'blighted ovum' [egg]. We never heard anything about a 'blighted sperm.' This new data suggests that both may be responsible. That is not unreasonable," he concludes, "given that it takes both an egg and a sperm to create a baby!"

WAR BABIES

What happens when mothers-to-be become the victims of starvation? Now three generations after World War II, we are still learning the disturbing answers.

Jared Diamond

Contributing editor Jared Diamond is a professor of physiology at the UCLA School of Medicine. In June he wrote about the search for eternal youth [for Discover*].*

*I*t is easy to write now that each person got 400 calories a day. In practice it was quite another thing. . . . People sought food everywhere in the streets and the surrounding countryside. Anything edible was picked up in this way, and they were lucky who found a potato or two or a handful of greens. . . . People dropped from exhaustion in the streets and many died there. Often people were so fatigued that they were unable to return home, before curfew; so they hid in barns or elsewhere to sleep and there died. . . . Older people, who lacked the strength to go searching for food, stayed at home in bed and died.
—Famine and Human Development: The Dutch Hunger Winter of 1944–1945

Among the homey images I recall from my wife's pregnancy are the bigger-than-usual milk cartons in the refrigerator and her vitamin bottles on the kitchen counter. To our generation the value of good nutrition for pregnant women seems obvious. But what makes us so sure? After all, we can't run experiments on people to prove it. Starving hundreds of pregnant women and then comparing their kids with well-nourished cousins would be absolutely unthinkable.

Yet such an inhuman experiment was indeed once conducted. By imposing a famine on part of the population of the Netherlands during the last seven months of World War II, the Nazis effectively reduced 40,000 pregnant women to starvation. These cruel circumstances resulted in a study of the effects of prenatal nutrition that was grimly well-designed, complete with a control group: while these women were starving, other mothers-to-be in the same society were eating comparatively healthy rations.

Years later, when the babies who survived had grown into adults, epidemiologists could distinguish the different effects of prenatal and postnatal nutrition; they could even discern the effects of malnutrition at different stages of pregnancy, for at the time the famine took hold, some women were further along in their pregnancy than others. Even now we are still learning what toll was exacted by the events of 45 years ago. Only recently have researchers learned that the famine's effects reached far beyond its immediate victims: now that girls born to the starved Dutch women have grown up and had children of their own, it's become apparent that some of these children too are marked by the deprivations suffered years earlier by their grandmothers!

Today we accept without question that proper nutrition is important for maintaining our health as adults and even more important for the development of our children. The evidence seems most persuasive when we look at the malnourished Third World and see shorter life spans, lowered resistance to disease, and high infant mortalities. But even in the industrialized world we can readily see the positive effects of a good diet. For one thing, today's adults tend to be taller than their parents; the difference approaches six inches in Japan. On average, too, people who are poor, with comparatively limited access to food, are shorter and less healthy than their wealthier countrymen. Moreover, it is not just physical health that seems to be at risk. Many tests of mental function suggest that poor nutrition in childhood may affect learning ability throughout life.

One might speculate that if we are so susceptible to the effects of poor nutrition as children, we must be especially sensitive to those effects while we're still in the womb, when our brain and body are forming. And, indeed, many studies have shown an association between poor nutrition, low weight at birth, and poor physical and mental performance later on. Yet it's not easy to prove that inadequate prenatal nutrition itself is the culprit. Sadly, babies poorly nourished in the womb are likely to be poorly nourished after birth as well. Furthermore, diet may not be the only thing influencing their health. Access to medical care, schooling, and stimulation outside school may play a part.

1. GENETIC AND PRENATAL INFLUENCES

Figuring out just how big a role prenatal malnutrition plays in this miserable chain of events, then, is difficult at best. But the starvation in the Nazi-occupied Netherlands nearly half a century ago offers some thought-provoking answers.

The Dutch tragedy was the result of one of the most controversial decisions of World War II. After the Allied forces invaded Normandy and liberated France in the summer of 1944, our generals debated two strategies for completing Germany's defeat: to advance northeastward from France into Germany's Ruhr industrial region or to push eastward into the Saar. Had all our resources been concentrated on a single strategy, either might have succeeded. In fact both advances were attempted at once, and both ground to a standstill.

The northern advance hinged on the famous Battle of Arnhem, which inspired the film *A Bridge Too Far*. On September 17, 1944, British paratroops were dropped on the Dutch city of Arnhem to take command of a crucial bridge over the Rhine; other Allied forces, meanwhile, tried to join them from the south. Dutch railroad workers courageously called a general strike to impede the Nazis' efforts to bring up reinforcements. But stiff Nazi resistance forced the Allies to retreat, on September 25, after heavy losses. The Allies then shifted their military effort away from the Netherlands, most of which remained under German occupation until May 1945.

In retaliation for the Dutch strike an embargo on transport in the Netherlands, including transport of food, was ordered by the notorious Nazi Reichskommissar Seyss-Inquart, later tried and hanged at Nuremberg. The predictable result of the embargo, which began in October 1944, was a famine that became progressively worse as stored food supplies were exhausted and that was not lifted until the Netherlands was liberated the following spring. Because an unusually severe winter hampered relief efforts, the famine became known as the Dutch Hunger Winter.

Intake dropped as low as 400 calories a day, down from an already-reduced daily ration of 1,500 calories. Still, some people were better off than others. The hunger was milder in the farming regions of the north and south; it was most severe in the large industrial cities of the west, such as Amsterdam, Rotterdam, and The Hague. Those people with enough strength went to the countryside to seek food, including tulip bulbs, in the fields. The hunger was also somewhat selective by social class: people of higher socioeconomic status were able to use money, property, and influence to obtain additional food.

Altogether 10,000 people starved to death, and malnutrition contributed to the deaths of countless others. Adults in the famine cities who survived lost, on average, 15 to 20 percent of their body weight. Some women weighed less at the end of their pregnancy than at its inception.

When the Allies finally liberated the Netherlands in early May 1945, they rushed in food, and conditions quickly improved. But by then 40,000 fetuses had been subjected to the hardships of famine. Depending on their date of conception, these babies were exposed at various stages of gestation, for periods as long as seven months. For example, babies conceived in April 1944 and born in early January 1945 were exposed to the starvation just in the last trimester of pregnancy; those conceived in February 1945 and born in November 1945 were exposed only in the first trimester. Babies unlucky enough to be conceived in August 1944 and born in May 1945 spent their entire second and third trimesters inside increasingly malnourished mothers.

In the late 1960s four researchers at Columbia University School of Public Health—Zena Stein, Mervyn Susser, Gerhart Saenger, and Francis Marolla, all of whom had studied malnutrition in urban ghettos—realized that much might be learned from the now-grown babies of the Dutch Hunger Winter. The outcomes of pregnancies in the stricken cities of the west could be compared with those in towns to the north or south, outside the worst-hit area. In addition, the results of pregnancies during the famine could be compared with those that occurred before and after it.

Hospital records and birth registries yielded statistics on the health of the wartime mothers and their newborns. And at least for the boys, follow-up information on those same children as young adults could be extracted from the records of the Dutch military draft system. Virtually all boys at age 19 were called up for an exam that recorded their height and weight, medical history, results of mental-performance tests, level of schooling completed, and father's occupation; the latter served as a rough indicator of socioeconomic status.

A starving mother was forced to unconsciously "choose" whether to devote the few available calories to her own body or to her fetus.

These studies provided some important insights, the first of which concerned the famine's effect on fertility. During the winter of 1944 conceptions quickly declined to one-third the normal level. This suggests that the women's fertility became impaired as their fat reserves, already depleted due to reduced wartime rations, were rapidly used up. The decline was more pronounced for wives of manual workers than of nonmanual workers, presumably because the former had less means to buy their way out of starvation.

The Dutch results agree with other evidence that body weight affects our reproductive physiology. Women in German concentration camps often ceased to menstruate (while low sperm counts and impotence were common among male inmates). Moreover, studies have shown that girls begin menstruating earlier in well-fed industrialized nations than in underfed Third World countries. The same trend applies to the present generation of American women compared with their less well nourished grandmothers. All these pieces of evidence suggest that a woman's fertility is dependent on having sufficient body weight to support conception.

Among the famine babies themselves, the most obvious effects were seen in those who were exposed during the last trimester, which is normally the period when a fetus undergoes its most rapid weight gain: these babies had markedly lower average birth weights (6 pounds 10 ounces) than those born before the famine began (7 pounds 6 ounces). Starvation during the third trimester also resulted in babies who were born slightly shorter and with smaller head circumferences, indicating slightly slower than normal growth of the bones and brain. But the main impact was to retard the growth of muscle and fat.

The prefamine pregnancies had taken place while wartime rations still hovered around 1,500 daily calories—meager for a pregnant woman, who normally requires 2,500 calories a day. Medical records showed that these expectant mothers lost weight themselves but were able to maintain a normal birth weight for their babies. Once rations dropped below 1,500 calories, however, babies began to share the impact. And eventually, as the famine wore on and severe starvation struck, all further weight loss was suffered by the baby rather than the mother. Birth weight recovered quickly when food supplies improved, though: babies born three months after the famine's end had normal weights.

Both during and right after the Hunger Winter there was a sharp rise in infant deaths in the Netherlands' hard-hit cities. For babies exposed to famine only in the first trimester, the rate of stillbirth nearly doubled. Those babies had been conceived just three months before the famine's end, and so they in fact completed most of their gestation inside mothers who were relatively well nourished. Yet malnutrition during those first three months had evidently planted a slow-fuse time bomb that went off at birth.

Still greater, however, was the effect on babies exposed during the second, and especially the third, trimesters. Those babies had a higher-than-normal death rate in their first week of life, and the rate continued to climb until they were at least three months old. Some of these babies died of malnutrition itself, others succumbed to normal childhood infections to which they had lowered resistance. Fortunately, once the famine babies reached the age of one year, their increased risk of death disappeared.

Let's now see how the babies who survived the perils of birth and early infancy were faring 19 years later, when the boys were called up for the draft. In many respects these young men were similar to any others their age. Their height, for example, showed all the usual effects of socioeconomic factors, including family size and diet: sons of manual workers averaged nearly an inch shorter than sons of wealthier fathers, children from families with many mouths to feed were shorter than only children, and later-born sons were shorter than first-born sons. The common thread is that children who have access to less food end up shorter. But postnatal, rather than prenatal, nutrition was the culprit here. If you picked any given group—say, sons of manual workers—the young men whose mothers were starved during pregnancy were no shorter than their peers.

Records from the Dutch draft exams also allowed the Columbia researchers to see if poor nutrition in pregnancy might cause lasting mental deficits as well as physical ones. Experiments with rats had shown that offspring of mothers that are starved in pregnancy end up with fewer-than-normal brain cells and learning disabilities. So when the researchers compared the grown-up famine babies' performance on tests of mental proficiency with the performance of those who had received better prenatal nourishment, they expected to find poorer scores for those who had been starved during gestation.

No such result was forthcoming. The draft exam, which included tests of verbal, arithmetic, clerical, and mechanical skills, clearly showed the effects of social environment, which were parallel to the physical effects already mentioned—thus, sons of manual laborers, sons from large families, and sons born late into a family of several children tended to score below other young men. But no effect whatsoever could be attributed to prenatal starvation. One possible explanation is that our brain has enough extra cells to preserve mental function even if some of our cells are lost. At any rate, whatever effects can be attributed to nutrition must be due to nutrition after birth, not before it.

The genetic interests of the fetus are served by saving itself. Hence we evolve as fetuses to be parasites commandeering our mother's nutrients.

This, then, was the good news, such as it was. Those starved children who made it to adulthood were no worse off than their better-nourished counterparts. However, the medical records of the male famine babies who never made it to a draft physical did reveal one consequence of prenatal starvation—and it was sobering. Fetuses exposed to famine during their first three months in the womb were twice as likely as others to have defects of the central nervous system, such as spina bifida (in which the spine fails to close properly) and hydrocephalus (a related condition, characterized by fluid accumulating in the brain). The birth defects, it now appears, almost certainly arose from starvation during the first trimester, when the nervous system was being laid down.

Just how did a lack of food have such a dire result? Animal experiments have raised the suspicion that such defects can arise from a deficiency of the B vitamin folic acid early in pregnancy. A year ago this finding was confirmed for humans in a study of 22,776 pregnant women in Boston. Babies born to mothers who took multivitamins including folic acid during the first six weeks of pregnancy had a nearly fourfold lower frequency of central nervous system defects than did babies born to women who did not take such supplements. Brands of multivitamins that lacked folic acid, or multivitamins taken only after the seventh week of pregnancy, offered no protection.

All the results from the Dutch famine studies that I've discussed so far describe the effects of starvation on mothers and their children. But recent findings have raised disturbing questions about the famine's effect on a third generation. By now the famine babies are 45 or 46, and most of the girls have long since had children of their own; the "girls" themselves are women at the end of their reproductive careers. More than 100 of these women happened to have had their babies in the same Amsterdam hospital in which they themselves were born, which makes for an easy comparison of birth records. An examination of those records has revealed something very odd: it turns out that those women who were themselves fetuses in their first and second trimester during the Dutch Hunger Winter gave birth to underweight babies. That is, the babies were somehow affected by the starvation of their grandmothers many decades earlier.

This result might have been easier to understand if the mothers themselves had been underweight at birth or were small as adults. Neither was true. Recall that starvation in the first or second trimester produced babies with normal birth weights. Only third-trimester starvation led to small babies. Yet, paradoxically, when these small babies later became mothers, they gave birth to normal-size babies. It was the women who were themselves normal size at birth who became mothers of underweight infants.

Somehow the grandmothers' suffering programmed their children in utero so that the grandchildren would be affected. This astonishing result will undoubtedly inspire experiments aimed at identifying the still-unknown cellular mechanism. But what is indisputable is that the Dutch famine left its harsh imprint on at least three generations.

From the perspective of evolutionary biology, the famine posed to the bodies of pregnant mothers an agonizing dilemma. What would you do in a situation threatening both your life and your child's life if anything you did to help one would hurt the other? Think quickly: If you see a car about to crash head-on into your car, do you throw yourself in front of your child sitting strapped in the seat beside you or do you try to protect yourself instead? Now let's make the choice more agonizing: What if your child's subsequent survival hinges on your own? You've all heard the airlines' standard safety announcement that in the event of a loss of cabin pressure, place the oxygen mask on yourself first, *then* place the mask on your child. In that situation, you have to help yourself first, because you'll be in no state to help your child if you are unconscious.

Similarly a mother starving in the Netherlands in 1944 was forced to unconsciously "choose" whether to devote the few available calories to her own body or to her fetus. This is a classic example of a conflict between two genetically related individuals. Natural selection favors the individual who passes on his or her genes to the most descendants. The genetic interests of the fetus are served by saving itself, and hence we evolve as fetuses to be parasites on our mother, commandeering her nutrients as efficiently as possible. But the mother's genetic interests are served by passing her genes to offspring. She gains nothing if her nutritional sacrifices kill not only herself but her child. Perhaps she would be best off, from an evolutionary point of view, if she sacrificed that fetus and tried again later. Yet there is no certainty that she will have another chance later.

The outcome of the Dutch famine indicates that natural selection struck a compromise. When the famine began, a mother's body at first accepted the full brunt, losing weight while preserving the weight of the fetus. In the next stage of famine both the fetus and the mother shared the hardship. In the last stage all weight loss came at the expense of the fetus, because any more weight loss by the mother would have threatened the mother's survival and thereby the survival of her child.

These pregnant women had no say in how their body allocated its precious resources, of course. Natural selection proceeded along its inexorable journey oblivious to any human agony or ethical dilemma. To ask whether the decisions it made were wise, whether they were somehow the "right" decisions, is irrelevant. The choices were arrived at in accordance with the cold logic of evolution and nothing more.

But what about the decisions that created such cruel conditions in the first place? What about the reasoning that even today, in the guise of wartime expediency, can compel one group of people to consciously impose starvation on another and thus scar the lives of unborn generations? For that matter, what about the reduction of social programs in our own society that might subject untold numbers of children, both before and after birth, to the dangers of malnutrition simply by failing to ensure proper nourishment for them and their mothers? The lessons of the Dutch Hunger Winter are there for the learning. We can ignore them only at our children's, and our grandchildren's, expense.

NATURE OR NURTURE?

■

Old chestnut, new thoughts

Few questions of human behaviour are more controversial than this: are people programmed by their genes, or by their upbringing? There is no simple answer, but the academic world is starting to hear a lot more from the genes brigade—on both sides of the political spectrum

ARE criminals born or made? Is homosexuality a preference or a predisposition? Do IQ tests measure innate abilities or acquired skills?

For the past 50 years, respectable academic opinion, whenever it has deigned to deal with such layman's questions, has come down firmly for nurture over nature. Nazism discredited even the mildest attempts to produce genetic explanations of human affairs. And economic growth after the second world war encouraged most western governments to imagine that they could eliminate social problems by a mixture of enlightened planning and generous spending—that, in effect, they could steer (even change) human nature.

In this atmosphere, the social sciences flourished as never before. Sociologists made lucrative careers producing "nurture" explanations of everything from school failure to schizophrenia. Geneticists stuck to safe subjects such as fruit flies and honey bees, rather than risk being accused of a fondness for jackboots and martial music.

The fashion is beginning to change. The failure of liberal reforms to deliver the Great Society has cast doubt on the proposition that better nurture can deliver better nature. The failure of sociologists to find even a few of the purported (Freudian or social) causes of schizophrenia, homosexuality, sex differences in criminal tendencies and the like has undermined their credibility. And a better understanding of how genes work has made it possible for liberals who still believe in the perfectibility of man to accept genetic explanations. In at least one case—homosexuality—it is now the liberals who espouse nature and their opponents who point to nurture.

The pro-nature people are still a minority in universities. But they are a productive and increasingly vocal minority—and one which is beginning to increase its influence in the media. Open the American newspapers and you can read left-inclined pundits like Micky Kaus arguing that income inequality is partly the result of genetic differences. Turn on the television and you can see intelligent, unbigoted people claiming that male homosexuals have a different brain structure from heterosexual men.

This is only the beginning. Richard Herrnstein, a professor of psychology at Harvard University, and Charles Murray, a controversial critic of the welfare state, are collaborating on a study of the implications of biological differences for public policy. The book will highlight the tension between America's egalitarian philosophy and the unequal distribution of innate abilities.

The reaction of orthodox opinion has been scathing. America's National Institutes of Health provoked such an angry response to its decision to finance a conference on genetics and crime that it decided to withdraw the money. Mr Murray lost the patronage of the Manhattan Institute, a New York-based think-tank, when he decided to study individual differences and social policy.

Even in these days of politically correct fetishes, on no other subject is the gulf between academics and ordinary people so wide. Even the most hopeful of parents know that the sentiment "all men are created equal" is a pious dream rather than a statement of fact. They know full well that, say, one of their sons is brighter, or more musical or more athletic than another; they see, despite their best attentions, that girls turn every toy into a doll and boys turn every toy into a weapon; they rarely persist in believing that each and all of these differences is the result of early encouragement or training. They know that even if full equality of opportunity could be guaranteed, equality of outcome could not. Ability is not evenly distributed.

But parents' opinions are unscientific. Not until 1979 did a few academics begin to catch up. In that year the Minnesota Centre for Twin and Adoption Research began to contact more than 100 sets of twins and triplets who had been separated at birth and reared apart, mostly in the United States and Britain.

The centre subjected each pair to thorough psychological and physiological tests. If two twins are identical (or "monozygotic"), any differences between them are due to the environment they were reared in; so a measure of heritability can be attached to various mental features. The study concluded that about 70% of the variance in IQ was explained by genetic factors. It also found that on a large number of measures of personality and temperament—notably personal interests and social attitudes—identical twins reared apart are about as similar as identical twins reared together.

The Minnesota study represents the respectable end of an academic spectrum that stretches all the way through to outright racists. If IQ is 70% inherited, then perhaps much of the IQ difference between

From *The Economist,* December 26, 1992–January 8, 1993, pp. 33-34, 36. © 1993 by The Economist, Ltd. Distributed by The New York Times Special Features.

races is also inherited. The logic does not necessarily follow, since the differences could all lie in the 30% that is nurture; but still it is a hypothesis worth testing—at least for those prepared to risk being called politically incorrect.

Unfortunately, because there are no black-white pairs of identical twins, nobody has yet found a way to test whether racial differences in IQ are genetic. It would require getting 100 pairs of black parents and 100 pairs of white parents to rear their children on identical incomes in an identical suburb and send the children of 50 of each to the same good school and 50 of each to a bad one. Impossible.

This means that racial differences in IQ tend to attract scientists with dubious motives and methods. With increasing enthusiasm over the past decade, some psychologists have disinterred a technique already consigned to the attic by their Victorian predecessors: using physiological data to measure intellectual skill.

Arthur Jensen, a professor of educational psychology at the University of California, Berkeley, has assembled a large body of results purportedly demonstrating that IQ is closely correlated with speed of reaction, a theory abandoned around 1900. He claims that intelligence is correlated with the rate at which glucose is consumed in the brain, the speed of neural transmission and a large number of anatomical variables such as height, brain size and even head size.

Jean Philippe Rushton, a professor of psychology at the University of Western Ontario, Canada, has revived craniometry, the Victorian attempt to correlate head size with brain power. (In "The Adventure of the Blue Carbuncle", one of Arthur Conan Doyle's most ingenious Christmas stories, Sherlock Holmes deduces that a man is an intellectual from the size of his hat: "It is a question of cubic capacity . . . a man with so large a brain must have something in it.")

Mr Rushton has studied data on the head sizes of thousands of American servicemen, gathered to make sure that army helmets fit. Adjusting the raw data for variables such as body size, he argues that men have bigger craniums than women, that the well-educated have bigger craniums than the less educated, and that orientals have bigger craniums than whites, who have bigger craniums than blacks.

Mr Rushton has done wonders for the protest industry. David Peterson, a former premier of Ontario, called for his dismissal. Protesters likened him to the Nazis and the Ku Klux Klan. The Ontario Provincial police even launched an investigation into his work. An embarrassed university establishment required Mr Rushton to give his lectures on videotape.

Even if you could conclude that blacks have lower IQs than whites after the same education, it is not clear what the policy prescription would be. Presumably, it would only add weight to the argument for positive discrimination in favour of blacks, so as to redress an innate inferiority with a better education. The "entitlement liberalism" that prevails in American social policy and finds its expression in employment quotas and affirmative-action programmes already assumes that blacks need preferential rather than equal treatment. Indeed, to this way of thinking, merit is less important than eliminating group differences and promoting social integration.

The gene of Cain

Compared with the study of racial differences, the study of the genetics of criminality is only slightly more respectable. Harvard's Mr Herrnstein teamed up in the early 1980s with James Wilson, a political scientist, to teach a class on crime. The result was "Crime and Human Nature" (1985), a bulky book which argues that the best explanation for a lot of predatory criminal behaviour—particularly assault and arson—may be biological rather than sociological.

Certainly, a Danish study of the children of criminals adopted into normal households lends some support to the idea that a recidivist criminal's son is more likely to be a criminal than other sons brought up in the same household. But Mr Herrnstein and Mr Wilson then spoil their case with another Victorian throwback to "criminal types"—people with low verbal intelligence and "mesomorphic" (short and muscular) bodies who, they believe, are more likely to be criminal.

One reason such work strikes horror into sociologists is that it suggests an obvious remedy: selective breeding. Mr Herrnstein has suggested that the greater fertility of stupid people means that the wrong kind of selective breeding is already at work and may be responsible for falling academic standards. "We ought to bear in mind", Mr Herrnstein ruminates gloomily about America, "that in not too many generations differential fertility could swamp the effects of anything else we may do about our economic standing in the world." Luckily for Mr Herrnstein, studies reveal that, despite teenage parents in the inner cities, people of high social status are still outbreeding those of low social status. Rich men have more surviving children—not least because they tend to have more wives—than poor men.

In one sense, it is plain that criminality is innate: men resort to it far more than women. Martin Daly and Margo Wilson, of McMaster University in Canada, have compared the homicide statistics of England and Wales with those of Chicago. In both cases, the graphs are identical in

shape, with young men 30 times as likely as women of all ages to commit homicide. It is perverse to deny the connection between testosterone and innate male aggressiveness. But it is equally perverse to ignore the fact that the scales of the two graphs are utterly different: young men in Chicago are 30 times as likely to kill as young men in England and Wales—which has nothing to do with nature and much to do with nurture. The sexual difference is nature; the national difference is nurture.

The most successful assault on the nurturist orthodoxy, however, has come not over race, or intelligence, or crime, but over sex. In the 1970s the nurturists vigorously repulsed an attack on their cherished beliefs by the then fledgling discipline of sociobiology. Sociobiology is the study of how animal behaviour evolves to fit function in the same way that anatomy does.

When sociobiologists started to apply the same ideas to human beings, principally through Edward Wilson of Harvard University, a furore broke out. Most of them retreated, as geneticists had done, to study animals again. Anthropologists insisted that their subject, mankind, was basically different from animals because it was not born with its behaviour but learnt it.

In the past few years, however, a new assault from scientists calling themselves Darwinian psychologists has largely refuted that argument. Through a series of experiments and analyses, they have asserted that (a) much sophisticated behaviour is not taught, but develops autonomously; and (b) learning is not the opposite of instinct, but is itself a highly directed instinct.

The best example of this is language. In 1957 Noam Chomsky of the Massachusetts Institute of Technology (MIT) argued that all human languages bear a striking underlying similarity. He called this "deep structure", and argued it was innate and not learnt. In recent years Steven Pinker of MIT and Paul Bloom of the University of Arizona have taken this idea further. They argue that human beings have a "language organ", specially designed for learning grammatical language. It includes a series of highly specific inbuilt assumptions that enable them to learn grammar from examples, without ever being taught it.

Hence the tendency to learn grammatical language is human nature. But a child reared in isolation does not start to speak Hebrew unaided. Vocabulary, and accent, are obviously 100% nurture. In this combination of nature and nurture, argue the Darwinian psychologists, language is typical of most human traits. Learning is not the opposite of instinct; people have innate instincts to learn certain things and not others.

This is heresy to sociologists and anthropologists, who have been reared since Emile Durkheim to believe the human mind is a *tabula rasa*—a blank slate upon which any culture can be written. To this, John Tooby and Leda Cosmides of the University of California at Santa Barbara, two leading thinkers on the subject, have replied: "The assertion that 'culture' explains human variation will be taken seriously when there are reports of women war parties raiding villages to capture men as husbands."

Nor will the Darwinian psychologists concede that to believe in nature is to be a Hobbesian fatalist and that to believe in nurture is to be a Rousseau-ist believer in the perfectibility of man. Many totalitarians are actually nurturists: they believe that rearing people to worship Stalin works. History suggests otherwise.

The making of macho

Physiologists have also begun to add weight to the nature side of the scale with their discovery of how the brain develops. The brain of a fetus is altered by the child's genes, by its and its mother's hormones and, after birth, by its learning. Many of the changes are permanent; so as far as the adult is concerned, they are all "nature", though many are not genetic. For example, the human brain is feminine unless acted upon by male hormones during two bursts—one in the womb and another at puberty. The hormone is nurture, in the sense that it can be altered by injections or drugs taken by the mother. But it is nature in the sense that it is a product of the body's biology.

This discovery has gradually altered the views of many psychologists about sex and education. An increasing number recognise that the competitiveness, roughness, mathematical ability and spatial skills of boys are the product of their biology (genes and hormones) not their family, and that the character-reading, verbal, linguistic and emotional interest and skills of girls are also biological. Hence girls get a better early education when kept away from boys. This conclusion, anathema to most practising educational psychologists, is increasingly common among those who actually do research on it.

Indeed, radical feminism is increasingly having to recognize the biological theme that underlies its claims. Feminists demand equality of opportunity, but they also routinely argue that women bring different qualities to the world: consensus-seeking, uncompetitive, caring, gentle qualities that inherently domineering men lack. Women, they argue, should be in Parliament or Congress in representative numbers to "represent the woman's point of view", which assumes that men cannot.

Many homosexuals have already crossed the bridge to nature. When sociobiologists first suggested that homosexuality might be biological, they were called Nazis and worse. But in the past few years things have turned around completely. The discovery that the identical twin of a homosexual man has an odds-on chance of being homosexual too, whereas a non-identical twin has only a one-in-five chance, implies that there are some influential genes involved. And the discovery that those parts of the brain that are measurably different in women and men are also different in heterosexuals and homosexuals adds further weight to the idea that homosexuality is as natural as left-handedness. That is anathema to pro-family-value conservatives, who believe that homosexuality is a (misguided) personal choice.

Assuming that the new hereditarians are right and that many human features can be related to genes (or, more likely, groups of genes), it might one day be possible to equip each member of the species with a compact disc telling him which version of each of the 50,000-100,000 human genes he has. He might then read whether he was likely to have a weight problem, or be any good at music, whether there was a risk of schizophrenia or a chance of genius, whether he might go manic-depressive or be devoutly religious. But he could never be sure. For beside every gene would be an asterisk referring to a footnote that read thus: "This prediction is only valid if you are brought up by two Protestant, middle-class, white parents in Peoria, Illinois."

TRENDS IN BEHAVIORAL GENETICS

EUGENICS REVISITED

Scientists are linking genes to a host of complex human disorders and traits, but just how valid—and useful—are these findings?

John Horgan, *senior writer*

"How to Tell If Your Child's a Serial Killer!" That was the sound bite with which the television show *Donahue* sought to entice listeners February 25. On the program, a psychiatrist from the Rochester, N.Y., area noted that some men are born with not one Y chromosome but two. Double-Y men, the psychiatrist said, are "at special risk for antisocial, violent behavior." In fact, the psychiatrist had recently studied such a man. Although he had grown up in a "Norman Rockwell" setting, as an adult he had strangled at least 11 women and two children.

"It is not hysterical or overstating it," Phil Donahue told his horrified audience, "to say that we are moving toward the time when, quite literally, just as we can anticipate . . . genetic predispositions toward various physical diseases, we will also be able to pinpoint mental disorders which include aggression, antisocial behavior and the possibility of very serious criminal activity later on."

Eugenics is back in fashion. The message that genetics can explain, predict and even modify human behavior for the betterment of society is promulgated not just on sensationalistic talk shows but by our most prominent scientists. James D. Watson, co-discoverer of the double-helix structure of DNA and former head of the Human Genome Project, the massive effort to map our entire genetic endowment, said recently, "We used to think that our fate was in our stars. Now we know, in large part, that our fate is in our genes."

Daniel E. Koshland, Jr., a biologist at the University of California at Berkeley and editor of *Science*, the most influential peer-reviewed journal in the U.S., has declared in an editorial that the nature/nurture debate is "basically over," since scientists have shown that genes influence many aspects of human behavior. He has also contended that genetic research may help eliminate society's most intractable problems, including drug abuse, homelessness and, yes, violent crime.

Some studies cited to back this claim are remarkably similar to those conducted over a century ago by scientists such as Francis Galton, known as the father of eugenics. Just as the British polymath studied identical twins in order to show that "nature prevails enormously over nurture," so do modern researchers. But the primary reason behind the revival of eugenics is the astonishing successes of biologists in mapping and manipulating the human genome. Over the past decade, investigators have identified genes underlying such crippling diseases as cystic fibrosis, muscular dystrophy and, this past spring, Huntington's disease. Given these advances, researchers say, it is only a matter of time before they can lay bare the genetic foundation of much more complex traits and disorders.

The political base for eugenics has also become considerably broader in recent years. Spokespersons for the mentally ill believe demonstrating the genetic basis of disorders such as schizophrenia and manic depression—and even alcoholism and drug addiction—will lead not only to better diagnoses and

treatments but also to more compassion toward sufferers and their families. Some homosexuals believe society will become more tolerant toward them if it can be shown that sexual orientation is an innate, biological condition and not a matter of choice.

But critics contend that no good can come of bad science. Far from moving inexorably closer to its goals, they point out, the field of behavioral genetics is mired in the same problems that have always plagued it. Behavioral traits are extraordinarily difficult to define, and practically every claim of a genetic basis can also be explained as an environmental effect. "This has been a huge enterprise, and for the most part the work has been done shoddily. Even careful people get sucked into misinterpreting data," says Jonathan Beckwith, a geneticist at Harvard University. He adds, "There are social consequences to this."

The skeptics also accuse the media of having created an unrealistically optimistic view of the field. Richard C. Lewontin, a biologist at Harvard and a prominent critic of behavioral genetics, contends that the media generally give much more prominent coverage to dramatic reports—such as the discovery of an "alcoholism gene"—than to contradictory results or retractions. "Skepticism doesn't make the news," Lewontin says. "It only makes the news when you find a gene." The result is that spurious findings often become accepted by the public and even by so-called experts.

The claim that men with an extra Y chromosome are predisposed toward violence is a case in point. It stems from a survey in the 1960s that found more extra-Y men in prison than in the general population. Some researchers hypothesized that since the Y chromo-

From *Scientific American*, June 1993, pp. 122-128, 130-131. © 1993 by Scientific American, Inc. All rights reserved. Reprinted by permission.

"EERIE" PARALLELS between identical twins raised apart—such as Jerry Levey (*left*) and Mark Newman, who both became firefighters—are said to support genetic models of human behavior. Yet skeptics say the significance of such coincidences has been exaggerated.

some confers male attributes, men with an extra Y become hyperaggressive "supermales." Follow-up studies indicated that while extra-Y men tend to be taller than other men and score slightly lower on intelligence tests, they are otherwise normal. The National Academy of Sciences concluded in a report published this year that there is no evidence to support the link between the extra Y chromosome and violent behavior.

Minnesota Twins

No research in behavioral genetics has been more eagerly embraced by the press than the identical-twin studies done at the University of Minnesota. Thomas J. Bouchard, Jr., a psychologist, initiated them in the late 1970s, and since then they have been featured in the *Washington Post, Newsweek,* the *New York Times* and other publications worldwide as well as on television. *Science* has favorably described the Minnesota team's work in several news stories and in 1990 published a major article by the group.

The workers have studied more than 50 pairs of identical twins who were separated shortly after birth and raised in different households. The assumption is that any differences between identical twins, who share all each other's genes, are caused by the environment; similarities are attributed to their shared genes. The group estimates the relative contribution of genes to a given trait in a term called "heritability." A trait that stems entirely from genes, such as eye color, is defined as 100 percent heritable. Height is 90 percent heritable; that is, 90 percent of the variation in height is accounted for by genetic variation, and the other 10 percent is accounted for by diet and other environmental factors.

The Minnesota group has reported finding a strong genetic contribution to practically all the traits it has examined. Whereas most previous studies have estimated the heritability of intelligence (as defined by performance on intelligence tests) as roughly 50 percent, Bouchard and his colleagues arrived at a figure of 70 percent. They have also found a genetic component underlying such culturally defined traits as religiosity, political orientation (conservative versus liberal), job satisfaction, leisure-time interests and proneness to divorce. In fact, the group concluded in *Science,* "On multiple measures of personality and temperament...monozy-

gotic twins reared apart are about as similar as are monozygotic twins reared together." (Identical twins are called monozygotic because they stem from a single fertilized egg, or zygote.)

The researchers have buttressed their statistical findings with anecdotes about "eerie," "bewitching" and "remarkable" parallels between reunited twins. One case involved Oskar, who was raised as a Nazi in Czechoslovakia, and Jack, who was raised as a Jew in Trinidad. Both were reportedly wearing shirts with epaulets when they were reunited by the Minnesota group in 1979. They also both flushed the toilet before as well as after using it and enjoyed deliberately sneezing to startle people in elevators.

Some other celebrated cases involved two British women who wore seven rings and named their firstborn sons Richard Andrew and Andrew Richard; two men who both had been named Jim, named their pet dogs Toy, married women named Linda, divorced them and remarried women named Betty; and two men who had become firefighters and drank Budweiser beer.

Other twin researchers say the significance of these coincidences has been greatly exaggerated. Richard J. Rose of Indiana University, who is collaborating on a study of 16,000 pairs of twins in Finland, points out that "if you bring together strangers who were born on the same day in the same country and ask them to find similarities between them, you may find a lot of seemingly astounding coincidences."

Rose's collaborator, Jaakko Kaprio of the University of Helsinki, notes that the Minnesota twin studies may also be biased by their selection method. Whereas he and Rose gather data by combing birth registries and sending questionnaires to those identified as twins, the Minnesota group relies heavily on media coverage to recruit new twins. The twins then come to Minnesota for a week of study—and, often, further publicity. Twins who are "interested in publicity and willing to support it," Kaprio says, may be atypical. This self-selection effect, he adds, may explain why the Bouchard group's estimates of heritability tend to be higher than those of other studies.

One of the most outspoken critics of

the Minnesota twin studies—and indeed all twin studies indicating high heritability of behavioral traits—is Leon J. Kamin, a psychologist at Northeastern University. In the 1970s Kamin helped to expose inconsistencies and possible fraud in studies of separated identical twins conducted by the British psychologist Cyril Burt during the previous two decades. Burt's conclusion that intelligence was mostly inherited had inspired various observers, notably Arthur R. Jensen, a psychologist at the University of California at Berkeley, to argue that socioeconomic stratification in the U.S. is largely a genetic phenomenon.

In his investigations of other twin studies, Kamin has shown that identical twins supposedly raised apart are often raised by members of their family or by unrelated families in the same neighborhood; some twins had extensive contact with each other while growing up. Kamin suspects the same may be true of some Minnesota twins. He notes, for example, that some news accounts suggested Oskar and Jack (the Nazi and the Jew) and the two British women wearing seven rings were reunited for the first time when they arrived in Minnesota to be studied by Bouchard. Actually, both pairs of twins had met previously. Kamin has repeatedly asked the Minnesota group for detailed case histories of its twins to determine whether it has underestimated contact and similarities in upbringing. "They've never responded," he says.

Kamin proposes that the Minnesota twins have particularly strong motives to downplay previous contacts and to exaggerate their similarities. They might want to please researchers, to attract more attention from the media or even to make money. In fact, some twins acquired agents and were paid for appearances on television. Jack and Oskar recently sold their life story to a film producer in Los Angeles (who says Robert Duvall is interested in the roles).

Even the Minnesota researchers caution against overinterpretation of their work. They agree with their critics that high heritability should not be equated with inevitability, since the environment can still drastically affect the expression of a gene. For example, the genetic disease phenylketonuria, which causes profound retardation, has a heritability of 100 percent. Yet eliminating the amino acid phenylalanine from the diet of affected persons prevents retardation from occurring.

Such warnings tend to be minimized in media coverage, however. Writers often make the same inference that Koshland did in an editorial in *Science:* "Bet-

ter schools, a better environment, better counseling and better rehabilitation will help some individuals but not all." The prime minister of Singapore apparently reached the same conclusion. A decade ago he cited popular accounts of the Minnesota research in defending policies that encouraged middle-class Singaporeans to bear children and discouraged childbearing by the poor.

Smart Genes

Twin studies, of course, do not indicate which specific genes contribute to a trait. Early in the 1980s scientists began developing powerful ways to unearth that information. The techniques stem from the fact that certain stretches of human DNA, called polymorphisms, vary in a predictable way. If a polymorphism is consistently inherited together with a given trait—blue eyes, for example—then geneticists assume it either lies near a gene for that trait or actually is the gene. A polymorphism that merely lies near a gene is known as a marker.

In so-called linkage studies, investigators search for polymorphisms co-inherited with a trait in families unusually prone to the trait. In 1983 researchers used this method to find a marker linked to Huntington's disease, a crippling neurological disorder that usually strikes carriers in middle age and kills them within 10 years. Since then, the same technique has pinpointed genes for cystic fibrosis, muscular dystrophy and other diseases. In association studies, researchers compare the relative frequency of polymorphisms in two unrelated populations, one with the trait and one lacking it.

Workers are already using both methods to search for polymorphisms associated with intelligence, defined as the ability to score well on standardized intelligence tests. In 1991 Shelley D. Smith of the Boys Town National Institute for Communication Disorders in Children, in Omaha, and David W. Fulker of the University of Colorado identified polymorphisms associated with dyslexia in a linkage study of 19 families exhibiting high incidence of the reading disorder.

Behavioral Genetics: A Lack-of-Progress Report

CRIME: Family, twin and adoption studies have suggested a heritability of 0 to more than 50 percent for predisposition to crime. (Heritability represents the degree to which a trait stems from genetic factors.) In the 1960s researchers reported an association between an extra Y chromosome and violent crime in males. Follow-up studies found that association to be spurious.

MANIC DEPRESSION: Twin and family studies indicate heritability of 60 to 80 percent for susceptibility to manic depression. In 1987 two groups reported locating different genes linked to manic depression, one in Amish families and the other in Israeli families. Both reports have been retracted.

SCHIZOPHRENIA: Twin studies show heritability of 40 to 90 percent. In 1988 a group reported finding a gene linked to schizophrenia in British and Icelandic families. Other studies documented no linkage, and the initial claim has now been retracted.

ALCOHOLISM: Twin and adoption studies suggest heritability ranging from 0 to 60 percent. In 1990 a group claimed to link a gene—one that produces a receptor for the neurotransmitter dopamine—with alcoholism. A recent review of the evidence concluded it does not support a link.

INTELLIGENCE: Twin and adoption studies show a heritability of performance on intelligence tests of 20 to 80 percent. One group recently unveiled preliminary evidence for genetic markers for high intelligence (an IQ of 130 or higher). The study is unpublished.

HOMOSEXUALITY: In 1991 a researcher cited anatomic differences between the brains of heterosexual and homosexual males. Two recent twin studies have found a heritability of roughly 50 percent for predisposition to male or female homosexuality. These reports have been disputed. Another group claims to have preliminary evidence of genes linked to male homosexuality. The data have not been published.

Two years ago Robert Plomin, a psychologist at Pennsylvania State University who has long been active in behavioral genetics, received a $600,000 grant from the National Institute of Child Health and Human Development to search for genes linked to high intelligence. Plomin is using the association method, which he says is more suited than the linkage technique to identifying genes whose contribution to a trait is relatively small. Plomin is studying a group of 64 schoolchildren 12 to 13 years old who fall into three groups: those who score approximately 130, 100 and 80 on intelligence tests.

Plomin has examined some 25 polymorphisms in each of these three groups, trying to determine whether any occur with greater frequency in the "bright" children. The polymorphisms have been linked to genes thought to have neurological effects. He has uncovered several markers that seem to occur more often in the highest-scoring children. He is now seeking to replicate his results in another group of 60 children; half score above 142 on intelligence tests, and half score less than 74 (yet have no obvious organic deficiencies). Plomin presented his preliminary findings at a meeting, titled "Origins and Development of High Ability," held in London in January.

At the same meeting, however, other workers offered evidence that intelligence tests are actually poor predictors of success in business, the arts or even advanced academic programs. Indeed, even Plomin seems ambivalent about the value of his research. He suggests that someday genetic information on the cognitive abilities of children might help teachers design lessons that are more suited to students' innate strengths and weaknesses.

But he also calls his approach "a fishing expedition," given that a large number of genes may contribute to intelligence. He thinks the heritability of intelligence is not 70 percent, as the Minnesota twin researchers have claimed, but 50 percent, which is the average finding of other studies, and at best he can only find a gene that accounts for a tiny part of variance in intelligence. "If you wanted to select on the basis of this, it would be of no use whatsoever," he remarks. These cautions did not prevent the *Sunday Telegraph,* a London newspaper, from announcing that Plomin had found "evidence that geniuses are born not made."

Evan S. Balaban, a biologist at Harvard, thinks Plomin's fishing expedition is doomed to fail. He grants that there may well be a significant genetic compo-

nent to intelligence (while insisting that studies by Bouchard and others have not demonstrated one). But he doubts whether investigators will ever uncover any specific genes related to high intelligence or "genius." "It is very rare to find genes that have a specific effect," he says. "For evolutionary reasons, this just doesn't happen very often."

The history of the search for markers associated with mental illness supports Balaban's view. Over the past few decades, studies of twins, families and adoptees have convinced most investigators that schizophrenia and manic depression are not caused by psychosocial factors—such as the notorious "schizophrenogenic mother" postulated by some Freudian psychiatrists—but by biological and genetic factors. After observing the dramatic success of linkage studies in the early 1980s, researchers immediately began using the technique to isolate polymorphic markers for mental illness. The potential value of such research was enormous, given that schizophrenia and manic depression each affect roughly one percent of the global population.

They seemed to have achieved their first great success in 1987. A group led by Janice A. Egeland of the University of Miami School of Medicine claimed it had linked a genetic marker on chromosome 11 to manic depression in an Amish population. That same year another team, led by Miron Baron of Columbia University, linked a marker on the X chromosome to manic depression in three Israeli families.

The media hailed these announcements as major breakthroughs. Far less attention was paid to the retractions that followed. A more extensive analysis of the Amish in 1989 by a group from the National Institute of Mental Health turned up no link between chromosome 11 and manic depression. This year Baron's team retracted its claim of linkage with the X chromosome after doing a new study of its Israeli families with more sophisticated markers and more extensive diagnoses.

Schizophrenic Results

Studies of schizophrenia have followed a remarkably similar course. In 1988 a group headed by Hugh M. D. Gurling of the University College, London, Medical School announced in *Nature* that it had found linkage in Icelandic and British families between genetic markers on chromosome 5 and schizophrenia. In the same issue, however, researchers led by Kenneth K. Kidd of Yale University reported seeing no such

linkage in a Swedish family. Although Gurling defended his result as legitimate for several years, additional research has convinced him that it was probably a false positive. "The new families showed no linkage at all," he says.

These disappointments have highlighted the problems involved in using linkage to study mental illness. Neil Risch, a geneticist at Yale, points out that linkage analysis is ideal for studying diseases, such as Huntington's, that have distinct symptoms and are caused by a single dominant gene. Some researchers had hoped that at least certain subtypes of schizophrenia or manic depression might be single-gene disorders. Single-gene mutations are thought to cause variants of breast cancer and of Alzheimer's disease that run in families and are manifested much earlier than usual. But such diseases are rare, Risch says, because natural selection quickly winnows them out of the population, and no evidence exists for distinct subtypes of manic depression or schizophrenia.

Indeed, all the available evidence suggests that schizophrenia and manic depression are caused by at least several genes—each of which may exert only a tiny influence—acting in concert with environmental influences. Finding such genes with linkage analysis may not be impossible, Risch says, but it will be considerably more difficult than identifying genes that have a one-to-one correspondence to a trait. The difficulty is compounded by the fact that the diagnosis of mental illness is often subjective—all the more so when researchers are relying on family records or recollections.

Some experts now question whether genes play a significant role in mental illness. "Personally, I think we have overestimated the genetic component of schizophrenia," says E. Fuller Torrey, a psychiatrist at St. Elizabeth's Hospital in Washington, D.C. He argues that the evidence supporting genetic models can be explained by other biological factors, such as a virus that strikes in utero. The pattern of incidence of schizophrenia in families often resembles that of other viral diseases, such as polio. "Genes may just create a susceptibility to the virus," Torrey explains.

The Drink Link

Even Kidd, the Yale geneticist who has devoted his career to searching for genes linked to mental illness, acknowledges that "in a rigorous, technical, scientific sense, there is very little proof that schizophrenia, manic depression" and other psychiatric disorders have a genetic origin. "Virtually all the evidence supports a genetic explanation, but there are always other explanations, even if they are convoluted."

The evidence for a genetic basis for alcoholism is even more tentative than that for manic depression and schizophrenia. Although some studies discern a genetic component, especially in males, others have reached the opposite conclusion. Gurling, the University College investigator, found a decade ago that identical twins were slightly *more* likely to be discordant for alcoholism than fraternal twins. The drinking habits of some identical twins were strikingly different. "In some cases, one drank a few bottles a day, and the other didn't drink at all," Gurling says.

Nevertheless, in 1990 a group led by Kenneth Blum of the University of Texas Health Science Center at San Antonio announced it had discovered a genetic marker for alcoholism in an association study comparing 35 alcoholics with a control group of 35 nonalcoholics. A page-one story in the *New York Times* portrayed the research as a potential watershed in the diagnosis and treatment of alcoholism without mentioning the considerable skepticism aroused among other researchers.

The Blum group claimed that its marker, called the A1 allele, was associated with a gene, called the D2 gene, that codes for a receptor for the neurotransmitter dopamine. Skeptics noted that the A1 allele was actually some 10,000 base pairs from the dopamine-receptor gene and was not linked to any detectable variation in its expression.

Since the initial announcement by Blum, three papers, including an additional one by Blum's group, have presented more evidence of an association between the A1 allele and alcoholism. Six groups have found no such evidence (and received virtually no mention in the popular media).

In April, Risch and Joel Gelernter of Yale and David Goldman of the National Institute on Alcohol Abuse and Alcoholism analyzed all these studies on the A1 allele in a paper in the *Journal of the American Medical Association.* They noted that if Blum's two studies are cast aside, the balance of the results shows

BRAIN OF SCHIZOPHRENIC (*right*) appears different from the brain of his identical twin in these magnetic resonance images. Such findings suggest that factors that are biological but not genetic—such as viruses—may play a significant role in mental illness.

The Huntington's Disease Saga: A Cautionary Tale

The identification of the gene for Huntington's disease, which was announced in March, was hailed as one of the great success stories of modern genetics. Yet it provides some rather sobering lessons for researchers seeking genes linked to more complex human disorders and traits.

The story begins in the late 1970s, when workers developed novel techniques for identifying polymorphisms, sections of the human genome that come in two or more forms. Investigators realized that by finding polymorphisms linked—always and exclusively—to diseases, they could determine which chromosome the gene resides in. Researchers decided to test the polymorphism technique on Huntington's disease, a devastating neurological disorder that affects roughly one in 10,000 people. Scientists had known for more than a century that Huntington's was caused by a mutant, dominant gene. If one parent has the disease, his or her offspring have a 50 percent chance of inheriting it.

One of the leaders of the Huntington's effort was Nancy Wexler, a neuropsychologist at Columbia University whose mother had died of the disease and who therefore has a 50 percent chance of developing it herself. She and other researchers focused on a poor Venezuelan village whose inhabitants had an unusually high incidence of the disease. In 1983, through what has now become a legendary stroke of good fortune, they found a linkage with one of the first polymorphisms they tested. The linkage indicated that the gene for Huntington's disease was somewhere on chromosome 4.

The finding led quickly to a test for determining whether offspring of carriers—either in utero or already born—have inherited the gene itself. The test requires an analysis of blood samples from several members of a family known to carry the disease. Wexler herself has declined to say whether she has taken the test.

Researchers assumed that they would quickly identify the actual gene in chromosome 4 that causes Huntington's disease. Yet it took 10 years for six teams of workers from 10 institutions to find the gene. It is a so-called expanding gene, which for unknown reasons gains base pairs (the chemical "rungs" binding two strands of DNA) every time it is transmitted. The greater the expansion of the gene, researchers say, the earlier the onset of the disease. The search was complicated by the fact that workers had no physical clues about the course of the disease to guide them. Indeed, Wexler and others emphasize that they still have no idea how the gene actually causes the disease; treatments or cures may be years or decades away.

The most immediate impact of the new discovery will be the development of a better test for Huntington's, one that requires blood only from the person at risk

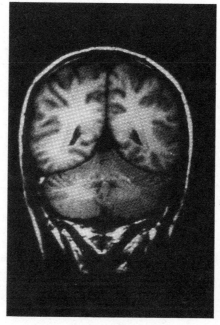 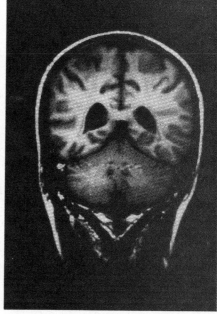

NANCY WEXLER helped to find the gene responsible for Huntington's disease by studying a population in Venezuela that has been ravaged by the disorder.

and not other family members. By measuring the length of the mutant gene, the test might also predict more accurately when carriers will show symptoms.

As difficult as it was to pinpoint the gene for Huntington's, it will be almost infinitely harder to discover genes for behavioral disorders, says Evan S. Balaban, a biologist at Harvard University. Unlike Huntington's disease, he notes, disorders such as schizophrenia and alcoholism cannot be unambiguously diagnosed. Furthermore, they stem not from a single dominant gene but from many genes acting in concert with environmental effects. If researchers do find a statistical association between certain genes and a trait, Balaban says, that knowledge may never be translated into useful therapies or tests. "What does it mean to have a 10 percent increased risk of alcoholism?" he asks.

no association between the D2 receptor and alcoholism, either in the disorder's milder or most severe forms. "We therefore conclude that no physiologically significant association" between the A1 allele and alcoholism has been proved, the group stated. "It's a dead issue," Risch says.

Gelernter and his colleagues point out that association studies are prone to spurious results if not properly controlled. They suggest that the positive findings of Blum and his colleagues may have derived from a failure to control for ethnic variation. The limited surveys done so far have shown that the incidence of the A1 allele varies wildly in different ethnic groups, ranging from 10 percent in certain Jewish groups to about 50 percent in Japanese.

Blum insists that the ethnic data, far from undermining his case, support it,

since those groups with the highest prevalence of the A1 allele also exhibit the highest rates of "addictive behavior." He contends that the only reason the Japanese do not display higher rates of alcoholism is that many also carry a gene that prevents them from metabolizing alcohol. "They're pretty compulsive," explains Blum, who recently obtained a patent for a genetic test for alcoholism.

These arguments have been rejected even by Irving I. Gottesman of the University of Virginia, who is a strong defender of genetic models of human behavior. He considers the papers cited by Blum to support his case to be ambiguous and even contradictory. Some see an association only with alcoholism that leads to medical complications or even death; others discern no association with alcoholism but only with "polysubstance abuse," including cigarette smoking. "I think it is by and large

garbage," Gottesman says of the alleged A1-alcoholism link.

By far the most controversial area of behavioral genetics is research on crime. Last fall complaints by civil-rights leaders and others led the National Institutes of Health to withdraw its funding from a meeting entitled "Genetic Factors in Crime: Findings, Uses and Implications." The conference brochure had noted the "apparent failure of environmental approaches to crime" and suggested that genetic research might yield methods for identifying and treating potists, notably Richard J. Herrnstein, a psychologist at Harvard, have made this assertion. Others reject this view but insist biological research on attributes linked to violent crime, such as aggression, may still have some value. "People who are unwilling to address genetic and biochemical factors are just putting their heads in the sand," says Goldman, the alcoholism expert. "It is not fair to say that just because there have been geneticists who have had a very narrow view of this in the past, we shouldn't explore this now."

In fact, investigations of the biology of violent crime continue, albeit quietly. Workers at City of Hope Hospital in Duarte, Calif., claim to have found an association between the A1 allele—the alleged alcoholism marker—and "criminal aggression." Last year a group led by Markus J. P. Kruesi of the University of Illinois at Chicago presented evidence of an association between low levels of the neurotransmitter serotonin and disruptive-behavior disorders in children. Kruesi concedes there is no way to determine whether the serotonin levels are genetically influenced. In fact, the serotonin levels might be an effect—a reaction to an environmental trauma—rather than a cause. "This might be a scar marker," he says.

One reason such research persists is that studies of families, twins and adoptees have suggested a genetic component to crime. Glenn D. Walters, a psychologist at the Federal Correctional Institution in Schuylkill, Pa., recently reviewed 38 of these studies, conducted from the 1930s to the present, in the journal *Criminology*. His meta-analysis turned up a small genetic effect, "but nothing to get excited about." He observes that "a lot of the research has not been very good" and that the more recent, better-designed studies tended to turn up less evidence. "I don't think we will find any biological markers for crime," he says. "We should put our resources elsewhere."

"Better Breeding"

Fairly or not, modern genetics research is still haunted by the history of eugenics. "It offers a lot of cautionary lessons," says Daniel J. Kevles, a historian at the California Institute of Technology, who wrote the 1985 book *In the Name of Eugenics*. The British scientist Francis Galton, cousin to Charles Darwin, first proposed that human society could be improved "through better breeding" in 1865 in an article entitled "Hereditary Talent and Character." He coined the term "eugenics," from the Greek for "good birth," in 1883.

Galton's proposal had broad appeal. The American sexual libertarian John Humphrey Noyes bent eugenics into an ingenious argument for polygamy. "While the good man will be limited by his conscience to what the law allows," Noyes said, "the bad man, free from moral check, will distribute his seed beyond the legal limit."

A more serious advocate was the biologist Charles B. Davenport, founder of Cold Spring Harbor Laboratory and of the Eugenics Record Office, which gathered information on thousands of American families for genetic research. After demonstrating the heritability of eye, skin and hair color, Davenport went on to "prove" the heritability of traits such as "pauperism," criminality and "feeble-mindedness." In one monograph, published in 1919, he asserted that the ability to be a naval officer is an inherited trait, composed of subtraits for thalassophilia, or love of the sea, and hyperkineticism, or wanderlust. Noting the paucity of female naval officers, Davenport concluded that the trait is unique to males.

Beginning in the 1920s the American Eugenics Society, founded by Davenport and others, sponsored "Fitter Families Contests" at state fairs around the U.S. Just as cows and sheep were appraised by judges at the fairs, so were human entrants (such as the family shown above at the 1925 Texas State Fair). Less amusingly, eugenicists helped to persuade more than 20 U.S. states to authorize sterilization of men and women in prisons and mental hospitals, and they urged the federal government to restrict the immigration of "undesirable" races.

No nation, of course, practiced eugenics as enthusiastically as Nazi Germany, whose program culminated in "euthanasia" ("good death") of the mentally and physically disabled as well as Jews, Gypsies, Catholics and others. As revelations of these atrocities spread after World War II, popular support for eugenics programs waned in the U.S. and elsewhere.

Gay Genes

The ostensible purpose of investigations of mental illness, alcoholism and even crime is to reduce their incidence. Scientists studying homosexuality have a different goal: simply to test whether homosexuality is innate, as many homosexuals have long professed. That claim was advanced by a report in *Science* in 1991 by Simon LeVay of the Salk Institute for Biological Studies in San Diego. LeVay has acknowledged both that he is gay and that he believes evidence of biological differences between homosexuals and heterosexuals will encourage tolerance toward gays.

LeVay, who recently left the Salk Institute to found the Institute of Gay and Lesbian Education, focused on a tiny neural structure in the hypothalamus, a region of the brain known to control sexual response. He measured this structure, called the interstitial nucleus, in autopsies of the brains of 19 homosexual males, 16 heterosexual males and six heterosexual women. LeVay found that the interstitial nucleus was almost twice as large in the heterosexual males as in the homosexual males or in the women. He postulated that the interstitial nucleus "is large in individuals oriented toward women"—whether male or female.

Of course, LeVay's finding only addresses anatomic differences, not necessarily genetic ones. Various other researchers have tried to establish that homosexuality is not just biological in its origin—caused, perhaps, by hormonal influences in utero—but also genetic. Some have sought evidence in experiments with rats and other animals. A group headed by Angela Pattatucci of the National Cancer Institute is studying a strain of male fruit flies—which wags have dubbed either "fruity" or "fruitless"—that court other males.

In December 1991 J. Michael Bailey of Northwestern University and Richard C. Pillard of Boston University announced they had uncovered evidence of a genetic basis for male homosexuality in humans. They studied 161 gay men, each of whom had at least one identical or fraternal twin or adopted brother. The researchers determined that 52 percent of the identical twins were both homosexual, as compared with 22 percent of the fraternal twins and 11 percent of the adopted brothers.

Bailey and Pillard derived similar results in a study of lesbians published this year in the *Archives of General Psychiatry*. They compared 147 gay women with identical or fraternal twins or adopted sisters: 48 percent of the identical twins were both gay, versus 16 percent of the fraternal twins (who share only half each other's genes) and 6 percent of the adopted sisters. "Both male and female sexual orientation appeared to be influenced by genetic factors," Bailey and Pillard concluded.

This conclusion has disturbed some of Bailey and Pillard's own subjects. "I have major questions about the validity of some of the assumptions they are making," says Nina Sossen, a gay woman living in Madison, Wis., whose identical twin is heterosexual. Her doubts are shared by William Byne, a psychiatrist at Columbia University. He notes that in their study of male homosexuality Bailey and Pillard found more concordance between unrelated, adopted brothers than related (but non-twin) brothers. The high concordance of the male and female identical twins, moreover, may stem from the fact that such twins are often dressed alike and treated alike—indeed, they are often mistaken for each other—by family members as well as by others.

"The increased concordance for homosexuality among the identical twins could be entirely accounted for by the increased similarity of their developmental experiences," Byne says. "In my opinion, the major finding of that study is that 48 percent of identical twins who were reared together were discordant for sexual orientation."

Byne also criticizes LeVay's conclusion that homosexuality must be biological—although not necessarily genetic—because the brains of male homosexuals resemble the brains of women. That assumption, Byne points out, rests on still another assumption, that there are significant anatomic differences between heterosexual male and female brains. But to date, there have been no replicable studies showing such sexual dimorphism.

Byne notes that he has been suspected of having an antigay motive. Two reviewers of an article he recently wrote criticizing homosexuality research accused him of having a "right-wing agenda," he says. He has also been contacted by conservative groups hoping he will speak out against the admittance of homosexuals to the military. He emphasizes that he supports gay rights and thinks homosexuality, whatever its cause, is not a "choice." He adds that genetic models of behavior are just as likely to foment bigotry as to quell it.

"Hierarchy of Worthlessness"

Despite the skepticism of Byne and others, at least one group, led by Dean Hamer of the National Cancer Institute, is searching not merely for anatomic or biochemical differences in homosexuals but for genetic markers. Hamer has done a linkage study of numerous small families, each of which has at least two gay brothers. He says his study has turned up some tentative findings, and he plans to submit his results soon. Hamer's colleague Pattatucci is planning a similar study of lesbians.

What purpose will be served by pinpointing genes linked to homosexuality? In an information sheet for prospective participants in his study, Hamer expresses the hope that his research may "improve understanding between people with different sexual orientations." He adds, "This study is not aimed at developing methods to alter either heterosexual or homosexual orientation, and the results of the study will not allow sexual orientation to be determined by a blood test or amniocentesis."

Yet even Pillard, who is gay and applauds Hamer's work, admits to some concern over the potential uses of a genetic marker for homosexuality. He notes that some parents might choose to abort embryos carrying such a marker. Male and female homosexuals might then retaliate, he says, by conceiving children and aborting fetuses that lacked such a gene.

Balaban, the Harvard biologist, thinks the possible dangers of such research—assuming it is successful—outweigh any benefits. Indeed, he sees behavioral genetics as a "hierarchy of worthlessness," with twin studies at the bottom and linkage studies of mental illness at the top. The best researchers can hope for is to find, say, a gene associated with a slightly elevated risk of schizophrenia. Such information is more likely to lead

to discrimination by insurance companies and employers than to therapeutic benefits, Balaban warns.

His colleague Lewontin agrees. In the 1970s, he recalls, insurance companies began requiring black customers to take tests for sickle cell anemia, a genetic disease that primarily affects blacks. Those who refused to take the test or who tested positive were denied coverage. "I feel that this research is a substitute for what is really hard—finding out how to change social conditions," Lewontin remarks. "I think it's the wrong direction for research, given that we have a finite amount of resources."

Paul R. Billings, a geneticist at the California Pacific Medical Center, shares some of these concerns. He agrees that twin studies seem to be inherently ambiguous, and he urges researchers seeking markers for homosexuality to consider what a conservative government—led by Patrick Buchanan, for example—might allow to be done with such information. But he believes some aspects of behavioral genetics, particularly searches for genes underlying mental illness, are worth pursuing.

In an article published in the British journal *Social Science and Medicine* last year, Billings and two other scientists offered some constructive criticism for the field. Researchers engaged in association and linkage studies should establish "strict criteria as to what would constitute meaningful data." Both scientists and the press should emphasize the limitations of such studies, "especially when the mechanism of how a gene acts on a behavior is not known." Billings and his colleagues strive to end their article on a positive note. "Despite the shortcomings of other studies," they say, "there is relatively good evidence for a site on the X chromosome which is associated with [manic depression] in some families." This finding was retracted earlier this year.

Development During Infancy and Early Childhood

No period in human development has received more attention during the past quarter century than infancy. Much of this research has been stimulated by Jean Piaget, the Swiss developmental theorist, who argued that the many abilities of the infant evolved slowly over the first 2 years as a product of the combined forces of maturation and experience. A major portion of this research has focused on infants' perceptual skills and cognitive abilities. These studies have made it quite apparent that infants are far from the passive, unknowing beings they were once thought to be. In fact, many of these abilities appear so early that Piaget's views are now being strongly challenged. In "A New Perspective on Cognitive Development in Infancy," a leading researcher, Jean Mandler, advances a competing view that the perceptual and cognitive abilities of the infant are more a part of the basic endowment of the child than a product of learning and practice. "The Amazing Minds of Infants" further explores the remarkable competencies revealed by babies in recent studies of memory, language, and understanding of the physical world.

The many skills of the newborn multiply dramatically over the first several years of life, transforming the physically helpless infant into a child who, by age 3 years or even earlier, is capable of thinking, communicating, and skillfully solving problems. Knowledge of the readiness to learn that is now so evident in infants and toddlers has brought with it questions about the best ways to nurture early intellectual and social development. As Bruce Bower notes in "A Child's Theory of Mind," knowledge about mental states and attitudes changes substantially throughout childhood. There is a continuing debate revolving around the clashing explanations of how and why change takes place. Then, David and Barbara Bjorklund address the ability of preschoolers to remember. According to "I Forget," young children's memory abilities do grow at a rapid pace. Developments in recall memory, selective attention, and memory for routines improve dramatically during the preschool period.

Cultures differ widely in their definition of appropriate roles for the two sexes. For more than a century, scientists have been debating the source of gender differences. As gender research has become more sophisticated, it has also become more controversial. However, most scientists agree that the sexes are more alike than different, with greater variation within each sex than between the sexes. Are boys really better at math and girls more verbal? Are girls really kinder and gentler and boys more aggressive? "Sizing Up the Sexes" examines recent research on this topic and puts forth the argument that hormonal differences and brain structure play a far more important role in gender differences than has been assumed in the past.

"The Day Care Generation" considers a critical problem in the United States: the lack of quality child-care facilities for children. Over 50 percent of working mothers have children under the age of 6. This statistic underlines the magnitude of the problem and the urgent need for effective solutions. Parents must choose among various day care options without the aid of any "industry-wide" standards, knowing that day care centers are operated with practically no federal or state regulations or guidelines to ensure quality. The article identifies a number of key factors to consider in evaluating day care arrangements and reviews some of the studies that have played an important role in the national debate over early child care.

Looking Ahead: Challenge Questions

How have scientists' views about the competencies of the infant changed in the past several decades?

What effect does work have on the development of attachment relationships between mother and infant, or the effectiveness of discipline in school-age children? Does society have a responsibility to provide supplementary care for children of working mothers? Does industry have this responsibility?

Why has so much effort been devoted to the study of sex differences in the past several decades? How would you summarize in brief the general feelings of this body of research?

A New Perspective on Cognitive Development in Infancy

Jean M. Mandler

Jean Mandler received her Ph.D. from Harvard in 1956. She is currently professor of psychology and cognitive science at the University of California, San Diego. Her interests are cognition and cognitive development, with emphasis on the representation of knowledge. She has done research on how our knowledge of stories, events, and scenes is organized and the way in which such organization affects remembering. In recent years her research has concentrated on conceptual development in infancy and early childhood. Preparation of this article was supported by an NSF grant. Address: Department of Cognitive Science D-015, University of California, San Diego, La Jolla, CA 92093.

Over the past decade something of a revolution has been taking place in our understanding of cognitive development during infancy. For many years one theory dominated the field—that of the Swiss psychologist Jean Piaget. Piaget's views on infancy were so widely known and respected that to many psychologists at least one aspect of development seemed certain: human infants go through a protracted period during which they cannot yet think. They can learn to recognize things and to smile at them, to crawl and to manipulate objects, but they do not yet have concepts or ideas. This period, which Piaget called the sensorimotor stage of development, was said to last until one-and-a-half to two years of age. Only near the end of this stage do infants learn how to represent the world in a symbolic, conceptual manner, and thus advance from infancy into early childhood.

Piaget formulated this view of infancy primarily by observing the development of his own three children—few laboratory techniques were available at the time. More recently, experimental methods have been devised to study infants, and a large body of research has been accumulating. Much of the new work suggests that the theory of a sensori-motor stage of development will have to be substantially modified or perhaps even abandoned (Fig. 1). The present article provides a brief overview of Piaget's theory of sensorimotor development, a summary of recent data that are difficult to reconcile with that theory, and an outline of an alternative view of early mental development.

In Piaget's (1951, 1952, 1954) theory, the first stage of development is said to consist of sensorimotor (perceptual and motor) functioning in an

Recent research suggests that infants have the ability to conceptualize much earlier than we thought

organism that has not yet acquired a representational (conceptual) capacity. The only knowledge infants have is what things look and sound like and how to move themselves around and manipulate objects. This kind of sensorimotor knowledge is often termed procedural or implicit knowledge, and is contrasted with explicit, factual (conceptual) knowledge (e.g., Cohen and Squire 1980; Schacter 1987; Mandler 1988). Factual knowledge is the kind of knowledge one can think about or recall; it is usually considered to be symbolic and propositional. Some factual information may be stored in the form of images, but these are also symbolic, in the sense that they are constructed from both propositional and spatial knowledge. Sensorimotor knowledge, on the other hand, is subsymbolic knowledge; it is knowing *how* to recognize something or use a motor skill, but it does not require explicitly knowing *that* something is the case. It is the

kind of knowledge we build into robots in order to make them recognize and manipulate objects in their environment, and it is also the kind of knowledge we ascribe to lower organisms, which function quite well without the ability to conceptualize facts. It is the kind of knowledge that tends to remain undisturbed in amnesic patients, even when their memory for facts and their personal past is severely impaired.

In the case of babies, the restriction of functioning to sensorimotor processing implies that they can neither think about absent objects nor recall the past. According to Piaget, they lack the capacity even to form an image of things they have seen before; a fortiori, they have no capacity to imagine what will happen tomorrow. Thus, the absence of a symbolic capacity does not mean just that infants cannot understand language or reason; it means that they cannot remember what they did this morning or imagine their mother if she is not present. It is, in short, a most un-Proustian life, not thought about, only lived (Mandler 1983).

According to Piaget, to be able to think about the world requires first that perceptual-motor schemas of objects and relations among them be formed. Then, symbols must be created to stand for these schemas. Several aspects of Piaget's formulation account for the slow course of both these developments. First, on the basis of his observations Piaget assumed that the sensory modalities are unconnected at birth, each delivering separate types of information. Thus, he thought that one of the major tasks of the first half of the sensorimotor stage is to construct schemas integrating the information from initially disconnected sights, sounds, and touches. Until this integration is

50

From *American Scientist*, Vol. 78, No. 3, May/June 1990, pp. 236-243. Reprinted by permission of *American Scientist*, journal of Sigma Xi, The Scientific Research Society.

accomplished, stable sensorimotor schemas of three-dimensional, solid, sound-producing, textured objects cannot be formed and hence cannot be thought about.

In addition, babies must learn about the causal interrelatedness of objects and the fact that objects continue to exist when not being perceived. Piaget thought that these notions were among the major accomplishments of the second half of the sensorimotor stage. He suggested that they derive from manual activity—for example, repeated covering and uncovering, poking, pushing, and dropping objects while observ-

represent bottles in their absence.

All the anticipatory behavior that Piaget observed throughout the first 18 months was accounted for in similar terms. Signs of anticipation of future events became more wide-ranging and complex but did not seem to require the use of images or other symbols to represent what was about to happen. Rather, Piaget assumed that an established sensorimotor schema set up a kind of imageless expectation of the next event, followed by recognition when the event took place. He used strict criteria for the presence of imagery—for example, verbal recall of the past

Figure 1. According to the Swiss psychologist Jean Piaget, babies like the author's 8-month-old grandson shown here have learned to recognize people, and their smile is a sign of that recognition. However, Piaget believed that babies have not yet learned to think at such an early age and thus cannot recall even the most familiar people in their lives when those people are not present. Recent research suggests that this view may be mistaken and that babies such as this one are already forming concepts about people and things in their environment.

William James described the perceptual world of the infant as a "blooming, buzzing confusion."

ing the results. Handling objects leads to understanding them; it allows the integration of perceptual and motor information that gives objects substantiality, permanence, and unique identities separate from the self. Since motor control over the hands is slow to develop, to the extent that conceptual understanding requires physical interaction with objects, it is necessarily a late development. Much of the first year of life, then, is spent accomplishing the coordination of the various sources of perceptual and motor information required to form the sensorimotor object schemas that will then be available to be conceptualized.

According to Piaget, the development of the symbolic function is itself a protracted process. In addition to constructing sensorimotor schemas of objects and relations, which form the basic content or meaning of what is to be thought about, symbols to refer to these meanings must be formed. Piaget assumed that the latter development has its precursors in the expectancies involved in conditioning. For example, the sight of a bottle can serve as a signal that milk will follow, and babies soon learn to make anticipatory sucking movements. This process, essentially the same as that involved in Pavlovian conditioning, does not imply a symbolic function; there is no indication that the baby can use such signals to

(which implies the ability to represent absent events to oneself) or rapid problem-solving without trial and error. Neither of these can be ascribed merely to running off a practiced sensorimotor schema, but they require instead some representation of information not perceptually present.

Piaget did not observe recall or covert problem-solving until the end of the sensorimotor period. One might think that the fact that infants begin to acquire language during the latter part of the first year would be difficult to reconcile with a lack of symbolic capacity. However, Piaget characterized early words as imitative schemas, no different in kind from other motor schemas displayed in the presence of familiar situations.

Imitation, in fact, plays an important role in this account, because it provides the source of the development of imagery. Piaget assumed that images are not formed merely from looking at or hearing something, but arise only when what is being perceived is also analyzed. The attempt to imitate the actions of others provides the stimulus for such analysis to take place. Although infants begin to imitate early, it was not until near the end of the first year or beyond that Piaget found his children able to imitate novel actions or actions involving parts of their bodies they could not see themselves, such as blinking or sticking out their

tongues. He took this difficulty as evidence that they could not form an image of something complex or unobserved until detailed analysis of it had taken place; it is presumably during this analysis that imagery is constructed. Piaget's study of imitation suggested that such analysis, and therefore the formation of imagery, was a late development in infancy. To complete the process of symbol formation, then, the anticipatory mechanisms of sensorimotor schemas become speeded up and appear as images of what will occur, thus allowing genuine representation. Finally, by some mechanism left unspecified, these newly created images can be used to represent the world independent of ongoing sensorimotor activity.

All these developments—constructing sensorimotor schemas, establishing a coherent world of objects and events suitable to form the content of ideas, learning to imitate and to form images that can be used to stand for things—are completed in the second half of the second year, and result in the child's at last being able to develop a conceptual system of ideas. Images can now be used to recall the past and to imagine the future, and even perceptually present objects can begin to be interpreted conceptually as well as by means of motor interactions with them. With the onset of thought, an infant is well on the way to becoming fully human.

This theory of the sensorimotor foundations of thought has come under attack from two sources. One is experimental work suggesting that a stable and differentiated perceptual world is established much earlier in infancy than Piaget realized. The other is recent work suggesting that recall and other forms of symbolic activity (presumably mediated by imagery) occur by at least the second half of the first year. I will discuss each of these findings in turn.

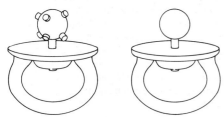

Figure 2. The old idea that the senses are unconnected at birth and are gradually integrated through experience is contradicted by an experiment using bumpy and smooth pacifiers to study the visual recognition of an object that has been experienced only tactilely. A one-month-old infant is habituated to one of the two kinds of pacifiers in its mouth without being allowed to see it. The pacifier is then removed, and the infant is shown both kinds of pacifiers. Infants look longer at the nipple they felt in their mouth. (After Meltzoff and Borton 1979.)

Perceptual development

The notion that the senses are unconnected at birth and that they become integrated only through experience is an old idea that was popularized by William James's (1890) description of the perceptual world of the infant as a "blooming, buzzing confusion." Recent work, however, suggests that either the senses are interrelated at birth or the learning involved in their integration is extremely rapid. There is evidence for integration of auditory and visual information as well as of vision and touch in the first months of life. What follows is a small sample of the research findings.

From birth, infants turn their heads to look at the source of a sound (Wertheimer 1961; Mendelson and Haith 1976). This does not mean that they have any particular expectations of what they will see when they hear a given sound, but it does indicate a mechanism that would enable rapid learning. By four months, if one presents two films of complex events not seen before and accompanied by a single sound track, infants prefer to look at the film that matches the sound (Spelke 1979). Perhaps even more surprising, when infants are presented with two films, each showing only a speaker's face, they will choose the correct film, even when the synchrony between both films and the soundtrack is identical (Kuhl and Meltzoff 1988). In addition, one-month-olds can recognize visually presented objects that they have only felt in their mouths (Fig. 2; Meltzoff and Borton 1979; Walker-Andrews and Gibson 1986). Such data suggest either that the output of each sensory transducer consists in part of the same amodal pattern of information or that some central processing of two similar patterns of information is accomplished. In either case, the data strongly support the view that there is more order and coherence in early perceptual experience than Piaget or James realized.

In addition to sensory coordination, a good deal of information about the nature of objects is provided by the visual system alone, information to which young infants have been shown to be sensitive. For example, it used to be thought that infants have difficulty separating objects from a background, but it ap-

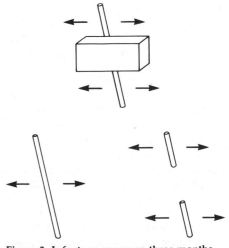

Figure 3. Infants as young as three months can use the perception of relative movement to determine object boundaries. They are habituated to the display shown at the top, which represents a rod moving back and forth behind a block of wood. Then they are tested with the two displays on the bottom: the rod moving as it did before, but with no block in front, or the two pieces of the rod that were visible behind the block, also moving as they did before. Infants tend to continue to habituate to the whole moving rod—that is, they cease to look at it, indicating that it is familiar to them. They prefer to look at the broken rod, indicating that they consider it something new. If the same experiment is done with a stationary rod behind a block, infants exhibit no preference when presented with a whole stationary rod or a broken stationary rod. (After Kellman and Spelke 1983.)

pears that such confusion is a rare event, not the norm. Infants may not "see" that a cup is separable from a saucer without picking it up, but in general they do not have difficulty determining the boundaries of objects. They use information from motion to parse objects from the perceptual surround long before they are able to manipulate them manually. At an age as young as three months, they can use the relative motion of objects against both stationary and moving backgrounds to determine the objects' boundaries (Fig. 3; Kellman and Spelke 1983; Spelke 1988). Even stationary objects are seen as separate if they are spatially separated, whether in a plane or in depth. Infants also use motion to determine object identity, treating an object that moves behind a screen and then reappears as one object rather than two (Spelke and Kestenbaum 1986).

Other work by Spelke and by

Baillargeon (Baillargeon et al. 1985; Baillargeon 1987a; Spelke 1988) shows that infants as young as four months expect objects to be substantial, in the sense that the objects cannot move through other objects nor other objects through them (Fig. 4), and permanent, in the sense that the objects are assumed to continue to exist when hidden. Finally, there is evidence that by six months infants perceive causal relations among moving objects (Leslie 1988) in a fashion that seems to be qualitatively the same as that of adults (Michotte 1963).

From this extensive research program, we can conclude that objects are seen as bounded, unitary, solid, and separate from the background, perhaps from birth but certainly by three to four months of age. Such young infants obviously still have a great deal to learn about objects, but the world must appear both stable and orderly to them, and thus capable of being conceptualized.

Conceptual development

It is easier to study what infants see than what they are thinking about. Nevertheless, there are a few ways to assess whether or not infants are thinking. One way is to look for symbolic activity, such as using a gesture to refer to something else. Piaget (1952) himself called attention to a phenomenon he called motor recognition. For example, he observed his six-month-old daughter make a gesture on catching sight of a familiar toy in a new location. She was accustomed to kicking at the toy in her crib, and when she saw it across the room she made a brief, abbreviated kicking motion. Piaget did not consider this true symbolic activity, because it was a motor movement, not a purely mental act; nevertheless, he suggested that his daughter was referring to, or classifying, the toy by means of her action. In a similar vein, infants whose parents use sign language have been observed to begin to use conventional signs at around six to seven months (Prinz and Prinz 1979; Bonvillian et al. 1983; see Mandler 1988 for discussion).

Another type of evidence of conceptual functioning is recall of absent objects or events. Indeed, Piaget accepted recall as irrefutable evidence

of conceptual representation, since there is no way to account for recreating information that is not perceptually present by means of sensorimotor schemas alone; imagery or other symbolic means of representation must be involved. Typically we associate recall with verbal recreation of the past, and this, as Piaget observed, is not usually found until 18 months or older. But recall need not be verbal—and indeed is usually not when we think about past events—so that in principle it is possible in preverbal infants.

One needs to see a baby do something like find a hidden object after a delay or imitate a previously observed event. Until recently, only diary studies provided evidence of recall in the second half of the first year—for example, finding an object hidden in an unfamiliar location after

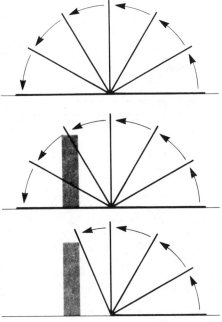

Figure 4. Shown here is a procedure used to demonstrate four- and five-month-olds' memory for the location of a hidden object. At the top is a screen moving through a 180° rotation, to which infants viewing from the right are habituated by repetition. Following habituation, a box is placed behind the screen, and the infants see two test events: an impossible (*middle*) and a possible event (*bottom*). In the impossible event, the screen continues to rotate 180°, moving "magically" through the hidden box (which the experimenter has surreptitiously removed). In the possible event, the screen rotates only to the point where it would hit the box. The infants' surprise at the impossible event demonstrates that they remember an object they cannot see. (After Baillargeon 1987a.)

a 24-hour delay (Ashmead and Perlmutter 1980). Now, however, similar phenomena are beginning to be demonstrated in the laboratory. Meltzoff (1988) showed that nine-month-olds could imitate actions that they had seen performed 24 hours earlier. Each action consisted of an unusual gesture with a novel object—for example, pushing a recessed button in a box (which produced a beeping sound)—and the infants were limited to watching the experimenter carry it out; thus, when they later imitated the action, they could not be merely running off a practiced motor schema in response to seeing the object again. Control subjects, who had been shown the objects but not the actions performed on them, made the correct responses much less frequently. We have replicated this phenomenon with 11-month-olds (McDonough and Mandler 1989).

Because of the difficulties that young infants have manipulating objects, it is not obvious that this technique can be used with infants younger than about eight months. One suspects, however, that if nine-month-olds can recall several novel events after a 24-hour delay, somewhat younger infants can probably recall similar events after shorter delays.

There is a small amount of data from a procedure that does not require a motor response and that, although using quite short delays, suggests recall-like processes. Baillargeon's experiments on object permanence, mentioned earlier, use a technique that requires infants to remember that an object is hidden behind a screen. For example, she has shown that infants are surprised when a screen appears to move backward through an object they have just seen hidden behind it (see Fig. 4). In her experiments with four- and five-month-olds, the infants had to remember for only about 8 to 12 seconds that there was an object behind the screen (Baillargeon et al. 1985; Baillargeon 1987a). However, in more recent work with eight-month-olds, Baillargeon and her colleagues have been successful with a delay of 70 seconds (Fig. 5; Baillargeon et al. 1989). This kind of performance seems to require a representational capacity not attributable to sensorimotor schemas. Not only is an absent

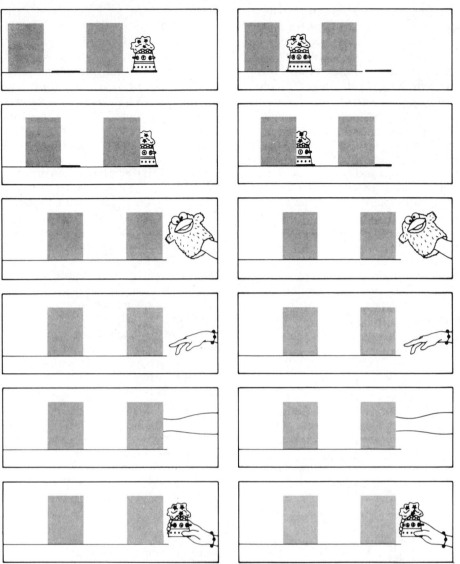

Figure 5. Another procedure involving possible *(left)* and impossible events *(right)* elicits meaningful responses from eight-month-old infants after a delay of 70 seconds. Moving from top to bottom, an object is hidden respectively behind the right or left of two screens; puppets and hand tiptoes are used to keep infants attentive during the delay period; the experimenter reaches behind the right screen and brings the hidden object into view from behind it. (The object was placed there surreptitiously as part of the impossible event.) Surprise at the impossible event indicates memory of the place where the object was hidden. The apparent recall suggests a kind of conceptual functioning that goes beyond the sensorimotor functioning described by Piaget. (After Baillargeon et al. 1989.)

object being represented, but the information is rather precise—for example, Baillargeon (1987b) found that infants remembered not only that an object was hidden but where it was located and how tall it was.

Where do concepts come from?

The data described above indicate that the theory of an exclusively sensorimotor stage of development, in which babies cannot yet represent the world conceptually, is in need of considerable revision. There does not

appear to be a protracted period during which infants have no conception of objects or events and cannot represent them in their absence. A great deal of information is available to and used by infants from an early age, even before they have developed the motor coordination enabling manual exploration that Piaget thought was crucial to conceptual development.

Indeed, a good deal of evidence suggests that we have tended to confuse infants' motor incompetence with conceptual incompetence. Piaget was particularly influenced in his theorizing by the difficulties that

children as old as a year have finding a hidden object, especially when it is hidden in more than one location a number of times in succession. The phenomena he demonstrated have been replicated many times, but it now appears that much of the difficulty infants have in such situations is due not to a lack of understanding of object permanence but to other factors. For example, repeatedly hiding an object in different locations can be confusing and leads to perseverative responding to the same place (see Diamond 1985; Mandler 1988, in press).

If a conceptual system of knowledge has begun to be formed by at least six months and perhaps earlier, where does it come from? Piaget's theory of a transformation of well-developed action schemas into conceptual thought cannot account for conceptual knowledge occurring before the action schemas themselves have developed. On the other hand, perceptual schemas about objects and events develop early. What is needed, then, is some mechanism for transforming these schemas into concepts, or ideas, about what is being perceived, preferably a mechanism that can operate as soon as perceptual schemas are formed.

Little has been written about this problem. One approach is to assume that even young infants are capable of redescribing perceptual information in a conceptual format. I have suggested a mechanism that might accomplish this (Mandler 1988): perceptual analysis, a process by which one perception is actively compared to another and similarities or differences between them are noted. (Such analysis, like other sorts of concept formation, requires some kind of vocabulary; this aspect, still little understood, is discussed below.) The simplest case of perceptual analysis occurs when two simultaneously presented objects are compared, or a single object is compared to an already established representation (i.e., one notes similarities or differences between what one is looking at and what one recalls about it). It is the process by which we discover that sugar bowls have two handles and teacups only one, or that a friend wears glasses. Unless we have engaged in this kind of analysis (or someone has told us), the information will not be accessible for us to think about. Much of the time, of course, we do not make such comparisons, which is why we often can recall few details of even recent experiences.

Although it is analytic, perceptual analysis consists primarily of simplification. Our perceptual system regularly processes vast amounts of information that never become accessible to thought. For example, we make use of a great deal of complex information every time we recognize a face: proportions, contours, subtle shading, relationships among various facial features, and so on. Yet little of this information is available to our thought processes. Few people are aware of the proportions of the human face—it is not something they have ever conceptualized. Even fewer know how they determine whether a face is male or female (this categorization depends on subtle differences in proportions). For the most part we do not even have words to describe the nuances that our perceptual apparatus uses instantly and effortlessly to make such a perceptual categorization.

For us to be able to think about such matters, the information must be reduced and simplified into a conceptual format. One way this redescription is done is via language; someone (perhaps an artist who has already carried out the relevant analytic process) conceptualizes aspects of a face for us. The other way is to look at a face and analyze it ourselves, such as noting that the ears are at the same level as the eyes. The analysis is often couched in linguistic form, but it need not be. Images can be used, but these, in spite of having spatial properties, have a major conceptual component (e.g., Kosslyn 1983).

An infant, of course, does not have the benefit of language, the means by which older people acquire much of their factual knowledge. So if infants are to transform perceptual schemas into thoughts, they must be able to analyze the perceptual information they receive. The perceptual system itself cannot decide that only animate creatures move by themselves or that containers must have bottoms if they are to hold things, and so forth. These are facts visually observed, but they are highly simpli-

Infants whose parents use sign language have been observed to begin to use conventional signs at around six to seven months

fied versions of the information available to be conceptualized.

The notion of perceptual analysis is similar to the process that Piaget theorized as being responsible for the creation of images. He thought that this kind of analysis does not even begin until around eight or nine months and does not result in imagery until later still. However, he had no evidence that image formation is such a late-developing process, and his own description of his children's imitative performance as early as three or four months strongly suggests that the process of perceptual analysis had begun. For example, he observed imitation of clapping hands at that time, a performance that would seem to require a good deal of analysis, considering the difference between what infants see and what they must do. In many places in his account of early imitation, Piaget

noted that the infants watched him carefully, studying both their own and his actions. Other developmental psychologists have commented on the same phenomenon. For example, Werner and Kaplan (1963) noted that infants begin "contemplating" objects at between three and five months. Ruff (1986) has documented intense examination of objects at six months (the earliest age she studied).

To investigate contemplation or analysis of objects experimentally is not easy. A possible measure is the number of times an infant looks back and forth between two objects that are presented simultaneously. Janowsky (1985), for example, showed that this measure increased significantly between four and eight months. At four months infants tend to look first at one object and then the other; at eight months they switch back and forth between the two a

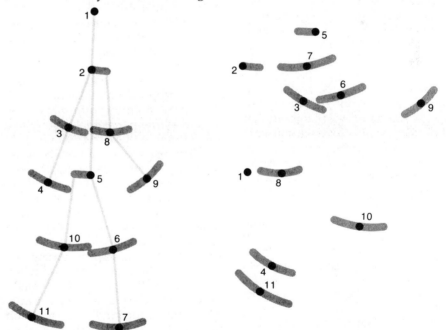

Figure 6. An equally subtle ability is involved in this demonstration of three-month-olds' responses to biological as opposed to nonbiological motion. The infants watch videotapes of computer-generated displays. On the left is a display of 11 point-lights moving as if attached to the head and major joints of a person walking. The motion vectors drawn through each point represent the perceived motions of the display; the lines connecting points, like the numbers and vectors, are not visible to the infants. The display on the right is identical to the normal walker except that the relative locations of the point-lights are scrambled. Correspondingly numbered points in the two displays undergo identical motions. Infants show greater interest in the scrambled display, indicating that they consider it novel. (After Bertenthal et al. 1987.)

good many times. Fox and his colleagues (1979) have reported a similar phenomenon. Interestingly, Janowsky found that the differences in looking back and forth are not associated with differences in total looking time, the rate at which infants habituate to objects (cease to look at them), or accuracy of recognition. So the looking back and forth must serve some other function. I would suggest that it is a comparison process, by which one object is being contrasted with the other.

A vocabulary for concepts

Assuming that perceptual analysis can lead to concept formation, it is still necessary to formulate the vocabulary in which the resulting concepts are couched. But here we face one of the major stumbling blocks in psychological theory: the problem of specifying conceptual primitives (see Smith and Medin 1981). Perhaps because of its difficulty, it has been largely ignored by developmental psychologists, in spite of the fact that any theory of conceptual development must resolve the issue of what the earliest concepts are like, no matter when they may first be formed. Leslie (1988) has offered an analysis of the primitives involved in early causal concepts, and people working on language acquisition have speculated about semantic primitives. For example, Slobin (1985) points out that children must already have concepts of objects and events, as well as relational notions about them, in order for language to be acquired. Since language comprehension begins at around nine to ten months (and perhaps earlier for sign language), some kind of conceptual system must be well established by that time. But we have almost no information as to its character.

Help may come from recent studies by cognitive linguists (e.g., Fauconnier 1985; Johnson 1987; Lakoff 1987). Although the primary goal of these theorists is to understand how language works, their analyses of the root concepts expressed in language may be of use in our search for babies' earliest concepts. For example, Lakoff and Johnson have proposed that image schemas—notions derived from spatial structure, such

as trajectory, up-down, container, part-whole, end-of-path, and link—form the foundation of the conceptualizing capacity. These authors suggest that image schemas are derived from preconceptual perceptual structures, forming the core of many of our concepts of objects and events and of their metaphorical extensions to abstract realms. They demonstrate in great detail how many of our most complex concepts are grounded in such primitive notions. I would characterize image schemas as simplified redescriptions of sensorimotor schemas, noting that they seem to be reasonably within the capacity of infant conceptualization.

The potential usefulness of image schemas as conceptual primitives can be illustrated by the example of the container schema. According to Johnson and Lakoff, the structural elements of this image schema are "interior," "boundary," and "exterior." It has a bodily basis likely to be appreciated by quite young infants, and a perceptual basis that seems to require minimal redescription of the object schemas described earlier. It also has a simple binary logic—either in or not-in; if A is in B and B is in C, then A is in C—that may or may not be the sensorimotor basis of the Boolean logic of classes, as Lakoff suggests, but is certainly a characteristic of concepts as opposed to percepts. (The conceptual system tends to reduce the continuous information delivered by the perceptual system to a small number of discrete values.)

The use of such an image schema might be responsible for the better performance nine-month-old infants show on hiding tasks when a container is used rather than cloths or screens (Freeman et al. 1980). Current work by Baillargeon (pers. com.) suggests that at approximately the same age infants are surprised when containers without bottoms appear to hold things. Of course, these are only fragments of the kind of information needed to document the development of the idea of a container, but

they indicate how we might go about tracking the early establishment of simple concepts.

A more complex concept that may also be acquired relatively early in infancy is that of animacy. Consider some possible sources for such a concept. We know that infants differentiate biological from nonbiological motion as early as three months (Fig. 6; Berthenthal et al. 1987). This perceptual differentiation, although an excellent source of information, does not constitute a concept by itself; it is an accomplishment similar to categorizing male and female faces, which infants have learned to do by six months (Fagan and Singer 1979). As discussed earlier, such perceptual categorization is not accessible for purposes of conceptual thought unless it has been redescribed in conceptual terms. An infant needs to conceptualize some differences between categories of moving objects, such as noting that one type starts up on its own and (sometimes) responds to the infant's signals, whereas the other type does not. An image schema of a notion such as beginning-of-path could be used to redescribe the perceptual information involved in initiation of motion. A link schema (whose elements are two entities and some kind of path between them) could be used to describe the observation of responsivity to self. From such simple foundations might arise a primitive concept of animal, a concept that we have reason to believe is present in some form by at least the end of the first year of life (Golinkoff and Halperin 1983; Mandler and Bauer 1988).

These are some examples of how a conceptual system might emerge from a combination of perceptual input and some relatively simple redescriptions of that input. I have suggested that a mechanism of perceptual analysis could enable such redescription, with the terms of the redescription being derived from spatial structure. The mechanism would not require an extended period of

---

A good deal of evidence suggests that we have tended to confuse infants' motor incompetence with conceptual incompetence

---

exclusively sensorimotor functioning but would allow conceptualization of the world to begin early in infancy. The data I have summarized indicate that babies do indeed begin to think earlier than we thought. Therefore, it seems safe to assume that they either are born with or acquire early in life the capacity to form concepts, rather than to assume that conceptual functioning can occur only as an outcome of a lengthy sensorimotor stage.

References

Ashmead, D. H., and M. Perlmutter. 1980. Infant memory in everyday life. In *New Directions for Child Development: Children's Memory*, vol. 10, ed. M. Perlmutter, pp. 1–16. Jossey-Bass.

Baillargeon, R. 1987a. Object permanence in 3.5- and 4.5-month-old infants. *Devel. Psychol.* 23:655–64.

———. 1987b. Young infants' reasoning about the physical and spatial properties of a hidden object. *Cognitive Devel.* 2:179–200.

Baillargeon, R., J. De Vos, and M. Graber. 1989. Location memory in 8-month-old infants in a nonsearch AB task: Further evidence. *Cognitive Devel.* 4:345–67.

Baillargeon, R., E. S. Spelke, and S. Wasserman. 1985. Object permanence in five-month-old infants. *Cognition* 20:191–208.

Bertenthal, B. I., D. R. Proffitt, S. J. Kramer, and N. B. Spetner. 1987. Infants' encoding of kinetic displays varying in relative coherence. *Devel. Psychol.* 23:171–78.

Bonvillian, J. D., M. D. Orlansky, and L. L. Novack. 1983. Developmental milestones: Sign language and motor development. *Child Devel.* 54:1435–45.

Cohen, N. J., and L. R. Squire. 1980. Preserved learning and retention of pattern-analyzing skills in amnesia: Dissociation of knowing how and knowing that. *Science* 210:207–10.

Diamond, A. 1985. The development of the ability to use recall to guide action, as indicated by infants' performance on AB. *Child Devel.* 56:868–83.

Fagan, J. F., III, and L. T. Singer. 1979. The role of simple feature differences in infant recognition of faces. *Infant Behav. Devel.* 2:39–46.

Fauconnier, G. 1985. *Mental Spaces*. MIT Press.

Fox, N., J. Kagan, and S. Weiskopf. 1979. The growth of memory during infancy. *Genetic Psychol. Mono.* 99:91–130.

Freeman, N. H., S. Lloyd, and C. G. Sinha. 1980. Infant search tasks reveal early concepts of containment and canonical usage of objects. *Cognition* 8:243–62.

Golinkoff, R. M., and M. S. Halperin. 1983. The concept of animal: One infant's view. *Infant Behav. Devel.* 6:229–33.

James, W. 1890. *The Principles of Psychology*. Holt.

Janowsky, J. S. 1985. Cognitive development and reorganization after early brain injury. Ph.D. diss., Cornell Univ.

Johnson, M. 1987. *The Body in the Mind: The Bodily Basis of Meaning, Imagination, and Reason*. Univ. of Chicago Press.

Kellman, P. J., and E. S. Spelke. 1983. Perception of partly occluded objects in infancy. *Cognitive Psychol.* 15:483–524.

Kosslyn, S. M. 1983. *Ghosts in the Mind's Machine: Creating and Using Images in the Brain*. Norton.

Kuhl, P. K., and A. N. Meltzoff. 1988. Speech as an intermodal object of perception. In *Perceptual Development in Infancy: The Minnesota Symposia on Child Psychology*, vol. 20, ed. A. Yonas, pp. 235–66. Erlbaum.

Lakoff, G. 1987. *Women, Fire, and Dangerous Things: What Categories Reveal about the Mind*. Univ. of Chicago Press.

Leslie, A. 1988. The necessity of illusion: Perception and thought in infancy. In *Thought without Language*, ed. L. Weiskrantz, pp. 185–210. Clarendon Press.

Mandler, J. M. 1983. Representation. In *Cognitive Development*, ed. J. H. Flavell and E. M. Markman, pp. 420–94. Vol. 3 of *Manual of Child Psychology*, ed. P. Mussen. Wiley.

———. 1988. How to build a baby: On the development of an accessible representational system. *Cognitive Devel.* 3:113–36.

———. In press. Recall of events by preverbal children. In *The Development and Neural Bases of Higher Cognitive Functions*, ed. A. Diamond. New York Academy of Sciences Press.

Mandler, J. M., and P. J. Bauer. 1988. The cradle of categorization: Is the basic level basic? *Cognitive Devel.* 3:247–64.

McDonough, L., and J. M. Mandler. 1989. Immediate and deferred imitation with 11-month-olds: A comparison between familiar and novel actions. Poster presented at meeting of the Society for Research in Child Development, Kansas City.

Meltzoff, A. N. 1988. Infant imitation and memory: Nine-month-olds in immediate and deferred tests. *Child Devel.* 59:217–25.

Meltzoff, A. N., and R. W. Borton. 1979. Intermodal matching by human neonates. *Nature* 282:403–04.

Mendelson, M. J., and M. M. Haith. 1976. The relation between audition and vision in the newborn. *Monographs of the Society for Research in Child Development*, no. 41, serial no. 167.

Michotte, A. 1963. *The Perception of Causality*. Methuen.

Piaget, J. 1951. *Play, Dreams and Imitation in Childhood*, trans. C. Gattegno and F. M. Hodgson. Norton.

———. 1952. *The Origins of Intelligence in Children*, trans. M. Cook. International Universities Press.

———. 1954. *The Construction of Reality in the Child*, trans. M. Cook. Basic Books.

Prinz, P. M., and E. A. Prinz. 1979. Simultaneous acquisition of ASL and spoken English (in a hearing child of a deaf mother and hearing father). Phase I: Early lexical development. *Sign Lang. Stud.* 25:283–96.

Ruff, H. A. 1986. Components of attention during infants' manipulative exploration. *Child Devel.* 57:105–14.

Schacter, D. L. 1987. Implicit memory: History and current status. *J. Exper. Psychol.: Learning, Memory, Cognition* 13:501–18.

Slobin, D. I. 1985. Crosslinguistic evidence for the language-making capacity. In *The Crosslinguistic Study of Language Acquisition*, vol. 2, ed. D. I. Slobin, pp. 1157–1256. Erlbaum.

Smith, E. E., and D. L. Medin. 1981. *Categories and Concepts*. Harvard Univ. Press.

Spelke, E. S. 1979. Perceiving bimodally specified events in infancy. *Devel. Psychol.* 15:626–36.

———. 1988. The origins of physical knowledge. In *Thought without Language*, ed. L. Weiskrantz, pp. 168–84. Clarendon Press.

Spelke, E. S., and R. Kestenbaum. 1986. Les origines du concept d'objet. *Psychologie française* 31:67–72.

Walker-Andrews, A. S., and E. J. Gibson. 1986. What develops in bimodal perception? In *Advances in Infancy Research*, vol. 4, ed. L. P. Lipsitt and C. Rovee-Collier, pp. 171–81. Ablex.

Werner, H., and B. Kaplan. 1963. *Symbol Formation*. Wiley.

Wertheimer, M. 1961. Psychomotor coordination of auditory and visual space at birth. *Science* 134:1692.

The Amazing Minds of Infants

Looking here, looking there, babies are like little scientists, constantly exploring the world around them, with innate abilities we're just beginning to understand.

Text by **Lisa Grunwald**
Reporting by **Jeff Goldberg**

Additional reporting: **Stacey Bernstein, Anne Hollister**

A light comes on. Shapes and colors appear. Some of the colors and shapes start moving. Some of the colors and shapes make noise. Some of the noises are voices. One is a mother's. Sometimes she sings. Sometimes she says things. Sometimes she leaves. What can an infant make of the world? In the blur of perception and chaos of feeling, what does a baby know?

Most parents, observing infancy, are like travelers searching for famous sites: first tooth, first step, first word, first illness, first shoes, first full night of sleep. Most subtle, and most profound of all, is the first time the clouds of infancy part to reveal the little light of a human intelligence.

For many parents, that revelation may be the moment when they see their baby's first smile. For others, it may be the moment when they watch their child show an actual

---

At three months, babies can learn—and remember for weeks—visual sequences and simple mechanical tasks.

---

preference—for a lullaby, perhaps, or a stuffed animal. But new evidence is emerging to show that even before those moments, babies already have wonderfully active minds.

Of course, they're not exactly chatty in their first year of life, so what—and how—babies truly think may always remain a mystery. But using a variety of ingenious techniques that interpret how infants watch and move, students of child development are discovering a host of unsuspected skills. From a rudimentary understanding of math to a

sense of the past and the future, from precocious language ability to an innate understanding of physical laws, children one year and younger know a lot more than they're saying.

MEMORY

Does an infant remember anything? Penelope Leach, that slightly scolding doyenne of the child development field, warns in *Babyhood* that a six- to eight-month-old "cannot hold in his mind a picture of his mother, nor of where she is." And traditionally psychologists have assumed that infants cannot store memories until, like adults, they have the language skills needed to form and retrieve them. But new research suggests that babies as young as three months may be taking quite accurate mental notes.

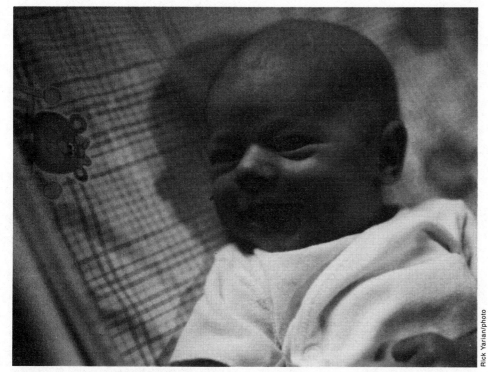
Babies show an unexpected ability to remember surprisingly intricate details.

Rick Yarian/photo

In his lab at the University of Denver, psychologist Marshall Haith has spent much of the past four years putting infants into large black boxes where they lie and look up at TV screens. The program they see is a Haith invention: a sequence of colorful objects appearing on different sides of the monitor. Using an infrared camera linked to a computer, Haith follows the babies' eye movements and has found that after only five tries the babies can anticipate where the next object will appear. With a little more practice, they can foresee a four-step sequence. And up to two weeks later, most can still predict it. Says Haith: "The babies are not just looking. They're analyzing, creating little hypotheses."

Similar findings by Carolyn Rovee-Collier, a psychologist at Rutgers University, suggest that infants can remember surprisingly intricate details. In a typical experiment, she places a baby in a crib beneath an elaborate mobile, ties

one of the baby's ankles to it with a satin ribbon, then observes as the baby kicks and—often gleefully—makes it move. When, weeks later, the baby's feet are left untied and the mobile is returned to the crib, the baby will try to kick again, presumably recalling the palmy days of kicking the last time. But if the mobile's elements are changed even slightly, the baby will remain unmoved—and unmoving. "When we change things," explains Rovee-Collier, "it wipes out the memory. But as soon as we bring back what had become familiar and expected, the memory comes right back. What we've learned from this is that even at two and a half months, an infant's memory is very developed, very specific and incredibly detailed."

Rachel Clifton, a psychologist at the University of Massachusetts, says that an infant's experience at six months can be remembered a full two years later. Clifton stumbled upon her findings while researching motor and hearing

skills. Three years ago she placed 16 six-month-olds in a pitch-dark room with objects that made different sounds. Using infrared cameras like Haith's, she observed how and when the infants reached for the objects. Later, realizing she had created a unique situation that couldn't have been duplicated in real life, she wondered if the babies would remember their experience. Two years after the original experiment, collaborating with psychologist Nancy Myers, she brought the same 16 children back to the lab, along with a control group of 16 other two-and-a-half-year-olds. Amazingly, the experimental group showed the behavior they had at six months, reaching for objects and showing no fear. Fewer control-group toddlers reached for the objects, and many of them cried.

Says Myers: "For so long, we didn't think that infants could rep-

At five months, babies have the raw ability to add.

resent in their memories the events that were going on around them, but put them back in a similar situation, as we did, and you can make the memory accessible."

MATH

At least a few parental eyebrows—and undoubtedly some expectations—were raised by this recent headline in *The New York Times:* "Study Finds Babies at 5 Months Grasp Simple Mathematics." The story, which reported on the findings of Karen Wynn, a psychologist at the University of Arizona, explained that infants as young as five months had been found to exhibit "a rudimentary ability to add and subtract."

Wynn, who published her research in the renowned scientific journal *Nature,* had based her experiments on a widely observed phenomenon: Infants look longer at things that are unexpected to them, thereby revealing what they do expect, or know. Wynn enacted addition and subtraction equations for babies using Mickey Mouse dolls. In a typical example, she had the babies watch as she placed a doll on a puppet stage, hid it behind a screen, then placed a second doll behind the screen (to represent one plus one). When she removed the screen to reveal three, not two, Mickey Mouse dolls, the infants stared longer at such incorrect outcomes than they had at correct ones. Wynn believes that babies' numerical understanding is "an innate mechanism, somehow built into the biological structure."

Her findings have been met with enthusiasm in the field—not least from Mark Strauss at the University of Pittsburgh, who a decade ago found that somewhat older babies could distinguish at a glance the difference between one, two, three and four balls—nearly as many objects as adults can decipher without counting. Says Strauss: "Five-month-olds are clearly thinking about quantities and applying numerical concepts to their world."

Wynn's conclusions have also inspired skepticism among some researchers who believe her results may reflect infants' ability to perceive things but not necessarily an ability to know what they're perceiving. Wynn herself warns parents not to leap to any conclu-

sions, and certainly not to start tossing algebra texts into their children's cribs. Still, she insists: "A lot more is happening in infants' minds than we've tended to give them credit for."

LANGUAGE

In an old stand-up routine, Robin Williams used to describe his son's dawning ability as a mimic of words—particularly those of the deeply embarrassing four-letter variety. Most parents decide they can no longer speak with complete freedom when their children start talking. Yet current research on language might prompt some to start censoring themselves even earlier.

At six months, babies recognize their native tongue.

At Seattle's University of Washington, psychologist Patricia Kuhl has shown that long before infants actually begin to learn words, they can sort through a jumble of spoken sounds in search of the ones that have meaning. From birth to four months, according to Kuhl, babies are "universal linguists" capable of distinguishing each of the 150 sounds that make up all human speech. But by just six months, they have begun the metamorphosis into specialists who recognize the speech sounds of their native tongue.

In Kuhl's experiment babies listened as a tape-recorded voice repeated vowel and consonant combinations. Each time the sounds changed—from "ah" to "oooh," for example—a toy bear in a box

was lit up and danced. The babies quickly learned to look at the bear when they heard sounds that were new to them. Studying Swedish and American six-month-olds, Kuhl found they ignored subtle variations in pronunciation of their own language's sounds—for instance, the different ways two people might pronounce "ee"—but they heard similar variations in a foreign language as separate sounds. The implication? Six-month-olds can already discern the sounds they will later need for speech. Says Kuhl: "There's nothing external in these six-month-olds that would provide you with a clue that something like this is going on."

By eight to nine months, comprehension is more visible, with babies looking at a ball when their mothers say "ball," for example. According to psychologist Donna Thal at the University of California, San Diego, it is still impossible to gauge just how many words babies understand at this point, but her recent studies of slightly older children indicate that comprehension may exceed expression by a factor as high as a hundred to one. Thal's studies show that although some babies are slow in starting to talk, comprehension appears to be equal between the late talkers and early ones.

PHYSICS

No, no one is claiming that an eight-month-old can compute the trajectory of a moon around a planet. But at Cornell University, psychologist Elizabeth Spelke is finding that babies as young as four months have a rudimentary knowledge of the way the world works—or should work.

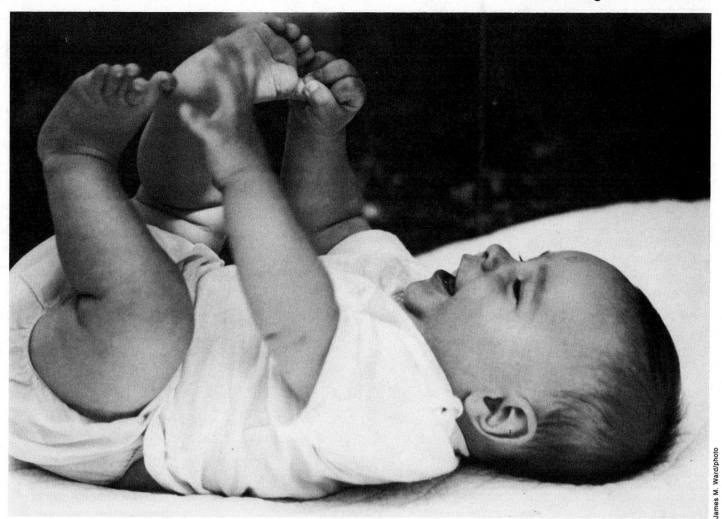

Babies learn how physical objects behave by moving their body parts.

Babies have a built-in sense of how objects behave.

Spelke sets her young subjects up before a puppet stage, where she shows them a series of unexpected actions: a ball seems to roll through a solid barrier, another seems to leap between two platforms, a third seems to hang in midair. Like Karen Wynn with her math experiments, Spelke measures the babies' looking time and has recorded longer intervals for unexpected actions than for expected ones. Again like Wynn, Spelke be-

lieves that babies must have some "core" knowledge—in this case, about the way physical objects behave. Says Spelke: "At an age when infants are not able to talk about objects, move around objects, reach for and manipulate objects, or even see objects with high resolution, they appear to recognize where a moving object is when it has left their view and make inferences about where it should be when it comes into sight again."

The notion of an infant's possessing any innate mechanism—other than reflexes like sucking that fade with time—would have shocked the shoes off the pioneers of child development research, who believed, as some still do, that

what we know can be learned only through experience. But the belief in biologically programmed core knowledge lies at the heart of the current research—not only with math and physics but with other cognitive skills as well. Indeed, Carnegie Mellon's Mark Johnson believes that the ability of infants to recognize the human face is not learned, as previously thought, but is present at birth. Studying infants, some only 10 minutes old, Johnson has observed a marked preference for pictures of faces to pictures of blank ovals or faces with scrambled features. He believes that we are born with a "template" of the human face that aids our survival by helping us recognize our meal ticket.

EMOTIONS: THE SHY AND THE LIVELY

A growing number of researchers believe early temperament may indicate later troubles.

One thing that infants are *not* good at is hiding what they feel. Fear, glee, rage, affection: Long before babies start talking, emotions tumble out of them in gestures, tears and belly laughs. But measuring infant temperament—finding a way to quantify its traits—has always been harder than measuring skills.

Around the country, researchers are now combining questionnaires filled in by parents, home visits by trained observers, and newly devised lab tests to explore the mystery of temperamenat. Concentrating on babies older than eight months (the age at which the full range of infant emotions has emerged), investigators have designed more than 50 experimental situations to provoke emotions from fear to sadness, from interest to pleasure. Most children's reactions fall within an average range on such tests. But there are babies on either extreme, and psychologist Nathan Fox at the University of Maryland has begun to explore their responses. Putting his babies in electroencephalogram (EEG) helmets, he has found that particularly inhibited babies show a distinctive brain-wave pattern, which others believe may predict later emotional problems, including depression. Although some scientists agree that early behavior can predict later temperament, other researchers argue that enduring character traits are the exception, not the rule. For psychiatrist Stanley Greenspan of Bethesda, Md., the ability of infants to change is an article of faith. Specializing in babies as young as three months, Greenspan says he can treat what he calls the garden-variety problems of sleep disorders, tan-

Long before babies begin talking, emotions are graphically expressed in their gestures and facial expressions.

trums and anger in a few sessions. (Don't imagine tiny couches for infant patients; although the babies are closely observed, it's the parents who often get treatment.) For more severe problems, such as suspected learning disorders, he recommends more intensive early intervention—often involving a team of therapists—and has found that this can make a huge difference: "Babies who were very scared, shy and inhibited can completely change and become very assertive, outgoing and confident over a number of months."

The University of Washington's Mary Rothbart has compared infants in Japan, the Netherlands and the U.S. and notes that northern European mothers are most prone to ignore their babies' fussiness with

a stiff-upper-lip approach. When tested at one year by having their mothers leave a room, the Dutch babies are the most distressed and ignore their mothers upon their return. Psychologists call this response an "insecure attachment relationship," and some regard it as an early warning of later anxiety disorders. Says Rothbart: "In the process of soothing a baby, you're helping to teach it to shift its attention away from negative sensations. Adults with anxiety disorders may never have learned to do this." Tellingly, when Dutch mothers were instructed to soothe and play with their fussy babies, the follow-up sessions showed positive results. "With intervention," concludes Rothbart, "you can turn things around."

TAKING INFANTS SERIOUSLY

The ultimate question becomes, should education begin at three months?

One question that might leap to the minds of parents newly informed of their infants' skills is a simple one: So what? What does it mean if children really have these unexpected abilities?

Pointing to the findings on memory that she has published with partner Rachel Clifton, Nancy Myers suggests that if memories of the babies' experience allowed them to be unafraid in the pitch-black room, then exposing children to a wide variety of events and places may make them more accepting of similar situations later on. "I don't want to say that mothers should make an extreme effort to stimulate their babies," Myers says, "but taking a baby to different places, allowing him to see and smell different things, is an important means of establishing familiarity. It will allow the baby to feel freer in the future."

But what about other kinds of skills: Should infants' innate abilities with language or math be consciously nurtured and pushed along?

In Philadelphia, instructors at the Institutes for the Achievement of Human Potential have been coaching parents since 1963 to teach their babies to read from birth. Touting "genetic potential," their program recommends that parents write out on cards everything from "nose" to "kiss" to "Mommy." The new findings about infants' skills have hardly gone unnoticed at the Institutes, where director Janet Doman says: "For the past thirty years, we've been saying that children can learn at very early ages. It's nice to know that science is finally validating what we've known all along."

Yet many of the scientists performing the experiments question the value of such intensive efforts. Says Rutgers's Carolyn Rovee-Collier: "Most of us agree that an infant could be taught to recognize letters and numbers. But the problem is that parents who do these kinds of programs start investing a lot in their infants and become very bound up in their success. It puts great strain on the infants and the parents."

University of Denver psychologist Marshall Haith agrees: "Babies are born prepared to take on the world. We've got to get away from the feeling that we've got this wonderful brain sitting there and we've got to keep pumping information into it. Nature wouldn't have done anything so stupid."

To most researchers, the moral of the story seems to be: Respect your baby, but don't go nuts. "Don't waste your child's fun months," says Karen Wynn, who says her findings about math "should be viewed as no more than a new insight for parents who have young children." Says the University of Pittsburgh's Mark Strauss: "Ideally, we can tell parents a lot more about subtle things they can watch happening in their infants, and that will make watching and getting involved more fun."

A Child's Theory of Mind

Mental life may change radically around age 4

BRUCE BOWER

If you think kids say the darnedest things, get a load of what they think.

Consider a group of preschoolers shown a box that they all agree appears to contain candy. Each child gets a chance to fling open the receptacle, but only a stash of crayons greets their hungry glares. If asked by an experimenter what someone else will think the box contains upon first seeing it, 4- and 5-year-olds typically grin at the trick and exclaim "Candy!"

They realize, in their devilish way, that the shape and design of the box at first create a false belief.

Yet most 3-year-olds react entirely differently to the trick box. After falling for the sweet deception, they insist that a newcomer will assume crayons lie within the container. If an adult enters the room, peers into the box, and does an obvious double take, 3-year-olds still maintain that the grown-up expected to find crayons. What's more, the same youngsters confidently assert that they, too, initially thought the box held crayons.

Of course, 3-year-olds cherish cantankerous and contrary remarks, but further experiments indicate that a deeper process orchestrates their explanations of the world.

Observe, for instance, preschoolers given some toys purchased at a novelty store: a large sponge shaped and painted to look like a rock, a "sucker" egg made of chalk, and a green cardboard cat covered by a removable red filter that makes it appear black. Give them plenty of time to examine the objects. Most 4- and 5-year-olds separate each object's real qualities from its apparent attributes; they note, for instance, that the sponge only looks like a rock.

But those obstinate 3-year-olds find such subtleties about as appealing as going to bed early. In their minds, an object possesses either real or apparent characteristics, but not both at the same time. For instance, some assert that the phony rock looks like a sponge and really is a sponge, while the cat looks black and really is black.

These findings emerge from research conducted over the past decade to examine how children reach an understanding of the mind's trappings, such as beliefs, desires, intentions, and emotions. Some investigators contend that this hybrid of developmental and cognitive psychology explores the ways in which children construct "theories of mind." Others argue that the research illuminates the origins of "folk psychology," or people's shared assumptions about how the mind works.

Whatever terminology they use, scientists generally agree that knowledge about mental states and attitudes changes substantially throughout childhood. Debate revolves around a number of clashing explanations of how and why that change takes place.

"There's a genuine argument now over whether a fundamental shift occurs in children's understanding of their own and others' minds between ages 3 and 5," says John H. Flavell, a psychologist at Stanford University and an early explorer of how preschoolers understand thinking.

The March BEHAVIORAL AND BRAIN SCIENCES contains two opposing reviews of research on children's understanding of the mind, as well as 60 written comments from an international group of investigators.

Swiss psychologist Jean Piaget launched the study of how youngsters conceptualize mental life more than 50 years ago. He argued that infants use a few basic reflexes, such as sucking objects that enter their mouths and following moving objects with their eyes, but extract no other meaning from the environment. Preschoolers make themselves the center of the universe, in Piaget's theory; they fail to grasp that other people have different viewpoints and different sources of knowledge. A full appreciation of mental states as experienced by oneself and others blooms in later childhood and adolescence, Piaget held.

Today, researchers contend that more goes on in the heads of babies and young children than Piaget imagined. "Theory of mind" advocates argue that infants possess a primitive sense of being like others; soon thereafter, children assemble a succession of progressively more sophisticated predictions about the types of thought that coordinate behavior in particular situations. This process resembles the accumulation of knowledge through theory testing in science, they propose.

In 1978, investigations into children's theories of mind got a major boost from a controversial article in which two researchers suggested that chimpanzees theorize about mental states. To test this assertion, scientists began to look at whether chimps and children attribute false beliefs to others. Chimps showed little talent for viewing the world from another's misleading perspective, but children at different ages yielded intriguing results that spurred continued research.

Some investigators now suggest that an

From *Science News*, Vol. 144, No. 3, July 17, 1993, pp. 40-41. Reprinted with permission from *Science News*, the weekly newsmagazine of science. © 1993 by Science News, Inc.

innate brain mechanism allows even very young children to begin theorizing about mental states. Others view the child's emerging understanding of the mind as a by-product of a maturing brain that manipulates many types of information in increasingly complex ways.

Another school of thought regards commonsense notions about mental life as socially and culturally learned tools for dealing with others rather than as theories for making predictions about people.

And a final account emphasizes intuition as the driving force behind children's take on the mind. In this view, preschoolers first imagine having the desires or beliefs of another person and then mentally simulate what that person would do and feel.

Alison Gopnik, a psychologist at the University of California, Berkeley, champions an influential version of the theory of mind approach known as the "theory theory." Individuals gradually construct commonsense psychological beliefs as a way of explaining themselves and others, according to Gopnik. On the basis of their experience, children theorize that invisible mental entities, such as beliefs and desires, exist and operate in lawful ways, she contends. Youngsters modify or discard a favored theory if it encounters too many difficulties or continually leads them astray in social situations, just as scientists drop or modify a theory that cannot account for or predict key phenomena, the Berkeley psychologist posits.

"The same mental capacities that children use to understand the mind have been applied to science by adults. It's not that children are little scientists, but scientists are big children," she says, chuckling at the implication.

However, the nature of these proposed psychological launching pads for abstract thought remains hazy. Gopnik presents a rough outline of what researchers know about the development of an understanding of the mind.

Even infants display a vague notion of internal psychological states, she asserts. For example, studies find that babies deftly mimic adult facial expressions and gaze in the direction they see others looking.

From around 18 months to 3 years, children learn to distinguish between mental and physical events, Gopnik notes. They know the difference between, say, an imagined dog and a real dog, and begin to engage in pretense and make-believe games. Their talk includes words for perceptions, such as "see," "look," and "taste," and emotions, such as "happy,"

"love," and "want." By age 3, most also use words such as "know," "think," and "remember."

In Gopnik's opinion, 3-year-olds retain a fascination with "silly" states that stand apart from the real world, such as dreams and make-believe. They also assume that beliefs and other mental states apprehend the world directly, just as their eyes see whatever lies in front of them. They do not assume that a person holds a belief about the contents of a box; in the 3-year-old's theory, the person's belief corresponds to what the box holds. Thus, the typical youngster says the box contains candy when assessing its appearance. But the same child sheds that assumption upon seeing its contents and acquires a belief that the box has always held crayons and other people share that knowledge.

A theory of mental states as direct conduits to reality, rather than as representations of what may or may not exist,

also sometimes causes children to confuse appearance with reality, as in encounters with spongy rocks and chalky eggs.

Further evidence suggests that 3-year-olds assign either total knowledge or absolute ignorance to mental states, Gopnik says. In other words, they fail to appreciate that belief comes in degrees. For instance, in contrast to 4-year-olds, 3-year-olds show no preference for information offered by people who express certainty about what a box contains versus people citing doubts about what the box holds.

Some investigators argue that 3-year-olds know enough about false beliefs to attempt to deceive others. A child at that age who breaks an expensive lamp may, when asked by his mother if he touched the lamp, quickly utter "No." But Gopnik maintains that

Don't just sit there, think something

Children know much about the mind by age 4, but their conception of how people think still diverges sharply from that of older children and adults, according to a report in the April CHILD DEVELOPMENT. Beginning around age 7, youngsters tend to conclude that mental activity goes on continuously in a waking mind. Younger children, in contrast, assume that the mind switches on when it has a job to do and switches off at the conclusion of a task, leaving the mental landscape blank.

A 4-year-old who attributes complex meaning to beliefs and other mental states, as proposed by "theory of mind" researchers, at the same time fails to realize that people lead continuous inner lives and experience a "stream of consciousness," contend John H. Flavell, a psychologist at Stanford University, and his colleagues.

In one trial conducted by Flavell's team, groups of 20 children at ages 3, 4, and 6 to 7 years, as well as 20 adults, stated whether they believed a female experimenter entertained any thoughts or ideas in three situations: waiting quietly in a chair facing a blank wall, looking at pictures on the wall, and attempting to explain how someone got a big pear into a small glass bottle. Participants indicated the absence of thought by selecting a drawing of a woman's head underneath an empty "thought bubble" (commonly used to indicate the thoughts of cartoon characters) and signaled the presence of

thought by choosing a portrayal of a woman's head under a thought bubble containing three asterisks.

Warm-up tests established that all of the participants viewed the asterisks as representing ongoing thoughts or ideas.

Only one of the 3-year-olds attributed mental activity to a waiting person. That number increased to four in the 4-year-olds, 11 in the 6- to 7-year-olds, and 19 in the adults. In contrast, at least 13 members of each age group granted thoughts to a person looking at pictures or trying to explain the pear-bearing bottle.

In further trials with 4-year-olds, most of these youngsters contended that people can voluntarily empty their minds of all thoughts and ideas for a few minutes and that the mind of a waiting person "was not doing anything."

And in unpublished results, Flavell's group finds that not until about age 7 do children consistently recall thoughts they just had while contemplating a problem.

Preschoolers may seldom reflect on their own and others' thoughts and probably experience problems when they try, Flavell suggests. Prior studies directed by Flavell suggest that at around age 7 kids realize that one thought triggers another in a chain reaction, a person's facial expression may contradict inner thoughts, and some psychological states linger indefinitely, such as worries that a monster will emerge from the dark at night.

— B. Bower

researchers cannot yet say whether the denial signals a conscious attempt to manipulate mother's beliefs or a learned strategy for avoiding punishment, devoid of any deeper understanding of why it might work.

By age 4 or 5, at least in Western cultures, children come to the conclusion that people form beliefs and other mental states *about* the world, Gopnik holds. These youngsters entertain notions of false belief, distinguish between real and apparent qualities of the same object, and recognize changes in their own beliefs, she says.

Moreover, 5-year-olds usually understand that individuals may perceive an object in different ways depending on their line of sight. They also recognize that beliefs dictate a person's emotional reactions to particular situations, such as an adult's expression of surprise at discovering crayons in a candy box.

"By 5 years of age, children have acquired a remarkable understanding of the mind, in many ways quite like that of adults, and certainly very different from that of 2- or even 3-year-olds," Gopnik contends.

Although adults generally believe that each person uses direct knowledge of his or her own mental states to make educated guesses about how others think, research with children suggests otherwise, she adds. At any given stage of development, children make the same inferences about their own minds and those of other people, Gopnik argues.

When confronting false beliefs, she points out, 3-year-olds make errors about their own immediately past beliefs, such as saying they thought the box contained crayons all along, and commit a similar blunder in claiming that a newcomer believes the box holds crayons.

In contrast, 3-year-olds perform much better when dealing with "silly" mental states that bear no relation to the real world. For example, in one study directed by Gopnik, 3-year-olds knew they had first pretended that an imaginary glass contained hot chocolate and then had imagined that the same glass was full of lemonade. Children at this age also realize that other people may engage in pretense and change the details of an imagined situation.

Arriving at an adult-like, abstract account of thought requires a child to continually tinker with and sometimes replace theories about how the mind works, Gopnik says. Other psychologists, including Henry M. Wellman of the University of Michigan in Ann Arbor and Josef Perner of the University of Sussex in Brighton, England, currently direct investigations aimed at shedding further light on these theories.

In an ironic twist, relatively stable theories of mind rapidly become second nature after age 5 and foster the false impression that we directly experience our own mental states rather than making well-practiced inferences about what we believe, want, and feel, Gopnik asserts. Master chess players experience a similar warping of perception, she says. After years of practice, their consideration of numerous potential moves during a match occurs so quickly and effortlessly that they report only a sensation of reacting to the competing forces and powers on the chessboard rather than making a step-by-step analysis of the proper move.

Other researchers argue that a child's ability to theorize about mental life depends on a specialized brain mechanism that exerts its influence by around age 2, when children begin to use pretense. Contrary to Gopnik's proposal, 4-year-olds probably do not overhaul their assumptions about mental states, argues Alan M. Leslie, a psychologist at the University of London in England. Instead, he says, their new treatment of false belief and other psychological concepts reflects a maturing capacity to parcel out different sources of information in their minds.

For instance, unlike many 3-year-olds, 4-year-olds also realize that an out-of-date photograph — say, a picture of candy in a cupboard that is now bare — represents a past state of affairs that has changed.

Leslie and his colleagues propose that young children easily slip into and out of pretend play because the brain's "theory-of-mind mechanism" allows them to grasp that people hold invisible attitudes about the veracity of a fictional state of affairs. Hence, even 2-year-olds understand that if mother pretends a banana is a telephone, she won't serve the telephone for lunch and call up father on the banana.

The same brain mechanism allows 3- to 4-year-olds to understand that a person behaves according to potentially misleading beliefs, hopes, or other attitudes held about people and objects, Leslie asserts.

Autistic children provide an example of what happens when apparent brain damage destroys the theory-of-mind mechanism, he contends. Studies conducted by Leslie and University of London coworkers Uta Frith and Simon Baron-Cohen indicate that autistic youngsters fail to develop any rules of thumb for understanding how mental states cause behavior. Autistic children cannot conceive that they or others hold false beliefs, and they find it difficult to understand deception, according to the British investigators.

As a result, symptoms of autism revolve around the absence of imagination, an inability to communicate with others, and a poverty of social skills, Leslie suggests.

Philip D. Zelazo of the University of Toronto and Douglas Frye of New York University, both psychologists, take a different approach. They hold that a 4-year-old's altered conception of mental states depends on the emergence of a general ability to reason first from one perspective and then from another, incompatible perspective.

One experiment conducted by Zelazo and Frye required children to place cards in various locations according to their colors and then sort the same cards according to their shapes. Three-year-olds succeeded at the first set of rules but could not immediately switch to the alternate rules; 4- and 5-year-olds performed well at sorting cards both by color and by shape.

Other investigators doubt that commonsense notions of the mind spring either from specific theories or a more general versatility at manipulating information.

Instead, children possess a powerful innate tendency to make sense of their own and other's actions by telling stories about those deeds, argues Jerome Bruner, a psychologist at New York University. Myths, oral stories, books, and other cultural influences on family and social life shape the ways in which children arrive at a personal understanding of belief, deception, and the rest of mental life, he asserts. Bruner expands on this notion in his book *Acts of Meaning* (1990, Harvard University Press).

If Bruner's argument is correct, children in the United States and Sri Lanka, or in other contrasting cultures, should report striking differences in their assumptions about the mind. To date, virtually all evidence regarding children's understanding of the mind comes from Western cultures, Gopnik points out.

Another explanation of folk psychology rests on a child's powers of imagination. Three-year-olds have trouble imagining mental states that contradict their own current mental states, and thus exhibit difficulty with false-belief tests, holds Alvin I. Goldman, a philosopher at the University of Arizona in Tucson. By age 4, children can imagine having the beliefs and desires of another person; they then mentally simulate that person's resulting feelings and behaviors, Goldman argues.

Paul L. Harris, a psychologist at the University of Oxford in England, agrees. In some studies, 3-year-olds accurately report their psychological experience and understand that mental states refer to the real world, according to Harris. When asked to visualize an imaginary object, 3-year-olds understand the direction to "make a picture in your head" and describe the mind as a container which at times displays pictures of nonexistent things, he notes.

Children apparently adopt such metaphors as a way of capturing their inner psychological experiences and improving their mental simulations of how others think, Harris asserts.

In addition, he says, 3-year-olds perform much better on false-belief tasks when an experimenter presents a situation in words rather than in actions.

For instance, an experimenter may tell 3-year-olds that an object that apparently belongs in one box has been secretly transferred to another box, rather than showing them the transfer. The children then look in both boxes to verify the transfer. Compared with same-age counterparts who only observe the transfer, these youngsters are much more likely to realize that an uninformed newcomer will guess the object's location incorrectly.

A verbal description makes it easier for 3-year-olds to imagine the object in its initial location and to ignore the knowledge that they saw the object in an unexpected box, Harris holds.

Still, Gopnik argues, the presence of an underlying theory best accounts for the wide range of understanding about the mind achieved by children around age 4. What's more, considerable research already suggests that adults often remain unaware of the unconscious mental states that direct their attitudes and judgments (SN: 3/28/92, p.200), adding to the likelihood that children also lack direct access to their own mental states and must construct theories to explain mental life, she points out.

Unfortunately, much remains unclear about the origins of theories and the reasons for their change in childhood as well as in science, Gopnik acknowledges.

"The scientist's ability to learn about the world is still almost as mysterious as the child's," she maintains. "Nevertheless, reducing two mysteries to one is an important advance, and a great deal more than we usually achieve."

"I Forget"

Kids remember a lot more than they know—or tell us. What are
the keys that unlock those precious memories?

**David F. Bjorklund, Ph.D.,
and Barbara R. Bjorklund**

David F. Bjorklund, Ph.D., and **Barbara R. Bjorklund** are the authors of the *Parents Book of Discipline* (Ballantine) and *Looking at Children* (Brooks/Cole).

ur friend Marie laughed when we told her that we were doing a research project on preschoolers' memory abilities. "Preschoolers' memory?" she said with a quizzical look on her face. "Well, if Jonathan is any example, it'll be a very short project."

Marie went on to tell us about her four-year-old son's recent school trip to a fire station. "How was your day?" she asked after school.

"Okay," Jonathan answered.

She tried again: "What did you do at school today?"

"Nothing much," he said.

Thinking she might have been mistaken about the date of the trip, Marie asked, "Wasn't this the day you were going to the fire station?"

"Yeah, we did," Jonathan replied.

"Well, tell me about it!" she prompted.

"We went on a bus and we saw the fire engine and we ate lunch at the park. Lisa gave me her cookies."

For all parents, this exchange has a familiar ring to it. Surely Jonathan remembers more about his field trip to the fire station than the bus ride and lunch in the park. For example, he probably learned a lot of new things and has many details of the morning tucked away in his memory. But deciding which tidbits to tell his mother first and which words to use to tell them is a difficult task.

How memory works.

There are many aspects of memory that a young child needs to master. First the event must be attended and perceived. Then the child must make some sense of that event so that it can be represented in his mind and recalled later on. If a child doesn't tune in to the important aspects of an event or cannot make sense of what he experienced, there is really nothing for the child to draw on.

Once the youngster has managed to accomplish all of this, the trick is to retrieve the memory, translate the mental picture he has in his head, and bring it to consciousness. The child must then find a way to explain that experience to another person. Broken down into its components, the process of remembering is quite complicated. It is understandable that young children, like Jonathan, often have a hard time doing it.

"Give me a hint!"

One thing that helps jog the memory is a cue. If someone asked you the name of Walter Mondale's running mate in the 1984 election, you might not be able to recall the name immediately. But if that person then told you that the first name of Mondale's running mate was Geraldine, you would no doubt snap your fingers and say, "Ferraro! I knew that all the time."

Children need cues too. According to Wolfgang Schneider, Ph.D.—professor of educational psychology at the University of Wuerzburg, in Germany, and coauthor, with Michael Pressley, of *Memory Development Between Two and Twenty* (Springer-Verlag)—young children have more difficulty retrieving information from their memory than they do storing it. To help them out, we need to use careful questioning techniques, involving a large dose of hints or cues. According to Schneider, the younger children are, the more hints they need to recall information. Robyn Fivush, Ph.D.—associate professor of psychology at Emory University, in Atlanta—and Nina R. Hamond, Ph.D., explain in *Knowing and Remembering in Young Children* (Cambridge University Press) that "younger children recall as much information as older children do, but they need more memory questions in order to do so." In other words, if Marie had asked Jonathan more specific questions when she picked him up, she might have gotten better answers. "Tell me about your trip to the fire station" would have been a good opener. "Did you see the fire fighters' clothes and boots? Did they have a spotted dog like the one we saw on TV? Did you get to see the fire engine? Did the fire chief talk to you?" Any of these questions, with the appropriate follow-up, would have had a better chance of winning detailed answers from a four-year-old than "How was your day?"

What to remember?

Preschoolers also have trouble selecting what to remember. Most adults know to watch the players on the field play ball at a baseball game. We automatically pay less attention to the field-maintenance staff, the players on the bench, and most of the other spectators. Young children do not always tune in to what adults view as the main point of the event. At a baseball game, they may spend more time watching the hot-dog vendors, the bat boys, and the second-base umpire.

We discovered this when we took our five-year-old grandson, Nicholas, to his first play—a community production of *Little Shop of Horrors*. He reported to his mother that the highlight of the afternoon was the punch and cookies that they served at "halftime." After some pointed questioning, she found that he remembered a lot about the play. But the punch and cookies were clearly his strongest recollection.

This reminded us of the family trip we took many years ago to the west coast of Florida, which included a tour of the Ringling Art Museum, in Sarasota. Our son, Derek, a typical five-year-old, wasn't interested in the paintings and sculpture that were featured in the building and gardens. The "art" that captured *his* attention was the pattern on the wood parquet floors. Years later we were amazed that he remembered details of the trip to Sarasota, specifically the patterned floor at "some museum."

Children's perspective of the world is unique, and we respect their sense of wonder at parquet floors and punch and cookies. Life's little details are important to young children. But we need to help them pay attention also to the salient features of events so that their memories of an experience don't exclude the baseball players, the actors on stage, and the art at a museum.

To prepare for an outing, try giving your youngster a child's-eye view of what you expect to happen. Keep it short and simple. Before a recent trip to the Boston Aquarium with our three-year-old grandson, Jeffrey, we told him that we were going to visit a big tank where a lot of fish lived. We told him we would also see some penguins and some other water animals. He would be able to touch some of the water animals if he wanted to, but he didn't have to. This simple summary of the events told him that the fish and water animals were the main topics of interest. No doubt he would also be interested in other children, the vending machines, and so on—which was okay—but the special thing about the trip was the fish and other water animals. A stop at the gift shop for postcards gave us a few more memory aides so that Jeffrey could tell his big brother all about his trip, which he did with reasonable accuracy after a few hints.

Total recall . . . sort of.

One thing that children tend to remember well is recurring events—what typically happens on a day-to-day basis. For example, research by Katherine Nelson, Ph.D.—professor of developmental psychology at the Graduate Center of the City University of New York, in New York City—and her colleagues has shown that preschool children remember novel information in the context of familiar events, such as a special clown cake served at a birthday party. Similarly, in a study by Robyn Fivush and Nina Hamond, two-and-a-half-year-olds—even when questioned about special events, such as a trip to the beach, a camping trip, and a ride on an airplane—tended to recall what adults would consider to be routine information. Take, for instance, the following conversation between an adult and a child about a camping trip, reported by Fivush and Hamond. The child first recalled sleeping outside, which is unusual, but then remembered very routine things:

Interviewer: You slept outside in a tent? Wow, that sounds like fun.
Child: And then we waked up and eat dinner. First we eat dinner, then go to bed, and then wake up and eat breakfast.
Interviewer: What else did you do when you went camping? What did you do . . . after breakfast?
Child: Umm, in the night, and went to sleep.

It seems strange that a child would talk about such routine tasks as waking up, eating, and going to bed when so many new and exciting things must have happened on the trip. But the younger the child, the more she may need to embed novel events in familiar routines. According to Fivush and Hamond's study, everything is new to two-year-olds, and they are constantly learning about their surroundings "so that they can anticipate and predict the world around them. In order to understand novel experience, young children may need to focus on what is familiar about this event, what makes [it] similar to events already known about, rather than what is distinctive or unusual about this event."

Just as strange—or at least surprising—is the accuracy with which children recall long-ago events. For example, two-and-a-half-year-old Katherine, upon seeing an ice cube wrapped in a washcloth, began a detailed account of a bee sting that she had received well over six months earlier, complete with time of day, where she had been when the incident occurred, and what her mother had done to soothe the pain.

This is all the more remarkable because Katherine had begun to talk only six months before, and the accurate account that she was now giving was far more detailed than she could have given at the time of the sting. But this and other impressive acts of long-term memory by young children are always prompted by a very specific cue, in this case the wrapped ice cube. Rarely will a three-year-old who is sitting pensively recount, out of the blue, an event that happened long ago. But with the proper prompt, a flood of information may gush forth.

We're amazed at young children's feats of long-term memory because they're clearly not able to learn as much or as quickly as older children. But learning and remembering are different. According to Charles Brainerd, Ph.D., professor of educational psychology at the University of Arizona, in Tucson, "Despite what our common sense tells us, research shows that learning does not have much to do with what we later remember or forget. A child who can't learn a four-line poem on Tuesday may have a very firm memory of what she had for dinner at Grandma's last month."

Teaching kids to remember.

The ability to remember is not usually thought of as a skill that we need to teach our children. Most of us think that it will simply develop with age: Children grow taller, run faster, and remember more with every birthday. It is true, to a certain extent, that a two-year-old cannot hold in her mind the number of things that a five-year-old can. And much of the trouble that preschoolers get into can be attributed to their forgetting. Young children really do forget to put away their toys, to wash their hands and face, and to return the pretty bracelet to Mommy's bedroom. The best thing that parents can do is to have realistic expectations of what their child can remember, and to be patient. When you're giving instructions, a handy rule of thumb is not to give your child more things to remember than her age. "Go get your shoes and your gloves" is enough for a two-year-old. Three-year-olds can handle three items ("Remember to brush your teeth, comb your hair, and put on your shirt"); most four-year-olds, four related items ("Call your brother for dinner, put away your tricycle, and bring in your jump rope and doll"). In fact, giving children one item less than their age increases the chances that the instructions will be followed.

Parents can play an important role in improving their child's memory. Judith Hudson, Ph.D., an associate professor of psychology at Rutgers University, in New Brunswick, New Jersey, and coeditor of *Knowing and Remembering in Young Children*, believes that children learn how to remember by interacting with their parents. She writes that "remembering can be viewed as an activity that is at first jointly carried out by parent and child and then later performed by the child alone."

In most families, Hudson explains, parents begin talking with young children about things that happened in the past. They ask questions such as, "Where did we go this morning?" "What did we see at the zoo?" "Who

went with us?" and "What else did we see?" From these exchanges, children learn that the important facts to remember about events are who, what, when, and where. These conversations help children learn to notice the important details of their experiences and to store their memories in an organized way so that they can easily be recalled.

In studying these exchanges between parents and preschoolers, Hudson found that parents do more than just ask the right questions; they also give the right answers when the child cannot remember. By providing the missing information, Hudson explains, parents help their child learn that if she is having difficulty recalling information, they will help her retrieve it.

A good example of this is a conversation that we overheard while riding on the Metro in Washington, D.C. A young mother and her daughter, who appeared to be around two, were returning home after a trip to the zoo.

Mother: Brittany, what did we see at the zoo?

Brittany: Elphunts.

Mother: That's right! We saw elephants. What else?

Brittany: *(Shrugs and looks at her mother.)*

Mother: Panda bear? Did we see a panda bear?

Brittany: *(Smiles and nods.)*

Mother: Can you say "panda bear"?

Brittany: Panda bear.

Mother: Good! Elephants and panda bears. What else?

Brittany: Elphunts.

Mother: That's right, elephants. And also a gorilla.

Brittany: Gorilla!

The importance of these hand-holding conversations has been shown in research by Hilary Horn Ratner, Ph.D., professor of psychology at Wayne State University, in Detroit. She observed two- and three-year-olds interacting with their mothers at home and recorded the number of times that the mother asked the child about past events. Ratner then tested the children's memories; those whose mothers had asked them many questions about past events showed better memory abilities both at that time and a year later.

Thinking about thinking.

The fact is that preschoolers simply don't think much about their thinking—if at all. They are still in that nice stage of mental life when remembering and learning "just happen." It will be many years before they are able to evaluate their memory ability and to think of how to make it work better.

When parents tell their preschoolers to "think harder" or "remember better," they are wasting their words. But through daily interactions—by not only asking their preschoolers questions that involve memory but also showing them how to answer—parents serve as memory teachers. Their children are then able to use these memory questions later on as they try to recall the details of specific events. Subtly, and almost effortlessly, parents help their children develop the memory, thinking, and learning skills that will be so useful to them throughout their lives.

Sizing Up The Sexes

Scientists are discovering that gender differences have as much to do with the biology of the brain as with the way we are raised

CHRISTINE GORMAN

What are little boys made of?
What are little boys made of?
Frogs and snails
And puppy dogs' tails,
That's what little boys are made of.

What are little girls made of?
What are little girls made of?
Sugar and spice
And all that's nice,
That's what little girls are made of.
—Anonymous

Many scientists rely on elaborately complex and costly equipment to probe the mysteries confronting humankind. Not Melissa Hines. The UCLA behavioral scientist is hoping to solve one of life's oldest riddles with a toybox full of police cars, Lincoln Logs and Barbie dolls. For the past two years, Hines and her colleagues have tried to determine the origins of gender differences by capturing on videotape the squeals of delight, furrows of concentration and myriad decisions that children from 2 1/2 to 8 make while playing. Although both sexes play with all the toys available in Hines' laboratory, her work confirms what most parents (and more than a few aunts, uncles and nursery-school teachers) already know. As a group, the boys favor sports cars, fire trucks and Lincoln Logs, while the girls are drawn more often to dolls and kitchen toys.

But one batch of girls defies expectations and consistently prefers the boy toys. These youngsters have a rare genetic ab-

normality that caused them to produce elevated levels of testosterone, among other hormones, during their embryonic development. On average, they play with the same toys as the boys in the same ways and just as often. Could it be that the high levels of testosterone present in their bodies before birth have left a permanent imprint on their brains, affecting their later behavior? Or did their parents, knowing of their disorder, somehow subtly influence their choices? If the first explanation is true and

biology determines the choice, Hines wonders, "Why would you evolve to want to play with a truck?"

Not so long ago, any career-minded researcher would have hesitated to ask such questions. During the feminist revolution of the 1970s, talk of inborn differences in the behavior of men and women was distinctly unfashionable, even taboo. Men dominated fields like architecture and engineering, it was argued, because of social, not hormonal, pressures. Women did the vast majority

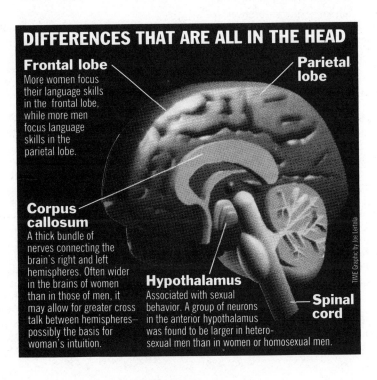

DIFFERENCES THAT ARE ALL IN THE HEAD

Frontal lobe
More women focus their language skills in the frontal lobe, while more men focus language skills in the parietal lobe.

Parietal lobe

Corpus callosum
A thick bundle of nerves connecting the brain's right and left hemispheres. Often wider in the brains of women than in those of men, it may allow for greater cross talk between hemispheres—possibly the basis for woman's intuition.

Hypothalamus
Associated with sexual behavior. A group of neurons in the anterior hypothalamus was found to be larger in heterosexual men than in women or homosexual men.

Spinal cord

TIME Graphic by Joe Lertola

of society's child rearing because few other options were available to them. Once sexism was abolished, so the argument ran, the world would become a perfectly equitable, androgynous place, aside from a few anatomical details.

But biology has a funny way of confounding expectations. Rather than disappear, the evidence for innate sexual differences only began to mount. In medicine, researchers documented that heart disease strikes men at a younger age than it does women and that women have a more moderate physiological response to stress. Researchers found subtle neurological differences between the sexes both in the brain's structure and in its functioning. In addition, another generation of parents discovered that, despite their best efforts to give baseballs to their daughters and sewing kits to their sons, girls still flocked to dollhouses while boys clambered into tree forts. Perhaps nature is more important than nurture after all.

Even professional skeptics have been converted. "When I was younger, I believed that 100% of sex differences were due to the environment," says Jerre Levy, professor of psychology at the University of Chicago. Her own toddler toppled that utopian notion. "My daughter was 15 months old, and I had just dressed her in her teeny little nightie. Some guests arrived, and she came into the room, knowing full well that she looked adorable. She came in with this saucy little walk, cocking her head, blinking her eyes, especially at the men. You never saw such flirtation in your life." After 20 years spent studying the brain, Levy is convinced: "I'm sure there are biologically based differences in our behavior."

Now that it is O.K. to admit the possibility, the search for sexual differences has expanded into nearly every branch of the life sciences. Anthropologists have debunked Margaret Mead's work on the extreme variability of gender roles in New Guinea. Psychologists are untangling the complex interplay between hormones and aggression. But the most provocative, if as yet inconclusive, discoveries of all stem from the pioneering exploration of a tiny 3-lb. universe: the human brain. In fact, some researchers predict that the confirmation of innate differences in behavior could lead to an unprecedented understanding of the mind.

Some of the findings seem merely curious. For example, more men than women are lefthanded, reflecting the dominance of the brain's right hemisphere. By contrast, more women listen equally with both ears while men favor the right one.

Other revelations are bound to provoke more controversy. Psychology tests, for instance, consistently support the notion that men and women perceive the world in subtly different ways. Males excel

EMOTIONS

FEMALE INTUITION: THERE MAY BE SOMETHING TO IT

Do women really possess an ability to read other people's hidden motives and meanings? To some degree, they do. When shown pictures of actors portraying various feelings, women outscore men in identifying the correct emotion. They also surpass men in determining the emotional content of taped conversation in which the words have been garbled. This ability may result from society's emphasis on raising girls to be sensitive. But some researchers speculate that it has arisen to give women greater skill in interpreting the cues of toddlers before they are able to speak.

MALE INSENSITIVITY: IT'S A CULTURAL RELIC

If men seem less adept at deciphering emotions, it is a "trained incompetence," says Harvard psychologist Ronald Levant. Young boys are told to ignore pain and not to cry. Some anthropologists argue that this psychic wound is inflicted to separate boys from their mothers and prepare them for warfare. Many men, says Levant, can recognize their emotions only as a physical buzz or tightness in the throat—a situation that can be reversed, he insists, with training.

at rotating three-dimensional objects in their head. Females prove better at reading emotions of people in photographs. A growing number of scientists believe the discrepancies reflect functional differences in the brains of men and women. If true, then some misunderstandings between the sexes may have more to do with crossed wiring than cross-purposes.

Most of the gender differences that have been uncovered so far are, statistically speaking, quite small. "Even the largest differences in cognitive function are not as large as the difference in male and female height," Hines notes. "You still see a lot of overlap." Otherwise, women could never read maps and men would always be lefthanded. That kind of flexibility within the sexes reveals just how complex a puzzle gender actually is, requiring pieces from biology, sociology and culture.

Ironically, researchers are not entirely sure how or even why humans produce two sexes in the first place. (Why not just one—or even three—as in some species?)

What is clear is that the two sexes originate with two distinct chromosomes. Women bear a double dose of the large X chromosome, while men usually possess a single X and a short, stumpy Y chromosome. In 1990 British scientists reported they had identified a single gene on the Y chromosome that determines maleness. Like some kind of biomolecular Paul Revere, this master gene rouses a host of its compatriots to the complex task of turning a fetus into a boy. Without such a signal, all human embryos would develop into girls. "I have all the genes for being male except this one, and my husband has all the genes for being female," marvels evolutionary psychologist Leda Cosmides, of the University of California at Santa Barbara. "The only difference is which genes got turned on."

Yet even this snippet of DNA is not enough to ensure a masculine result. An elevated level of the hormone testosterone is also required during the pregnancy. Where does it come from? The fetus' own undescended testes. In those rare cases in which the tiny body does not respond to the hormone, a genetically male fetus develops sex organs that look like a clitoris and vagina rather than a penis. Such people look and act female. The majority marry and adopt children.

The influence of the sex hormones extends into the nervous system. Both males and females produce androgens, such as testosterone, and estrogens—although in different amounts. (Men and women who make no testosterone generally lack a libido.) Researchers suspect that an excess of testosterone before birth enables the right hemisphere to dominate the brain, resulting in lefthandedness. Since testosterone levels are higher in boys than in girls, that would explain why more boys are southpaws.

Subtle sex-linked preferences have been detected as early as 52 hours after birth. In studies of 72 newborns, University of Chicago psychologist Martha McClintock and her students found that a toe-fanning reflex was stronger in the left foot for 60% of the males, while all the females favored their right. However, apart from such reflexes in the hands, legs and feet, the team could find no other differences in the babies' responses.

One obvious place to look for gender differences is in the hypothalamus, a lusty little organ perched over the brain stem that, when sufficiently provoked, consumes a person with rage, thirst, hunger or desire. In animals, a region at the front of the organ controls sexual function and is somewhat larger in males than in females. But its size need not remain constant. Studies of tropical fish by Stanford University neurobiologist Russell Fernald reveal that certain cells in this tiny region of the brain swell markedly in an individual male whenever he comes to dominate a school. Unfortunately for the piscine pasha, the cells will also shrink if he loses control of his harem to another male.

Many researchers suspect that, in humans too, sexual preferences are controlled by the hypothalamus. Based on a study of 41 autopsied brains, Simon Le-Vay of the Salk Institute for Biological Studies announced last summer that he had found a region in the hypothalamus that was on average twice as large in heterosexual men as in either women or homosexual men. LeVay's findings support the idea that varying hormone levels before birth may immutably stamp the developing brain in one erotic direction or another.

These prenatal fluctuations may also steer boys toward more rambunctious behavior than girls. June Reinisch, director of the Kinsey Institute for Research in Sex, Gender and Reproduction at Indiana University, in a pioneering study of eight pairs of brothers and 17 pairs of sisters ages 6 to 18 uncovered a complex interplay between hormones and aggression. As a group, the young males gave more belligerent answers than did the females on a multiple-choice test in which they had to imagine their response to stressful situations. But siblings who had been exposed in utero to synthetic antimiscarriage hormones that mimic testosterone were the most combative of all. The affected boys proved significantly more aggressive than their unaffected brothers, and the drug-exposed girls were much more contentious than their unexposed sisters. Reinisch could not determine, however, whether this childhood aggression would translate into greater ambition or competitiveness in the adult world.

PERCEPTION

HE CAN READ A MAP BLINDFOLDED, BUT CAN HE FIND HIS SOCKS?

It's a classic scene of marital discord on the road. Husband: "Do I turn right?" Wife, madly rotating the map: "I'm not sure where we are." Whether men read maps better is unclear, but they do excel at thinking in three dimensions. This may be due to ancient evolutionary pressures related to hunting, which requires orienting oneself while pursuing prey.

IF LOST IN A FOREST, WOMEN WILL NOTICE THE TREES

Such prehistoric pursuits may have conferred a comparable advantage on women. In experiments in mock offices, women proved 70% better than men at remembering the location of items found on a desktop—perhaps reflecting evolutionary pressure on generations of women who foraged for their food. Foragers must recall complex patterns formed of apparently unconnected items.

While most of the gender differences uncovered so far seem to fall under the purview of the hypothalamus, researchers have begun noting discrepancies in other parts of the brain as well. For the past nine years, neuroscientists have debated whether the corpus callosum, a thick bundle of nerves that allows the right half of the brain to communicate with the left, is

larger in women than in men. If it is, and if size corresponds to function, then the greater crosstalk between the hemispheres might explain enigmatic phenomena like female intuition, which is supposed to accord women greater ability to read emotional clues.

These conjectures about the corpus callosum have been hard to prove because the structure's girth varies dramatically with both age and health. Studies of autopsied material are of little use because brain tissue undergoes such dramatic changes in the hours after death. Neuroanatomist Laura Allen and neuroendocrinologist Roger Gorski of UCLA decided to try to circumvent some of these problems by obtaining brain scans from live, apparently healthy people. In their investigation of 146 subjects, published in April, they confirmed that parts of the corpus callosum were up to 23% wider in women than in men. They also measured thicker connections between the two hemispheres in other parts of women's brains.

Encouraged by the discovery of such structural differences, many researchers have begun looking for dichotomies of function as well. At the Bowman Gray Medical School in Winston-Salem, N.C., Cecile Naylor has determined that men and women enlist widely varying parts of their brain when asked to spell words. By monitoring increases in blood flow, the neuropsychologist found that women use both sides of their head when spelling while men use primarily their left side. Because the area activated on the right side is used in understanding emotions, the women apparently tap a wider range of experience for their task. Intriguingly, the effect

LANGUAGE

IN CHOOSING HER WORDS, A WOMAN REALLY USES HER HEAD

For both sexes, the principal language centers of the brain are usually concentrated in the left hemisphere. But preliminary neurological studies show that women make use of both sides of their brain during even the simplest verbal tasks, like spelling. As a result, a woman's appreciation of everyday speech appears to be enhanced by input from various cerebral regions, including those that control vision and feelings. This greater access to the brain's imagery and depth may help explain why girls often begin speaking earlier than boys, enunciate more clearly as tots and develop a larger vocabulary.

IF JOHNNY CAN'T READ, IS IT BECAUSE HE IS A BOY?

Visit a typical remedial-reading class, and you'll find that the boys outnumber the girls 3 to 1. Stuttering affects four times as many boys as girls. Many researchers have used these and other lopsided ratios to support the argument that males, on average, are less verbally fluent than females. However, the discrepancy could also reflect less effort by teachers or parents to find reading-impaired girls. Whatever the case, boys often catch up with their female peers in high school. In the past few years, boys have even begun outscoring girls on the verbal portion of the Scholastic Aptitude Test.

occurred only with spelling and not during a memory test.

Researchers speculate that the greater communication between the two sides of the brain could impair a woman's performance of certain highly specialized visual-spatial tasks. For example, the ability to tell directions on a map without physically having to rotate it appears stronger in those individuals whose brains restrict the process to the right hemisphere. Any crosstalk between the two sides apparently distracts the brain from its job. Sure enough, several studies have shown that this mental-rotation skill is indeed more tightly focused in men's brains than in women's.

But how did it get to be that way? So far, none of the gender scientists have figured out whether nature or nurture is more important. "Nothing is ever equal, even in the beginning," observes Janice Juraska, a biopsychologist at the University of Illinois at Urbana-Champaign. She points out, for instance, that mother rats lick their male offspring more frequently than they do their daughters. However, Juraska has demonstrated that it is possible to reverse some inequities by manipulating environmental factors. Female rats have fewer nerve connections than males into the hippocampus, a brain region associated with spatial relations and memory. But when Juraska "enriched" the cages of the females with stimulating toys, the females developed more of these neuronal connections. "Hormones do affect things—it's crazy to deny that," says the researcher. "But there's no telling which way sex differences might go if we completely changed the environment." For humans, educational enrichment could perhaps enhance a woman's ability to work in three dimensions and a man's ability to interpret emotions. Says Juraska: "There's nothing about human brains that is so stuck that a different way of doing things couldn't change it enormously."

Nowhere is this complex interaction between nature and nurture more apparent than in the unique human abilities of speaking, reading and writing. No one is born knowing French, for example; it must be learned, changing the brain forever. Even so, language skills are linked to specific cerebral centers. In a remarkable series of experiments, neurosurgeon George Ojemann of the University of Washington has produced scores of detailed maps of people's individual language centers.

First, Ojemann tested his patients' verbal intelligence using a written exam. Then, during neurosurgery—which was performed under a local anesthetic—he asked them to name aloud a series of objects found in a steady stream of black-and-white photos. Periodically, he touched different parts of the brain with an electrode that temporarily blocked the activity of that region. (This does not hurt because the brain has no sense of pain.) By noting when his patients made mistakes, the surgeon was able to determine which sites were essential to naming.

Several complex sexual differences emerged. Men with lower verbal IQs were more likely to have their language skills located toward the back of the brain. In a number of women, regardless of IQ, the naming ability was restricted to the frontal lobe. This disparity could help explain why strokes that affect the rear of the brain seem to be more devastating to men than to women.

Intriguingly, the sexual differences are far less significant in people with higher verbal IQs. Their language skills developed in a more intermediate part of the brain. And yet, no two patterns were ever identical. "That to me is the most important finding," Ojemann says. "Instead of these sites being laid down more or less the same in everyone, they're laid down in subtly different places." Language is scattered randomly across these cerebral centers, he hypothesizes, because the skills evolved so recently.

What no one knows for sure is just how hardwired the brain is. How far and at what stage can the brain's extraordinary flexibility be pushed? Several studies suggest that the junior high years are key. Girls show the same aptitudes for math as boys until about the seventh grade, when more and more girls develop math phobia. Coincidentally, that is the age at which boys start to shine and catch up to girls in reading.

By one account, the gap between men and women for at least some mental skills has actually started to shrink. By looking at 25 years' worth of data from academic tests, Janet Hyde, professor of psychology and women's studies at the University of Wisconsin at Madison, discovered that overall gender differences for verbal and mathematical skills dramatically decreased after 1974. One possible explanation, Hyde notes, is that "Americans have changed their socialization and educational patterns over the past few decades. They are treating males and females with greater similarity."

Even so, women still have not caught up with men on the mental-rotation test. Fascinated by the persistence of that gap, psychologists Irwin Silverman and Marion Eals of York University in Ontario wondered if there were any spatial tasks at which women outperformed men. Looking at it from the point of view of human evolution, Silverman and Eals reasoned that while men may have developed strong spatial skills in response to evolutionary pressures to be successful hunters, women would have needed other types of visual skills to excel as gatherers and foragers of food.

The psychologists therefore designed a test focused on the ability to discern and later recall the location of objects in a complex, random pattern. In series of tests, student volunteers were given a minute to study a drawing that contained such unrelated objects as an elephant, a guitar and a cat. Then Silverman and Eals presented their subjects with a second drawing containing additional objects and told them to cross out those items that had been added and circle any that had moved. Sure enough, the women consistently surpassed the men in giving correct answers.

What made the psychologists really sit up and take notice, however, was the fact that the women scored much better on the mental-rotation test while they were menstruating. Specifically, they improved their scores by 50% to 100% whenever their estrogen levels were at their lowest. It is not clear why this should be. However, Silverman and Eals are trying to find out if women exhibit a similar hormonal effect for any other visual tasks.

Oddly enough, men may possess a similar hormonal response, according to new research reported in November by Doreen Kimura, a psychologist at the University of Western Ontario. In her study of 138 adults, Kimura found that males perform better on mental-rotation tests in the spring, when their testosterone levels are low, rather than in the fall, when they are higher. Men are also subject to a daily cycle, with testosterone levels lowest around 8 p.m. and peaking around 4 a.m. Thus, says June Reinisch of the Kinsey Institute: "When people say women can't be trusted because they cycle every month, my response is that men cycle every day, so they should only be allowed to negotiate peace treaties in the evening."

Far from strengthening stereotypes about who women and men truly are or how they should behave, research into innate sexual differences only underscores humanity's awesome adaptability. "Gender is really a complex business," says Reinisch. "There's no question that hormones have an effect. But what does that have to do with the fact that I like to wear pink ribbons and you like to wear baseball gloves? Probably something, but we don't know what."

Even the concept of what an innate difference represents is changing. The physical and chemical differences between the brains of the two sexes may be malleable and subject to change by experience: certainly an event or act of learning can directly affect the brain's biochemistry and physiology. And so, in the final analysis, it may be impossible to say where nature ends and nurture begins because the two are so intimately linked.

—*Reported by*
J. Madeleine Nash/Los Angeles

The Day Care Generation

Pat Wingert
and Barbara Kantrowitz

Meryl Frank is an expert on child care. For five years she ran a Yale University program that studied parental leave. But after she became a new mother two years ago, Frank discovered that even though she knew about such esoteric topics as staff-child ratios and turnover rates, she was a novice when it came to finding someone to watch her own child. Frank went back to work part time when her son, Isaac, was 5 months old, and in the two years since then she has changed child-care arrangements *nine* times.

Her travails began with a well-regarded day-care center near her suburban New Jersey home. On the surface, it was great. One staff member for every three babies, a sensitive administrator, clean facilities. "But when I went in," Frank recalls, "I saw this line of cribs and all these babies with their arms out crying, wanting to be picked up. I felt like crying myself." She walked out without signing Isaac up and went through a succession of other unsatisfactory situations—a babysitter who couldn't speak English, a woman who cared for 10 children in her home at once—before settling on a neighborhood woman who took Isaac into her home. "She was fabulous," Frank recalls wistfully. Three weeks after that babysitter started, she got sick and had to quit. Frank advertised for help in the newspaper and got 30 inquiries but no qualified babysitter. (When Frank asked one prospective nanny about her philosophy of discipline, the woman replied: "If he touched the stove, I'd punch him.") A few weeks later she finally hired her 10th babysitter. "She's a very nice young woman," Frank says. "Unfortunately, she has to leave in

May. And I just found out I'm pregnant again and due in June."

That's what happens when a *pro* tries to get help. For other parents, the situation can be even worse. Child-care tales of woe are a common bond for the current generation of parents. Given the haphazard state of day care in this country, finding the right situation is often just a matter of luck. There's no guarantee that a good thing will last. And always, there's the disturbing question that lurks in the back of every working parent's mind: *what is this doing to my kids?*

The simple and unsettling answer is, nobody really knows for sure. Experts say they're just beginning to understand the ramifications of raising a generation of youngsters outside the home while their parents work. Mothers in this country have always had jobs, but it is only in the past few years that a majority have gone back to the office while their children are still in diapers. In the past, most mothers worked out of necessity. That's still true for the majority today, but they have also been joined by mothers of all economic classes. Some researchers think we won't know all the answers until the 21st century, when the children of today's working mothers are parents themselves. In the meantime, results gathered so far are troubling.

Some of the first studies of day care in the 1970s indicated that there were no ill effects from high-quality child care. There was even evidence that children who were out of the home at an early age were more independent and made friends more easily. Those results received wide attention and reassured many parents. Unfortunately, they don't tell the whole story. "The problem is that much of the day care available

Child care has immediate problems. But what about the long-term effect it will have on kids?

---

in this country is not high quality," says Deborah Lowe Vandell, professor of educational psychology at the University of Wisconsin. The first research was often done in university-sponsored centers where the child-care workers were frequently students preparing for careers as teachers. Most children in day care don't get such dedicated attention.

Since the days of these early studies, child care has burgeoned into a $15 billion-a-year industry in this country. Day-care centers get most of the attention because they are the fastest-growing segment, but they account for only a small percentage of child-care arrangements. According to 1986 Census Bureau figures, more than half of the kids under 5 with working mothers were cared for by nonrelatives: 14.7 percent in day-care centers and 23.8 percent in family day care, usually a neighborhood home where one caretaker watches several youngsters. Most of the rest were in nursery school or preschool.

Despite years of lobbying by children's advocates, there are still no federal regulations covering the care of young children. The government offers consumers more guidance choosing breakfast cereal than child care. Each state makes its own rules, and they vary from virtually no governmental supervision to strict enforcement of complicated licensing procedures for day-care centers. Many child-development experts recommend that each caregiver be responsible for no more than three infants under the age of 1. Yet only three states—Kansas, Maryland and Massachusetts—require that ratio. Other states are far more lax. Idaho, for example, allows one caregiver to look after as many as 12 children of any age (including babies). And in 14 states there are absolutely no training requirements before starting a job as a child-care worker.

Day-care centers are the easiest to supervise and inspect because they usually operate openly. Family day care, on the other hand, poses big problems for regulatory agencies. Many times, these are informal arrangements that are hard to track down. Some child-care providers even say that regulation would make matters worse by imposing confusing rules that would keep some potential caregivers out of business and intensify the shortage of good day care.

No wonder working parents sometimes feel like pioneers wandering in the wilderness. The signposts point every which way. One set of researchers argues that babies who spend more than 20 hours a week in child care may grow up maladjusted. Other experts say the high turnover rate among poorly paid and undertrained child-care workers has created an unstable environment for youngsters who need dependability and consistency. And still others are worried about health issues—the wisdom of putting a lot of small children with limited immunities in such close quarters. Here's a synopsis of the current debate in three major areas of concern.

There's no question that the care of the very youngest children is by far the most controversial area of research. The topic so divides the child-development community that a scholarly journal, Early Childhood Research Quarterly, recently devoted two entire issues to the subject. Nobody is saying that mothers ought to stay home until their kids are ready for college. Besides that, it would be economically impossible; two thirds of all working women are the sole support of their families or are married to men who earn less than $15,000 a year. But as the demographics have changed, psychologists are taking a second look at what happens to babies. In 1987, 52 percent of mothers of children under the age of 1 were working, compared with 32 percent 10 years earlier. Many experts believe that day-care arrangements that might be fine for 3- and 4-year-olds may be damaging to infants.

Much of the dispute centers on the work of Pennsylvania State University psychologist Jay Belsky. He says mounting research indicates that babies less than 1 year old who receive nonmaternal care for more than 20 hours a week are at a greater risk of developing insecure relationships with their mothers; they're also at increased risk of emotional and behavioral problems in later childhood. Youngsters who have weak emotional ties to their mothers are more likely to be aggressive and disobedient as they grow older, Belsky says. Of course, kids whose mothers are home all day can have these problems, too. But Belsky says that mothers who aren't with their kids all day long don't get to know their babies as well as mothers who work part time or not at all. Therefore, working mothers may not be as sensitive to a baby's first attempts at communication. In general, he says, mothers are more attentive to these crucial signals than babysitters. Placing a baby in outside care increases the chance that an infant's needs won't be met, Belsky says. He also argues that working parents have so much stress in their lives that they have little energy left over for their children. It's hard to find the strength for "quality time" with the kids after a 10- or 12-hour day at the office. (It is interesting to note that not many people are promoting the concept of quality time these days.)

Work by other researchers has added weight to Belsky's theories. Wisconsin's Vandell studied the day-care histories of 236 Texas third graders and found that youngsters who had more than 30 hours a week of child care during infancy had poorer peer relationships, were harder to discipline and had poorer work habits than children who had been in part-time child care or exclusive maternal care. The children most at risk were from the lowest and highest socioeconomic classes, Vandell says, probably because poor youngsters usually get the worst child care and rich parents tend to have high-stress jobs that require long hours away from home. Vandell emphasizes that her results in the Texas study may be more negative than those for the country as a whole because Texas has minimal child-care regulation. Nonetheless, she thinks there's a "serious problem" in infant care.

Other experts say there isn't enough information yet to form any definitive conclusions about the long-term effects of infant

Who's Minding the Children?

Even with the sharp rise in working mothers, most children are still cared for at home—their own or someone else's.

Percent of Mothers Working

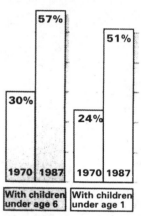

	With children under age 6	With children under age 1
1970	30%	24%
1987	57%	51%

SOURCE: CHILD CARE INC.

Day Care
WHO LOOKS AFTER CHILDREN UNDER AGE 5 WHILE THEIR MOTHERS WORK

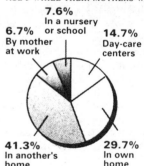

7.6% In a nursery or school
6.7% By mother at work
14.7% Day-care centers
41.3% In another's home
29.7% In own home

SOURCE: U.S. CENSUS BUREAU

Day care that might be fine for 3- or 4-year-olds may be damaging to infants

care. "There is no clear evidence that day care places infants at risk," says Alison Clarke-Stewart, a professor of social ecology at the University of California, Irvine. Clarke-Stewart says that the difference between the emotional attachments of children of working and of nonworking mothers is not as large as Belsky's research indicates. She says parents should be concerned but shouldn't overreact. Instead of pulling kids out of any form of day care, parents might consider choosing part-time work when their children are very young, she says.

For all the controversy over infant care, there's little dispute over the damaging effects of the high turnover rate among caregivers. In all forms of child care, consistency is essential to a child's healthy development. But only the lucky few get it. "Turnover among child-care workers is second only to parking-lot and gas-station attendants," says Marcy Whitebook, director of the National Child Care Staffing Study. "To give you an idea of how bad it is, during our study, we had tiny children coming up to our researchers and asking them, 'Are you my teacher?' "

The just-released study, funded by a consortium of not-for-profit groups, included classroom observations, child assessments and interviews with staff at 227 child-care centers in five cities. The researchers concluded that 41 percent of all child-care workers quit each year, many to seek better-paying jobs. In the past decade, the average day-care-center enrollment has nearly doubled, while the average salaries for child-care workers have decreased 20 percent. Typical annual wages are very low: $9,931 for full-time, year-round employment ($600 less than the 1988 poverty threshold for a family of three). Few child-care workers receive any benefits.

Parents who use other forms of day care should be concerned as well, warns UCLA psychologist Carollee Howes. Paying top dollar for au pairs, nannies and other in-home caregivers doesn't guarantee that they'll stay. Howes conducted two studies of 18- to 24-month-old children who had been cared for in their own homes or in family day-care homes and found that most had already experienced two or three changes in caregivers and some had had as many as six. In her research, Howes found that the more changes children had, the more trouble they had adjusting to first grade.

The solution, most experts agree, is a drastic change in the status, pay and training of child-care workers. Major professional organizations, such as the National Association for the Education of Young Children, have recommended standard accreditation procedures to make child care more of an established profession, for everyone from workers in large for-profit centers to women who only look after youngsters in their neighborhood. But so far, only a small fraction of the country's child-care providers are accredited. Until wide-scale changes take place, Whitebook predicts that "qualified teachers will continue to leave for jobs that offer a living wage." The victims are the millions of children left behind.

When their toddlers come home from day care with a bad case of the sniffles, parents often joke that it's "schoolitis"—the virus that seems to invade classrooms from September until June. But there's more and more evidence that child care may be hazardous to a youngster's health.

A recent report from the Centers for Disease Control found that children who are cared for outside their homes are at increased risk for both minor and major ailments because they are exposed to so many other kids at such a young age. Youngsters who spend their days in group settings are more likely to get colds and flu as well as strep throat, infectious hepatitis and spinal meningitis, among other diseases.

Here again, the state and federal governments aren't doing much to help. A survey released this fall by the American Academy of Pediatrics and the American Public Health Association found that even such basic health standards as immunization and hand washing were not required in child-care facilities in half the states. Inspection was another problem. Without adequate staff, states with health regulations often have difficulty enforcing them, especially in family day-care centers.

Some experts think that even with strict regulation, there would still be health problems in child-care centers, especially among infants. "The problem is that caretakers are changing the diapers of several kids, and it's difficult for them to wash their hands frequently enough [after each diaper]," says Earline Kendall, associate dean of graduate studies in education at Belmont College in Nashville, Tenn. Kendall, who has operated four day-care centers herself, says that very young babies have the most limited immunities and are the most vulnerable to the diseases that can be spread through such contact. The best solution, she thinks, would be more generous leave time so that parents can stay home until their kids are a little older.

Despite the compelling evidence about the dark side of day care, many experts say there's a great reluctance to discuss these problems publicly. "People think if you say anything against day care, you're saying young parents shouldn't work, or if they do work, they're bad parents," says Meryl Frank, who is now a consultant on family and work issues. "For a lot of parents, that's just too scary to think about. But we have to be realistic. We have to acknowledge that good day care may be good for kids, but bad day care is bad for kids."

There is a political battle as well. Belsky, who has become a lightning rod for controversy among child-development professionals, says "people don't want working mothers to feel guilty" because "they're afraid the right wing will use this to say that only mothers can care for babies, so women should stay home." But, he says, parents should use these problems as evidence to press for such changes as paid parental leave, more part-time jobs and higher-quality child care. The guilt and anxiety that seem to be part of every working parent's psyche aren't necessarily bad, Belsky says. Parents who worry are also probably alert to potential problems—and likely to look for solutions.

Child-Care Checklist

Questions to ask at day-care centers:

■ What are the educational and training backgrounds of staff members?

■ What is the child-staff ratio for each age? Most experts say it should be no more than 4:1 for infants, 5:1 for 18 months to 2 years, 8:1 for 2 to 3 years, 10:1 for 3 to 4 years and 15:1 for 5 to 6 years.

■ What are the disciplinary policies?

■ Are parents free to visit at any time?

■ Are the center's facilities clean and well maintained?

■ Are child-safety precautions observed? Such as heat covers on radiators, childproof safety seals on all electrical outlets?

■ Are staff members careful about hygiene? It's important to wash hands between diaper changes in order to avoid spreading diseases.

■ Are there facilities and staff for taking care of sick children?

■ Is there adequate space, indoors and out, for children to play?

■ Most important of all, do the children look happy and cared for? Trust your instincts.

Development During Childhood

- **Social and Emotional Development (Articles 18–23)**
- **Cognitive and Language Development (Articles 24–26)**
- **Developmental Problems (Articles 27 and 28)**

The transition to childhood brings many new and difficult challenges to parents in promoting healthy social and emotional growth in their children while encouraging and supporting effective cognitive and language development. The subsection *Social and Emotional Development* begins with a review of perspectives on the factors that promote an effective sense of right and wrong and the self-discipline to function in accordance with the dictates of society. "The Good, the Bad, and the Difference" reviews several competing contemporary accounts. Though they differ in important respects, all agree that parents do play a major role in inculcating moral standards in their children.

One set of issues that parents have to resolve focuses on the role that television plays in the household. Some see television as a source of information for children. Others regard it as a "plug-in drug" and a ready model for aggressive behavior. Do televised acts of aggression desensitize children to violence? Even worse, does it instigate violent behavior in some children? While the findings cited in "TV Violence—What Influence on Young Minds?" raise concerns of this nature, some authorities dispute the practical implications of these claims.

Parents also have to contend with their children's pleas for an array of ever-popular toys associated with action figures and violent actions. As described in "A Push for PG-Rated Playthings," toy companies are coming under increasing pressure by consumer groups and governmental bodies to establish warning labels for toys associated with violence. Some toy manufacturers and distributors are now showing concern over the part they are taking in the promotion of violence through the sale of these products.

The next selection, "Your Loving Touch," examines the importance of touch in human development. Americans are not an especially touch-oriented culture, often refraining from physical contact. However, many child specialists stress the benefits of affectionate physical contact at all age levels.

Every family experiences interpersonal dynamics. Are the effects of birth order potent enough to control the patterning of these dynamics? Put another way, is ordinal position in the family a powerful determinant of behavior? The issue is a thorny one. Most older children and adults acknowledge that their parents' expectations and behaviors were influenced by the birth order of the children. However, whether these practices result in predictable effects on personality is controversial. Nonetheless, consideration of the possible influences of birth order, as discussed in "Places Everyone," is instructive in sensitizing us to family dynamics.

All life transitions create some degree of stress. Although some children react to stress by striking out against the perceived source, and others respond by withdrawing and attempting to isolate themselves, some children seem to take stress-producing situations in stride. These "invulnerable" or "resilient" children, as pointed out in "The Miracle of Resiliency," have developmental histories that may include extreme poverty or chronic family stress. Most people would consider both factors to be highly damaging to the growth of personal and social competence. Yet these hardy children do not become victims; instead, they develop effective interpersonal skills. Without question, studies of these children contribute importantly to our understanding of personality and social development.

The articles in the *Cognitive and Language Development* subsection focus on developmental changes in learning ability and on the acquisition of language. A great deal of knowledge has accumulated in the past 3 decades about children's learning styles, much of it stimulated by the work of the famous developmental theorist Jean Piaget. Piaget stressed the need for the child to play an active role in the learning process—taking a position that contrasts dramatically with the traditional "sit still and listen" method of teaching that is all too familiar to most of us. In Piaget's view, young children learn best when given the opportunity to actively engage objects and concepts.

Language development actually begins long before the child's first spoken word. But that milestone, which typically occurs between about 10 and 14 months of age, stands as a dramatic announcement by the child that language acquisition is indeed underway. Many, perhaps most, parents wonder what they can do to help their child in the mastery of his or her native language.

The *Developmental Problems* subsection addresses issues relating to the socialization and education of children who are handicapped as a result of drug use by their mothers during pregnancy, or by genetic anomalies, severe disabilities such as cerebral palsy, and deficits of unknown origin. "Clipped Wings" describes the effects of prenatal exposure to drugs, alcohol, and smoking by the mother. Exposure to any of these can result in low birth weight. As babies, they are likely to be inattentive, socially withdrawn, and hyperactive. By school age, these children are at a higher risk for failure. However, early intervention can greatly improve the intellectual functioning of these children and their ability to cope with the demands of structured school settings.

"Of a Different Mind" describes the characteristics associated with Williams syndrome, a genetic disorder that has been receiving close scrutiny by a number of leading behavioral and brain scientists because of the unusual pattern of abilities it yields: linguistic ability is in some respects unusually well developed, while mental functions are significantly delayed. As a result, this disorder is providing a fertile ground for studying the relation between language abilities and other mental functions such as planning, reasoning, and deduction.

Looking Ahead: Challenge Questions

Children who are described as resilient are an enigma. How would you explain such strength of personality in the face of so many potentially disruptive influences in their lives? What coping mechanisms seem to provide resilient children with such strength of character?

A substantial number of children enter the public school system with learning impairments caused by the mother's use of alcohol, tobacco, and drugs. How are educators helping these children to overcome their disabilities?

What role should parents play in instilling moral values in their children?

To what extent are parents responsible for the pace of language growth in their young children, and how can they best support the child to acquire effective communicative skills?

Sentiment is growing for restructuring the primary grades to reflect the ways in which young children learn. How high a priority would you place on efforts to bring about these changes?

Do parents treat the eldest child in the family differently than they treat the other children? If so, what personality characteristics might be fostered by differential expectations and experiences?

What is the probable cause of Williams syndrome and how do children with this disorder differ from normally developing children?

The Good, The Bad And The DIFFERENCE

Barbara Kantrowitz

Like many children, Sara Newland loves animals. But unlike most youngsters, she has turned that love into activism. Five years ago, during a trip to the zoo, the New York City girl learned about the plight of endangered species, and decided to help. With the aid of her mother, Sara—then about 4 years old—baked cakes and cookies and sold them on the sidewalk near her apartment building. She felt triumphant when she raised $35, which she promptly sent in to the World Wildlife Fund.

A few weeks later, triumph turned into tears when the fund wrote Sara asking for more money. "She was devastated because she thought she had taken care of that problem," says Polly Newland, who then patiently told her daughter that there are lots of big problems that require continual help from lots of people. That explanation worked. Sara, now 9, has expanded her causes. Through her school, she helps out at an inner-city child-care center; she also regularly brings meals to homeless people in her neighborhood.

A sensitive parent can make all the difference in encouraging—or discouraging—a child's developing sense of morality and values. Psychologists say that not only are parents important as role models, they also have to be aware of a child's perception of the world at different ages and respond appropriately to children's concerns. "I think the capacity for goodness is there from the start," says Thomas Lickona, a professor of education at the State University of New York at Cortland and author of "Raising Good Children." But, he says, parents must nurture those instincts just as they help their children become good readers or athletes or musicians.

That's not an easy task these days. In the past, schools and churches played a key role in fostering moral development. Now, with religious influence in decline and schools wavering over

A sensitive parent is crucial in encouraging a child's sense of morality and values

the way to teach values, parents are pretty much on their own. Other recent social trends have complicated the transmission of values. "We're raising a generation that is still groping for a good future direction," says psychologist William Damon, head of Brown University's education department. Many of today's parents were raised in the '60s, the age of permissiveness. Their children were born in the age of affluence, the '80s, when materialism was rampant. "It's an unholy combination," says Damon.

These problems may make parents feel they have no effect on how their children turn out. But many studies show that parents are still the single most important influence on their children. Lickona says that the adolescents most likely to follow their consciences rather than give in to peer pressure are those who grew up in "authoritative" homes, where rules are firm but clearly explained and justified—as opposed to "authoritarian" homes (where rules are laid down without explanation) or "permissive" homes.

The way a parent explains rules depends, of course, on the age of the child. Many adults assume that kids see right and wrong in grown-up terms. But what may be seen as "bad" behavior by an adult may not be bad in the child's eyes. For example, a young child may not know the difference between a fanciful tale and a lie, while older kids—past the age of 5—do know.

Many psychologists think that in children, the seeds of moral values are emotional, not intellectual. Such traits as empathy and guilt—observable in the very young—represent the beginning of what will later be a conscience. Even newborns respond to signs of distress in others. In a hospital nursery, for example, a bout of crying by one infant will trigger wailing all around. Research on children's attachment to their mothers shows that babies who are most secure (and those whose mothers are most responsive to their needs) later turn out to be leaders in school: self-directed and eager to learn. They are also most likely to absorb parental values.

The first modern researcher to describe the stages of a child's moral development was Swiss psychologist Jean Piaget. In his groundbreaking 1932 book, "The Moral Judgment of the Child," he described three overlapping phases of childhood, from 5 to 12. The first is the "morality of constraint" stage: children accept adult rules as absolutes. Then comes the "morality of cooperation," in which youngsters think of morality as equal treatment. Parents of siblings will recognize this as the "If he got a new Ninja Turtle, I want one, too," stage. In the third, kids can see complexity in moral situations. They can understand extenuating circumstances in which strict equality might not necessarily mean fairness ("He got a new Ninja Turtle, but I got to go to the ball game, so it's OK.")

Although Piaget's conclusions have been expanded by subsequent researchers, his work forms the basis for most current theories of moral development. In a study begun in the 1950s, Lawrence Kohlberg, a Harvard professor, used "moral dilemmas" to define six phases. He began with 50 boys who were 10, 13 and 16. Over the next 20 years, he asked them their reactions to carefully constructed dilemmas. The most famous concerns a man named Heinz, whose wife was dying of cancer. The boys were told, in part, that a drug that might save her was a form of radium discovered by the town pharmacist. But the pharmacist was charging 10 times the cost of manufacture for the drug and Heinz could not afford it—although he tried to borrow money from everyone he knew. Heinz begged the pharmacist to sell it more cheaply, but he refused. So Heinz, in desperation, broke into the store and stole the drug. Kohlberg asked his subjects: Did Heinz do the right thing? Why?

Kohlberg and others found that at the first stage, children base their answers simply on the likelihood of getting caught. As they get older, their reasons for doing the right thing become more complex. For example, Lickona says typical 5-year-olds want to stay out of trouble. Kids from 6 to 9 characteristically act out of self-interest; most 10- to 13-year-olds crave social approval. Many 15- to 19-year-olds have moved on to thinking about maintaining the social system and being responsible.

Over the years, educators have used these theories to establish new curricula at schools around the country that emphasize moral development. The Lab School, a private preschool in Houston, was designed by Rheta DeVries, a student of Kohlberg's. The teacher is a "companion/guide," not an absolute authority figure. The object of the curriculum is to get kids to think about why they take certain actions and to think about consequences. For example, if two children are playing a game and one wants to change the rules, the teacher would ask the other child if that was all right. "Moral development occurs best when children live in an environment where fairness and justice is a way of life," says DeVries.

Not everyone agrees with the concept of moral development as a series of definable stages. Other researchers say that the stage theories downplay the role of emotion, empathy and faith. In "The Moral Life of Children," Harvard child psychiatrist Robert Coles tells the story of a 6-year-old black girl named Ruby, who braved vicious racist crowds to integrate her New Orleans school—and then prayed for her tormentors each night before she went to bed. Clearly, Coles says, she did not easily fall into any of Kohlberg's or Piaget's stages. Another criticism of stage theorists comes from feminist psychologists, including Carol Gilligan, author of "In a Different Voice." Gilligan says that the stages represent only *male* development with the emphasis on the concepts of justice and rights, not female development, which, she says, is more concerned with responsibility and caring.

But many psychologists say parents can use the stage theories to gain insight into their children's development. At each phase, parents should help their children make the right decisions about their behavior. In his book, Lickona describes a typical situation involving a 5-year-old who has hit a friend over the head with a toy while playing at the friend's house. Lickona suggests that the parents, instead of simply punishing their son, talk to him about why he hit his friend (the boy played with a toy instead of with him) and about what he could do next time instead of hitting. The parents, Lickona says, should also discuss how the friend might have felt about being hit. By the end of the discussion, the child should realize that there are consequences to his behavior. In Lickona's example, the child decides to call his friend and apologize—a positive ending.

For older children, Lickona suggests family "fairness meetings" to alleviate tension. If, for example, a brother and sister are constantly fighting, the parents could talk to both of them about what seem to be persistent sources of irritation. Then, youngsters can think of ways to bring about a truce—or at least a cease-fire.

Children who learn these lessons can become role models for other youngsters—and for adults as well. Sara Newland tells her friends not to be scared of homeless people (most of them rush by without even a quick glance, she says). "Some people think, 'Why should I give to them?'" she says. "But I feel that you should give. If everyone gave food, they would all have decent meals." One recent evening, she and her mother fixed up three plates of beef stew to give out. They handed the first to the homeless man who's always on their corner. Then, Sara says, they noticed two "rough-looking guys" down the block. Sara's mother, a little scared, walked quickly past them. Then, she changed her mind and asked them if they'd like some dinner. "They said, 'Yes, God bless you'," Sara recalls. "At that moment, they weren't the same people who were looking through a garbage can for beer bottles a little while before. It brought out a part of them that they didn't know they had."

With TESSA NAMUTH *in New York and* KAREN SPRINGEN *in Chicago*

TV violence— what influence on young minds?

Robert A. Hamilton

Robert A. Hamilton is a freelance writer who lives in Franklin, Connecticut.

Children see more than 30,000 violent deaths on TV by age 18. How much does this violence affect their behavioral patterns? The debate rages on.

For people who grew up in the early years of broadcasting, violence on television consisted of someone getting shot on a dusty Western street. The victim would clutch his bloodless chest, gasp a few last words to impart some moral lesson, and fall asleep.

Today, movie makers are competing for new ways to shock us. Actors are being blown apart by bombs, chopped to pieces with chainsaws, hacked to death with broadswords, eaten alive by aliens, or ripped apart on the rack. With dramatic advances in special effects, each of these torture-deaths seems surprisingly realistic. And there is a growing trade in "snuff films," where the people are supposed to be actually killed on screen.

It's now estimated that children living in a home with cable television and a videocassette recorder will be exposed to huge doses of violence. In fact, they will view more than 30,000 violent deaths, and 40,000 attempted murders, by the time they turn 18.

As the body count continues to rise, more and more health professionals are asking how this is affecting the mental health of our children.

Violence — a way of life? "The children we see today are a lot more preoccupied with violence than those we saw even five years ago," says Daniel Koenigsberg, M.D., chief of Child Psychiatry at the Hospital of Saint Raphael. "They're not scared by it, as much as they are accepting of it, and interested in it. Further, they're talking about violence more. I infer from that that they're being exposed to it more, by watching more television. Today, of course, there is much more violence on TV."

Children from age three or younger, but even as old as ages four to eight, cannot easily determine whether television violence is real, Koenigsberg says. Because of this blurring, he adds, it is more anxiety-provoking to witness it.

"I would say the percentage of children we see who are preoccupied and interested in violence has more than doubled in the last five years," Koenigsberg says. "Previously, it was only a fraction of the kids. Now, more than half the young patients we see have some kind of problem related to aggression or violence."

"What is on television, in terms of social values, is pretty deviant," says James H. Watt, professor of Communications Sciences at the University of Connecticut. "Television is not real life, but to a child who's not getting a lot of instruction on moral values, there is a danger of learning to behave that way," he says.

Douglas M. Wills, a spokesman for the National Association of Broadcasters, downplays the effects of television viewing on violence. "There have been sociologists who have tried to establish a link between viewing violence on television, and subsequent violence on the part of the viewer," Wills says. "But there has yet to be any sort of causal link established."

In addition, he says, last December CBS, NBC and ABC adopted voluntary guidelines designed to limit television violence. "Broadcasters have responded in every way to the concerns of the community, and concerns of the lawmakers."

More must be done But there is a growing feeling that more should be done. After a two-year-old boy was beaten to death by two ten-year-olds in England this year, people rioting in the streets blamed it on the increasing savagery of television shows. In this country, too, people are growing more concerned about televised violence.

"It's become a public health issue," says Wally Bowen, executive director of Citizens for Media Literacy. This national organization recently devoted an entire issue of its newsletter to the subject.

Bowen says his crusade has found allies in public health professionals, who see television linked not only to violence, but also to teen pregnancy, drug and alcohol abuse, smoking, and a host of other ills. That is because of the way television shows deal with those problems.

"A whole gamut of social ills has a media component; we've got to come to grips with that," Bowen says. "People are starting to wake up to how much power our media culture has in terms of shaping our consciousness. This is going to be the decade of media 'literacy'."

From 1980 to 1992, the federal government relaxed many of the controls on industry, including television. That might be changing. One of President Clinton's first acts was to commission a report to Congress, *Ready to Learn*, that will examine the impact of television, including television violence.

Studies of the link have progressed considerably since 1972, when the U.S. Surgeon General issued his first report on television violence. Jerome L. Singer, a psychologist and researcher with the Yale University Family Television Research and Consultation Center, is helping prepare *Ready to Learn*. He says one study followed people for more than 20 years, from age ten to age 30. Children who were heavy viewers turned out to be more aggressive, and were more likely to have been arrested, he says.

"You could argue that children who are more aggressive inherently, also like to watch more aggressive television," Singer says. But other studies establish an even firmer link.

TV access might increase violence One Canadian study looked at one town that had no access to television and compared it to two towns that did. Initially, the town with no television had a demonstrably lower level of violence. "Once television was introduced, however, there was an increase in aggressive behavior," Singer says.

Brandon S. Centerwall, M.D., a Seattle physician, published an article in the June 10, 1992 issue of the *Journal of the American Medical Association*. He compared homicide rates in the United States and Canada (where television was introduced by 1945) to those in South Africa, where TV was banned until 1975 for security reasons. In the U.S. and Canada, the homicide rate rose more than 90 percent from 1945 to 1974, while in South Africa it declined 7 percent. Eight years after television was introduced, however, South Africa's homicide rate had increased 56 percent.

"Although television broadcasting was prohibited prior to 1975, white South Af-

rica had well-developed book, newspaper, radio and cinema industries," Centerwall wrote. "Therefore, the effect of television could be isolated from that of other media influences."

Centerwall reports that he also looked at a number of other factors, including economic conditions, alcohol abuse, and the availability of firearms. "None provided a viable explanation for the observed homicide trends," he says.

Centerwall estimates that, had television never been invented, there would be 10,000 fewer murders, 70,000 fewer rapes, and 700,000 fewer serious assaults each year in the United States.

More disturbing, studies have found a ten- to 15-year delay between television's influence and subsequent increases in violence. This might mean that children exposed to more television violence today might possibly become more violent 15 to 20 years from now.

One question that has to be addressed is how children who watch television become violent. There are several theories, says Watt. Most laypeople believe that the continued exposure to violence inures children to aggression, and makes them more likely to do something aggressive themselves, Watt says.

"Desensitization is one of the issues we have to address," Watt says. But there are several other theoretical "models" under investigation by researchers.

Monkey see; monkey do One theory is called "observational learning." This holds that if you see someone wrestling on television, or fighting in a bar, or karate-kicking someone in an alley, you learn that it is appropriate behavior, and are likely to mimic it.

Another is "arousal". Seeing violence, the child becomes excited, because he or she is seeing activity that is prohibited normally. Then, the child is more likely to act out aggressive tendencies because of "excitation transfer." This could explain how young people seeing a movie about gang violence get into fights in the parking lot when the movie lets out.

Theories about how television viewing affects our behavior are important, because they could ultimately show the way to manage children's viewing habits. "The critical factor is control through the parents," Singer says. "Parents should be monitoring what their children are watching, as well as how much they are watching."

To bring children back to reality, experts say, parents should watch television with their children, and intervene at ap-

propriate points. It could be an offhand comment designed to underscore the fact that television violence is just fantasy: "Can you imagine how much that would have hurt if they were *really* fighting?" Or, "Nobody could take a punch like that and get up so quickly."

Teachers speak out Teachers deal with the impact of television every day, and are often among the advocates for changes in the way we watch. "Television can be very positive, if you set some rules and the whole family watches," says

TV, or not TV (regulation)?

Douglas M. Wills, spokesman for the National Association of Broadcasters, says calls for federal control of television violence are not going to solve any problems. "Any time the federal government decides to become the programming czar for television, you're asking for problems of censorship," Wills says.

That, however, does not mean people can't have an impact on what they watch. Wills notes that most of the top 100 rated shows on television today are sitcoms and hour-long dramas that contain little, if any, violence. The reason? Television has to provide what people want to watch. He says if you see a show that offends you, or if you see a show on another channel that you would like to see locally, pick up the phone and call the station.

"Program managers and station managers and general managers respond to those kinds of calls," Wills says. "It's not in the station's interest to alienate large numbers of viewers. Goodwill is only a part of it — their income depends on attracting as many viewers as possible."

Wills says people should make their views known to the station in the fall, before TV executives go to the big syndication conferences and select the shows they're going to air in the coming year.

At the same time, don't be surprised if a local channel airs some shows that might shock a few people on late-night time slots. "There should be a place and time for adult fare, provided what's being shown is not gratuitous," Wills says.

Lidia Choma, principal of a magnet school in New Haven. "But that's not typically the way it's used. TV doesn't do anything for their critical thinking skills, and their view of the world is one that is violent and unrealistic."

Alfred A. Karpinski, principal at Tilford W. Miller Elementary School in Wilton, says statistics show that for every hour children spend in school, they spend an hour and 20 minutes watching television. So he began a program to develop "critical viewing skills." This program teaches children how news shows are produced, what commercials are designed to do, how to separate fantasy from reality, and how docudramas can be more fiction than fact.

Karpinski notes that when students learn how to interpret novels, they are directed to look at the use of words, the construction of certain images, and the repetition of certain phrases. In critical viewing, children learn how lighting, music, the placement of actors on the set, and other factors will affect how you feel about a character, or a concept. "Before we had this kind of training, we found that even among the second graders there were children having difficulty distinguishing between fantasy and reality," Karpinski says.

He adds, "Schools might be print-domi-nated, but as educators we have to be aware of the role, and the impact, that television has on them outside of school. It's a major part of their lives, and we can't ignore it."

The debate goes on Not all experts are convinced that what children learn from television violence is transferred to long-term behaviors. In fact, Watt says, if you put 100 children in a room and expose them to violent behavior, you cannot predict with any accuracy how an individual will react.

"It's probably safe to say that kids are desensitized to television violence by the time they've seen their 14,000th murder on television," Watt says. "It's another thing, certainly, to say that's going to influence how they act in real life."

Until research shows a stronger link, Watt says, it is too soon to demand changes in public policy. People who are calling for regulation of television violence, he says, would be imposing rules on the majority for a problem that might affect only a handful of people in the country.

"If you look at millions of children, you're probably going to find one or two who are extremely susceptible to that kind of influence," Watt says. "But you can't make public policy based on the response of a minuscule minority."

He adds, "After looking at 25 years of research, my observation is that the best thing a parent can do is monitor, and restrict, what their children are watching. But it is very unlikely that a child watching a violent show — with his or her parents also watching — will then leave the house and commit a violent act. It's the kids who are on their own, who have very little parental guidance of any kind, who are in danger from their exposure to television violence. A child who is socially well-adapted shouldn't have that problem."

Others are not so sure. Wally Bowen says he is encouraged by the fact that some schools, and parents, are seeking to develop critical viewing skills.

"We're not trying to force people to go back to a primitive way of life; we just want people to realize that the television is not just a piece of furniture," Bowen says. "The TV set is the most powerful story-teller ever invented," he adds. "You wouldn't invite a stranger into your house and let him sit down and tell your children stories without you being present in the room. But that's exactly what a lot of parents do with television, and we still don't know for sure how much influence this 'stranger' has on children."

A Push for PG-Rated Playthings

Some companies are starting to soften the violence in toyland. Such self-policing only goes so far, though, because gore sells big—especially with hot summer movie tie-ins.

Denise Gellene

Times Staff Writer

In the film "Last Action Hero," houses explode, cars crash and dead bodies turn up in swimming pools and parking garages, on roof tops—even in a tar pit.

This is the stuff that toys are made of. But children seeking to re-create movieland-style mayhem with the "Last Action Hero" toy line are in for a surprise. The eight-inch plastic figures of star Arnold Schwarzenegger come with ropes, axes, hooks and dynamite—but no guns.

The toy, marketed to children considered too young to see Columbia's PG-13 movie, also comes with this message printed on the box: "In real life, guns and violence are a big mistake . . . never play with real guns."

Mattel's somewhat kinder, gentler super-hero signals a change in the way make-believe violence is being marketed to children, a potentially groundbreaking shift that is emerging at some companies this summer.

For years, the industry has resisted pressure to limit violence because shoot-'em-up toys are very successful. However, increased concern about violent entertainment—leading to this week's historic agreement by TV networks to issue viewer warnings—is causing at least a few toy companies to act.

Sega of America has announced plans to rate its video games the way Hollywood rates movies, to help parents make suitable choices for children. Electronic Arts, a leading maker of video and computer games, said this week that it also is considering a ratings system.

The move by manufacturers to curb violence in toys is not widespread, and some prominent companies, like Hasbro—the maker of G.I. Joe—argue there is no need for reforms. (Unlike the television industry, the toy business does not face congressional regulation.)

Several events in the past year have nonetheless created pressure for change:

• Toys R Us in Canada has refused to sell "Night Trap," a Sega game that depicts bloody attacks on young women.

• In Britain, the same game came under attack on the floor of Parliament. Sega says it will work with the government to develop a rating for "Night Trap."

• In Hawaii, state lawmakers narrowly defeated legislation that would have required retailers to post warnings that so-called "war toys"—action figures, video games and even water pistols—"increase anger and violence in children."

"The toy industry doesn't lead, it follows," said Carolyn Shapiro, editor of the trade magazine, Toy & Hobby World. "If things change outside the industry, it responds. . . . This may be the start of a trend."

Controversy about violent toys probably has been around since kids picked up slingshots. In the past 30 years, researchers have observed children's play with war toys and their subsequent behavior. Studies have demonstrated that children exhibit aggression after playing with guns and action figures.

For more than a decade, pacifist organizations have rallied to no avail against such toy tough guys as Rambo, an action figure based on the movie. Its maker, now-defunct Coleco Industries, did not drop Rambo until kids dropped it for the next super-hero.

In the '90s, a stream of carjackings, drive-by shootings and other crimes involving teen-agers have fueled the perception that violence is out of control. "As a society, we're reaching our limit for violence," said Dr. Carole Lieberman, a UCLA psychiatrist, who has testified before Congress on the issue. "There is a growing perception that violent entertainment is not OK."

There is intense disagreement in the industry over where to draw the line when it comes to violent toys. Video game firms are sharply divided over how to use an advanced technology that brings film-quality realism to deadly duels. Toy companies appear split over how to transform the themes of violent films into acceptable products for young children.

A look at the toys linked to this summer's action films highlights the differences: A Hasbro unit is selling a line of toys based on Universal's scary, blockbuster film "Jurassic Park" compete with wounded dinosaurs and people. On the other hand, Mattel not only took away the guns from its "Last Action Hero" line, but labeled the toys "stunt" instead of "action" figures.

The confusion reflects America's paradoxical relationship with violent entertainment. In a February poll conducted by the Times Mirror Center on People and the Press, a majority of Americans denounced violent TV while admitting that they spend a lot of time watching it.

The situation with violent toys is just as muddled. Much-maligned "war toys" are big sellers. Helped along by lines based on "Terminator 2" and "Batman Returns"—both violent films—action figure sales rose last year to nearly $500 million. They were snapped up mostly by children ages 4 to 9.

Sales expectations are high for the "Jurassic Park" action figures. Prospects for "Last Action Hero" toys are less certain because the movie is doing poorly. In fact, a trade magazine on Thursday said Mattel had stopped production of the toy line, but company officials denied the report.

Make-believe violence also sells when it comes to video games, which brought in $4 billion last year, a 50% increase. The bestseller was "Street Fighter II," a fast-paced martial arts game, which rang up a record $160 million for Nintendo of America. About two-thirds of video game sales are to children under 15.

Marketing experts say children, especially boys under 9, seek out violent toys because they give them a sense of control and power lacking in their lives. "It all comes down to physical dominance. . . . When you put a gun in a character's hand, it has all the more power," said Dan Acuff, president of Youth Marketing Systems, a Glendale consulting firm.

Acuff said parents buy the toys because "their children are begging for them. Parents know their children will play with them, and keep occupied."

No company is proposing to take violence out of play. The video game companies are discussing a system that would alert buyers about violence, but not eliminate it. Schwarzenegger's plastic alter-ego cannot shoot its enemies, but it can blow them up with dynamite; the toy comes with directions on how to hurl it. Mattel has been reluctant to say whether it will incorporate anti-gun messages with subsequent action figures.

Skeptics wonder whether toy makers are struck with an attack of conscience or "political correctness." Lieberman, the UCLA psychiatrist, called rating systems and anti-gun warnings "public relations ploys."

However, Roy Takumi, the Hawaiian legislator who sponsored the failed toy labeling law, sees the changes in the industry as an important first step.

"I think toy companies are beginning to get the message," he said. "I don't want to see these toys banned. But I think consumers should be warned about the violence in toys."

The first test of Sega's rating system will come this fall, when the arcade game "Mortal Kombat" arrives on cartridges for the Nintendo and Sega home systems.

"Mortal Kombat" owes its popularity to "fatality moves," skillful maneuvers that allow players to finish opponents with bloody blows. Take it from 11-year-old Damien Vansen, a regular at Family Arcade near Los Angeles City College:

"You can do fatality moves and actually watch the characters die. In other games, you can't see that as well."

Sega intends to include the popular moves in its version of the game, to be rated MA-13, the equivalent of PG-13, meaning it is suitable for teenagers and adults. Nintendo plans to eliminate the moves from its game because its corporate standards do not permit blood or explicit violence.

The irony is that Nintendo expects to lose $6 million in potential sales because its game lacks the fatality moves. Sega has said it does not believe its rating system will hurt sales.

"If Sega really wants to limit violence, there is an answer: Don't sell the game," said Perin Kaplan, a Nintendo spokeswoman.

For all the concern and studies of their potential effect, it isn't known whether violent toys and video games cause any harm.

UCLA psychiatrist Lieberman contends that violent toys pick up where violent TV shows or films leave off, numbing children to the horror of real violence. "The effect is cumulative," she said.

Jeffery Derevensky, a child psychologist at Montreal's McGill University, contends that violent toys are harmless if played with in moderation. The biggest concern about "war toys" is that they might interest children in seeing movies that are too scary or violent.

In the case of "Last Action Hero," representatives of Mattel and Schwarzenegger argue that the toy softens the impact of the film, which depicts 57 death scenes, about one every two minutes. Schwarzenegger's publicist said it was assumed that children would see the movie because the star is so popular with the grade-school set.

"Arnold realizes the children will see the film. That is why he insisted that no weapons be included with the toy. Particularly a toy that bears his image," said Schwarzenegger publicist Charlotte Parker. She described the dynamite as "survival equipment."

The companies involved with "Jurassic Park" have gone to extraordinary lengths to discourage young children from attending the scary PG-13 film, despite the curiosity-raising parade of dinosaurs, trading cards, action figures, sticker books and video games.

The film's director, Steven Spielberg, said he considered the movie too scary for his four children, all under 9. Universal rep-

resentatives advised parents to take the film's rating seriously. They surveyed theater crowds and found that few young children were attending. Representatives of MCA-Universal and Kenner Products, manufacturer of the action figures, declined comment.

Despite such caveats, do all the kid-friendly promotions end up confusing parents?

It's lunchtime at the McDonald's in Temple City and the chain's "Jurassic Park" promotion is in full swing. Parents and toddlers entering the restaurant are greeted by a kid-size cardboard cutout of a toothy *Tyrannosaurus rex*. Above the counter,

"dino-fry" containers—there's that *T. Rex* again—are displayed. Out at the McPlayground, preschoolers cling to mothers who cling to plastic souvenir cups depicting *T. Rex*, this time snarling at an overturned car.

Robin Giammuta of Upland explains that she is collecting the cups for her sons, ages 2 and 4. "They just love dinosaurs, from Barney"—the star of the PBS kids' show—"to Jurassic Park," she said. "I haven't decided whether to take them [to the movie] yet."

She is surprised to learn the film is rated PG-13: "Look at all the stuff for kids."

Your Loving Touch

The hugs, cuddles, and kisses you give your children will benefit them throughout their lives.

Janice T. Gibson, Ed.D.

Janice T. Gibson, Ed.D., is a contributing editor of *Parents* Magazine.

Like most mothers, I remember vividly the births of my two children, Robin and Mark. Each time I cuddled my newborn children in my arms—snuggling them gently against my skin and caressing them with my hands and lips—I felt peace and an extraordinarily personal happiness. For each child, born four years apart, it took only an instant for me to fall in love! My joy made me want to continue cuddling and, in the process, strengthened a learned need to hug. Years later, when Mark was in fourth grade, I would hide behind the kitchen door and nab him for a hug when he came home from school. (He always put up with me, except in front of his friends.) And when Robin dressed for the prom, I zipped her gown, patted her on the shoulders, and wrapped my arms around her before she left with her date.

The power of touch.

Affectionate physical contact is meaningful at all age levels. Everyone needs affection, especially when frightened, insecure, or overtired. But particularly for children who cannot yet talk or understand words, cuddling and other forms of affectionate touch convey strong nonverbal messages and serve as important means of communication. When your baby is tired and snuggles in your arms, the gentle body-to-body contact relaxes him and communicates, "You're special. I love you."

Cuddling teaches infants about their environment and the people in it. They explore by touching with their fingers and tongue. Since touching is a reciprocal act, by cuddling your child you teach him to cuddle back. And by responding to his actions, you teach your baby to feel good about himself.

As your child grows older and snuggles with you after a frightening experience, a gentle hug that says "You are safe" will relieve him of his anxiety and help him to feel secure. If during a tantrum he lets you pick him up and hold him on your lap, he will be able to calm down and gain control of his emotions. Furthermore, your affectionate touch can help if your child misbehaves. If he hits his baby brother, for example, you can hold him on your lap as you tell him, "Hitting your brother is not okay." These words, together with the affectionate actions, tell him that although his behavior is not acceptable, you still love him. And when your child exhibits positive behavior, by praising him with a hug and a kiss or an enthusiastic high five, you will convey the message "I'm proud of you."

Why touch is so important.

Physical affection is crucial to a child's development. First of all, parents form strong affectional ties to their children by cuddling and touching them. Gary Johnson, of Delavan, Wisconsin, recalls how he felt after the birth of his first child, Jake: "I got to hold him in my arms for the first twenty minutes of his life. From those first moments together, I never felt strange with him. He was this little helpless creature who needed to be held, cuddled, and protected."

Whether an attachment such as the one Gary describes occurs immediately or over time, it increases the probability that parents will respond to their children's needs. Later, this strong attachment increases the child's psychological well-being.

For babies whose parents don't respond to their signals for close bodily contact, the result is what Mary Ainsworth, Ph.D., professor of psychology emeritus at the University of Virginia, in Charlottesville, has termed "anxious avoidance attachment." She and her colleagues found that babies whose mothers seldom pick them up to comfort them, and who rebuff their attempts to snuggle and cuddle, eventually learn to mask their emotions. When these babies are anxious and upset and most want their mother, they will avoid her so as not to risk being rejected again. "These babies often become adults who don't trust people and find it difficult to form close attachments," remarks Ainsworth. Thus the cycle becomes vicious and self-perpetuating.

The results of a recently completed 36-year study further demonstrate that the effects of parental affection are lifelong. In 1951 a team of psychologists from Harvard University, in Cambridge, Massachusetts, studied 379 five-year-olds in Boston. They asked the children's mothers about their own and their husband's child-rearing practices, including how the mothers responded when their child cried and whether they played with him; whether the father hugged and kissed the child when he came home from work; and whether he spent free time with the child. The researchers found that kindergartners whose parents were warm and affectionate and cuddled them frequently were happier, played better, and had fewer feeding, behavior, and bed-wetting problems than did their peers raised by colder and more reserved parents.

In a 1987 follow-up study involving 76 of the original subjects, researchers found that as adults, those who were raised by warm, nurturing parents tended to have longer, happier marriages and better relationships with close friends than did adult peers whose early child rearing was not so warm. According to psychologist Carol Franz, Ph.D., one of the study's researchers, "Affectionate touching was always associated with a lot of warmth. The more warmth parents exhibited, the more socially adjusted their child was at midlife."

Cuddling barriers.

Most parents provide what their babies need and want. Holding, carrying, rocking, and caressing are part of child rearing in most societies. Infant massage, in which babies are systematically touched and stroked in caring ways, is practiced throughout the world. In some countries, such as India, mothers massage with scented oils. And in China, moms not only massage their youngsters but also use acupuncture to relax them.

But in contrast with people from other countries, Americans, in general, aren't "touchy." In my own cross-cultural studies of child rearing, I've found that although mothers and fathers in the United States are basically as affectionate as other parents, they tend to refrain from physical expressions of love. Although a baby's need for constant physical attention is obvious, the need is less obvious for older children and adults. Consequently, as U.S. children grow older, touching becomes less a part of parent-child interaction.

Some parents are uncomfortable behaving affectionately because they are afraid that it will spoil their children. Far from spoiling children, however, it teaches them to trust you and to view the world as a safe place to explore. Youngsters whose parents pick them up and hug them when they are hurt, frightened, or insecure develop feelings of security that make it easier for them to do things on their own.

Although there has been a lot of talk about how much more involved dads are today, many fathers still have

a problem touching their children affectionately. Ronald Levant, Ed.D., former director of Boston University's Fatherhood Project and coauthor of *Between Father and Child* (Penguin), explains that today's generation of men have been raised to be like their fathers, who were the family breadwinners, and as a result they have grown up to be stoic. "As boys, they did not learn the basic psychological skills that girls did—such as self-awareness and empathy—which are necessary to nurture and care for children."

Furthermore, when dads do give their children affection, they tend to give more hugs and kisses to their daughters than to their sons. Why? Some fathers think that cuddling is not masculine and that too much physical affection will turn boys into "sissies." One dad admitted that when his wife was pregnant with their first child, he secretly hoped for a girl. "My father was not a very tactile person. We mostly shook hands. So I was concerned that if I had a son, I'd be too reserved. I was afraid to touch a son." Levant assures, however, that boys who are cuddled by their dads will not become "sissies" but will learn to be nurturing themselves. And more good news: The fathers of this generation are recognizing that they missed affection from their dads and, says Levant, are "breaking the old molds" of masculine reserve.

Some women also feel uncomfortable kissing and hugging their children because their parents weren't comfortable showing affection. One mother says that on the surface, her parents were warm and loving and she was well taken care of, "but I was rarely touched, hugged, or kissed." She wasn't comfortable cuddling with her children until she went into therapy and talked about her feelings. Now, she says, "I don't even think about it anymore. Hugging comes very naturally."

The high rate of divorce today, and the large number of single-parent homes in which the head of the household must work outside the home, also make it more difficult for some parents to provide the physical affection that their children may want or need at any given time. The recent concern raised by the specter of child abuse hasn't made it easier either. Highly publicized cases of purported sexual abuse of children by caregivers or estranged parents make

some adults afraid that cuddling and touching may be construed as sexual and harmful. So what can be done? Although it is critical to protect children from sexual abuse, it is equally important to show all children that they are loved and needed. Children need healthy affection, and parents need to find ways to provide it.

● ● ●

Some parents are uncomfortable behaving affectionately with their children because they are afraid it will spoil them. On the contrary, it will help them develop feelings of security.

● ● ●

There are 1,001 ways to demonstrate affection, and not everyone needs to do it the same way. Parents who aren't comfortable giving their children big hugs and kisses shouldn't feel obliged to do so. Patting on the hand or back—or giving a squeeze—plus some loving words, can convey affection if it is done in a meaningful way.

Cuddling comfort.

Like some parents, some children are uncomfortable about being held closely, not because they don't want affection, but because they are uncomfortable feeling physically constrained. For such children, you can stroke their shoulders or back gently, give them lots of kisses, or tickle them gently so that they don't feel entrapped. Eventually they may even like to be cuddled. Gary Johnson's four-year-old daughter, Hallie, and one-year-old son, Nate, weren't as cuddly from the beginning with their father as was their older brother, Jake. But now Hallie is "Daddy's little girl and a permanent fixture on my lap." And Nate has just recently started to want Gary to cuddle him. "It's a real thrill to me to have him reach out for a hug from Dad," he says.

3. CHILDHOOD: Social and Emotional Development

If you work outside the home and are away for most of the day, be sure that your caregiver supplies all the physical love your child needs. The Johnsons were concerned about leaving their kids in somebody else's care. "Becky and I believe that kids need plenty of physical love and affection, and we were afraid that someone else might not give them enough," says Gary. So they searched carefully. "We were fortunate to find a warm, loving, and wonderful caregiver. We can tell the kids are happy."

When peers become important to your child, he may start to shun your affections, particularly if his friends are present. Statements of rejection, such as "Yuck, Mom, don't kiss me" and "Leave my hair alone," do sting, but they signal that your child is growing up and striving for independence. Because he still needs your affection, you might try hugging him at bedtime when his friends aren't around.

As boys and girls reach puberty, touching becomes charged with sexual meaning, making it hard for many adolescents even to acknowledge the desire to touch or be touched in non-sexual ways. Parents should respect their teens' discomfort. When a hug may be too threatening, you can still express your love with a squeeze of the hand or a pat on the back.

If you are divorced, your child needs love from both you and your ex-spouse, even more than before the separation. So, if possible, work together with your ex-spouse to help your child to understand that both of you care. Sometimes boys raised in fatherless households, interpreting the loss of their father as making them the "man of the house," decide that permitting their mother to hug or kiss them makes them less manly. Mothers should respect these feelings but should not stop showing affection: A hug at bedtime or a lingering pat on the arm while going over homework will do wonders.

A recent experience underscored the message for me that even in adulthood, we still need, and benefit from, touch. It was while my now adult children and I were mourning their father's death. We stood silently for some minutes in a circle, our arms around one another, holding on tightly. The feel of our bodies touching consoled us and gave us strength. It convinced us, in a very concrete way, that we would be able to get on with our lives.

PLACES EVERYONE

THE FIRSTBORN IS A PERFECTIONIST, THE MIDDLE CHILD REBELLIOUS, AND THE LAST BORN A CHARMER. DOES BIRTH ORDER PREDICT YOUR PERSONALITY?

Stephen Harrigan

Stephen Harrigan is a novelist and screenwriter who lives in Austin, Texas. His newest novel, Water and Light, *is published by Houghton Mifflin.*

A few months ago, when I was in Los Angeles, I paid a call on my older brother at the gleaming new downtown office building where he works. I gave my name at the reception booth in the lobby, and then ascended the many floors to his corner office in an elevator that glided upward as silently as a spider on a thread.

He was standing there to greet me, dressed in a gray suit, when the doors opened on the 56th floor. As ever, he was three inches taller, and quicker on the draw with his handshake. My older brother's name is Jim, though I have noticed that professionally he goes by the commanding initials J.P. As he led me on a tour of his building, past works of corporate art, through conference rooms and executive dining rooms while I trailed along with my untied shoelace flapping on the marble floor, it occurred to me that even in childhood—when he was Jimmy and I was Stevie—somehow I had already perceived him as J.P.

Decades of adulthood, I realized, had not bred the younger brother out of me. Nor could I expect it to. There is a school of thought—and a cottage industry to go with it—that decrees that birth order is destiny. We are who we are because of who was there ahead of us when we were born, and who came behind. In my own case, one might argue, the scenario was so predictable it could have been plotted on a graph. "The younger brother of a brother," wrote psychologist Walter To-

The younger brother has lived with an older, taller, smarter, more perfect boy than himself as far back as he can remember.

man, "has lived with an older, taller, smarter, stronger, more perfect boy than himself as far back as he can remember." In order to avoid the hopeless task of competing against Jim, I became in many ways his opposite—a process that is known in psycho-jargon as sibling deidentification. Where he was authoritative, I was cunningly acquiescent. Where he was athletic, I was bookish. Without either of us consciously knowing it, I conceded him the title of standard-bearer, conservator, defender of the realm—then scouted out the terrain and found my own dreamy path.

It is intoxicatingly simple, this idea that our place in the family is the fount of our strengths and failings, our drives and our fears. If we know our place in the family, the birth order gurus suggest in their hyper-friendly self-help books, we know ourselves. If you're one of the 44 percent of the population who's first or only born, you were the early recipient of the brunt of your parents' attention and expectations. That means you're likely to be hard driving, demanding, doggedly responsible. Oldest children tend to spend more time with adults, so it's natural that they grow up faster, eager to invest themselves with leadership and grave responsibility. (All seven Mercury astronauts were firstborns.) If you are an only child, you are supposed to be just as much a perfectionist as a firstborn, but intransigent and finicky as well, since you never experienced the tempering trauma of dethronement by a younger sibling.

Middle children, like me, are the hardest to nail down, but in general we are seen as the victims of benign neglect, the ones with the fewest pictures in the family photo album. To cope with that lack of attention, we became rebellious and secretive, relying on friends for the companionship that somehow eluded us within the family. And because we never got our parents all to ourselves, we learned to compromise. By the time we were out of childhood, we were already seasoned diplomats.

Youngest children may smolder with

thwarted ambition (like Joseph in the Old Testament, who dreamed of himself as a sheaf of wheat that suddenly stood upright in a field, commanding obeisance from the lesser sheaves representing his ten brothers), but typically by the time they were born their parents had exhausted their expectations on all the siblings ahead of them, and were content to pamper the youngest without condition. Last borns are described variously as clowns, cutups, and mascots.

Birth order experts are full of breezy observations and prescriptions. They tell us we should marry into relationships that roughly duplicate our old sibling connections. So if we are the youngest brother of sisters we should marry the oldest sister of brothers, or if we are the youngest sister of brothers we should marry the oldest brother of sisters. We are advised that the secret to good parenting is to use birth order to understand the behavior of our own children—the supercharged firstborn, the mediating middle child, the restless last born.

When viewed through the birth order lens, human nature all at once seems marvelously comprehendable. Of *course* Hilary Clinton and Henry Kissinger are firstborns! Of *course* Katie Couric and Richard Simmons are youngest children! Firstborn, second born, last born—thinking of ourselves in these terms, we seem to snap immediately into place.

But is it true? Are the insights we receive from pondering birth order any more authentic than those we find in a daily horoscope, or in the lugubrious responses from a Ouija board?

"What could make more sense?" psychologist Kevin Leman asked one bright morning as we left his Tucson office to go out in search of breakfast. "A theory based on the dynamics between parents and children and between children and their siblings. It's not just that you're number one or number two. It's more complex than that. You have to take the whole family into account. But you *can* use birth order to get a quick handle on people."

Leman is the reigning pooh-bah of birth order, the author of *The Birth Order Book,* which bears the confident subtitle *Why You Are the Way You Are,* as well as *Growing Up Firstborn: The Pressure and Privilege of Being Number One.* His books are found in that vast self-help section of the nineties bookstore devoted to co-dependency, addiction, miscarriage, Cinderella complexes, and books by both sexes on what's wrong with men.

CELEBRATED SIBLINGS

AS A PSYCHOLOGICAL THEORY, birth order may be full of holes. But it's hard to resist guessing someone's place in the family by looking for clues in his or her personality. Here's a chance to put your intuition to the test.

1
WHO CAME FIRST?

Circle the eldest of these famous family members.

A. Dick and Tommy Smothers
B. Jimmy and Billy Carter
C. David and Ricky Nelson
D. Eva and Zsa Zsa Gabor
E. Joan and Jackie Collins
F. Randy and Dennis Quaid
G. Jeff and Beau Bridges
H. Groucho, Harpo, and Chico Marx

BONUS: Who are the two remaining Marx brothers and were they older or younger than the others?

2
SIBLING SAYS:

Match these personalities to their quotes about their kin.

__Yogi Bera   __Warren Beatty
__Cher   __Meryl Streep
__Diane Keaton   __Edward Kennedy
__Joan Rivers   __Diane Sawyer
__Charlie Sheen __Candice Bergen

A. "My sister was older by three years, and prettier, and things always seemed easier for her . . . She was vivacious and popular. I was the loner, full of self-doubt and deadly serious in my inch-thick glasses."

B. "It was like having a whole army of mothers around me. While it seemed I could never do anything right with my brothers, I could never do anything wrong with my sisters."

C. "I always wanted to look like [my younger sister], who has blond hair and green eyes . . . We've always been alike in a lot of ways. But we were very different in that she was good in school and I hated it."

D. "During high school I wanted to be a baseball player because nobody else in the family played baseball. [My father acted, and my brother wrestled and played soccer.] So I thought, 'If I could just excel at baseball, they'll think I'm something.'"

E. "I have a younger brother and two younger sisters . . . As a kid, I was always the exhibitionist of the family, constantly trying out for talent contests and school plays and always covering up my supersensitivity by being funny."

F. "Every now and then a reporter who thinks he is Freud asks me if being the youngest is why I made it . . . I almost always say yes—[but] I don't think it had anything to do with it."

G. "I was a rather bossy big sister. I would push my little brothers around—after all, that's what they were there for. When we made home movies, I was always the director. I'd dress my brothers in costumes and order them about."

H. "I get my drive from being the second child and a fat child. My sister was smarter and better than I was in every way. I think what I do embarrasses her terribly because I'm so unladylike."

I. "I was fifteen when my brother was born. He was a child of light, while I was a child of shadows . . . I even forgave him for inheriting my mother's beautiful singing voice."

J. "I don't talk about my sister."

ANSWERS
1. **Who Came First?** A: Though he portrays the whining younger brother, Tommy is the firstborn. B: Jimmy was the overachieving firstborn and Billy the beer-guzzling baby. C: David was four years older. D: Though both claim to be younger than official records indicate, Zsa Zsa is the elder of the two. E: Joan is Jackie's senior. F: Randy Quaid is older. G: Beau is older by eight years. H: Chico is two years older than Harpo, who is two years older than Groucho. BONUS: Gummo and Zeppo; three and 11 years younger than Groucho.

2. **Sibling Says:** A: Diane Sawyer B: Edward Kennedy C: Cher D: Charlie Sheen E: Diane Keaton F: Yogi Bera G: Meryl Streep H: Joan Rivers I: Candice Bergen J: Warren Beatty

—Steven Finch

Needless to say, Leman's office is not a dark Freudian lair, but a sunny enclave on the second floor of an office strip. Leman himself is as uncomplicated as his book titles suggest. Sandy-haired and clean-shaven, he was wearing jeans the day I met him. (As a last born, he can't stand to wear a suit.)

Leman told me he first heard about birth order when he was a graduate student at the University of Arizona, and the theory had the force of an epiphany. "All I could think about was my family—my firstborn sister who has clear vinyl runners on the carpet and whose children are always color coordinated; my older brother, who bears my father's name; and then me, the baby of the family."

As we approached his car, Leman pointed to his personalized licence plates, which bore the message ZAP ASU. "Now that's a typical thing for a baby of the family to do," he said. "Out here in Tucson, we hate ASU because they're the University of Arizona's rivals. To me it's worth it to pay twenty-five dollars a year to have people pull up and honk.

"Have you ever seen me on TV?" Leman asked as we drove off to the restaurant. "I'm funny. You'll find that most comedians—Steve Martin, Eddie Murphy, Goldie Hawn—are last borns."

Leman has promoted his ideas on most of the major talk shows and in various business seminars, where he advises executives on how to use birth order information as a strategic tool. If you own a car dealership, for example, you'd want to know that a last born might very well be the star of the sales force, but would be a disaster in the general-manager slot, which should go to a firstborn.

"I was on 'Jenny Jones' last week," he said. "Producers love to do this kind of thing: They bring out three siblings and make me guess which one is which. I was in good form that day. I nailed them, which made me feel like Mickey Mantle in 1956. I felt so confident I took a stab at Jenny herself. I guessed that she was a baby girl, since she was overflowing with affection, and I was right."

He turned to me, sized me up for a moment, and said, "I'd say you're the firstborn son with an older sister."

"Actually," I confessed, "second-born son with a younger sister."

"Hmmmm," Leman said.

"MOST OF THIS STUFF on birth order," complains Harold Mosak, a clinical psy-chologist who teaches a course on the subject at the Adler School of Professional Psychology in Chicago, "is just psychological pap that depends on popular notions and misconceptions. People who want to understand themselves rush to this stuff just like they rush to astrology."

Even Alfred Adler, the founding father of birth order theory, believed that the idea could be carried too far.

"There has been some misunderstanding," he wrote in 1918, "of my custom of classification according to position in the family. It is not, of course, the child's number in the order of successive births which influences his character, but the situation into which he is born and the way he interprets it." Adler recognized that classifying people by birth order was overly simplistic. But, in retrospect, his basic observations on the subject still have the sort of ringing self-evidence that is often associated with ideas of genius. He pointed out, for instance, that second-born children often have dreams in which they picture themselves running after trains and riding in bicycle races. "Sometimes this hurry in his dreams is sufficient by itself to allow us to guess that the individual is a second child."

Adler was convinced that his own life was shaped by his birth order. Born in 1870 in Penzing, a suburb of Vienna, he was the second of six children. He was a sickly boy who felt hopelessly over-shadowed by his older brother. "One of my earliest recollections," he wrote, "is of sitting on a bench, bandaged up on account of rickets, with my healthy elder brother sitting opposite me. He could run, jump, and move about quite effortlessly, while for me movement of any sort was a strain and an effort." Even when he was an old man, Adler was haunted by the robust power of his older brother. "He is *still* ahead of me!" he lamented near the end of his life.

Adler's resentment of his older brother's authority invested him with a re-bellious streak that would leave its stamp on the burgeoning science of psychology. He began his career as a physician, and was keenly interested in the influence of environment on physical and mental health. In 1902, his brilliance brought him to the attention of Sigmund Freud, who was then refining his theories of the un-conscious mind and consolidating his position as the high priest of psycho-analysis. Freud was 13 years older than Adler, and in his authoritarian cast of mind a classic firstborn who was used to ruling his younger siblings. ("I am by temperament nothing but a conquistador," he once admitted to a friend.)

Adler was asked to join Freud's famous weekly discussion group that later be-came known as the Vienna Psychological Society. Over the course of ten years Adler contributed greatly to the insights and even the terminology of Freud's work (the term *inferiority complex*, for instance, was first coined by Adler).

But the firstborn Freud, sensing a rival, began to hound and berate his colleague. Adler, still suffering from his lifelong re-sentment at being number two, bristled and left the sanctum. "Why should I al-ways do my work under your shadow?" he asked Freud in a parting shot.

Adler took a small group of followers with him and started his own rival mental health dynasty. His ideas were simpler and more pragmatic than Freud's. The hallmark of what he called individual psy-chology was a conviction that people do not live in a gloomy, deterministic uni-verse, subject to unconscious drives they cannot control. Adler's focus was on get-ting his patients up and running, showing them what was wrong with their lives and then allowing them to make a choice to either sink into despair or become pro-ductive members of society.

Today, Adlerians—such as Kevin Leman—are a distinct minority in a men-tal health industry still largely influenced by Freudian thought, but it is they who have kept the concept of birth order alive.

Even the Adlerians have found, howev-er, that it's tricky to prove that birth order counts for much. Since Adler's death, various studies *have* turned up some inter-esting observations. Last borns are more likely to write their autobiographies (what better way to be noticed?). They also are statistically more inclined to alco-holism. It turns out that more firstborns seek psychological counseling. Renowned baseball players have tended to be middle and youngest children (by conditioning, perhaps, they're more drawn to team sports). And firstborn girls are overrepresented among striptease artists.

By and large, though, the idea that birth order is directly related to personality has proven to be as ungraspable as it is enticing. "Birth order influence is a disappointment," says Jules Angst, a psychologist from Zurich. "It doesn't explain a lot."

Angst arrived at this conclusion after surveying, with his colleague Cecile Ernst, 34 years of birth order research, from 1946 to 1980. Ernst and Angst came away unimpressed. In short, birth order didn't consistently predict which sibling is most likely to be an extrovert, feel pain, take risks, lack self-esteem, select certain marriage partners, feel guilt, adopt conservative political views, get frustrated easily, need autonomy, or suffer psychological problems. Only a few of the studies they considered gave even marginal support to the idea that birth order influence is a factor in shaping personality, and most of these, Angst says, were fraught with "methodological fallacies."

"Most serious researchers have stopped talking about birth order," says Toni Falbo, an educational psychologist at the University of Texas in Austin. "If you look at all the factors that lead to a particular outcome in shaping someone's personality, on a good day, birth order might account for one percent."

The big problem with assessing birth order is the almost impossible task of getting a clear focus on what it is that's being studied. A family is a densely woven fabric made up of innumerable threads, some of which are apparent and some of which are not. Even if you could extract that one birth order thread out of the carpet—leaving in place a background of other powerful influences like socioeconomic status, race, class, values, aspirations, disease, death, ancestral history—you would still have a great deal of untangling to do.

Take, as an example, a family with four siblings. The children might have been born one after another at regular intervals, in which case their birth order positions would be fairly clear. But what if they came along in sets of two that were separated by a wide gap of years? Wouldn't the third child be likely to develop the characteristics of a firstborn, and might not the second child share the same last born traits of the fourth child? What if the firstborn was a boy, and all the rest were girls? Wouldn't the oldest girl develop a firstborn personality in relation to her sisters? How would an oldest son turn out if he were haunted by the knowledge of a "phantom" older brother lost to an early death?

The permutations of gender, spacing, and circumstance are so endless and complicating that it hardly seems worthwhile trying to sort through them. For Kevin Leman, however, they're just more spice for the stew.

"Every time another child is born," he says, "the entire environment changes. How parents interact with each child as it enters the family circle determines in great part that child's final destiny.

"Now the reason I guessed that you're a firstborn son with an older sister," he explained to me on the way to the restaurant that morning, "is because you seem to have a nice, easygoing demeanor. Which tells me one of two things: You have sisters above you in the family, or you have a good relationship with your mother. Now one of those things has to be true or you can get out of the car and walk.

"Also," he went on, "you're a reporter. Reporters are almost always firstborns. On my last tour I was interviewed by ninety-two people. Out of the ninety-two, eighty-seven were firstborns. Same thing with pilots. If you want to have fun on the flight home, stick your head into the cockpit and ask, 'How are the firstborns today?' Eighty-eight percent of them are. And librarians! Firstborns are voracious readers. I challenge you to call thirty librarians and find out their birth orders."

Over breakfast, Leman sketched his own history as a last born goofball. He was a poor student and behavior problem in high school, he said, and when he managed to find a college that would take him, he was more or less kicked out in his third semester. Leman was working as a janitor when he met his wife, Sande, who as fate would have it was a firstborn and therefore ideally suited to the task of shaping him up. Leman also credits his wife with helping him find a sustaining belief in God, the ultimate firstborn.

Leman related all this with good humor and a certain commonsense gravity, which made him seem less superficial than I had expected. But it was clear that his last born traits had prepared him well for the role of pop psychologist. Not only was he gleeful in his disregard for the academics who might consider him a lightweight ("Academia! You want to talk about an unreal world?"), he was also still enough of a showboat to put his birth order knowledge to use as a kind of parlor game.

Just then, for instance, he was trying to guess the birth order of our waiter.

"Okay, Eric," Leman said, glancing at the waiter's name tag. "Give me a description of your mom or dad. Either one."

"Well," Eric said, "my dad is very shy."

"How about little boy Eric? Age five to twelve?"

"Well, I guess some people would have said I was a mama's boy."

"Hmmmm. And when you grew up, did you marry a firstborn, middle child, or baby?"

"Baby. She's the last of four kids."

"So," Leman said. "I bet you're a firstborn son."

Eric smiled. "You got it," he said, and went back to the kitchen.

"What tipped you off?" I asked Leman.

"Two things. First, did you notice the way he came out and wanted our order right away? He was impatient, he didn't want to fool with us. The other thing was *very*. He described his father as 'very shy.' So he probably sees things in black or white—not much gray. That's definitely a firstborn trait."

I went home impressed, willing to overlook Leman's misreading of my own birth order. If the Great Birth Order Theory did not quite bear up under the weight of evidence, it was still tantalizing enough to my imagination to *seem* true. That, surely, is what keeps it alive. Scientific scrutiny may erode the birth order stereotype, but we tend to shore it up again whenever we meet a supercharged eldest child or a last born who is lost in the ozone.

I called 30 librarians. It turned out that only 18 of them were firstborns or only children. As I had come to expect when dealing with the notion that birth order rules our lives, I was neither convinced nor resoundingly disabused. As a middle child, I could see only shades of gray.

the MIRACLE OF RESILIENCY

DAVID GELMAN

There are sharp differences in the way children bear up under stress
—

A prominent child psychiatrist, E. James Anthony, once proposed this analogy: there are three dolls, one made of glass, the second of plastic, the third of steel. Struck with a hammer, the glass doll shatters; the plastic doll is scarred. But the steel doll proves invulnerable, reacting only with a metallic ping.

In life, no one is unbreakable. But child-health specialists know there are sharp differences in the way children bear up under stress. In the aftermath of divorce or physical abuse, for instance, some are apt to become nervous and withdrawn; some may be illness-prone and slow to develop. But there are also so-called resilient children who shrug off the hammer blows and go on to highly productive lives. The same small miracle of resiliency has been found under even the most harrowing conditions—in Cambodian refugee camps, in crack-ridden Chicago housing projects. Doctors repeatedly encounter the phenomenon: the one child in a large, benighted brood of five or six who seems able to take adversity in stride. "There are kids in families from very adverse situations who really do beautifully, and seem to rise to the top of their potential, even with everything else working against them," says Dr. W. Thomas Boyce, director of the division of behavioral and developmental pediatrics at the University of California, San Francisco. "Nothing touches them; they thrive no matter what."

Something, clearly, has gone right with these children, but what? Researchers habitually have come at the issue the other way around. The preponderance of the literature has to do with why children fail, fall ill, turn delinquent. Only recently, doctors realized they were neglecting the equally important question of why some children *don't* get sick. Instead of working backward from failure, they decided, there might be as much or more to be learned from studying the secrets of success. In the course of looking at such "risk factors" as poverty, physical impairment or abusive parents, they gradually became aware that there were also "protective factors" that served as buffers against the risks. If those could be identified, the reasoning went, they might help develop interventions that could change the destiny of more vulnerable children.

At the same time, the recognition that many children have these built-in defenses has plunged resiliency research into political controversy. "There is a danger among certain groups who advocate nonfederal involvement in assistance to children," says Duke University professor Neil Boothby, a child psychologist who has studied children in war zones. "They use it to blame people who don't move out of poverty. Internationally, the whole notion of resiliency has been used as an excuse not to do anything."

The quest to identify protective factors has produced an eager burst of studies in the past 10 or 15 years, with new publications tumbling off the presses every month. Although the studies so far offer no startling insights, they are providing fresh perspectives on how nature and nurture intertwine in childhood development. One of the prime protective factors, for example, is a matter of genetic luck of the draw: a child born with an easygoing disposition invariably handles stress better than one with a nervous, overreactive temperament. But even highly reactive children can acquire resilience if they have a consistent, stabilizing element in their young lives—something like an attentive parent or mentor.

The most dramatic evidence on that score comes not from humans but from their more researchable cousins, the apes. In one five-year-long study, primate researcher Stephen Suomi has shown that by putting infant monkeys in the care of supportive mothers, he could virtually turn their lives around. Suomi, who heads the Laboratory of Comparative Ethology at the National Institute of Child Health and Human Development, has been comparing "vulnerable" and "invulnerable" monkeys to see if there are useful nurturing approaches to be learned. Differences of temperament can be spotted in monkeys before they're a week old. Like their human counterparts, vulnerable monkey infants show measurable increases in heart rate and stress-hormone production in response to threat situations. "You see a fairly consistent pattern of physiological arousal, and also major behavioral differences," says Suomi. "Parallel patterns have been found in human-developmental labs, so we feel we're looking at the same phenomenon."

Left alone in a regular troop, these high-strung infants grow up to be marginal figures in their troops. But by putting them in the care of particularly loving, attentive foster mothers within their first four days of life, Suomi turns the timid monkeys into social lions. Within two months, they become bold and outgoing. Males in the species Suomi has been working with normally leave their native troop at puberty and eventually work their way into a new troop. The nervous, vulnerable individuals usually are the last to leave home. But after being "cross-fostered" to loving mothers, they develop enough confidence so that they're first to leave.

Once on their own, monkeys have complicated (but somehow familiar) patterns of alliances. Their status often depends on whom they know and to whom they're related. In squabbles, they quickly generate support among friends and family members. The cross-fostered monkeys grow very adept at recruiting that kind of support. It's a knack they somehow get through interaction with their foster mothers, in which they evidently pick up coping styles as well as information. "It's essentially a social-learning phenomenon," says Suomi. "I would argue that's what's going on at the human level, too. Evidently, you can learn styles in addition to specific information."

In the long run, the vulnerable infants not only were turned around to normality, they often rose to the top of their hierarchies; they became community leaders. Boyce notes there are significant "commonalities" between Suomi's findings and studies of vulnerable children. "The implications are that vulnerable children, if placed in the right social environment, might become extraordinarily productive and competent adult individuals," he says.

Children, of course, can't be fostered off to new parents or social conditions as readily as monkeys. Most resiliency research is based on children who have not had such interventions in their lives. Nevertheless, some of the findings are revealing. One of the definitive studies was conducted by Emmy E. Werner, a professor of human development at the University of California, Davis, and Ruth S. Smith, a clinical psychologist on the Hawaiian island of Kauai. Together,

they followed 698 children, all descendants of Kauaiian plantation workers, from their birth (in 1955) up to their early 30s. About half the children grew up in poverty; one in six had physical or intellectual handicaps diagnosed between birth and age 2. Of the 225 designated as high risk, two thirds had developed serious learning or behavior problems within their first decade of life. By 18 they had delinquency records, mental-health problems or teenage pregnancies. "Yet one out of three," Werner and Smith noted, "grew into competent young adults who loved well, worked well, played well and expected well."

Some of the protective factors the two psychologists identified underscore the nature-nurture connection. Like other researchers, they found that children who started out with robust, sunny personalities were often twice lucky: not only were they better equipped to cope with life to begin with, but their winning ways made them immediately lovable. In effect, the "nicer" the children, the more readily they won affection—both nature and nurture smiled upon them. There were also other important resiliency factors, including self-esteem and a strong sense of identity. Boyce says he encounters some children who even at 2 or 3 have a sense of "presence" and independence that seem to prefigure success. "It's as if these kids have had the 'Who am I' questions answered for them," he says.

One of the more intriguing findings of the Kauai research was that resilient children were likely to have characteristics of both sexes. Boys and girls in the study tended to be outgoing and autonomous, in the male fashion, but also nurturant and emotionally sensitive, like females. "It's a little similar to what we find in creative children," observes Werner. Some other key factors were inherent in the children's surroundings rather than their personalities. It helped to have a readily available support network of grandparents, neighbors or relatives. Others note that for children anywhere, it doesn't hurt at all to be born to well-off parents. "The advantage of middle-class life is there's a safety net," says Arnold Sameroff, a developmental psychologist at Brown University's Bradley Hospital. "If you screw up, there's someone to bail you out."

In most cases, resilient children have "clusters" of protective factors, not just one or two. But the sine qua non, according to Werner, is a "basic, trusting relationship" with an adult. In all the clusters in the Kauai study, "there is not one that didn't include that one good relationship, whether with a parent, grandparent, older sibling, teacher or mentor—someone consistent enough in that person's life to say, 'You count,' and that sort of begins to radiate other support in their lives." Even children of abusive or schizophrenic parents may prove resilient if they have had at least one caring adult looking out for them—someone, as Tom Boyce says, "who serves as a kind of beacon presence in their lives."

Such relationships do the most good when they are lasting. There is no lasting guarantee for resiliency itself, which is subject to change, de-

Researchers can spot differences of temperament in monkeys before they're a week old

pending on what sort of ups and downs people encounter. Children's ability to cope often improves naturally as they develop and gain experience, although it may decline after a setback in school or at home. Werner notes that around half the vulnerable children in the Kauai study had shaken off their previous problems by the time they reached their late 20s or early 30s. "In the long-term view, more people come through in spite of circumstances. There is an amazing amount of recovery, if you don't focus on one particular time when things are falling apart."

Ironically, this "self-righting" tendency has made the resiliency issue something of a political football. Conservatives have seized on the research to bolster their case against further social spending. "It's the politics of 'It's all within the kid'," says Lisbeth Schorr, a lecturer in social medicine at Harvard Medical School whose book, "Within Our Reach: Breaking the Cycle of Disadvantage," has had a wide impact in the field. "The conservative argument against interventions like Operation Head Start and family-support programs is that if these inner-city kids and families just showed a little grit they would pull themselves up by their own bootstraps. But people working on resilience are aware that when it comes to environments like the inner city, it really doesn't make a lot of sense to talk about what's intrinsic to the kids, because the environment is so overwhelming."

So overwhelming, indeed, that some researchers voice serious doubts over how much change can be brought about in multiple-risk children. Brown's Sameroff, who has been dealing with poor inner-city black and white families in Rochester, N.Y., says the experience has left him "more realistic" about what is possible. "Interventions are important if we can target one or two things wrong with a child. So you provide psychotherapy or extra help in the classroom, then there's a lot better chance." But the children he deals with usually have much more than that going against them—not only poverty but large families, absent fathers, drug-ridden neighborhoods and so on. "We find the more risk factors the worse the outcome," says Sameroff. "With eight or nine, *nobody* does well. For the majority of these children, it's going to involve changing the whole circumstance in which they are raised."

Others are expressing their own reservations, as the first rush of enthusiasm in resiliency research cools somewhat. "A lot of the early intervention procedures that don't follow through have been oversold," says Emmy Werner. "Not every-

There are kids from adverse situations who do beautifully and seem to rise to their potential

one benefited equally from such programs as Head Start." Yet, according to child-development specialists, only a third of high-risk children are able to pull through relatively unaided by such interventions. Says Werner: "At least the high-risk children should be guaranteed basic health and social programs."

Interestingly, when Suomi separates his vulnerable monkeys from their foster mothers at 7 months—around the same time that mothers in the wild go off to breed, leaving their young behind—the genes reassert themselves, and the monkeys revert to fearful behavior. According to Suomi, they do recover again when the mothers return and their new coping skills seem to stay with them. Yet their experience underscores the frailty of change. Boyce, an admirer of Suomi's work, acknowledges that the question of how lasting the effects of early interventions are remains open. But, he adds, programs like Head Start continue to reverberate as much as 15 years later, with reportedly higher school-completion rates and lower rates of delinquency and teen pregnancies.

Boyce recalls that years ago, when he was at the University of North Carolina, he dealt with an 8-year-old child from an impoverished, rural black family, who had been abandoned by his mother. The boy also had "prune-belly syndrome," an anomaly of the abdominal musculature that left him with significant kidney and urinary problems, requiring extensive surgery. But he also had two doting grandparents who had raised him from infancy. They showered him with love and unfailingly accompanied him on his hospital visits. Despite his physical problems and loss of a mother, the boy managed to perform "superbly" in school. By the age of 10, when Boyce last saw him, he was "thriving."

Children may not be as manageable or resilient as laboratory monkeys. If anything, they are more susceptible in the early years. But with the right help at the right time, they can overcome almost anything. "Extreme adversity can have devastating effects on development," says psychologist Ann Masten, who did some of the groundbreaking work in the resiliency field with her University of Minnesota colleague Norman Garmezy. "But our species has an enormous capacity for recovery. Children living in a hostile caregiving environment have great difficulty, but a lot of ability to recover to better functioning if they're given a chance. That's a very important message from the resiliency literature." Unfortunately, the message may not be getting through to the people who can provide that chance.

Toddler Talk

New research shows that when you stimulate your child's language development, you stimulate her mind.

Chris Ravashiere Medvescek

Chris Ravashiere Medvescek is a mediator and freelance writer living in Tucson, Arizona. She has two children.

"I'll cry to the moon!"

Four-year-old Jason meant it, too. Language, in all its poetic possibilities, sprang forth to keep Mom from turning off the light at bedtime.

Where did Jason learn to say this? His mom and dad had never used such a phrase (although they certainly enjoyed hearing it). And who had taught him that words could be useful substitutes for wails?

Jason didn't really "learn" this. Nobody deliberately "taught" him. He simply had acquired one of the most complex and highly abstract systems in all of life: language.

"You don't have to learn to use language. You can't prevent it from happening," says Susan Curtiss, Ph.D., a linguist studying language and brain function at the University of California at Los Angeles Medical Center. "It's part of the biological phenomenon of growing as a human being, like 'learning' to walk."

Language acquisition—what most of us call learning to talk—is really a lifelong process. But by far the most intense advancement occurs during the "toddler talk" years, roughly between the ages of two and five. It is a time of poetic phrases, charming mispronunciations, and garbled syntax. By the end, a child will have moved from silly statements ("Ducks eat me!") to complete sentences ("The ducks are eating my bread").

"They will have reached their goal," says Naomi Baron, Ph.D., linguist and author of several books on children's language, including *Growing Up With Language* (Addison-Wesley). "They now can form complex abstract sentences.

How does this happen? If language is acquired instinctively, what is the parents' role? And what does toddler talk reveal about the complex communication system children are gaining as they move from being burbling babies to fluent speakers?

Parents who take the time to answer these questions will be repaid many times over. Toddler talk, shared with a caring, attentive adult, builds bonds of trust and love. And ultimately, parents will have helped their children academically as well. Because language is expressed thought, stimulating language means stimulating the mind. And the beauty of it is, you probably already know how to do it.

How parents help.

Because language acquisition is too important to leave to chance, nature has programmed parents into the process. "Helping children learn to talk is not something we do consciously, even if we sometimes con-sciously try," says Judith Creighton, Ph.D., a child-development specialist and coauthor of *Learning to Talk Is Child's Play* (Communication Skill Builders). "We instinctively go along with their budding ability."

For example, parents routinely name things for their children, obligingly providing them with the vocabulary necessary to build sentences. Naming objects actually helps establish a core concept: Words represent reality. It is the first abstract step toward mastering language.

"Simplification" is another language aid that comes easily even to those who aren't parents. The use of short sentences that generally match the child's verbal skills ("Want a drink? Here you go!") stimulates "the child's comfortable and timely development of language," says Creighton.

By "repeating" and "expanding," parents naturally facilitate their child's speech development. Their conversations often go something like this:

Child: Doggie.
Parent: Doggie bark.
Child: Doggie bark.
Parent: The doggie is barking.

As parents repeat what they hear and add a few words, they mold their child's language, explains Naomi Baron. In doing so, parents also are tacitly giving their child permission to practice talking, are building parent-child trust, and, most important, are saying, "I'm listening."

Through "parallel talk" and "snap-

From *Parents*, December 1992, pp. 73-77. © 1992 by Gruner & Jahr USA Publishing. Reprinted from *Parents* Magazine by permission.

shotting," parents act as language tour guides. In the first instance, parents describe their own actions: "I'm putting milk on your cereal right now." In the second, parents create a verbal snapshot of what their child is doing: "Oh, you're building a tall tower! You're using red and yellow blocks." Either tactic has the effect of "pouring language on top of experience," says Judith Creighton, which is the most effective way to learn language.

Pretty simple stuff, yet these unsophisticated, unconscious strategies are all basic to language acquisition. Applied conscientiously by interested parents, they lead to an invaluable activity for building language and thinking skills: conversation.

Studies show that even parent-infant conversation lays a foundation for creative and critical thought, reading, writing, decision making, and problem solving. A program for poverty-level toddlers that encouraged their mothers to talk to them resulted in an average eighteen-point increase in the children's IQ scores. In addition, the children became more cooperative and attentive, asked more questions, and demonstrated an increase in their vocabulary.

Talking *with*, not *at*, children is the key: asking questions, pausing for an answer (verbal or nonverbal), then responding. No matter how limited your child's vocabulary, your efforts invite her to stretch her language and, therefore, her mind.

The best avenue for conversation is play. "Language and play are very closely linked. Both are symbolic activities," says Jill Heerboth, a pediatric speech-language pathologist in Tucson, Arizona. "If parents want to help their children with language, they should play with them."

Play provides perfect opportunities for parents to use the tactics that encourage children to speak. There are many objects, actions, and concepts to name, as well as comments to repeat and expand upon. "You're making the car go fast," a parent watching his toddler roll a toy vehicle might say. Picking up some blocks nearby, the parent could add, "I'm building a big house."

Just like grown-ups, toddlers respond best when you talk about the things that interest them. "Pay attention to what your child thinks is important," advises Creighton. "Is she stacking blocks? Sorting by color or size? Watch and listen, then try out a few neutral comments: 'I see you're using all the blue blocks.' If the reply comes back, 'It's getting tall,' change direction to focus on stacking.

"This leads naturally to true communication: 'I listen to you, you listen to me,' " adds Creighton. Insisting that children talk about your focus only shuts them down. Sometimes, though, kids are too busy to talk. By describing what they're doing and remaining attentive without demanding a reply, you can create a relaxed atmosphere that usually will lead to later exchanges.

Asking questions can provide lots of conversational fodder—provided that they are the right ones, observes Heerboth. Being asked, "What's this? What color is it? How many are there?" feels more like a test than a talk, and kids will tune out. But open and sincere questions, such as "What should we do next?" and "Why did that happen?" prolong discussion.

Parents can mix in questions with their repetitions and expansions. Linguists call this "scaffolding," or building a structure around your child's language to encourage further growth:

Child: *(Pointing to his drawing)* A looong line.

Parent: You made a looong line. Where is it going?

Encourage reasoning through "what," "why," and "what if" questions, especially when your child shows signs that he is ready mentally. "When children start using because or if clauses, such as, 'My teddy's crying because he's hungry,' " says Heerboth, "they're showing they now understand cause and effect and are ready to reason."

From nonsense to sense.

Okay—you're holding up your end of the conversation. What are your pint-size partners doing with theirs? Most likely they are valiantly throwing together everything they know about language in the hope of coming up with something that makes sense to you.

Imagine an American tourist in Mexico City desperately calling up every remembered bit of high school Spanish to order a meal in a restaurant. A few words, a little grammar, and a lot of pointing—coupled with a concrete topic (food) and a mutual desire to communicate—have fed more than one hungry tourist. Naomi

---

When a Child Makes a Mistake

Toddler talk can be really cute, but . . . to correct or not to correct, that is the question. Below are a few words on the subject from the experts:

•**Move and move on.** When your child says something incorrectly ("What it be?"), repeat in the proper form ("What is it?"), then move on with the conversation. If your child wants help (that is, if he can't pronounce a word or convey what he's trying to say), by all means help him.

•**They'll learn when they're ready.** All the correcting in the world means nothing until a child is developmentally ready and able to say a word the right way. So keep modeling without demeaning or nagging your child. Remember, children want to be fluent speakers.

•**Word for word won't work.** Having your child repeat after you "the right way" will have no impact on her learning.

•**Don't overdo it.** Children may restrict their talking around people who correct them too frequently. Don't let corrections overpower free-and-easy conversation, which is a much more effective teaching tool.

•**Use mirroring.** With a four-or five-year-old, repeat his statement exactly as you heard it, then pause momentarily at allow him to correct it. Or say the sentence right up to the problem word, then pause for his correction. Maintain a friendly, nonjudgmental attitude, and offer to help your child when needed.

•**Pay attention to the bottom line.** Can the child communicate what she's trying to say? If yes, then can't worry too much about grammar and vocabulary—it will come.

—C.R.M.

Baron calls this process "managing on a linguistic shoestring."

Toddlers are out there on a shoestring, dangling at the limit of their abilities, bravely trying to bring that sentence in on a wing and a prayer. To do so, they all use basically the same strategies and acquire new skills in basically the same order.

Children first acquire a vast collection of single words, then begin using them in two-word phrases ("Mommy eat"); they then string them together in a telegraphic, "Cookie Monster" fashion: "Me so hungry!" From the age of about two and a half to five years, they acquire grammatical morphemes—words or parts of words that add meaning to their sentences. All English-speaking children—including those with hearing or language disorders—learn the same number of morphemes in the same general order, although at different rates.

The first one that children learn is "ing," as in walking or eating. This is followed by the prepositions "in" and "on," then "s" to form plurals. The last morphemes to be acquired are "is" and "were" and contractions ("*That's* Daddy"; "*We're* home").

Practice makes perfect.

Acquiring morphemes is one thing. Using them, and the rest of vocabulary and grammar, is another. Kids broadly rely on three basic grammatical strategies—"analogies," "scissors and paste," and "potshots"—when putting together what they know, explains Baron. These strategies would pass unnoticed but for the errors kids make in using them. Mistakes are your clue that your child is actively practicing the art of language.

When four-year-old Jason protested he wasn't sleepy, his mom replied, "Well, just rest, then."

"But I'm not resty, either," he moaned. Jason was creating a language "analogy." His strategy: If "sleep" can become "sleepy," then "rest" can become "resty."

As children learn grammatical structures and morphemes, they look for consistency among the rules. Hence, Ryan, at three and a half, yelled, "Go down in the hole. Even downer!" (low, lower; down, downer). Sometimes the analogy is correct but the context is wrong: "Can I listen in your ears?" asked Nick, three, doctor kit in hand (look, eyes; listen, ears).

"I can't get out!" wailed Rosie. Actually, she wasn't having trouble getting out of the wading pool—in fact, she didn't want to get out at all! But to say, "I don't want to get out," required more linguistic dexterity than she possessed at age three. So she simply pasted a negative onto the front of her sentence and hoped for the best.

Preschoolers rely on the "scissors and paste" strategy when asking questions and expressing negatives, two very complicated undertakings in English. They just paste the question or negative at the beginning of the sentence ("Why you go home?" "No eat dinner"). As children progress, they put the words in a more grammatically correct order, but there may still be glitches: "That dog not go away," Sarah, three, noted apprehensively.

Locating the right word to paste onto a sentence is challenging, especially when kids try to use words that sound similar. Ever willing to try, preschoolers puzzle this out and go with their best guess: "What are we going?" "Where does it do?" Some thoughts just have to come out, no matter what they sound like. "Are you still have any of these candies before?" in-

---

When a Child Doesn't Say Much

According to experts, there may be several explanations as to why a child is slow to begin speaking, ranging from birth order to personal style to poor hearing. Children with older siblings tend to talk less (since their big brother or sister may communicate for them), as do naturally shy children.

For some kids (especially preemies), the coordination needed to vocalize speech sounds and syllables may be slow to develop. Poor hearing—sometimes caused by chronic ear infections—is a common culprit; if it's undetected, children miss out on a critical period of language development.

Check with your pediatrician.

As a rule of thumb, if your child hasn't started using two-word phrases by the time he is two to two and a half, or if you are simply worried, check with your pediatrician. He or she may recommend hearing- and language-assessment testing. If a hearing problem is ruled out, there are many ways to encourage your child to speak, according to child-development specialist Judith Creighton.

First, Creighton recommends, parents should accept body language, actions, and gestures as dialogue. (In this example a boy is working on a puzzle.)
Parent: You're putting it all together. (Child tries to force a piece into the wrong space.)
Parent: Oh, no, it won't fit. (Child throws the piece away.)
Parent: You don't want that piece. Good-bye! (Child fits another piece in the right space.) It fits! You did it! (Child smiles broadly.)

Often you will hear your child repeat what you have said earlier. (Child pulling on his shoe: "It fits!") Encourage him to use language that you've modeled. For instance, after showing your child how a toy works, you might suggest that he show someone else how to play with it. Also, ask rhetorical questions: "I wonder what that little kitty is thinking?" The child can consider the question without being put on the spot.

Empathize with your child.

Because children know more than they can convey, they often become frustrated and throw temper tantrums. In these cases, "Children won't hear reason, but they will hear the language of their own feelings," says Creighton. "You can say, 'I see that you're crying, and I guess you're feeling very frustrated.' This is another way to give children language to express and control the world around them." Empathy does not mean giving in or coddling, only acknowledging that you understand what your child is experiencing.

If your child is upset, try verbalizing his feelings or playing twenty questions: "Can you tell me with words?" "Show me with your hands?" "Take me to where it is?" Both tactics model language and encourage him to be a full, if nonverbal, partner. Knowing that in time your child will be able to articulate his thoughts and feelings will make his slow start easier to manage. —C.R.M.

quired a very excited recipient of a new kind of candy. Huh? That must be some candy! " 'Potshots' provide a lifeline for preschoolers who have important thoughts to express but who lack control over the plethora of grammatical detail," says Baron.

While grammatical oddities can last for months as preschoolers figure out the rules (for example, saying "goed" instead of "went"), a potshot is a one-time affair. The child grabs whatever language is handy and throws it out the door. "Then it won't be any more gooder," protested Susan when her mom cut her

sandwich in half. "I gots both twos together," crowed Nick, his arms full of Daddy's shoes. Often a child cannot reconstruct the potshot even when asked to immediately afterward.

Because we seek meaning from language, Baron observes, parents often overlook their children's potshots. Like good conversational partners, parents listen to their children's thoughts, not their words.

The journey to fluency—part nature, part nurture—lasts, as Jason says, just "a couple little whiles." The charm of toddler talk soon is replaced with a first-grader's precision and reasoning, so take advantage of

this time. When you slow down enough to become a conversational partner to a preschooler, your reward is a magical glimpse of the world through his eyes.

"Just step back, stop worrying, and enjoy the thrill of your child's discovering and developing his language skills," advises Susan Curtiss. "It's full of fascinating parts. To think that we can have this system that allows us to represent the world, that we can carry ideas and notions around in our head and communicate them to someone else—it's really pretty miraculous."

Young Children's Moral Understanding: Learning About Right and Wrong

Cary A. Buzzelli

Cary A. Buzzelli, Ph.D., is currently associate professor of Early Childhood Education at the University of Alabama at Birmingham. A former preschool teacher, Cary studies how classroom interactions influence young children's moral understanding.

Early childhood educators have long valued children's social and emotional development. An important aspect of this interest has been helping children develop an understanding of right and wrong. Until recently, however, little research has examined the development of *moral* understanding in young children. This gap in the research has left teachers and parents wondering about their role in guiding children's understanding of right and wrong.

In this review, what early childhood educators have learned about moral development from Piaget, Kohlberg, and Freud will first be acknowledged. A growing body of recent research indicating that moral understanding emerges earlier—during the first few years of life—and is related to a different set of relationships and factors than those described by Piaget, Kohlberg, and Freud will then be reviewed. These new findings examine how changes in children's cognitive, social, and emotional abilities, as well as changes in their family relationships, influence the development of moral understanding.

Reviewing current research will enable us to address the following questions:
• How and when do children develop an understanding of standards and of right and wrong?
• How do children's interactions with parents and siblings contribute to the development of moral understanding?
• How do children's interactions with teachers and peers influence their understanding of right and wrong?
• What can parents and teachers do to nurture children's moral understanding?

*This is one of a regular series of Research in Review columns. The column in this issue was edited by **Laura E. Berk,** Ph.D., professor of psychology at Illinois State University.*

Robert Maust

It will not startle many caregivers, teachers, and parents to learn that developing mental and language abilities, deep identification with parents, and adults' approval or disapproval of their behavior help toddlers begin to form behavior (moral) standards. But did you know that a feeling of mastery of a goal attained and developing capacity to feel empathy for others are involved, too?

Past views: Piaget, Kohlberg, and Freud

Many early childhood educators' knowledge of moral development comes from the cognitive developmental theories of Piaget (1932) and Kohlberg (1969) or the psychoanalytic theory of Freud (1961). In these theories, children younger than four to six years of age were considered "premoral" because their judgments of moral violations are

From *Young Children*, Vol. 47, No. 6, September 1992, pp. 47-53. © 1992 by Cary A. Buzzelli, Department of Curriculum and Instruction, School of Education, Indiana University. Reprinted by permission of the author.

> As early as the second year of life, children begin to use standards in evaluating their own behavior and the behavior of others, an achievement that marks the beginning of moral understanding.

based on compliance with parental authority (Piaget referred to this as *heteronomy*), avoidance of punishment (which Kohlberg called an *obedience orientation*), or the absence of a sense of conscience (Freud believed that conscience, or the *superego,* did not emerge until around four to six years of age) (Zahn-Waxler & Kochanska, 1990; Killen, 1991).

Recent research

Much current research is based on the premise that regardless of one's theoretical approach to moral judgment, two features are crucial in the development of children's moral understanding: (1) children's developing understanding of the standards and rules of their social world, and (2) children's growing understanding of the feelings of others who share their social world (Dunn, 1987).

The emergence of standards

As early as the second year of life, children begin to use standards in evaluating their own behavior and the behavior of others, an achievement that marks the beginning of moral understanding (Kagan, 1984; Dunn, 1988). Two researchers in this area are Jerome Kagan and Sharon Lamb. Kagan believes that as the result of maturing cognitive and affective abilities, and of experiences with significant adults in our lives, we invent and believe in a set of moral principles (Kagan, 1984).

These principles take their first form as standards that arise from several sources: (1) adult approval and disapproval of children's behaviors, (2) children's feeling of mastery of a goal attained through their efforts, (3) children's developing capacity to feel empathy for others in distress, (4) children's identification with parents, and (5) children's developing cognitive and linguistic abilities.

In his research, Kagan found that beginning around 18 months of age, children show concern over broken or flawed toys. At about the same time, children begin to infer the causes of events. Kagan believes that children will show concern if they infer that the toy was broken through actions they deem as wrong or bad or from behaviors disapproved of by their parents. The disapproval of parents is one source of standards.

Most parents expect their children to have an awareness of behavior standards by age three and to regulate their behavior according to the standards by age seven (Kagan, 1984). For children, meeting an age-appropriate standard provides a sense of mastery and pleasant feelings about themselves. Children's feelings of mastery serve as a second source of standards and a means

through which children adopt the behaviors adults want socialized.

A third source of standards emerges during the second and third years, as children show awareness of others' distress and attempt to offer aid and comfort to them. These developments have been superbly documented by Carolyn Zahn-Waxler and Marion Radke-Yarrow (Zahn-Waxler & Radke-Yarrow, 1982; Radke-Yarrow, Zahn-Waxler, & Chapman, 1983). For example, children begin at around 18 months to offer comfort to another by giving that person what is comforting to themselves, such as a blanket or a favorite toy. Between the ages of two and three, children understand that other children in distress are comforted more by their own mother or blanket than by something that another child can offer. With the ability to empathize, children come to understand that actions that hurt others are violations of standards.

By age four, identification becomes a fourth source of standards. As Freud's description of the Oedipal conflict suggests, children develop a strong desire to identify with and emulate parents. Current research suggests, however, that children accept parental standards and abide by them not out of fear of punishment (as Freud's Oedipal theory implies) but rather out of a desire to be like parents who have established a warm and loving relationship with them.

> Most parents expect their children to have an awareness of behavior standards by age three and to regulate their behavior according to the standards by age seven.

Like Kagan, Lamb found an increasing awareness of standards in children during the second year of life (1991). In her research, Lamb examined occurrences of a variety of morally related acts. These included awareness of standards, interest in flawed objects and events that differ from what is expected, and use of moral vocabulary (e.g., "good," "bad"). Results indicated a peak in occurrence around 17 to 18 months of age, followed by a slight decline. Lamb concluded that around 18 months, children may have an increased sensitivity to morally related events that may be independent of mothers' socialization attempts. She hypothesized that children's moral sense, which appears to emerge during the second half of the second year, may be mediated by yet another set of sources: their developing cognitive, linguistic, and affective abilities. The emergence of the ability to make inferences about intentionality and causality, to use symbols and make mental representations, to express two-word utterances, and to feel empathy may, in combination, provide the maturational preparedness needed by children to nurture and support an awareness of others' standards and to act prosocially toward others (Lamb, 1991).

Both Kagan's and Lamb's research point to the importance of maturational processes in the development of moral understanding. For Kagan, the appreciation of standards may be a universal process "built into" each of us, with the specific virtues we develop being dependent on the social context in which we live (Kagan, 1984). According to Lamb (1991), emerging abilities in cognition, language, and affective expression provide the "maturational preparedness" supportive of children's increased sensitivity to moral events around 17 to 18 months of age.

Development of early moral emotions

Robert Emde and colleagues (Emde, Johnson, & Easterbrooks, 1987; Emde & Buchsbaum, 1990) also believe that empathy may be a universal process that provides early moral development with a maturational

The emergence of the ability to make inferences about intentionality and causality, to use symbols and make mental representations, to express two-word utterances, and to feel empathy may, in combination, provide the maturational preparedness needed by children to nurture and support an awareness of others' standards and to act positively toward others.

basis. In reformulating early moral development from a psychoanalytic perspective, however, Emde examines the contribution of an additional set of moral emotions—pride, shame, and guilt—and the influence of motivational conflicts within the caregiving relationship.

During the one- to three-year age period, conflicts involving opposing motives between parent and child first arise. It is no mere coincidence that as the toddler becomes more willful and able to say "No!" more often and more emphatically, parents become increasingly focused on teaching standards, enforcing rules, and using other types of discipline. Conflicts between children and caregivers take on special meaning not only because they represent constraints on the child but also because the conflicts are emotionally charged. Through such encounters, pride, shame, and guilt emerge.

Pride is experienced by the child when a standard or rule has been successfully applied in a given situation, resulting in a positive self-evaluation. Conversely, shame is felt when a rule has been violated, resulting in a negative self-evaluation. The child indicates an awareness of having done something wrong by certain behaviors, such as an aversion of gaze. "Hurt feelings" occur when a prohibi-

tion is given by a parent, particularly if delivered in an angry tone, resulting in the child looking "hurt." Hurt feelings may be a forerunner of guilt (Emde et al., 1987).

Emde believes that these early moral emotions are significant for the following reasons: (1) they are based on relationships and occur as part of a shared experience with parents; (2) they are indications of children's awareness and knowledge of standards—the early do's and don'ts; and (3) they involve some sense of conflict or dilemma (Emde et al., 1987). It is thus within shared emotional experiences, under the watchful eyes of a parent or caregiver, that children begin to internalize what is and is not appropriate and experience significant emotions as a result of their compliance or transgression of the standard.

Developing standards within the family

Dunn (1988) acknowledges that affective experiences within family relationships make important contributions to children's moral understanding. According to Dunn, however, cognitive changes in children's developing sense of self and of others play an equally important role.

During the second and third years of life, many changes occur in children's understanding of the feelings, thoughts, intentions, and behavior of others. These changes are the result of children's experiences as observers of and participants in family discussions, routines, and activities. Dunn suggests that these changes are also intimately related to children's growing appreciation of standards and social rules and of what hurts and comforts others (Dunn, 1988). Three behaviors in particular point to children's growing knowledge of social and moral rules: (1) involvement in family conflict, especially teasing of siblings and parents; (2) discussions with the mother about feelings and inner states; and (3) appeals to the mother for help.

During the second year, children begin to tease others—usually an older sibling, but sometimes a parent. To tease, children must know what upsets and annoys others. Besides demonstrating an awareness of the feelings of others, teasing reflects an early understanding of family standards and of prohibited actions.

Young children's understanding of moral and social rules and of others' feelings are learned not only in conflict situations but also through family conversations. When examining young children's discussions with their mothers concerning the feelings and inner states of a new sibling, Dunn and Kendrick (1982) found that frequent references to the sibling's feelings were related to more affectionate and friendly behavior between children. Similarly, Dunn, Bretherton, and Munn (1987) found that the more mothers discussed feelings with toddlers, the more likely toddlers were to refer to their own feelings.

Around age three, children come to understand that they are accountable to others for their actions, particularly prohibited actions. This becomes obvious in how children expect others to respond to their compliance with or transgression of social and moral rules. For example, young children will seek aid and comfort from their mother if a sibling has acted in an aggressive or teasing manner toward them; however, they rarely do so if they acted in such a manner toward their sibling (Dunn, 1988).

Dunn's work shows that information about rules and standards, about what to do and not do, is conveyed to children through participation in a variety of family experiences, only a small number of which are disciplinary encounters.

During the one- to three-year age period, conflicts involving opposing motives between parent and child first arise. It is no mere coincidence that as the toddler becomes more willful and able to say "No!" more often and more emphatically, parents become increasingly focused on teaching standards, enforcing rules, and using other types of discipline. Conflicts between children and caregivers take on special meaning not only because they represent constraints on the child but also because the conflicts are emotionally charged. Through such encounters, pride, shame, and guilt emerge.

Children's understanding of their social world

According to another group of researchers, children's ability to distinguish between moral and social-conventional rules and events is central to the development of standards and moral understanding.

Moral transgressions are acts that violate others' rights, are unfair to others, or cause physical or emotional harm to others, such as hitting, teasing, or taking the property of another. Social-conventional transgressions violate rules and norms of appropriate and acceptable ways of acting in social settings, such as home or school, and include impolite and inappropriate acts. Social rules are made and agreed on by individuals for the purpose of maintaining social order (Smetana, 1983; Turiel, 1983).

The social-cognitive domain approach proposes that children classify their knowledge of people and social events into distinct domains (Smetana, 1983; Turiel, 1983). The domains "develop out of qualitatively different interactions with different classes of objects, events, and persons" (Smetana, 1983, p. 132). Much of the research using this approach has investigated how children make distinctions between moral and social-conventional events (Nucci & Nucci, 1982; Smetana, 1983; Turiel, 1983).

Researchers have found that children use a number of criteria to judge their own behavior and that of others. On the basis of these criteria, children make distinctions between moral and social-conventional events. The criteria include (1) permissibility (Is the act right or wrong?), (2) generalizability (Is the act wrong in other places or for other people?), (3) rule contingency (Would the act be wrong if there were no rule against it?), (4) authority contingency (Is the act wrong if a parent or teacher doesn't see it?), and (5) seriousness (Is the act a little wrong or very wrong?) (Turiel, Killen, & Helwig, 1987).

Moral transgressions are judged by children as more generalizably wrong, independent of rules and authority, and more serious and punishable than social-conventional transgressions (Nucci, 1982; Smetana, 1983; Turiel, 1983). Children as young as 34 months of age have been shown to judge moral transgressions as more generalizably wrong than social-conventional transgressions. By three-and-a-half years of age, moral transgressions are judged as more serious, more generalizably wrong, and more independent of rules and authority than social-conventional transgressions (Smetana & Braeges, 1990). Thus, the ability to distinguish between moral and social transgressions emerges early in development.

According to these researchers, domains are constructed by children through qualitatively different interactions with adults, peers, and events (Smetana, 1983; Turiel, 1983). The rightness or wrongness of an act and the evaluation of the act as a moral or social transgression are cognitive inferences that children make based upon the consequences of the act. "The child need not be told that the act is a rule violation or that it is wrong; she will construct this knowledge from her experience of the event" (Smetana, 1983, p. 134).

Observational research shows that toddlers' (Smetana, 1989), preschoolers' (Nucci, 1985), and school-age children's (Nucci & Nucci, 1982) responses to moral transgressions include emotional reactions, attempts to retaliate, attempts to enlist the aid of an adult, and references to the harmful consequences of the actions on others. Adults' responses include indicating to the transgressor the consequences of the act on the victim (Nucci, 1985).

Violations of social conventions are not seen as intrinsically wrong because alternative methods can be used to achieve the same result. For example, there is no intrinsic basis for children having to be seated before a snack is served. It is possible that in other preschools, children eat snacks standing up (Smetana, 1983). Research indicates that with age, children increasingly respond to violations of social conventions, such as eating a snack standing up, by making reference to rules, norms, and social expectations (Nucci & Nucci, 1982). Adults' responses to social conventional transgressions include references to the act as disruptive and/or against the rules (Nucci, 1985). This evidence supports the view that children make cognitive inferences about what is moral from different types of interactions with adults and peers.

Two other factors may influence children's understanding of moral transgressions: the nature of children's interactions with peers and children's perceptions of others' moral knowledge. Buzzelli (in press) found that peer-rejected children rated moral transgressions committed by others as more serious than those committed by themselves, while popular children rated the transgressions as equally serious. The data suggest that peer-rejected children may focus more on the effects of others' behavior on themselves, whereas popular children pay just as much attention to the effects of their own behavior on others. These results support the idea that increased negative treatment from peers may influence peer-rejected children's moral judgments.

Children's inferences may also be influenced by their perceptions of others' moral knowledge. Buzzelli (1991) found that first and second grade children rated transgressions committed by younger children as less wrong than those committed by a same-age peer or an older child, whereas kindergartners and preschoolers rated transgressions as equally wrong whether committed by a young child, a same-age peer, or an older child. The first and second graders reasoned that the younger child would not know better, whereas the preschoolers did not show the ability to consider other children's moral knowledge.

It may be found that peer-rejected children rate moral transgressions committed by others as more serious than those committed by themselves, while popular children rate the transgressions as equally serious.

Finally, researchers have found that some cultural groups may not make as sharp a distinction between moral rules and social conventions as do others. Fowler (1992) reported that low-income Caucasian, African-American, and Asian-American children do not make the same distinctions between moral and social events as do upper-income Caucasian children. Similar findings are reported by Shweder, Mahapatra, and Miller (1987) for Indian Brahmin children and adults. Teachers must understand that not all children are presented with environments that help them sort out moral from social events in the same way.

Conclusions: Implications for parents and teachers

Each of the different perspectives described in the preceding sections suggests ways that parents and teachers can support children's early moral understanding.

• **First**, adults must acknowledge and value young children's emerging morally relevant abilities, including increasingly sophisticated cognitive and language skills, which provide the foundation for moral understanding. Current research also suggests that children's appreciation of standards (Kagan, 1984) and their empathetic sensitivity to others' distress may be "built-in" universal processes (Kagan, 1984; Emde & Buchsbaum, 1990). If

parents and teachers know that children possess these abilities, they are better able to view the abilities as strengths of children and build upon them in nurturing moral understanding.

• **Second**, adults need to set clear and appropriate standards and expectations for young children's behavior (Kagan, 1984; Emde & Buchsbaum, 1990). Children demonstrate their knowledge of these standards by conforming to them; by their behavior during occasions of noncompliance, such as teasing (Dunn, 1988); and through their expressions of pride, shame, and guilt (Emde et al., 1987).

• **Third**, children's construction of moral and social-conventional domains reflects qualitatively different experiences with people and events (Turiel, 1983). Parents and teachers support children's moral understanding when they respond to children's transgressions in ways that are consistent with the type of transgression (Nucci, 1982, 1985). By commenting on how actions may cause others harm or distress, adults offer information consistent with children's inferences of moral events. Likewise, references to maintaining social order and norms of behavior confirm children's inferences about social-conventional events (Nucci, 1985).

Early childhood educators play a central role in structuring children's social experiences with other children. Recent research by DeVries, Reese-Learned, and Morgan (1991) documents how early childhood educators and the curricula they select create sociomoral atmospheres in classrooms that may encourage or discourage interactions supportive of young children's moral understanding. Extensive naturalistic observations were conducted in three early childhood classrooms, each implementing a curriculum representing a distinct orientation to early childhood education: constructivist (based on Piaget's notions of children as active learners who construct knowledge), Direct Instruction in Arithmetic, Reading, and Language (DISTAR), based on a behaviorist view of teachers as transmitters of knowledge to children through teacher-directed activities, and an eclectic program that included some characteristics of both constructivist and DISTAR programs. The results showed that children in the constructivist classroom were more cooperative with one another and used more negotiation strategies to solve conflicts than children in the other two classrooms.

As early childhood educators, we know that from their earliest years young children possess sophisticated abilities and understandings of their social world. Likewise, we know that young children are very impressionable and that they look to the adults around them as examples and guides. Therefore, our efforts to nurture young children's moral understanding, to ensure that they develop the knowledge and reasoning skills necessary to make decisions, and to help them discern what is good and right must take into account the variety of views expressed here.

References

Buzzelli, C.A. (1991, April). *Children's perceptions of other children's moral knowledge.* Paper presented at the annual meeting of the American Educational Research Association, Chicago, IL.

Buzzelli, C.A. (in press). Popular and rejected children's social reasoning: Linking social status and social knowledge. *Journal of Genetic Psychology.*

DeVries, R., Reese-Learned, H., & Morgan, P. (1991). Sociomoral development in direct instruction, eclectic, and constructivist kindergartens: A study of children's enacted interpersonal understanding. *Early Childhood Research Quarterly, 6*(4), 473–519.

Dunn, J. (1987). The beginnings of moral understanding: Development in the second year. In J. Kagan & S. Lamb (Eds.), *The emergence of morality in young children* (pp. 91–111). Chicago: University of Chicago Press.

Dunn, J. (1988). *The development of social understanding.* Cambridge, MA: Cambridge University Press.

Dunn, J., & Kendrick, C. (1982). *Siblings: Love, envy and understanding.* Cambridge, MA: Harvard University Press.

Dunn, J., Bretherton, I., & Munn, P. (1987). Conversations about feeling states between mothers and their young children. *Developmental Psychology, 23,* 132–139.

Emde, R.N., & Buchsbaum, H.K. (1990). "Didn't you hear my mommy?": Autonomy with connectedness in moral self emergence. In D. Cicchetti & M. Beeghly (Eds.), *The self in transition: Infancy to childhood* (pp. 35–60). Chicago: University of Chicago Press.

Emde, R.N., Johnson, W.F., & Easterbrooks, M.A. (1987). The do's and don'ts of early moral development: Psychoanalytic tradition and current research. In J. Kagan & S. Lamb (Eds.), *The emergence of morality in young children* (pp. 245–276). Chicago: University of Chicago Press.

Fowler, R.C. (1992, April). *Social and moral conceptions of Caucasian-, African-, and Chinese-American preschoolers.* Paper presented at the annual meeting of the American Educational Research Association, San Francisco, CA.

Freud, S. (1961). The ego and the id. In J. Strachey (Ed.), *The standard edition of the complete psychological works of Sigmund Freud* (Vol. 19, pp. 3–66). London: Hogarth Press. (Original work published 1923)

Kagan, J. (1984). *The nature of the child.* New York: Basic Books.

Killen, M. (1991). Social and moral development in early childhood. In W. Kurtines & J. Gewirtz (Eds.), *Handbook of moral behavior and development: Vol. 2. Research* (pp. 115–138). Hillsdale, NJ: Lawrence Erlbaum Associates.

Kohlberg, L. (1969). Stage and sequence: The cognitive-developmental approach to socialization. In D.A. Goslin (Ed.), *Handbook of socialization theory and research* (pp. 347–480). Chicago: Rand McNally and Co.

Lamb, S. (1991). First moral sense: Aspects of and contributions to a beginning morality in the second year of life. In W.M. Kurtines & J.L. Gewirtz (Eds.), *Handbook of moral behavior and development: Vol. 2. Research* (pp. 171–189). Hillsdale, NJ: Lawrence Erlbaum Associates.

Nucci, L.P. (1982). Conceptual development in the moral and social domains: Implications for values education. *Review of Educational Research, 52,* 93–122.

Nucci, L.P. (1985). Social conflict and the development of children's moral and conventional concepts. In M. Berkowitz (Ed.), *Peer conflict and psychological growth: New directions in child development* (No. 29, pp. 55–71). San Francisco: Jossey-Bass.

Nucci, L.P., & Nucci, M.S. (1982). Children's social interactions in the context of moral and conventional transgressions. *Child Development, 53,* 403–412.

Piaget, J. (1965). *The moral judgment of the child* (M. Gabain, Trans.). New York: Free Press. (Original work published 1932)

Radke-Yarrow, M., Zahn-Waxler, C., & Chapman, M. (1983). Children's prosocial dispositions and behavior. In P.H. Mussen (Ed.), *Handbook of child psychology: Vol. 4. Socialization, personality, and social development* (pp. 469–545). New York: Wiley.

Shweder, R.A., Mahapatra, M., & Miller, J.G. (1987). Culture and moral development. In J. Kagan & S. Lamb (Eds.), *The emergence of morality in young children* (pp. 1–90). Chicago: University of Chicago Press.

Smetana, J.G. (1983). Social-cognitive development: Domain distinctions and coordinations. *Developmental Review, 3,* 131–147.

Smetana, J.G. (1989). Toddlers' social interactions regarding moral and conventional transgressions in the home. *Developmental Psychology, 25,* 499–508.

Smetana, J.G., & Braeges, J.L. (1990). The development of toddlers' moral and conventional judgments. *Merrill-Palmer Quarterly, 36,* 329–346.

Turiel, E. (1983). *The development of social knowledge: Morality and convention.* Cambridge, MA: Cambridge University Press.

Turiel, E., Killen, M., & Helwig, C. (1987). Morality: Its structure, functions, and vagaries. In J. Kagan & S. Lamb (Eds.), *The emergence of morality in young children* (pp. 155–243). Chicago: University of Chicago Press.

Zahn-Waxler, C., & Kochanska, G. (1990). The origins of guilt. In R.A. Thompson (Ed.), *Nebraska symposium on motivation: Vol. 36. Socioemotional development* (pp. 183–285). Lincoln: University of Nebraska Press.

Zahn-Waxler, C., & Radke-Yarrow, M. (1982). The development of altruism: Alternative research strategies. In N. Eisenberg-Berg (Ed.), *The development of prosocial behavior* (pp. 109–137). New York: Academic Press.

Understanding Bilingual/Bicultural Young Children

Lourdes Diaz Soto

Dr. Lourdes Diaz Soto is Assistant Professor of Early Childhood Education at The Pennsylvania State University. A former preschool teacher, she studies the learning environments of culturally and linguistically diverse young children.

E arly childhood educators have long created exciting and enriching environments for young children but may find an additional challenge when attempting to meet the needs of bilingual/bicultural learners. Teachers currently working with young linguistically and culturally diverse children have asked questions such as: "I feel confident with the art, music and movement activities I have implemented, but how can I best address the needs of speakers of other languages? Are there specific educational strategies that I should incorporate to enhance second language learning? What practical applications can I gain from the research evidence examining second language learning and successful instructional approaches in bilingual early childhood education?"

This review examines:

● demographic and educational trends pointing to the growing numbers of bilingual/bicultural young children in America today

● misconceptions about young children learning a second language

● successful educational approaches in early childhood bilingual education

● practical applications of existing research which can be readily implemented by early childhood educators.

Demographic and educational trends

Although the reliability of statistics over the past nine years describing the size and characteristics of the non-English language background (NELB) population has been questioned (Wong Fillmore, in press), it is clear from existing data and projections that language minority students comprise an increasing proportion of our youngest learners. The number of NELB children aged birth to 4 years old rose steadily from 1.8 million (1976) to a projected 2.6 million in 1990, while the number of children aged 5 to 14 are projected to rise from 3.6 million to 5.1 million in the year 2000 (Oxford, 1984). Additional evidence points to "minority" enrollments, which include culturally diverse learners, ranging from 70 percent to 96 percent in the nation's 15 largest school districts (Hodgkinson, 1985).

Immigrant children from diverse, developing nations such as Haiti, Vietnam, Cambodia, El Salvador, Guatemala, Honduras, and Laos are entering classrooms which are usually unprepared to receive them. La Fontaine (1987) estimates that two-thirds of school-age, language-minority children may not be receiving the language assistance needed to succeed in school. This situation is bound to intensify with the projected increases in total school-age population of language-

---

> ## More and more bilingual/bicultural children are appearing in early childhood classrooms across the country.

From *Young Children*, Vol. 42, No. 2, January 1991, pp. 30-36. © 1991 by The National Association for the Education of Young Children, 1834 Connecticut Avenue, NW, Washington, DC. Reprinted by permission.

minority students, ranging from 35 percent to 40 percent by the year 2000 (Oxford, 1984). Existing demographic data provides evidence that meeting the educational needs of bilingual/bicultural young children is an important mandate for our schools.

The field of Bilingual Early Childhood Education has evolved from two educational domains, contributing to differing philosophies and practices. The elementary domain has, with some exceptions, largely emphasized formal language learning instruction; while the early childhood domain has emphasized a variety of approaches including natural language acquisition. Based upon existing bilingual research and what we know about how young children develop, a supportive, natural, language-rich environment, affording acceptance and meaningful interactions, appears optimal.

Early childhood educators are faced with a recurrent challenge, however, when programs earmarked for speakers of other languages are continually viewed as compensatory, or incorporate deficit philosophies. The practice of many instructional programs has been to develop English proficiency at the expense of the native language. The latter approach is called "subtractive" (Lambert, 1975) because the language learning process substitutes one language for another. This form of "bilingual education" may be a misnomer, since it continues to foster monolingualism (Snow & Hakuta, 1987).

Language learning and cultural enhancement need to be viewed as a resource, and not as a deficiency. Garcia (1986) has suggested that early childhood bilingualism includes the following characteristics:
● the child is able to comprehend and produce linguistic aspects of two languages
● the child is exposed naturally to two systems of language as used in the form of social interaction during early childhood
● both languages are developed at the same time.
Garcia (1983) notes that definitions of early childhood bilingualism must consider linguistic diversity, as well as social and cognitive parameters. Teachers of young children need a broad educational framework because a child's social, mental, and emotional worlds are an integral part of language learning.

Simplistic categorizations of bilingual children are not appropriate, since a variety of dimensions and possibilities exist for individual learners. Both experienced and novice bilingual/bicultural educators have noted differing educational terminology, reflecting the political mood of the nation. The table on page 32 illustrates the variety of terms in use. For example, the term "limited English proficient" (LEP) often cited in the literature points to a child's limitation rather than strength. The definitions proposed by Snow (1987) provide both clarity and recency, and are presented in the table in an attempt to show the range of concepts related to second language education. Casanova (1990) introduced the term "speakers of other languages" (SOL), helping to portray a positive attribute. The addition of the term "speakers of other languages" seems especially useful because there is ample documentation of the existence of both bilingual and multilingual young children in our schools.

Educators need to think in terms of "additive" (Lambert, 1975) bilingualism by incorporating practices which will enhance, enrich, and optimize educational opportunities for second language learners. Minimum standards and compensatory approaches are likely to sustain the existing educational difficulties faced by second language learners, speakers of other languages (SOL), and monolingual (EO) learners currently being deprived of a second language.

Misconceptions about young learners

A variety of misconceptions about second language acquisition and young learners exists (McLaughlin, 1984). **One misconception is that young children acquire language more easily than adults.** This idea was borne of the assumption that children are biologically programmed to acquire languages.

Although we know that early, simultaneous bilingualism will not harm young children's language development, and that they are capable of acquiring a second language without explicit instructions, it is a myth to think that children find the process "painless" (Hakuta, 1986).

Experimental research comparing young children and adults in second language learning has consistently indicated poorer performance by young children, except in pronunciation. Factors leading to the impression that young children acquire languages more easily are that children have fewer inhibitions, and greater frequency of social interactions (McLaughlin, 1984).

A second, related misconception states that the younger the child, the more quickly a second language is acquired. There is no evidence of a critical period for second language learning with the possible exception of accent (Hakuta, 1986). Studies reported by Krashen, Long, and Scarcella (1979), which examine rate of second language acquisition, favor adults. In addition,

---

Table. **Explanation of Terms Used in Second Language Education**

Linguistic minority student	*speaks the language of a minority group, e.g., Vietnamese*
Linguistic majority student	*speaks language of the majority group, i.e., English in the U.S.*
Limited English proficient	*any language background (LEP) student who has limited speaking skills in English as a second language*
Non-English proficient (NEP)	*has no previous experience learning English; speaks only the home language*
English Only (EO)	*is monolingual English speaker*
Fluent English proficient	*speaks both English and another language at home. This student speaks English fluently, e.g., ethnically diverse student born in the U.S., who speaks a second language at home.*

(Adapted from Snow, 1987)

adolescent learners acquire a second language faster than younger learners. Young children who receive natural exposure to a second language, however, are likely to eventually achieve higher levels of second language proficiency than adults.

It may be that "threshold levels" (Cummins, 1977; Skutnabb-Kangas, 1977) of native language proficiency are needed by young language minority learners in order to reap the benefits of

It is not true that young children learn a new language more quickly and easily than adults.

becoming bilingual. Young children, as a rule, will eventually catch up to, and surpass, most adults, but we need to provide them with a necessary gift of time.

A third misconception is that there is a single path to acquiring a second language in childhood. Wong Fillmore's (1976, 1985, 1986) research emphasizes the complex relationship among individual differences in young second language learners. Wong Fillmore (1985) suggests that three interconnected processes, including the social, linguistic, and cognitive domains, are responsible for variability in language learning. Learner characteristics contribute substantially to differential second language learning in children, but the relationship between learner characteristics and outcomes is not simple. No one characteristic can determine language learning (e.g., gregariousness) because variables such as situations, input, and interactions are also important (Wong Fillmore, 1986).

The research viewing individual differences points to the fact that young learners' second language acquisition abilities vary a great deal and are dependent upon social situations. Teachers of young children need to be cognizant of these variabilities by becoming keen observers of existing knowledge and abilities (Genishi, 1989). The assessment of language is a complex en-

deavor, and informal observations and teacher documentation can be extremely valuable tools. Readers are referred to Genishi and Dyson (1984) for a practical and sensitive review of how to assess progress in second language acquisition.

The second language learning process cannot be isolated from the young child's cultural learning. Ethnographic studies examining linguistically and culturally diverse children have found that classroom patterns also need to be culturally responsive, since differing approaches may work well with diverse children. For instance, Phillips (1972) found that Native American children were more willing to participate in group speaking activities than non-Native American children. Also, Au and Jordan (1981) found that reading and test scores improved when teachers incorporated narrative speech patterns such as talk story and overlapping speech into classroom routines with native Hawaiian children. Young children need to develop a positive and confident sense of biculturalism.

A great deal of trial and error takes place when a young child acquires a second language (McLaughlin, 1984). Learning to walk may serve as an example of another skill where exploration and experimentation are necessary. Young children progress at their own rate and persist until the skill is mastered. An accepting attitude is necessary during the trial and error phases of language acquisition. Rigid instructional practices emphasizing grammar construction are not appropriate because they can confuse and interfere with the natural developmental progression of second language acquisition (Felix, 1978, Lightbrown, 1977). The developmentally appropriate instructional practices advocated by NAEYC (Bredekamp, 1987) apply to second language learners as well. Young bilingual/bicultural children experience the same developmental progressions, with additional challenges involving second language/cultural learning.

Successful instructional approaches

In the United States, bilingual education is typically defined as an educational program for language minority students, in which instruction is provided in the child's primary language

while the child acquires sufficient English skills to function academically. As noted earlier, an *additive* approach focuses on enrichment by the addition of a second language while supporting the native language, and a *subtractive* approach teaches a second language as a replacement, often at the expense of the native language. Programs that offer no aid to students learning a second language are referred to as "sink or swim" or "submersion" efforts (Snow, 1987). While it is beyond the scope of this paper to examine the pervasive "English Only" attitudes in our nation today, it should be noted that bilingual instruction is controversial, and that the sociopolitical climate has often prompted the needs of young bilingual/bicultural children to be overlooked. It is also often the case that programs purporting to include bilingual approaches, in truth, emphasize English only, and a "sink or swim" approach.

Nevertheless, three bilingual education approaches are prevalent for preschoolers and early elementary school students (Ovando & Collier, 1985). The **transitional** approach is widespread and emphasizes the rapid development of English language skills, so the student can participate in the mainstreamed setting as soon as possible. Native language instruction is used initially but the major focus is generally to quickly transfer the learner to the mainstreamed setting. We need to look carefully at these programs in light of Cummins' (1979, 1984, 1985) research, emphasizing the need for learners to obtain optimal levels of native language proficiency.

The **maintenance/developmental** approach emphasizes the development of language skills in the home language, with an additional goal of English mastery. This strategy enhances the child's native language and allows learners to gain concepts in the native language while introducing English as a Second Language (ESL). Children are usually served by additional "pull out" English as a Second Language (ESL) instruction from teachers trained in ESL methods.

The **two-way** bilingual approach serves both the language majority and the language minority, expecting both groups of learners to become bilingual, and to experience academic success. An advantage of the two-way bilingual approach is that children are afforded an opportunity to participate in culturally and linguistically diverse intergroup relations. Recent research points to long-term attitudinal effects from this newly emerging bilingual approach (Collier, 1989).

The role of Head Start in Bilingual Early Childhood Education needs to be acknowledged in light of exemplary service for over 25 years (U.S. Department of Health and Human Services, 1990). Soledad Arenas (1980) describes a bilingual early childhood Head Start effort initiated by Administration for Children, Youth and Families (ACYF). Four contracts were awarded throughout the nation, including: Un Marco Abierto at the High/Scope Center in Ypsilanti, Michigan; Nuevas Fronteras de Aprendizaje at the University of California; Alerta at Columbia University; and Amanecer in San Antonio, Texas. Each program differed considerably, but was based upon an additive philosophy, and serviced Spanish-speaking Head Start children. The evaluation conducted by Juarez and Associates (1980), viewing the impact of the programs over a three-and-a-half year period, found the bilingual preschool curricula to be effective for both Spanish and English preferring young children. In addition, the evaluation concluded that parent and teacher attitudes were favorable, that models can be implemented in differing geographical locations, and that dual language strategies were most related to positive child outcomes.

An important and thorough review of bilingual education research involving 23 different programs found that preschool, elementary, and middle school children who were enrolled in the bilingual programs reviewed, outperformed children on a variety of standardized measures in nonbilingual programs, regardless of the language used for testing (Willig, 1985). Also, research examining bilingualism and cognitive competence favors the attainment of higher levels of bilingual proficiency (Barrik & Swain, 1974; Cummins & Gulutson, 1974; Cummins & Mulcahy, 1976; Duncan & De Avila, 1979; Lessler & Quinn, 1982; Peal & Lambert, 1962; Skutnabb-Kangas, 1977; Hakuta, 1986). Advanced bilingualism has been found to be associated with cognitive flexibility and divergent thinking (Hakuta, 1986). These are powerful findings in an era when the usefulness of bilingual approaches continues to be questioned.

It has been suggested that successful programs progress from native language instruction to initial second language learning, to a stage of enrichment and eventually a return to the native language instruction via the incorporation of literature and social studies, in order to incorporate a healthy sense of biculturalism (Krashen & Biber, 1988). The three components of successful programs serving limited English proficient children reviewed by Krashen and Biber include:

● high-quality subject matter instruction in the native language without concurrent translation
● development of literacy in the native language
● comprehensible input in English

The Carpinteria Preschool Program (Keatinge, 1984; Krashen & Biber, 1988) is particularly interesting because of the emphasis on native language instruction. The children in this program received instruction in Spanish, yet outperformed comparison learners on a test of conversational English (Bilingual Syntax Measure), and exceeded published norms on tests of school readiness (School Readiness Inventory), and academic achievement (California Achievement Test). This particular program supports Cummins' (1984) contention that learners need to obtain a "threshold level" or optimal level of native language proficiency. It appears that native language instruction actually gave students an advantage in their acquisition of a second language.

What can we conclude from this discussion? In an attempt to summarize selected research findings regarding second language acquisition and successful approaches to bilingual education, a list of practical classroom applications is proposed.

Practical applications for teachers of young children

As a caretaker in a decision-making capacity, the early childhood educator plays a critical role in the lives of linguistically and culturally diverse young children. The early childhood setting becomes a home away from home, the first contact with non-family members, the first contact with culturally different people, and the first experience with non-native speakers. A teacher's attitude and knowledge base is crucial in setting the educational goals of acceptance and appreciation of diversity (Ramsey, 1987). The possibilities are endless for teachers of young children who, as role models, are in a unique position to establish the tone, or "classroom climate," through decision making, collaboration, interactions, and activities.

Teachers of young children are currently implementing a variety of educationally sound strategies. In addition, based upon the recent research, and what we know about young children, we can:

1. Accept individual differences with regard to language-learning time frames. It's a myth to think that young children can learn a language quickly and easily. Avoid pressures to "rush" and "push out" children to join the mainstream classrooms. Young children need time to acquire, explore, and experience second language learning.

2. Accept children's attempts to communicate, because trial and error are a part of the second language learning process. Negotiating meaning, and collaboration in conversations, is important. Children should be given opportunities to practice both native and newly established language skills. Adults should not dominate the conversations; rather, children should be listened to. Plan and incorporate opportunities for conversation such as dramatic play, storytime, puppetry, peer interactions, social experiences, field trips, cooking and other enriching activities.

3. Maintain an additive philosophy by recognizing that children need to acquire new language skills instead of replacing existing linguistic skills. Afford young children an opportunity to retain their native language and culture. Allow young learners ample social opportunities.

4. Provide a stimulating, active, diverse linguistic environment with many opportunities for language use in meaningful social interactions. Avoid rigid or didactic grammatical approaches with young children. Children enjoy informal play experiences, dramatizations, puppetry, telephone conversations, participation in children's literature, and social interactions with peers.

5. Incorporate culturally responsive experiences for all children. Valuing each child's home culture and incorporating meaningful/active participation will enhance interpersonal skills, and contribute to academic and social success.

6. Use informal observations to guide the planning of activities, interactions, and conversations for speakers of other languages.

3. CHILDHOOD: Cognitive and Language Development

7. Provide an **accepting** classroom climate that values culturally and linguistically diverse young children. We know that young children are part of today's natural resources, capable of contributing to tomorrow's multicultural/multilingual society.

References

Arenas, S. (1980, May/June). Innovations in bilingual/multicultural curriculum development. *Children Today.* Washington, DC: U.S. Government Printing Office No. 80–31161.

Au, K., & Jordan, C. (1981). Teaching reading to Hawaiian children: Finding a culturally appropriate solution. In H.T. Trueba & G.P. Guthrie (Eds.), *Culture and the bilingual classroom: Studies in classroom ethnography.* Cambridge, MA: Newbury House.

Baker, C. (1988). *Key issues in bilingualism and bilingual education.* Clevedon, Avon, England: Multilingual Matters, Ltd.

Barrik, H., & Swain M. (1974). English-French bilingual education in the early grades: The Elgin study. *Modern Language Journal, 58,* 392–403.

Bredekamp, S. (1987). (Ed.). *Developmentally appropriate practice in early childhood programs serving children from birth through age 8.* Washington, DC: NAEYC.

Casanova, U. (1990). *Shifts in bilingual education policy and the knowledge base.* Tuscon, AZ: Research Symposia of the National Association of Bilingual Educators.

Dulay, H., & Burt, M. (1974). Natural sequences in child second language acquisition. *Language Learning, 24,* 37–53.

Duncan, S.E., & DeAvila, E. (1979). Bilingualism and cognition: Some recent findings. *NABE Journal, 4,* 15–50.

Escobedo, T. (1983). *Early childhood bilingual education. A Hispanic perspective.* New York: Teachers College Press, Columbia University.

Felix, S.W. (1978). Some differences between first and second language acquisition. In C. Waterson & C. Snow (Eds.), *The development of communication.* New York: Wiley.

Garcia, E. (1983). *Early childhood bilingualism.* Albuquerque: University of New Mexico.

Garcia, E. (1986). Bilingual development and the education of bilingual children during early childhood. *American Journal of Education, 11,* 96–121.

Collier, V. (1989). Academic achievement, attitudes, and occupation among graduates of two-way bilingual classes. Paper presented at the American Educational Research Association, San Francisco, California.

Contreras, R. (1988). *Bilingual education.* Bloomington, IN: Phi Delta Kappa.

Cook, V.J. (1973). The comparison of language development in native children and foreign adults. *International Review of Applied Linguistics in Language Teaching, 11,* 13–29.

Cummins, J. (1977). Cognitive factors associated with intermediate levels of bilingual skills. *Modern Language Journal, 61,* 3–12.

Cummins, J. (1979). Linguistic interdependence and the educational development of bilingual children. *Review of Educational Research, 49*(2), 222–251.

Cummins, J. (1984). *Bilingualism and special education: Issues in assessment and pedagogy.* Clevedon, Avon, England: Multilingual Matters, Ltd.

Cummins, J. (1985). The construct of language proficiency in bilingual education. In James Alatis & John Staczek (Eds.), *Perspectives on bilingualism and bilingual education* (pp. 209–231). Washington, DC: Georgetown University.

Cummins, J., & Gulutson, M. (1974). Some effects of bilingualism on cognitive functioning. In S. Carey (Ed.), *Bilingualism, biculturalism and education.* Edmonton: University of Alberta.

Cummins, J., & Mulcahy, R. (1978). Orientation to language in Ukrainian-English bilingual children. *Child Development, 49,* 1239–1242.

Genishi, C. (1984). *Language assessment in the early years.* Norwood, NJ: Ablex.

Genishi, C. (1989). Observing the second language learner: An example of teachers' learning. *Language Arts, 66*(5), 509–515.

Hakuta, K. (1986). *Mirror of language. The debate of bilingualism.* New York: Basic.

Hodgkinson, H. (1985). *All one system: Demographics of education, kindergarten through graduate school.* Washington, DC: Institute for Educational Leadership, Inc.

Juarez & Associates (1980). Final report of an evaluation of the Head Start bilingual/bicultural curriculum models. Washington, DC: U.S. Department of Health and Human Services. No. 105–77–1048.

Keatinge, R.H. (1984). An assessment of the pinteria preschool Spanish immersion program. *Teacher Education Quarterly, 11,* 80–94.

Kessler, C., & Quinn, M. (1982). Cognitive development on bilingual environments. In B. Hartford, A. Valdman, & C. Foster (Eds.), *Issues in international bilingual education.* New York: Plenum.

Krashen, S., & Biber, D. (1988). *On course: Bilingual education's success in California.* Sacramento: California Association for Bilingual Education.

La Fontaine, H. (1987). *At-risk children and youth—The extra educational challenges of limited English-proficient students.* Washington, DC: Summer Institute of the Council of Chief State School Officers.

Lightbron, P. (1977). French second language learners: What they're talking about. *Language Learning, 27,* 371–381.

McLaughlin, B. (1984). *Second-language acquisition on childhood: Volume 1: Preschool children.* Hillsdale, NJ: Erlbaum.

Ovando, C., & Collier, V. (1985). *Bilingual and ESL classrooms.* New York: McGraw-Hill.

Oxford, C., et al. (1984). *Demographic projections of non-English background and limited English-proficient persons in the United States in the year 2000.* Rosslyn, VA: InterAmerica Research Associates.

Peal, E., & Lambert, W. (1962). The revelations of bilingualism to intelligence. *Psychological Monographs, 76*(27), 1–23.

Phillips, S. (1972). Participation structures and communicative competence: Warm Springs children in community and classroom. In C. Cazden, V. John, & D. Hymes, (Eds.), *Functions of language in the classroom.* New York: Teachers College, Columbia University.

Ramsey, P. (1987). *Teaching and learning in a diverse world.* New York: Teachers College Press, Columbia University.

Skutnabb-Kangas, T. (1977). *Bilingualism or not: The education of minorities.* Clevedon, Avon, England: Multilingual Matters, Ltd.

Sleeter, C., & Grant, C. (1987). An analysis of multicultural education in the United States. *Harvard Educational Review, 57*(4), 421–444.

Snow, M. (1987). *Common terms in second language education: Center for Language Education and Research.* Los Angeles: University of California.

Snow, C., & Hakuta, K. (1987). *The costs of monolingualism.* Unpublished monograph, Cambridge, MA: Harvard University.

Soto, L.D. (in press). Alternate research paradigms in bilingual education research. In R. Padilla and A. Benavides (Eds.), *Critical perspectives on bilingual education research.* Phoenix: Bilingual Review/Press.

Soto, L.D. (in press). Success stories. In C. Grant (Ed.), *Research directions for multicultural education.* Bristol, PA: Falmer Press.

Swain, M. (1987). Bilingual education: Research and its implications. In M. Long and J. Richards (Eds.), *Methodology in TESOL.* Cambridge, MA: Newbury House.

U.S. Department of Health and Human Services. (1990). Head Start: A child development program. Washington, DC: Office of Human Development Services, Administration for Children, Youth and Families.

Willig, A. (1985). A meta-analysis of selected studies on the effectiveness of bilingual education. *Review of Educational Research, 55*(3), 269–317.

Wong Fillmore, L. (1976). *The second time around: Cognitive and social strategies.* Unpublished doctoral dissertation, Stanford University, Stanford, CA.

Wong Fillmore, L. (1985). *Second language learning in children: A proposed model.* Proceedings of a conference on issues in English language development, Arlington, VA. ERIC Document 273149.

Wong Fillmore, L. (in press). Language and cultural issues in early education. In S. Kagan (Ed.), *The care and education of America's young children: Obstacles and opportunities.* The 90th yearbook of the National Society for the Study of Education.

Wong Fillmore, L., & Valadez, C. (1986). **Teaching bilingual learners. In M. Wittrock** (Ed.), *Handbook of research on teaching.* New York: Macmillan.

CLIPPED WINGS

*The Fullest Look Yet at How
Prenatal Exposure to Drugs, Alcohol, and Nicotine
Hobbles Children's Learning*

LUCILE F. NEWMAN AND STEPHEN L. BUKA

Lucile F. Newman is a professor of community health and anthropology at Brown University and the director of the Preventable Causes of Learning Impairment Project. Stephen L. Buka is an epidemiologist and instructor at the Harvard Medical School and School of Public Health.

SOME FORTY thousand children a year are born with learning impairments related to their mother's alcohol use. Drug abuse during pregnancy affects 11 percent of newborns each year—more than 425,000 infants in 1988. Some 260,000 children each year are born at below normal weights—often because they were prenatally exposed to nicotine, alcohol, or illegal drugs.

What learning problems are being visited upon these children? The existing evidence has heretofore been scattered in many different fields of research—in pediatric medicine, epidemiology, public health, child development, and drug and alcohol abuse. Neither educators, health professionals, nor policy makers could go to one single place to receive a full picture of how widespread or severe were these preventable causes of learning impairment.

In our report for the Education Commission of the States, excerpts of which follow, we combed these various fields to collect and synthesize the major studies that relate prenatal exposure to nicotine, alcohol, and illegal drugs* with various indexes of students' school performance.

The state of current research in this area is not always as full and satisfying as we would wish. Most of what

exists is statistical and epidemiological data, which document the frequency of certain high-risk behaviors and correlate those behaviors to student performance. Such data are very interesting and useful, as they allow teachers and policy makers to calculate the probability that a student with a certain family history will experience school failure. But such data often cannot control for the effects of other risk factors, many of which tend to cluster in similar populations. In other words, the same mother who drinks during her pregnancy may also use drugs, suffer from malnutrition, be uneducated, a teenager, or poor—all factors that might ultimately affect her child's school performance. An epidemiological study generally can't tell you how much of a child's poor school performance is due exclusively to a single risk factor.

Moreover, the cumulative damage wrought by several different postnatal exposures may be greater than the damage caused by a single one operating in isolation. And many of the learning problems that are caused by prenatal exposure to drugs can be compounded by such social factors as poverty and parental disinterest and, conversely, overcome if the child lives in a high-quality postnatal environment.

All of these facts make it difficult to isolate and interpret the level and character of the damage that is caused by a single factor. Further, until recently, there was little interest among researchers in the effects of prenatal alcohol exposure because there was little awareness that it was affecting a substantial number of children. The large cohort of children affected by crack is just now entering the schools, so research on their school performance hasn't been extensive.

What does clearly emerge from the collected data is that our classrooms now include many students whose ability to pay attention, sit still, or fully develop their visual, auditory, and language skills was impaired even before they walked through our schoolhouse doors. On the

---

*The full report for the ECS also addressed the effect on children's learning of fetal malnutrition, pre- and postnatal exposure to lead, and child abuse and neglect.

From *American Educator,* Spring 1991, pp. 27-33, 42. Adapted from "Every Child a Learner: Reducing Risks of Learning Impairment During Pregnancy and Infancy," supported by the Exxon Educational Foundation, published by the Education Commission of the States.

3. CHILDHOOD: Developmental Problems

brighter side, the evidence that many of these impairments can be overcome by improved environmental conditions suggests that postnatal treatment is possible; promising experiments in treatment are, in fact, under way and are outlined at the end of this article.

1. Low Birthweight

The collection of graphs begins with a set on low birthweight, which is strongly associated with lowered I.Q. and poor school performance. While low birthweight can be brought on by other factors, including maternal malnutrition and teenage pregnancy, significant causes are maternal smoking, drinking, and drug use.

Around 6.9 percent of babies born in the United States weigh less than 5.5 pounds (2,500 grams) at birth and are considered "low-birthweight" babies. In 1987, this accounted for some 269,100 infants. Low birthweight may result when babies are born prematurely (born too early) or from intrauterine growth retardation (born too small) as a result of maternal malnutrition or actions that restrict blood flow to the fetus, such as smoking or drug use.

In 1987, about 48,750 babies were born at very low birthweights (under 3.25 lbs. or 1,500 grams). Research estimates that 6 to 8 percent of these babies experience major handicaps such as severe mental retardation or cerebral palsy (Eilers et al., 1986; Hack and Breslau, 1986). Another 25 to 26 percent have borderline I.Q. scores, problems in understanding and expressing language, or other deficits (Hack and Breslau, 1986; Lefebvre et al., 1988; Nickel et al., 1982; Vohr et al., 1988). Although these children may enter the public school system, many of them show intellectual disabilities and require special educational assistance. Reading, spelling, handwriting, arts, crafts, and mathematics are difficult school subjects for them. Many are late in developing

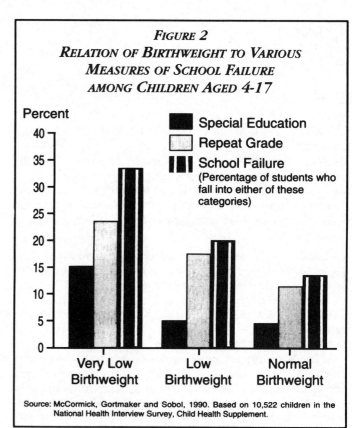

FIGURE 2
RELATION OF BIRTHWEIGHT TO VARIOUS MEASURES OF SCHOOL FAILURE AMONG CHILDREN AGED 4-17

Source: McCormick, Gortmaker and Sobol, 1990. Based on 10,522 children in the National Health Interview Survey, Child Health Supplement.

their speech and language. Children born at very low birthweights are more likely than those born at normal weights to be inattentive, hyperactive, depressed, socially withdrawn, or aggressive (Breslau et al., 1988).

New technologies and the spread of neonatal intensive care over the past decade have improved survival rates of babies born at weights ranging from 3.25 pounds to 5.5 pounds. But, as Figures 2 and 3 show, those born at low birthweight still are at increased risk of school failure. The increased risk, however, is very much tied to the child's postnatal environment. When the data on which Figure 2 is based are controlled to account for socioeconomic circumstances, very low-birthweight babies are approximately twice, not three times, as likely to repeat a grade.

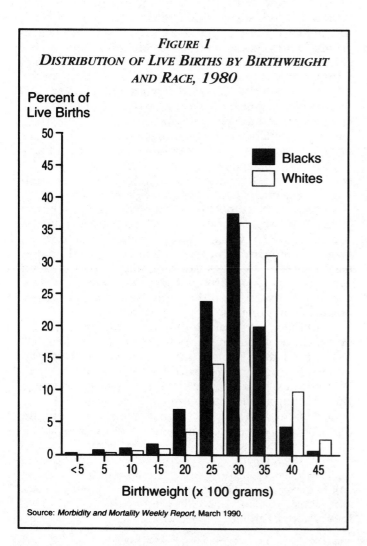

FIGURE 1
DISTRIBUTION OF LIVE BIRTHS BY BIRTHWEIGHT AND RACE, 1980

Source: *Morbidity and Mortality Weekly Report*, March 1990.

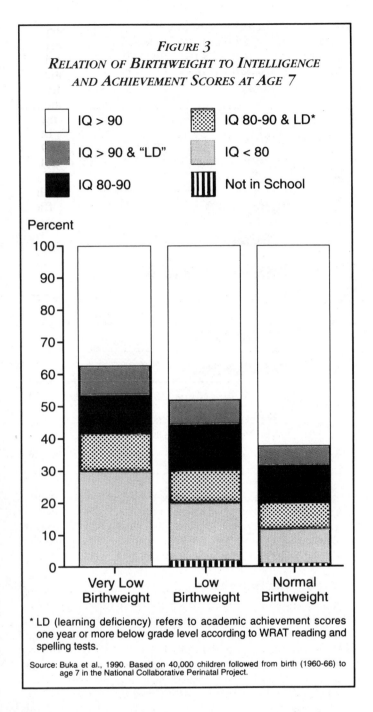

FIGURE 3
RELATION OF BIRTHWEIGHT TO INTELLIGENCE
AND ACHIEVEMENT SCORES AT AGE 7

IQ > 90

IQ > 90 & "LD"

IQ 80-90

IQ 80-90 & LD*

IQ < 80

Not in School

Percent

Very Low Birthweight   Low Birthweight   Normal Birthweight

* LD (learning deficiency) refers to academic achievement scores one year or more below grade level according to WRAT reading and spelling tests.

Source: Buka et al., 1990. Based on 40,000 children followed from birth (1960-66) to age 7 in the National Collaborative Perinatal Project.

to, among other problems, frequent hospitalization and school absence (Streissguth, 1986). A growing number of new studies has shown that children of smokers are smaller in stature and lag behind other children in cognitive development and educational achievement. These children are particularly subject to hyperactivity and inattention (Rush and Callahan, 1989).

Data from the National Collaborative Perinatal Project on births from 1960 to 1966 measured, among other things, the amount pregnant women smoked at each prenatal visit and how their children functioned in school at age seven. Compared to offspring of nonsmokers, children of heavy smokers (more than two packs per day) were nearly twice as likely to experience school failure by age seven (see Figure 4). The impact of heavy smoking is apparently greater the earlier it occurs during pregnancy. Children of women who smoked heavily during the first trimester of pregnancy were more than twice as likely to fail than children whose mothers did not smoke during the first trimester. During the second and third trimesters, these risks decreased. In all of these analyses, it is difficult to differentiate the effects of exposure to smoking before birth and from either parent after birth; to distinguish between learning problems caused by low birthweight and those caused by other damaging effects of smoking; or, to disentangle the effects of smoke from the socioeconomic setting of the smoker. But it is worth noting that Figure 4 is based on children born in the early sixties, an era when smoking mothers were fairly well distributed across socioeconomic groups.

One study that attempted to divorce the effects of smoking from those of poverty examined middle-class children whose mothers smoked during pregnancy (Fried and Watkinson, 1990) and found that the infants showed differences in responsiveness beginning at one week of age. Later tests at 1, 2, 3, and 4 years of age showed that on verbal tests "the children of the heavy smokers had mean test scores that were lower than those born to lighter smokers, who in turn did not perform as well as those born to nonsmokers." The study also indicated that the effects of smoke exposure, whether in the womb or after birth, may not be identifiable until later ages when a child needs to perform complex cognitive functions, such as problem solving or reading and interpretation.

3. Prenatal Alcohol Exposure

Around forty thousand babies per year are born with fetal alcohol effect resulting from alcohol abuse during pregnancy (Fitzgerald, 1988). In 1984, an estimated 7,024 of these infants were diagnosed with fetal alcohol syndrome (FAS), an incidence of 2.2 per 1,000 births (Abel and Sokol, 1987). The three main features of FAS in its extreme form are facial malformation, intrauterine growth retardation, and dysfunctions of the central nervous system, including mental retardation.

There are, in addition, about 33,000 children each year who suffer from less-severe effects of maternal alcohol use. The more prominent among these learning impairments are problems in attention (attention-deficit disorders), speech and language, and hyperactivity. General

Indeed, follow-up studies of low-birthweight infants at school age have concluded that "the influence of the environment far outweighs most effects of nonoptimal prenatal or perinatal factors on outcome" (Aylward et al., 1989). This finding suggests that early assistance can improve the intellectual functioning of children at risk for learning delay or impairment (Richmond, 1990).

2. Maternal Smoking

Maternal smoking during pregnancy has long been known to be related to low birthweight (Abel, 1980), an increased risk for cancer in the offspring (Stjernfeldt et al., 1986), and early and persistent asthma, which leads

3. CHILDHOOD: Developmental Problems

school failure also is connected to a history of fetal alcohol exposure (Abel and Sokol, 1987; Ernhart et al., 1985). Figure 5 shows the drinking habits of women of child-bearing age by race and education.

When consumed in pregnancy, alcohol easily crosses the placenta, but exactly how it affects the fetus is not well known. The effects of alcohol vary according to how far along in the pregnancy the drinking occurs. The first trimester of pregnancy is a period of brain growth and organ and limb formation. The embryo is most susceptible to alcohol from week two to week eight of development, a point at which a woman may not even know she is pregnant (Hoyseth and Jones, 1989). Researchers have yet to determine how much alcohol it takes to cause problems in development and how alcohol affects each critical gestational period. It appears that the more alcohol consumed during pregnancy, the worse the effect.

And many of the effects do not appear until ages four to seven, when children enter school.

Nearly one in four (23 percent) white women, eighteen to twenty-nine, reported "binge" drinking (five

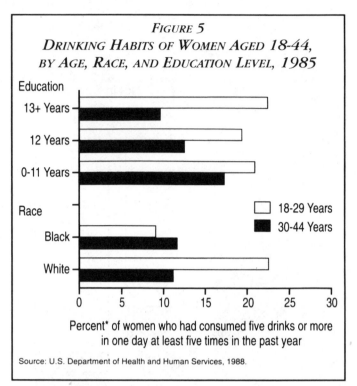

FIGURE 5
DRINKING HABITS OF WOMEN AGED 18-44, BY AGE, RACE, AND EDUCATION LEVEL, 1985

Percent* of women who had consumed five drinks or more in one day at least five times in the past year

Source: U.S. Department of Health and Human Services, 1988.

drinks or more a day at least five times in the past year). This was nearly three times the rate for black women of that age (about 8 percent). Fewer women (around 3 percent for both black and white) reported steady alcohol use (two drinks or more per day in the past two weeks).

4. Fetal Drug Exposure

The abuse of drugs of all kinds—marijuana, cocaine, crack, heroin, or amphetamines—by pregnant women affected about 11 percent of newborns in 1988—about 425,000 babies (Weston et al., 1989).

Cocaine and crack use during pregnancy are consistently associated with lower birthweight, premature birth, and smaller head circumference in comparison with babies whose mothers were free of these drugs (Chasnoff et al., 1989; Cherukuri et al., 1988; Doberczak et al., 1987; Keith et al., 1989; Zuckerman et al., 1989). In a study of 1,226 women attending a prenatal clinic, 27 percent tested positive for marijuana and 18 percent for cocaine. Infants of those who had used marijuana weighed an average of 2.8 ounces (79 grams) less at birth and were half a centimeter shorter in length. Infants of mothers who had used cocaine averaged 3.3 ounces (93 grams) less in weight and .7 of a centimeter less in length and also had a smaller head circumference than babies of nonusers (Zuckerman et al., 1989). The study concluded that "marijuana use and cocaine use during pregnancy are each independently associated with impaired fetal growth" (Zuckerman et al., 1989).

In addition, women who use these substances are like-

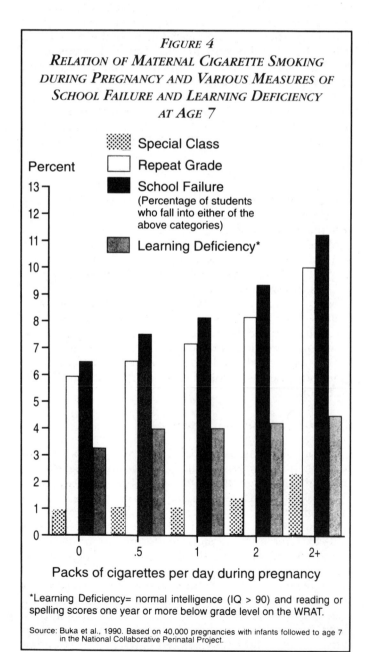

FIGURE 4
RELATION OF MATERNAL CIGARETTE SMOKING DURING PREGNANCY AND VARIOUS MEASURES OF SCHOOL FAILURE AND LEARNING DEFICIENCY AT AGE 7

Special Class
Repeat Grade
School Failure
(Percentage of students who fall into either of the above categories)
Learning Deficiency*

Packs of cigarettes per day during pregnancy

*Learning Deficiency= normal intelligence (IQ > 90) and reading or spelling scores one year or more below grade level on the WRAT.

Source: Buka et al., 1990. Based on 40,000 pregnancies with infants followed to age 7 in the National Collaborative Perinatal Project.

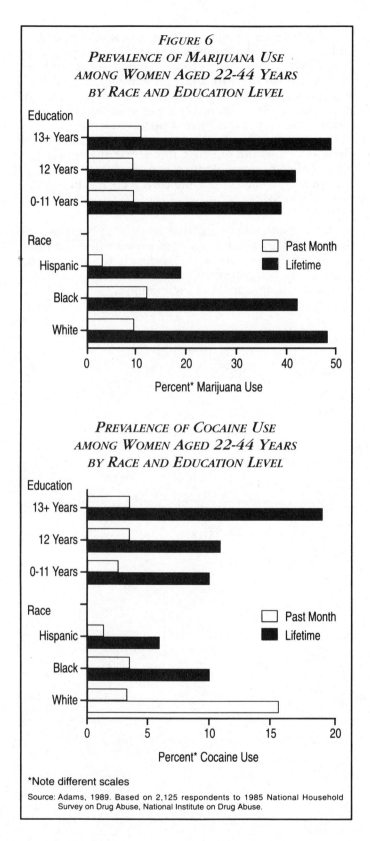

FIGURE 6
PREVALENCE OF MARIJUANA USE
AMONG WOMEN AGED 22-44 YEARS
BY RACE AND EDUCATION LEVEL

PREVALENCE OF COCAINE USE
AMONG WOMEN AGED 22-44 YEARS
BY RACE AND EDUCATION LEVEL

*Note different scales

Source: Adams, 1989. Based on 2,125 respondents to 1985 National Household Survey on Drug Abuse, National Institute on Drug Abuse.

aged nearly a pound (14.6 ounces or 416 grams) smaller than those born to women who had normal weight gain and did not use cigarettes, marijuana, and cocaine (see Table 1). The effect of these substances on size is more than the sum of the risk factors combined.

Like alcohol use, drug use has different effects at different points in fetal development. Use in very early pregnancy is more likely to cause birth defects affecting organ formation and the central nervous systems. Later use may

TABLE 1		
INFANT WEIGHT DIFFERENCES ASSOCIATED WITH SUBSTANCE ABUSE		
Substance Use During Pregnancy at One Prenatal Clinic:		
N = 1,226 Marijuana (n = 330) (27%) Cocaine (n = 221) (18%)		
		Birthweight difference:
Marijuana users only vs. non-users		− 2.8 oz.
Cocaine users only vs. non-users		− 3.3 oz.
Combination users (marijuana, cocaine, one pack of cigarettes a day, low maternal weight gain) vs. non-users		−14.6 oz.

Source: Zuckerman et al., 1989.

result in low birthweight due to either preterm birth or intrauterine growth retardation (Kaye et al., 1989; MacGregor et al., 1987; Petitti and Coleman, 1990). While some symptoms may be immediately visible, others may not be apparent until later childhood (Weston et al., 1989; Gray and Yaffe, 1986; Frank et al., 1988).

In infancy, damaged babies can experience problems in such taken-for-granted functions as sleeping and waking, resulting in exhaustion and poor development. In childhood, problems are found in vision, motor control, and in social interaction (Weston et al., 1989). Such problems may be caused not only by fetal drug exposure but also by insufficient prenatal care for the mother or by an unstimulating or difficult home environment for the infant (Lifschitz et al., 1985).

WHAT CAN be done to ameliorate the condition of children born with such damage? Quite a bit, based on the success of supportive prenatal care and the results of model projects that have provided intensive assistance to both baby and mother from the time of birth. These projects have successfully raised the I.Q. of low- and very-low birthweight babies an average of ten points or more—an increase that may lift a child with below-average intelligence into a higher I.Q. cate-

ly to smoke and to gain less weight during pregnancy, two factors associated with low birthweight. The cumulative effect of these risk factors is demonstrated by the finding that infants born to women who gained little weight, who had smoked one pack of cigarettes a day, and who tested positive for marijuana and cocaine aver-

gory (i.e., from retarded to low average or from low average to average). Generally known as either educational day care or infant day care, these programs provide a developmentally stimulating environment to high-risk babies and/or intensive parent support to prepare the parent to help her child.

In one such program based at the University of California/Los Angeles, weekly meetings were held among staff, parents, and infants over a period of four years. By the project's end, the low-birthweight babies had caught up in mental function to the control group of normal birthweight children (Rauh et al., 1988). The Infant Health and Development Project, which was conducted in eight cities and provided low-birthweight babies with pediatric follow-up and an educational curriculum with family support, on average increased their I.Q. scores by thirteen points and the scores of very-low birthweight children by more than six points. Another project tar-

geted poor single teenage mothers whose infants were at high risk for intellectual impairment (Martin, Ramey and Ramey, 1990). One group of children was enrolled in educational day care from six and one-half weeks of age to four and one-half years for five days a week, fifty weeks a year. By four and one-half years, the children's I.Q. scores were in the normal range and ten points higher than a control group. In addition, by the time their children were four and one-half, mothers in the experimental group were more likely to have graduated from high school and be self-supporting than were mothers in the control group.

These studies indicate that some disadvantages of poverty and low birthweight can be mitigated and intellectual impairment avoided. The key is attention to the cognitive development of young children, in conjunction with social support of their families.

Of a different mind

Williams syndrome: in the twilight zone of life

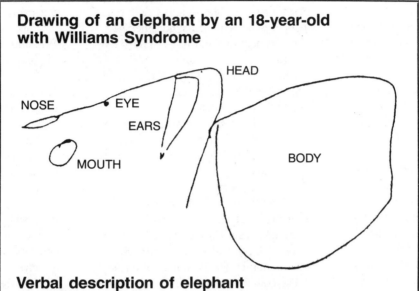

Drawing of an elephant by an 18-year-old with Williams Syndrome

NOSE EYE HEAD EARS MOUTH BODY

Verbal description of elephant

And what an elephant is, it is one of the animals. And what the elephant does, it lives in the jungle. It can also live in the zoo. And what it has, it has long gray ears, fan ears, ears that can blow in the wind. It has a long trunk that can pick up grass, or pick up hay... If they're in a bad mood it can be terrible... If the elephant gets mad it could stomp; it could charge. Sometimes elephants can charge, like a bull can charge. They have big long tusks. They can damage a car... It could be dangerous. When they're in a pinch, when they're in a bad mood it can be terrible. You don't want an elephant as a pet. You want a cat or a dog or a bird...

Susan Duerksen

Staff Writer

Annette Augustine loves to read and reread poetry, savoring the meaning of each word. She's perceptive and quick in conversation and expresses deep concern for the well-being of others, whether a hospitalized friend or the homeless.

However, she can't add and subtract well enough to make change for a dollar. She can barely write legibly and can't drive.

At 21, she's living with a companion in a program for the handicapped and thinking of moving back to her parents' home in Poway because even semi-independent life is overwhelming her.

Annette has a genetic disorder called Williams syndrome, a bizarre collection of what scientists call "peaks and valleys of abilities."

Asked what she knows about Williams syndrome, Annette provides a typical example of its characteristics: She can't quite define the essence of the disorder, but she can talk about it extensively.

"Williams syndrome is another person being exactly like me, the same hair, same eyes, same hands," she said. A little later she added, "I don't do things normally like other people

do. I do work slower. I can scribble my name and even that doesn't look correct. I make curved lines when I try to make a circle. Bad hand-motor control."

She also has the distinctive Williams syndrome look: facial features usually described as elfin, including wide-spaced eyes, a pug nose and full lips. Annette also has the heart defect that afflicts many people with the syndrome: a narrowing of the heart's main artery that can cause very high blood pressure.

Williams syndrome has been known only since 1961, when a cardiologist in New Zealand, Dr. J. C. P. Williams, wrote about four mentally retarded, elfin-looking patients with that heart condition.

A national association of Williams parents—formed in San Diego a decade ago—now includes 1,800 families. However, experts believe there are many more people with Williams in this country, perhaps one in every 20,000 to 50,000, most of whom are probably considered mentally retarded. About 80 parents and 30 Williams syndrome youngsters are gathering in San Diego Saturday for the annual meeting of the national association's western region.

What fascinates scientists about the disorder is its highly unusual dichotomy between language skills and other mental functions, lending credence to the theory developed in studies of stroke patients and others that language is somehow separated in the brain from other thinking and knowing.

At the Salk Institute in La Jolla, linguist and neuroscientist Dr. Ursula Bellugi is working with a growing band of specialists to probe the brains and abilities of people with Williams syndrome, looking for clues to how all our brains are organized.

"It's a good puzzle," Bellugi said. "It's going to keep us busy for a while. We're still at the tip of the iceberg."

Masters of fluid speech

Verbal expression and outgoing friendliness are the standout features of people with Williams syndrome. Although most of them test mildly retarded on IQ tests and are late talkers as children, they have astounding vocabularies and fluid, sophisticated speech.

They are master storytellers, embellishing either fictional tales or past experiences with plenty of voice modulation and strong expressions of feeling and wonder.

"They're in the twilight zone of retardation, but they're not exactly retarded," said Eleanor Semel, a San Diego educational psychologist who runs a hotline for Williams families. "Their ability to use idioms and analogies is highly developed. They're terrific at storytelling, sometimes far superior to average kids.

"Their ability to read facial expressions is uncanny. They're sensitive to others. They're sweet, they're kindly, they're empathetic, they're cooperative, they're very industrious and eager to please."

Language skills and sociability may be linked, researchers say. While they fail many tests involving pictures and size and space judgments, people with Williams syndrome exceed at recognizing and interpreting faces.

But their brains hit the brakes when faced with other mental tasks like planning, reasoning, solving puzzles or drawing.

When people with Williams syndrome try to draw what they see, the result usually is a scattered, haphazard collage of the parts rather than the whole. For some reason, they see the trees and not the forest, Bellugi said.

A drawing of a bicycle by a San Diego 11-year-old with Williams shows the chain stretched out under the wheels, the fishlike body of the rider under the chain and the pedals off to the side.

Bellugi has been testing Williams adolescents since 1984 and recently began studying infants and children as well, as part of a larger federally funded study of language development.

Much of the testing so far has compared Williams teens to others of the same ages and IQs with Down's syndrome, a major cause of mental retardation.

The differences are startling. When asked to name all the animals he could think of in a timed test, an adolescent with Down's syndrome said, "dogs, cats, fish, bird, fish." A Williams youngster of the same age and IQ replied, "brontosaurus, pteranodon, brontosaurus rex, dinosaurs, elephant, dog, cat, lion, baby hippopotamus, ibex, whale, bull, yak, zebra, puppy, kitten, tiger, koala, dragon."

Magnetic resonance scans show that the brain is about 85 percent of normal size in both Williams and Down's syndrome, but certain portions such as the cerebellum remain normal size in Williams.

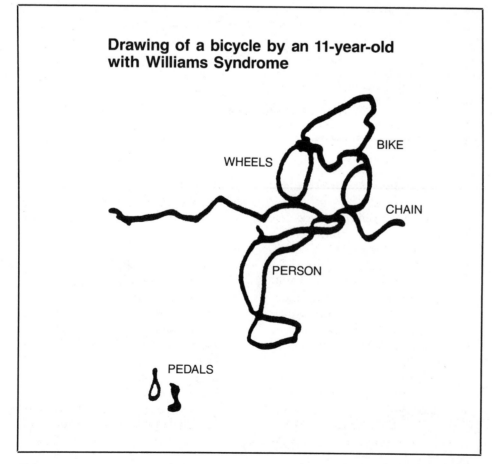

Drawing of a bicycle by an 11-year-old with Williams Syndrome

WHEELS

BIKE

CHAIN

PERSON

PEDALS

The studies indicate that the cerebellum, known as the center of muscle coordination, might also be involved in language processing, said Dr. Paul Wang, a pediatrician working with Bellugi.

For some people with Williams syndrome, the language skills include an aptitude for foreign languages, including sign language. The youngsters who come to Bellugi's lab for testing are fascinated by two deaf researchers who work there, Wang said.

"They'll wander over to the deaf people who are signing and stand there in rapt attention," he said. "They pick up some of the signs and they remember it. They seem to be interested in language of all sorts."

Musical talent apparently is another peak in the varied Williams landscape. Gloria Lenhoff, a 37-year-old Costa Mesa woman with Williams, might be the ultimate example of both skills. She sings opera and folk songs in six languages, with the recent addition of Chinese, and plays the accordion. She has performed at colleges, movie premieres and conferences, and was the subject of a 1988 public television movie.

"She can't add three and four. Her handwriting is barely legible and she has the social skills of a sweet 9-year-old," said her father, Howard Lenhoff. "But she can hear an aria and sing it back. She has perfect pitch."

Gloria doesn't read a note of music, but sings and plays from memory. She also speaks a little of many languages, including Greek and Yiddish, her father said.

When Gloria is asked to explain how she learns languages so quickly, her answer contains a slight miswording that is a common trait of Williams speech:

"I just hear them when people speak them and I try to say it in the dialogue," she said, apparently meaning 'dialect.'

Bellugi has recorded "unexpected word choices" among her test subjects that sometimes sound confused and sometimes almost poetically creative. "I'll have to evacuate the glass," one said before pouring out her milk. And another, "I'm so worry-hearted."

A genetic link

Williams syndrome is believed to be caused by a defect in a dominant gene, said Dr. Colleen Morris, a University of Nevada geneticist, because two families have been found in which a parent and child both have the syndrome and the other parent does not.

Morris is conducting what she calls "a needle in the haystack search" for the gene involved. The search is focused on finding the gene that causes the rare aorta defect common in Williams syndrome, on the theory that that gene and the Williams gene are closely linked or possibly the same.

Seven families have been found with cases of the aorta narrowing in multiple generations, and three of them include a person with Williams syndrome, Morris said. There are no such multigenerational families for tracing Williams syndrome because few people with the disorder have had children.

The culprit may be a gene involved in calcium metabolism, Morris said. Scientists are exploring whether the high levels of calcium found in the blood of infants with Williams may cause a neurotransmitter imbalance in the central nervous system.

Another part of the mystery is an ultrasensitivity to sound, sometimes exhibited as particularly sharp hearing and sometimes as aversion to sounds that don't bother most people.

"Williams syndrome is a constellation of findings," Morris said. "I believe there's a single gene that affects many parts of the body."

Falling in the middle

Mental functioning in Williams varies greatly, including some people with borderline normal intelligence. Semel said some Williams adults do well in people-oriented jobs such as nurses aide, senior citizen caretaker or home products sales. She said the education system has failed many of them by placing them where they don't fit in classes with Down's syndrome or developmentally disabled children.

Diane Niles, of San Diego, said she "almost had to sue the school system" to get her son, Justin Filley, into an individualized program at the Urban Skills Center in Southeast San Diego, which contracts with local schools to take students they can't appropriately serve.

Within regular schools, Niles said, "the choice was, you're learning disabled or mentally retarded. He was constantly falling in the middle."

Niles founded the national parents' group, with another local mother, after Justin was diagnosed with Williams syndrome at age 3. Now 16, Justin said he still has a hard time learning, but added, "My teachers are my friends, too, because they taught me a lot of things."

A devoted rock music fan, he reads rock magazines and books about rock stars, and plays the drums. He and 19-year-old friend Greg Crisell, who also has Williams syndrome and who plays the bass, are forming a band.

"We're not disabled," Greg said. "We're not in wheelchairs. I feel normal."

Greg is an Eagle Scout, rides a moped, works part-time as a grill cook and favors reading and composition classes at school. Talking with Justin and Annette, he listens intently as they discuss their feelings and experiences, and asks for explanations or more detail with the insight of a practiced interviewer.

"He's sharp as a tack," said his mother, Toni Crisell, "but he has areas that aren't there."

When Justin had trouble articulating his belief that Williams is not such a bad condition, Annette politely helped out.

"Regular people are special and so are Williams kids," she said.

"That's a good point, right there," Justin agreed emphatically. "We love people."

"No one should hate us because we have this syndrome," Annette continued. "People out in the community should know there are Williams kids and they have to learn to love us and appreciate us."

Family, School, and Cultural Influences on Development

- Parenting (Articles 29–32)
- Stress and Maltreatment (Articles 33–36)
- Cultural Influences (Articles 37–39)
- Education (Articles 40–42)

The articles in the *Parenting* subsection touch upon a number of the formidable issues that today's parents face. As we approach the middle of the last decade of the twentieth century, parents as well as children are perhaps subject to more sources of psychological stress than at any time in the recent past. Some of the chief sources of parental stress stem from single parenting, the decline of intergenerational families, and the increase in teenage mothers and fathers. These factors and others have strained the support services available for families in our society. Families that are stressed may turn to expedient rearing techniques even when they are aware of "expert" opinion. One such expediency is the use of physical punishment in order to discipline children. However, physical punishment is an ineffective form of discipline that teaches lack of self-control and the use of aggression in order to control someone else's behavior. Today, childrearing advice seems to have struck a middle road between strict and permissive approaches. Parents are encouraged to cuddle their infants, to provide their children with ample love, to use reason as the major disciplinary technique, and to encourage verbal interaction—all in an environment where rules are clearly spelled out and enforced. Suggestion, persuasion, and explanation have become the preferred techniques of rule enforcement, rather than spanking or withdrawal of love.

William Galston, an educator with strong interests in public policy and the family, is the author of the first subsection selection. In "Putting Children First," Galston discusses the need for appropriate actions in the public and private sector to promote the well-being of children and families as they are buffeted about in our rapidly changing society.

"Same Family, Different Lives" by Bruce Bower describes some recent attempts to disentangle the effects of environment versus genetics. In other words, the article examines the nature-nurture controversy.

Part of parenting is spending time with your kids. However, as "Can Your Career Hurt Your Kids?" points out, with the decreasing number of mothers who stay home and the increasing number of single-parent families, parents are spending less time with their kids. Many of these children are in some sort of day care, especially the younger ones, but as they get older, a large number become latchkey children. This article looks at the advantages and disadvantages of day care, examines possible effects of leaving adolescents on their own, and considers the consequences for family relationships of parents coming home too tired to interact with their children. In all walks of life, fathers are disappearing in ever increasing numbers. "Bringing Up Father" notes that the importance of a father in the family is more essential than ever. A very strong message sent to today's American males is that they are not up to the job of fatherhood.

The *Stress and Maltreatment* subsection points out that, taken to extremes, severe disciplinary techniques can spill over into physical abuse. What are the long-term consequences of physical, psychological, and sexual abuse? We often assume that abused children become maladjusted and abusing parents. However, as discussed in "The Lasting Effects of Child Maltreatment," the story is not that simple. Many, perhaps most, abused children become well-adjusted adults. Similarly, most abusing adults were not targets of abuse as children. Other factors, such as poverty, play a major role in determining the outcome of earlier experiences.

The articles "Helping Children Cope with Violence" and "Children of Violence" point out that children who grow up with real-world violence all around them may become desensitized as their exposure to violence increases. Many of these children suffer post-traumatic stress disorder and may exhibit a number of different symptoms such as aggression, indifference, or inability to concentrate. However, some proportion of children reared under highly negative conditions show an amazing resiliency in their ability to survive. Experts believe that early intervention can be crucial in helping children recover from violent incidents in which they have been an observer or a participant.

Children as well as parents are subject to a variety of stressors in society today. Many young children are being pushed too hard and too fast academically; poor children suffer from peer pressures and are more likely to be abused and neglected; children experiment with drugs and alcohol at an earlier age. Divorce is one of the more common major sources of stress. Regardless of who wins custody, children do not have an easy time adjusting to the separation of their parents. Suggestions for helping children to cope often require a level of parental cooperation that may be unrealistic. The results of a longitudinal study of the effects of divorce on children, presented in "Children after Divorce," indicate that the psychological effects may be longer lasting than previously thought. In spite of forces threatening to tear families apart, however, the influence of the family on the life of an individual remains strong and pervasive.

Three selections comprise the *Cultural Influences* subsection. In the article "Why Kids Have a Lot to Cry About," David Elkind draws attention to the family in the current "postmodern" age. In his view, our long-held culture has failed us as we have witnessed in this century rampant warfare between nations, a breakdown of traditional faith, governmental instability, and disintegration of the traditional family structure.

School expands a child's social network beyond the neighborhood peer group and often presents new social adjustment problems. In "Alienation and the Four Worlds of Childhood," Urie Bronfenbrenner draws attention to the increase in disorganized families and environment, which contribute to alienation from family, friends, school, and work.

The final article in this section, "Culture, Race Too Often Ignored in Child Studies," is a summary of a symposium discussion that took place at the 1990 meeting of the Society for Research in Child Development, a key organization for child research specialists. The participants stressed the need for more careful and more systematic consideration of ethnicity and cultural factors in conducting research on development.

In the *Education* subsection, the article "Tracked to Fail" notes that among those who are at risk to fail are children who acquire negative labels at a very early age based on criteria such as reading ability or developmental test scores. The article shows how labels tend to stick all through school, regardless of the child's ability.

Additional aspects of contemporary education are addressed in two final selections. Americans are both mystified and impressed by the educational achievements of Asian children. How do they do it? Are Asian children smarter than American children? Apparently not. Then what accounts for the spectacular performance of Asian children in school? As described in "Learning from Asian Schools," a panel of experts who recently visited schools in three Asian countries and in the United States found there is nothing mysterious about the success of Asian school children. It is a matter of effective teaching methods and highly supportive parents operating in cultural settings in which education ranks as a top priority.

Looking Ahead: Challenge Questions

It is relatively easy to blame teen pregnancy and teen substance abuse on the disorganization of the American family. It is far more difficult to suggest effective solutions to the problems. What changes do you believe should be instituted in American society to resolve such problems as divorce, child abuse, teen pregnancy, racism, sexism, and substance abuse?

What are some of the pros and cons associated with maternal employment when the children are young?

It is abundantly clear that parents can cross the line between discipline and abuse. Is it also possible for parents to cross the line in the other direction—by providing too well for their children? Are abused children unlikely, somewhat likely, or very likely to become abusing parents?

What is the basis for the assertion that family experiences may increase the differences rather than the similarities among the children?

Will you raise your children the way your parents raised you? If not, how would you do it differently, and why?

Are sex differences in intellectual abilities, aggressiveness, and emotionality as common as is often claimed?

Why do Asian children dramatically outperform U.S. children in school achievement? This pattern also holds for Asian immigrants to the United States. What accounts for their high levels of success?

PUTTING CHILDREN FIRST

WILLIAM A. GALSTON

William A. Galston, the author most recently of Liberal Purposes: Goods, Virtues, and Diversity in the Liberal State *(Cambridge University Press), teaches at the University of Maryland, College Park. He is an advisor to the Washington, D.C.–based Progressive Policy Institute and a co-editor of* The Responsive Community, *a new journal that seeks a better balance between rights and responsibilities. This article is an expanded version of an essay that appeared in the December 2, 1991, issue of* The New Republic, *with material drawn from* Putting Children First: A Progressive Family Policy for the 1990s *by Elaine Ciulla Kamarck and William A. Galston, published by the Progressive Policy Institute.*

THE AMERICAN family has changed dramatically in the past generation, and it is children who have paid the price. From Ozzie and Harriet to the Simpsons, from one breadwinner to two, from child-centered nuclear families that stayed together for the sake of the children to the struggling one-parent families of today; the revolution in the American family has affected us all. Divorce rates have surged, and child poverty has risen alarmingly. The signs are everywhere around us that America's children are suffering—economically, educationally, and emotionally. Although this fact is obvious, indeed increasingly obtrusive, it has hardly been discussed by intellectuals and policy elites until quite recently. Several broad forces—racial conflict, feminism, the culture of individual rights—help explain this odd silence.

The story begins in 1965, with the publication of Daniel Patrick Moynihan's *The Negro Family: The Case for National Action,* which identified the breakdown of the black family as a growing obstacle to racial progress. Although intended as the analytical backdrop to major federal initiatives, it was received as a call for quietism, even as a subtle relegitimation of racism. Black civil rights leaders and white liberal scholars argued that the emphasis on family structure would inevitably divert attention from economic inequalities and would justify "blaming the victims" for the consequences of discrimination. As William Julius Wilson has argued, this enraged response had the consequence of suppressing public debate over, and serious scholarly inquiry into, the relation between black family structure and the problems of the ghetto poor—suppressing it for an entire generation.

Feminism also contributed to the silence. The postwar American women's movement began as a criticism of the 1950s family. "Liberation" meant leaving the domestic sphere for the world of work outside the home. It also meant denying traditional theories of gender difference that seemed to legitimate inequalities of resources, power, and self-respect. To be equal was to be the same: to compete on the same terms as men, with the same focus on individual separateness and independence. As Sylvia Ann Hewlett argues, the unquestionable moral force of the feminist movement muted the voices of those who, though dubious about its denial of gender differences and deeply concerned about its consequences for the well-being of children, did not wish to be accused of a disguised effort to ratify the patriarchal or chauvinist status quo.

Then there was the cultural upheaval of the 1960s, which yielded an ethic of self-realization through incessant personal experimentation, the triumph of what has been termed "expressive individualism." An increasingly influential therapeutic vocabulary emphasized the constraints that relations could impose on personal growth and encouraged adults to turn inward toward the self's struggles for sovereignty, to view commitments as temporary or endlessly renegotiable—to behave, in effect, like adolescents. This vocabulary was anything but hospitable to the discourse of parental continuity, commitment, and self-sacrifice.

A related legacy of the generation just past has been an impoverishment of moral vocabulary. What some regard as a descent into relativism is more accurately

Reprinted with permission from the Summer 1992 issue of the *American Educator,* pp. 8-13, 44-46, the quarterly journal of the American Federation of Teachers.

characterized as the relentless expansion of morality understood as the articulation of the rights of individuals. This development is not alien to the American experience, and it is not wholly to be deplored. Rights, after all, do support self-respect and offer protection against evils. Still, we now know that there is a difficulty: Although systems of rights can guide some spheres of life tolerably well, they can obscure and distort others. In particular, the effort to understand family relations as the mutual exercise of rights led to a legal and emotional cul-de-sac.

IN RECENT years, however, the climate has changed. Debates within the black community, and among social democrats as well as conservatives, have helped to relegitimate the discussion of the links between family structure and a range of social ills. To acknowledge such links, it is not necessary to sever the causal connections between structural inequalities at the political and economic level and disintegration at the family level, or to focus exclusively on the "culture of poverty." The point is, rather, that the cultural effects of past discrimination can take on a life of their own, that they can persist even in the face of changing opportunity structures.

The women's movement is changing, too. In place of equality understood as sameness, feminists such as Sara Ruddick, Carol Gilligan, and Jean Bethke Elshtain have embraced categories of difference, nurturance, and care. Martha Albertson Fineman insists that public policy "recognize and accommodate the positive and lasting nature of mothers' ties to their children." Surely this style of feminist argument will prove far more compatible with traditional understandings of the family than anyone could have predicted a decade ago.

And even broader cultural changes are under way, provoked by demographic shifts. Baby boomers who delayed marriage until their thirties have discovered that the moral universe of their young adulthood is not a suitable place for parents with young children. Others have discovered that the casting off of binding relationships is not necessarily the path to liberation and happiness. A generation that once devoted itself to the proliferation of rights and the expression of individuality has begun haltingly to explore counterbalancing notions of responsibility and community; several polls have documented rapid shifts during the past two years in public attitudes toward a range of family issues.

The most important shift is a welcome expansion of concern beyond narrow bounds of race and class. For too long, worries about children and families focused on such issues as teenage pregnancy, dire deprivation, and collapsing marriage rates. These are serious problems, but they are disproportionately characteristic of the ghetto poor. Such measurements, in other words, enabled the American middle class, scholars as well as citizens, to believe that families and children were someone else's problem. But with increased attention to the clash between work and family, to parental time deficits, and to the impact of divorce, the middle class can no longer sustain such an illusion. The decay of the family is its problem, too. The children of the middle class are also at risk; and its choices can be just as shortsighted, self-

There is growing recognition that we must place the family at the center of our thinking about social issues and children at the center of our thinking about the family.

indulgent, and harmful to the young as any ever contemplated in the culture of poverty.

THESE RECENT trends are at last producing important changes at the level of national politics. For decades, the revolution in the American family evoked a polarized reaction: Liberals talked about structural economic pressures facing families and avoided issues of personal conduct, and conservatives did just the reverse. Liberals habitually reached for bureaucratic responses, even when they were counter-productive, and conservatives reflexively rejected government programs even when they would work.

Both are wrong. Traditional conservatives' support for families is largely rhetorical; their disregard for new economic realities engenders a policy of unresponsive neglect—expressed for example, in President Bush's misguided veto of the Family Leave Act. Conversely, traditional liberals' unwillingness to acknowledge that intact two-parent families are the most effective units for raising children has led them into a series of policy cul-de-sacs.

Recently, however, this clash of conflicting world-views has begun to give way to a new spirit of accommodation. As E.J. Dionne Jr. has observed, recent proposals for pro-family tax reform reflect the realization that both values and dollars count. Many younger conservatives are addressing social problems long neglected by their movement. Many younger Democrats, meanwhile, are looking for new forms of nonbureaucratic, choice-based public activism as a supplement to the frequently cumbersome and intrusive institutions of the welfare state. There is growing recognition that we must place the family at the center of our thinking about social issues and children at the center of our thinking about the family. We need policies that support and compensate families as they carry out their critical social role—providing for the economic and moral well-being of children. As we will see, a large body of evidence supports the conclusion that in the aggregate, the intact two-parent family is best suited to this task. Making this premise our point of departure takes us toward policies that *reinforce* families and away from bureaucratic approaches that seek to *replace* family functions.

To avoid misunderstanding, I want to make it clear that a general preference for the intact two-parent family does not mean that this is the best option in every case. Nor does it mean that all single-parent families are somehow dysfunctional; that proposition would diminish the achievements of millions of single parents who are struggling successfully against the odds to provide good homes for their children. Rather, the point is that at the level of statistical aggregates and society-wide phenomena, significant differences do emerge between one-parent and two-parent families, differences that can and should shape our understanding of social policy.

I DO NOT mean to suggest that the renewed emphasis on the family is solely the product of cultural and ideological change. Equally important is a broad process of social learning—a growing (and increasingly painful) awareness of the consequences of the choices that we already have made, individually and collectively, over the past generation.

The economic facts are distressing. As Hewlett summarizes the data: Among all children eighteen years and under, one in five is poor, nearly twice the poverty rate for the elderly; among children younger than six, the rate is almost one in four; among children in families headed by adults younger than thirty, one in three; among black children, almost one in two. And noneconomic trends are no less stark. In the past quarter-century, the amount of time that parents spend with their children has dropped by 40 percent, from thirty hours a week to just seventeen; and there is no evidence that these remaining shreds of parental availability represent "quality time." On the contrary: As social historian Barbara Whitehead reports, "Increasingly, family schedules are intricate applications of time-motion principles."

These stress-filled lives reflect changes in the economy that have prompted momentous shifts in the labor force in this country. Since 1973, under the pressure of declining productivity and mounting international competition, family incomes have stagnated while the relative costs of a middle-class existence—in particular, of homeownership, health care, and higher education—have soared. Wage prospects have grown increasingly dismal, especially for young people with no more than a high school education. The surge of women into the work force may have begun three decades ago as a cultural revolt against household roles experienced as stifling, but it has been sustained by increasingly urgent economic necessity. Today two-thirds of all mothers with children younger than eighteen do at least some work outside the home, as do more than one-half of all mothers with children under five.

For tens of millions of American families, the second income means the difference between keeping and losing a tenuously maintained middle-class way of life. To be sure, some adjustments at the margin are possible: Young families can live in smaller houses and stop eating at restaurants. Still, the hope of many moral traditionalists that the 1950s family can somehow be restored flies in the face of contemporary market forces. The tension between remunerative work and family time will not be overcome in the foreseeable future—unless increased income from nonmarket sources allows parents with young children to do less work outside the home. Many thoughtful conservatives are coming to the realization that they must choose between their vision of a well-ordered family and their desire for smaller, less costly government.

THESE TENSIONS and others have clearly taken their toll. Test scores are down, and not just the much-discussed SATs. At BellSouth in Atlanta, for example, only about 10 percent of job applicants can pass exams that test basic learning ability, versus 20 percent a decade ago. Theft, violence, and the use of illicit drugs are far more prevalent among teenagers than they were thirty years ago; and the rate of suicide among teenagers has tripled.

It is tempting to dismiss these data as one sided, or to interpret them as mere cyclical variations within longer-term stability. After all, virtually every generation in every culture has complained of a decline of the family. But this is an alibi. We must face the fact that the conditions we take for granted are the product of a social revolution that has rapidly unfolded over just the past three decades. And at the heart of this revolution lie changes in family structure.

In thirty years, the percentage of children born outside of marriage has quintupled, and now stands at 18 percent for whites and 63 percent for blacks. In this same period, the divorce rate has tripled, as has the percentage of children living with only one parent. Of white children born in the early 1950s, 81 percent lived continuously until the age of seventeen with their two biological parents; the projected rate for children born in the early 1980s is 30 percent. The corresponding rate for black children has fallen from 52 percent in the 1950s to only 6 percent today.

These structural shifts are responsible for a substantial portion of child poverty. As David Ellwood has observed, "[t]he vast majority of children who are raised entirely in a two-parent home will never be poor during childhood. By contrast, the vast majority of children who spend time in a single-parent home will experience poverty." As Ellwood showed in *Poor Support,* in any given year, fully 50 percent of children in one-parent families will experience poverty, versus 15 percent for those in two-parent families; 73 percent of children from one-parent families will experience poverty at some point during their childhood, versus 20 percent for children from two-parent families; 22 percent of children from one-parent families will experience persistent poverty (seven years or more), versus only 2 percent from two-parent families.

These data suggest that the best anti-poverty program for children is a stable, intact family. And this conclusion holds even for families headed by younger parents with very modest levels of educational attainment. For married high school graduates with children, the 1987 poverty rate was 9 percent, versus more than 47 percent for families headed by female high school graduates. Even for married high school dropouts with children, the poverty rate was 25 percent, versus more than 81 percent for families headed by female high school dropouts. Overall, Frank Furstenberg Jr. and Andrew Cherlin conclude, the differences in family structure go "a long way toward accounting for the enormous racial disparity in poverty rates. Within family types, black families are still poorer than white families; but the racial gap in poverty shrinks considerably when the marital status of the household head is taken into account."

> *'The vast majority of children who are raised entirely in a two-parent home will never be poor during childhood. By contrast, the vast majority of children who spend time in a single-parent home will experience poverty.'*

TO BE SURE, the causal arrow could point in the opposite direction: differences in family structure might be thought to reflect differences in economic status. Wilson offered an influential statement of this counterthesis in *The Truly Disadvantaged:* Reduced black marriage rates reflect dramatically higher rates of black male unemployment, which reduces the "male marriageable pool"—under the assumption that "to be marriageable a man needs to be employed." But the most recent research offers only modest support for this hypothesis. Robert Mare and Christopher Winship find that changes in employment rates among young black males account for only 20 percent of the decline in their marriage rates since 1960; they speculate that the various family disruptions of the past three decades may be self-reinforcing.[1] Though Wilson continues to defend the validity of his thesis for the hard-hit central cities of the Northeast and Midwest, he is now willing to say that "the decline in marriage among inner-city blacks is not simply a function of the proportion of jobless men . . . it is reasonable to consider the effects of weaker social structures against out-of-wedlock births."

Along with family non-formation, family breakup is a potent source of poverty, especially among children. According to a recently released Census Bureau study by Susan Bianchi, who identified and tracked twenty thousand households, it turns out that after their parents separate or divorce, children are almost twice as likely to be living in poverty as they were before the split. The gross income of the children and their custodial parent (usually the mother) dropped by 37 percent immediately after the family breakup (26 percent after adjustment for the decline in family size) and recovered only slightly after sixteen months. These findings support the arguments of scholars who have long contended that divorce under current law spells economic hardship for most custodial parents and their minor children.

As Furstenberg and Cherlin show in their admirably balanced survey of current research, there are at least three sets of reasons for this outcome: Many women bargain away support payments in return for sole custody of their children or to eliminate the need to deal with their former spouses; when awarded, child support payments are on average pitifully inadequate; and many fathers cough up only a portion (at best) of their required payments. A Census Bureau report from the mid-1980s showed that of mothers with court-ordered support payments, only half received all of what they were owed, a quarter received partial payments, and the remaining quarter got nothing at all.

IF THE economic effects of family breakdown are clear, the psychological effects are just now coming into focus. As Karl Zinsmeister summarizes an emerging consensus, "There is a mountain of scientific evidence showing that when families disintegrate children often end up with intellectual, physical, and emotional scars that persist for life. . . . We talk about the drug crisis, the education crisis, and the problems of teen pregnancy and juvenile crime. But all these ills trace back predominantly to one source: broken families."

As more and more children are reared in one-parent families, it becomes clear that the economic consequences of a parent's absence (usually the father) may pale beside the psychological consequences—which include higher than average levels of youth suicide, low intellectual and educational performance, and higher than average rates of mental illness, violence, and drug use.

Nowhere is this more evident than in the longstanding and strong relationship between crime and one-parent families. In a recent study, Douglas Smith and G. Roger Jarjoura found that "neighborhoods with larger percentages of youth (those aged 12 to 20) and areas with higher percentages of single-parent households also have higher rates of violent crime."[2] The relationship is so strong that controlling for family configuration erases the relationship between race and crime and between low income and crime. This conclusion shows up time and time again in the literature; poverty is far from the sole determinant of crime.

While the scarcity of intact families in the ghetto is largely a function of the failure of families to form in the first place, in the larger society the central problem is family disintegration, caused primarily by divorce. This pervasive phenomenon has effects that are independent of economics. It is to these studies that we now turn.

In 1981, John Guidubaldi, then president of the National Association of School Psychologists, picked a team of 144 psychologists in thirty-eight states, who gathered long-term data on seven hundred children, half from intact families, the other half children of divorce. Preliminary results published in 1986 showed that the effects of divorce on children persisted over time and that the psychological consequences were significant even after correcting for income differences.[3]

The problems engendered by divorce extend well beyond vanishing role models. Children need authoritative rules and stable schedules, which harried single parents often have a hard time supplying. As Guidubaldi puts it, "One of the things we found is that children who had regular bedtimes, less TV, hobbies and after-school activities—children who are in households that are orderly and predictable—do better than children who [did] not. I don't think we can escape the conclusion that children need structure, and oftentimes the divorce household is a chaotic scene."

The results of the Guidubaldi study have been confirmed and deepened by Judith Wallerstein's ten-year study of sixty middle-class divorced families. Among her key findings:

• Divorce is almost always more devastating for children than for their parents.

• The effects of divorce are often long lasting. Children are especially affected because divorce occurs during their formative years. What they see and experience becomes a part of their inner world, their view of themselves, and their view of society.

• Almost half the children entered adulthood as worried, underachieving, self-deprecating, and sometimes angry young men and women.

• Adolescence is a period of grave risk for children in divorced families; those who entered adolescence in the immediate wake of their parents' divorces had a particularly bad time. The young people told us time and again how much they needed a family structure, how much they wanted to be protected, and how much they yearned for clear guidelines for moral behavior.[4]

Furstenberg and Cherlin offer a nuanced, but ultimately troubling, account of the noneconomic consequences of divorce. For most children, it comes as an "unwelcome shock," even when the parents are openly quarreling. In the short-term, boys seem to have a harder time coping than girls, in part because of an "escalating cycle of misbehavior and harsh response between mothers and sons." Girls more typically respond with internalized disruption rather than external behavior—with heightened levels of anxiety, withdrawal, and depression that may become apparent only years later. These differences reflect the fact that divorce almost always means disrupted relations with the father. It is difficult to overstate the extent of the disruption that typically occurs. Even in the period relatively soon after divorce, only one-sixth of all children will see their fathers as often as once a week, and close to one-half will not see them at all. After ten years, almost two-thirds will have no contact.

These findings are less than self-interpreting, Furstenberg and Cherlin point out, because they must be compared with the effects on children of intact but troubled families. On the one hand, various studies indicate that the children of divorce do no worse than children in families in which parents fight continuously. On the other hand, a relatively small percentage of divorces result from, and terminate, such clearly pathological situations. There are many more cases in which there is little open conflict, but one or both partners feels unfulfilled, bored, or constrained. Indeed, the onset of divorce in these families can intensify conflict, particularly as experienced by children. As Nicholas Zill observes, "Divorces tend to generate their own problems."

Given the profound psychological effects of divorce, it is hardly surprising to discover what teachers and administrators have known for some time: One of the major reasons for America's declining educational achievement is the disintegrating American family. And if we continue to neglect the crisis of the American family, we will have undercut current efforts at educational reform.

Untangling just what it is about family structure that makes for high or low educational achievement is a dif-

ficult task. Clearly the economics of the family have a great deal to do with achievement; children from poor families consistently do less well than do children from non-poor or well-to-do families. Nevertheless, income is clearly not the whole story. When studies control for income, significant differences in educational achievement appear between children from single-parent families and children from intact families.

For example, a study conducted under the auspices of the National Association of Elementary School Principals and the Institute for Development of Educational Activities shows that family background has an important effect on educational achievement above and beyond income level—especially for boys. Lower-income girls with two parents, for instance, score higher on achievement tests than do higher-income boys with one parent. At the very bottom of the achievement scale are lower-income boys with one parent.[5]

WHAT SHOULD be our response to these developments? The recent literature suggests three broad possibilities. First, we may applaud, with Judith Stacey, the demise of the traditional (rigid, patriarchal) family and the rise of "postmodern" (flexible, variegated, female-centered) arrangements, which are allegedly far more consistent with egalitarian democracy. Second, we may accept Jan Dizard and Howard Gadlin's suggestion that moral change (in the direction of autonomy) and economic change (in the direction of a two-earner, postindustrial economy) have rendered obsolete the older model of the private family; in its place, they advocate a dramatically expanded public sphere on the Swedish model that assumes many of the private family's functions. And third, there is the response, neither postmodern nor socialist, that might be called neotraditional.

It goes something like this. A primary purpose of the family is to raise children well, and for this purpose stably married parents are best. Sharply rising rates of divorce, unwed mothers, and runaway fathers do not represent "alternative lifestyles." They are, instead, most truly characterized as patterns of adult behavior with profoundly negative consequences for children. Families have primary responsibility for instilling traits such as discipline, ambition, respect for the law, and regard for others; and it is a responsibility that cannot be discharged as effectively by auxiliary social institutions such as public schools. This responsibility entails a sphere of legitimate parental authority that should be bolstered—not undermined—by society. It requires personal sacrifice and the delay of certain forms of gratification on the part of parents. It means that government should devote substantial resources to stabilizing families and to enhancing their child-rearing capacity. But at the same time it must minimize bureaucratic cost, complexity, and intrusiveness, working instead to broaden family choice, opportunity, and responsibility.

The willingness to join the languages of economics and morals, and to consider new approaches to old goals, is increasingly characteristic of public discussion of the family. As Barbara Whitehead notes, this approach suffuses the recent report of the National Commission on Children. The volume edited by David Blankenhorn, Steven Bayme, and Jean Bethke Elshtain is particularly strong along the moral dimension. To be sure, it is easy for this stance to give the appearance of ineffectual exhortation. The editors of *The New York Times* assert that the commission's final report "swims in platitudes." Still, there are eminently practical ways of embedding moral concerns in policies and institutions. Richard Louv argues for moral change focused on the community as much as the individual. He urges us to reweave the tattered "web" of social relationships—parent-school ties, neighborhoods, communal child care arrangements, and the like—that provide a supportive environment for families and help nurture children. Although Louv emphasizes the importance of civil society, he does not imagine that the web can be adequately repaired without major changes in public policy.

Here Louv joins an emerging consensus that differs over details but not over essentials. The point is not to be driven to make a false choice between moral and economic concerns, but rather to combine them in a relation of mutual support. It might well be argued, for example, that the government has a responsibility not to tax away the money that families need to raise children. Four decades ago, the United States had a disguised family allowance: In 1948 the personal exemption was $600 (42 percent of per-capita personal income), while today's personal exemption is only 11 percent of per-capita income. This meant that a married couple at the median income with two minor dependents paid only 0.3 percent of their 1948 income in federal income taxes, compared to today's 9.1 percent. The 1948 couple's total tax bill (federal, state, and Social Security) was 2 percent of personal income. Today that total comes to about 30 percent.

Thus, one proposal now gaining support is to raise the personal exemption from the current $2,050 to at least $4,000, and perhaps eventually to $7,500. To make this more affordable, the bulk of the increase could be targeted to young children, and the increase could be phased out for upper-income taxpayers. Another approach, endorsed by the National Commission on Children, would create a $1,000 tax credit for each child; low-income families that owe no taxes would receive a cash payment for the amount of the credit. (To avoid potentially perverse incentives, this proposal should be coupled with a broader program of welfare reform.)

Reducing the tension between work and family will take changes in the private as well as the public sector. Hewlett, Louv, and many others argue for a "family-oriented workplace" with far more adaptable schedules: more flexible hours, greater opportunities for working at home and communicating by computer, for part-time employment, and for job sharing. Resistance to these changes reflects primarily the ignorance or the obduracy of middle-aged male managers, not negative impact on corporate balance sheets. Much the same is true of unpaid leave for parents following the birth of a child. Studies at the state level indicate that the costs and disruptive effects of such leaves, even when legally mandatory, are minimal. President Bush's opposition to federal

family leave legislation is increasingly indefensible.

Adequate reward for labor force participation represents another important link between morals and public policy. If we believe that the presence of a parent who works outside the home furnishes a crucial moral example for his or her children, then surely the community has a responsibility to ensure that full-time work by a parent provides a nonpoverty family income. As Robert Shapiro of the Progressive Policy Institute has argued, the most efficient way to accomplish this goal would be to expand the Earned Income Tax Credit and tie it to family size.

This emphasis on the use of the tax code to promote family opportunity and responsibility is characteristic of a political outlook that has been called "neoprogressive." This is not to suggest that traditional liberal approaches are in every case misguided. Some of them—prenatal care, WIC (the nutrition program for poor women, infants, and children), childhood immunization, and Head Start—efficiently promote the well-being of children and families, and the political consensus supporting their expansion now stretches from KidsPac (a liberal, children-oriented political action committee) and the Children's Defense Fund to the Bush administration and the corporate-based Committee for Economic Development. And yet the neoprogressives are more willing than the traditional liberals to re-examine the programs of the past and to distinguish between what works and what doesn't.

IF THE PRIVATE and public sectors must assume greater responsibility for the well-being of families with children, so must parents. In particular, the moral obligation to help support one's biological children persists regardless of one's legal relationship to them, and the law is fully justified in enforcing this obligation. The 1988 Family Support Act requires states to collect the Social Security numbers of both parents (married or unmarried) at birth, to increase efforts to establish contested paternity, to use (as at least rebuttable presumptions) their guidelines concerning appropriate levels of child support, and to move toward collecting all new support awards through automatic payroll deductions.

These are steps in the right direction, but they don't go far enough. Mary Ann Glendon has argued powerfully that a "children first" principle should govern our spousal support and marital property law:

> The judges' main task would be to piece together, from property and income and inkind personal care, the best possible package to meet the needs of children and their physical guardian. Until the welfare of the children had been adequately secured in this way, there would be no question of, or debate about, "marital property." All assets, no matter when or how acquired, would be subject to the duty to provide for the children.[6]

Moreover, the state-level reforms mentioned above do nothing to address what is in many cases the chief impediment to support collection: fathers moving from state to state to slow or avoid apprehension. Conflicting state laws and a morass of administrative complexity discourage mothers from pursuing their claims across jurisdictions. Ellwood and others have called for the federalization of the system, with payroll deductions remitted to, and support payments drawn from, a centralized national fund. The U.S. Commission on Interstate Child Support, created by Congress to develop a blueprint for reform, is considering this idea.

Even when child support is collected regularly from absent parents who can afford to provide it, payments are typically set too low to avoid tremendous disruption in the lives of custodial mothers and their children. Writing from very different perspectives, Lenore Weitzman, Martha Albertson Fineman, and Furstenberg and Cherlin converge on the conclusion that the laws and the practices of many states leave men in a far more favorable situation after divorce. Furstenberg and Cherlin cite approvingly a proposal to require noncustodial fathers to pay a fixed proportion of their income, 17 percent to 34 percent, depending on the number of minor children; the adoption of this standard nationwide would raise total child support due by roughly two-thirds. Fineman advocates a need-based approach that would (she argues) yield better results for women and children than would ostensibly egalitarian standards.

During the past generation, the presumption in favor of awarding mothers custody of their children has been replaced in many cases by the presumption of equal claims. This development has generated a rising number of joint custody arrangements that do not, on average, work out very well. It has also worsened the post-divorce economic status of custodial mothers and their children: Because women tend to view custody as a paramount issue, they often compromise on economic matters to avoid the custody battle made possible by the new, supposedly more egalitarian, legal framework. And here, too, scholars from various points on the ideological spectrum are converging on the conclusion that the traditional arrangement had much to recommend it. They propose a "primary caretaker" standard: judges should be instructed to award custody of young children to the parent who has (in the words of a leading advocate) "performed a substantial majority of the [direct] caregiving tasks for the child."

THESE AND similar proposals will help custodial mothers and their children pick up the pieces after divorce, but they will do little to reduce the incidence of divorce. For Furstenberg and Cherlin, this is all that can be done: "We are inclined to accept the irreversibility of high levels of divorce as our starting point for thinking about changes in public policy." Hewlett is more disposed to grasp the nettle. While rejecting a return to the fault-based system of the past, she believes that the current system makes divorce too easy and too automatic.

Government should send a clearer moral signal that families with children are worth preserving. In this spirit, she suggests that parents of minor children seeking divorce undergo an eighteen-month waiting period, during which they would be obliged to seek counseling and to reach a binding agreement that truly safeguards their children's future.

The generation that installed the extremes of self-expression and self-indulgence at the heart of American culture must now learn some hard old lessons about commitment, self-sacrifice, the deferral of gratification, and simple endurance. It will not be easy. But other sorts of gratifications may be their reward. Perhaps the old morality was not wrong to suggest that a deeper kind of satisfaction awaits those who accept and fulfill their essential human responsibilities.

REFERENCES

[1] Mare, Robert D. and Winship, Christopher, "Socio-economic Change and the Decline of Marriage for Blacks and Whites." In *The Urban Underclass,* edited by Christopher Jencks and Paul Peterson. Washington, D.C.: The Brookings Institute, 1991.

[2] Smith, Douglas A., Jarjoura, G. Roger, "Social Structure and Criminal Victimization." In *Journal of Research in Crime and Delinquency,* Vol. 25, No. 1, February 1988.

[3] Guidubaldi, J., Cleminshaw, H.K., Perry, J.D., Nastasi, B.K., and Lightel, J., "The Role of Selected Family Environment Factors in Children's Post-Divorce Adjustment." In *Family Relations,* Vol. 35, 1986.

[4] Wallerstein, Judith S., and Blakeslee, Sandra, *Second Chances: Men, Women, and Children a Decade after Divorce.* New York: Ticknor and Fields, 1989.

[5] Sally Banks Zakariya, "Another Look at the Children of Divorce," *Principal Magazine,* September 1982, p. 35. See also, R.B. Zajonc, "Family Configuration and Intelligence," *Science,* Vol. 192, April 16, 1976, pp. 227-236. In a later and more methodologically sophisticated study, the authors try to define more completely what it is about two-parent families that make them better at preparing students for educational success. Income clearly stands out as the most important variable; but the close relationship between one-parent status, lower income, and lack of time for things like homework help and attendance at parent teacher conferences—to name a few of the variables considered—led the authors to say that "the negative effects of living in a one-parent family work primarily through other variables in our model." Ann M. Milne, David E. Myers, Alvin S. Rosenthal, and Alan Ginsburg, "Single Parents, Working Mothers, and the Educational Achievement of School Children," *Sociology of Education,* 1986, Vol. 59 (July), p. 132.

[6] Glendon, Mary Ann, *Abortion and Divorce in Western Law.* Cambridge, MA: Harvard University Press, 1987 (pp. 93-95).

Same Family, Different Lives

Family experiences may make siblings different, not similar

BRUCE BOWER

Psychologists uncovered a curious feature of military morale during World War II. Those in branches of the service handing out the most promotions complained the most about their rank. The investigators cited "relative deprivation" as an explanation for the trend — it's not what you have, but what you have compared with others in the same situation.

Relative deprivation achieves a more profound influence through the daily battles and negotiations that constitute life in the nuclear family, maintain researchers in human behavioral genetics. Each child in a family harbors an exquisite sensitivity to his or her standing with parents, brothers and sisters, and thus essentially grows up in a unique psychological environment, according to these investigators. The result: Two children in the same family grow to differ from one another in attitudes, intelligence and personality as much as two youngsters randomly plucked from the population at large.

While one-of-a-kind experiences and perceptions of family life combine with each child's genetic heritage to create pervasive sibling differences, shared genes — which account for half the genes possessed by all siblings save for identical twins — foster whatever similarities they display, argue scientists who apply behavioral genetics to child development.

The emphasis on children's diverse experiences cultivating sibling differences seems ironic coming from scientists dedicated to estimating the genetic contribution to individual development. Yet behavioral genetic data provide a compelling antidote to the increasingly influential notion among psychiatrists that defective genes and broken brains primarily cause mental disorders, asserts psychologist Robert Plomin of Pennsylvania State University in University Park, a leading researcher in human behavioral genetics. Ongoing studies also challenge the assumption of many developmental psychologists that important family features, such as parental education, child-rearing styles and the quality of the marital relationship, affect all siblings similarly, Plomin adds.

"What runs in families is DNA, not shared experiences," Plomin contends. "Significant environmental effects are specific to each child rather than common to the entire family."

In a further challenge to child development researchers, Plomin and psychologist Cindy S. Bergeman of the University of Notre Dame (Ind.) contend that genetic influences substantially affect common environment measures, such as self-reports or experimenter observations of family warmth and maternal affection. "Labeling a measure environmental does not make it environmental," they conclude in the September BEHAVIORAL AND BRAIN SCIENCES. "We need measures ... that can capture the individual's active selection, modification and creation of environments."

Not surprisingly, the trumpeting of "non-shared" sibling environments and the questioning of traditional measures of the family milieu have drawn heated rebukes from some psychologists. In particular, critics claim that behavioral genetics studies rely on statistical techniques that inappropriately divvy up separate genetic and environmental effects on individual traits, rather than examining more important interactions between genes and environment.

Human behavioral genetics use family, adoption and twins studies to estimate the importance of genes and environment to individual development. Family studies assess the similarity among genetically related family members on measures of intelligence, extroversion, verbal ability, mental disturbances and other psychological traits. Adoption studies obtain psychological measures from genetically related individuals adopted by different families, their biological parents, and their adoptive parents and siblings. Researchers assume that similar scores between adoptees and biological parents reflect a greater genetic contribution, while adoptees showing similarity to adoptive parents and their children illuminate environmental effects. Twin studies compare the resemblance of identical twins on various measures to the resemblance of fraternal twins on the same measures. If heredity shapes a particular trait, identical twins display more similarity for it than fraternal twins, behavioral geneticists maintain.

Psychologist John C. Loehlin of the University of Texas at Austin directed a twin study published in 1976 that greatly influenced human behavioral genetics. Averaging across a broad range of personality measures obtained from 514 identical and 336 fraternal pairs of twins culled from a national sample of high school seniors, Loehlin's group found a correlation of 0.50 for identical twins and 0.28 for fraternal twins.

Correlations numerically express associations between two or more variables. The closer to 1.0 a correlation figure reaches, the more one variable resembles another — say, one twin's IQ and the corresponding twin's IQ. A correlation of zero between twin IQs would signify a complete lack of resemblance, with twin pairs as different in intelligence scores as randomly selected pairs of youngsters.

The Texas researchers doubled the difference between identical and fraternal twin correlations to obtain a "heritability estimate" of 0.44, or 44 percent, an estimate of how much genes contribute to individual differences. This means that genes accounted for just under half of the individual personality differences observed in the sample of twins. Thus, environment accounted for slightly more than half of the twin's personality variations.

A further finding intrigued the scientists. The correlation on personality measures for identical twins only reached 0.50, suggesting the environment orchestrated one-half of their personality differences. Since these twins carried matching sets of genes and grew up in the same families, only "non-shared" family experiences could account for such differences, Loehlin's group argued.

Subsequent twin and adoption studies carried out in Colorado, Minnesota, Sweden and England confirmed the importance of the non-shared environment for most aspects of personality, as well as intelligence and mental disorders such as schizophrenia, Plomin asserts. He and psychologist Denise Daniels of Stanford University reviewed much of this data in the March 1987 BEHAVIORAL AND BRAIN SCIENCES, followed by a book on the subject written with Penn State psychologist Judy Dunn titled *Separate Lives: Why Siblings Are So Different* (1990, Basic Books).

All the correlations and heritability estimates boil down to a simple point, Plomin maintains: Allegedly shared family influences, such as parent's emotional warmth or disciplinary practices, get filtered through each child's unique perceptions and produce siblings with strikingly diverse personalities. For example, a shy 9-year-old who gets picked on by schoolmates will react differently to an emotional, permissive mother than a gregarious 7-year-old sibling who attracts friends easily.

Many factors divide sibling's perceptions of family life, Plomin says, including age spacing, peer and school experiences, accidents, illnesses, random events and — to a lesser extent — birth order and sex differences.

Each sibling's temperament and behavior also generate specific perceptions and responses from parents that further shape non-shared environments, he argues.

As researchers in molecular genetics vigilantly pursue genes that predispose people to a variety of mental disorders, psychiatrists should not neglect the importance of the environment specific to each child in a family, contends Plomin and two colleagues — psychiatrist David Reiss of George Washington University in Washington, D.C., and psychologist E. Mavis Hetherington of the University of Virginia in Charlottesville — in the March AMERICAN JOURNAL OF PSYCHIATRY.

The three researchers bluntly warn psychiatrists enamored of the new genetic techniques that biology alone cannot explain the development of serious mental disorders. For example, a large, ongoing study in Sweden — conducted by Plomin and several other researchers — has found that when one identical twin develops schizophrenia, the other twin contracts the disorder about one-third of the time. Heredity shoulders considerable responsibility for fomenting schizophrenia, Plomin acknowledges, but an individual's experience of family life, peers and chance events plays at least as strong a role in triggering the devastating fragmentation of thought and emotion that characterizes the disorder.

Research directed by George Washington's Reiss, and described in his article with Plomin and Hetherington, suggests non-shared experiences protect some siblings, but not others, from alcoholism when one or both parents drink alcohol uncontrollably. Family members often shield the protected child from alcoholic behavior during that child's most cherished family practices, such as Christmas celebrations, Reiss' team finds. In this way, the protected sibling gradually learns to minimize brushes with the corrosive effects of alcoholism within and outside the family, the investigators observe. Upon reaching adolescence and adulthood, the protected sibling maintains limited family contacts to avoid the influence of an alcoholic parent and often marries a non-alcoholic person.

Given the importance of non-shared environments, developmental researchers need to study more than one child per family and devise better measures of children's perceptions of family experiences, Plomin contends. He and Bergeman find that several self-report tests currently used to assess the home environment largely ignore unique individual experiences within the family and rely on measures that show substantial genetic influence. In one case they cite,

unpublished data from a study of 179 reared-apart twin pairs (both identical and fraternal) and 207 reared-together twin pairs indicate that genes account for one-quarter of the individual differences plumbed by the widely used Family Environment Scales, which is generally regarded to measure environmental influences. These scales include ratings of emotional warmth, conflict, cohesion and cultural pursuits within the family.

Even the time children spend watching television — a seemingly vacuum-sealed environmental measure employed in many studies — significantly stems from genetically influenced characteristics, Plomin and his colleagues argue in the November 1990 PSYCHOLOGICAL SCIENCE. Parental restrictions do not exert strong effects on children's television viewing, since about 70 percent of parents put no limits on how much time their offspring can spend watching the tube, they state.

Plomin's team tested 220 adopted children three times, at 3, 4 and 5 years of age, as well as their biological and adoptive parents, younger adopted and non-adopted siblings, and control families with no adopted children. Biological parents and their children adopted by others spent a surprisingly similar amount of time watching television, indicating an important genetic influence on the behavior, Plomin's team asserted. Shared home environment, such as the television viewing habits of parents, also influenced children's television time, but to a lesser extent.

The results do not imply that some people follow a genetic imperative to sit glassy-eyed in front of the television for hours, day after day. "We can turn the television on or off as we please, but turning it off or leaving it on pleases individuals differently, in part due to genetic factors," the investigators conclude.

Some scientists who have long labored to understand family influences on psychological development take no pleasure in the conclusions of behavioral genetics researchers. Psychologist Lois W. Hoffman of the University of Michigan in Ann Arbor offers a critique of research highlighting sibling differences in the September PSYCHOLOGICAL BULLETIN.

Behavioral genetics tends to overestimate sibling differences because it concentrates on self-reports of personality traits, rather than on observations of coping skills and social behavior typically relied upon by developmental psychologists, Hoffman holds. A child may exaggerate differences from siblings on self-reports, whereas behavioral observations by experimenters may turn up sibling similarities in aggression or other attributes, she maintains.

Even in behavioral genetics research, significant sibling similarities apparently due to shared family environment turn up in political and religious beliefs and in general interests such as music, Hoffman adds.

Some family environments may more easily produce similarities among siblings than others, she argues. When both parents share the same values, attitudes and child-rearing styles, the chances increase that their pattern of behavior will rub off on all their children, in Hoffman's opinion.

Behavioral genetics researchers also incorrectly assume that only strong correlations between the personalities of adoptive parents and their adopted children reflect an environmental influence, the Michigan psychologist contends. Parental influences can weaken parent-child correlations on all sorts of personality measures, she points out. For instance, domineering, powerful parents may produce an anxious child, and an extremely self-assured, professionally successful parent may make a child feel inadequate.

Behavioral genetics comes under additional fire for its reliance on statistics that treat genetic and environmental influences on personality separately. This approach simply lacks the statistical power to pick up the interactions between genes and environment that primarily direct physical and psychological development, rendering current research in human behavioral genetics meaningless, argues Canadian psychologist Douglas Wahlsten of the University of Alberta in Edmonton. Much larger samples might begin to pick up such interactions, he adds.

Behavioral geneticists rely on statistics derived from a technique known as analysis of variance (ANOVA). This method is used throughout psychology to calculate whether a significant relationship, or correlation, exists between experimental variables by comparing variations in individual scores from a group's average value. Statisticians developed ANOVA in the 1920s as a way to estimate whether different types and amounts of fertilizer substantially increased the yield of various agricultural crops.

When applied to human personality and behavior, an ANOVA-based approach treats heredity and environment as mutually exclusive influences on personality, Wahlsten argues. Psychologists possess no conclusive test of interactions between genes and environments. But evidence of their interplay — as in the widely accepted theory that specific genes combine with particular family experiences to produce a psychotic disorder — may begin to emerge in behavioral genetics studies employing samples of 600 or more individuals, Wahlsten maintains. Mathematical formulas used in conjunction with ANOVA stand a better chance of ferreting out gene-environment interactions in extremely large samples, Wahlsten concludes in the March 1990 BEHAVIORAL AND BRAIN SCIENCES.

Psychologist Daniel Bullock of Boston University takes a bleaker view of ANOVA, citing its neglect of the intertwined forces guiding personality development. "The special status of ANOVA in psychology is an utter anachronism," he contends. "Many past claims by behavioral geneticists are unreliable."

Plomin rejects such charges. "To say that genetic and environmental effects interact and therefore cannot be disentangled is wrong," he states.

Twin and adoption studies consistently find strong separate effects of genes and non-shared environments on personality and other developmental measures, even when researchers painstakingly seek out possible interactions of nature and nurture, Plomin points out. Investigators may devise more sensitive statistical tests to illuminate cooperative ventures between genes and family experiences, but that will not invalidate the insights of behavioral genetics, he maintains.

That includes the discovery that what parents do similarly to two children does not importantly influence personality or problem behavior in the long run; rather, each child's perceptions of what goes on in the family prove critical. Appreciating the differences of offspring based on their individual qualities, with minimal preferential treatment of one child over another, seems a good general rule for concerned parents, Plomin says. Parents should recognize that siblings as well as "only children" harbor a keen sensitivity to their standing within the family, he adds.

"If we are reasonable, loving, but not perfect parents, the children will grow up to be themselves — all different but okay," says psychologist Sandra Scarr of the University of Virginia, a behavioral genetics researcher. "Children experience us as different parents, depending on their own characteristics, and we simply cannot make them alike or easily spoil their chances to be normal adults."

CAN YOUR CAREER HURT YOUR KIDS?

Mommy often gets home from work too tired to talk. Daddy's almost never around. Says one expert: "We can only guess at the damage being done to the very young."

Kenneth Labich

BECAUSE CHILDREN are the future, America could be headed for bad bumps down the road. Some of the symptoms are familiar—rising teenage suicides and juvenile arrest rates, average SAT scores lower than 30 years ago. But what is the disease festering beneath that disturbing surface? Says Alice A. White, a clinical social worker who has been counseling troubled children in Chicago's prosperous North Shore suburbs for nearly two decades: "I'm seeing a lot more emptiness, a lack of ability to attach, no sense of real pleasure. I'm not sure a lot of these kids are going to be effective adults."

Not all children, or even most of them, are suffering from such a crisis of the spirit. In fact, some trends are headed in a promising direction. For example, drug use among young people has fallen sharply since the 1970s. But a certain malaise does seem to be spreading. Far more and far earlier than ever before, kids are pressured to take drugs, have sex, deal with violence. In a world ever more competitive and complex, the path to social and economic success was never more obscure.

And fewer traditional pathfinders are there to show the way. Divorce has robbed millions of kids of at least one full-time parent. With more and more women joining the work force, and many workaholic parents of both sexes, children are increasingly left in the care of others or allowed to fend for themselves. According to a University of Maryland study, in 1985 American parents spent on average just 17 hours a week with their children.

This parental neglect would be less damaging if better alternatives were widely available, but that is decidedly not the case. Families that can afford individual child care often get good value, but the luxury of

a compassionate, full-time, \$250-a-week nanny to watch over their pride and joy is beyond the reach of most American parents. They confront a patchwork system of informal home arrangements and more structured day care centers. In far too many cases, parents with infants or toddlers cannot feel secure about the care their children get. Says Edward Zigler, a professor of child development at Yale, who has spent much of his career fighting the abuses of child care: "We are cannibalizing children. Children are dying in this system, never mind achieving optimum development."

For older children with no parental overseer, the prospects can be equally bleak. Studies are beginning to show that preteens and teenagers left alone after school, so-called latchkey children, may be far more prone than other kids to get involved with alcohol and illegal drugs.

For some experts in the field, the answer to all this is to roll back the clock to an idyllic past. Mom, dressed in a frilly apron, is merrily stirring the stew when Dad gets home from work. Junior, an Eagle Scout, and Sally—they call her Muffin—greet him with radiant smiles. Everybody sits down for dinner to talk about schoolwork and Mom's canasta party.

For others more in touch with the economic temper of the times—especially the financial realities behind the rising number of working mothers—the solution lies in improving the choices available to parents. Government initiatives to provide some financial relief may help, but corporations could make an even greater difference by focusing on the needs of employees who happen to be parents. Such big companies as IBM and Johnson & Johnson have taken the lead in dealing with employee child care problems, and many progressive corporations are discovering the benefits of greater

flexibility with regard to family issues. At the same time, an array of professional child care organizations has sprung up to help big corporations meet their employees' demands.

Without doubt, helping improve child care is in the best interest of business—today's children, after all, are tomorrow's labor pool. Says Sandra Kessler Hamburg, director of education studies at the Committee for Economic Development, a New York research group that funnels corporate funds into education projects: "We can only guess at the damage being done to very young children right now. From the perspective of American business, that is very, very disturbing. As jobs get more and more technical, the U.S. work force is less and less prepared to handle them."

The state of America's children is a political mine field, and threading through the research entails a lot of gingerly probing as well as the occasional explosion. Much work in the field is contradictory, and many additional longer-range studies need to be done before anyone can say precisely what is happening.

Moreover, any researcher who dwells on the problems of child care—of infants in particular—risks being labeled antiprogressive by the liberal academic establishment. If the researcher happens to be male, his motives may seem suspect. If he says babies are at risk in some child care settings, he may be accused of harboring the wish that women leave the work force and return to the kitchen. Much valid research may be totally ignored because it has been deemed politically incorrect.

For example: Jay Belsky, a Penn State professor specializing in child development, set off a firestorm in 1986 with an article in *Zero to Three*, an influential journal that summarizes existing academic re-

REPORTER ASSOCIATE *Jung Ah Pak*

search. His conclusions point to possible risks for very small children in day care outside the home. Though he scrupulously threw in a slew of caveats and even went so far as to confess a possible bias because his own wife stayed home with their two children, Belsky came under heavy attack. Feminist researchers called his scholarship into question. Says Belsky: "I was flabbergasted by the response. I felt like the messenger who got shot."

Belsky's critics charged, among other things, that he had ignored studies that document some more positive results from infant day care. Since then, for example, a study conducted by researchers at the University of Illinois and Trinity College in Hartford, Connecticut, found that a child's intellectual development may actually be helped during the second and third years of life if the mother works. The study, which tracked a nationwide sample of 874 children from ages 3 to 4, determined that the mental skills of infants in child care outside the home were lower than those of kids watched over by their mothers during the first year, but then picked up enough at ages 2 and 3 to balance out.

Whatever the merits of his critics' assault, Belsky presents a disturbing picture of the effects on infants of nonparental child care outside the home. In a 1980 study he cited in the article, involving low-income women in the Minneapolis-St. Paul area, infants in day care were disproportionately likely to avoid looking at or approaching their mothers after being separated from them for a brief period.

ANOTHER STUDY, conducted in 1974, concluded that 1-year-olds in day care cried more when separated from their mothers than those reared at home; still another, in 1981, found that day care infants threw more temper tantrums. To at least some extent, the observations seem to apply across socioeconomic boundaries. A 1985 University of Illinois study of infants from affluent Chicago families showed that babies in the care of full-time nannies avoided any sort of contact with their mothers more often than those raised by moms during their first year.

An infant's attachment, or lack of it, to the mother is especially crucial because it can portend later developmental problems. In the Minnesota study, toddlers who had been in day care early on displayed less enthusiasm when confronted with a challenging task. They were less likely to follow their mothers' instructions and less persistent in dealing with a difficult problem. Another study, which took a look at virtually all 2-year-olds on the island of Bermuda, found more poorly adjusted children among the early day care group regardless of race, IQ, or socioeconomic status.

Researchers in Connecticut investigating 8- to 10-year-old children in 1981 found higher levels of misbehavior and greater withdrawal from the company of others among those who had been in day care as infants, no matter what the educational level of their parents. In a study of kindergarten and first-grade children in North Carolina, the early day care kids were found more likely than others to hit, kick, push, threaten, curse, and argue with their peers.

What we should take away from the research, says an unrepentant Belsky, is this: "There is an accumulating body of evidence that children who were cared for by people other than their parents for 20 or more hours per week during their first year are at increased risk of having an insecure relationship with their parents at age 1—and at increased risk of being more aggressive and disobedient by age 3 to 8."

Belsky adds several "absolutely necessary caveats": First, the results of all these studies must be viewed in light of the added stress that many families experience when both parents work and of the fact that affordable high-quality day care is not always available. Belsky agrees with some of his academic opponents that the quality of day care matters. His second warning: The results of these studies are generalizations and do not apply to every single child. Third, he says, nobody really knows what causes underlie the findings.

Research on older children who spend at least part of the day on their own is far less controversial, though no less disturbing. A recent study by the American Academy of Pediatrics focused on substance abuse by nearly 5,000 eighth-graders around Los Angeles and San Diego. The sample cut across a wide range of ethnic and economic backgrounds and was split about half and half between boys and girls. The researchers concluded that 12- and 13-year-olds who were latchkey kids, taking care of themselves for 11 or more hours a week, were about twice as likely as supervised children to smoke, drink alcohol, and use marijuana. About 31% of the latchkey kids have two or more drinks at a time; only about 17% of the others do. Asked whether they expected to get drunk in the future, 27% of the latchkey kids and 15% of the others said yes.

Increasingly, isolation from parents is a problem even when the family is physically together. Beginning in infancy, children are highly attuned to their parents' moods. And when parents have little left to give to their offspring at the end of a stressful day, the kids' disappointment can be crushing. Says Eleanor Szanton, executive director of the National Center for Clinical Infant Programs, a nonprofit resource center in Virginia: "What happens between parents and children during the first hour they are reunited is as important as anything that happens all day. If the mother is too exhausted to be a mother, you've got a problem."

When children become adolescents and begin to test their wings by defying their parents' authority, stressed-out families may break down completely because no strong relationship between parents and children has developed over the years. In high-achiever families, says Chicago social worker Alice White, family life can become an ordeal where children must prove their worth to their parents in the limited time available. Conversation can be a series of "didjas"—Didja ace that test, win the election, score the touchdown? What's missing is the easygoing chatter, the long, relaxed conversations that allow parents and children to know each other.

White says that many of today's kids don't understand how the world works because they haven't spent enough time with their parents to understand how decisions are made, careers are pursued, personal relationships are formed. She finds herself spending more and more time acting as a surrogate mother for the seemingly privileged kids she counsels, advising them on everything from sexual issues to recipes for a small dinner party. Says White: "The parents serve as a model of success, but the kids are afraid they won't get there because nobody has shown them how."

JUST ABOUT EVERYONE in the child-development field agrees that all this adds up to a discouraging picture, but opinions vary wildly as to what ought to be done about it—and by whom. For a growing band of conservative social thinkers, the answer is simple: Mothers ought to stay home. These activists, working at private foundations and conservative college faculties, rail against what they see as the permissiveness of recent decades. They save their most lethal venom for organized child care, blaming it for everything from restraining kids' free will to contributing to major outbreaks of untold diseases. One conservative researcher, Bryce Christensen of the Rockford Institute in Illinois, has likened day care to the drug Thalidomide. Day care, he writes, is "a new threat to children that not only imperils the body, but also distorts and withers the spirit."

Gary L. Bauer, president of a conservative Washington research outfit called the Family Research Council, is among the most visible of these social activists. Bauer, a domestic-policy adviser in the Reagan White House, believes strongly that the entry of great numbers of women into the work force has harmed America's children. He says the importance of bonding between a mother and her children became clear to him and his wife one morning several years ago when they were dropping their 2-year-old daughter at a babysitter's home. The child went immediately to the sitter, calling her "Mommy." That was something of an epiphany for Bauer's wife, Carol: She quit her job as a government employment counselor soon after and has since stayed home to raise the couple's three children.

Still, the dual-career trend continues. No

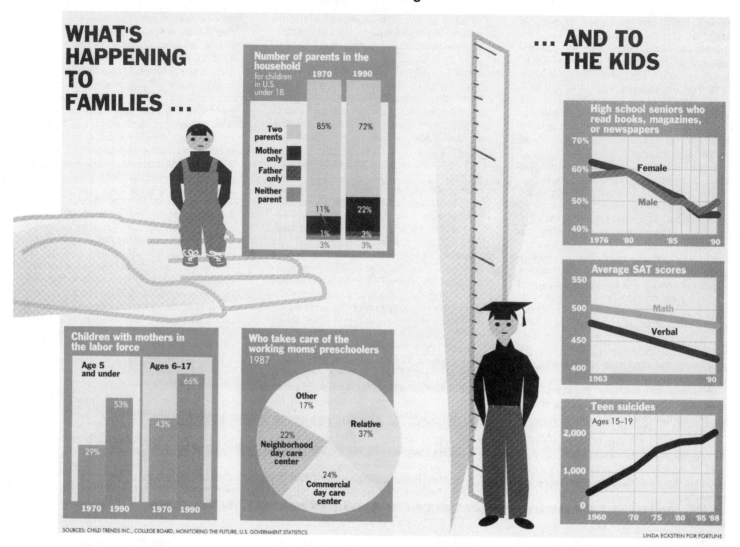

WHAT'S HAPPENING TO FAMILIES ...

... AND TO THE KIDS

Number of parents in the household
for children in U.S. under 18

	1970	1990
Two parents	85%	72%
Mother only	11%	22%
Father only	1%	3%
Neither parent	3%	3%

Children with mothers in the labor force

	Age 5 and under	Ages 6–17
1970	29%	43%
1990	53%	66%

Who takes care of the working moms' preschoolers
1987

- Other 17%
- Relative 37%
- Neighborhood day care center 22%
- Commercial day care center 24%

High school seniors who read books, magazines, or newspapers
Female / Male — 1976, '80, '85, '90 (40%–70%)

Average SAT scores
Math / Verbal — 1963 to '90 (400–550)

Teen suicides
Ages 15–19 — 1960, '70, '75, '80, '85, '88 (0–2,000)

SOURCES: CHILD TRENDS INC., COLLEGE BOARD, MONITORING THE FUTURE, U.S. GOVERNMENT STATISTICS

LINDA ECKSTEIN FOR FORTUNE

wonder. Most American families could not afford to forfeit a second income, a fact that renders the conservatives' yearning for a simpler past quixotic at best. Real weekly earnings for workers declined 13% from 1973 to 1990. So in most cases two paychecks are a necessity. Also, about a quarter of American children—and about half of black children—live in single-parent homes. Those parents are nearly all women. Though some receive child support or other income, their wages are usually their financial lifeblood. About half the mothers who have been awarded child support by the courts do not get full payments regularly.

From the standpoint of the national economy, a mass exodus of women from the work force would be a disaster: There simply won't be enough available males in the future. Women now make up over 45% of the labor force, and they are expected to fill about 60% of new jobs between now and the year 2000.

EVEN IF a child's welfare were the only consideration, in many cases full-time motherhood might not be the best answer. Children whose mothers are frustrated and angry about staying home might be better off in a high-quality day care center. And many kids may well benefit from the socializing and group activities available in day care. A mother and child alone together all day isn't necessarily a rich environment for the child.

In the end, the short supply of high-quality day care is the greatest obstacle to better prospects for America's children. Experts agree on what constitutes quality in child care—a well-paid and well-trained staff, a high staff-child ratio, a safe and suitable physical environment. They also generally concur that if those criteria are met, most children will not just muddle through but prosper. Says Barbara Reisman, executive director of the Child Care Action Campaign, a nonprofit educational and advocacy organization in New York: "Despite all the questions that have been raised, the bottom line is that if the quality is there, and the parents are comfortable with the situation, the kids are going to be fine."

But even tracking, much less improving, child care quality is a monumental task. Something like 60% of the approximately 11 million preschool kids whose mothers work are taken care of in private homes. That can be a wonderful experience: Grandma or a warm-hearted neighbor spends the day with the wee ones baking cookies and imparting folk wisdom. Or it can be hellish. Yale's Edward Zigler speaks in horror of the home where 54 kids in the care of a 16-year-old were found strapped into car seats all day. Low pay and the lack of status associated with organized day care centers make it tough to recruit and retain qualified workers. A study by a research group called the Child Care Employee Project in Oakland revealed an alarming 41% annual turnover rate at day care operations across the U.S. One big reason: an average hourly salary of $5.35. Says Zigler: "We pay these people less than we do zoo keepers—and then we expect them to do wonders."

The experts have floated various schemes to make more money available. The Bush Administration has offered $732 million in block grants to the states for child care and has also proposed increasing the modest tax credits (current maximum: $1,440) for lower-income parents using most kinds of day care. Another current idea: increase the personal exemption. If it had kept pace with inflation since 1950, it would be about $7,000 instead of $2,050. Zigler has proposed that couples be allowed to dip into their Social Security accounts for a short while when their children are young. Under his plan families would be limited to tapping the accounts for up to three years per child, and their retirement benefits would be reduced or delayed proportionately. Zigler would also limit the amount of money withdrawn to some reasonable maximum.

Under all these proposals, parents—especially women—could more easily afford to pay for high-quality day care, scale back their work hours, or even stay at home longer with a newborn if they wished. A 1989 Cornell University study found that about two-thirds of mothers who work full time would cut their hours if they didn't need the extra income. In other surveys, even greater percentages of working mothers with infants say they would reduce their hours or stay home if money were no problem.

In his recent book, *Child Care Choices*, Zigler presents some innovative notions about improving care for older children. He would start organized classes in the public school system beginning at age 3, and keep schools open in the afternoon and early evening for the use of kids with working parents. School libraries, gyms, music rooms, and art rooms would be available. Says Zigler: "All you need is a traffic cop." The city of Los Angeles and the entire state of Hawaii have begun after-school programs along these lines.

BUSINESS has a crucial role to play in helping employees who are parents cope with their responsibilities. The U.S. Congress is currently considering legislation that would guarantee 12 weeks of unpaid leave in the event of a family illness or the birth of a child. According to a study conducted by economics professors at Cornell University and the University of Connecticut, the costs of allowing such leaves for most workers is less than letting them quit and hiring permanent replacements. Companies can provide big-time relief with smaller gestures as well: making a telephone available to assembly-line workers so they can check up on their latchkey kids, say, or letting office workers slip out for a parent-teacher conference without a hassle.

As the competition for good workers heats up, many companies will be forced to grapple with the problems working parents face, or risk losing desirable employees. Says Douglas Besharov, a resident scholar at the American Enterprise Institute in Washington: "If you need workers, you will do what has to be done."

Many corporations have already taken the plunge. IBM, among other companies, offers employees a free child-care referral service; IBM uses 250 different organizations. The company has also pledged $22 million over five years to improve the quality of day care available in the towns and cities where most of its employees live. Johnson & Johnson provides an array of goodies: one-year unpaid family care leaves, an extensive referral network, dependent care reimbursement accounts so that employees can pay child care expenses with pretax dollars, and up to $2,000 toward the cost of adoption.

J&J also supports an on-site day care center at its headquarters in New Brunswick, New Jersey. The company subsidizes part of the cost, but employees using the center still pay $110 to $130 a week depending on the age of the child. Depending on the region, average charges for a preschooler range from $67 to $115 a week. Infant care can cost up to $230 a week, and the affluent few with a full-time nanny pay $200 to $600.

Some smaller companies are paying attention as well. American Bankers Insurance Group, based in Miami, maintains a day care center for employees' children ages 6 weeks to 5 years. After that the child can attend a company-run private school for an additional three years. The school takes care of the child from 8 A.M. to 6:15 P.M. and keeps its doors open during school holidays and summer vacations.

The child care business is growing rapidly. Approximately 77,000 licensed child care centers now serve about four million children daily. Financially troubled Kinder-Care Learning Centers of Montgomery, Alabama, is the industry giant, with 1,257 centers around the country and revenues of $396 million a year. The runner-up is a Kansas City, Missouri, outfit called La Petite Academy Inc. It operates about 750 centers and did $201 million worth of business in 1990.

ServiceMaster, the widely diversified management company based near Chicago, jumped into the field last year and now runs three centers in suburban office parks, with four more under construction. The beauty part of the business is that ServiceMaster typically gets some form of financial help from a landlord or corporate client—reduced rent or lower occupancy costs—and then charges market rates for its services.

Parents working at companies such as Sears, Abbott Laboratories, Ameritech, and Mobil pay about $140 to $150 a week for infants and about $95 a week for 3- to 5-year-olds. ServiceMaster executives consider this a business with splendid growth prospects: They plan to open another half-dozen centers by the end of 1991 and then begin expanding beyond the Chicago area.

Child-development experts admire a relatively new and growing company, Bright Horizons Children's Centers of Cambridge,

Massachusetts, for the innovative on-site day care it provides for major corporations including IBM, Prudential, and Dun & Bradstreet. Founded in 1986 by Linda Mason and her husband, Roger Brown, both former economic development workers in Africa, Bright Horizons now operates 38 centers up and down the East Coast. In most cases the corporate client donates space for child care in or near its office building, providing Bright Horizons with a handsome cost advantage. Fees can be steep—up to $225 per week for infants—but companies often subsidize the payments for employees low on the wage scale.

Because the centers are close to the workplace, parents are encouraged to drop in throughout the day. Bright Horizons' teaching staff members earn up to $20,000 per year, far more than most day care centers pay, plus a full benefits package. They can pursue a defined career track and move into management ranks if they qualify. As a result, turnover runs at a relatively low 16% to 24%.

Brown and Mason concede that many children might be damaged by second-rate child care, but they contend that parents rarely have anything to fear from the kind of high-quality attention their centers provide. Says Mason: "It's very much like health care. If you can afford to pay for it, you can receive the best child care in the world in this country."

For business, helping employees find their way through the child care thicket makes increasing sense—and not only as a method of keeping today's work force happy. More and more companies with an eye on the future recognize the importance of early childhood development, and many are alarmed by the discouraging signals they see in the upcoming generation of workers. At BellSouth in Atlanta, for instance, only about one job applicant in ten passes a battery of exams that test learning ability; ten years ago, twice as many did. Even those who make it through the tests often require extensive training and carry heavy personal baggage: A startling 70% of BellSouth's unmarried employees support at least one child.

More companies are finding that they have to help employees cope not just with their children but also with the gamut of life's vicissitudes. Says Roy Howard, BellSouth's senior vice president for corporate human resources: "Business used to feel that you ought to leave your personal problems at home. We can no longer afford to take that view." The psychic welfare of workers—and of their children—is increasingly a legitimate management concern, and companies that ignore it risk their employees' future as well as their own.

BRINGING UP FATHER

The message dads get is that they are not up to the job. And a record number don't stick around—even as fathers are needed more than ever.

NANCY R. GIBBS

"I don't have a dad," says Megan, 8, a tiny blond child with a pixie nose who gazes up at a visitor and talks of her hunger. "Well, I do have a dad, but I don't know his name. I only know his first name, Bill."

Just what is it that fathers do?

"Love you. They kiss you and hug you when you need them. I had my mom's boyfriend for a while, but they broke up." Now Megan lives with just her mother and older brother in Culver City, California.

What would you like to do with your dad?

"I'd want him to talk to me." She's hurting now. "I wish I had somebody to talk to. It's not fair. If two people made you, then you should still be with those two people." And she's sad. "I'm not so special," she says, looking down at the floor. "I don't have two people."

She imagines what it would be like for him to come home from work at night.

"It would be just like that commercial where the kids say, 'Daddy, are you all right?'" She smiles, dreaming. "The kids show the daddy that they care for him. They put a thermometer in his mouth. They think he's sick because he came home early. They are sitting on the couch watching TV, and it's like, wow, we can play with Dad!"

Megan thinks her father is in the Navy now. "One day when I get older, I'm gonna go back to Alabama and try to find him."

More children will go to sleep tonight in a fatherless home than ever in the nation's history. Talk to the experts in crime, drug abuse, depression, school failure, and they can point to some study somewhere blaming those problems on the disappearance of fathers from the American family. But talk to the fathers who do stay with their families, and the story grows more complicated. What they are hearing, from their bosses, from institutions, from the culture around them, even from their own wives, very often comes down to a devastating message: We don't really trust men to be parents, and we don't really need them to be. And so every day, everywhere, their children are growing up without them.

Corporate America, for a start, may praise family life but does virtually nothing to ease it. Managers still take male workers aside and warn them not to take a paternity leave if they want to be taken seriously. On TV and in movies and magazine ads, the image of fathers over the past generation evolved from the stern, sturdy father who knew best to a helpless Homer Simpson, or some ham-handed galoot confounded by the prospect of changing a diaper. Teachers call parent conferences but only talk to the mothers. When father arrives at the doctor's office with little Betsy, the pediatrician offers instructions to pass along to his wife, the caregiver presumptive. The Census Bureau can document the 70 million mothers age 15 or older in the U.S. but has scant idea how many fathers there are. "There's no interest in fathers at all," says sociologist Vaughn Call, who directs the National Survey of Families and Households at the University of Wisconsin. "It's a nonexistent category. It's the ignored half of the family."

Mothers themselves can be unwitting accomplices. Even women whose own progress in public life depends on sharing the workload in private life act as "gatekeepers" in the home, to use Harvard pediatrician T. Berry Brazelton's description. Dig deeply into household dynamics, and the tensions emerge. Women say they need and want their husbands to be more active parents but fear that they aren't always reliable. Men say they might like to be more involved, but their wives will not make room for them, and jealously guard their domestic power.

Most troubling of all to some social scientists is the message men get that being a good father means learning how to mother. Among child-rearing experts, the debate rages over whether men and women parent differently, whether there is some unique contribution that each makes to the emotional health of their children. "Society sends men two messages," says psychologist Jerrold Lee Shapiro, father of two and the author of *A Measure of the Man,* his third book on fatherhood. "The first is, We want you to be involved, but you'll be an inadequate mother. The second is, You're invited into the birthing room and into the nurturing process—but we don't want all of you. We only want your support. We're not really ready as a culture to accept men's fears, their anger or their sadness. This is the stuff that makes men crazy. We want men to be the protectors and providers, but we are scared they won't be if they become soft."

So now America finds its stereotypes crushed in the collision between private needs and public pressures. While some commend the nurturing nature of the idealized New Father, others cringe at the idea

From *Time,* June 28, 1993, pp. 52-56, 58, 61. © 1993 by Time Inc. Magazine Company. Reprinted by permission.

of genderless parenting and defend the importance of men being more than pale imitations of mothers. "If you become Mr. Mom," says Shapiro, "the family has a mother and an assistant mother. That isn't what good fathers are doing today." And fathers themselves wrestle with memories of their own fathers, vowing to do it differently, and struggling to figure out how.

THE DISAPPEARING DAD

Well into the 18th century, child-rearing manuals in America were generally addressed to fathers, not mothers. But as industrialization began to separate home and work, fathers could not be in both places at once. Family life of the 19th century was defined by what historians call the feminization of the domestic sphere and the marginalization of the father as a parent. By the 1830s, child-rearing manuals, increasingly addressed to mothers, deplored the father's absence from the home. In 1900 one worried observer could describe "the suburban husband and father" as "almost entirely a Sunday institution."

What alarms modern social scientists is that in the latter part of this century the father has been sidelined in a new, more disturbing way. Today he's often just plain absent. Rising divorce rates and out-of-wedlock births mean that more than 40% of all children born between 1970 and 1984 are likely to spend much of their childhood living in single-parent homes. In 1990, 25% were living with only their mothers, compared with 5% in 1960. Says David Blankenhorn, the founder of the Institute for American Values in New York City: "This trend of fatherlessness is the most socially consequential family trend of our generation."

Credit Dan Quayle for enduring the ridicule that opened the mainstream debate over whether fathers matter in families. In the year since his famous Murphy Brown speech, social scientists have produced mounting evidence that, at the very least, he had a point. Apart from the personal politics of parenting, there are larger social costs to reckon in a society that dismisses fathers as luxuries.

Studies of young criminals have found that more than 70% of all juveniles in state reform institutions come from fatherless homes. Children from broken families are nearly twice as likely as those in two-parent families to drop out of high school. After assessing the studies, economist Sylvia Hewlett suggested that "school failure may well have as much to do with disintegration of families as with the quality of schools."

Then there is the emotional price that children pay. In her 15 years tracking the lives of children of divorced families, Judith Wallerstein found that five years af-

ter the split, more than a third experienced moderate or severe depression. After 10 years a significant number of the young men and women appeared to be troubled, drifting and underachieving. At 15 years many of the thirtyish adults were struggling to create strong love relationships of their own. Daughters of divorce, she found, "often experience great difficulty establishing a realistic view of men in general, developing realistic expectations and exercising good judgment in their choice of partners."

For boys, the crucial issue is role modeling. There are psychologists who suggest that boys without fathers risk growing up with low self-esteem, becoming overly dependent on women and emotionally rigid. "Kids without fathers are forced to find their own ways of doing things," observes Melissa Manning, a social worker at the Boys and Girls Club of Venice, Cali-

It Takes Two

WOMEN'S VOICES ARE MORE SOOTHING. THEY CAN READ THE SIGNALS A CHILD SENDS BEFORE HE OR SHE CAN TALK. BUT AS TIME PASSES, THE STRENGTHS THAT FATHERS MAY BRING TO CHILD REARING BECOME MORE IMPORTANT.

fornia. "So they come up with their own ideas, from friends and from the gangs. Nobody is showing them what to do except to be drunk, deal drugs or go to jail." Then there are the subtler lessons that dads impart. Attorney Charles Firestone, for instance, recently decided it was time to teach his 11-year-old son how to play poker. "Maybe it will help if he knows when to hold 'em, when to fold 'em," he says.

THE ANTI-FATHER MESSAGE

Given the evidence that men are so vital to a healthy home, the anti-father messages that creep into the culture and its institutions are all the more troubling. Some scholars suggest that fatherhood is by its very biological nature more fragile than motherhood, and needs to be encouraged by the society around it. And yet for all the focus on the New Father (the kind who skips the corporate awards dinner to attend the school play), the messages men receive about how

they should act as parents are at best mixed and often explicitly hostile.

Employers that have been slow to accommodate the needs of mothers in their midst are often even more unforgiving of fathers. It is a powerful taboo that prevents men from acknowledging their commitment to their children at work. A 1989 survey of medium and large private employers found that only 1% of employees had access to paid paternity leave and just 18% could take unpaid leave. Even in companies like Eastman Kodak, only 7% of men, vs. 93% of women, have taken advantage of the six-year-old family-leave plan.

Those who do soon discover the cost. "My boss made me pay a price for it emotionally," says a prominent Washington executive who took leaves for both his children. "He was very generous with the time, but he never let me forget it. Every six seconds he reminded me what a great guy he was and that I owed him really, really big. You don't get a lot of points at the office for wanting to have a healthy family life." Men, like women, are increasingly troubled by the struggle to balance home and work; in 1989, asked if they experienced stress while doing so, 72% of men answered yes, compared with 12% a decade earlier, according to James Levine of the Fatherhood Project at the Families and Work Institute of New York City.

Many men will freely admit that they sometimes lie to employers about their commitments. "I announced that I was going to a meeting," shrugged a Washington journalist as he left the office in midafternoon one day recently. "I just neglected to mention that the 'meeting' was to watch my daughter play tennis." Now it is the fathers who are beginning to ask themselves whether their careers will stall and their incomes stagnate, whether the glass ceiling will press down on them once they make public their commitment as parents, whether today's productivity pressures will force them to work even harder with that much less time to be with their kids. In the higher reaches of management, there are not only few women, there are also few men in dual-income families who take an active part in raising their children. "Those who get to the top today," says Charles Rodgers, owner of a 10-year-old family-research organization in Brookline, Massachusetts, called Work/Family Directions, "are almost always men from what used to be the traditional family, men with wives who don't work outside the home."

Many men insist that they long to veer off onto a "daddy track." In a 1990 poll by the Los Angeles *Times,* 39% of the fathers said they would quit their jobs to have more time with their kids, while another survey found that 74% of men said they would rather have a daddy-track job than a fast-track job. But in real life, when they are not talking to pollsters, some fathers recognize the power of their atavistic impulses to earn bread and compete, both of which often leave them ambivalent about their obligations as fathers.

George Ingram, 48, lives on Capitol Hill with his sons Mason, 15, and Andrew, 10. He is the first to admit that single fatherhood has not helped his career as a political economist. "We're torn between working hard to become Secretary of State and nurturing our kids," he says. "You make the choice to nurture your kids, and people think it's great. But does it put a crimp on your career? Yes, very definitely. When I finish this process, I will have spent 15 years on a professional plateau." Ingram finds that his colleagues accept his dual commitments, his leaving every night before 6, or by 5 if he has a soccer practice to coach. In fact they are more accepting of his choices than those of his female colleagues. "I get more psychic support than women do," he says. "And I feel great about spending more time with my kids than my father did."

MATERNAL GATEKEEPERS

The more surprising obstacle men say, arises in their own homes. Every household may be different, every division of labor unique, but sociologists do find certain patterns emerging when they interview groups of men and women about how they view one another's parenting roles. Men talk about their wife's unrealistic expectations, her perfectionism, the insistence on dressing, feeding, soothing the children in a certain way. "Fathers, except in rare circumstances, have not yet become equal partners in parenthood," says Frank Furstenberg, professor of sociology at the University of Pennsylvania. "The restructuring of the father role requires support and encouragement from wives. Presumably, it is not abnormal for wives to be reluctant to give up maternal prerogatives."

Many men describe in frustration their wife's attitude that her way of doing things is the only way. "Dad is putting the baby to bed," says Levine. "He's holding his seven-month-old on his shoulders and walking around in circles. Mom comes in and says, 'She likes it better when you just lay her down on her stomach and rub her back.' Dad gets mad that Mom is undermining his way of doing things, which he thinks works perfectly well."

In most cases, it is still the mother who carries her child's life around in her head, keeping the mental daybook on who needs a lift to piano practice and who needs to get the poetry folder in on time. After examining much of the research on men's housework and child care, Sylvia Hewlett con-

cluded that married men's average time in household tasks had increased only 6% in 20 years, even as women have flooded the workplace. Psychologists Rosalind Barnett and Grace Baruch found that fathers were often willing to perform the jobs they were assigned but were not responsible for remembering, planning or scheduling them.

Women often respond that until men prove themselves dependable as parents, they can't expect to be trusted. A haphazard approach to family responsibilities does nothing to relieve the burdens women carry. "Men haven't been socialized to think about family appointments and how the household runs for kids," notes Marie Wilson of the Ms. Foundation for Women, who constantly hears of the hunger women feel for their husbands to participate more fully at home. "They don't really get in there and pay attention. Mothers often aren't sure they can trust them—not just to do it as they do it, but to do it at a level that you can get away with without feeling guilty."

Some women admit that their own feelings are mixed when it comes to relinquishing power within the family. "I can probably be overbearing at times as far as wanting to have it my way," says the 35-year-old wife of a St. Louis, Missouri, physician. "But I would be willing to relax my standards if he would be more involved. It would be a good trade-off." Here again the attitude is changing with each generation. Women under 35, researchers find, seem more willing than older women, whose own fathers were probably less engaged, to trust men as parents. Also, as younger women become more successful professionally, they are less fearful of relinquishing power at home because their identity and satisfaction come from many sources.

THE NEW FATHER

The redefinition of fatherhood has been going on in virtually every arena of American life for well over 20 years. As women worked to broaden their choices at home and work, the implicit invitation was for men to do likewise. As Levine has observed, Dr. Spock had carefully revised his advice on fathers by 1974. The earlier version suggested that fathers change the occasional diaper and cautioned mothers about "trying to force the participation of fathers who get gooseflesh at the very idea of helping to take care of a baby." The new version of *Baby and Child Care*, by contrast, offered a prescription for the New Fatherhood: "The father— any father—should be sharing with the mother the day-to-day care of their child from birth onward ... This is the natural way for the father to start the relationship, just as it is for the mother."

By the '80s, bookstores were growing fat with titles aimed at men: *How to Father,*

Expectant Father, Pregnant Fathers, The Birth of a Father, Fathers Almanac and *Father Power.* There were books about child-and-father relations, like *How to Father a Successful Daughter,* and then specific texts for part-time fathers, single fathers, stepfathers and homosexual fathers. Bill Cosby's *Fatherhood* was one of the bestselling books in publishing history, and *Good Morning, Merry Sunshine,* by Chicago *Tribune* columnist Bob Greene, a journal about his first year of fatherhood, was on the New York *Times* best-seller list for almost a year. Parents can now pick up *Parents' Sports,* a new magazine dedicated to reaching the dad market with stories on the joys of soccer practice.

Institutions were changing too. In his book *Fatherhood in America,* published this month, Robert L. Griswold has traced the history of a fast-changing role that today not only allows men in the birthing room (90% of fathers are in attendance at their child's birth) but also offers them

Mixed Emotions

"WE'RE NOT READY TO ACCEPT MEN'S FEARS . . . OR THEIR SADNESS. WE WANT MEN TO BE THE PROTECTORS . . . BUT WE ARE SCARED THEY WON'T BE IF THEY BECOME SOFT."

postpartum courses in which new fathers learn how to change, feed, hold and generally take care of their infant. Some fathers may even get in on the pregnancy part by wearing the "empathy belly," a bulge the size and weight of a third-trimester fetus. Suddenly available to men hoping to solidify the father-child bond are "Saturday with Daddy Outings," special songfests, field trips and potlucks with dads. Even men behind bars could get help: one program allows an inmate father to read children's stories onto cassette tapes that are then sent, along with the book and a Polaroid picture of Dad, to his child.

"It's become cool to be a dad," says Wyatt Andrews, a correspondent for CBS News who has three children: Rachel, 8, Averil, 7, and Conrad, 5. "Even at dinner parties, disciplinary techniques are discussed. Fathers with teenagers give advice about strategies to fathers with younger kids. My father was career Navy. I don't think he ever spent two seconds thinking about strategies of child rearing. If he said anything, it was 'They listen to me.'"

BRING BACK DAD

These perceptual and behavioral shifts have achieved enough momentum to trigger a backlash of their own. Critics of the New Fatherhood are concerned that something precious is being lost in the revolution in parenting—some uniquely male contribution that is essential for raising healthy kids. In a clinical argument that sends off political steam, these researchers argue that fathers should be more than substitute mothers, that men parent differently than women and in ways that matter enormously. They say a mother's love is unconditional, a father's love is more qualified, more tied to performance; mothers are worried about the infant's survival, fathers about future success. "In other words, a father produces not just children but socially viable children," says Blankenhorn. "Fathers, more than mothers, are haunted by the fear that their children will turn out to be bums, largely because a father understands that his child's character is, in some sense, a measure of his character as well."

When it comes to discipline, according to this school of thought, it is the combination of mother and father that yields justice tempered by mercy. "Mothers discipline children on a moment-by-moment basis," says Shapiro. "They have this emotional umbilical cord that lets them read the child. Fathers discipline by rules. Kids learn from their moms how to be aware of their emotional side. From dad, they learn how to live in society."

As parents, some psychologists argue, men and women are suited for different roles at different times. The image of the New Fatherhood is Jack Nicholson surrounded by babies on the cover of *Vanity Fair*, the businessman changing a diaper on the newly installed changing tables in an airport men's room. But to focus only on infant care misses the larger point. "Parenting of young infants is not a natural activity for males," says David Popenoe, an associate dean of social studies at Rutgers University who specializes in the family. He and others argue that women's voices are more soothing; they are better able to read the signals a child sends before he or she can talk. But as time passes, the strengths that fathers may bring to child rearing become more important.

"At a time when fatherhood is collapsing in our society," warns Blankenhorn, "when more children than ever in history are being voluntarily abandoned by their fathers, the only thing we can think of talking about is infant care? It's an anemic, adult-centered way of looking at the problem." Why not let mothers, he says, do more of the heavy lifting in the early years and let fathers do more of the heavy lifting after infancy when their special skills have more relevance? As children get older, notes William Maddox, director of research and policy at the Washington-based Family Research Council, fathers become crucial in their physical and psychological development. "Go to a park and watch father and mother next to a child on a jungle gym," he said. "The father encourages the kid to challenge himself by climbing to the top; the mother tells him to be careful. What's most important is to have the balance of encouragement along with a warning."

This notion that men and women are genetically, or even culturally, predisposed to different parenting roles strikes other researchers as misguided. They are quick to reject the idea that there is some link between X or Y chromosomes and, say, conditional or unconditional love. "To take something that is only a statistical tendency," says historian E. Anthony Rotundo, "and turn it into a cultural imperative—fathers must do it this way and mothers must do it that way—only creates problems for the vast number of people who don't fit those tendencies, without benefiting the children at all." While researchers have found that children whose fathers are involved in their early rearing tend to have higher IQs, perform better in school and even have a better sense of humor, psychologists are quick to say this is not necessarily a gender issue. "It has to do with the fact that there are two people passionately in love with a child," says Harvard's Brazelton.

The very fact that psychologists are arguing about the nature of fatherhood, that filmmakers are making movies based entirely on fatherlove, that bookstores see a growth market in father guides speaks not only to children's well-being but to men's as well. As much as families need fathers, men need their children in ways they are finally allowed to acknowledge, to learn from them all the secrets that children, with their untidy minds and unflagging hearts, have mastered and that grownups, having grown up, long to retrieve.

—Reported by Ann Blackman/Washington, Priscilla Painton/New York and James Willwerth/Los Angeles

THE LASTING EFFECTS OF CHILD MALTREATMENT

Raymond H. Starr, Jr.

Raymond H. Starr, Jr., is a developmental psychologist on the faculty of the University of Maryland, Baltimore County. He has been conducting research with maltreated children and their families for more than sixteen years and was also a founder and first president of the National Down Syndrome Congress.

Every day, the media contain examples of increasingly extreme cases of child abuse and neglect and their consequences. The cases have a blurring sameness. Take, for example, the fourteen-year-old crack addict who lives on the streets by selling his body. A reporter befriends him and writes a vivid account of the beatings the boy received from his father. There is the pedophile who is on death row for mutilating and murdering a four-year-old girl. His record shows a sixth-grade teacher threatened to rape and kill him if he told anyone what the teacher had done to him. There is the fifteen-year-old girl who felt that her parents didn't love her. So she found love on the streets and had a baby she later abandoned in a trash barrel. And there are the prostitutes on a talk show who tell how the men their mothers had trusted sexually abused them as children. These and hundreds more examples assault us and lead us to believe that abused children become problem adolescents and adults.

Are these incidents the whole story? Case examples are dramatic, but have you ever wondered how such maltreatment changes the course of a child's life? In this sound-bite era, most of us rarely stop to think about this important question. We seldom ask why trauma should play such an important role in shaping the course of a child's life.

To examine these questions, we need to understand what psychologists know about the course of lives and how they study them—the subject of the field of life-span developmental psychology.

LIFE-SPAN DEVELOPMENT

Understanding why people behave the way they do is a complex topic that has puzzled philosophers, theologians, and scientists. The course of life is so complex that we tend to focus on critical incidents and key events. Most of us can remember a teacher who played an important role in our own development, but we have to consider that other teachers may have been important. If his seventh-grade civics teacher, Ms. Jones, is the person Bill says showed him the drama of the law, leading him to become a lawyer, does this mean that his sixth-grade English teacher, Ms. Hazelton, played no role in his career choice? An outside observer might say that Ms. Hazelton was the key person because she had a debate club and Bill was the most able debater in his class.

Case descriptions fascinate us, but it is hard to divine the reasons for life courses from such examples. It is for this reason that scientists studying human behavior prefer to use prospective studies. By following people from a certain age, we can obtain direct evidence about the life course and factors that influence it. However, most of our information comes from retrospective studies in which people are asked what has happened to them in the past and how it relates to their present functioning.

Life-span developmental theory seeks to explain the way life events have influenced individual development. Of necessity, such explanations are complex; lives themselves are complex. They are built on a biological foundation, shaped by genetic characteristics, structured by immediate events, and indirectly influenced by happenings that are external to the family. As if this were not complex enough, contemporary theory holds that our interpretation of each event is dependent on the prior interactions of all these factors.

Hank's reaction to the loss of his wife to cancer will differ from George's reaction to his wife's death from a similar cancer. Many factors can contribute to these differing reactions. Hank may have grown up with two parents who were loving and attentive, while George may never have known his father. He may have had a mother who was so depressed that from the time he was two, he had lived in a series of foster homes, never knowing a secure, loving, consistent parent.

MALTREATED CHILDREN AS ADULTS

Research has shown that there is a direct relation between a child's exposure to negative emotional, social, and environmental events and the presence of problems during adulthood. Psychiatrist Michael Rutter compared young women who were removed from strife-filled homes and who later came back to live with their parents to women from more harmonious homes.[1] The women from discordant homes were more likely to become pregnant as teens, were less skilled in parenting their children, and had unhappy marriages to men who also had psychological and social problems. Adversity begat adversity.

Do the above examples and theoretical views mean that abused and neglected children will, with great certainty, become adults with problems? Research on this issue has focused on three questions: First, do maltreated children grow up to maltreat their children? Second, are yesterday's maltreated children today's criminals? Third, are there more general effects of abuse and neglect on later psychological and social functioning? A number of research studies have examined these questions.

The cycle of maltreatment. It makes logical sense that we tend to raise our own children as we ourselves were raised. Different theoretical views of personality development suggest that this should be the case. Psychoanalytic theorists think that intergenerational transmission of parenting styles is unconscious. Others, such as learning theorists, agree that transmission occurs but differ about the mechanism. Learning parenting skills from our parents is the key mode by which child-rearing practices are transmitted from one generation to the next, according to members of the latter group of theorists.

Research suggests that the correspondence between being maltreated as a child and becoming a maltreating adult is far from the one-to-one relationship that has been proposed. Studies have focused on physical abuse; data are not available for either sexual abuse or neglect. In one recent review, the authors conclude that the rate of intergenerational transmission of physical abuse is between 25 percent and 35 percent.[2] Thus, it is far from certain that an abused child will grow up to be an abusive parent. Physical abuse should be seen as a risk factor for becoming an abusive adult, not as a certainty. Many abusive adults were never abused when they were children.

Researchers have also taken a broader approach by examining the cycle of family violence. Sociologist Murray Straus surveyed a randomly selected national sample of families about the extent of violence between family members.[3] Members of the surveyed families were asked about experiences of violence when they were children and how much husband-wife and parent-child violence there had been in the family in the prior year.

Straus concluded that slightly fewer than 20 percent of parents whose mothers had been violent toward them more than once a year during childhood were abusive toward their own child. The child abuse rate for parents with less violent mothers was less than 12 percent. Having or not having a violent father was less strongly related to whether or not fathers grew up to be abusive toward their own children. Interestingly, the amount of intergenerational transmission was higher if a parent was physically punished by his or her opposite-sex parent.

Straus also found that the abusive adults in his study did not have to have been abused in childhood to become abusive adults. A violent home environment can lead a nonabused child to become an abusive adult. Boys who saw their fathers hit their mothers were 38 percent more likely to grow up to be abusive than were boys who never saw their father hit their mother (13.3 vs. 9.7 percent). Similarly, mothers who saw their mothers hit their fathers were 42 percent more likely to become abusive mothers (24.4 vs. 17.2 percent). Straus views seeing parents fight as a training ground for later child abuse.

To summarize, this evidence suggests that maltreatment during childhood is but one of many factors that lead to a person's becoming an abusive parent. Being abused as a child is a risk marker for later parenting problems and not a cause of such difficulties. It accounts for, at most, less than a third of all cases of physical abuse. Research suggests that a number of other factors, such as stress and social isolation, also play a role as causes of child abuse.[4]

Maltreatment and later criminality. Later criminal behavior is one of the most commonly discussed consequences of child abuse. Research on this subject has examined the consequences of both physical abuse and sexual abuse. Maltreatment has been linked to both juvenile delinquency and adult criminality.

It is difficult to do research on this topic. Furthermore, the results of studies must be carefully interpreted to avoid overstating the connection between maltreatment and criminality. For example, researchers often combine samples of abused and neglected children, making it hard to determine the exact effects of specific forms of maltreatment.

Two types of study have typically been done. Retrospective studies examine the family backgrounds of criminals and find the extent to which they were maltreated as children. It is obvious that the validity of the results of such studies may be compromised by the criminals' distortion of or lack of memory concerning childhood experiences. Prospective studies, in which a sample of children is selected and followed through childhood and into adolescence or adulthood, are generally seen as a more valid research strategy. Such studies are expensive and time-consuming to do.

One review of nine studies concluded that from 8 to 26 percent of delinquent youths studied retrospectively had been abused as children.[5] The rate for prospective studies was always found to be less than 20 percent. In one of the best studies, Joan McCord analyzed case records for more than 250 boys, almost 50 percent of whom had been abused by a parent.[6] Data were also collected when the men were in middle age. McCord found that 39 percent

> *Research has shown that there is a direct relation between a child's exposure to negative emotional, social, and environmental events and the presence of problems during adulthood.*

of the abused boys had been convicted of a crime as juveniles, adults, or at both ages, compared to 23 percent of a sample of 101 men who, as boys, had been classified as loved by their parents. The crime rate for both sets of boys is higher than would be expected because McCord's sample lived in deteriorated, urban areas where both crime and abuse are common.

Researchers have also examined the relationship between abuse and later violent criminality. Research results suggest that there is a weak relationship between abuse and later violence. For example, in one study, 16 percent of a group of abused children were later arrested —but not necessarily convicted—as suspects in violent criminal cases.[7] This was twice the arrest rate for nonabused adolescents and adults. Neglected children were also more likely to experience such arrests. These data are higher than would be the case in the general population because the samples contained a disproportionately high percentage of subjects from low-income backgrounds.

The connection between childhood sexual abuse and the commission of sex crimes in adolescence and adulthood is less clear. Most of the small number of studies that have been done have relied upon self-reports of childhood molestation made by convicted perpetrators. Their results show considerable variation in the frequency with which childhood victimization is reported. Incidence figures range from a low of 19 percent to a high of 57 percent. However, we should look at such data with suspicion. In an interesting study, perpetrators of sex crimes against children were much less likely to report that they had been sexually abused during their own childhood when they knew that the truthfulness of their answers would be validated by a polygraph examination and that lies were likely to result in being sent to jail.[8] Thus, people arrested for child sexual abuse commonly lie, claiming that they were abusing children because they themselves had been victims of sexual abuse as children.

To summarize, there is a link between childhood abuse and later criminality. Although some studies lead to a conclusion that this relationship is simple, others suggest that it is really quite complex. The latter view is probably correct.

The case of neglect is an example of this complexity. Widom, in her study discussed above, found that 12 percent of adolescents and adults arrested for violent offenses were neglected as children and 7 percent experienced both abuse and neglect (compared to 8 percent of her nonmaltreated control adolescents and adults).

These data raise an interesting question: Why is neglect, typically considered to be a nonviolent offense, linked to later criminality? Poverty seems to be the mediating factor. Neglect is more common among impoverished families. Poor families experience high levels of frustration, known to be a common cause of aggression. Similarly, we know that lower-class families are, in general, more violent.[9] For these reasons, all the forms of maltreatment we have considered make it somewhat more likely that a maltreated child will grow up to commit criminal acts.

Maltreatment in context. Research suggests that maltreatment during childhood has far-reaching consequences. These are best seen as the results of a failure to meet the emotional needs of the developing child. Indeed, in many cases, the trust the child places in the parent is betrayed by the parent.

This betrayal has been linked to many and varied consequences. The greatest amount of research has focused on the long-term effects of sexual abuse. Studies have looked at samples that are representative of the normal population and also at groups of adults who are seeking psychotherapy because of emotional problems. The most valid findings come from the former type of study. One review of research concluded that almost 90 percent of studies found some lasting effect of sexual abuse.[10]

Sexual abuse has been linked to

a wide variety of psychological disturbances. These include depression, low self-esteem, psychosis, anxiety, sleep problems, alcohol and drug abuse, and sexual dysfunction (including a predisposition to revictimization during adulthood). As was true for the research reviewed in the preceding two sections of this article, any particular problem is present in only a

---

Psychoanalytic theorists think that intergenerational transmission of parenting styles is unconscious.

---

minority of adult survivors of childhood sexual victimization.

We know less about the long-term effects of physical abuse. Most of the limited amount of available research has used data obtained from clinical samples. Such studies have two problems. First, they rely on retrospective adult reports concerning events that happened during childhood. Second, the use of such samples results in an overestimate of the extent to which physical abuse has long-term consequences. Compared with a random sample of the general population, clinical samples contain individuals who are already identified as having emotional difficulties, regardless of whether or not they have been abused.

Researchers in one study found that more than 40 percent of inpatients being treated in a psychiatric hospital had been sexually or physically abused as children, usually by a family member.[11] Also, the abuse was typically chronic rather than a onetime occurrence. The abused patients were almost 50 percent more likely to have tried to commit suicide, were 25 percent more likely to have been violent toward others, and were 15 percent more likely to have had some involvement with the criminal justice system than were other patients at the same hospital who had not experienced childhood maltreatment.

Much research remains to be done in this area. We know little about the long-term consequences of particular forms of abuse. The best that we can say is that many victims of physical and sexual abuse experience psychological trauma lasting into adulthood.

The lack of universal consequences. The above analysis suggests that many victims of childhood maltreatment do *not* have significant problems functioning as adults. Researchers are only beginning to ask why many adult victims apparently have escaped unsullied. Factors that mediate and soften the influence of abuse and neglect are called buffers.

The search for buffers is a difficult one. Many of the negative outcomes that have been discussed in the preceding sections may be the result of a number of factors other than maltreatment itself. For example, abused children commonly have behavior problems that are similar to those that have been reported in children raised by drug addicts or adults suffering from major psychological disturbances. Abused children do not exhibit any problems that can be attributed only to abuse. A given behavior problem can have many causes.

One view of the way in which buffers act to limit the extent to which physical abuse is perpetuated across succeeding generations has been proposed by David Wolfe.[12] He believes that there is a three-part process involving the parent, the child, and the relationships between

ating factors that work at this level include normal developmental changes in child behavior, parental attendance at child management classes, and the development of parental ability to cope with the child's escalating annoying actions. Finally, additional compensatory factors work to limit the ongoing use of aggression as a solution to parenting problems.

One study compared parents who broke the cycle of abuse to those who did not.[13] Mothers who were not abusive had larger, more supportive social networks. Support included help with child care and financial assistance during times of crisis. Mothers who did not continue the abusive cycle also were more in touch with their own abuse as children and expressed

---

The amount of intergenerational transmission was higher if a parent was physically punished by his or her opposite-sex parent.

Parents may realize that researchers are indeed correct when they say that physical punishment is an ineffective way of changing child behavior. In addition, children may respond positively to parental use of nonaggressive disciplinary procedures and, at a broader level, society or individuals in the parents' circle of friends may inhibit the use of physical punishment by making their disapproval known. Parents who were abused as children are therefore less likely to abuse their own children if any or all of these mediating factors are present.

Research suggests that the factors

doubts about their parenting ability. This awareness made them more able to relive and discuss their own negative childhood experiences.

To summarize, investigators have gone beyond just looking at the negative consequences of childhood maltreatment. They are devoting increasing attention to determining what factors in a child's environment may inoculate the child against the effects of maltreatment. While research is starting to provide us with information concerning some of these mediating influences, much more work needs to be done before we can specify the most important mediators and know how they exert their influences.

Physical abuse should be seen as a risk factor for becoming an abusive adult, not as a certainty.

---

the two. In the first stage, factors predisposing a parent to child abuse (including stress and a willingness to be aggressive toward the child) are buffered by such factors as social support and an income adequate for the purchase of child-care services. Next, Wolfe notes that children often do things that annoy parents and create crises that may lead to abuse because the parent is unprepared to handle the child's provocative behavior. Amelior-

mentioned by Wolfe and other influences all can work to buffer the adult effects of childhood maltreatment. These include knowing a nurturing, loving adult who provides social support, intellectually restructuring the maltreatment so that it is not seen so negatively, being altruistic and giving to others what one did not get as a child, having good skills for coping with stressful events, and getting psychotherapy.

CONCLUSIONS

We know much about the intergenerational transmission of childhood physical and sexual abuse. Research suggests that abused children are (1) at an increased risk of either repeating the acts they experienced with their own children or, in the case of sexual abuse, with both their own and with unrelated children; (2) more likely to be involved with the criminal justice system as adolescents or adults; and (3) likely to suffer longlasting emotional effects of abuse even if they do not abuse their own children or commit criminal acts.

This does not mean that abused chil-

People arrested for child sexual abuse commonly lie, claiming that they were abusing children because they themselves had been victims of sexual abuse as children.

dren invariably grow up to be adults with problems. Many adults escape the negative legacy of abuse. They grow up to be normal, contributing members of society. Their escape from maltreatment is usually related to the presence of factors that buffer the effects of the physical blows and verbal barbs.

The knowledge base underlying these conclusions is of varied quality. We know more about the relationship of physical and sexual abuse to adult abusiveness and criminality, less about long-term psychological problems and buffering factors, and almost nothing about the relationship of neglect to any of these outcomes. Almost no research has been done on neglect, a situation leading to a discussion of the reasons behind our "neglect of neglect."[14] Our ignorance is all the more surprising when we consider that neglect is the most common form of reported maltreatment.

The issues involved are complex. We can no longer see the development of children from a view examining such simple cause-effect relationships as exemplified by the proposal that abused children grow up to be abusive adults. Contemporary de-

velopmental psychology recognizes that many interacting forces work together to shape development. Children exist in a context that contains their own status as biological beings, their parents and the background they bring to the task of child-rearing, the many and varied environments such as work and school that exert both direct and indirect influences on family members, and the overall societal acceptance of violence.

Advances in research methods allow us to evaluate the interrelationships of all the above factors to arrive at a coherent view of the course of development. Appropriate studies are difficult to plan and expensive to conduct. Without such research, the best that we can do is to continue performing small studies that give us glimpses of particular elements of the picture that we call the life course.

Research is necessary if we are to develop and evaluate the effectiveness of child maltreatment prevention and treatment programs. Our existing knowledge base provides hints that are used by program planners and psychotherapists to find families where there is a high risk of

maltreatment and to intervene early. But when such hints are all we have to guide us in working to break the cycle of maltreatment, there continues to be risk of intergenerational perpetuation.

1. Michael Rutter, "Intergenerational Continuities and Discontinuities in Serious Parenting Difficulties," in *Child Maltreatment: Theory and Research on the Causes and Consequences of Child Abuse and Neglect*, ed., Dante Cicchetti and Vicki Carlson (New York: Cambridge University Press, 1989), 317–348.

2. Joan Kaufman and Edward Zigler, "Do Abused Children Become Abusive Adults?" *American Journal of Orthopsychiatry* 57 (April 1987): 186–192.

3. Murray A. Straus, "Family Patterns and Child Abuse in a Nationally Representative American Sample," *Child Abuse and Neglect* 3 (1979): 213–225.

4. Raymond H. Starr, Jr., "Physical Abuse of Children," in *Handbook of Family Violence* ed. Vincent B. Van Hasselt, et al. (New York: Plenum Press, 1988): 119–155.

5. Cathy Spatz Widom, "Does Violence Beget Violence? A Critical Examination of the Literature," *Psychological Bulletin* 106 (1989): 3–28.

6. Joan McCord, "A Forty-year Perspective on Effects of Child Abuse and Neglect," *Child Abuse and Neglect* 7 (1983): 265–270. Joan McCord, "Parental Aggressiveness and Physical Punishment in Long-term Perspective," in *Family Abuse and Its Consequences*, ed. Gerald T. Hotaling, et al. (Newbury Park, Calif.: Sage Publishing, 1988): 91–98.

7. Cathy Spatz Widom, "The Cycle of Violence," *Science*, 14 April 1989.

8. Jan Hindman, "Research Disputes Assumptions about Child Molesters," *National District Attorneys' Association Bulletin* 7 (July/August 1988): 1.

9. Murray A. Straus, Richard J. Gelles, and Suzanne K. Steinmetz, *Behind Closed Doors: Violence in the American Family* (New York: Anchor Press, 1980).

10. David Finkelhor and Angela Browne, "Assessing the Long-term Impact of Child Sexual Abuse: A Review and Conceptualization," in *Family Abuse and Its Consequences*, ed. Gerald T. Hotaling, et al.: 270–284.

11. Elaine (Hilberman) Carmen, Patricia Perri Rieker, and Trudy Mills, "Victims of Violence and Psychiatric Illness," *American Journal of Psychiatry* 141 (March 1984): 378–383.

12. David A. Wolfe, *Child Abuse: Implications for Child Development and Psychopathology* (Newbury Park, Calif.: Sage Publishing, 1987).

13. Rosemary S. Hunter and Nancy Kilstrom, "Breaking the Cycle in Abusive Families," 136 (1979): 1320–22.

14. Isabel Wolock and Bernard Horowitz, "Child Maltreatment as a Social Problem: The Neglect of Neglect," *American Journal of Orthopsychiatry* 54 (1984); 530–543.

Helping Children Cope With Violence

Lorraine B. Wallach

Lorraine B. Wallach, M.A., is one of the founders of the Erikson Institute in Chicago and is presently a faculty member there. Her recent work includes staff training around issues of children and violence.

Children who grow up in violent communities are at risk for pathological development because growing up in a constant state of apprehension makes it difficult to establish trust, autonomy, and social competence.

V iolence is epidemic in the United States today. The murder rate in this country is the fifth highest in the world. It is 10 times higher than England's and 25 times that of Spain. For many inner-city children, violence has become a way of life. In a study of more than 1,000 children in Chicago, 74% of them had witnessed a murder, shooting, stabbing, or robbery (Kotulak, 1990; Bell, 1991). Almost half (47%) of these incidents involved friends, family members, classmates, or neighbors. Forty-six percent of the children interviewed reported that they had personally experienced at least one violent crime. These figures are similar to those found in other U.S. urban areas, such as Baltimore (Zinsmeister, 1990), Los Angeles County (Pynoos & Eth, 1985), and New Orleans (Osofsky, Wewers, Hann, Fick, & Richters, 1991).

Children are exposed to several kinds of violence, including child abuse and domestic violence. And there are communities where violence is endemic, where gang bangers, drug dealers, petty crimi-

nals, and not-so-petty criminals rule the streets. For children living in these conditions, feelings of being safe and secure do not exist.

Children who are not designated victims of assault can be unintended victims. Shoot-outs between gangs and drive-by shootings result in the wounding, and often killing, of innocent bystanders. In addition, the psychological toll of living under these conditions is immeasurable. The children in these neighborhoods see violence and hear it discussed. They are surrounded by danger and brutality.

Child abuse, other domestic violence, and neighborhood violence can harm development

The effects of this kind of violence on children are widespread and can permeate all areas of development, beginning in infancy and continuing through childhood. The first task a baby faces is the development of trust—trust

in the caregiving environment and eventually in himself. Achieving a sense of trust is compromised by growing up in a violent community. Many families find it difficult to provide infants with support, love, and affection in a consistent and predictable manner when they live in a constant state of apprehension—not knowing when they are going to be victims of violence. Toddlers have difficulty developing a sense of autonomy when their families cannot help them explore their environments because their surroundings are filled with danger. Preschoolers, too, are inhibited from going out into the world. Just at the age when they should be expanding their social contacts and finding out about people beyond the family, they are restricted by the dangers lurking outside. Many children living in high-rise housing projects and other dangerous neighborhoods are cooped up inside all day because it is unsafe to go out-of-doors. The situation is even more tragic when children experience violence within the family. Where can a child find protection when she is victimized within her own home? Although domestic violence occurs in *every* kind of neighborhood, the effects may be even more damaging when compounded by the harmful effects of growing up in *violent* neighborhoods.

Children who grow up under conditions that do not allow them to develop trust in people and in themselves or learn to handle day-to-day problems in socially acceptable ways are at risk for pathological development; they are at risk for resorting to violent behaviors themselves. The anger that is instilled in children when they are mistreated or when they see their mothers or siblings mistreated is likely to be incorporated into their personality structures. Children learn by identifying with the people they love. They also identify with the people who have power and control. When children see and experience abuse and violence as a way of life, when the people who are responsible for them behave without restraint, the children often learn to behave in the same manner.

Another serious problem for children living in chaotic communities is that the protectors and the dangerous people may be one and the same. The police, who are supposed to be protectors, are often seen as dangerous by community members. In his book *There Are No Children Here,* Alex Kotlowitz (1991) describes how a young man who is idolized by his housing project community be-

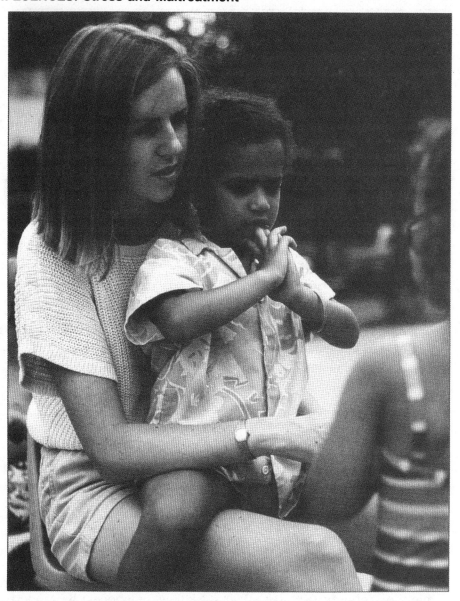

It is particularly important for children who come from chaotic environments to have firm but appropriate limits, even though children who feel powerless may try to provoke adults into a battle of wills in an effort to make themselves feel important.

The young child's protectors and the dangerous people in her life may be one and the same.

cause he is successful, has graduated from high school, is not caught up in gangs, and is still his own person is mistakenly killed by the police. What do children think when their idol is gunned down by the people who are supposed to protect them?

Children are confused when they cannot tell the good guys from the bad guys. Their teachers and the media tell them that drug dealers are bad and are the cause of the problems in the community, but the children may know

that cousins or friends or even older brothers are dealing. Some people have likened the inner city, especially housing projects, to war zones; but in a war the enemy is more often than not on the outside, and usually everyone knows who he is.

Children growing up with violence face risks other than becoming violent themselves. Children who live with danger develop defenses against their fears, and these defenses can interfere with their development. When children have to defend themselves constantly from outside or inside dangers, their energies are not available for other, less immediately urgent tasks, such as learning to read and write and do arithmetic and learning about geography and history and science. In addition to not having enough energy to devote to schoolwork, there is evidence that specific cognitive functions such as memory and a sense of time can be affected by experiencing trauma (Terr, 1981).

Boys and girls who are victims of abuse and who see abusive behavior in their families can grow up feeling as if they are responsible for what is happening. Young children cannot always differentiate between what is real and what is part of their inner lives. The literature on divorce has made clear that many children believe that they have caused the breakup of the family, even though it had nothing to do with them (Wallerstein & Kelly, 1980; Hetherton, Cox, & Cox, 1982). Children who feel guilty about the violence in their families often perceive themselves as being bad and worthless. Feelings of worthlessness can lead children to the idea that they

When children have to defend themselves constantly from inside and outside dangers, there is little energy for schoolwork. There is also evidence that specific cognitive functions such as memory and a sense of time can be affected.

are not capable of learning, which leads, in turn, to a lack of motivation to achieve in school.

Children who experience trauma may have difficulty seeing themselves in future roles that are meaningful. Lenore Terr (1983), in her study of the schoolchildren of Chowchilla who were kidnapped in their school bus, found that the views of their future lives were limited and often filled with anticipation of disaster. Children who cannot see a decent future for themselves cannot give their all to the present task of learning and becoming socialized.

Living in unpredictably frightening situations makes children feel as if they have no control over their lives. We know that young children need to feel as if they can direct some parts of their lives, but children who are victims of violence learn that they have no say in what happens to them. This sense of helplessness interferes with the development of autonomy.

It is difficult for children to keep on growing and maturing when they have been traumatized because an almost universal reaction of children to traumatic occurrences is regression. Children slip back to stages at which they felt more secure. This is particularly true when they have only a tenuous hold on their current status.

What makes some children more resilient than others, and what can we do?

As depressing as all this sounds, however, it does not mean that all children who experience violence are doomed. It is known that some children are more resilient and withstand trauma and stress better than others. If a child has an easy temperament and makes a good fit with his primary caregiver, he or she is more likely to be off to a good start. Some lucky children are born to strong parents who can withstand the ravages of poverty and community violence and still provide some security and hope for their children. Children are shaped not only by their parents' behavior but also by their parents' hopes, expectations, motivations, and view of the future—including their children's future.

It is important to remember that children are malleable, that what happens in the early years is im-

A kindergarten teacher in a Chicago public school was discussing her dilemma concerning two boys in her classroom. All of the children were at their tables, engaged in drawing, when the teacher noticed these boys crawling under the tables, pretending to have guns. When one of the boys saw the teacher watching them, he reassured her, "Don't worry, we're just playing breaking into an apartment." The teacher questioned whether she should let the play continue or offer a more socially acceptable view of behavior. How should she react? A Head Start teacher in the group said that the boy who was taking the lead in this game had been in her class the year before, and that his family's apartment had been burglarized. The boy had been very frightened and, after that experience, had changed from a confident, outgoing youngster to a quiet and withdrawn child. Here it was a year later, and he was just beginning to play out his experience. He was becoming the aggressor in the play instead of the helpless victim. And he was regaining some of his old confidence.

portant, but that many children can overcome the hurts and fears of earlier times. Many can make use of positive experiences that occur both inside and outside their families. Child care centers, recreation programs, and schools can be resources for children and offer them alternative perceptions of themselves, as well as teaching them skills. One of the things that help determine the resiliency of children is the ability to make relationships and to make use of the people in their environments, people who provide to children what they do not get in their families or who supplement what their families cannot offer.

Child care professionals can help offset the negative effects of violence in the lives of young children by providing that supplement. Although teachers, social workers, and human service personnel cannot cure all of the hurts experienced by children today, they can make a difference.

1. The first thing they need to do is to make sure that their programs provide opportunities for children to develop meaningful relationships with caring and knowledgeable adults. Teachers and other staff members can offer each child a chance to form an important relationship with one of them, a relationship within which the child can learn that there are people in the world who can be of help. The best thing to offer children at risk is caring people, people who are available both physically and emotionally.

Some years ago the famous Chicago analyst Franz Alexander (1948) coined the term *corrective emotional experience* to explain the curative power of therapy, and that term best describes what child care professionals can do for children at risk. A corrective emotional experience means having a relationship with another person that touches one's deepest core—not a relationship that

is superficial or intellectual, but one that engages the emotions. It means having a relationship within which a person can redo old patterns and ties. It means feeling safe enough within a relationship to risk making basic changes in one's psychic structure. Children cannot be forced into these kinds of relationships; they can only be offered the opportunities with the hope that they take advantage of them.

Some children attach easily, and it does not take much effort on the part of the adults for these children to form attachments; these are usually the children who have had a good relationship in their past. Other children have not been lucky enough to have had the kind of relationship that makes them want to seek out others and repeat this satisfying experience; these children need more help in forming ties and trusting alliances.

What can adults do to stimulate relationships with children who do not come easily to this task? They can look into themselves and see if they are ready

for this kind of relationship—a relationship that makes demands on their emotions, their energies, and their time. Relationships with children who have inordinate needs and who do not have past experiences in give-and-take partnerships are not 50–50 propositions; adults must meet these children more than halfway.

2. Child care professionals can organize their schedules and their time with the children so that they provide as much consistency as possible. Attachment can be encouraged by reducing the number of people a child encounters during the day and by maximizing the amount of meaningful time and activity the child has with one adult. In this way each child is allowed to form an attachment to one person. There are several models—including therapeutic centers, child-life programs, and primary-care nursing—that use relationship as the principal tool in their interventions. Establishing significant relationships with the children who

A nine-year-old boy in a shelter for battered women told a story about his recurring dream. This is what he said: "I dreamed of someone taking me away. He was dressed like a lady, but he had a moustache. I went inside the house. It was dark. The lights were out, and there were people inside having a party. It was ugly. They were eating worms and they asked me to try one. I took one and threw it away. Then I opened the door, and the light came on in there, and I saw there were no more ghosts, and I saw I was sleeping. When I dream like that, I become afraid."

It was obvious that the boy was expressing his fears, but the exact meaning of the details was not evident—not until one of the child care workers who knew the mother reported that the abusive father was bisexual and brought his male sexual partners to the family's apartment. It then became clear that in addition to struggling with feelings about an abusive father, the boy was also frightened and confused about the meaning of his father's behavior and probably about his own sexual identification. In this case the child was able to tell about a disturbing dream through the telling of a story, and the adults were able to understand it with additional information about his family.

have suffered from trauma is the most important thing that can be done, and it is the basis for all of the work that follows. What is this other work?

3. Child care professionals must provide structure and very clear expectations and limits. All children, especially young children, need to know where they stand, but it is particularly important for children who come from chaotic environments to have firm but appropriate limits. It should be noted that they do not take to this kind of structure easily. It is not something they have experienced before, and the newness of it may cause anxiety and tension, just as any new situation does.

Some children see the structure of a new setting as an opportunity to assert themselves and force the adults into power struggles. Children who feel powerless may try to provoke adults into a battle of wills in an effort to make themselves feel important. But even though some of the neediest children may rebel against structure, no matter how benign, it is important to provide it so that the boundaries are clear.

4. Early childhood professionals should offer children many opportunities to express themselves within the confines of a comfortable and consistent schedule, with clear expectations about behavior. Children need to air their emotions; they need to tell their stories. They can do this in several activities that can be a part of any good program for children.

Josephine, the child of an abused mother, told a story about a girl with red eyes who bit and scratched her mother because she was angry at her and the devil got into her body. The child care worker listened and accepted her story, thereby accepting the child's feelings. In subsequent sessions, after establishing a more trusting relationship with the child, the worker told her a story about the same little girl who told the devil not to bother her and who talked to her mother about how she was going to try harder to be nicer. By using the same characters and theme, she offered the little girl another way of relating to her mother. At the same time, the mother's worker helped her understand her own anger and supported her in trying to alter her behavior toward her daughter.

Except for life-sustaining activities, play is, of course, the most universal activity of children

Through play, children learn about the physical and social world. As they play, children develop a map of the world, a map that helps them make sense of the complexities that define the world today. Play, in the context of a corrective experience, offers children who live with chaos and violence a chance to redraw their world map.

Play provides an avenue for children to express their feelings. Children who are angry or hurt can take their anger out on toys, dolls, and stuffed animals. Children who feel isolated or lonely can find solace in pretending to live in a world with lots of friends. Children who are frightened can seek safety within a game by pretending to be big and strong. In other words, children can play out their own scenarios, changing their real life situations to their own design. They can invent happy endings. They can reverse roles and become the big—instead of the small—people. They can become the aggressors rather than the victims.

Play also allows children to repeat some of the bad things in their lives. Some people think that children want to forget the frightening or horrible things that they have experienced and try to put these events out of their minds. Some people think that children's play reflects only happy experiences; and many times it does. But some children gain strength from repeating situations that were overwhelming to them, as a way of trying to come to terms with the experiences.

Traumatic events have a way of staying with us. Sometimes they are repeated in dreams. Adults may review these events by talking about them with their friends

Children may feel guilty about the violence in their families, perceive themselves as being bad and worthless, feel as if they have no control over their lives, and have difficulty seeing themselves in future roles that are meaningful; they often slip back to stages at which they felt more secure.

and even with strangers. Adults, through discussion—and children, through play—gain control over trauma by repeating it again and again. Repetition allows the trauma victim to absorb the experience little by little, come to grips with what happened, and learn to accept it or live with it.

Expressive art is very therapeutic

In addition to being given many opportunities for dramatic play, children can benefit from a chance to paint and draw. Just as some children make sad or frightening events into happy occasions in their play, others may draw pictures of happy times, even when they are living in far-from-happy circumstances. They draw pictures of nice houses with flowers and trees and sunshine. Others draw pictures that are, or that represent, disturbing things in their lives. They draw angry or violent pictures and find solace in expressing their feelings through art and conquering their fears by putting them on paper.

Storytelling can bridge to valuable conversation

Storytelling is another way in which children can handle difficult situations and express their inner thoughts. Sharing the telling of stories can be an excellent way to open up communication between adults and children. It can establish rapport between the two and lay the basis for further discussions of a child's difficulties. It is easier for the adult to under-

stand stories than to interpret drawings or play, and the adult is able to engage a child in a conversation about her or his story.

This does not mean that the stories children tell can be accepted verbatim. Just as play and drawing allow children to express themselves symbolically, so do stories offer them a chance to communicate an idea or feeling without acknowledging its closeness to reality. Adults often cannot understand a child's story without having some outside information about the child's life.

If we understand what children are telling us through their stories, we can help them by participating with them in storytelling. Gardner (1971) used this method in his therapy with children. After the child told a story, Gardner told the same story but with a different, healthier ending. Although teachers are not therapists, they can engage children in joint storytelling sessions and offer alternative endings to the stories told by the children.

Collaboration with families is critically important

Direct work with children is invaluable, but if it can be combined with help for parents, its effectiveness can be increased. Young children are best understood in the context of their families and communities. Professionals need to know the facts about a child's life situation, and that information can be gained from the adults who know the child well.

In addition to obtaining information from parents, the most ef-

fective help for a child is in collaboration with help for the family. Because the child is entwined with his family for many years, it is important to make changes in his familial relationships, if possible; even small changes can be important.

It is not possible for teachers and other child specialists to also be social workers and parent therapists. The person who makes contact with a child, however, is often in a good position to establish a working alliance with the child's parents. This alliance can then be used to refer parents to community agencies, clinics, churches, or self-help groups for

Not all children who experience violence are doomed.

the support, guidance, or therapy that they need. Making a good referral takes skill and patience. It cannot be done quickly, which means that teachers and child care workers must have the time to talk to parents and to make home visits if necessary. They must have time to establish contact with families as an essential part of their work with children who suffer the consequences of violence.

The problems spelled out here are formidable. They will not be easy to solve, but professionals who see children on a daily basis can be an important part of the solution. They cannot cure all of the ills and solve all of the problems that confront children today, but they can offer these children a chance to face and accept their feelings and to see alternative ways of relating to others. If child care professionals can help some—not all, but some—children find alternatives to destructive behavior, be it toward themselves or others, they have helped break the cycle of violence.

The best thing to offer children at risk is caring people, people who are available both physically and emotionally—a relationship that touches one's deepest core.

References

Alexander, F. (1948). *Fundamentals of psychoanalysis.* New York: W.W. Norton.

Bell, C. (1991). Traumatic stress and children in danger. *Journal of Health Care for the Poor and Underserved, 2*(1), 175–188.

Gardner, R. (1971). *Therapeutic communication with children: The mutual storytelling technique.* New York: Science House.

Hetherton, E.M., Cox, M., & Cox, R. (1982). Effects of divorce on parents and children. In M. Lamb (Ed.), *Non-traditional families.* Hillsdale, NJ: Lawrence Erlbaum.

Kotlowitz, A. (1991). *There are no children here.* New York: Doubleday.

Kotulak, R. (1990, September 28). Study finds inner-city kids live with violence. *Chicago Tribune,* pp. 1, 16.

Osofsky, J., Wewers, S., Hann, D., Fick, A., & Richters, J. (1991). *Chronic community violence: What is happening to our children?* Manuscript submitted for publication.

Pynoos, R., & Eth, S. (1985). Children traumatized by witnessing personal violence: Homicide, rape or suicide behavior. In S. Eth & R. Pynoos (Eds.), *Posttraumatic stress disorder in children* (pp. 19–43). Washington, DC: American Psychiatric Press.

Terr, L. (1981). Forbidden games: Posttraumatic child's play. *Journal of American Academy of Child Psychiatry, 20,* 741–760.

Terr, L. (1983). Chowchilla revisited: The effects of psychic trauma four years after a schoolbus kidnapping. *American Journal of Psychiatry, 140,* 1543–1550.

Wallerstein, J.S., & Kelley, J.B. (1980). *Surviving the breakup: How children and parents cope with divorce.* New York: Basic Books.

Zinsmeister, K. (1990, June). Growing up scared. *The Atlantic Monthly,* pp. 49–66.

CHILDREN
of
VIOLENCE

What Happens to Kids Who Learn as Babies to Dodge Bullets and Step Over Corpses on the Way to School?

LOIS TIMNICK

Lois Timnick is a Times staff writer. Lilia Beebe contributed to this report.

THE morning after a 19-year-old gang member was gunned down at a phone box at 103rd and Grape streets in Watts, his lifeless body lay in a pool of blood on the sidewalk as hundreds of children walked by, lunch boxes and school bags in hand, on their way to the 102nd Street Elementary School. A few months later, during recess, kindergartners at the school dropped to the ground as five shots were fired rapidly nearby, claiming another victim. On still another occasion, an outdoor school assembly was disrupted by the crackle of gunshots and wailing sirens as students watched a neighborhood man scuffle with police officers.

Terrifying occurrences such as these have brought together six youngsters, ages 6 through 11, who sit in a circle around a box of Kleenex in a colorful classroom. The children are a bit fidgety and shy at first, as a psychiatric social worker asks if anyone would like to share a recent event that made them sad. With hesitation, then with the words spilling out, each tells his story—pausing frequently to grab a tissue to wipe away the tears.

"They shoot somebody every day," begins Lester Ford, who is 9 and lives with his mother and brother in the vast Jordan Downs housing project across from the school. When he's playing outside and hears gunshots, the solemn child says softly, "I go in and get under the bed and come out after the shooting stops."

He says he has lost seven relatives. "My daddy got knifed when he got out of jail," Lester explains, and suddenly tears begin streaming down his face. "My uncle got shot in a fight—there was a bucket of his blood. And I had two aunties killed—one of them was pushed off the freeway and there were maggots on her."

Sitting next to Lester, 11-year-old Trevor Dixon, whose mother and father died of natural causes, puts a comforting arm around his friend. "We don't come outside a lot now," he says of himself and his twin sister. "It's like the violence is coming down a little closer."

When it's her turn, 8-year-old Danielle Glover peers through thick glasses and says matter-of-factly: "Just three people [in my family] died." At night their ghosts haunt her, she says. "I been seein' two of them."

This is grief class at the 102nd Street Elementary School, and it is one of the front lines in the battle against violence in South-Central Los Angeles and other urban war zones.

Experts and mental health professionals are just beginning to learn what happens to children like Lester, Trevor and Danielle as they grow into adulthood: **Even if these children of violence survive the drugs, the gangs and the shootings, they might not survive the psychological effects of the constant barrage.**

Though therapists are finding encouraging signs of resiliency, they believe that no child who is victimized, witnesses violent crime or simply grows up in its maelstrom escapes unscathed. Despite a fragmented and sometimes underfunded approach, these researchers are developing therapies to address the problem.

Two years ago, 102nd Street school principal Melba Coleman, the school guidance counselor and the school psychologist had seen some children regress to bed-wetting, others become overly withdrawn or hostile and good students struggle to concentrate. They called on the Los Angeles Unified School District's mental health center, and social worker Deborah Johnson, to develop a way to help the kids overcome their experiences.

So far, 30 children have participated in the weekly hour-long class, which is thought to be the first regular grief and loss program for elementary school students in the nation. They are encouraged to talk about life, death and ways to keep safe in an unsafe world. The hope is that, by sharing their thoughts and emotions with others, the children will come to terms with their feelings of loss, anger and confusion before long-term, irreversible problems develop. And it seems to be working.

Says Kentral Brim, 10, whose two older brothers were killed and who barely escaped injury himself during a gang fight that broke out at Martin Luther King Jr./Drew Medical Center: "I was getting mad and fighting." With the group's help, the neatly dressed, polite young boy says, "I settled down."

SETTLING DOWN IS hard in South-Central Los Angeles, in the shadow of the famous Watts Towers and within a few blocks of four squalid public housing projects. Sleepless nights are punctuated by gunshots, sirens and hovering police helicopters. Liquor stores are routinely robbed. Children as young as 6 are recruited as drug-runners. Some babies' first words and gestures are the names and hand signs of their parents' gangs. The color of a T-shirt can determine whether someone lives or dies, and the most important lesson of childhood is that survival depends on hitting the ground when the inevitable shooting starts. Some families are so fearful that whenever gang warfare flares up, they live behind closed curtains with the lights off, sleeping and eating on the floor to avoid stray bullets.

The scope of violence in South-Central Los Angeles is horrifying. In the first seven months of this year, there have been 237 homicides, 413 rapes, 5,864 robberies and 9,068 aggravated assaults in one of the most turbulent areas of the city. Thirty-five of the homicide victims were under 18. A study headed last year by Dr. Gary Ordog at King/Drew Medical Center found that 34 children under 10 years old were treated there for gunshot wounds between 1980 and 1987. Records showed none in earlier years.

Perhaps most telling of all is the fact that 90% of children taken to the psychiatric clinic at the hospital have witnessed some act of violence, a recent UCLA survey found.

"How can children see all that [violence] and *not* be affected?" asks Gwen Bozart, a third-grade teacher at Compton Avenue Elementary School. Especially when such violence takes place against a landscape of deprivation and failure. Standardized school test scores in South-Central Los Angeles are far below the average for the rest of the city and state. The dropout rate in some high schools is nearly twice that of the rest of the district. More than half the adult population is unemployed. And mental health professionals say depression and suicide attempts are disproportionately high among a despairing population that is barely surviving.

"There's just so much stress that an individual can take before he is completely overwhelmed," notes UCLA child psychiatrist Gloria Johnson Powell, who grew up in the tough Roxbury section of Boston and this fall will establish a center at Harvard University to focus on the special needs of minority children. Often, Powell points out, inner-city children witness violence at home as well as at school and in the streets. They frequently endure abusive family relationships and watch endless hours of romanticized TV violence. "[Many of] these children have daily stress from the time they wake up until they go to bed," she says.

Researchers have found that youngsters growing up in a war-zone environment such as South-Central Los Angeles are likely to become anxious or depressed. Youngsters who have been direct victims or who have witnessed, say, the brutal murder of a parent, are most likely to suffer post-traumatic stress disorder, today's term for a cluster of symptoms recognized in soldiers and others for many years but given labels such as "shellshock" or "combat neurosis."

In children, post-traumatic stress disorder takes the form of reliving the violent experience repeatedly in play, nightmares and sudden memories that intrude during class or other activities. Kids with the disorder can be easily startled, apathetic, hopeless or possessed by a fear of death. Many children regress to early childhood behaviors such as clinginess, become extremely irritable and develop stomachaches and headaches that have no organic cause.

They play differently, too, going beyond the roughhousing that is part of normal child development. Such traumatized children tend to be more aggressive and more willing to take risks—wrestling to hurt companions, for example, or jumping from high places. Others can become inhibited, forsaking sports they used to enjoy; still others might re-enact a gruesome event in play. (The popular childhood game of ring-around-the-rosy with its "ashes, ashes, all fall down" is thought to have originated as a response to the bubonic plague, when children watched people die and saw streets filled with corpses.) A psychiatrist tells of a child who, after having witnessed the stabbing of her mother, painted her hands red with her paintbrush.

Most devastating perhaps for school-age children, post-traumatic stress disorder reduces the ability to concentrate and remember, resulting in poor school performance. But it doesn't stop there. Principal Coleman says the teachers at the 102nd Street school identified about 10% of the school's more than 1,200 youngsters as showing "high risk" behaviors and notes that these children also interfere with the others' ability to learn. "High risk" behaviors, which include repeatedly cursing at and hitting adults, are thought to be early signs that a child could become a social misfit.

Older children sometimes cope by affecting an indifference to the violence around them, experts say. They exhibit an emotional denial that can cripple all of their relationships. The seeming indifference is evident in random conversations with South-Central Los Angeles children over the last year. One group spoke dispassionately of finding a murdered woman's mutilated body—"Her eyeball was in her shoe," a child said. Another group, when told about a fatal shooting, appeared less interested in the victim than in the details of his shiny new truck and its equipment. And, when asked for class field-trip ideas, an 11-year-old boy suggested, "How about the cemetery?"

Other conversations reveal further emotional distancing: Several 8-year-olds discussing whether the murder of a lifeguard was justified because he had ordered someone to get out of the pool agreed that, as one child explained, "Yeah, he [the killer] shudda done it." To them, killing seemed a reasonable response to a perceived insult. A 16-year-old girl at Jordan High School, ticking off the

'The more kids are exposed to violence, the more desensitized they become.'

names of at least nine people who had been shot recently, put it this way: "The ones [bodies] I see in the street that are killed, that don't mean nothin' to me anymore."

Such callous talk among children alerts mental health professionals to underlying emotional difficulties. "You're not going to be very trusting [as an adult] if you observe or have close to you violent behavior," says Santa Monica therapist Ruth Bettelheim, a former consultant to Head Start and daughter of noted child psychologist Bruno Bettelheim. "You tend to keep your distance psychologically—making close and intimate relationships difficult. And that isolation fuels depression, which is already there because of previous losses."

But, Bettelheim says, some children are able to overcome these problems if the adults and children around them can offer support. "It's old psychology wisdom that the same fire that melts butter hardens steel," she adds, so the very violence that spells destruction for one child might make a strong survivor out of another.

Psychiatrist William Arroyo, acting director of the Los Angeles County/USC child-adolescent psychiatric clinic, has studied refugee children from Central America and children from inner-city areas as well. He acknowledges that supportive parents, schools and neighborhoods can serve as buffers against stressful environments, then shakes his head sadly at the fact that South-Central Los Angeles offers so little: Many households are chaotic and headed by uneducated welfare mothers, nutrition and prenatal care are poor, mental health programs are scarce, and Watts doesn't even have a YMCA, where kids can participate in structured activities instead of hanging out and getting into trouble.

"The more they are exposed to violence, the more desensitized they become until it's no longer horrifying but merely an occurrence in daily living," Arroyo says. "We are *very* concerned about those who already have psychiatric disorders and those who have poor impulse control, who then witness violence either in real life or on television. If youngsters learn that the way of succeeding in everyday tasks includes maiming or killing community members, stealing and generally engaging in sorts of behavior that larger society calls criminal, we'll see a larger population of these types."

THE CALENDAR SAYS it happened more than five years ago. But Ana Anaya Gonzalez, now nearly 16, still pictures it clearly. Even when she tries to forget, her scarred body and recurring nightmares have been constant reminders.

It was a winter Friday afternoon in South-Central Los Angeles, just as children were being dismissed from the 49th Street Elementary School. A deranged neighborhood resident fired 57 times at the playground from his second-story window across the street, killing two people and injuring 13 others.

Ana, a fifth-grader at the time, remembers that she was playing on the monkey bars while her sister, Rosa, went back inside to get her sweater.

"I thought it sounded like gunfire, but a friend said, 'No, it's firecrackers.' Then a bullet hit the ground near me, and everybody dropped. I fell on my knees. I couldn't feel my legs, but I didn't know I was hit."

Inside the school, Rosa's teacher pushed her to the floor and fell on top of her to protect her. A passing jogger spotted the sniper, shouted to him to stop and, seeing that Ana was moving, threw himself over her. He was hit by the next round of gunfire and died two months later.

"I was wearing a pink dress," Ana says, "and when I saw it was full of blood, I tried to scream to a teacher in the doorway to help me. He looked at me and then turned around and closed the door."

Ana spent five months in the hospital. She lost a kidney, still suffers leg pain, cannot bend backward and experiences stomach discomfort when she eats. A single bullet wound scars her back; surgical incisions mark her abdomen.

She also suffers from post-traumatic stress disorder, according to Dr. Quinton C. James, the psychiatrist who treated her and several others injured in the sniper attack. "Whether you're talking about violence in Belfast, Beirut or South-Central Los Angeles, I think it all has an impact, although you never know how it will manifest itself in a particular child. Up to a point, one child may adapt with no [apparent] impairment, while for another it may impair [his] ability to function adequately, socially and academically," says James, the former chief of child/adolescent services at the Augustus Hawkins Mental Health Center (a part of King/Drew Medical Center) who now works with the School Mental Health Center and the Centinela Child Guidance Clinic in Inglewood.

Immediately after the attack, mental health professionals from the school district, the Los Angeles County Mental

Art Therapy: Drawing From Experience

Pictures from several schools, clockwise from top, depict a classmate's suicide; a man killing his baby; the "cemetery where baby is"; sadness about a classmate who drowned.

EVEN WHEN children can't verbalize the effect that violence has on them, they sometimes express it by drawing pictures full of blood, guns and knives, says Dr. Spencer Eth, acting chief of psychiatry of the West Los Angeles Veteran's Administration Medical Center and medical director of a trauma unit associated with Cedars-Sinai Medical Center.

Eth worked with the crisis team that responded to the shooting at the 49th Street Elementary School. He says that when children too traumatized to talk are told, "Just draw about anything you want," their pictures reveal much about what's on their minds. This enables therapists to ask children to tell a story, which usually has some connection with the trauma they have suffered.

For example, after a boy threatened to jump off the roof at an elementary school as his horrified classmates watched, children spontaneously made drawings that depicted the incident and the hospital where they imagined the boy was taken.

Says Eth: "Drawing is one of the most effective techniques we have for getting a child to open up and confront difficult feelings—the first step in healing." —L.T.

Health Department, County-USC and UCLA medical centers and the Cedars-Sinai Psychological Trauma Center and various university and private consultants volunteered to help students, as well as parents and teachers. Over the next several weeks, using art therapy (see box above) and in-depth discussions of the shooting, the experts helped those who had witnessed the attack deal with its shattering effects. Social workers continued to work with the children several days a week for the next year.

A month after the shooting, a team headed by Dr. Robert Pynoos, an associate professor of psychiatry at the UCLA School of Medicine, returned to see how the children were doing. Those most severely affected reported feeling stressed, upset and afraid just from thinking about the shooting, and fearful that it might happen again. They complained of jumpiness, nightmares, loss of interest in activities, difficulty paying attention in school and other disturbances. Those who had experienced other violence, an unexpected death or physical injury during the preceding year described having renewed thoughts and images of that event—even if they were not directly exposed to the playground shooting. Many were depressed or grieving a year later, the team found.

"You can cope with it," James says he told Ana at the start of her psychotherapy. "There are things that happen in life, but you don't have to be defeated by them. You'll have physical scars, emotional scars, but you have to accept that it happened and that we don't know why. . . . The thing is you're still alive . . . and there is something you can do. We'll find out together; I'll help you, and so will your family and other relatives, people at school and other agencies."

With her determination and the help of intense psychotherapy, Ana's condition improved. After seeing James every day for the first month she was hospitalized and five days a week for the next four months, she was able to return to finish sixth grade at the 49th Street school, although she never again ventured onto the playground.

Ana continues to progress, but memories of the shooting plague her, James says. As recently as last February—on the anniversary of the incident—she told James: "I still feel the same way. I get scared about things. . . . I get nervous and start crying about the past."

Though she knows the sniper killed himself, Ana occasionally feels as if he is stalking her. She is sometimes afraid to be alone and sleeps in a bed with Rosa. Until recently, she has had a recurring nightmare: A man is chasing her and shoots her. "I wake up when he shoots me and can't go back to sleep."

Formerly an excellent student, Ana has had trouble concentrating, has required a tutor and is working at about average academic level—although her grades are improving at Jefferson High School, where she is now a junior.

Other members of Ana's family are dealing with the shooting as well. Rosa, now 14, appears withdrawn and more traumatized than Ana, perhaps because she has received less therapy, James says. She was reluctant to return to school, avoids discussing the attack and remains fearful and anxious.

Their mother, Esperanza "Blanca" Gonzalez, a waitress who has four other children, suffered a nervous breakdown and had to be hospitalized briefly.

"I feel sick for Ana," Gonzalez says. "She's very nervous and restless in the classroom. She's lost a lot of her spirit." Gonzalez knows that her daughter "cries every night . . . and is sad much of the time," but she says the family cannot afford psychotherapy.

The Gonzalezes live in the same neighborhood, still frightened by the gunshots they hear in the night. "I still get scared," Ana says. "When I hear the shots outside, sometimes I feel like they are shooting at me."

Ana's mother says she remains bitter about the police department's failure to respond to previous complaints about the sniper's brandishing and firing guns. "Until we see blood, we can't do anything about him," she says officers told neighbors.

On the outside, Ana is a pretty, dark-haired teen-ager who appears bubbly, caught up in plans with her girlfriends for her upcoming Sweet 16 birthday party. She landed a summer job selling theater tickets and says she goes to dances and parties as much as possible.

She is talkative—but not about the shooting. "It's not going to change anything to talk about it," she says, then adds, "but I would like to go back to therapy because I like to draw the pictures about what happened. I get too nervous now, and I think talking with the doctor helps."

James adds that Ana is one of the lucky ones, a child whose outlook is much brighter for having a "very supportive network." Without caring family, friends and school person-

nel, she might have become another trauma victim unable to envision a future. But Ana has career hopes, "like maybe becoming a doctor. I liked how they worked when I was in the hospital."

WHILE EDUCATORS and mental health professionals work closely with youngsters in the classroom, researchers continue studying—and in some cases, debating—how violence affects the young.

The first attempts to evaluate scientifically the phenomenon investigated children during wartime. Studies by Anna Freud and others after World War II suggested that children are minimally affected by war and sometimes find it exciting. This work has now been largely debunked. After studying the survivors of Belfast, Cambodia and Beirut, most experts contend instead that the effects of trauma can be masked, delayed or minimized—but never eliminated.

Some experts such as UCLA's Pynoos have found that exposure to violence can cause physiological changes in a child's developing brain stem, altering the brain's chemistry and causing personality changes—such as reduced impulse control, an attraction to danger or a debilitating sense of fear.

But whatever the theory, almost all the experts speak with awe of the emotional strength children possess, even those youngsters from the bleakest backgrounds.

One of the few studies exploring the roots of resilience in young children followed nearly 700 Hawaiian children over a 30-year period, ending in 1985. The study, conducted by Emmy Werner, a child psychologist at the University of California, Davis, found that one out of every four children classified as "high risk" infants had developed into a competent, confident and caring young adult. Some seemed to have a natural strength, but for others, the scales tipped from vulnerability to resilience because the children found strong emotional support at home, school, work or church.

Raiford Woods, manager of the Jordan High Student Health Clinic, sees examples of resiliency every day in the heart of Los Angeles' most violent neighborhood. With or without outside support, some of "these kids are marvelous and have the psychological strength to survive," he says. "You compare a kid from Watts to one from Orange County or Westwood; he can handle twice as much pressure."

Studies and observations like this form the basis for the widely held belief among experts that early intervention is essential—that anti-gang programs must begin in junior high, that grade-school children need support to get them off to a good start and make them less vulnerable, that "drug babies" and preschoolers need special care. And a growing number of programs seek to apply this premise in young lives.

"Some [older children] are lost causes," psychiatrist James says. "We have to focus our attention on those coming along. I met with some youngsters who all told me they'd already been in jail. 'Doc, you're wasting your time with us,' one said. 'You work with our little brothers and sisters.' "

A few Los Angeles programs focus on prevention, others with helping youngsters cope after the damage has been done. The Los Angeles Unified School District, for instance, offers a kindergarten intervention project in which children who are identified as having social problems often stemming from exposure to violence, are assigned a volunteer "special friend" to act as a companion and confidant.

Preschoolers known to have been prenatally exposed to drugs are the focus of a new program at the Salvin Special Education Center, where early childhood specialists try to interrupt behaviors, often violent, that are forerunners of school failure.

At Jordan High School, alone in the district, all ninth-graders are required to take a violence prevention course. Among other things, the course stresses how to avoid fights, how to be manly without being macho and how to deal positively with anger.

UCLA's Program in Trauma, Violence and Sudden Bereavement responds to requests for assistance from cities across the United States where extreme acts of violence—such as sniper attacks, hostage-taking and shootings—have occurred. The Cleveland Elementary School in Stockton asked for assistance after the mass shooting in January. (While these incidents are obviously traumatic, experts say, they differ significantly from the chronic violence experienced in the inner city.) The program also trains mental health professionals, provides counseling and studies children who have witnessed violence in the home or community. Likewise, the Psychological Trauma Center affiliated with Cedars-Sinai Medical Center provides psychological assistance to schools where tragedy has struck.

'These children have stress from the time they wake up until they go to bed.'

Effective ways of coping with a reality that can't be erased are not likely to lie with any single approach, the experts say. Nor can therapy ignore the web of problems that make dealing with violence even worse. Success lies in the cooperative efforts of the police, mental health and health services, schools, churches and concerned parents, and in solutions that address violence as well as drug abuse, poverty and single-parent homes.

Early-prevention programs are important, such as camp programs that give children an opportunity to see the world outside their everyday existence and television. Parents, especially mothers, need exposure to alternatives, with programs that give them a break from the draining responsibil-ity of caring for several children around the clock, on limited resources and without male support. And ways to bring fathers into the system also need to be found.

For two years, the 102nd Street school program has focused mainly on grief and loss. Run by the school staff, the class is based on the theory that, with the support of their peers, troubled children can learn to deal with feelings they might otherwise suppress or act out at school or at home.

The program's pilot group began with social worker Johnson reading a story about a young boy who flew kites with his uncle. The uncle dies—"and there was not a dry eye in the room," Johnson remembers—but at the end, the boy goes out alone with his kite and remembers the good times they had shared. "That set the stage for the rest," she says.

"Our focus is on recognizing and expressing feelings, getting them to come to grips with the fact that they've experienced a loss and leading toward an acceptance that loss is something we all experience," says Johnson, who has spent most of the past 15 years working with disadvantaged children and their families and responding to violent crises at various schools.

Activities in the grief class include using a "feeling board," on which children draw or write whatever they want. Children play a game in which they make faces in a mirror to reflect different feelings, and they perform relaxation exercises such as deep breathing and stretching. They also listen to soft music while they visualize a place that makes them feel good. And they plant small gardens, which helps instill in them a sense of responsibility while symbolizing the beginning, growth and end of all life.

The program has not been scientifically evaluated. Some participants remain deeply troubled and have required referrals for outside counseling, and a few families have moved in hopes that memories will fade faster in a new setting. But teachers say the attitude, behavior and academic performance of most of the youngsters have improved markedly.

It is those little ones who are maturing and progressing amid daily bloodshed who give hope to Johnson and her colleagues.

"Even though all these horrible things are happening, there is a resilience there. These children and their families do respond to interventions. They have strengths even though life circumstances don't allow them to live outside this war zone," she says. "They've seen a lot, but for some some reason they're still children, still trying to walk the tightrope between the craziness of the adult world and a carefree kind of kid world."

CHILDREN AFTER DIVORCE

WOUNDS THAT DON'T HEAL

Judith S. Wallerstein

Judith S. Wallerstein is a psychologist and author of "Second Chances: Men, Women & Children a Decade After Divorce," published by Ticknor & Fields. This article, adapted from the book, was written with the book's co-author, Sandra Blakeslee, who is a regular contributor to The New York Times.

As recently as the 1970's, when the American divorce rate began to soar, divorce was thought to be a brief crisis that soon resolved itself. Young children might have difficulty falling asleep and older children might have trouble at school. Men and women might become depressed or frenetic, throwing themselves into sexual affairs or immersing themselves in work.

But after a year or two, it was expected, most would get their lives back on track, at least outwardly. Parents and children would get on with new routines, new friends and new schools, taking full opportunity of the second chances that divorce brings in its wake.

These views, I have come to realize, were wishful thinking. In 1971, working with a small group of colleagues and with funding from San Francisco's Zellerback Family Fund, I began a study of the effects of divorce on middle-class people who continue to function despite the stress of a marriage breakup.

That is, we chose families in which, despite the failing marriage, the children were doing well at school and the parents were not in clinical treatment for psychiatric disorders. Half of the families attended church or synagogue. Most of the parents were college educated. This was, in other words, divorce under the best circumstances.

Our study, which would become the first ever made over an extended period of time, eventually tracked 60 families, most of them white, with a total of 131 children, for 10, and in some cases 15, years after divorce. We found that although some divorces work well— some adults are happier in the long run, and some children do better than they would have been expected to in an unhappy intact family—more often than not divorce is a wrenching, long-lasting experience for at least one of the former partners. Perhaps most important, we found that for virtually all the children, it exerts powerful and wholly unanticipated effects.

Our study began with modest aspirations. With a colleague, Joan Berlin Kelly—who headed a community mental-health program in the San Francisco area—I planned to examine the short-term effects of divorce on these middle-class families.

We spent many hours with each member of each of our 60 families—hearing their first-hand reports from the battleground of divorce. At the core of our research was the case study, which has been the main source of the fundamental insights of clinical psychology and of psychoanalysis. Many important changes, especially in the long run, would be neither directly observable nor easily measured. They would become accessible only through case studies: by examining the way each of these people processed, responded to and integrated the events and relationships that divorce brings in its wake.

We planned to interview families at the time of decisive separation and filing for divorce, and again 12 to 18 months later, expecting to chart recoveries among men and women and to look at how the children were mastering troubling family events.

We were stunned when, at the second series of visits, we found family after family still in crisis, their wounds wide open. Turmoil and distress had not noticeably subsided. Many adults were angry, and felt humiliated and rejected, and most had not gotten their lives back together. An unexpectedly large number of children were on a downward course. Their symptoms were worse than they had been immediately after the divorce. Our findings were absolutely contradictory to our expectations.

Dismayed, we asked the Zellerbach Fund to support a follow-up study in the fifth year after divorce. To our surprise, interviewing 56 of the 60 families in our original study, we found that although half the men and two-thirds of the women (even many of those suffering economically) said they were more content with their lives, only 34 percent of the children were clearly doing well.

Another 37 percent were depressed, could not concentrate in school, had trouble making friends and suffered a wide range of other behavior problems. While able to function on a daily basis, these children were not recovering, as everyone thought they would. Indeed most of them were on a downward course. This is a powerful statistic, considering that these were children who were functioning well five years before. It would be hard to find any other group of children—except, perhaps, the victims of a natural disaster—who suffered such a rate of sudden serious psychological problems.

The remaining children showed a mixed picture of good achievement in some areas and faltering achievement in others; it was hard to know which way they would eventually tilt.

The psychological condition of these children and adolescents, we found, was related in large part to the overall quality of life in the post-divorce family, to what the adults had been able to build in place of the failed marriage. Children tended to do well if their mothers and fathers, whether or not they remarried, resumed their parenting roles, managed to put their differences aside, and allowed the children a continuing relationship with both parents. Only a handful of kids had all these advantages.

We went back to these families again in 1980 and 1981 to conduct a 10-year follow-up. Many of those we had first interviewed as children were now adults. Overall, 45 percent were doing well; they had emerged as competent, compassionate and courageous people. But 41 percent were doing poorly; they were entering adulthood as worried, underachieving, self-deprecating and sometimes angry young men and women. The rest were strikingly uneven in how they adjusted to the world; it is too soon to say how they will turn out.

At around this time, I founded the Center for the Family in Transition, in Marin County, near San Francisco, which provides counseling to people who are separating, divorcing or remarrying. Over the years, my colleagues and I have seen more than 2,000 families—an experience that has amplified my concern about divorce. Through our work at the center and in the study, we have come to see divorce not as a single circumscribed event but as a continuum of changing family relationships—as a process that begins during the failing marriage and extends over many years. Things are not getting better, and divorce is not getting easier. It's too soon to call our conclusions definitive, but they point to an urgent need to learn more.

It was only at the 10-year point that two of our most unexpected findings became apparent. The first of these is something we call the sleeper effect.

A divorce-prone society is producing its first generation of young adults, men and women so anxious about attachment and love that their ability to create enduring families is imperiled.

The first youngster in our study to be interviewed at the 10-year mark was one who had always been a favorite of mine. As I waited for her to arrive for this interview, I remembered her innocence at age 16, when we had last met. It was she who alerted us to the fact that many young women experience a delayed effect of divorce.

As she entered my office, she greeted me warmly. With a flourishing sweep of one arm, she said, "You called me at just the right time. I just turned 21!" Then she startled me by turning immediately serious. She was in pain, she said.

She was the one child in our study who we all thought was a prime candidate for full recovery. She had denied some of her feelings at the time of divorce, I felt, but she had much going for her, including high intelligence, many friends, supportive parents, plenty of money.

As she told her story, I found myself drawn into unexpected intricacies of her life. Her trouble began, typically, in her late teens. After graduating from high school with honors, she was admitted to a respected university and did very well her freshman year. Then she fell apart. As she told it, "I met my first true love."

The young man, her age, so captivated her that she decided it was time to have a fully committed love affair. But on her way to spend summer vacation with him, her courage failed. "I went to New York instead. I hitchhiked across the country. I didn't know what I was looking for. I thought I was just passing time. I didn't stop and ponder. I just kept going, recklessly, all the time waiting for some word from my parents. I guess I was testing them. But no one—not my dad, not my mom—ever asked me what I was doing there on the road alone."

She also revealed that her weight dropped to 94 pounds from 128 and that she had not menstruated for a year and a half.

"I began to get angry," she said. "I'm angry at my parents for not facing up to the emotions, to the feelings in their lives, and for not helping me face up to the feelings in mine. I have a hard time forgiving them."

I asked if I should have pushed her to express her anger earlier.

She smiled patiently and said, "I don't think so. That was exactly the point. All those years I denied feelings. I thought I could live without love, without sorrow, without anger, without pain. That's how I coped with the unhappiness in my parents' marriage. Only when I met my boyfriend did I become aware of how much feeling I was sitting on all those years. I'm afraid I'll lose him."

It was no coincidence that her acute depression and anorexia occurred just as she was on her way to consummate her first love affair, as she was entering the kind of relationship in which her parents failed. For the first time, she confronted the fears, anxieties, guilt and concerns that she had suppressed over the years.

Sometimes with the sleeper effect the fear is of betrayal rather than commitment. I was shocked when another young woman—at the age of 24, sophisticated, warm and friendly—told me she worried if her boyfriend was even 30 minutes late, wondering who he was with and if he was having an affair with another woman. This fear of betrayal occurs at a frequency that far exceeds what one might expect from a group of people randomly selected from the population. They suffer minute to minute, even though their partners may be faithful.

In these two girls we saw a pattern that we documented in 66 percent of the young women in our study between the ages of 19 and 23; half of them were seriously derailed by it. The sleeper effect occurs at a time when these young women are making decisions with long-term implications for their lives. Faced with issues of commitment, love and sex in an adult context, they are aware that the game is serious. If they tie in with the wrong man, have children too soon, or choose harmful life-styles, the effects can be tragic. Overcome by fears and anxieties, they begin to make connections between these feelings and their parents' divorce:

"I'm so afraid I'll marry someone like my dad."

"How can you believe in commitment when anyone can change his mind anytime?"

"I am in awe of people who stay together."

We can no longer say—as most experts have held in recent years—that girls are generally less troubled by the divorce experience than boys. Our study strongly indicates, for the first time, that girls experience serious effects of divorce at the time they are entering young adulthood. Perhaps the risk for girls and boys is equalized over the long term.

When a marriage breaks down, men and women alike often experience a diminished capacity to parent. They may give less time, provide less discipline and be less sensitive to their children, since they are themselves caught up in the maelstrom of divorce and its aftermath. Many researchers and clinicians find that parents are temporarily unable to separate their children's needs from their own.

In a second major unexpected finding of our 10-year study, we found that fully a quarter of the mothers and a fifth of the fathers had not gotten their lives back on track a decade after divorce. The diminished parenting continued, permanently disrupting the child-rearing functions of the family. These parents were chronically disorganized and, unable to meet the challenges of being a parent, often leaned heavily on their children. The child's role became one of warding off the serious depression that threatened the parents' psychological functioning. The divorce itself may not be solely to blame but, rather, may aggravate emotional difficulties that had been masked in the marriage. Some studies have found that emotionally disturbed parents within a marriage produce similar kinds of problems in children.

These new roles played by the children of divorce are complex and unfamiliar. They are not simple role reversals, as some have claimed, because the child's role becomes one of holding the parent together psychologically. It is more than a caretaking role. This phenomenon merits our careful attention, for it affected 15 percent of the children in our study, which means many youngsters in our society. I propose that we identify as a distinct psychological syndrome the "overburdened child," in the hope that people will begin to recognize the problems and take steps to help these children, just as they help battered and abused children.

One of our subjects, in whom we saw this syndrome, was a sweet 5-year-old girl who clearly felt that she was her father's favorite. Indeed, she was the only person in the family he never hit. Preoccupied with being good and helping to calm both parents, she opposed the divorce because she knew it would take her father away from her. As it turned out, she also lost her mother who, soon after the divorce, turned to liquor and sex, a combination that left little time for mothering.

A year after the divorce, at the age of 6, she was getting herself dressed, making her own meals and putting herself to bed. A teacher noticed the dark circles under her eyes, and asked why she looked so tired. "We have a new baby at home," the girl explained. The teacher, worried, visited the house and discovered there was no baby. The girl's story was designed to explain her fatigue but also enabled her to fantasize endlessly about a caring loving mother.

Shortly after this episode, her father moved to another state. He wrote to her once or twice a year, and when we saw her at the five-year follow-up she pulled out a packet of letters from him. She explained how worried she was that he might get into trouble, as if she were the parent and he the child who had left home.

"I always knew he was O.K. if he drew pictures on the letters," she said. "The last two really worried me because he stopped drawing."

Now 15, she has taken care of her mother for the past 10 years. "I felt it was my responsibility to make sure that Mom was O.K.," she says. "I stayed home with her instead of playing or going to school. When she got mad, I'd let her take it out on me."

I asked what her mother would do when she was angry.

"She'd hit me or scream. It scared me more when she screamed. I'd rather be hit. She always seemed so much bigger when she screamed. Once Mom got drunk and passed out on the street. I called my brothers, but they hung up. So I did it. I've done a lot of things I've never told anyone. There were many times she was so upset I was sure she would take her own life. Sometimes I held both her hands and talked to her for hours I was so afraid."

In truth, few children can rescue a troubled parent. Many become angry at being trapped by the parents' demands, at being robbed of their separate identity and denied their childhood. And they are saddened, sometimes beyond repair, at seeing so few of their own needs gratified.

Since this is a newly identified condition that is just being described, we cannot know its true incidence. I suspect that the number of overburdened children runs much higher than the 15 percent we saw in our study, and that we will begin to see rising reports in the next few years—just as the reported incidence of child abuse has risen since it was first identified as a syndrome in 1962.

The sleeper effect and the overburdened-child syndrome were but two of many findings in our study. Perhaps most important, overall, was our finding that divorce has a lasting psychological effect on many children, one that, in fact, may turn out to be permanent.

Children of divorce have vivid memories about their parents' separation. The details are etched firmly in their minds, more so than those of any other experiences in their lives. They refer to themselves as children of divorce, as if they share an experience that sets them apart from all others. Although many have come to agree that their parents were wise to part company, they nevertheless feel that they suffered from their parents' mistakes. In many instances, conditions in the post-divorce family were more stressful and less supportive to the child than conditions in the failing marriage.

If the finding that 66 percent of the 19- to 23-year-old young women experienced the sleeper effect was most unexpected, others were no less dramatic. Boys, too, were found to suffer unforeseen long-lasting effects. Forty percent of the 19- to 23-year-old young men in our study, 10 years after divorce, still had no set goals, a limited education and a sense of having little control over their lives.

In comparing the post-divorce lives of former husbands and wives, we saw that 50 percent of the women and 30 percent of the men were still intensely angry at their former spouses a decade after divorce. For women over 40 at divorce, life was lonely throughout the decade; not one in our study remarried or sustained a loving relationship. Half the men over 40 had the same problem.

In the decade after divorce, three in five children felt rejected by one of their parents, usually the father—whether or not it was true. The frequency and duration of visiting made no difference. Children longed for their fathers, and the need increased during adolescence. Thirty-four percent of the youngsters went to live with their fathers during adolescence for at least a year. Half returned to the mother's home disappointed with what they had found. Only one in seven saw both mother and father happily remarried after 10 years. One in two saw their mother or their father undergo a second divorce. One in four suffered a severe and enduring drop in the family's standard of living and went on to observe a lasting discrepancy between their parents' standards of living.

We found that the children who were best adjusted 10 years later were those who showed the most distress at the time of the divorce—the youngest. In general, pre-schoolers are the most frightened and show the most dramatic symptoms when marriages break up. Many are afraid that they will be abandoned by both parents and they have trouble sleeping or staying by themselves. It is therefore surprising to find that the same children 10 years later seem better adjusted than their older siblings. Now in early and mid-adolescence, they were rated better on a wide range of psychological dimensions than the older children. Sixty-eight percent were doing well, compared with less than 40 percent of older children. But whether having been young at the time of divorce will continue to protect them as they enter young adulthood is an open question.

Our study shows that adolescence is a period of particularly grave risk for children in divorced families. Through rigorous analysis, statistical and otherwise, we were able to see clearly that we weren't dealing simply with the routine angst of young people going through transition but rather that, for most of them, divorce was the single most important cause of enduring pain and anomie in their lives. The young people told us time and again how much they needed a family structure, how much they wanted to be protected, and how much they yearned for clear guidelines for moral behavior. An alarming number of teenagers felt abandoned, physically and emotionally.

For children, divorce occurs during the formative years. What they see and experience becomes a part of their inner world, influencing their own relationships 10 and 15 years later, especially when they have witnessed violence between the parents. It is then, as these young men and women face the developmental task of establishing love and intimacy, that they most feel the lack of a template for a loving relationship between a man and a woman. It is here that their anxiety threatens their ability to create new, enduring families of their own.

As these anxieties peak in the children of divorce throughout our society, the full legacy of the rising divorce rate is beginning to hit home. The new families being formed today by these children as they reach adulthood appear particularly vulnerable.

Because our study was such an early inquiry, we did not set out to compare children of divorce with children from intact families. Lacking fundamental knowledge about life after the breakup of a marriage, we could not know on what basis to build a comparison or control group. Was the central issue one of economics, age, sex, a happy intact marriage—or would any intact marriage do? We began, therefore, with a question—What is the nature of the divorce experience?—and in answering it we would generate hypotheses that could be tested in subsequent studies.

This has indeed been the case. Numerous studies have been conducted in different regions of the country, using control groups, that have further explored and validated our findings as they have emerged over the years. For example, one national study of 699 elementary school children carefully compared children six years after their parents' divorce with children from intact families. It found—as we did—that elementary-age boys from divorced families show marked discrepancies in peer relationships, school achievement and social adjustment. Girls in this group, as expected, were hardly distinguishable based on the experience of divorce, but, as we later found out, this would not always hold up. Moreover, our findings are supported by a litany of modern-day statistics. Although one in three children are from divorced families, they account for an inordinately high proportion of children in mental-health treatment, in special-education classes, or referred by teachers to school psychologists. Children of divorce make up an estimated 60 percent of child patients in clinical treatment and 80 percent—in some cases, 100 percent—of adolescents in inpatient mental hospital settings. While no one would claim that a cause and effect relationship has been established in all of these cases, no one would deny that the role of divorce is so persuasively suggested that it is time to sound the alarm.

All studies have limitations in what they can accomplish. Longitudinal studies, designed to establish the impact of a major event or series of events on the course of a subsequent life, must always allow for the influence of many interrelated factors. They must deal with chance and the uncontrolled factors that so often modify the sequences being followed. This is particularly true of children, whose lives are influenced by developmental changes, only some of which are predictable, and by the problem of individual differences, about which we know so little.

Our sample, besides being quite small, was also drawn from a particular population slice—predominately white, middle class and relatively privileged suburbanites.

Despite these limitations, our data have generated working hypotheses about the effects of divorce that can now be tested with more precise methods, including appropriate control groups. Future research should be aimed at testing, correcting or modifying our initial findings, with larger and more diverse segments of the population. For example, we found that children—especially boys and young men—continued to need their fathers after divorce and suffered feelings of rejection even when they were visited regularly. I would like to see a study comparing boys and girls in sole and joint custody, spanning different developmental stages, to see if greater access to both parents counteracts these feelings of rejection. Or, does joint custody lead to a different sense of rejection—of feeling peripheral in both homes?

It is time to take a long, hard look at divorce in America. Divorce is not an event that stands alone in childrens' or adults' experience. It is a continuum that begins in the unhappy marriage and extends through the separation, divorce and any remarriages and second divorces. Divorce is not necessarily the sole culprit. It may be no more than one of the many experiences that occur in this broad continuum.

Profound changes in the family can only mean profound changes in society as a whole. All children in today's world feel less protected. They sense that the institution of the family is weaker than it has ever been before. Even those children raised in happy, intact families worry that their families may come undone. The task for society in its true and proper perspective is to strengthen the family—all families.

A biblical phrase I have not thought of for many years has recently kept running through my head: "Watchman, what of the night?" We are not I'm afraid, doing very well on our watch—at least for our children. We are allowing them to bear the psychological, economic and moral brunt of divorce.

And they recognize the burdens. When one 6-year-old boy came to our center shortly after his parents' divorce, he would not answer questions; he played games instead. First he hunted all over the playroom for the sturdy Swedish-designed dolls that we use in therapy. When he found a good number of them, he stood the baby dolls firmly on their feet and placed the miniature tables, chairs, beds and, eventually, all the playhouse furniture on top of them. He looked at me, satisfied. The babies were supporting a great deal. Then, wordlessly, he placed all the mother and father dolls in precarious positions on the steep roof of the doll house. As a father doll slid off the roof, the boy caught him and, looking up at me, said, "He might die." Soon, all the mother and father dolls began sliding off the roof. He caught them gently, one by one.

"The babies are holding up the world," he said.

Although our overall findings are troubling and serious, we should not point the finger of blame at divorce per se. Indeed, divorce is often the only rational solution to a bad marriage. When people ask whether they should stay married for the sake of the children, I have to say, "Of course not." All our evidence shows that children exposed to open conflict, where parents terrorize or strike one another, turn out less well-adjusted than do children from divorced families. And although we lack systematic studies comparing children in divorced families with those in unhappy intact families, I am convinced that it is not useful to provide children with a model of adult behavior that avoids problem-solving and that stresses martyrdom, violence or apathy. A divorce undertaken thoughtfully and realistically can teach children how to confront serious life problems with compassion, wisdom and appropriate action.

Our findings do not support those who would turn back the clock. As family issues are flung to the center of our political arena, nostalgic voices from the right argue for a return to a time when divorce was more difficult to obtain. But they do not offer solutions to the wretchedness and humiliation within many marriages.

Still we need to understand that divorce has consequences—we need to go into the experience with our eyes open. We need to know that many children will suffer for many years. As a society, we need to take steps to preserve for the children as much as possible of the social, economic and emotional security that existed while their parents' marriage was intact.

Like it or not, we are witnessing family changes which are an integral part of the wider changes in our society. We are on a wholly new course, one that gives us unprecedented opportunities for creating better relationships and stronger families—but one that also brings unprecedented dangers for society, especially for our children.

WAAAH!

Why kids have a lot to cry about

David Elkind, Ph.D.

David Elkind, Ph.D., professor of child study at Tufts University, is the author of more than 400 articles. He is perhaps best known for his books The Hurried Child; All Grown Up and No Place to Go *and* Ties That Stress: Childrearing in a Postmodern Society. *He is an active consultant to government agencies, private foundations, clinics, and mental-health centers.*

"MOMMY," THE FIVE-YEAR-OLD GIRL asked her mother, "why don't you get divorced again?" Her thrice-married mother was taken aback and said in return, "Honey, why in the world should I do that?" To which her daughter replied, "Well, I haven't seen you in love for such a long time."

This young girl perceives family life and the adult world in a very different way than did her counterpart less than half a century ago. Likewise, the mother perceives her daughter quite differently than did a mother raising a child in the 1940s. Although this mother was surprised at her daughter's question, she was not surprised at her understanding of divorce, nor at her familiarity with the symptoms of romance.

As this anecdote suggests, there has been a remarkable transformation over the last 50 years in our children's perceptions of us, and in our perceptions of our children. These altered perceptions are a very small part of a much larger tectonic shift in our society in general and in our families in particular. This shift is nothing less than a transformation of the basic framework, or paradigm, within which we think about and thus perceive our world. To understand the changes in the family, the perceptions of family members, and of parenting that have been brought about, we first have to look at this broader "paradigm shift" and what it has meant for family sentiments, values, and perceptions.

FROM MODERN TO POSTMODERN

Without fully realizing it perhaps, we have been transported into the postmodern era. Although this era has been called "postindustrial" and, alternatively, "information age," neither of these phrases is broad enough to encompass the breadth and depth of the changes that have occurred. The terms modern and postmodern, in contrast, encompass all aspects of society and speak to the changes in science, philosophy, architecture, literature, and the arts—as well as in industry and technology—that have marked our society since mid-century.

THE MODERN AND THE NUCLEAR FAMILY

The modern era, which began with the Renaissance and spanned the Industrial Revolution, was based upon three related assumptions. One was the idea of *human progress*—the notion that the natural direction of human and societal development is toward a more equitable, peaceful, and harmonious world in which every individual would be entitled to life, liberty, and the pursuit of happiness. A

From *Psychology Today,* May/June 1992, pp. 38-41, 80-83. © 1992 by Sussex Publishers, Inc. Reprinted by permission.

We are so caught up in our perception of kids' competence that we teach five-year-olds about AIDS and child abuse, and give them toys that simulate pregnancy and dismemberment.

second assumption is *universality*. There were, it was taken as given, universal laws of nature of art, science, economics, and so on that transcended time and culture. The third basic assumption was that of *regularity*—the belief that the world is an orderly place, that animals and plants, geological layers and chemical elements could be classified in an orderly hierarchy. As Einstein put it, "God does not play dice with the universe!"

These assumptions gave a unique character and distinctiveness to modern life. Modern science, literature, architecture, philosophy, and industry all embodied these premises. And they were enshrined in the Modern Family as well. The modern nuclear family, for example, was seen as the end result of a progressive evolution of family forms. Two parents, two or three children, one parent working and one staying home to rear the children and maintain the home was thought to be the ideal family form toward which all prior, "primitive" forms were merely preliminary stages.

SENTIMENTS OF THE NUCLEAR FAMILY

The Modern Family was shaped by three sentiments that also reflected the underlying assumptions of modernity. One of these was Romantic Love. In premodern times, couples married by familial and community dictates. Considerations of property and social position were paramount. This community influence declined in the modern era, and couples increasingly came to choose one another on the basis of mutual attraction. This attraction became idealized into the notion that "Some enchanted evening, you will meet a stranger" for whom you and only you were destined ("You were meant for me, I was meant for you"), and that couples would stay together for the rest of their lives, happily "foreveraftering."

A second sentiment of the Modern Family was that of Maternal Love—the idea that women have a maternal "instinct" and a need to care for children, particularly when they are small. The idea of a maternal instinct was a thoroughly modern invention that emerged only after modern medicine and nutrition reduced infant mortality. In premodern times, infant mortality was so high that the young were not even named until they were two years old and stood a good chance of surviving. It was also not uncommon for urban parents to have their infants "wet-nursed" in the country. Often these

infants died because the wet-nurse fed her own child before she fed the stranger, and there was little nourishment left. Such practices could hardly be engaged in by a mother with a "maternal instinct."

The third sentiment of the Modern Family was Domesticity, a belief that relationships within the family are always more powerful and binding than are those outside it. The family was, as Christopher Lasch wrote, "a haven in a heartless world." As a haven, the nuclear family shielded and protected its members from the evils and temptations of the outside world. This sentiment also extended to the family's religious, ethnic, and social-class affiliations. Those individuals who shared these affiliations were to be preferred, as friends and spouses, over those with different affiliations.

PARENTING THE INNOCENT

The modern perceptions of parenting, children, and teenagers grew out of these family sentiments. Modern parents, for example, were seen as intuitively or instinctively knowledgeable about child-rearing. Professional help was needed only to encourage parents to do "what comes naturally." In keeping with this view of parenting was the perception of children as innocent and in need of parental nurturance and protection. Teenagers, in turn, were seen as immature and requiring adult guidance and direction. Adolescence, regarded as the age of preparation for adulthood, brought with it the inevitable "storm and stress," as young people broke from the tight nuclear family bonds and became socially and financially independent.

These modern perceptions of parenting

and of children and youth were reinforced by the social mirror of the media, the law and the health professions. Motion pictures such as the Andy Hardy series (starring Mickey Rooney) depicted a teenage boy getting into youthful scrapes at school and with friends from which he was extricated by his guardian the judge, played by Harlan Stone. Fiction similarly portrayed teenagers as immature young people struggling to find themselves. Mark Twain's Huck Finn was an early version of the modern immature adolescent, while J. D. Salinger's Holden Caulfield is a modern version.

Modern laws, such as the child-labor laws and compulsory-education statutes were enacted to protect both children and adolescents. And the health professions attributed the mental-health problems of children and youth to conflicts arising from the tight emotional bonds of the nuclear family.

POSTMODERNITY AND THE POSTMODERN FAMILY

The postmodern view has largely grown out of the failure of modern assumptions about progress, universality, and regularity. Many of the events of this century have made the idea of progress difficult to maintain. Germany, one of the most educationally, scientifically, and culturally advanced countries of the world, engaged in the most heinous genocide. Modern science gave birth to the atomic bomb that was dropped on Hiroshima and Nagasaki. Environmental degradation, pollution, population explosions, and widespread famine can hardly be reconciled with the notion of progress.

Secondly, the belief in universal principles has been challenged as the "grand" theories of the modern era—such as those of Marx, Darwin, and Freud——are now recognized as limited by the social and historical contexts in which they were elaborated. Modern theorists believed that they could transcend social-historical boundaries; the postmodern worker recognizes that he or she is constrained by the particular discourse of narrative in play at the time. Likewise, the search for abiding ethical, moral, and religious universals is giving way to a recognition that there are many different ethics, moralities, and religions, each of which has a claim to legitimacy.

Finally, the belief in regularity has given way to a recognition of the importance of irregularity, indeterminacy, chaos, and fuzzy logic. There is much in nature, such as the weather, that remains unpredictable—not because it is perverse, but only because the weather is affected by non-regular events. Sure regularity appears, but irregularity is now seen as a genuine phenomenon in its own right. It is no longer seen, as it was in the modern era, as the result of some failure to discover an underlying regularity.

In place of these modern assumptions, a new, postmodern paradigm with its own basic premises has been invented. The assumption of progress, to illustrate, has given way to the presumption of *difference*. There are many different forms and types of progress, and not all progressions are necessarily for the better. Likewise, the belief in universals has moved aside for the belief in *particulars*. Different phenomena may have different rules and principles that are not necessarily generalizable. For example, a particular family or a particular class of children is a non-replicable event that can never be exactly duplicated and to which universal principles do not apply. Finally, the assumption of regularity moved aside to make room for the principle of *irregularity*. The world is not as orderly and as logically organized as we had imagined.

As the societal paradigm has shifted, so has the structure of the family. The ideal nuclear family, thought to be the product of progressive social evolution, has given way to what might be called the *Permeable Family* of the postmodern era. The Permeable Family encompasses many different family forms: traditional or nuclear, two-parent working, single-parent, blended, adopted child, test-tube, surrogate mother, and co-parent families. Each of these is valuable and a potentially successful family form.

Rapid social change is a catastrophe for children and youths, who require stability and security for healthy growth and development.

The family is permeable in other ways as well. It is no longer isolated from the larger community. Thanks to personal computers, fax and answering machines, the workplace has moved into the homeplace. The homeplace, in turn, thanks to childcare facilities in office buildings and factories, has moved into the workplace. The home is also permeated by television, which brings the outside world into the living room and bedrooms. And an ever-expanding number of TV shows (*Oprah, Donahue, Geraldo, and Sally Jessy Raphael*), all detailing the variety of family problems, brings the living room and the bedroom into the outside world.

Quite different sentiments animate the postmodern Permeable Family than animated the modern nuclear family. The transformation of family sentiments came about in a variety of ways, from the civil-rights movement, the women's movement, changes in media, and laws that were part of the postmodern revolution. Because there is a constant interaction between the family and the larger society, it is impossible to say whether changes in the family were brought about by changes in society or vice versa. Things moved in both directions.

For a number of reasons, the Modern Family sentiment of Romantic Love has been transformed in the Postmodern era into the sentiment of *Consensual Love*. In contrast to the idealism and perfectionism of Romantic Love, consensual love is realistic and practical. It recognizes the legitimacy of premarital relations and is not premised on long-term commitment. Consensual Love is an agreement or contract between the partners; as an agreement it can be broken. The difference between Romantic Love and Consensual Love is summed up in the prenuptial agreement, which acknowledges the possible rupture of a marriage——before the marriage actually occurs. The current emphasis upon safe sex is likewise a symptom of consensual, not romantic, love.

The Modern Family sentiment of ma-

ternal love has yielded to other changes. Today, more than 50 percent of women are in the workforce, and some 60 percent of these women have children under the age of six. These figures make it clear that non-maternal and non-parental figures are now playing a major role in child-rearing. As part of this revision of child-rearing responsibilities, a new sentiment has emerged that might be called *shared parenting*. What this sentiment entails is the understanding that not only mothers, but fathers and professional caregivers are a necessary part of the child-rearing process. Child-rearing and childcare are no longer looked upon as the sole or primary responsibility of the mother.

The permeability of the Postmodern Family has also largely done away with the Modern Family sentiment of domesticity. The family can no longer protect individuals from the pressures of the outside world. Indeed, the impulse of the Permeable Family is to move in the other direction. Permeable Families tend to thrust children and teenagers forward to deal with realities of the outside world at ever earlier ages. This has resulted in what I have called the "hurrying" of children to grow up fast. Much of the hurrying of children and youth is a well-intentioned effort on the part of parents to help prepare children and youth for the onrush of information, challenges, and temptations coming at them through the now-permeable boundaries of family life.

POSTMODERN PARENTS
OF KIDS WITHOUT INNOCENCE

These new, postmodern sentiments have given rise to new perceptions of parenting, of children, and of adolescents. Now that parenting is an activity shared with non-parental figures, we no longer regard it as an instinct that emerges once we have become parents; it is now regarded as a matter of learned *technique*.

Postmodern parents understand that doing "what comes naturally" may not be good for children. There are ways to say things to children that are less stressful than others. There are ways of disciplining that do not damage the child's sense of self esteem. The problem for parents today is to choose from the hundreds of books and other media sources bombarding them with advice on child-rearing. As one mother said to me, "I've read your books and they sound okay, but what if you're wrong?"

With respect to children, the perception of childhood innocence has given way to the perception of childhood competence. Now that children are living in Permeable Families with—thanks to television—a steady diet of overt violence, sexuality, substance abuse, and environmental degradation, we can no longer assume they are innocent. Rather, perhaps to cover our own inability to control what our children are seeing, we perceive them as competent to deal with all of this material. Indeed, we get so caught up in this perception of competence that we teach four- and five-year-olds about AIDS and child abuse and provide "toys" that simulate pregnancy or the dismemberment that accidents can cause unbuckled-up occupants. And the media reinforce this competence perception with films such as *Look Who's Talking* and *Home Alone*.

If children are seen as competent, teenagers can no longer be seen as immature. Rather they are now seen as sophisticated in the ways of the world, knowledgeable about sex, drugs, crime, and much more. This is a convenient fiction for parents suffering a time-famine. Such parents can take the perception of teenage sophistication as a rationale to abrogate their responsibility to provide young people with limits, guidance, and supervision. Increasingly, teenagers are on their own. Even junior and senior high schools no longer provide the social programs and clubs they once did.

This new perception of teenagers is also reflected in the social mirror of media, school and law. Postmodern films like *Risky Business* (in which teenager runs a bordello in the parents' home) and *Angel* (demure high school student by day, avenging hooker by night) are a far cry from the Andy Hardy films. Postmodern TV sitcoms such as *Married with Children* and *Roseanne* present images of teenage sophistication hardly reconcilable with the teenagers portrayed in modern TV shows such as *My Three Sons* or *Ozzie and Harriet*. Postmodern legal thinking is concerned with protecting the *rights* of children and teenagers, rather than protecting children themselves. Children and teenagers can now sue their parents for divorce, visitation rights, and for remaining in the United States when the family travels overseas.

REALITY IS HERE TO STAY

The postmodern perceptions of children as competent and of teenagers as sophisticated did not grow out of any injustices nor harm visited upon children and youth. Rather they grew out of a golden era for young people that lasted from the end of the last century to the middle of this one. Society as a whole was geared to regard children as innocent and teenagers as immature, and sought to protect children and gradually inculcate teenagers into the ways of the world.

In contrast, the perceptions of childhood competence and teenage sophistication have had detrimental effects upon children and youth. Indeed, these perceptions have placed children and teenagers under inordinate stress. And it shows. On every measure that we have, children and adolescents are doing less well today than they did a quarter century ago, when the new postmodern perceptions were coming into play. While it would be unwise to attribute all of these negative effects to changed perceptions alone—economics and government policy clearly played a role—it is also true that government policy and economics are affected by the way young people are perceived.

The statistics speak for themselves. There has been a 50-percent increase in obesity in children and youth over the past two decades. We lose some ten thousand teenagers a year in substance-related accidents, not including injured and maimed. One in four teenagers drinks to excess every two weeks, and we have two million alcoholic teenagers.

Teenage girls in America get pregnant at the rate of one million per year, twice the rate of the next Western country, England. Suicide has tripled among teenagers in the last 20 years, and between five and six thousand teenagers take their own lives each year. It is estimated that one out of four teenage girls manifests at least one symptom of an eating disorder, most commonly severe dieting. The 14- to 19-year-old age group has the second-highest homicide rate of any age group.

These are frightening statistics. Yet they are not necessarily an indictment of the postmodern world, nor of our changed perceptions of children and youth. We have gone through enormous social changes in a very brief period of time. No other society on Earth changes, or can change, as rapidly as we do. That is both our strength and our weakness. It has made us, and will keep us, the leading industrial nation in the world because we are more flexible than any other society, including Japan.

But rapid social change is a catastrophe for children and youth, who require stability and security for healthy growth and development. Fortunately, we are now moving toward a more stable society. A whole generation of parents was caught in the transition between Modern and Postmodern Family sentiments; among them, divorce, open marriage, and remarriage became at least as commonplace as the permanent nuclear family. The current generation of parents have, however, grown up with the new family sentiments and are not as conflicted as their own parents were.

As a result, we are slowly moving back to a more realistic perception of both children and teenagers, as well as toward a family structure that is supportive of all family members. We are moving towards what might be called the *Vital Family*. In the Vital Family, the modern value of togetherness is given equal weight with the Postmodern Family value of autonomy. Children are seen as *growing into competence* and as still needing the help and support of parents. Likewise, teenagers are increasingly seen as *maturing into sophistication*, and able to benefit from adult guidance, limits, and direction.

These new perceptions pop up in the media. Increasingly, newspapers and magazines feature articles on the negative effects pressures for early achievement have upon children. We are also beginning to see articles about the negative effects the demands for sophistication place upon teenagers. A number of recent TV shows (such as *Beverly Hills 90210*) have begun to portray children and youth as sophisticated, but also as responsible and accepting of adult guidance and supervision. There is still much too much gratuitous sex and violence, but at least there are signs of greater responsibility and recognition that children and adolescents may not really be prepared for everything we would like to throw at them.

After 10 years off traveling and lecturing all over the country, I have an impression is that the American family is alive and well. It has changed dramatically, and we are still accommodating to the changes. And, as always happens, children and youths are more harmed by change than are adults. But our basic value system remains intact. We do have a strong Judeo-Christian heritage; we believe in hard work, democracy, and autonomy. But our sense of social and parental responsibility, however, was temporarily deadened by the pace of social change. Now that we are getting comfortable in our new Permeable Family sentiments and perceptions, we are once again becoming concerned with those who are young and those who are less fortunate.

As human beings we all have a need to become the best that we can be. But we also have a need to love and to be loved, to care and to be cared for. The Modern Family spoke to our need to belong at the expense, particularly for women, of the need to become.

The Permeable Family, in contrast, celebrates the need to become at the expense of the need to belong, and this has been particularly hard on children and youth. Now we are moving towards a Vital Family that ensures both our need to become and our need to belong. We are not there yet, but the good news is, we are on our way.

ALIENATION

AND THE FOUR WORLDS OF CHILDHOOD

The forces that produce youthful alienation are growing in strength and scope, says Mr. Bronfenbrenner. And the best way to counteract alienation is through the creation of connections or links throughout our culture. The schools can build such links.

Urie Bronfenbrenner

Urie Bronfenbrenner is Jacob Gould Shurman Professor of Human Development and Family Studies and of Psychology at Cornell University, Ithaca, N.Y.

To be alienated is to lack a sense of belonging, to feel cut off from family, friends, school, or work—the four worlds of childhood.

At some point in the process of growing up, many of us have probably felt cut off from one or another of these worlds, but usually not for long and not from more than one world at a time. If things weren't going well in school, we usually still had family, friends, or some activity to turn to. But if, over an extended period, a young person feels unwanted or insecure in several of these worlds simultaneously or if the worlds are at war with one another, trouble may lie ahead.

What makes a young person feel that he or she doesn't belong? Individual differences in personality can certainly be one cause, but, especially in recent years, scientists who study human behavior and development have identified an equal (if not even more powerful) factor: the circumstances in which a young person lives.

Many readers may feel that they recognize the families depicted in the vignettes that are to follow. This is so because they reflect the way we tend to look at families today: namely, that we see parents as being good or not-so-good without fully taking into account the circumstances in their lives.

Take Charles and Philip, for example. Both are seventh-graders who live in a middle-class suburb of a large U.S. city. In many ways their surroundings seem similar; yet, in terms of the risk of alienation, they live in rather different worlds. See if you can spot the important differences.

CHARLES

The oldest of three children, Charles is amiable, outgoing, and responsible. Both of his parents have full-time jobs outside the home. They've been able to arrange their working hours, however, so that at least one of them is at home when the children return from school. If for some reason they can't be home, they have an arrangement with a neighbor, an elderly woman who lives alone. They can phone her and ask her to look after the children until they arrive. The children have grown so fond of this woman that she is like another grandparent—a nice situation for them, since their real grandparents live far away.

Homework time is one of the most important parts of the day for Charles and his younger brother and sister. Charles's parents help the children with their homework if they need it, but most of the time they just make sure that the children have a period of peace and quiet—without TV—in which to do their work. The children are allowed to watch television one hour each night—but only after they have completed their homework. Since Charles is doing well in school, homework isn't much of an issue, however.

Sometimes Charles helps his mother or father prepare dinner, a job that everyone in the family shares and enjoys. Those family members who don't cook on a given evening are responsible for cleaning up.

Charles also shares his butterfly collection with his family. He started the collection when he first began learning about butterflies during a fourth-grade science project. The whole family enjoys picnicking and hunting butterflies together, and Charles occasionally asks his father to help him mount and catalogue his trophies.

Charles is a bit of a loner. He's not a very good athlete, and this makes him somewhat self-conscious. But he does have one very close friend, a boy in his class who lives just down the block. The two boys have been good friends for years.

Charles is a good-looking, warm, happy young man. Now that he's beginning to be interested in girls, he's gratified to find that the interest is returned.

PHILIP

Philip is 12 and lives with his mother, father, and 6-year-old brother. Both of his parents work in the city, commuting more than an hour each way. Pandemonium strikes every weekday morning as

From *Phi Delta Kappan*, February 1986, pp. 430-436. Reprinted by permission of the author and Phi Delta Kappan.

171

the entire family prepares to leave for school and work.

Philip is on his own from the time school is dismissed until just before dinner, when his parents return after stopping to pick up his little brother at a nearby day-care home. At one time, Philip took care of his little brother after school, but he resented having to do so. That arrangement ended one day when Philip took his brother out to play and the little boy wandered off and got lost. Philip didn't even notice for several hours that his brother was missing. He felt guilty at first about not having done a better job. But not having to mind his brother freed him to hang out with his friends or to watch television, his two major after-school activities.

The pace of their life is so demanding that Philip's parents spend their weekends just trying to relax. Their favorite weekend schedule calls for watching a ball game on television and then having a cookout in the back yard. Philip's mother resigned herself long ago to a messy house; pizza, TV dinners, or fast foods are all she can manage in the way of meals on most nights. Philip's father has made it clear that she can do whatever she wants in managing the house, as long as she doesn't try to involve him in the effort. After a hard day's work, he's too tired to be interested in housekeeping.

Philip knows that getting a good education is important; his parents have stressed that. But he just can't seem to concentrate in school. He'd much rather fool around with his friends. The thing that he and his friends like to do best is to ride the bus downtown and go to a movie, where they can show off, make noise, and make one another laugh.

Sometimes they smoke a little marijuana during the movie. One young man in Philip's social group was arrested once for having marijuana in his jacket pocket. He was trying to sell it on the street so that he could buy food. Philip thinks his friend was stupid to get caught. If you're smart, he believes, you don't let that happen. He's glad that his parents never found out about the incident.

Once, he brought two of his friends home during the weekend. His parents told him later that they didn't like the kind of people he was hanging around with. Now Philip goes out of his way to keep his friends and his parents apart.

THE FAMILY UNDER PRESSURE

In many ways the worlds of both

> Institutions that play important roles in human development are rapidly being eroded, mainly through benign neglect.

teenagers are similar, even typical. Both live in families that have been significantly affected by one of the most important developments in American family life in the postwar years: the employment of both parents outside the home. Their mothers share this status with 64% of all married women in the U.S. who have school-age children. Fifty percent of mothers of preschool children and 46% of mothers with infants under the age of 3 work outside the home. For single-parent families, the rates are even higher: 53% of all mothers in single-parent households who have infants under age 3 work outside the home, as do 69% of all single mothers who have school-age children.[1]

These statistics have profound implications for families — sometimes for better, sometimes for worse. The determining factor is how well a given family can cope with the "havoc in the home" that two jobs can create. For, unlike most other industrialized nations, the U.S. has yet to introduce the kinds of policies and practices that make work life and family life compatible.

It is all too easy for family life in the U.S. to become hectic and stressful, as both parents try to coordinate the disparate demands of family and jobs in a world in which everyone has to be transported at least twice a day in a variety of directions. Under these circumstances, meal preparation, child care, shopping, and cleaning — the most basic tasks in a family — become major challenges. Dealing with these challenges may sometimes take precedence over the family's equally important child-rearing, educational, and nurturing roles.

But that is not the main danger. What

threatens the well-being of children and young people the most is that the external havoc can become internal, first for parents and then for their children. And that is exactly the sequence in which the psychological havoc of families under stress usually moves.

Recent studies indicate that conditions at work constitute one of the major sources of stress for American families.[2] Stress at work carries over to the home, where it affects first the relationship of parents to each other. Marital conflict then disturbs the parent/child relationship. Indeed, as long as tensions at work do not impair the relationship between the parents, the children are not likely to be affected. In other words, the influence of parental employment on children is indirect, operating through its effect on the parents.

That this influence is indirect does not make it any less potent, however. Once the parent/child relationship is seriously disturbed, children begin to feel insecure — and a door to the world of alienation has been opened. That door can open to children at any age, from preschool to high school and beyond.

My reference to the world of school is not accidental, for it is in that world that the next step toward alienation is likely to be taken. Children who feel rootless or caught in conflict at home find it difficult to pay attention in school. Once they begin to miss out on learning, they feel lost in the classroom, and they begin to seek acceptance elsewhere. Like Philip, they often find acceptance in a group of peers with similar histories who, having no welcoming place to go and nothing challenging to do, look for excitement on the streets.

OTHER INFLUENCES

In contemporary American society the growth of two-wage-earner families is not the only — or even the most serious — social change requiring accommodation through public policy and practice in order to avoid the risks of alienation. Other social changes include lengthy trips to and from work; the loss of the extended family, the close neighborhood, and other support systems previously available to families; and the omnipresent threat of television and other media to the family's traditional role as the primary transmitter of culture and values. Along with most families today, the families of Charles and Philip are experiencing the unraveling and disintegration of social institutions that in the past were central to the health and well-being of children and their parents.

Notice that both Charles and Philip come from two-parent, middle-class families. This is still the norm in the U.S. Thus neither family has to contend with two changes now taking place in U.S. society that have profound implications for the future of American families and the well-being of the next generation. The first of these changes is the increasing number of single-parent families. Although the divorce rate in the U.S. has been leveling off of late, this decrease has been more than compensated for by a rise in the number of unwed mothers, especially teenagers. Studies of the children brought up in single-parent families indicate that they are at greater risk of alienation than their counterparts from two-parent families. However, their vulnerability appears to have its roots not in the single-parent family structure as such, but in the treatment of single parents by U.S. society.[3]

In this nation, single parenthood is almost synonymous with poverty. And the growing gap between poor families and the rest of us is today the most powerful and destructive force producing alienation in the lives of millions of young people in America. In recent years, we have witnessed what the U.S. Census Bureau calls "the largest decline in family income in the post-World War II period." According to the latest Census, 25% of all children under age 6 now live in families whose incomes place them below the poverty line.

COUNTERING THE RISKS

Despite the similar stresses on their families, the risks of alienation for Charles and Philip are not the same. Clearly, Charles's parents have made a deliberate effort to create a variety of arrangements and practices that work against alienation. They have probably not done so as part of a deliberate program of "alienation prevention" — parents don't usually think in those terms. They're just being good parents. They spend time with their children and take an active interest in what their children are thinking, doing, and learning. They control their television set instead of letting it control them. They've found support systems to back them up when they're not available.

Without being aware of it, Charles's parents are employing a principle that the great Russian educator Makarenko employed in his extraordinarily success-

ful programs for the reform of wayward adolescents in the 1920s: "The maximum of support with the maximum of challenge."[4] Families that produce effective, competent children often follow this principle, whether they're aware of it or not. They neither maintain strict control nor allow their children total freedom. They're always opening doors — and then giving their children a gentle but firm shove to encourage them to move on and grow. This combination of support and challenge is essential, if children are to avoid alienation and develop into capable young adults.

From a longitudinal study of youthful alienation and delinquency that is now considered a classic, Finnish psychologist Lea Pulkkinen arrived at a conclusion strikingly similar to Makarenko's. She found "guidance" — a combination of love and direction — to be a critical predictor of healthy development in youngsters.[5]

No such pattern is apparent in Philip's family. Unlike Charles's parents, Philip's parents neither recognize nor respond to the challenges they face. They have dispensed with the simple amenities of family self-discipline in favor of whatever is easiest. They may not be indifferent to their children, but the demands of their jobs leave them with little energy to be actively involved in their children's lives. (Note that Charles's parents have work schedules that are flexible enough to allow one of them to be at home most afternoons. In this regard, Philip's family is much more the norm, however. One of the most constructive steps that employers could take to strengthen families would be to enact clear policies making such flexibility possible.)

But perhaps the clearest danger signal in Philip's life is his dependence on his peer group. Pulkkinen found heavy reliance on peers to be one of the strongest predictors of problem behavior in adolescence and young adulthood. From a developmental viewpoint, adolescence is a time of challenge — a period in which young people seek activities that will serve as outlets for their energy, imagination, and longings. If healthy and constructive challenges are not available to them, they will find their challenges in such peer-group-related behaviors as poor school performance, aggressiveness or social withdrawal (sometimes both), school absenteeism or dropping out, smoking, drinking, early and promiscuous sexual activity, teenage parenthood, drugs, and juvenile delinquency.

This pattern has now been identified in a number of modern industrial societies, including the U.S., England, West Germany, Finland, and Australia. The pattern is both predictable from the circumstances of a child's early family life and predictive of life experiences still to come, e.g., difficulties in establishing relationships with the opposite sex, marital discord, divorce, economic failure, criminality.

If the roots of alienation are to be found in disorganized families living in disorganized environments, its bitter fruits are to be seen in these patterns of disrupted development. This is not a harvest that our nation can easily afford. Is it a price that other modern societies are paying, as well?

A CROSS-NATIONAL PERSPECTIVE

The available answers to that question will not make Americans feel better about what is occurring in the U.S. In our society, the forces that produce youthful alienation are growing in strength and scope. Families, schools, and other institutions that play important roles in human development are rapidly being eroded, *mainly through benign neglect.* Unlike the citizens of other modern nations, we Americans have simply not been willing to make the necessary effort to forestall the alienation of our young people.

As part of a new experiment in higher education at Cornell University, I have been teaching a multidisciplinary course for the past few years titled "Human Development in Post-Industrial Societies." One of the things we have done in that course is to gather comparative data from several nations, including France, Canada, Japan, Australia, Germany, England, and the U.S. One student summarized our findings succinctly: "With respect to families, schools, children, and youth, such countries as France, Japan, Canada, and Australia have more in common with each other than the United States has with any of them." For example:

• The U.S. has by far the highest rate of teenage pregnancy of any industrialized nation — twice the rate of its nearest competitor, England.
• The U.S. divorce rate is the highest in the world — nearly double that of its nearest competitor, Sweden.
• The U.S. is the only industrialized society in which nearly one-fourth of all infants and preschool children live in families whose incomes fall below the

poverty line. These children lack such basics as adequate health care.

• The U.S. has fewer support systems for individuals in all age groups, including adolescence. The U.S. also has the highest incidence of alcohol and drug abuse among adolescents of any country in the world.[6]

All these problems are part of the unraveling of the social fabric that has been going on since World War II. These problems are not unique to the U.S., but in many cases they are more pronounced here than elsewhere.

WHAT COMMUNITIES CAN DO

The more we learn about alienation and its effects in contemporary post-industrial societies, the stronger are the imperatives to counteract it. If the essence of alienation is disconnectedness, then the best way to counteract alienation is through the creation of connections or links.

For the well-being of children and adolescents, the most important links must be those between the home, the peer group, and the school. A recent study in West Germany effectively demonstrated how important this basic triangle can be. The study examined student achievement and social behavior in 20 schools. For all the schools, the researchers developed measures of the links between the home, the peer group, and the school. Controlling for social class and other variables, the researchers found that they were able to predict children's behavior from the number of such links they found. Students who had no links were alienated. They were not doing well in school, and they exhibited a variety of behavioral problems. By contrast, students who had such links were doing well and were growing up to be responsible citizens.[7]

In addition to creating links within the basic triangle of home, peer group, and school, we need to consider two other structures in today's society that affect the lives of young people: the world of work (for both parents and children) and the community, which provides an overarching context for all the other worlds of childhood.

Philip's family is one example of how the world of work can contribute to alienation. The U.S. lags far behind other industrialized nations in providing child-care services and other benefits designed to promote the well-being of children and their families. Among the most needed benefits are maternity and paternity leaves, flex-time, job-sharing

> Caring is surely an essential aspect of education in a free society; yet we have almost completely neglected it.

arrangements, and personal leaves for parents when their children are ill. These benefits are a matter of course in many of the nations with which the U.S. is generally compared.

In contemporary American society, however, the parents' world of work is not the only world that both policy and practice ought to be accommodating. There is also the children's world of work. According to the most recent figures available, 50% of all high school students now work part-time — sometimes as much as 40 to 50 hours per week. This fact poses a major problem for the schools. Under such circumstances, how can teachers assign homework with any expectation that it will be completed?

The problem is further complicated by the kind of work that most young people are doing. For many years, a number of social scientists — myself included — advocated more work opportunities for adolescents. We argued that such experiences would provide valuable contact with adult models and thereby further the development of responsibility and general maturity. However, from their studies of U.S. high school students who are employed, Ellen Greenberger and Lawrence Steinberg conclude that most of the jobs held by these youngsters are highly routinized and afford little opportunity for contact with adults. The largest employers of teenagers in the U.S. are fast-food restaurants. Greenberger and Steinberg argue that, instead of providing maturing experiences, such settings give adolescents even greater exposure to the values and lifestyles of their peer group. And the adolescent peer group tends to emphasize immediate gratification and consumerism.[8]

Finally, in order to counteract the

mounting forces of alienation in U.S. society, we must establish a working alliance between the private sector and the public one (at both the local level and the national level) to forge links between the major institutions in U.S. society and to re-create a sense of community. Examples from other countries abound:

• Switzerland has a law that no institution for the care of the elderly can be established unless it is adjacent to and shares facilities with a day-care center, a school, or some other kind of institution serving children.

• In many public places throughout Australia, the Department of Social Security has displayed a poster that states, in 16 languages: "If you need an interpreter, call this number." The department maintains a network of interpreters who are available 16 hours a day, seven days a week. They can help callers get in touch with a doctor, an ambulance, a fire brigade, or the police; they can also help callers with practical or personal problems.

• In the USSR, factories, offices, and places of business customarily "adopt" groups of children, e.g., a day-care center, a class of schoolchildren, or a children's ward in a hospital. The employees visit the children, take them on outings, and invite them to visit their place of work.

We Americans can offer a few good examples of alliances between the public and private sectors, as well. For example, in Flint, Michigan, some years ago, Mildred Smith developed a community program to improve school performance among low-income minority pupils. About a thousand children were involved. The program required no change in the regular school curriculum; its principal focus was on building links between home and school. This was accomplished in a variety of ways.

• A core group of low-income parents went from door to door, telling their neighbors that the school needed their help.

• Parents were asked to keep younger children out of the way so that the older children could complete their homework.

• Schoolchildren were given tags to wear at home that said, "May I read to you?"

• Students in the high school business program typed and duplicated teaching materials, thus freeing teachers to work directly with the children.

• Working parents visited school classrooms to talk about their jobs and about how their own schooling now helped them in their work.

WHAT SCHOOLS CAN DO

As the program in Flint demonstrates, the school is in the best position of all U.S. institutions to initiate and strengthen links that support children and adolescents. This is so for several reasons. First, one of the major — but often unrecognized — responsibilities of the school is to enable young people to move from the secluded and supportive environment of the home into responsible and productive citizenship. Yet, as the studies we conducted at Cornell revealed, most other modern nations are ahead of the U.S. in this area.

In these other nations, schools are not merely — or even primarily — places where the basics are taught. Both in purpose and in practice, they function instead as settings in which young people learn "citizenship": what it means to be a member of the society, how to behave toward others, what one's responsibilities are to the community and to the nation.

I do not mean to imply that such learnings do not occur in American schools. But when they occur, it is mostly by accident and not because of thoughtful planning and careful effort. What form might such an effort take? I will present here some ideas that are too new to have stood the test of time but that may be worth trying.

Creating an American classroom. This is a simple idea. Teachers could encourage their students to learn about schools (and, especially, about individual classrooms) in such modern industrialized societies as France, Japan, Canada, West Germany, the Soviet Union, and Australia. The children could acquire such information in a variety of ways: from reading, from films, from the firsthand reports of children and adults who have attended school abroad, from exchanging letters and materials with students and their teachers in other countries. Through such exposure, American students would become aware of how attending school in other countries is both similar to and different from attending school in the U.S.

But the main learning experience would come from asking students to consider what kinds of things *should* be happening — or not happening — in American classrooms, given our nation's values and ideals. For example, how should children relate to one another and to their teachers, if they are doing things in an *American* way? If a student's idea seems to make sense, the American tradition of pragmatism makes the next step obvious: try the idea to see if it works.

The curriculum for caring. This effort also has roots in our values as a nation. Its goal is to make caring an essential part of the school curriculum. However, students would not simply learn about caring; they would actually engage in it. Children would be asked to spend time with and to care for younger children, the elderly, the sick, and the lonely. Caring institutions, such as daycare centers, could be located adjacent to or even within the schools. But it would be important for young caregivers to learn about the environment in which their charges live and the other people with whom their charges interact each day. For example, older children who took responsibility for younger ones would become acquainted with the younger children's parents and living arrangements by escorting them home from school.

Just as many schools now train superb drum corps, they could also train "caring corps" — groups of young men and women who would be on call to handle a variety of emergencies. If a parent fell suddenly ill, these students could come into the home to care for the children, prepare meals, run errands, and serve as an effective source of support for their fellow human beings. Caring is surely an essential aspect of education in a free society; yet we have almost completely neglected it.

Mentors for the young. A mentor is someone with a skill that he or she wishes to teach to a younger person. To be a true mentor, the older person must be willing to take the time and to make the commitment that such teaching requires.

We don't make much use of mentors in U.S. society, and we don't give much recognition or encouragement to individuals who play this important role. As a result, many U.S. children have few significant and committed adults in their lives. Most often, their mentors are their own parents, perhaps a teacher or two, a coach, or — more rarely — a relative, a neighbor, or an older classmate. However, in a diverse society such as ours, with its strong tradition of volunteerism, potential mentors abound. The schools need to seek them out and match them with young people who will respond positively to their particular knowledge and skills.

The school is the institution best suited to take the initiative in this task, because the school is the only place in which all children gather every day. It is also the only institution that has the right (and the responsibility) to turn to the community for help in an activity that represents the noblest kind of education: the building of character in the young.

There is yet another reason why schools should take a leading role in rebuilding links among the four worlds of childhood: schools have the most to gain. In the recent reports bemoaning the state of American education, a recurring theme has been the anomie and chaos that pervade many U.S. schools, to the detriment of effective teaching and learning. Clearly, we are in danger of allowing our schools to become academies of alienation.

In taking the initiative to rebuild links among the four worlds of childhood, U.S. schools will be taking necessary action to combat the destructive forces of alienation — first, within their own walls, and thereafter, in the life experience and future development of new generations of Americans.

1. Urie Bronfenbrenner, "New Worlds for Families," paper presented at the Boston Children's Museum, 4 May 1984.
2. Urie Bronfenbrenner, "The Ecology of the Family as a Context for Human Development," *Developmental Psychology*, in press.
3. Mavis Heatherington, "Children of Divorce," in R. Henderson, ed., *Parent-Child Interaction* (New York: Academic Press, 1981).
4. A.S. Makarenko, *The Collective Family: A Handbook for Russian Parents* (New York: Doubleday, 1967).
5. Lea Pulkkinen, "Self-Control and Continuity from Childhood to Adolescence," in Paul Baltes and Orville G. Brim, eds., *Life-Span Development and Behavior*, Vol. 4 (New York: Academic Press, 1982), pp. 64-102.
6. S.B. Kamerman, *Parenting in an Unresponsive Society* (New York: Free Press, 1980); S.B. Kamerman and A.J. Kahn, *Social Services in International Perspective* (Washington, D.C.: U.S. Department of Health, Education, and Welfare, n.d.); and Lloyd Johnston, Jerald Bachman, and Patrick O'Malley, *Use of Licit and Illicit Drugs by America's High School Students — 1975-84* (Washington, D.C.: U.S. Government Printing Office, 1985).
7. Kurt Aurin, personal communication, 1985.
8. Ellen Greenberger and Lawrence Steinberg, *The Work of Growing Up* (New York: Basic Books, forthcoming).

Culture, race too often ignored in child studies

Tina Adler

Monitor staff

SEATTLE

Child development researchers have not paid enough attention to both the environmental conditions in which children grow up and their cultural and racial identities, researchers said at an ethics symposium at the biennial meeting of the Society for Research in Child Development (SRCD) here. As a result of these and other oversights, they said they fear the findings may not apply to a wide population or get at the core of what makes children tick.

Although research practices per se are not unethical, many researchers are not sufficiently informed about cultural and racial influences and that can cause them to develop faulty studies, the researchers suggested. And there are ethical implications when the studies' findings are applied that need to be examined, said psychologist Celia Fisher. Researchers at the symposium outlined their opinions of the problems with studies and how the problems evolved.

For example, the speakers said that studies too often do not include subjects from different cultural and racial backgrounds. As a result, these studies' findings don't apply to those different groups. And that means researchers are not able to design good interventions or help those children as well as they might.

Researchers identified other problems with child development studies. For instance, too many researchers don't describe their subjects' racial or socioeconomic background in the studies. They often overlook the very powerful influence of the environment on children. Also, many studies are too short to find out if children could be helped by a specific intervention. More attention needs to be given to the special needs of high-risk children, who are increasingly the subjects of child development research.

Many child development researchers don't study minority infants who are not at a high risk for developmental problems, said Fisher, who is at Fordham University. As a result, little is known about healthy minority children. That may not violate any ethical code but is unjust because it makes it hard to design good interventions for them when needed, she said.

"At present, most data on low-risk infants cannot be generalized beyond the behaviors of white, middle-class families," she said.

In one recent review of infant studies in major child development journals, Fisher found that almost half of the 102 articles "did not report cultural background or ethnicity of their sample." Of those that did, seven studies looked only at minority subjects, 26 examined only whites and nine included mixed samples.

The studies were no better in their treatment of socioeconomic status, she said. Also, of the studies that do report race, many just look at whites.

In an interview, Fisher offered several possible explanations for these findings.

Researchers may be looking at mixed groups, but not reporting the ethnic make-up of their subject pool because of a notion from the 1960s that it would be derogatory, she said. Researchers who look at whites only and neglect to say so may assume readers will think that if no race is specified, the subjects are white.

Others may not describe the racial or economic backgrounds of their subjects, or not use a varied subject pool, because "some people assume there are universal aspects of development and don't see any need to test cultural differences," she said.

Still other researchers may want to include a more varied pool than they can get access to. Some communities, such as the college campus or surrounding community where researchers get their subjects from, are populated primarily by one race. Also, researchers tend to get infant subjects by reading birth announcements and calling the parents, who are often middle-class, she said.

Funding plays a role as well in limiting the scope of research. Federal and state agencies tend to support projects that look at social problems. That results in more research on poor people, including lower class minorities, she said. As a result, normative data for healthy, middle-class minorities doesn't exist, she said.

These problems are being addressed "little by little," she said. "It's very slow, but the attendance at our [SRCD] symposium was indicative of the interest people have in this."

It is critical to look at children's socioeconomic and cultural background, because poverty is a much stronger predictor of how children will develop than all other factors combined, said Lewis P. Lipsitt, executive director for science at the American Psychological Association and a Brown University child research psychologist. Yet not enough research is being done on the environment's influence, he said at the conference.

Many people still think that tests are the best predictors of children's outcomes, he said.

"Our society is too test-happy. . . . We overlook the processes and mechanisms that got [the test taker] to that point in the first place," he said in an interview.

T. Berry Brazelton, a pediatrician at Harvard Medical School, agreed, saying that the trouble with most assessment scales is that the environment is the best predictor of outcome, particularly for high-risk children. Brazelton developed the scale named after him that measures very young infants' development.

The most exciting findings right now are coming from neuropsychological work, said Brazelton. Researchers are discovering that children's minds and bodies can bounce back from a variety of insults, such as the abuses of poverty, better than scientists had realized. This makes intervention even more important, he said.

Both federal and private agencies that fund research make poor decisions at times about what they will and won't fund. The reason for the poor decisions concerning behavioral science is, in part, "because there are natural human biases against studying human behavior," he said. For example, agencies are reluctant to fund surveys on people's sexual behavior. Also, behavioral science research proposals on crib death, the leading cause of death for babies, have been poorly funded.

In addition, review committees are at times closed-minded about the reasonableness of research proposals in general, and about the rights of researchers to do studies, Lipsitt said.

"Review committees act as though

the mere act of research is an imposition on humans," he said. Instead, they need to operate from the viewpoint that "people have the right to benefit from research results, and thus from the research enterprise. We need data on human behavior in order to help people."

Psychologist Michael Lewis of the Robert Wood Johnson Medical School also decried the limitations put on researchers. Researchers are often forced to implement interventions with limited funds and to end them too soon. As a result, it appears that many interventions don't work, he said. That leads some policy makers to conclude that the people whom the interventions are designed for can't really be helped, he said.

As a result, researchers' work may inadvertently support what he calls a "conservative world view," which holds that change is relatively difficult.

Some policy-makers and researchers also fall prey to viewing interventions in general as cures that last forever, Lewis said. That is like thinking you can go to confession "once in 1962 and that should save your soul forever," Lewis said.

Interventions are too often falsely assumed by researchers and policy-makers to work equally well for all kids, such as shy and extroverted kids. Instead of looking at the aggregate results for all children and deciding if an intervention works, researchers should see which children it worked or did not work for, and then design another program for the latter group.

The goals of an intervention also have to be reconsidered, he said.

"We've decided that smarter is the most important outcome, but why didn't we choose happier?" Lewis said. Emotional outcomes need more attention, he believes. He pointed out that suicide is the third leading cause of death for children.

Asked in an interview where the money would come from for interventions with a limitless expense account, Lewis said if the United States has billions of dollars for the Persian Gulf

war, it can find money for thorough interventions and evaluations.

Much of what he discussed is published in a chapter in *Ethics in Applied Developmental Psychology: Emerging Issues in an Emerging Field,* published in 1990 by Abelex Publishing Corporation and edited by Celia Fisher.

Researchers are becoming increasingly aware of ethical issues as they turn their focus to high-risk babies. In studying this group, researchers are faced with ethical dilemmas that are not part of the picture in studies of low-risk children, Fisher said. For example, researchers can't just study high-risk children and not help them. And the parents' desperate need for help may influence researchers' responses.

"When research enters the lives of vulnerable families, ethical concerns . . . play an increasingly central role in research design and implementation," Fisher said.

As part of the design and implementation of a study, researchers need to promote participants' welfare and their right to make decisions about their lives, she said. They also need to ensure that the knowledge gained from the study is applicable to a wide group by not just studying one racial or socio-economic group, for example. The study's finding should also be distributed widely, she wrote in a paper presented at the conference.

"Informed consent is seen by many as the major means of protecting the rights of research participants," she wrote. But for participants to be truly informed, the information needs to be tailored to their cognitive level, language ability, cultural background and to their societal expectations, she wrote.

Finally, she said, researchers may uncover a variety of developmental problems, psychological distress or maltreatment when studying high-risk children. Researchers need to make clear to the parents what of this information they will share with them and others during the course of the study.

Tracked to Fail

In today's schools, children who test poorly may lose the chance for a quality education. Permanently.

Sheila Tobias

Sheila Tobias is the author of Breaking the Science Barrier *(1992),* Succeed With Math *(1987) and* Overcoming Math Anxiety *(1978).*

No one who has ever read Aldous Huxley's anti-utopian novel, *Brave New World,* can forget the book's opening scene, a tour of the "Hatchery and Conditioning Centre." There human embryos in their first hours of existence are transformed into Alphas, Betas, Gammas, Deltas and Epsilons—the five social classes that collectively meet the economy's manpower needs. Arrested in their development, the Gamma, Delta and Epsilon embryos are programmed *in vitro* for a lower-class future. After "birth," whatever individuality remains with these pre-ordained proletarians will be conditioned out of each child, until there is no one in this brave new world who does not grow up accepting and even loving his bleak servitude.

Huxley's totalitarian embryology may seem fanciful to us, but his real message was political, not technological. Huxley understood, as he wrote in the foreword to the 1946 edition of *Brave New World,* that any "science of human differences" would enable the authorities to assess the relative capacities of each of us and then assign everybody his or her appropriate place in society. Huxley's vision of the modern state, with its desire for social control, implies that the discovery that ability can be measured will suggest that it *should* be. Similarly, the knowledge that people can be sorted by ability will lead irresistibly to the belief that they ought to be.

Today, many educators contend that a "science of human differences" does exist in the form of standardized tests for intelligence and ability. And, as Huxley foresaw, the pressures have grown to put these discriminating instruments to use. Education in this country is becoming a process of separating the "gifted" from the "average," the "intelligent" from the "slow"—one is tempted to say, the wheat from the chaff. From an early age, children are now ranked and sorted (a process known variably as tracking, ability grouping or screening) as they proceed through school. Those who test well are encour-

aged and expected to succeed and offered the most challenging work. Those who do not, get a watered-down curriculum that reflects the system's minimal expectations of them.

All this is a far cry from the vision of schooling that America's founding educators had in mind. Horace Mann, the father of American public education and the influential first secretary of the Massachusetts board of education from 1837 to 1848, thought public education would be "the great equalizer" in a nation of immigrants. For over a century now, Mann's egalitarian vision, translated into educational policy, has helped millions of immigrants to assimilate and to prosper here. But this vision is now threatened by a competing view of individual potential—and worth. We are becoming a society where test-taking skills are the prerequisites for a chance at getting a good education, and where hard work, hope and ambition are in danger of becoming nothing more than meaningless concepts.

A poor showing on tests was once a signal to all concerned—child, teacher, parents—that greater effort was needed to learn, or to teach, what was required. It didn't mean that a child *couldn't* learn. But the damaging assumption behind testing and tracking as they are now employed in many schools is that *only* those who test well are capable of learning what is needed to escape an adult life restricted to menial, dead-end jobs. This new message imparted by our schools is profoundly inegalitarian: that test-measured ability, not effort, is what counts. What many students are learning is that they are *not* equal to everybody else. Gammas, Deltas and Epsilons shouldn't even try to compete with Alphas. Alphas are better, *born* better, and it is impossible for others to catch up. What's tragic about this change is not just that it's unjust—but that it's untrue.

A Lifetime of Testing

In a private Los Angeles primary school, a 4-year-old is being taught to play a game-like test he is going to have to pass to show that he is ready for kindergarten. This is the first in an endless series of evaluations that will determine who he is, what he can learn and how far he will go in school. Just before the test begins, the counselor hands him the red plastic cube he will use. But he doesn't need her cube. He has taken this test so often, as his parents drag him around from his preschool admissions screenings, that when the time comes to play, he pulls his *own* bright red cube out of his pocket. Whether or not he is ready for this particular school, he is more than ready for the test.

Each year after this child's admission to kindergarten, he will take "norm-referenced tests" to show his overall achievement against those of his age group and "criterion-referenced tests," which examine the specific skills he is supposed to have learned in each grade. Even if he and his parents are not told his test scores (a practice that varies from school to school), ability-grouping in elementary school will soon let him know where he stands. "By the second or third grade," says Susan Harter, a psychology professor at the University of Denver who studies social development in children, "children know precisely where they stand on the 'smart or dumb' continuum, and since most children at this age want to succeed in school, this knowledge profoundly affects their self-esteem."

The point is that today "smart or dumb" determinations are made very early. "Those who come to school knowing how to read or who learn very quickly are pronounced bright," says Jeannie Oakes, author of *Keeping Track: How Schools Structure Inequality.* "Those for whom reading is still a puzzle at the end of the first grade are judged slow." And these early decisions stick. As children proceed through the elementary grades, more and more of their course work is grouped by ability. By ninth grade, 80% to 90% of students are in separate classes determined by whether they are judged to be "fast," "average" or "slow."

Magnifying Our Differences

Tracking in all its variants is rarely official policy, and the validity and fairness of standardized testing have long been under fire. Nevertheless, both tracking and testing are becoming more common. As a result, argues University of Cincinnati education professor Joel Spring (in unwitting resonance with Huxley), education in America has become a "sorting machine."

Moreover, the stunting effects of this machine may remain with students for a lifetime. "Adults can remember well into middle age whether they were 'sharks' or 'goldfish' in reading," says Bill Kelly, professor of education at Regis College in Denver. Students learn whether they have good verbal skills or mathematical ones. They learn whether or not they are musically or mechanically inclined, and so on. There are millions of adults who carry with them the conviction that they "can't do math" or play an instrument or write well. And it may all be the result of assessments made of them and internalized as children — long before they had any idea of what they wanted from life. Their sense of inadequacy may prevent them from exploring alternative careers or simply narrow their experiences.

Why are testing and tracking on the rise? Oakes, who has studied more than 13,000 junior- and senior-high-school students, their schools and their teachers, suggests that the answer has several components. They range from the focus on educational excellence during the last decade to widespread public confidence that testing is an accurate, appropriate way of gauging educational potential. Oakes also believes that testing and tracking comprise a not-so-subtle effort to resegregate desegregated schools. But they reflect as well a preference among teachers for "homogeneous groupings" of students, which are easier to teach than classes composed of students of varying abilities.

Whatever the motives, Oakes is convinced that the basic premise of the whole system is wrong. There is no way, she says, to determine accurately the potential of young or even older children by standardized tests. One key reason: Such examinations are always fine-tuned to point out differences, not similarities. They eliminate those items that everyone answers the same way — either right or wrong. Thus, small differences that may or may not measure ability in general are amplified to give the test makers what they want, namely ease of sorting. Test results, then, will make any group of individuals appear to be more different than they really are.

Benjamin Bloom, Distinguished Service Professor Emeritus of Education at the University of Chicago, agrees. "I find that many of the individual differences in school learning are man-made and accidental rather than fixed in the individual at the time of conception," he writes in his book *All Our Children Learning.* "When students are provided with unfavorable learning conditions, they become even more dissimilar." Bloom concedes that some longitudinal studies show that between grades 3 and 11, for example, children's rank in class remains virtually the same. But this is not because intelligence is fixed, he argues. It is the result of the unequal, unsupportive education the schools provide. So long as schools think there is little they can do about "learning ability," says Bloom, they will see their task as weeding out the poorer learners while encouraging the better learners to get as much education as they can.

Watered-Down Education

Research generated by Oakes and others supports Bloom, revealing that placement in a low track has a corroding impact on students' self esteem. Worse yet, because there are real differences not just in level but in the *content* of what is being taught, tracking may in fact contribute to academic failure.

Students in low-track courses are almost never exposed to what educators call "high-status knowledge," the kind that will be useful in colleges and universities. They do not read works of great literature in their English classes, Oakes's team found, and instead of critical-thinking skills and expository writing, low-track students are taught standard English usage and "functional literacy," which involves mainly filling out forms, job applications and the like. In mathematics, high-track students were exposed to numeration, computational systems, mathematical models, probability and statistics in high school. "In contrast," writes Oakes, "low-track classes focused grade after grade on basic computational skills and arithmetic facts" and sometimes on simple measurement skills and converting English to metric.

More generally, Oakes's team also found that high-track classes emphasize reasoning ability over simple memorization of disembodied facts. Low-track students, meanwhile, are taught by rote, with an emphasis on conformity. "Average" classes — the middle track — resembled those in the high track, but they are substantially "watered down."

Is this discriminatory system the only way to handle differences in ability among students? One innovative program is challenging that notion. Called "accelerated learning," it is the creation of Henry M. Levin, a professor of education and economics at Stanford University. Levin, an expert on worker-managed companies, decided to apply the principles of organizational psychology to an analysis of the crisis in education. He began with a two-year-study, during which he surveyed the literature on education and looked at hundreds of evaluations of at-risk students at elementary and middle schools. Fully one-third of all students, he estimated, were "educationally disadvantaged" in some way, were consigned to a low track and were falling farther and farther behind in one or more areas. These children needed remedial help, but that help, Levin writes, treated "such students and their educators as educational discards, marginal to mainstream education." For them, the pace of instruction was slowed to a crawl and progressed by endless repetition. The whole system seemed designed to demoralize and fail everyone who was a part of it. As Levin told one reporter, "As soon as you begin to talk about kids needing remediation, you're talking about damaged merchandise. And as soon as you have done that, you have lost the game."

To try to change the game, Levin designed and is helping to implement the Accelerated Schools Program. Now being tested in California, Utah, Missouri and (this fall) Illinois, the project accepts that elementary school children who are having academic problems *do* need special assistance, but it departs radically from traditional tracking in every other respect. First, Accelerated Schools are expected to have all their students learning at grade level by the time they reach the sixth grade. In other words, the remedial track exists only to get students off it. Collectively, the teachers and administrators at each school are allowed to design their own curricula, but they must create a clear set of measurable (and that means testable) goals for students to meet each year they are in the program. Finally, it is expected that the curriculum, whatever its specifics, will be challenging and fast-paced and will emphasize abstract reasoning skills and a sophisticated command of English.

Levin's program reflects the current administration's view that business practice has much to contribute to schooling. Levin wants schools to find a better way to produce what might be called their product — that is, children willing and able to get the quality education they will need in life. To do this, he recognizes that schools must offer better performance incentives to students, teachers and administrators. "Everyone benefits from the esprit de corps," explains Levin, "and the freedom to experiment with curriculum and technique — which we also encourage — is an incentive for teachers." By insisting upon school and teacher autonomy, the regular attainment of measurable goals and the development of innovative, engaging curricula, Accelerated Schools also hope to erase the stigma associated with teaching or needing remediation. The early results of this six-year test program are encouraging: The Hoover Elementary School in Redwood City, CA, one of the first schools to embark on the project, is reporting a 22 percentile increase in sixth-grade reading scores, actually outperforming state criteria. Both Levin and Ken Hill, the district superintendent, caution that these results are preliminary and the improved scores could be due to many factors other than the Accelerated Schools Program. But regardless of the program's measurable impact, Hill sees real changes in the school. "Teachers are now working with the kids on science projects and developing a literature-based reading program. There's a positive climate, and all the kids are learners."

Another alternative to tracking is what Bloom calls "mastery learning." He believes that it is the rate of learning, not the capacity to learn, that differentiates students with "high" or "low" abilities. This is a critical distinction, for we are rapidly approaching the day when all but the most menial jobs will require relatively complex reasoning and technical skills.

In a mastery class, children are given as much time as they need to become competent at a certain skill or knowledge level.

Teachers must take 10% to 15% more time with their classes and break the class down into small groups in which the fast learners help their peers along. In time, the slower students catch up both in the amount of knowledge acquired and in the rate at which they learn. Though slow students may start out as much as five times slower than their classmates, Bloom says, "in mastery classes, fast and slow students become equal in achievement and increasingly similar in their learning rates."

At present, fewer than 5% of the nation's schools are following either of these promising strategies, estimates Gary Fenstermacher, dean of the University of Arizona's College of Education. He is a firm believer that de-tracking in some form must be the educational wave of the future. "There are ethical and moral imperatives for us to do whatever we can to increase the equality of access to human knowledge and understanding," he says.

Second Class and Dropping Out

Until society responds to those ethical and moral imperatives, however, the educational system, with its testing, tracking and discriminatory labeling, will continue on its questionable course. Today, around 25% of America's teenagers — 40% to 60% in inner-city schools — do not graduate from high school, according to Jacqueline P. Danzberger of the Institute for Educational Leadership in Washington, DC. Most of the attrition occurs by the third year of high school, and many educators believe increased testing is a contributing factor.

Norman Gold, former director of research for the District of Columbia's public school system, says school dropouts are linked to the raising of standards (with no compensatory programs) in the late 1970s and the end of "social promotions" — the habit of routinely allowing failing students to move to a higher grade. "Studies show," he says, "that the risk of dropping out goes up 50% if a child fails one school year." Neil Shorthouse, executive director of Atlanta's Cities in Schools, which enrolls 750 teenagers on the point of dropping out, agrees. "Most of these kids quit school," he says of his students, "because they repeatedly get the message that they are bad students, 'unteachables.'"

Ending social promotions was long overdue. What purpose is served by graduating high-school students who can't read, write or do simple arithmetic? But schools have done little to help these failing students catch up. The present system is continuing to produce a whole class of people, particularly inner-city blacks and Hispanics, who have little economic role in our society. High school, Gold observes, has become an obstacle course that a significant number of young people are unable to negotiate. "We expect them to fail. We have to have greater expectations, and equally great support."

These failing students are missing what John Ogbu, an educational anthropologist at the University of California, Berkeley, calls "effort optimism," the faith that hard work will bring real rewards in life. Ogbu's ethnographic studies of black and Hispanic schoolchildren in Stockton, CA, suggest that one reason today's inner-city children do poorly in tests is that "they do not bring to the test situation serious attitudes and do not persevere to maximize their scores." The fault lies neither with their intelligence, Ogbu argues, nor with the absence of the "quasi-academic training" that middle-class children experience at home. Rather, it is **their lower caste status and the limited job prospects of their parents that lower their sights. Tracking formalizes this caste humiliation and leads to disillusionment about school and what school can do for their lives.**

What Parents Can Do

If you are worried that your own child is losing his or her enthusiasm for schoolwork as a result of being put in a lower, "dumber" track, Susan Harter of the University of Denver advises you to watch for the following signs of trouble:

Decline in intrinsic motivation, the kind of curiosity and involvement in school work that promises long-term academic success, and its replacement with *extrinsic* motivation, doing just enough to get by while depending too much on the teacher for direction and help.

Indifference to school and schoolwork; losing homework on the way to school, or homework assignments on the way back; delivering homework that is crumpled, dirty or incomplete.

Constant self-deprecation: "I'm no good." "I can't do long division."

Signs of helplessness: unwillingness to try a task, especially new ones; starting but not finishing work; difficulty in dealing with frustration.

Avoiding homework, or school, altogether. (The most frequent cause of truancy, says Olle Jane Sahler of the pediatrics department at the University of Rochester, is low self-esteem with regard to school subjects.)

Should parents whose kids have problems undertake compensatory home instruction? Sherry Ferguson and Lawrence E. Mazin, authors of *Parent Power: A Program to Help Your Child Succeed in School,* think so, not because parents can make their children "smart," but because they have the power to make their kids persistent, competitive and eager. Here are some specific steps parents can take at home to achieve this end, according to Abigail Lipson, Ph.D., a clinical psychologist at the Harvard University Bureau of Study Counsel:

Praise your child for effort, not just for achievement. Children learn about persistence from many contexts, not just academic ones, so praise your child for hard work at any task: developing a good hook shot, painting a picture, etc.

Ask your child to explain her homework, or the subjects she is studying at school, to you. Try to learn *from* your child, don't just instruct her.

Find a regular time when you and your child can work in the same space. When children are banished to their rooms to do homework, they are cut off from social interaction. It can be very lonely. Setting up a special study time together can help both (or all) of you focus on accomplishing difficult or onerous tasks. While your child is doing homework, you can balance your checkbook, pay bills, whatever.

Help your child find a learning activity he feels good about. If the subject is animals, go to a zoo. If it's cars, select some car books together from the library. Encourage him to pursue his natural interests.

Games of all kinds are good for teaching children about persistence and achievement. Competitive games emphasize strategies for competing effectively and fairly, while noncompetitive games provide children with a sense of accomplishment through perseverance.

—S.T.

Who Is "Smart"?
Who Will "Succeed"?

The consequences of increased testing and tracking are only now beginning to be felt. First there is personal trauma, both for students who do reasonably well but not as well as they would like, and for those who fail. "When a child is given to understand that his or her worth resides in what he or she achieves rather than in what he or she is, academic failure becomes a severe emotional trauma," David Elkind writes in *The Child and Society.*

But the most severe consequence may be what only dropouts are so far demonstrating—an overall decline in Ogbu's effort optimism. Its potential social effects extend well beyond the schoolroom. Intelligence and ability, says writer James Fallows, have become legally and socially acceptable grounds for discrimination, and both are measured by the testing and tracking system in our schools. Doing well in school has thus come to be the measure of who is intelligent and who has ability. Beyond that, Fallows writes, our culture increasingly accepts that "he who goes further in school will go further in life." Many of the best jobs and most prestigious professions are restricted to those with imposing academic and professional degrees, thus creating a monopoly on "positions of privilege."

At a time when our economy requires better-educated workers than ever before, can we afford to let abstract measures of ability curtail the educational aspirations and potential accomplishments of our children? Quite aside from questions of national prosperity, do we really want to become a culture whose fruits are not available to most of its citizens? Despite income disparities and more classism than many observers are willing to admit, there has always been the *belief* in America that success, the good life, is available to all who are willing to work for it. But with our current fixation on testing and tracking, and what Fallows calls credentialism, we may be abandoning that belief and, with it, the majority of our young people.

Creating Creative Minds

Schools are probably as likely to work against the development of creativity as in its favor, Messrs. Sternberg and Lubart maintain. But it doesn't have to be that way. For specifics, read on.

ROBERT J. STERNBERG
AND TODD I. LUBART

ROBERT J. STERNBERG is IBM Professor of Psychology and Education at Yale University, New Haven, Conn., where TODD I. LUBART is a graduate student in psychology. The preparation of this article was supported by a contract from the Army Research Institute, though the opinions are those of the authors. Requests for reprints should be addressed to Robert J. Sternberg, Department of Psychology, Yale University, Box 11A Yale Station, New Haven, CT 06520.

CREATIVITY is not simply inborn. On the contrary, schooling can create creative minds — though it often doesn't. To create creativity, we need to understand the resources on which it draws and to determine how we can help children develop these resources. In particular, we need to know how we can invest in our children's futures by helping them invest in their own creative endeavors.

We propose an "investment theory of creativity."[1] The basic notion underlying our theory is that, when making any kind of investment, including creative investment, people should "buy low and sell high." In other words, the greatest creative contributions can generally be made in areas or with ideas that at a given time are undervalued. Perhaps people in general have not yet realized the importance of certain ideas, and hence there is a potential for making significant advances. The more in favor an idea is, the less potential there is for it to appreciate in value, because the idea is already valued.

A theory of creativity needs to account for how people can generate or recognize undervalued ideas. It also needs to specify who will actually pursue these under-valued ideas rather than join the crowd and make contributions that, while of some value, are unlikely to turn around our existing ways of thinking. Such a theory will enable us and our children to invest in a creative future.[2] As is sometimes said, nothing is as practical as a good theory.

We hold that developing creativity in children — and in adults — involves teaching them to use six resources: intelligence, knowledge, intellectual style, personality, motivation, and environmental context. Consider each of these resources in turn.

INTELLIGENCE

Two main aspects of intelligence are relevant to creativity. These aspects, based on the triarchic theory of human intelligence, are the ability to define and

 From *Phi Delta Kappan,* April 1991, pp. 608-614. Reprinted by permission of the author and Phi Delta Kappan.

redefine problems and the ability to think insightfully.[3]

Problem definition and redefinition. Major creative innovations often involve seeing an old problem in a new way. For example, Albert Einstein redefined the field of physics by proposing the theory of relativity; Jean Piaget redefined the field of cognitive development by conceiving of the child as a scientist; Pablo Picasso redefined the field of art through his cubist perspective on the world.

In order to *re*define a problem, a student has to have the option of defining a problem in the first place. Only rarely do schools give students this luxury. Tests typically pose the problems that students are to solve. And if a student's way of seeing a problem is different from that of the test constructor, the student is simply marked wrong. Similarly, teachers typically structure their classes so that they, not the students, set the problems to be solved. Of course, textbooks work the same way. Even when papers or projects are assigned, teachers often specify the topics. Some teachers, who view themselves as more flexible, allow students to define problems for themselves. These same teachers may then proceed to mark students down when students' definitions of problems do not correspond to their own.

In the "thinking-skills movement," we frequently hear of the need for schools to emphasize more heavily the teaching of problem-solving skills. Educators are then pleased when students do not merely memorize facts but rather use the facts to solve problems. Certainly, there is much to be said for a problem-solving approach to education. But we need to recognize that creative individuals are often most renowned not for solving problems, but for posing them. It is not so much that they have found the "right" answers (often there are none); rather, they have asked the right questions — they recognized significant and substantial problems and chose to address them. One only has to open almost any professional journal to find articles that are the fruit of good problem solving on bad — or at least fairly inconsequential — problems.

If we are to turn schooling around and emphasize creative definition and redefinition of problems, we need to give our students some of the control we teachers typically maintain. Students need to take more responsibility for the problems they choose to solve, and we need to take less. The students will make mistakes and attempt to solve inconsequential or even

> **T**wo main aspects of intelligence — the ability to define and redefine problems and the ability to think insightfully — are relevant to creativity.

wrongly posed problems. But they learn from their mistakes, and, if we do not give them the opportunity to make mistakes, they will have no mistakes to learn from. Instead of almost always giving children the problems, we more often need to let them find the problems that they are to solve. We need to help them develop their skills in defining and redefining problems, not just in solving them.

Insight skills. Insight skills are involved when people perceive a high-quality solution to an ill-structured problem to which the solution is not obvious. Being truly creative involves "buying low" — that is, picking up on an idea that is out of favor. But just picking up on any idea that is out of favor is not sufficient. Insight is involved in spotting the *good* ideas. We have proposed a theory of insight whereby insights are of three kinds.[4]

The first kind of insight involves seeing things in a stream of inputs that most people would not see. In other words, in the midst of a stream of mostly irrelevant information, an individual is able to zero in on particularly relevant information for his or her purposes. For example, the insightful reader observes clues to an author's meaning that others may miss. An insightful writer is often one whose observations about human behavior, as revealed through writing, go beyond those of the rest of us.

The second kind of insight involves seeing how to combine disparate pieces

of information whose connection is nonobvious and usually elusive. For example, proving mathematical theorems requires seeing how to fit together various axioms and theorems into a coherent proof. Interpreting data from a scientific experiment often involves making sense of seemingly disparate pieces of information.

The third kind of insight involves seeing the nonobvious relevance of old information to a new problem. Creative analogies and metaphors are representative of this kind of insight. For example, the student of history comes to see how understanding events of long ago can help us understand certain events in the present. A scientist might recall a problem from the past that was solved by using a certain methodology and apply this methodology to a current scientific problem.

Problems requiring insightful solution are almost always ill-structured; that is, there are no readily available paths to solution. Rather, much of the difficulty in solving the problem is figuring out what the steps toward solution might be. For example, when James Watson and Francis Crick sought to find the structure of DNA, the nature of the problem was clear. The way in which to solve it was not clear at all.

Problems presented in schools, however, are usually well-structured; that is, there is a clear path — or several paths — to a prompt and expedient solution. In standardized tests, for example, there is always a path that guarantees a "correct" solution. The examinee's problem is, in large part, to find that guaranteed path. Similarly, textbook problems are often posed so that there can be an answer key for the teacher that gives the "correct" answers. Problems such as these are unlikely to require insightful thinking. One ends up trying to "psych out" the thought processes of the person who formulated the problem, rather than to generate one's own insightful thought processes.

While not exclusively limited to ill-structured problems, creative innovations tend to address such problems — not the well-structured ones that we typically use in school settings. If we want students to think insightfully, we need to give them opportunities to do so by increasing our use of ill-structured problems that allow insightful thinking. Project work is excellent in this regard, for it requires students not only to solve problems but also to structure the problems for themselves.

KNOWLEDGE

In order to make a creative contribution to a field of knowledge, one must, of course, have knowledge of that field. Without such knowledge, one risks rediscovering what is already known. Without knowledge of the field, it is also difficult for an individual to assess the problems in the field and to judge which are important. Indeed, during the past decade or so, an important emphasis in psychology has been on the importance of knowledge to expertise.

Schools can scarcely be faulted for making insufficient efforts to impart knowledge. Indeed, that seems to be their main function. Yet we have two reservations about the extent to which the knowledge they impart is likely to lead to creativity.

First, there is a difference between knowledge and usable knowledge. Knowledge can be learned in a way that renders it inert. Knowledge may be stored in the brain, but an individual may nonetheless be unable to use it. For example, almost every college undergraduate who majors in psychology takes a course in statistics as a part of that major. Yet

> ## Increased expertise in terms of knowledge in a given domain often comes at the expense of flexibility in that domain.

very few undergraduates who have taken statistics are able to use what they have learned in the design and analysis of scientific experiments. (At the secondary level, many physics and chemistry students are unable to use basic algebra when they need to apply it.) Undergraduates in psychology do fine as long as they are given highly structured problems in which it is obvious which statistical technique applies. But they have trouble when they have to figure out which technique to apply and when to ap-

There is a difference between knowledge and usable knowledge.

ply it. The context in which they acquired their knowledge is so different from the context in which they must use it that their knowledge is simply unavailable.

Our experience with knowledge learned in statistics courses is, we believe, the rule rather than the exception. Students do not generally learn knowledge in a way that renders it useful to them. To the contrary, they are likely to forget much of what they learn soon after they are tested on it. We have all had the experience of studying for an exam and then quickly forgetting what we studied. The information was learned in such a way as to make it useful in the context of a structured exam; once the exam is finished, so is that use of the knowledge.

Our second reservation about the knowledge that schools typically impart is that students are not taught in a way that makes clear to them why the information they are learning is important. Students do much better in learning if they believe that they can use what they learn. Foreign language provides a good example. People who need to use a foreign language learn it. Those who don't need it rarely retain much of it. Unless we show students why what they are learning should matter to them, we cannot expect them to retain what they are taught. Unfortunately, we often don't really know ourselves how students might use what we are teaching them. And if we don't know, how can we expect them to?

We also need to be concerned about the tradeoff that can develop between knowledge and flexibility. We have suggested that increased expertise in terms of knowledge in a given domain often comes at the expense of flexibility in that domain.[5] We can become so automatic about the way we do certain things that we lose sight of the possibility of other ways. We can become entrenched and have trouble going beyond our very comfortable perspective on things. Because creativity requires one to view things flexibly, there is a danger that, with increasing knowledge, one will lose creativity by losing the ability to think flex-

ibly about the domain in which one works. We need to recognize that sometimes students see things that we do not see — that they may have insights we have not had (and that initially we may not even recognize as insights). Teachers who have been doing the same thing year after year can become so self-satisfied and happy with the way they do things that they are closed to new ways of doing these things. They are unwilling to "buy low" — to try an idea that is different from those they have favored in the past.

On the one hand, we do not wish to underemphasize the importance of knowledge to creativity. On the other hand, we cannot overemphasize the importance of usable knowledge that does not undermine flexibility. Often we need to adopt the maintenance of flexibility as a goal to be achieved self-consciously. We might go to inservice training sessions, read new kinds of books, learn about a new domain of knowledge, seek to learn from our students, or whatever. If we want students to be creative, we have to model creativity for them, and we won't be able to do that if we seek to turn students' minds into safe-deposit boxes in which to store our assorted and often undigested bits of knowledge.

INTELLECTUAL STYLES

Intellectual styles are the ways in which people choose to use or exploit their intelligence as well as their knowledge. Thus intellectual styles concern not abilities, but how these abilities and the knowledge acquired through them are used in day-to-day interactions with the environment.

Elsewhere one of the authors has presented details of a theory of intellectual styles based on a notion of "mental self-government."[6] Hence we need not cover the theory in detail here. The basic idea is that people need to govern themselves mentally and that styles provide them with ways to do so. The ways in which people govern themselves are internal mirrors of the kinds of government we see in the external world.

Creative people are likely to be those with a legislative proclivity. A legislative individual is someone who enjoys formulating problems and creating new systems of rules and new ways of seeing things. Such a person is in contrast to an individual with an executive style: someone who likes implementing the systems, rules, and tasks of others. Both differ from an individual with a judicial style: someone who enjoys evaluating people, things, and rules. Thus the creative person not only has the ability to see things in new ways but likes to do so. The creative person is also likely to have a global — not just a local — perspective on problems. Seeing the forest despite all the trees is the mark of creative endeavor.

PERSONALITY

Creative people seem to share certain personality attributes. Although one can probably be creative in the short term without these attributes, long-term creativity requires most of them. The attributes are tolerance of ambiguity, willingness to surmount obstacles and persevere, willingness to grow, willingness to take risks, and courage of one's convictions.

Tolerance for ambiguity. In most creative endeavors, there is a period of time during which an individual is groping — trying to figure out what the pieces of the puzzle are, how to put them together, how to relate them to what is already known. During this period, an individual is likely to feel some anxiety — possibly even alarm — because the pieces are not forming themselves into a creative solution to the problem being confronted. Creative individuals need to be able to tolerate such ambiguity and to wait for the pieces to fall into place.

In many schools, most of the assignments students are given are due the next day or within a very short period of time. In such circumstances students cannot develop a tolerance for ambiguity, because they cannot spare the time to allow a situation to be ambiguous. If an assignment is due in a day or two, ambiguities need to be resolved quickly. A good way to help students develop a tolerance for ambiguity is to give them more long-term assignments and encourage them to start thinking about the assignments early on so that they can mull over whatever problems they face. Moreover, students need to realize that a period of ambiguity is the rule, not the exception, in creative work and that they should welcome this period as a chance to hatch their ideas, rather than dread it as a time when their ideas are not fully formed.

Willingness to surmount obstacles and persevere. Almost every major creative thinker has surmounted obstacles at one time or another, and the willingness not to be derailed is a crucial element of success. Confronting obstacles is almost a certainty in creative endeavor because

most such endeavors threaten some kind of established and entrenched interest. Unless one can learn to face adversity and conquer it, one is unlikely to make a creative contribution to one's field.

We need to learn to think of obstacles and the need to surmount them as part of the game, rather than as outside it. We should not think of obstacles as something only we have, but as something that everyone has. What makes creative people special is not that they have obstacles but how they face them.

Schools can be fairly good proving grounds for learning to surmount obstacles, because we face so many of them while we are in school (whether as students or as teachers). But students sometimes leave school with the feeling that society is more likely to get in the way of creativity than to support it. Sometimes they are right, of course. And ultimately, they may have to fight for their ideas, as creative people have done before them. However, training to overcome resistance to new ideas shouldn't be the main contribution of the schools to students' creativity.

Willingness to grow. When a person has a creative idea and is able to have others accept it, that person may be highly rewarded for the idea. It then becomes difficult to move on to still other ideas. The rewards for staying with the first idea are often great, and it feels comfortable to stick with that idea. At the same time, the person who has had a creative idea often acquires a deep-seated fear that his or her next idea won't be as good as the first one. Indeed, the phenomenon of "statistical" regression toward the mean would suggest that subsequent ideas actually will not be as good — that they will regress toward the mean. This is the same phenomenon that operates when the "rookie of the year" in baseball doesn't play as well in his second year as in his first or when a restaurant that seems outstanding when we first eat there isn't quite as good the second time. In short, there is a fair amount of pressure to stay with what one has and knows. But creativity exhibited over prolonged periods of time requires one to move beyond that first creative idea and even to see problems with what at one time may have seemed a superb idea. While schools often encourage the growth of a student's knowledge, such growth will by no means lead automatically to creativity, in part because schools do not encourage students to take risks with their newly acquired knowledge and abilities.

Willingness to take risks. A general principle of investment is that, on the average, greater return entails greater risk. For the most part, schools are environments that are not conducive to risk taking. On the contrary, students are as often as not punished for taking risks. Taking a course in a new area or in an area of weakness is likely to lead to a low grade, which in turn may dim a student's future prospects. Risking an unusual response on an exam or an idiosyncratic approach in a paper is a step likely to be taken only with great trepidation, because of the fear that a low or failing grade on a specific assignment may ruin one's chances for a good grade in the course. Moreover, there is usually some safe response that is at least good enough to earn the grade for which one is aiming.

In addition, many teachers are not themselves risk-takers. Teaching is not a profession that is likely to attract the biggest risk-takers, and hence many teachers may feel threatened by students who take large risks, especially if the teacher perceives those risks to be at his or her expense. Unfortunately, students' unwillingness to take risks derives from their socialization in the schools, which are environments that encourage conformity to societal norms. The result is often stereotyped thinking.

Courage of one's convictions and belief in oneself. There are times in the lives of almost all creative people when they begin to doubt their ideas — and themselves. Their work may not be achieving the recognition it once achieved, or they may not have succeeded in getting recognition in the first place. At these times, it is difficult to maintain a belief in one's ideas or in oneself. It is natural for people to go through peaks and valleys in their creative output, and there are times when creative people worry that their most recent good idea will end up being their final good idea. At such times, one needs to draw upon deep-seated personal resources and to believe in oneself, even when others do not.

Schools do teach some students to believe in themselves: namely, those who consistently receive high grades. But the skills one needs to earn high grades are often quite different from those one needs to be creative. Thus those who go out and set their own course may receive little encouragement, whereas those who play the game and get good grades may develop a confidence in themselves that, though justified, is not necessarily related to their past or potential creative contributions.

Those who most need to believe in themselves may be given every reason not to.

MOTIVATION

There is now good evidence to suggest that motivation plays an important part in creative endeavors. Two kinds of motivation are particularly important: intrinsic motivation and the motivation to excel. Both kinds of motivation lead to a focus on tasks rather than on the external rewards that performance of these tasks might generate.

Intrinsic motivation. Teresa Amabile has conducted and reviewed a number of studies suggesting the importance of intrinsic motivation to creativity.[7] People are much more likely to respond creatively to a task that they enjoy doing for its own sake, rather than a task that they carry out exclusively or even primarily for such extrinsic motivators as grades. Indeed, research suggests that extrinsic rewards undermine intrinsic motivation.[8]

There is little doubt as to the way in which most schools motivate students to-

> **T**here is little doubt as to the way in which most schools motivate students today: namely, through grades — the criterion of school success.

day: namely, through grades. Grades are the ultimate criterion of one's success in school, and, if one's grades are not good, love of one's work is unlikely to be viewed as much compensation. Therefore, many students chart a path in school that is just sufficient to get them an A. (If they put too much effort into a single course, they risk jeopardizing their performance in the other courses they are taking.) Students who once may have performed well for love of an intellectual challenge may come to perform well

only to get their next A. Whatever intrinsic motivation children may have had at the start is likely to be drummed out of them by a system that rewards extrinsically, not intrinsically.

Motivation to excel. Robert White identified as an important source of motivation a desire to achieve competence in one or more of a person's endeavors.[9] In order to be creative in a field, one generally will need to be motivated not only to be competent, but also to excel. The best "investors" are almost always those who put in the work necessary to realize their goals. Success does not just come to them — they work for it.

Schools vary in the extent to which they encourage students to excel. Some schools seem to want nothing more than for all their students to be at some average or "golden mean." Many schools, however, encourage excellence. Unfortunately, it is rare in our experience for the kind of excellence that is encouraged to be *creative* excellence. It may be excellence in grades, which generally does not require great creativity to attain; it may be excellence in sports or in extracurricular activities. There is nothing wrong with excellence of these kinds. Indeed, they are undoubtedly important in today's world. But seeking such excellences does not foster creativity — and may even interfere with it. When a student is simultaneously taking five or six courses, there is not much opportunity to spend the time or to expend the effort needed to be creative in any of them.

ENVIRONMENTAL CONTEXT

Creativity cannot be viewed outside an environmental context. What would be viewed as creative in one context might be viewed as trivial in another. The role of context is relevant to the creative enterprise in at least three different ways: in sparking creative ideas, in encouraging follow-up of these ideas, and in rewarding the ideas and their fruits.

Sparking creative ideas. Some environments provide the bases for lots of creative sparks, whereas other environments may provide the basis for none at all. Do schools provide environments for sparking creative ideas? Obviously, the answer to this question is necessarily subjective. Given the discussion above, we would have difficulty saying that they do. Schools provide environments that encourage learning about and dealing with existing concepts rather than inventing new ones. There is a lot of emphasis on

memorization and some emphasis on analysis, but there is little emphasis on creative synthesis. Indeed, it is difficult for us to remember more than a handful of tests we ever took in school that encouraged creative thinking. On the contrary, the tests students typically take reward them for spitting back what they have learned — or, at best, analyzing it in a fairly noncreative way.

Encouraging follow-up of creative ideas. Suppose a student has a genuinely creative idea and would like to pursue it within the school setting. Is there any vehicle for such follow-up? Occasionally, students will be allowed to pursue projects that encourage them to develop their creative thinking. But again, spending a great deal of time on such projects puts them at risk in their other courses and in their academic work. It is quite rare that any allowance is made whereby students can be excused from normal requirements in order to pursue a special interest of their own.

Evaluating and rewarding creative ideas. Most teachers would adamantly maintain that, when grading papers, they reward creativity. But, if the experience of other teachers is similar to that of the teachers with whom we have worked, they don't find a great deal of creativity to reward. And we sometimes worry whether they would recognize creativity in student work were they to meet it. Please note that we do not except ourselves from this charge. We have failed more than once to see the value of a student's idea when we first encountered it, only to see that value later on — after the student had decided to pursue some other idea, partly at our urging. Teachers genuinely believe that they reward creativity. But the rewards are few and far between.

Look at any school report card, and assess the skills that the report card values. You will probably not find creativity anywhere on the list. One of us actually analyzed the report cards given to children in several elementary schools. A number of skills were assessed. However, not a single one of the report cards assessed creativity in any field whatsoever. The creative child might indeed be valued by the teacher, but it would not show up in the pattern of check marks on the report card.

TEACHING FOR CREATIVITY

How can we help develop students' creativity in the classroom? Consider an example. A few weeks ago, one of us had the opportunity to teach a class of 9- and 10-year-olds in a New York City school. The children ranged fairly widely in abilities and came from various socioeconomic backgrounds. The guest teacher was asked to demonstrate how to "teach for thinking" and decided to do so in the context of teaching about psychology. However, he wanted to impart not merely a set of decontextualized "facts" about the field, but rather the way psychologists think when they develop ideas for creative scientific theory and research.

He didn't tell the students what problem they were going to solve or even offer them suggestions. Rather, he asked each of them to share with the class some aspect of human behavior — their own, their parents', their friends' — that intrigued them and that they would like to understand better. In other words, the students were asked to *define problems* rather than have the teacher do it for them. At first, no one said anything. The children may never have been asked to formulate problems for themselves. But the teacher waited. And then he waited some more (so as not to teach them that, if only they said nothing, he would panic and start to answer his own questions).

Eventually, one student spoke up, and then another, and then another. The ice broken, the children couldn't wait to contribute. Rather than adopting the executive and largely passive style to which they were accustomed, they were adopting a *legislative style* whereby they enjoyed and actively participated in the opportunity to create new ideas. And create ideas they did. Why do parents make children dress up on special occasions? Why do parents sometimes have unreasonable expectations for their children? Why do some siblings fight a lot while others don't? How do we choose our friends?

Because these problems were the children's own problems and not the teacher's, the children were *intrinsically motivated* to seek answers. And they came up with some very perceptive answers indeed. We discussed their ideas and considered criteria for deciding which potential experiment to pursue as a group. The criteria, like the ideas, were the students' own, not the teacher's. And the students considered such factors as *taking risks* in doing experiments, *surmounting obstacles to doing an experiment*, and so on.

The children entered the class with almost no formal knowledge about psychology. But they left it with at least a

rudimentary *procedural knowledge* of how psychologists formulate research. The teacher didn't give them the knowledge; they created it for themselves, in an environment that *sparked* and then *rewarded* creative ideas. To be sure, not all of the ideas were creative or even particularly good. But the students were encouraged to give it their best shot, and that's what they did.

> **E**ncouraged to do so, the middle-graders created knowledge for themselves, in an environment that *sparked* and then *rewarded* creative ideas.

The class didn't have time in one 75-minute period to complete the full design of an experiment. However, it did have time to demonstrate that even children can do the kind of creative work that we often reserve until graduate school. We can teach for creativity at any level, in any field. And if we want to improve our children and our nation, this is exactly what we need to do.

Does teaching for creativity actually work? We believe that it does. Moreover, the effectiveness of such teaching has been demonstrated.[10] After five weeks of insight training involving insight problems in language arts, mathematics, science, and social studies, students in grades 4 through 6 displayed significant and substantial improvements (from a pretest to a posttest) over an untrained control group on insight skills and general intelligence. In addition, the training transferred to insight problems of kinds not covered in the course, and, a year later, the gains were maintained. These children had improved their creative skills with only a relatively small investment of instructional time.

THOSE WHO invest are taught that most obvious of strategies: buy low and sell high. Yet few people manage to do so. They don't know when a given security is really low or when it is really high. We believe that those who work in the schools do not have much better success in fostering creativity. We often don't recognize creativity when we see it. And although most of us believe that we encourage it, our analysis suggests that schools are probably as likely to work against the development of creativity as in its favor. The conventional wisdom is likely correct: schools probably do at least as much to undermine creativity as to support it.

It is important to realize that our theory of creativity is a "confluence" theory: the elements of creativity work together interactively, not alone. The implication for schooling is that addressing just one — or even a few — of the resources we have discussed is not sufficient to induce creative thinking. For example, a school might teach "divergent thinking," encouraging students to see multiple solutions to problems. But children will not suddenly become creative in the absence of an environment that tolerates ambiguity, encourages risk taking, fosters task-focused motivation, and supports the other aspects of creativity that we have discussed.

It is also important to realize that obtaining transfer of training from one domain to another is at least as hard with creative thinking as with critical thinking. If you use trivial problems in your classroom (e.g., "What are unusual uses of a paper clip?"), you are likely to get transfer only to trivial problems outside the classroom. We are not enthusiastic about many so-called tests of creativity, nor about many training programs, because the problems they use are trivial. We would encourage the use of serious problems in a variety of disciplines in order to maximize the transfer of training. Better to ask students to think of unusual ways to solve world problems — or school problems, for that matter — than to ask them to think of unusual ways to use a paper clip!

Perhaps the greatest block to the enhancement of creativity is a view of the "ideal student" that does not particularly feature creativity. Paul Torrance used an "Ideal Child Checklist," composed of characteristics that had been found empirically to differentiate highly creative people from less creative people.[11] A to-

4. FAMILY, SCHOOL, AND CULTURAL INFLUENCES: Education

tal of 264 teachers in the state of New York ranked the items in terms of desirability. The teachers' rankings showed only a moderate relation with the rankings of 10 experts on creativity. The teachers supported more strongly than the experts such attributes as popularity, social skills, and acceptance of authority. The teachers disapproved of asking questions, being a good guesser, thinking independently, and risk taking. A replication of this study in Tennessee showed only a weak relation between the views of teachers and those of experts on creativity.[12] Clearly, to engender creativity, first we must value it!

Schools could change. They could let students define problems, rather than almost always doing it for them. They could put more emphasis on ill-structured rather than well-structured problems. They could encourage a legislative rather than (or in addition to) an executive style, by providing assignments that encourage students to see things in new ways. They could teach knowledge for use, rather than for exams; they could emphasize flexibility in using knowledge,

rather than mere recall. They could encourage risk taking and other personality attributes associated with creativity, and they could put more emphasis on motivating children intrinsically rather than through grades. Finally, they could reward creativity in all its forms, rather than ignore or even punish it.

But for schools to do these things, it would take a rather fundamental re*valuation* of what schooling is about. We, at least, would like to see that process start now. Rather than put obstacles in their paths, let's do all that we can to *value* and encourage the creativity of students in our schools.

1. Robert J. Sternberg, "A Three-Facet Model of Creativity," in idem, ed., *The Nature of Creativity* (New York: Cambridge University Press, 1988), pp. 125-47; and Robert J. Sternberg and Todd I. Lubart, "An Investment Theory of Creativity and Its Development," *Human Development*, vol. 34, 1991, pp. 1-31.
2. Herbert J. Walberg, "Creativity and Talent as Learning," in Sternberg, *The Nature of Creativity*, pp. 340-61.
3. Robert J. Sternberg, *Beyond IQ: A Triarchic Theory of Human Intelligence* (New York: Cambridge University Press, 1985); and idem, *The Triarchic Mind: A New Theory of Human Intelligence* (New York: Viking, 1988).
4. Janet E. Davidson and Robert J. Sternberg, "The Role of Insight in Intellectual Giftedness," *Gifted Child Quarterly*, vol. 28, 1984, pp. 58-64; and Robert J. Sternberg and Janet E. Davidson, "The Mind of the Puzzler," *Psychology Today*, June 1982, pp. 37-44.
5. Robert J. Sternberg and Peter A. Frensch, "A Balance-Level Theory of Intelligent Thinking," *Zeitschrift für Pädagogische Psychologie*, vol. 3, 1989, pp. 79-96.
6. Robert J. Sternberg, "Mental Self-Government: A Theory of Intellectual Styles and Their Development," *Human Development*, vol. 31, 1988, pp. 197-224; and idem, "Thinking Styles: Keys to Understanding Student Performance," *Phi Delta Kappan*, January 1990, pp. 366-71.
7. Teresa M. Amabile, *The Social Psychology of Creativity* (New York: Springer-Verlag, 1983).
8. Mark Lepper, David Greene, and Richard Nisbett, "Undermining Children's Intrinsic Interest with Extrinsic Rewards: A Test of the 'Overjustification' Hypothesis," *Journal of Personality and Social Psychology*, vol. 28, 1973, pp. 129-37.
9. Robert White, "Motivation Reconsidered: The Concept of Competence," *Psychological Review*, vol. 66, 1959, pp. 297-323.
10. Davidson and Sternberg, op. cit.
11. E. Paul Torrance, *Role of Evaluation in Creative Thinking* (Minneapolis: Bureau of Educational Research, University of Minnesota, 1964).
12. Bill Kaltsounis, "Middle Tennessee Teachers' Perceptions of Ideal Pupil," *Perceptual and Motor Skills*, vol. 44, 1977, pp. 803-6.

Learning from Asian Schools

American schools could benefit from the teaching styles and institutional structures used in Asia—many of which were pioneered here

Harold W. Stevenson

Harold W. Stevenson is professor of psychology at the University of Michigan, Ann Arbor. He received his Ph.D. from Stanford University. Since 1979, he has been conducting a series of cross-national studies of children's academic achievement. Stevenson has earned several distinctions, including a Guggenheim fellowship and the American Psychological Association's G. Stanley Hall award for research in developmental psychology.

During the past decade, it has become a truism that American students are not being adequately prepared to compete in a global economy. The latest research shows that the deficiencies become apparent as early as kindergarten and persist throughout the school years. These deficiencies have been most evident when the students are compared with their peers in East Asia. Yet contrary to popular stereotypes the high levels of achievement in Asian schools are not the result of rote learning and repeated drilling by overburdened, tense youngsters. Children are motivated to learn; teaching is innovative and interesting. Knowledge is not forced on children; instead the students are led to construct their own ways of representing this knowledge. The long school days in Asia are broken up by extensive amounts of recess. The recess in turn fosters a positive attitude toward academics.

My colleagues and I gained these insights in a series of five collaborative, large cross-national studies begun in 1980. We explored the children's experiences both at home and at school in the U.S., China, Taiwan and Japan. We found that there is nothing mysterious about the teaching styles and techniques used in Asian schools. Rather these societies embody many of the ideals Americans have for their own schools. They just happen to apply them in an interesting, productive way that makes learning enjoyable.

The vast cultural differences preclude direct translation of many of the practices and beliefs from those cultures to our own. But these comparative data have helped us realize how far Americans have strayed from the effective application of well-known teaching methods. The studies have revealed new perspectives about our own culture and fresh ideas about how our educational system might be improved. Indeed, simply increasing the length of school days would be meaningless if there were no change in the way American teachers are asked to perform their jobs.

Results from cross-national studies can be greatly distorted if the research procedures are not comparable in each area and if the test materials are not culturally appropriate. We avoided the first potential problem by selecting a full range of schools in five metropolitan areas: Minneapolis, Chicago, Sendai, Beijing and Taipei. These cities are similar in size and cultural status within their own countries. In each metropolitan region, we selected from 10 to 20 elementary schools that represented a range of students from different socioeconomic backgrounds. (Because socioeconomic status is not easy to define, we used the parents' educational level as the basis for selection.) We then randomly chose two first-grade and two fifth-grade classrooms in each school.

To avoid the difficulty in translating materials developed in one culture for use in another, we constructed our own tests. We began by compiling computer files of every concept and skill included in the students' mathematics textbooks and of every word and grammatical structure in their reading material. With these files, we were able to create test items that were relevant to each culture and that were at the appropriate levels of difficulty.

Armed with these materials, we administered mathematics and reading tests to thousands of students in the first- and fifth-grade classrooms. Later we randomly selected samples of six boys and six girls from each classroom for more in-depth testing and interviews. In one of the studies, we visited a total of 204 classrooms in 11 schools in Beijing, 10 in Taipei, 10 in Sendai and 20 in Chicago.

The test results confirmed what has become common knowledge: schoolchildren in Asia perform better academically than do those in the U.S. In mathematics the average scores of the Asian first graders were above the American average, but scores of some of the American schools were as high as some of those in Sendai and Taipei. By fifth grade, however, the American students lost much ground: the average score of only one of the Chicago-area schools was as high as the worst of the Asian schools. On a computation test, for example, only 2.2 percent of the Beijing first graders and 1.4 percent of the fifth graders scored as low as the mean for their Chicago counterparts. On a test of word problems, only 2.6 percent of the Beijing first graders and 10 percent of the fifth graders scored at or below corresponding American means.

The deficiencies of American children appear to build throughout the school years. When we compared the scores of kindergarten children and of first, fifth and 11th graders in Minneapolis, Sendai, and Taipei, we found a relative decline in the scores among the American students, improvement in Taiwan and steady high performance in Japan.

American students' shortcomings are not limited to mathematics. Although Americans performed the best on read-ing in the first grade, the Asian students had caught up by the fifth grade. The rise is remarkable when one considers the reading demands of Asian languages. Chinese students had to learn several thousand characters by the fifth grade, and Japanese students had to learn Chinese characters, two syllabaries (symbols for the syllables in Japanese) and the roman alphabet.

Because of the early onset and pervasiveness of cross-cultural differences in academic achievement, it seemed obvious that we would have to investigate attitudes, beliefs and practices related to children's success. We spent hundreds of hours observing in the classrooms, interviewed the teachers, children and mothers and gave questionnaires to the fathers.

American parents show a surprisingly high level of satisfaction with their children's level of academic performance. From kindergarten through the 11th grade, more than three times as many Minneapolis mothers as Asian mothers said they were very satisfied with their child's current level of achievement.

The U.S. students were also very positive about their abilities. More than 30 percent of the Chicago fifth graders considered themselves to be "among the best" in mathematics, in reading, in sports and in getting along with other children. Such self-ratings were significantly higher than those made by Sendai and Taipei children for mathematics and by Sendai children for reading. Taipei children gave the highest self-ratings for reading. Except for social skills, many fewer Beijing children gave themselves such positive ratings.

In another set of questions, we asked the mothers how well the school was educating their own children. More than 80 percent of the American mothers expressed a high level of satisfaction. Except at kindergarten, when mothers in all four societies were quite satisfied, Minneapolis mothers felt much better about their children's schools than did mothers in Taipei and Sendai.

Why should American mothers be so positive? One likely explanation is that they lack clear standards to which they can refer. No national or state curricula define what children should learn at each grade, and few mothers receive more than vague reports about their children's performance. American mothers also seem to place a lesser emphasis on academic achievement. In the U.S., childhood is a time for many different types of accomplishment. Doing well in school is only one of them.

Asian mothers, on the other hand, have told us repeatedly that their chil-

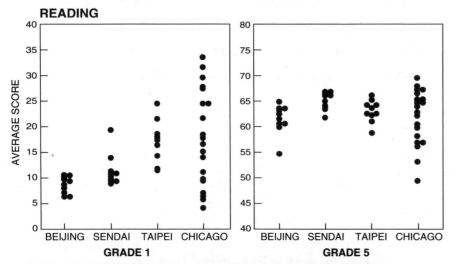

READING

MATHEMATICS

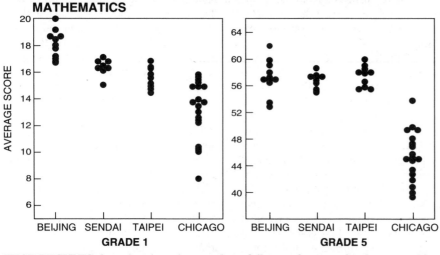

TEST RESULTS show that American students fail to perform at a level comparable to that of their peers in Asia. The data plotted are mean scores from various schools (dots). Although Americans performed best in reading in the first grade, they lost the advantage by the fifth grade. In mathematics, American students in both the first and fifth grades on average scored the poorest.

dren's primary task is to do well in school. The mothers' own job is to try to do everything possible to ensure that success. They regarded education as critical for their children's future. Thus, Asian mothers find it more difficult to be satisfied with moderate levels of performance.

The American mothers' contentment had clearly been transmitted to their children. Fifth graders were asked whether they agreed with the statement, "I am doing as well in school as my parents want me to." American children thought this statement was more true of them than did the Asian children. We obtained similar results when we asked the question in terms of their teachers' satisfaction.

The American mothers we interviewed apparently were not strongly impressed by recent criticisms of U.S. education. As far as they were concerned, the relatively poor academic showing of U.S. students did not reflect the abilities of their own children or their children's schools. For American mothers, problems existed at other schools and with other children. Our interviews revealed little evidence that American mothers were motivated to seek improvements in the quality of their children's education or that American children believed they were doing anything but a satisfactory job in school.

We explored academic motivation in another way by posing a hypothetical question to the children: "Let's say there is a wizard who will let you make a wish about anything you want. What would you wish?" The most frequent wishes fell into four categories: money; material objects, such as toys or pets; fantasy, such as wanting to be sent to the moon, or to have more wishes; and educational aspirations, such as doing well in school

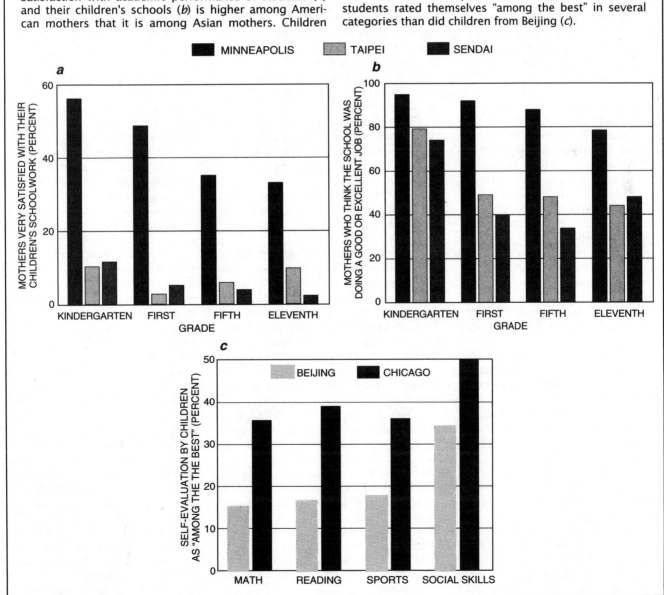

How Parents and Students See the System

Satisfaction with academic performance of students (*a*) and their children's schools (*b*) is higher among American mothers that it is among Asian mothers. Children seem to reflect their parents' attitudes: more American students rated themselves "among the best" in several categories than did children from Beijing (*c*).

■ MINNEAPOLIS   ▨ TAIPEI   ■ SENDAI

a

MOTHERS VERY SATISFIED WITH THEIR CHILDREN'S SCHOOLWORK (PERCENT)

KINDERGARTEN   FIRST   FIFTH   ELEVENTH
GRADE

b

MOTHERS WHO THINK THE SCHOOL WAS DOING A GOOD OR EXCELLENT JOB (PERCENT)

KINDERGARTEN   FIRST   FIFTH   ELEVENTH
GRADE

c

▨ BEIJING   ■ CHICAGO

SELF-EVALUATION BY CHILDREN AS "AMONG THE THE BEST" (PERCENT)

MATH   READING   SPORTS   SOCIAL SKILLS

or going to college. Almost 70 percent of the Chinese children focused their wishes on education. American children were more interested in receiving money and material objects. Fewer than 10 percent of the American children expressed wishes about education.

The enthusiasm Asian children express about school comes in part, of course, from the well-known societal emphasis on education. Several studies of immigrants have documented the willingness of Asian children to work hard [see "Indochinese Refugee Families and Academic Achievement," by Nathan Caplan, Marcella H. Choy and John K. Whitmore; SCIENTIFIC AMERICAN, February 1992]. This attitude stems from Confucian beliefs about the role of effort and ability in achievement. The malleability of human behavior has long been emphasized in Chinese writings, and a similar theme is found in Japanese philosophy. Individual differences in potential are deemphasized, and great importance is placed on the role of effort and diligence in modifying the course of human development.

In contrast, Americans are much more likely to point to the limitations imposed by an assumed level of innate ability. This belief has potentially devastating effects. When parents believe success in school depends for the most part on ability rather than effort, they are less likely to foster participation in activities related to academic achievement. Such parents may question whether spending time in academic pursuits after school is useful for children of presumed low ability. They may readily accept poor performance. Furthermore, if the parents believe the child has high ability, they may question whether such activities are needed.

It is relatively easy to demonstrate the greater emphasis placed by Americans on innate ability. One approach is to ask children to rate the importance of certain factors for doing well in school. Beijing children emphasized effort rather than ability. Chicago children thought both to be of near-equal importance.

In another approach we asked Taipei, Sendai and Minneapolis children to indicate the degree to which they agreed with the statement that "everybody in the class has about the same amount of ability in math." American children expressed less strong agreement than did the Chinese and Japanese children. Mothers follow the same pattern of re-

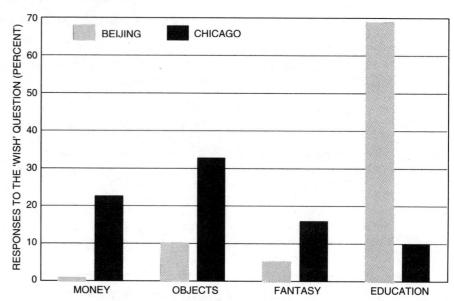

WISHFUL THINKING seems to reflect cultural priorities. Chicago children tended to wish for money and material objects, such as toys or pets. Beijing children wished for educational goals, such as going to college.

sponse. When asked about the degree to which they agreed that "any student can be good at math if he/she works hard enough," Minneapolis mothers expressed less agreement than did Sendai or Taipei mothers.

Children may work harder because they believe achievement depends on diligence. The idea that increased effort will lead to improved performance is an important factor in accounting for the willingness of Chinese and Japanese children, teachers and parents to spend so much time and effort on the children's academic work.

The enthusiasm for school also seems to come from the happy times that Asian children appear to have there. That these children regard school as pleasant—rather than as regimented, austere and demanding—surprises most Americans. Our stereotype is that the intense quest for academic excellence reduces the possibilities of making school a place that children enjoy. This clearly is not the case.

When we compare the daily routine in Asian and American schools, we realize how easy it is to overlook the constraints of American schools. Classes begin shortly after the students arrive, and the children leave just after their last class ends. Rarely is there more than a single recess. The lunch period—a potential time for play and social interaction—is usually limited to half an hour or less. As a consequence, American children spend most of their time at school in the classroom.

In contrast, the daily routine in Asian schools offers many opportunities for social experience. There are frequent recesses, long lunch periods and after-school activities and clubs. Such opportunities make up about one fourth of the time spent during the eight hours at school. The school day is longer in Asia mainly because of the time devoted to these nonacademic periods. Play, social interaction and extracurricular activity may not contribute directly to academic success, but they make school an enjoyable place. The enjoyment likely creates cooperative attitudes.

The relative lack of nonacademic activities in American schools is reflected in greater amounts of time spent in play after school. American mothers estimated that their elementary school children spend nearly 25 hours a week playing. We found this surprisingly high until we considered how little time was available for play at school. Estimates for Chinese children were much lower—their social life at school is reflected in the shorter amounts of time they play after returning home.

Chicago children also spent nearly twice as much time as Beijing children watching television. But compared with Americans, Japanese students from kindergarten through high school spent even more time watching television. The difference in this case appears to be that Japanese children are more likely to watch television after they had completed their homework.

American children were reported to

spend significantly less time than Asian children in doing homework and reading for pleasure—two pursuits that are likely to contribute to academic achievement. Mothers estimated that the Taipei children spent about four times as much time each day doing homework as did American children and over twice as much time as did Japanese children. American children were estimated to spend less time reading for pleasure than their Asian peers throughout their school years.

The enjoyment Asian students have at school may be the reason they appear to Western visitors as well behaved and well adjusted. These observations, however, have always been informal, and no data exist to support or refute them. So we decided to ask mothers and teachers in Beijing and Chicago about these matters. In particular, we questioned them about physical symptoms of tension, which we thought would be a good indicator of adjustment.

Chinese mothers reported fewer complaints by their children of stomachaches and headaches, as well as fewer requests to stay home from school than did American mothers. The Chinese mothers also more frequently described their children as happy and obedient. Only 4 percent of the Chinese mothers, but 20 percent of the American mothers, said their children encountered problems in getting along with other children.

The intense dedication of Chinese elementary school children to schoolwork did not appear to result in tension and maladjustment. Nor have we found patterns of psychological disturbance

among several thousand Chinese and Japanese 11th graders in self-evaluations of stress, depression, academic anxiety or psychosomatic complaints. Our data do not support the Western assumption that Asian children must experience extraordinary stress from their more demanding curriculum. The clear academic goals and the enthusiastic support given by family, teachers and peers may reduce the strain from working so hard.

The achievement of Asian students is facilitated by the extensive amount of attention teachers can give the children. Indeed, one of the biggest differences we found was the amount of time teachers had. Beijing teachers were incredulous after we described a typical day in American schools. When, they asked, did the teachers prepare their lessons, consult with one another about teaching techniques, grade the students' papers and work with individual students who were having difficulties? Beijing teachers, they explained, are responsible for classes for no more than three hours a day; for those with homeroom duties, the total is four hours. The situation is similar in Japan and Taiwan, where, according to our estimates, teachers are in charge of classes only 60 percent of the time they are at school.

Teaching is more of a group endeavor in Asia than it is in the U.S. Teachers frequently consult with one another, because, in following the national curriculum, they are all teaching the same lesson at about the same time. More

experienced teachers help newer ones. Head teachers in each grade organize meetings to discuss technique and to devise lesson plans and handouts. The group may spend hours designing a single lesson or discussing how to frame questions that will produce the greatest understanding from their pupils. They also have a teachers' room, where all the instructors have desks and where they keep their books and teaching materials. They spend most of the time there when not teaching.

American teachers have neither the time nor the incentive to share experiences with one another or to benefit from hearing about the successes and failures of other instructors. Each teacher's desk is in the classroom, and little space is allocated specifically for informal discussions and meetings. The teachers' room in American schools is typically a place to rest rather than to work. As a result, American teachers spend most of their time at school isolated in their own classrooms, with few opportunities for professional interaction or consultation.

With no national curriculum or guidelines, American schools typically develop their own agenda. In any year the curriculum may not be consistent within a city or even within a single school. Adding further to the diversity in the curricula among American classrooms is the fact that teachers are free to proceed through textbooks at any rate they wish, skipping the parts they do not find especially interesting or useful.

The demanding daily schedule places serious constraints on the ability of

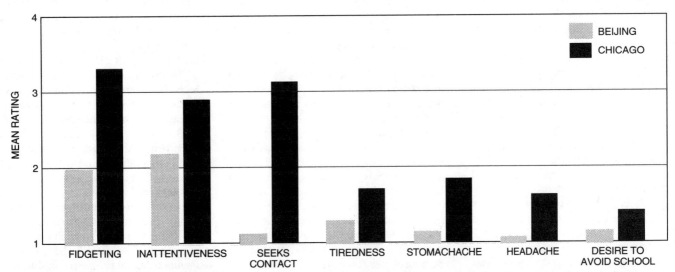

SYMPTOMS OF STRESS in U.S. classrooms exceed those in Asian schools. First-grade teachers in Chicago and Beijing estimated the frequency of physical complaints among students. They rated their impressions on a scale from 1 (seldom complained) to 5 (often complained). American schoolchildren expressed symptoms more often than did Beijing students.

American teachers to create exciting, well-organized lessons. They usually must prepare for their classes at home during evenings and weekends. Furthermore, they must cover all elementary school subjects, because teachers for specific academic subjects typically do not appear until junior high school. Evenings are not the most appropriate time to begin such a difficult task, for teachers are tired from the demands of school and their own affairs. There are, of course, excellent American teachers. And there are individual differences among Asian teachers. But what has impressed us in our observations and in the data from our studies is how remarkably well most East Asian teachers do their jobs.

Asian teachers can be described best as well-informed, well-prepared guides. They do not see themselves primarily as dispensers of information and arbiters of what is correct but rather as persons responsible for guiding students skillfully through the material. Each lesson typically begins with a statement of its purpose and ends with a summary of its content. The lesson follows a well-planned script in which children are led through a series of productive interactions and discussions. Teachers regard children as active participants in the learning process who must play an important role in producing, explaining and evaluating solutions to problems.

The skill shown by Asian teachers is not acquired in college. In fact, some teachers in China have only a high school education. The pattern for training teachers resembles that provided to other professionals: in-service training under the supervision of skilled models. Colleges are assumed to provide basic knowledge about subject matter, as well as about child development and theories of learning. But Asian instructors believe the art of teaching can be accomplished better in classrooms of elementary schools than in lecture halls of colleges. This approach stands in sharp contrast to that taken in the U.S., where teaching skill is generally thought to be best acquired through several specialized courses in teaching methods.

The skills employed by Asian teachers are also more effective in attracting and maintaining children's attention. We found Asian children listening to the teacher more frequently than American children—at least 80 percent of the time versus approximately 60 percent. This finding may also result from differences

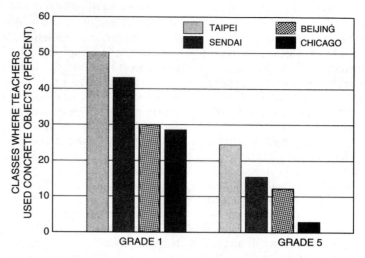

USING OBJECTS to teach young children is often more effective than verbal instruction. In mathematics classes, teachers in Asia use concrete materials more frequently than do American teachers.

in the number of recesses in Asian and American schools. Attention is more likely to falter after several hours of classes than it is if opportunities for play and relaxation precede each class, as is the case in Asian schools.

Another likely reason for the American children's lack of attention lies in the manner in which U.S. teachers often structure the lessons. Because of the time spent on seatwork—exercises or assignments children are to complete at their desks—and the way in which seatwork is used, American children have fewer opportunities to interact with the teacher than do children in Asian classrooms. American teachers rely more heavily on seatwork than do Asian teachers, which is not surprising. Giving children such tasks is one of the few ways American teachers can gain some free time in their grueling daily schedule.

In the U.S., teachers usually explain the concepts during the early part of the lesson and then assign seatwork during the later part. Asian teachers, on the other hand, intersperse brief periods of seatwork throughout the class period. Seatwork is a means of getting children to practice what they have just learned and of quickly spotting difficulties the children might be encountering. American teachers are less likely to take advantage of the diagnostic value of seatwork.

Children's attention also increases when they receive feedback. If students do not receive some type of acknowledgment from the teacher or some indication of whether their work is correct, they are more likely to lose interest. In a sur-

prisingly large number of classes, Chicago teachers failed to provide feedback to the children, especially when the children were doing seatwork. In nearly half of the 160 class periods we observed in the Chicago fifth grades, teachers failed to offer any type of evaluation as the children worked alone at their desks. In striking contrast, lack of such acknowledgment was practically never observed in Sendai and only infrequently in Taipei.

In addition, Asian teachers make more frequent use of materials that can be manipulated. Jean Piaget and other psychologists (as well as most parents and teachers) have discovered that young children enjoy manipulating concrete objects, which is often a more effective way to learn than is listening to verbal instruction. Even so, American teachers were much less likely than Asian teachers to provide concrete objects for manipulation in mathematics classes.

Finally, Asian teachers make the subjects interesting by giving them some meaningful relation to the children's everyday lives. In mathematics, word problems often serve this function. They can transform mathematics from a subject of dull computation to one requiring active problem solving. We found that American teachers were much less likely than Asian teachers to introduce word problems. Fifth-grade American teachers presented word problems in less than one out of five class periods; Sendai teachers included word problems in more than eight out of every 10 lessons. Similar differences emerged when we calculated how often children were asked to construct word problems themselves. This exercise rarely occurred in American classrooms.

Asian teachers are able to engage children's interest not because they have insights that are unknown in the U.S. but because they take well-known principles and have the time and energy to apply them with remarkable skill. They incorporate a variety of teaching techniques within each lesson, rely more frequently on discussion than on lectures, teach children how to make smooth transitions from one type of activity to another and seldom engage in irrelevant discussions—all approaches to teaching that American instructors would agree are reasonable and effective.

Perhaps the most pointed difference between the goals of Asian and American teachers emerged when we asked teachers in Beijing and Chicago what

they considered to be the most-important characteristics of a good instructor. "Clarity," said nearly half of the Beijing teachers. "Sensitivity to the needs of individuals" was the most common response of the Chicago teachers. Beijing teachers were also more likely to emphasize enthusiasm, and Chicago teachers were more likely to stress patience.

Have the goals of education diverged to such a degree in Eastern and Western cultures that American teachers see their main tasks as those of evaluating and meeting the needs of individuals, while Asian teachers can devote their attention to the process of teaching? If this is the case, the academic achievement of American children will not improve until conditions are as favorable as those provided in Asia. Clearly, a challenge in the U.S. is to create a greater cultural emphasis on education and academic success. But we must also make changes in their teaching schedules, so that they,

too, will be able to incorporate sound teaching practices into their daily routines.

FURTHER READING

PRESCHOOL IN THREE CULTURES: JAPAN, CHINA, AND THE UNITED STATES. J. J. Tobin, D. Y. H. Wu and D. H. Davidson. Yale University Press, 1989.

JAPANESE EDUCATIONAL PRODUCTIVITY. Edited by R. Leestma and H. J. Walberg. University of Michigan, Center for Japanese Studies, 1992.

LEARNING TO GO TO SCHOOL IN JAPAN: THE TRANSITION FROM HOME TO PRESCHOOL LIFE. L. Peak. University of California Press, 1992.

THE LEARNING GAP: WHY OUR SCHOOLS ARE FAILING AND WHAT WE CAN LEARN FROM JAPANESE AND CHINESE EDUCATION. H. W. Stevenson and J. W. Stigler. Summit Books, 1992.

Development During Adolescence and Early Adulthood

- Adolescence (Articles 43–46)
- Early Adulthood (Articles 47–49)

In some cultures, a ritualistic ceremony marks the transition to adulthood—a transition that occurs quickly, smoothly, and with relatively few problems. The onset of adulthood is more difficult to distinguish in modern industrial societies. In American culture the transition is vague. Does someone become an adult when he or she achieves the right to vote, the privilege of obtaining a driver's license, the ability to legally order an alcoholic drink in a bar, or the right to volunteer for the armed forces? The first selection in the *Adolescence* subsection, "The Thunder Years," addresses the relationship among parents and their teenagers. Bruce Baldwin suggests that while adolescence is construed as a time of stressful parent-child

relationships in our society, it need not be. Baldwin recommends strategies that parents can use to keep rebelliousness to a minimum.

Teenagers today are faced with temptations such as drugs, sex, and mobility at an earlier age than their predecessors and at the same time are less likely to get the guidance they need from adults, due to such factors as the high rate of single parent homes and working mothers. As a consequence, teen-related problems such as drug and alcohol use, teen pregnancy, dropping out of high school, and suicide occur at distressingly high rates. These issues are examined in "A Much Riskier Passage."

Former NBA basketball superstar Magic Johnson

shocked the world when he announced that he had tested HIV-positive. Predictions were made that, finally, teens would take the threat of AIDS seriously. Do they? Not enough to slow the rate of new infections, according to "Teenagers and AIDS." The problem is compounded in teens by their "It can't happen to me" attitude. This article surveys some of the approaches now being tried with teens in an attempt to fight this out-of-control epidemic.

Adolescence has its ups and downs, but some researchers argue that much of the storm and stress attributed to adolescence is exaggerated. Focusing on the negative aspects of adolescent behavior may create a set of expectations that the adolescent strives to fulfill. However, for some adolescents the transition to adulthood *is* fraught with despair, loneliness, and interpersonal conflict. The pressures of peer group, school, and family may produce conformity or may lead to rebellion against or withdrawal from friends, parents, or society at large.

Although much attention has been given to the problems of adolescence, developmentalists have shown far less interest in the early years of adulthood. The second subsection, *Early Adulthood*, includes articles that examine the pressures that peak as the individual separates from the family and assumes the independence and responsibilities of adulthood.

During early adulthood, individuals experience significant changes in their lives. Marriage, parenthood, divorce, single parenting, employment, and the effects of sexism may be powerful influences on ego development, self-concept, and personality. Negative emotions such as jealousy and envy subvert efforts to establish effective interpersonal relationships and often lead to hostility or isolation. "Proceeding with Caution" describes the "twentysomething generation," i.e., today's young adults who fall between 18 and 29 years of age. They are a "back-to-basics" group living in the shadow of the baby boomers. They have very few role models. They are staying single longer and living at home longer. Many are from families of divorce or were latchkey kids, and they do not want this for their own children—if they ever have any. This generation likes reinforcement—reviews, grades, performance evaluations, etc. They are the best-educated group in U.S. history—the means to a middle-class lifestyle. However, they are reluctant to make vocational commitments.

Parenting, though never easy, is stressful even for well-adjusted couples. And being a new parent today may be harder than in the past. As described in "Is There Love after Baby?" conflict over parental roles and division of labor (including child care) is responsible for much of the difficulty. The push for young mothers to return to the work force, combined with the isolation from extended families so common in our mobile society, compounds the child care issue and places additional stress on the couple's relationship.

Some individuals seem to grow stronger when confronted by the stresses of daily living, whereas others have great difficulty coping. The challenge for developmentalists is to discover the factors that contribute to one's ability to cope with stress and the natural crises of life with minimum disruption to the integrity of one's personality.

Looking Ahead: Challenge Questions

For some, the teen years are a largely joyous period in which a variety of challenges are successfully negotiated. For others, everything seems to come apart as many adolescents and young adults lose themselves in drugs or cults rather than confronting their problems and taking steps to develop self-control and self-reliance. What accounts for the victories of the first group and the failures of the second? What kinds of parenting techniques might have given the latter the self-esteem and coping skills to combat their self-doubts and loneliness?

Even for the well-adjusted, however, adolescence seems to be fraught with formidable difficulties these days. Is the nature of adolescence changing? If so, how? Do you think adolescence really continues into the late 20s, as some experts maintain? Why have the many programs to promote safe sexual practices in teens met with so little success?

Do the generations really differ as much as suggested in "Proceeding with Caution"? In your experience, do the characteristics of the "twentysomething" generation described in this article ring true? Or are people, regardless of similarities in age, too variable to categorize?

What do you or your married friends regard as the greatest challenges to successful adaptation that couples face in adapting to the birth of their first child?

The Thunder Years

After the wonder years, the winds of change bring adolescence. Here's how you and your teenager can weather the storm.

BRUCE A. BALDWIN

Dr. Bruce A. Baldwin is a practicing psychologist and author who heads Direction Dynamics in Wilmington, North Carolina, a consulting service specializing in promoting quality of life. This article has been taken from a chapter of Dr. Baldwin's book Beyond the Cornucopia Kids: How to Raise Healthy Achieving Children.

When you look back to your teenage years, do you remember the emotional highs and lows, the thrills and the fears, the sense of discovery? To you and your pals, the world was new. You had few worries about the future. Adventures were everywhere.

Now, as an adult, you remember the good times and the insecurities, and sometimes there's a lingering pain for the disappointments you experienced. If you're a parent, your thoughts often turn to your teenage children. You have hopes and fears for them. You think of all the heedless things you did, and you worry about your kids doing the same things. You hope they won't give you as many sleepless nights as you gave *your* parents. Deep down, though, you know that some things don't change with the years. One of them is that teenagers will be teenagers.

Early adolescents grow rapidly emotionally, socially, and, of course, physically. Their world is confusing and unstable, and that makes effective parenting frustrating. Add the present dangers that weren't there when you were growing up, and a volatile mix of strong emotions and parental protectiveness emerges. Part of the problem lies in the differences in perspective that lead to tension in parent-teenager relationships. Here's what this touchy "hassle factor" is all about.

> With their new "adult perspective" on life and living, teenagers develop acute sensitivity to being controlled.

What parents see. From the relative tranquility of childhood has suddenly emerged a physically larger, psychologically stronger, but still emotionally immature young adult. This young man or woman, more mobile and not as communicative as before, loudly and in no uncertain terms demands new privileges, complete freedom of choice, and personal rights. Because parents are rightly fearful of their teenagers' lack of experience and limited perspective, they resist lifting limits.

What adolescents see. With their new "adult perspective" on life and living, teenagers develop acute sensitivity to being controlled. They see themselves striving for independence from the domination of too-restrictive parents who are holding them back. Teenagers resist what they perceive to be the old-fashioned, out-of-touch, completely unreasonable, and dictatorial control of parents.

What's really going on. At this stage, early adolescents are beginning to separate emotionally from their parents. Although they do not realize it, their rebellion is actually a way to begin establishing an adult identity quite different from the childish dependency of earlier years. As the process of separation continues through testing and resistance, they gradually develop more emotional autonomy.

However uncomfortable for parents and teenagers, all of this behavior is entirely normal, and you must walk a fine line if you want to help a vulnerable young man or woman gain autonomy and independence from you. On the one hand, you must give more responsibility to a physically maturing and now mobile teenager. On the other hand, you must also provide enough structure to give that

From *USAir Magazine,* March 1993, pp. 14, 16-20. Adapted from B. A. Baldwin, *Beyond the Cornucopia Kids: How to Raise Healthy Achieving Children,* Direction Dynamics, Wilmington, NC, 1988. Book available from DIRECTION DYNAMICS, 309 Honeycutt Dr., Wilmington, NC 28412-7171 for $12.95 postpaid (NC residents add $0.66 sales tax).

adolescent personal security and to ensure his or her safety.

Your task as a parent is to provide protective custody in ways that your teenager can accept and respect (albeit grudgingly). It's not easy. You must retain perspective when your emotions may be overwhelming. You must remain strong even when you are tired and vulnerable. You must retain a depth of understanding when change occurs daily. And you must hold onto sound values despite intense pressure to give in to your teenager's demands. Learning more about the parent-teen relationship will help you remain calm and even thrive during these hectic times.

All parents of teenagers wrestle constantly with one question: How can they set reasonable limits that will provide their teenager with enough independence to grow toward maturity without being so lax or so controlling that they invite serious trouble?

Too many limits on your teenager will force him or her to become crafty and develop manipulative ways to circumvent your rules. Sometimes it can trigger outright rebelliousness and defiance. When you set too many restrictions on your teenager, you reinforce evading personal responsibility rather than accepting it. But too much freedom too fast is also dangerous. Gradually gaining freedom allows the teenager to make the continuous adjustments that are necessary as control from external sources (parents) is transferred to internal resources (self).

Work to create a reasonable balance between too much freedom too soon and too little independence too late. Monitor your teenager, and then adjust your rules as necessary. Your goal is to help him or her grow toward emotional maturity and personal responsibility while minimizing the risk of serious problems. While there are no pat ways to implement this process, here are some suggestions.

Do not use the "seniority system." In business, perks and privileges are often granted automatically on the basis of how many years you've been with the company, not necessarily competence or demonstrated responsibility. Individuals in such organizations don't have to work to earn new privileges—they just have to stay long enough. This is not a good

---

Your goal is to help your teenager grow toward personal responsibility and emotional maturity.

---

way to parent your teenager. Grant your adolescent new privileges based on maturity and demonstrated responsibility, not on how long he or she has been with the family. Each child is different in terms of how much responsibility can be handled and when.

Negotiate, don't mandate. Your adolescent desperately wants to be treated as an adult. Negotiate limits directly with your child from time to time. Sit down to talk about new privileges and responsibilities rather than unilaterally setting rules that invite rebellion or a power struggle.

Beware of "serial exceptions." If you too frequently grant well-rationalized exceptions to your rules, you run the risk that the exception will become the rule. While you must be reasonably flexible and respond to extenuating circumstances, be sure that your adolescent doesn't learn to manufacture these circumstances to gain the easy "just this once" exception.

Watch for "reversed awards." Albert was suspended from school for continual misbehavior. He received his reward when his parents decided that those three days would provide a wonderful time for a skiing trip. Nan found that the only time that she really got to talk to her parents was when she was in trouble. When she was good, she was virtually ignored. Be very conscious of what you are rewarding if you want your limits to be respected.

THE WAYS OF THE WORLD

The early adolescent years are disproportionately influential in shaping adjustment to the later responsibilities of adulthood. Patterns set during the teen years often last a lifetime, so you'll want to help your child develop positive ways of relating and coping. Although no two teenagers are exactly alike, here are a number of sound parenting guidelines that, when used consistently, will help you and your teenager. Discuss these with your teen, and make them an integral part of your family value system.

Insist on meeting your child's friends. It's very important that you have contact with your child's peer group. It could mean trouble if you know the friends' names but have never seen or met them, if your child always insists on going to meet friends somewhere else, or if your teenager and friends never spend time at your home. Make it a mandate for yourself to meet all of your teenager's friends and have them spend at least some time in your home.

Get to know the parents of your teenager's friends. There are several sound reasons for this suggestion. First, it's nice to know others who are dealing with the same parenting issues that you are. Second, when you get to know those parents (at least on the telephone), you already have a relationship, and it's easier to call if there's a problem. Third, you'll get a sense of how effectively these other parents parent, which helps you better protect your teenager if you find other parents' responses unsatisfactory.

Check arrangements with parents of your teenager's friends. Most teenagers attempt to pull a fast one at least once by saying they are going to a friend's house and then going somewhere else. Confront this kind of deceit early to avoid its becoming a pattern. Savvy parents spot-check such arrangements and invite friends' parents to do the same. Insist that your teenager call and check with you if there is any change in plans.

Stay in touch with the school and with your child's teachers. Dramatic changes in academic performance often occur during the teen years. There may be relationship or authority problems at school that sometimes don't show up at home because teenagers hide them or refuse to discuss them. A teacher's insight into a teen's behavior often can help parents become more aware and prevent emerging problems from getting worse. Make time to talk with teachers regularly.

Insist on reasonable family time together. Teenagers naturally want to spend more time with friends than with family. Responsible parents, however, don't let a teenager completely abandon or withdraw from the family. Although they may resist, teens need some quality time with their families for healthy emotional development to take place. Suggest that your teen invite a friend along on family outings.

Educate yourself and your teenager. The "if they don't know about it, they won't do it" approach doesn't work. Your teenager will become educated—either through parents who provide sound and up-to-date information or from peers who disseminate distortions and erroneous information. With educated awareness, your teenager will be in a much better position to make responsible choices. Inform, but don't preach.

Don't ask too many questions. Teenagers develop a tremendous sensitivity about privacy and their independence. They dislike constantly being questioned by their parents about their thoughts, feelings, actions, or plans. When there are too many questions, a teen's responses will become short and evasive. Sometimes this triggers more questions, and a vicious circle begins. Learn to converse casually with your adolescent without intrusive questioning. Patience and good listening

skills are absolutely crucial when dealing with teenagers.

Join or develop a support group for parents of teens. Parents are increasingly isolated and sometimes have no one with whom to discuss teen issues. In recent years, parenting support groups have formed through churches and under the auspices of PTO/PTA organizations. Find one or start one in your community.

If you suspect trouble, investigate immediately. Don't jump to unwarranted conclusions or confront your teenager with unsubstantiated accusations. You should, however, remain vigilant, sensitive, and aware of what is going on in his or her life. It helps to know what to look for in terms of emotional problems and drug use. If you suspect your teenager is in trouble, seek more information, then calmly bring your concerns to your son or daughter. Angry, irrational confrontations usually don't work, but an informed and mature approach just might.

Allow your teenager to be different. As part of the separation process, your teenager will adopt different language, dress, and behaviors. This is healthy, and you should accept it within reasonable limits. Adolescents need freedom to define personal values and directions. If you overreact to your teen's newfound career possibility (not going to college, becoming a rock star), you may inadvertently reinforce that option. Patience and an accepting openness help immeasurably, especially when communicated by secure parents who don't feel that a teenager has to conform or be exactly like them.

Do not impose your solutions on all your teenager's problems. Your teenager is becoming more emotionally self-sufficient and wants to deal with problems in a more independent way. If you insist on taking over and imposing your will, he or she will not learn judgment and may even become more evasive and private, or power struggles may erupt. Create a relationship with your teenager in which there is freedom to talk over problems openly. Help define options and

consequences, but let your teenager make the final decision. This way, you keep the relationship open, and your teenager will feel better about returning to you for advice.

For parents, early adolescence is a time of letting go. For energetic young adults, it's an age of many firsts: a first date, a driver's license, an awareness of emerging sexuality, the first prom, evenings out alone, a first real job. Vivid memories of your own adolescent experiences will rise up with each new step your teenager makes toward independence. These memories take on a bittersweet quality as you realize your son or daughter is growing up. Old memories and the new independence of teenagers can conspire to make life an emotional roller coaster for parents. Here are a few parenting "givens" that, once accepted, go far toward making these trying years easier.

A healthy sense of humor is one of the best coping mechanisms. A good sense of humor requires perspective and the ability to sort out what is typical and what signals real trouble.

The healthier your involvement during the preteen years, the easier it is to parent effectively during adolescence. Don't wait until puberty to begin teaching values, spending quality time together, and implementing discipline. Teenagers who have experienced a solid family life and effective parenting from day one find early adolescence emotionally easier, and so do their parents.

One child will give you much more trouble than any of the rest. Personality, placement in sibling order, and individual emotional needs can conspire to make the adolescent years immensely more difficult for one child than for another. With this child, you must be even more sensitive, patient, and strong, because his or her sensitivity, patience, and strength will be sorely tested.

Although your values are resisted, they do make a difference. You and your value system are very important to a teenager experiencing confusing changes and intense emotions. It's normal that you will be resisted; positive feedback won't be forthcoming. Over the long haul, however, your understanding and strength of conviction during these years will influence your teenager more significantly than you may ever know.

THE PATH OF GOOD INTENTIONS

Imagine the parent-teenager relationship in terms of a hurricane. Deep within the center of every hurricane is the eye. In this area there is relative calm, despite the intensity of the storm that swirls around it. At puberty, a teenager is inexorably swept up in the swift winds of change, and parents must remain calm and aware in the eye of a hurricane.

A healthy sense of humor is one of the best coping mechanisms. A good sense of humor requires perspective and the ability to sort out what is typical and what signals real trouble. As one parent said to another, "I know how to help you understand your teenager. Just keep in mind the six 'm's' of early adolescence: moody, mouthy, messy, me, money, and monosyllables." An ability to joke and smile will see you through the trying years.

A Much
RISKIER
PASSAGE

DAVID GELMAN

There was a time when teenagers believed themselves to be part of a conquering army. Through much of the 1960s and 1970s, the legions of adolescence appeared to command the center of American culture like a victorious occupying force, imposing their singular tastes in clothing, music and recreational drugs on a good many of the rest of us. It was a hegemony buttressed by advertisers, fashion setters, record producers suddenly zeroing in on the teen multitudes as if they controlled the best part of the country's wealth, which in some sense they did. But even more than market power, what made the young insurgents invincible was the conviction that they were right: from the crusade of the children, grown-ups believed, they must learn to trust their feelings, to shun materialism, to make love, not money.

In 1990 the emblems of rebellion that once set teenagers apart have grown frayed. Their music now seems more derivative than subversive. The provocative teenage styles of dress that adults assiduously copied no longer automatically inspire emulation. And underneath the plumage, teens seem to be more interested in getting ahead in the world than in clearing up its injustices. According to a 1989 survey of high-school seniors in 40 Wisconsin communities, global concerns, including hunger, poverty and pollution, emerged last on a list of teenage worries. First were personal goals: getting good grades and good jobs. Anything but radical, the majority of teens say they're happy and eager to get on with their lives.

One reason today's teens aren't shaking the earth is that they can no longer marshal the demographic might they once could. Although their sheer numbers are still growing, they are not the illimitably expanding force that teens appeared to be 20 years ago. In 1990 they constitute a smaller percentage of the total population (7 percent, compared with nearly 10 percent in 1970). For another thing, almost as suddenly as they became a highly visible, if unlikely, power in the world, teenagers have reverted to anonymity and the old search for identity. Author Todd Gitlin, a chronicler of the '60s, believes they have become "Balkanized," united less by a common culture than by the commodities they own. He says "it's impossible to point to an overarching teen sensibility."

But as a generation, today's teenagers face more adult-strength stresses than their predecessors did—at a time when adults are much less available to help them. With the divorce rate hovering near 50 percent, and 40 to 50 percent of teenagers living in single-parent homes headed mainly by working mothers, teens are more on their own than ever. "My parents let me do anything I want as long as I don't get into trouble," writes a 15-year-old high-schooler from Ohio in an essay submitted for this special issue of NEWSWEEK. Sociologists have begun to realize, in fact, that teens are more dependent on grown-ups than was once believed. Studies indicate that they are shaped more by their parents than by their peers, that they adopt their parents' values and opinions to a greater extent than anyone realized. Adolescent specialists now see real hazards in lumping all teens together; 13-year-olds, for instance, need much more parental guidance than 19-year-olds.

These realizations are emerging just when the world has become a more dangerous place for the young. They have more access than ever to fast cars, fast drugs, easy sex—"a bewildering array of options, many with devastating outcomes," observes Beatrix Hamburg, director of Child and Adolescent Psychiatry at New York's Mount Sinai School of Medicine. Studies indicate that while overall drug abuse is down, the use of lethal drugs like crack is up in low-income neighborhoods, and a dangerous new kick called ice is making inroads in white high schools. Drinking and smoking rates remain ominously high. "The use of alcohol appears to be normative," says Stephen Small, a developmental psychologist at the University of Wisconsin. "By the upper grades, everybody's doing it."

Sexual activity is also on the rise. A poll conducted by Small suggests that most teens are regularly having sexual intercourse by the 11th grade. Parents are generally surprised by the data, Small says. "A lot of parents are saying, 'Not my kids . . .' They just don't think it's happening." Yet clearly it is: around half a million teenage girls give birth every year, and sexually transmitted diseases continue to be a major problem. Perhaps the only comforting note is that teens who are given AIDS education in schools and clinics are more apt to use condoms—a practice that could scarcely be mentioned a few years ago, let alone surveyed.

One reliable assessment of how stressful life has become for young people in this country is the Index of Social Health for Children and Youth. Authored by social-policy analyst Marc Miringoff, of Fordham University at Tarrytown, N.Y., it charts such factors as poverty, drug-abuse and high-school dropout rates. In 1987, the latest year for which statistics are available, the index fell to its lowest point in two decades. Most devastating, according to Miringoff, were the numbers of teenagers living at poverty levels—about 55 percent for single-parent households—and taking their own lives. The record rate of nearly 18 suicides per 100,000 in 1987—a total of 1,901—was double that of 1970. "If you take teens in the '50s—the 'Ozzie and Harriet' generation—those kids lived on a less complex planet," says Miringoff. "They could be kids longer."

The social index is only one of the yardsticks used on kids these days. In fact, this generation of young people is surely one of the most closely watched ever. Social scientists are tracking nearly everything they do or think about, from dating habits (they prefer going out in groups) to extracurricular activities (cheerleading has made a comeback) to general outlook (45 percent think the world is getting worse and 62 percent believe life will be harder for them than it was for their parents). One diligent prober, Reed Larson of the University of Illinois, even equipped his 500 teen subjects with beepers so he could remind them to fill out questionnaires about how they are feeling, what they are doing and who they are with at random moments during the day. Larson, a professor of human development, and psychologist Maryse Richards of Loyola University, have followed this group since grade school. Although the results of the high-school study have not been tabulated yet, the assumption is that young people are experiencing more stress by the time they reach adolescence but develop strategies to cope with it.

Without doubt, any overview of teenage problems is skewed by the experience of the inner cities, where most indicators tilt sharply toward the negative. Especially among the minority poor, teen pregnancies continue to rise, while the institution of marriage has virtually disappeared. According to the National Center for Vital Statistics, 90 percent of black teenage mothers are unmarried at the time of their child's birth, although about a third eventually marry. Teenage mothers, in turn, add to the annual school-dropout rate, which in some cities reaches as high as 60 percent. Nationwide, the unemployment rate for black teenagers is 40 to 50 percent; in some cities, it has risen to 70 percent. Crack has become a medium of commerce and violence. "The impact of crack is worse in the inner city than anywhere else," says psychiatrist Robert King, of the Yale Child Study Center. "If you look at the homicide rate among young, black males, it's frighteningly high. We also see large numbers of young mothers taking crack."

Those are realities unknown to the majority of white middle-class teenagers. Most of them are managing to get through the adolescent years with relatively few major problems. Parents may describe them as sullen and self-absorbed. They can also be secretive and rude. They hang "Do Not Disturb" signs on their doors, make phone calls from closets and behave churlishly at the dinner table if they can bring themselves to sit there at all. An earlier beeper study by Illinois's Larson found that in the period between ages 10 and 15, the amount of time young people spend with their families decreases by half. "This is when the bedroom door becomes a significant marker," he says.

Yet their rebelliousness is usually overstated. "Arguments are generally about whether to take out the garbage or whether to wear a certain hairstyle," says Bradford Brown, an associate professor of human development at the University of Wisconsin. "These are not earth-shattering issues, though they are quite irritating to parents." One researcher on a mission to destigmatize teenagers is Northwestern University professor Ken Howard, author of a book, "The Teenage World," who has just completed a study in Chicago's Cook County on where kids go for help. The perception, says Howard, is that teenagers are far worse off than they really are. He believes their emotional disturbances are no different from those of adults, and that it is only 20 percent who have most of the serious problems, in any case.

The findings of broad-based studies of teenagers often obscure the differences in their experience. They are, after all, the product of varied ethical and cultural influences. Observing adolescents in 10 communities over the past 10 years, a team of researchers headed by Frances Ianni, of Columbia University's Teachers College, encountered "considerable diversity." A key finding, reported Ianni in a 1989 article in Phi Delta Kappan magazine, was that the people in all the localities reflected the ethnic and social-class lifestyles of their parents much more than that of a universal teen culture. The researchers found "far more congruence than conflict" between the views of parents and their teenage children. "We much more frequently hear teenagers preface comments to their peers with 'my mom says' than with any attributions to heroes of the youth culture," wrote Ianni.

For years, psychologists also tended to overlook the differences between younger and older adolescents, instead grouping them together as if they all had the same needs and desires. Until a decade ago, ideas of teen behavior were heavily influenced by the work of psychologist Erik Erikson, whose own model was based on older adolescents. Erikson, for example, emphasized their need for autonomy—appropriate, perhaps, for an 18-year-old preparing to leave home for college or a job, but hardly for a 13-year-old just beginning to experience the confusions of puberty. The Erikson model nevertheless was taken as an across-the-board prescription to give teenagers independence, something that families, torn by the domestic upheavals of the '60s and '70s, granted them almost by forfeit.

In those turbulent years, adolescents turned readily enough to their peers. "When there's turmoil and social change, teenagers have a tendency to break loose and follow each other more," says Dr. John Schowalter, president of the American Academy of Child and Adolescent Psychiatry. "The leadership of adults is somewhat splintered and they're more on their own—sort of like 'Lord of the Flies'."

That period helped plant the belief that adolescents were natural rebels, who sought above all to break free of adult influence. The idea persists to this day. Says Ruby Takanishi, director of the Carnegie Council on Adolescent Development: "The society is still permeated by the notion that adolescents are different, that their hormones are raging around and they don't want to have anything to do with their parents or other adults." Yet research by Ianni and others suggests the contrary. Ianni points also to studies of so-called invulnerable adolescents—those who develop into stable young adults in spite of coming from troubled homes, or other adversity. "A lot of people have attributed this to some inner resilience," he says. "But what we've seen in practically all cases is some caring adult figure who was a constant in that kid's life."

Not that teenagers were always so dependent on adults. Until the mid-19th century, children labored in the fields alongside their parents. But by the time they were 15, they might marry and go out into the world. Industrialization and compulsory education ultimately deprived them of a role in the family work unit, leaving them in a state of suspension between childhood and adulthood.

To teenagers, it has always seemed a useless period of waiting. Approaching physical and sexual maturity, they feel capable of doing many of the things adults do. But they are not treated like adults. Instead they must endure a prolonged childhood that is stretched out even more nowadays by the need to attend college—and then possibly graduate school—in order to make one's way in the world. In the family table of organization, they are mainly in charge of menial chores. Millions of teenagers now have part-time or full-time jobs, but those tend to be in the service industries, where the pay and the work are often equally unrewarding.

If teenagers are to stop feeling irrelevant, they need to feel needed, both by the family and by the larger world. In the '60s they gained some sense of empowerment from their visibility, their music, their sheer collective noise. They also joined and swelled the ranks of Vietnam War protesters, giving them a feeling of importance that evidently they have not had since. In the foreword to "Student Service," a book based on a 1985 Carnegie Foundation survey of teenagers' attitudes toward work and community service, foundation director Ernest Boyer wrote: "Time and time again, students complained that they felt isolated, unconnected to the larger world . . . And this detachment occurs at the very time students are deciding who they are and where they fit." Fordham's Miringoff goes so far as to link the rising suicide rate among teens to their feelings of disconnection. He recalls going to the 1963 March on Washington as a teenager, and gaining "a sense of being part of something larger. That idealism, that energy, was a very stabilizing thing."

Surely there is still room for idealism in the '90s, even if the causes are considered less glamorous. But despite growing instances of teenagers involving themselves in good works, such as recycling campaigns, tutorial programs or serving meals at shelters for the homeless, no study has yet detected anything like a national groundswell of volunteerism. Instead, according to University of Michigan social psychologist Lloyd Johnston, teens seem to be taking their cues from a culture that, up until quite recently at least, has glorified self-interest and opportunism. "It's fair to say that young people are more career oriented than before, more concerned about making money and prestige," says Johnston. "These changes are consistent with the Me Generation and looking for the good life they see on television."

Some researchers say that, indeed, the only thing uniting teenagers these days are the things they buy and plug into. Rich or poor, all have their Walkmans, their own VCRs and TVs. Yet in some ways, those marvels of communication isolate them even more. Teenagers, says Beatrix Hamburg, are spending "a lot of time alone in their rooms."

Other forces may be working to isolate them as well. According to Dr. Elena O. Nightingale, author of a Carnegie Council paper on teen rolelessness, a pattern of "age segregation" is shrinking the amount of time adolescents spend with grown-ups. In place of family outings and vacations, for example, entertainment is now more geared toward specific age groups. (The teen-terrorizing "Freddy" flicks and their ilk would be one example.) Even in the sorts of jobs typically available to teenagers, such as fast-food chains, they are usually supervised by people close to their age, rather than by adults, notes Nightingale. "There's a real need for places for teenagers to go where there's a modicum of adult involvement," she says.

Despite the riskier world they face, it would be a mistake to suggest that all adolescents of this generation are feeling more angst than their predecessors. Middle-class teenagers, at least, seem content with their lot on the whole: According to recent studies, 80 percent—the same proportion as 20 years ago—profess satisfaction with their own lives, if not with the state of the world. Many teenagers, nevertheless, evince wistfulness for what they think of as the more heroic times of the '60s and '70s—an era, they believe, when teenagers had more say in the world. Playwright Wendy Wasserstein, whose Pulitzer Prize-winning "The Heidi Chronicles" was about coming of age in those years, says she has noticed at least a "stylistic" nostalgia in the appearance of peace-sign earrings and other '60s artifacts. "I guess that comes from the sense of there having been a unity, a togetherness," she says. "Today most teens are wondering about what they're going to do when they grow up. We had more of a sense of liberation, of youth—we weren't thinking about getting that job at Drexel." Pop-culture critic Greil Marcus, however, believes it was merely the "self-importance" of the '60s generation—his own contemporaries—"that has oppressed today's kids into believing they've missed something. There's something sick about my 18-year-old wanting to see Paul McCartney or the Who. We would never have emulated our parents' culture."

But perhaps that's the point: the teens of the '90s do emulate the culture of their parents, many of whom are the very teens who once made such an impact on their own parents. These parents no doubt have something very useful to pass on to their children—maybe their lost sense of idealism rather than the preoccupation with going and getting that seems, so far, their main legacy to the young. Mom and Dad have to earn a living and fulfill their own needs—they are not likely to be coming home early. But there must be a time and place for them to give their children the advice, the comfort and, most of all, the feelings of possibility that any new generation needs in order to believe in itself.

With MARY TALBOT *and* PAMELA G. KRIPKE

The gender machine

Congress is looking for ways to remove old barriers to girls' success

Most adults still remember the prefeminist ditty about little girls being made of "sugar and spice and everything nice." And most who remember have long since dismissed it as an archaic old saw, a vestige of sexism long since eradicated. But while Americans have been busy celebrating their own sexual enlightenment over the past decades, scientists have continued to examine the nuances of gender and sex roles in the classroom, on the playing field and at home, and the latest research is far from encouraging. Despite the 20-year-old federal mandate for gender equity in schools, despite feminism's many effects and despite Hillary Rodham Clinton's ground-breaking activism in the White House, society's gender-sorting machinery still grinds away, steering girls forcefully into outdated female roles. Its grumblings can be heard throughout a girl's everyday world; at playtime, in television programming, even in the guiding words of well-intentioned parents and teachers. Its damage can be seen in the way girls hush up as they age, in the crisis of confidence most face as teens and in the often-diminished career aspirations of even the brightest young women.

Renewed crusade. This unsettling news from social scientists has left a generation of feminists aghast, and it is now spawning a massive national movement aimed at dismantling the gender-sorting machine and ensuring that girls have the opportunities everyone assumed they already had. Universities, foundations and women's groups have all joined the crusade, formulating programs to counter old stereotypes, foster self-esteem and encourage girls to venture into nontraditional fields. At the forefront of the drive is a nine-part piece of legislation entitled the Gender Equity in Education Act, cosponsored by more than 70 members of the House of Representatives and poised to move through Congress this fall. The bill is a response to various social forces working against girls, ranging from teacher indifference and discouragement to debilitating sexual harassment. While the measure has drawn the scorn of some critics who see it transforming girls and young women into a new class of victims, so far the bill has not met with a trace of opposition inside the halls of Congress.

Advocates of the legislation are adamant that their efforts have less to do with altruism than they do with a productive citizenry. "It's not only that these girls need us, it's that we absolutely need them," says Jane Daniels, head of a National Science Foundation effort to bring more girls into math and science. "How can we imagine, in this highly technical world, that our economy won't collapse if we fail to fully develop half our nation's brainpower?" The future awaiting today's schoolgirl not only will be devoid of many of the low-skilled jobs that 60 percent of women now hold, but it will demand three times the current number of women scientists, according to NSF projections.

Against such prospects, current findings on the typical girl's development look grim indeed. Girls participate in class discussions at only an eighth the rate that boys do, and researchers find links between this silence and the depression and suicidal feelings that strike girls three or four times more often than boys. Although the old myth that boys are more capable and interested in math and science has been disproved time and time again, many girls nevertheless believe they can't handle the subjects and drop out of those classes, even after earning exceptional grades. By the time high-school graduation approaches, young women are a minority in all advanced math and science courses; they are outnumbered 2 to 1 in computer classes and score 50 points lower than boys on the math portion of the Scholastic Aptitude Test. With the 21st century in sight, secretary and nurse still often top the list of girls' career aspirations.

Some efforts to chip away at girls' disincentives are already paying off. Through training efforts that include classroom videotapes, teachers have been able to spot how they inadvertently overlook or discourage their female students. With simple adjustments of style, teachers find that the girls in their classrooms change from silent witnesses into involved hand-raisers virtually overnight and that the 8-to-1 gender gap in participation simply vanishes. At least a few schools in all 50 states have hired gender-equity trainers, and the Gender Equity in Education Act would provide more federal dollars for such training.

A key factor in capturing and maintaining girls' interest and proficiency in science, math and computer classes appears to be a cooperative learning environment. In trying to find out why girls shied away from the classes, educators discovered that boys typically monopolize the computer monitors, science equipment and math contests, leaving even the brightest girls to lurk about in the corners of the classroom. By focusing on group projects, teachers were able to keep girls involved and enthusiastic. The NSF is currently funding 15 model programs, and the new legislation calls for added funds to encourage new ways of teaching math and science.

Spreading the word. The broader purpose of the Gender Equity Act is to institutionalize the idea of gender equity in the nation's public schools. An Office of Women's Equity at the education department, for example, would disseminate information on programs that work

 From *U.S. News & World Report*, August 2, 1993, pp. 42-44. © 1993 by U.S. News & World Report. Reprinted by permission.

for girls throughout the nation's schools and mandate that schools follow certain equity policies. "The law would put gender issues firmly in the mind of every school administrator," says Alicia Coro, head of the department's school-improvement programs. The Clinton administration is expected to declare its support for the proposal within the next few weeks.

Yet for all the signs of progress, a close look at girls' lives hints that many of the forces that inhibit them will not be easily countered with a new law or an experimental program. A landmark study by human development scholars Carol Gilligan of Harvard University and Lyn Mikel Brown of Colby College shows that even girls with "all the right" circumstances suffer a traumatic loss of confidence as they grow up. Gilligan's and Brown's recent book, "Meeting at the Crossroads," details a five-year study of 100 girls between 7 and 18 at a private, all-girls school in Ohio. Even though these girls had professional mothers as role models and did well academically, at the age of 11 or 12 their psychological development stalled. The girls began to repress emotions and opinions; they grew confused and uncertain, unable to speak their minds and were paralyzed at the thought of even minor conflict.

Extensive interviews revealed the source of such symptoms. The girls described poignantly how they had learned, even from mothers and female teachers, that a "good girl" attempts to please everyone, is too nice to express anger or cause conflict, politely lets the other person have the upper hand and thoughtfully puts her own needs last. As the girls left childhood and entered puberty, these messages intensified. To conform to the ideal, the girls explained how they silenced themselves, went through mental dissociations and even remained in harmful or abusive situations. Many girls spoke of "not really feeling like myself."

It is this pervasive cultural image of the "good girl" that is perhaps the most powerful gear of the gender-sorting machine, and the one that will undoubtedly prove hardest to shut down. Studies of a girl's first years of life show that from the day she is born, she is inundated with old-fashioned toys, clothes and rules of conduct. Child-development scholars Kay Bussey and Albert Bandura published a report in *Child Development* last fall showing that kids learn and internalize such stereotypes between the ages of 2 and 5, and that despite current applause for gender equality, children in the study "seem to be as stereotypically sex-typed as those of yesteryear."

Although the traditional feminine ideal, the sugar and spice, may seem innocuous enough, it is in fact potent, deterministic and harmful, psychologists are now saying. It is this ideal that keeps girls from studying "male" subjects even when the doors are opened to them, that leads girls to hide their intellect when around boys and that discourages girls from taking risks or mastering new challenges. "The very behaviors adults praise in girls—compliance, selflessness, silence—are the same behaviors that are going to drop them out of the competition in the work force," says Brown. "Virtually all the qualities needed to thrive in life—strength, courage, independence—also happen to be the stereotypic 'male' attributes."

But society's gender norms can change, and the legal and institutional efforts afoot may speed that process. "There was a time when long, flowing hair and cooking skills were the antithesis to masculinity," notes Heather Johnston Nicholson, research director for the nonprofit group Girls Inc. "Those days are gone." New fairy tales are crafted almost daily, featuring girl heroes and leaders. As they take root in popular culture, the idea of the damsel in distress may lose its allure and so, too, the notion that there are some things girls just can't do.

TEENAGERS AND AIDS

'Do you want to put your life in that other person's hands? Is that boy or girl worth dying for? I doubt it . . . Every one of my dreams was shattered, blown away.'

The din inside the downtown Seattle video arcade is overpowering: guns blasting away, bells ringing wildly. None of the 50 or so teens inside notices the tall kid with a Falcons cap who walks in. He steps up to two boys engrossed in a shooting game. "Hey, brothers, you using condoms?" he asks. They nod, barely looking his way. "Need some?" he says, shoving a handful toward them. The boys grab the condoms and stuff them into their pockets. The intruder isn't finished with them. "Know much about AIDS and HIV?" he continues, with the patter of a door-to-door salesman. "Yeah," they answer, in unison. "Then you know you can get it from unprotected sex and sharing needles?" They nod. He quickly hands them a brochure: "This will answer any other questions you have."

The kid in the Falcons cap is Kevin Turner and at 19, he is already an experienced warrior on the front lines of the battle against AIDS. He carries his weapon of choice, condoms, in a black leather bag strapped around his chest. Turner works for POCAAN (People of Color Against AIDS Network). Officially, he's a peer educator; unofficially, he's "Mr. Condom," on call 24 hours a day. He gives out hundreds of condoms every week and has been known to burst into conservations when he hears someone talking about sex. "You're going to use condoms, aren't you?" he'll ask. "Here, have a few."

It's a tough sell, even though it's literally a matter of life and death. A congressional report issued in April warned that HIV, the virus that causes AIDS, is "spreading unchecked among the nation's adolescents, regardless of where they live or their economic status." Since the beginning of the epidemic, more than 5,000 children and young adults have died of AIDS; it is now the sixth leading cause of death among 15- to 24-year-olds. No one knows exactly how many teens are HIV-positive, but during the past three years, the cumulative number of 13- to 24-year-olds diagnosed with AIDS increased 77 percent. By the end of last year, AIDS cases in that age group had been reported in almost every state and the District of Columbia. Nearly half of the afflicted teenagers come from just six places: New York, New Jersey, Texas, California, Florida and Puerto Rico.

No one has yet managed to screen a true cross section of any community's adolescents, but Dr. Lawrence D'Angelo has come close. Since late 1987, the Washington, D.C., pediatrician has tested virtually all the blood samples drawn from 13- to 20-year-olds at Children's National Medical Center, a large public hospital serving kids from all over the metropolitan area. Of the samples drawn between October 1987 and January 1989, one in 250 tested positive. During the next study period (through October 1991), the infection rate rose to one in 90. D'Angelo predicts that one sample in 50 will test positive this year.

Up to now, the majority of afflicted teens have been males, minorities and older adolescents—who, given the long incubation period, probably got the virus in their early teens. But the future holds the frightening prospect of much more widespread illness. A 1990 study of blood samples drawn from college students on 19 campuses found that one student in 500 tested positive. In 1991, the rate among 137,000 Job Corps participants was closer to one in 300. According to U.S. Surgeon General Antonia Novello, the ratio of female to male AIDS patients has doubled in the last four years, with females going from 17 percent of adolescent cases in 1987 to 39 percent of cases last year.

The virus is spreading because adolescent sexual behavior is risky. Some studies have suggested that up to a quarter of teenagers report engaging in rectal intercourse, sometimes to avoid pregnancy or to retain their virginity. But that practice is more likely to cause the cuts and tears that invite infection. Many adolescents also report having multiple partners, again increasing their chances of infection.

The most effective ammunition against AIDS for other high-risk groups—gays, drug users, hemophiliacs—has been education: blunt talk, reinforced by peer support groups. But this approach isn't working for teens. High-risk adults are free to seek any information they want. But teens are at the mercy of adults—parents, teachers, politi-

Kaye Brown, Houston
19 Years Old

AIDS also kills dreams.

At 18, Kaye Brown was ready for the world. The bubbly honor student was looking forward to life in the army. Last March, she signed up at a recruiting office in Houston and took a mandatory AIDS test. A week later she learned she was HIV-positive, and the world was no longer a sure thing. "I was really, really angry," she says. "My career had been snatched away from me."

Though doctors estimated that she had contracted the virus recently, they recommended that she get in touch with anyone she had had sex with in the previous year. The list was long. "It was easy for me to list the guys I had slept with," she says, "but when I counted 24, I was like, gosh!" Brown chose to tell them personally. One former partner said, "But you don't look like you're that way." Brown shot back, "What is *that way*? HIV doesn't mean that I'm dirty or low. It just means that I made a mistake." Her boyfriend couldn't cope with the news, and they split up. Not one man was willing to be tested. "They were too scared,"

Brown says.

Brown blames only herself; she never insisted on condoms. "It makes me angry that I allowed this to happen," she says. "Choices I made have stolen away the choices that I might have had in the future." Now she's turning her anger to good use by working at the AIDS Foundation Houston Inc., talking to teens. "Kids see people who have HIV as bad," she says. "I'm out there to prove that it does happen to good, everyday people." Most teenagers, says Brown, won't practice safe sex unless someone really close to them becomes ill. HIV, she tells them, "doesn't discriminate. It doesn't care how old you are or who you are." She refuses to put her life on hold, and next fall she'll attend Texas Southern University. She gobbles up romance novels ("If you can't live it, read it, " she jokes) and lives a day at a time: "That way, worry won't kill me before HIV does." AIDS, she says, has given her a purpose: "I feel responsible for educating other young people. That's my big mission; that's why I'm here."

cians—who often won't give young people the information they desperately need to make the right choices about their sexual behavior. Even in areas where AIDS is widely acknowledged as a serious problem, there's powerful resistance to frank discussion of teenage sexuality—as if avoiding the issue will make it go away. Many communities avoid the issue altogether, says Rep. Patricia Schroeder, because "they know they are going to raise a firestorm" about whether discussing sex and AIDS will "degenerate morals and values." Jerry Permenter, an AIDS educator in east Texas, has offered to teach in many schools in his area, but few have taken him up on his offer, and he is frustrated. "Some people don't want to talk about issues below the waistline," says Permenter. "That is the conservative mind-set that exists right now in east Texas and that is the mind-set that will bury the next generation."

Clearly, teenagers aren't getting the safe-sex message—either at home or in school. Although many adolescents say they use condoms, experts think most don't. According to the congressional study, only 47 percent of females and 55 percent of males used condoms the first time they had intercourse. Roger Bohman, who teaches a popular course on AIDS at the University of California, Los Angeles, takes surveys of students' condom use before and after the course. He found that students didn't really change their behavior—even when they knew all the dangers. Says Bohman: "They think it can't happen to them."

Teenagers' feelings of invulnerability make them even

more difficult to reach than other at-risk groups. Emotionally, they are still children and they still think they are going to be "rescued" from disaster. "We have a hard time gaining compliance from teens," says Dr. E. Richard Stiehm of the Los Angeles Pediatric AIDS Consortium. "They don't watch out for their own health care. I don't think it's ignorance of the consequences so much as the fallacy that it can only happen to someone else." Wendy Arnold, director of the Peer Education Program in Los Angeles, says that a typical attitude is: "I'm practically a virgin. He couldn't have HIV. He drives a nice car and I just had lunch with him."

That attitude is deadly. Bridgett Pederson always made her boyfriends use condoms until she met Alberto Gonzalez, then a 24-year-old bartender in Portland, Ore. Pederson, then 17, didn't protest when Gonzalez refused; he told her he was "safe." He was a clean, good-looking guy, so she went along. They began living together when she was 19; a year later, she says, he lost his job and they went to a plasma center to sell their blood. The doctors there told Pederson and Gonzalez that they were both HIV-positive. There was worse news to come. Gonzalez's brother told Pederson that Alberto had known for years that he had the virus—and had already infected a previous girlfriend, Shawn Hop. Armed with that information, Pederson went to the authorities and last October, Gonzalez became the first person in the nation to be convicted on assault charges for passing the virus. He's now in a detention center in Portland.

As for Pederson, she has a new mission: getting the

word out. She has become an AIDS activist, appearing on television and speaking to school groups. Her message is simple: "Don't trust someone, even someone you love, to come clean. People aren't always honest about their past sex life or HIV status. I'm a white, middle-class female who is well educated. I didn't fall into any of the high-risk groups, and it happened to me." Pederson, now 23, doesn't have any symptoms yet, but she knows her good health won't last forever. Although she's comfortable talking frankly to groups of teens about the virus, it was painful to visit Shawn Hop, Gonzalez's previous girlfriend, who died June 15. In her last days, Shawn was pale, gaunt and bedridden. Seeing her scared Pederson: "I wonder if I'm looking into my future."

Pederson's story is shocking—and when the young people she talks to hear it, they can't ignore the message. But AIDS educators say that while first-person testimony is important, teens also need careful instruction in how to prevent the disease. A recent study of 100 programs that reduced high-risk behavior among teens indicated that young people need more than good medical information, they also need training in how to stand up to peer pressure. Other reports indicate that each at-risk group has different needs. For example, heterosexual teenagers need to understand that they are not immune just because they're straight. Gay teens, on the other hand, need special support as they cope with accepting their sexuality and the possibility of disease. Dr. June Osborn, chair of the National Commission on AIDS, says that kids want frank answers from someone who is not judgmental or condemnatory. "They know their peers are sexually active and they know there's something out there they don't know enough about," she says. "They know the adult world is quarreling about condoms, and they are terribly eager to ask questions."

But getting those questions answered has not been simple—even in supposedly "liberal" areas of the country where AIDS among adults is openly discussed. For example, New York leads the nation in the number of AIDS cases among teenagers and the state's schools and health facilities have pioneered approaches to AIDS education. Since 1987, all public schools in New York have been required to include HIV/AIDS instruction as part of their sex-education and family-planning programs. And last fall, New York City became the first major city to begin giving out free condoms to high-school students despite pressure from religious groups and others opposed to the program.

But last May, after 92 of the city's 120 high schools had implemented condom-distribution plans, the city school board voted to bar a state-approved video and city-produced pamphlet used in the schools. The board members said the materials did not place enough emphasis on abstinence, and they required all AIDS educators to devote "substantially" more time and attention to abstinence than to other methods of prevention. The restric-

Wally Hansen, San Francisco, 24 Years Old

Getting a driver's license was a liberating experience for 16-year-old Wally Hansen, who grew up in a household so "normal [it was] almost like 'Leave It to Beaver'." He and some buddies in suburban Pinole, Calif., would cut classes and drive to the woods near a gay beach in San Francisco, where they would "frolic" with each other and the men they met there. Hansen never considered using a condom—this was the mid-'80s, when safe sex meant not getting caught by your parents.

Hansen eventually joined the air force. But in 1987, he was discharged after the service discovered he was a homosexual. Routine exit exams revealed the presence of the AIDS virus. Hansen, now 24, is almost certain he was first exposed to HIV during his hooky-playing days. Had he known about the growing epidemic, he says, he might have altered his behavior. He is convinced that education is the key to stopping the spread of AIDS among young people. The effort, he says, should begin in junior high. And since teenagers "are going to have sex no matter what," it's important, "especially in high school, to hand out condoms, anything." Hansen, an administrative assistant at the Bay Area Reporter, a gay paper in San Francisco, is active in the AIDS war. For two years he was a driver for Rubbermen, an organization that donates condoms to city bars, and now volunteers at AIDS fund-raisers.

But when it comes to his own health—and sometimes that of others—Hansen is reckless. He says he has used speed intermittently for two years. Though he knows that unprotected sex brings the risk of more infections with more strains of the AIDS virus, he doesn't always use a condom. He admits that many of his peers who are HIV-positive don't always inform their partners of their condition, in the assumption that they are infected, too. Some may see it as the behavior of the doomed, but to Hansen, "it basically comes down to what you think it's worth." He insists he wouldn't be happy if he restricted his activities. "I can only think positively. I do anything I want. I feel like I'd do more damage to myself by stressing my system out of worry." His family has taken his illness in stride. "My mom and dad told me they may not love the things I do," says Hansen, "but they love me." And that, sad to say, makes him luckier than many.

Krista Blake, Columbiana, Ohio
20 Years Old

In the fall of 1990, Krista Blake was 18 and looking forward to her first year at Youngstown State University in Ohio. She and her boyfriend were talking about getting married. Her life, she says, was "basic, white-bread America." Then she went to the doctor, complaining about a backache, and found out she had the AIDS virus.

Blake had been infected with HIV, the virus that causes AIDS, two years earlier by an older boy, a hemophiliac. "He knew that he was infected, and he didn't tell me," she says. "And he didn't do anything to keep me from getting infected, either." When she first heard the diagnosis, Blake felt as though she had just walked into a brick wall. Suddenly, she couldn't envision her future. She found herself thinking things like "There are 50 states out there. I don't want to just live and die in Ohio." Her doctor sent her to University Hospital in Cleveland, 90 minutes from home, for treatment. She has taken AZT and is now on the new antiviral DDI. Although she needed frequent transfusions to counteract the effects of AZT, she is relatively healthy. "I am living with AIDS, not dying from AIDS," she says. "I do all of the same things I used to do. That doesn't mean I can run the Boston Marathon, but my mind is still 20." She reads everything from Danielle Steel to "Life 101," a popular advice book. She makes a point of going out at least once very day, even if it's just down to the park to watch a softball game. "It gets those juices moving," she says.

Still, she doesn't know how long her good health will last—a month, a year, five years. She doesn't make long-term commitments. Blake and her fiancé broke off their engagement, because, she says, "I love him enough that I want him to have his options for a life open." However, they are still very good friends. Blake also dropped out of school. "A bachelor's degree wouldn't do much for me," she says with a rueful laugh.

Since the spring of 1991, Blake has spent as many as four or five days a week doing the one thing she believes is really important—talking to other teens about HIV and how to avoid infection. The first thing the kids ask about is her sex life. "I don't have a sex life," she tells them, "but that's because I don't have any energy to have a sex life." The kids usually start laughing. Then she says: "I have just so much energy and I have to decide, do I come out here and talk to you, or do I have sex? I pick what's important, and you won." After one presentation, a student came up to Blake and told her: "I had an uncle who came home at Easter one year, and he had AIDS. This was in 1988. My mom was afraid. We didn't go see him. She wouldn't let us go. He died the next year, at Easter. I never got to say goodbye to my uncle. Would it be OK if I came up and gave you a hug?"

LUCILLE BEACHY

tions went even further, requiring outside AIDS groups working with the schools to abide by the rules as well. The board's actions have been challenged by the New York Civil Liberties Union; to date, there has been no ruling. In the meantime, the city's AIDS educators complain that they can't work under censorship. "This is a disaster for us," says Cydelle Berlin, coordinator of the adolescent AIDS-prevention program at Mount Sinai Medical Center. "We're talking life and death. We can't submit our work to the sex police."

Sessions at clinics like Berlin's go far beyond technical descriptions of the virus—and discussions of abstinence seem beside the point. On one recent afternoon, 20-year-old Jerome Bannister held up a pink plastic penis for a group of inner-city teens. "Anybody wanna touch this?" he asked. "His name is Johnson." Bannister's 20-year-old partner, Diana Hernandez, flicked open a flesh-colored condom. "We've got a little friend here," she said. Bannister went next. "You wanna put a little jelly inside," he said, gesturing toward the condom. "There are a lot of nerve endings in the penis. That way you get that wet, hot feeling when it's in the vagina where it's warm. But lubrication's not only for that warm feeling. It's also a backup. If you use nonoxynol-9, it can kill the sperm—and the HIV virus." Many experts believe that nonoxynol-9 helps prevent transmission. Bannister and Hernandez then demonstrated exactly how to slip the condom on the penis. The team went through equally detailed descriptions of dental dams and the new female condom, which is inserted like a diaphragm. Their audience took the session very seriously, asking questions about where to buy condoms and grabbing handfuls of free samples.

Buying condoms isn't enough; kids also need help persuading partners to use them. Many AIDS programs focus on role-playing, giving teens practical strategies for dealing with social pressure. "All these kids want to do is fit in with their peers," says Dr. Marvin Belzer of Children's Hospital in Los Angeles. "If a young woman thinks she'll lose her boyfriend if she insists on condoms, and feels that he is the only reason she is somebody, she's not going to use them." There are mixed cultural messages to deal with, too. A boy who is told that having sex with multiple partners is dangerous is also being told that more sexual conquests make him more of a man. "In this society, if we want to make a difference, we have to stop the mixed message between parental and community values versus the values portrayed in the media," says Belzer.

Straight teens have a difficult time sorting out conflicting values; gay teens have even fewer resources—and they have to contend with cultural prejudices and their own mixed emotions about their emerging sexual identity. "Nobody wants to talk about male-to-male sex in the teen population," says Rene Durazzo of the San Francisco AIDS Foundation. AIDS experts say that prevention campaigns designed for older gay men don't help teenagers. "Education efforts to date assume youths have choices and are free agents," says Barry Lawlor of the Haight Ashbury Free Clinic in San Francisco. "Many youths do not have choices . . . They're new to sexual behavior and they can be exploited." The likelihood of exploitation increases among runaways who are desperate for money. "On the streets, when a teen says he's not going to have sex without a condom and the other guy says he'll pay $20 more if he does, that's a lot of pressure," Lawlor says. But even teens still at home take risks when they know they shouldn't. The need for love and affection overwhelms the fear of getting sick. Scott Miller, 24, of San Francisco, discovered he was HIV-positive in college. He says that when he was a teenager, his sense of self-worth was low; witnessing a particularly violent gay-bashing incident made him feel even more vulnerable. "Unsafe behavior was OK if it would make you my friend," he says. "If this person wouldn't want me because I wanted to use a condom, well, I'd rather have him like me."

Gay teens who discover they are HIV-positive must tell their parents—often in the same conservation—that they're gay and that they're infected. Sue Beardsley, a volunteer with Rest Stop, a San Francisco support center for people with AIDS, still remembers the phone call she got from 16-year-old David on the last night of his life. His family was thousands of miles away and he didn't want to be alone. She rushed to his hospital room; a few hours later he died in her arms. Beardsley telephoned David's mother to tell her that her son was gone. "My son David doesn't exist," the mother said. "He died a year ago." That was when David had told his mother he was gay.

Fear of such rejection compels many gay teens to keep both their sexual identity and their HIV status a secret. They're desperate for a "safe place" where they can talk freely. One such place is Bay Positives in San Francisco, a peer support group for HIV-positive young people. Jim Neiss, 21, a Bay Positives member, says that even though his family is behind him, he needs the group as well. "In the middle of the night, if I'm really upset or traumatized about something, I don't hesitate to call a member." They share a tragic bond: confronting the prospect of an unnaturally early death before they have even embarked on their adult lives. Support groups for adult AIDS sufferers often seem irrelevant because the adult agenda is so different. In adult groups, says therapist Julie Graham, a founder of Bay Positives, "People talk about stuff . . . they'll never have. Like wills. Young people with HIV often don't have enough material possessions to need a will. Or relationships. Young people with HIV feel like they're never going to get the chance to have a relationship."

Knowing that life will be short gives other HIV-positive young people a special sense of purpose. Amy Dolph grew up in the quintessential small town of Katy, Texas. In the spring of 1987, she seemed to be just a typical all-American girl: blond, blue-eyed, with nothing more serious on her mind than going steady and heading for college in the fall. But when she donated blood to help her ailing great-grandmother, she found out that the second man she slept with had given her HIV. She was shocked and confused. The last of her friends to lose her virginity, she didn't sleep around. "Every one of my dreams was shattered, blown away," she says. To this day she isn't sure how the man who infected her contracted the virus; she knew that he had been sexually active at an early age and had experimented with drugs. Later she found out that he was also bisexual. She is past the stage of blaming him but says she wishes she had known more and had understood that she could be at risk. "Back then we were always reading that you're only at high risk if you're this group, this group or this group," she says. "And you're at low risk if you're a sexually active heterosexual. And everyone saw that 'low risk' as 'no risk'."

Dolph, now 23, works with the AIDS Foundation Houston Inc. in its education program, traveling to urban and rural high schools and junior highs to talk about AIDS. She's trying to give the kids something she never got—a warning. She tells teenagers that they shouldn't allow their sex partners, no matter how close they are to them, to have control over when they're going to die. "Do you want to put your life in that other person's hands? Is that boy or girl worth dying for? I doubt it." Dolph doesn't dwell on the past and she doesn't look too far ahead into the future. Her present is full—and, for the moment, that has to be enough.

BARBARA KANTROWITZ *with* MARY HAGER *in Washington,*
GEOFFREY COWLEY *and* LUCILLE BEACHY *in New York,*
MELISSA ROSSI *in Seattle,* BRYNN CRAFFEY
in San Francisco,
PETER ANNIN *in Houston,* REBECCA CRANDALL
in Los Angeles
and bureau reports

Reaching the child within us

ASHLEY MONTAGU

The truth about the human species is that we are intended to remain in many ways childlike; we were never intended to grow "up" into the kind of adults most of us have become. We are designed—in body, spirit, feeling, and conduct—to grow and develop in ways that emphasize rather than minimize childlike traits. By learning to act more like a child, human beings can revolutionize their lives and become for the first time, perhaps, the kinds of creatures their heritage has prepared them to be—youthful all the days of their lives.

What are those traits of childhood behavior that are so valuable yet tend to disappear gradually as human beings grow older? We have only to watch children to see them clearly displayed: Curiosity is one of the most important; imaginativeness; playfulness; open mindedness; willingness to experiment; flexibility; humor; energy; receptiveness to new ideas; honesty; eagerness to learn; and perhaps the most pervasive and the most valuable of all, the need to love. Children ask questions endlessly: "Why?" "What is it?" "What's it for?" "How does it work?" They watch, and they listen. They want to know everything about everything. They can keep themselves busy for hours with the simplest toys, endowing sticks and stones and featureless objects with personalities and histories, imagining elaborate stories about them, building sagas that continue day after day, month after month. They play games endlessly, sometimes carefully constructing the rules, sometimes developing the game as they go along. They accept changes without defensiveness. When they try to accomplish something and fail, they are able to try it another way, and

Most adults draw back from the unfamiliar.

another, until they find a way that works. They laugh—babies smile and laugh before they can even babble—and children laugh from sheer exuberance and happiness. Unless they fear punishment, they tell the truth; they call the shots as they see them. And they soak up knowledge and information like sponges; they are learning all the time; every moment is filled with learning.

How many adults retain these qualities into middle age? Few. They tend to stop asking those questions that will elicit information. Not many adults, when confronted with something unfamiliar, ask, as children do: "What is it?" "What's it for?" "Why?" "How does it work?" Most adults draw back from the unfamiliar, perhaps because they are reluctant to reveal ignorance, perhaps because they have become genuinely indifferent to the interesting experiences of life and consider that absorbing something new is simply too much trouble.

Nor can most adults content themselves with simple playthings enriched by the imagination. Witness the enormous growth of industries that cater to the "leisure-time" and "recreational" activities of adults, that manufacture the toys grown-ups need to play: boats, cars, trailers, equipment for camping, hiking, running, tennis, and golf. The list seems endless.

Most adults have lost, too, the ability to laugh

from sheer happiness; perhaps they have lost happiness itself. Adulthood as we know it brings sobriety and seriousness along with its responsibilities. Most adults have also lost the ability to tell the simple truth; many appear to have lost the ability to discern a simple truth in the complex morass they live in.

Perhaps the saddest loss of all is the gradual erosion of the eagerness to learn. Most adults stop any

Celebrate midlife with a ritual

As part of my work as a learning consultant, I have held ritual ceremonies for people who were concerned about reaching midlife. Like many in their 40s and 50s, these people are regretful about losing opportunities and youthful energy, worried about bodily changes, and fearful of losing influence as they grow older. The ritual's purpose is to create a vehicle for expressing concerns and regrets, in the process releasing some of the pain caused by midlife worries as well as moving toward acceptance of growing older, and ultimately gaining new-found peace and empowerment.

I've found rituals to be a very moving experience for participants, and I encourage readers to try their own. Any imaginative person with good listening skills, compassion, experience with symbols, and guidance from resource materials can serve as facilitator. A partial list of resources includes Nancy Cunningham's book *Feeding the Spirit* (Resource Publishing, 160 E. Virginia St., #290, San Jose, CA 95112), Penina Adelman's *Miriam's Well* (Biblio Press, 27 W. 20th St., Room 1001, New York, NY 10011), and Gertrud Nelson's *To Dance with God* (Paulist Press, 997 Macarthur Blvd., Mahwah, NJ 07430).

The following is a brief description of a ceremony for a group of women who recently turned 40. In this particular ritual, the participants were six women who had been friends since high school and who got together a few times a year. We started the evening with a potluck dinner, which allowed people to shed the day's stresses and to renew their bonds. Since it was fall, we celebrated the concept of harvest with each person bringing a dish made from local produce.

We began the ceremony sitting in a circle, stretching and breathing deeply as one by one each woman spoke of a frustrating experience of the day she wanted to release: a fight with a child, arriving late for a meeting. We passed a sprig of sage—which in Indian rituals is used as a purifier—to signify the start of a special event in which we would speak from a deeper, more poetic place in ourselves. I talked about the emotional stages we'd explore (ones similar to those experienced with loss) of grieving, acceptance, and empowerment.

Then the women named all the things they disliked about being 40—varicose veins, wrinkles, needing to go to bed earlier—while tossing a ball to each other. The ball game brought a lightheartedness to the heartfelt disclosures. Ready now to go deeper,

we made a centerpiece out of a circle of gray fabric, on which each woman placed a stone she had brought. The women took turns being storytellers, slipping on a full-length black coat to symbolize loss and grieving. I asked them to dive deep inside themselves to find what it was that pained them most about aging, and to begin a story about what they discovered with the phrase "I never thought _____ would happen to me." Their stories revealed the feelings of betrayal midlife can bring. One spoke of priding herself on never needing glasses; yet a doctor recently suggested that "it's not too early to consider bifocals." Another said that she "feels so young, and yet two of my teeth have already died." Another lamented the fading of the passion that formerly inspired her to stay up all night to know its mystery and then to greet the dawn. And as each woman finished her lament, there was a chorus of, "Oh no! Not you, too!" We pounded the floor and wailed and laughed as these common experiences comforted us.

After some time spent writing in journals, which helped everyone process and pay tribute to the losses of midlife, each woman held the stone she had brought. I led a meditation on the agelessness and endurance of the stones, which have witnessed so much on the planet since their creation, and asked people to imagine that they could send their pain into their stone.

Next we changed the centerpiece to a cloth that symbolized harvest, and each woman added the ripe fruit or vegetable she had brought—a metaphor for the bounty that comes with aging—and commented on it. As an example, one noted that her ripe peach would have been hard and tasteless before; now its fragrance fills the air and it is lush and flavorful. Then each added a photo of a woman in her 40s whom she admired. Many photos were of women older than us, and we mused on how our sexist society is slow to recognize a woman for her accomplishments. One photo showed the wizened face of a native woman, another the mother of a participant who continued to have zest for life at 70.

Next we passed around an ear of corn—a symbol of physical nurturing for humans in almost every culture—as each woman told of something she was passing on to the next generation. Each reflected on the experiences and wisdom the years had brought: love of music, the ability to read a story aloud with drama, pride in ethnic heritage, helping people to believe in themselves.

Then, as the women laid on their backs listen-

conscious efforts to learn early in their adulthood, and thereafter never actively pursue knowledge or understanding of the physical world. It is as if they believed that they had learned all they needed to know by the age

---

ing to soothing background music, I led a meditation that reflected on each part of the body, thanking it for its gifts, e.g., strong arms and legs that take us on journeys, hands that carry out the creativity borne in the heart and mind.

Next, we reflected on other gifts that years and personal growth had brought: As we focused on one woman, each of her friends in turn held a mirror up to her, saying, "I see that the years have given you the gift of _____," gifts such as a great sense of humor, endurance, self-confidence, courage, and patience.

Finally, each woman shared some of the wisdom she had gained from life that could be helpful to others, and then we closed by taking hands and sending a squeeze around the circle, reminding everyone that she could reach back through time to get sustenance from this evening any time she encountered the turning-40 blues.

Rituals for people turning 50 have a different flavor. At this stage, people are generally more accepting of the aging process and more interested in sorting through the emerging patterns in their lives and celebrating the richness of the journey. Ritual components vary: One woman gathered friends and family and described how each person had been instrumental in her life. She made a hoop from the two ribbons each guest brought—one representing a quality they loved in her and the other representing a funny memory they shared. We talked about the three phases women pass through—maiden, creator/mother, and crone—and conjured up images of those in each of us through guided imagery. Another chose to reconnect with the child in her and thank that child for helping her become who she was, and we made masks to invite our own child out. Guests brought a poem or picture that reminded them of the woman who was having her 50th birthday.

Rituals offer a means of viewing life as a journey that offers us many opportunities for transformation. Any moment or event of importance to someone can be acknowledged and explored in a personalized ritual—spontaneous or planned. Thus, if someone you know wants to mark her midlife, consider going beyond those black balloons that say, "You're over the hill now."

—Kaia Svien
Special to Utne Reader

The later years can be the happiest of one's life.

of 18 or 22. At this time they begin to grow a shell around their pitiful store of knowledge; from then on they vigorously resist all attempts to pierce that shell with anything new. In a world changing so rapidly that even the most agile-minded cannot keep up, the effect of this shell building on a person is to develop a dislike of the unfamiliar. This hardening of the mind—psychosclerosis—is a long distance from a child's acceptance and flexibility and open-mindedness.

But the qualities of the child are ours to express for all time. Genius, said Baudelaire, is childhood recaptured. The fables we have inherited concerning aging are so old that many accept them as truths beyond refutation. Such myths constitute striking examples of the self-fulfilling prophecy. Senility is a disease, not an inevitable consequence of aging. Physical,

---

We are intended to remain childlike—curious, flexible, imaginative, playful, honest, open-minded.

physiological, and psychological changes do occur with aging. There is, however, no necessary connection between the aging of the body and the aging of the mind.

Recent research indicates that intellectual ability does not decrease through the eighth decade and that with exercise and training significant gains can be achieved. To remain intellectually active, intellectual stimulation is necessary, and that is what the quality of youthfulness is constantly encouraging: to remain in touch with reality, to soak up from the environment that for which the mind hungers.

The later years can be the happiest of one's life. Many of those who have achieved what others call old age have confessed to feeling embarrassingly young, as if such feeling were something anachronistic, an unexpected freshness. It is the kind of freshness that the long-distance runner experiences when at the peak of fatigue he experiences a second wind that takes him on to the finish line. This kind of freshness can be maintained throughout life; it is not too late to achieve it in one's later years. The earlier one has been encouraged in one's childlike qualities, however, the more likely is one to realize that feeling of unadulterated joy in being alive that the romping child so gloriously feels—perhaps without the physical romping, but with that gaiety of spirit that has enabled one to grow young more effectively and more happily than was ever before possible—the last of life, for which the first was made.

Life in the not-so-fast lane

The middle-aging of society will affect the way all Americans live—from the television they watch and the food they eat to the way they spend their precious free time. Here are some statistics to help you chart the course for this coming cultural revolution.

Percent growth in the number of Americans aged 35 to 44 between 1987 and 2000: 27%

Percent growth in the number of Americans aged 45 to 54 between 1987 and 2000: 59%

Percent growth in the number of Americans aged 25 to 34 between 1987 and 2000: -16%

Median age of the U.S. population in 1965: 28.1

Median age in 1985: 31.5

Projected median age in 2005: 37.8

Projected median age in 2030: 41.8

Projected median age in 2080: 43.9

Average annual expenditures for households in 1986: $24,000

Average annual expenditures for households whose head was aged 45 to 54 in 1986: $32,000

Number of companies offering long-term care insurance policies in 1984: 20

Number of companies offering long-term care insurance policies in 1987: 73

Percent of daily newspapers that assigned a reporter to an "aging" beat in 1987: 38

Percent of daily newspapers that carried a regular column on aging in 1987: 47

Number of subscribers to cable TV's Nostalgia Channel since 1985: 5 million

Percentage of luxury car owners who are aged 35 to 54: 41

Percentage of American Express gold card holders who are aged 35 to 54: 42

Number of people in work force per each retiree in 1985: 3.4

In 2030: 2.0

According to the Social Security Administration's intermediate forecast:

The year that Medicare will slip into deficit: 1993

The year that Medicare reserves will be depleted: 1998

The year the federal Social Security disability fund will be exhausted: 2034

The year the federal Social Security pension fund will go broke: 2050

Cost of the nation's disability fund, Medicare, and pension fund as a percent of the nation's taxable payroll in 1985: 14 percent

In 2055: 42 percent

Percent of 18- to 29-year-olds who prefer to spend their leisure time at home: 28

Percent of 30- to 44-year-olds who do: 45

Percent of 45- to 59-year-olds who do: 53

Percent of 18- to 29-year-olds who went to bed before midnight on New Year's Eve 1988: 13

Percent of 30- to 44-year-olds who did: 20

Percent of 45- to 59-year-olds who did: 26

Percent of women aged 18 to 34 who used hair coloring in 1986: 17

Percent of women aged 35 and over who did: 26

—Compiled by Blayne Cutler
Blayne Cutler is a contributing
editor to American Demographic *magazine.*

Statistics taken from a variety of sources, including Roper Organization polls and Interep Research. For a list of citations, send an SASE to Aging Facts, Utne Reader, 1624 Harmon Pl., Minneapolis, MN 55403.

Proceeding With Caution

The twentysomething generation is balking at work, marriage and baby-boomer values. Why are today's young adults so skeptical?

DAVID M. GROSS and
SOPHFRONIA SCOTT

They have trouble making decisions. They would rather hike in the Himalayas than climb a corporate ladder. They have few heroes, no anthems, no style to call their own. They crave entertainment, but their attention span is as short as one zap of a TV dial. They hate yuppies, hippies and druggies. They postpone marriage because they dread divorce. They sneer at Range Rovers, Rolexes and red suspenders. What they hold dear are family life, local activism, national parks, penny loafers and mountain bikes. They possess only a hazy sense of their own identity but a monumental preoccupation with all the problems the preceding generation will leave for them to fix.

This is the twentysomething generation, those 48 million young Americans ages 18 through 29 who fall between the famous baby boomers and the boomlet of children the baby boomers are producing. Since today's young adults were born during a period when the U.S. birthrate decreased to half the level of its postwar peak, in the wake of the great baby boom, they are sometimes called the baby busters. By whatever name, so far they are an unsung generation, hardly recognized as a social force or even noticed much at all. "I envision ourselves as a lurking generation, waiting in the shadows, quietly figuring out our plan," says Rebecca Winke, 19, of Madison, Wis. "Maybe that's why nobody notices us."

But here they come: freshly minted grownups. And anyone who expected they would echo the boomers who came before, bringing more of the same attitude, should brace for a surprise. This crowd is profoundly different from—even contrary to—the group that came of age in the 1960s and that celebrates itself each week on *The Wonder Years* and *thirtysomething*. By and large, the 18-to-29 group scornfully rejects the habits and values of the baby boomers, viewing that group as self-centered, fickle and impractical.

While the baby boomers had a placid childhood in the 1950s, which helped inspire them to start their revolution, today's twentysomething generation grew up in a time of drugs, divorce and economic strain. They virtually reared themselves. TV provided the surrogate parenting, and Ronald Reagan starred as the real-life Mister Rogers, dispensing reassurance during their troubled adolescence. Reagan's message: problems can be shelved until later. A prime characteristic of today's young adults is their desire to avoid risk, pain and rapid change. They feel paralyzed by the social problems they see as their inheritance: racial strife, homelessness, AIDS, fractured families and federal deficits. "It is almost our role to be passive," says Peter Smith, 23, a newspaper reporter in Ventura, Calif. "College was a time of mass apathy, with pockets of change. Many global events seem out of our control."

The twentysomething generation has been neglected because it exists in the shadow of the baby boomers, usually defined as the 72 million Americans born between 1946 and 1964. Members of the tail end of the boom generation, now ages 26 through 29, often feel alienated from the larger group, like kid brothers and sisters who disdain the paths their siblings chose. The boomer group is so huge that it tends to define every era it passes through, forcing society to accommodate its moods and dimensions. Even relatively small bunches of boomers made waves, most notably the 4 million or so young urban professionals of the mid-1980s. By contrast, when today's 18-to-29-year-old group was born, the baby boom was fading into the so-called baby bust, with its precipitous decline in the U.S. birthrate. The relatively small baby-bust group is poorly understood by everyone from scholars to marketers. But as the twentysomething adults begin their prime working years, they have suddenly become far more intriguing. Reason: America needs them. Today's young adults are so scarce that their numbers could result in severe labor shortages in the coming decade.

Twentysomething adults feel the opposing tugs of making money and doing good works, but they refuse to get caught up in the passion of either one. They reject 70-hour workweeks as yuppie lunacy, just as they shirk from starting another social revolution. Today's young adults want to stay in their own backyard and do their work in modest ways. "We're not trying to change things. We're trying to fix things," says Anne McCord, 21, of Portland, Ore. "We are the generation that is going to renovate America. We are going to be its carpenters and janitors."

This is a back-to-basics bunch that wishes life could be simpler. "We expect less, we want less, but we want less to be better," says Devin Schaumburg, 20, of Knoxville. "If we're just trying to pick up the pieces, put it all back together, is there a label for that?" That's a laudable notion, but don't hold your breath till they find their answer. "They are finally out there, saying 'Pay attention to us,' but I've never heard them think of a single thing that defines them," says Martha Farnsworth Riche, national editor of *American Demographics* magazine.

What worries parents, teachers and employers is that the latest crop of adults wants to postpone growing up. At a time when they should be graduating, entering the work force and starting families of their own, the twentysomething crowd is balking at those rites of passage. A prime reason is their recognition that the American Dream is much tougher to achieve after years of housing-price inflation and stagnant wages. Householders under the age of 25 were the only group during the 1980s to suffer a drop in income, a decline of 10%. One result: fully 75% of young males 18 to 24 years old are still living at home, the largest proportion since the Great Depression.

In a TIME/CNN poll of 18- to 29-year-olds, 65% of those surveyed agreed it will be harder for their group to live as comfortably as previous generations. While the majority of today's young adults think they have a strong chance of finding a well-paying and interesting job, 69% believe they will have more difficulty buying a house, and 52% say they will have less leisure time than their predecessors. Asked to describe their generation, 53% said the group is worried about the future.

Until they come out of their shells, the twentysomething/baby-bust generation will be a frustrating enigma. Riche calls them the New Petulants because "they can often end up sounding like whiners." Their anxious indecision creates a kind of ominous fog around them. Yet those who take a more sanguine view see in today's young adults a sophistication, tolerance and candor that could help repair the excesses of rampant individualism. Here is a guide for understanding the puzzling twentysomething crowd:

FAMILY: THE TIES DIDN'T BIND
"Ronald Reagan was around longer than some of my friends' fathers," says Rachel Stevens, 21, a graduate of the University of Michigan. An estimated 40% of people in

their 20s are children of divorce. Even more were latchkey kids, the first to experience the downside of the two-income family. This may explain why the only solid commitment they are willing to make is to their own children—someday. The group wants to spend more time with their kids, not because they think they can handle the balance of work and child rearing any better than their parents but because they see themselves as having been neglected. "My generation will be the family generation," says Mara Brock, 20, of Kansas City. "I don't want my kids to go through what my parents put me through."

That ordeal was loneliness. "This generation came from a culture that really didn't prize having kids anyway," says Chicago Sociologist Paul Hirsch. "Their parents just wanted to go and play out their roles—they assumed the kids were going to grow up all right." Absent parents forced a dependence on secondary relationships with teachers and friends. Flashy toys and new clothes were supposed to make up for this lack but instead sowed the seeds for a later abhorrence of the yuppie brand of materialism. "Quality time" didn't cut it for them either. In a survey to gauge the baby busters' mood and tastes, Chicago's Leo Burnett ad agency discovered that the group had a surprising amount of anger and resentment about their absentee parents. "The flashback was instantaneous and so hot you could feel it," recalls Josh McQueen, Burnett's research director. "They were telling us passionately that quality time was exactly what was not in their lives."

At this point, members of the twentysomething generation just want to avoid perpetuating the mistakes of their own upbringing. Today's potential parents look beyond their own mothers and fathers when searching for child-rearing role models. Says Kip Banks, 24, a graduate student in public policy at the University of Michigan: "When I raise my children, my approach will be my grandparents', much more serious and conservative. I would never give my children the freedoms I had."

MARRIAGE: WHAT'S THE RUSH? The generation is afraid of relationships in general, and they are the ultimate skeptics when it comes to marriage. Some young adults maintain they will wait to get married, in the hope that time will bring a more compatible mate and the maturity to avoid a divorce. But few of them have any real blueprint for how a successful relationship should function. "We never saw commitment at work," says Robert Higgins, 26, a graduate student in music at Ohio's University of Akron.

As a result, twentysomething people are staying single longer and often living together before marrying. Studying the 20-to-24 age group in 1988, the U.S. Census Bureau found that 77% of men and

61% of women had never married, up sharply from 55% and 35%, respectively, in 1970. Among those 25 to 29, the unmarried included 43% of men and 29% of women in 1988, vs. 19% and 10% in 1970. The sheer disposability of marriage breeds skepticism. Kasey Geoghegan, 20, a student at the University of Denver and a child of divorced parents, believes nuptial vows have lost their credibility. Says she: "When people get married, ideally it's permanent, but once problems set in, they don't bother to work things out."

DATING: DON'T STAND SO CLOSE
Finding a date on a Saturday night, let alone a mate, is a challenge for a generation that has elevated casual commitment to an art form. Despite their nostalgia for family values, few in their 20s are eager to revive a 1950s mentality about pairing off. Rick Bruno, 22, who will enter Yale Medical School in the fall, would rather think of himself as a free agent. Says he: "Not getting hurt is a big priority with me." Others are concerned that the generation is too detached to form caring relationships. "People are afraid to like each other," says Leslie Boorstein, 21, a photographer from Great Neck, N.Y.

For those who try to make meaningful connections—often through video dating services, party lines and personals ads—risks of modern love are greater than ever. AIDS casts a pall over a generation that fully expected to reap the benefits of the sexual revolution. Responsibility is the watchword. Only on college campuses do remnants of libertinism linger. That worries public-health officials, who are witnessing an explosion of sexually transmitted diseases, particularly genital warts. "There is a high degree of students who believe oral contraception protects them from the AIDS virus. It doesn't," says Wally Brewer, coordinator of a study of HIV infection on U.S. campuses. "Obviously it's a big educational challenge."

CAREERS: NOT JUST YET, THANKS
Because they are fewer in number, today's young adults have the power to wreak havoc in the workplace. Companies are discovering that to win the best talent, they must cater to a young work force that is considered overly sensitive at best and lazy at worst. During the next several years, employers will have to double their recruiting efforts. According to *American Demographics,* the pool of entry-level workers 16 to 24 will shrink about 500,000 a year through 1995, to 21 million. These youngsters are starting to use their bargaining power to get more of what they feel is coming to them. They want flexibility, access to decision making and a return to the sacredness of work-free weekends. "I want a work environment concerned about my personal growth," says Jennifer Peters, 22, one of the youngest candidates ever to be admitted to the State Bar of California. "I don't want to go to work and feel I'll be burned out two or three years down the road."

Most of all, young people want constant feedback from supervisors. In contrast with the baby boomers, who disdained evaluations as somehow undemocratic, people in their 20s crave grades, performance evaluations and reviews. They want a quantification of their achievement. After all, these were the children who prepped diligently for college-aptitude exams and learned how to master Rubik's Cube and Space Invaders. They are consummate game players and grade grubbers. "Unlike yuppies, younger people are not driven from within, they need reinforcement," says Penny Erikson, 40, a senior vice president at the Young & Rubicam ad agency, which has hired many recent college graduates. "They prefer short-term tasks with observable results."

Money is still important as an indicator of career performance, but crass materialism is on the wane. Marian Salzman, 31, an editor at large for the collegiate magazine *CV,* believes the shift away from the big-salary, big-city role model of the early '80s is an accommodation to the reality of a depressed Wall Street and slack economy. Many boomers expected to have made millions by the time they reached 30. "But for today's graduates, the easy roads to fast money have dried up," says Salzman.

Climbing the corporate ladder is trickier than ever at a time of widespread corporate restructuring. When recruiters talk about long-term job security, young adults know better. Says Victoria Ball, 41, director of Career Planning Services at Brown University: "Even IBM, which always said it would never lay off—well, now they're doing it too." Between 1987 and the end of this year, Big Blue will have shed about 23,000 workers through voluntary incentive programs.

Most of all, young workers want job gratification. Teaching, long disdained as an underpaid and underappreciated profession, is a hot prospect. Enrollment in U.S. teaching programs increased 61% from 1985 to 1989. And more graduates are expressing interest in public-service careers. "The glory days of Wall Street represented an extreme," says Janet Abrams, 29, a Senate aide who regularly interviews young people looking for jobs on Capitol Hill. "Now I'm hearing about kids going to the National Park Service."

Welcome to the era of hedged bets and lowered expectations. Young people increasingly claim they are willing to leave careers in middle gear, without making that final climb to the top. The leitmotiv of the new age: second place seems just fine. But young adults are flighty if they find their workplace harsh or inflexible. "The difference between now and then was that we had a higher threshold of unhappiness," says editor Salzman. "I always expected that a job would be 80% misery and 20% glory, but this generation refuses to pay its dues."

EDUCATION: NO DEGREE, NO DOLLARS Smart and savvy, the twenty-something group is the best-educated generation in U.S. history. A record 59% of 1988 high school graduates enrolled in college, compared with 49% in the previous decade. The lesson they have taken to heart: education is a means to an end, the ticket to a cherished middle-class lifestyle. "The saddest thing of all is that they don't have the quest to understand things, to understand themselves," says Alexander Astin, whose UCLA-based Higher Education Research Institute has been measuring changing attitudes among college freshman for 24 years.

Yet, a fact of life in the 1990s economy is that a college degree is mostly about survival. A person under 30 with a college degree will earn four times as much money as someone without it. In 1973 the difference was only twice as great. With the loss of well-paying factory jobs, there are fewer chances for less-educated young people to reach the middle class. Many dropouts quickly learn this and decide to return to school. But that decision costs money and sends many twentysomethings back to the nest. Others are flocking to the armed services. Private First Class Dorin Vanderjack, 20, of Redding, Calif., left his catering job at a Holiday Inn to join the Army. After two years of racking up credits at the local community college, he was ready for a four-year school and found the Army's offer of $22,800 in tuition assistance too tempting to turn down. "There's no possible way I could save that," he says. "This forced me to grow up."

WANDERLUST: LET'S GET LOST While the recruiters are trying to woo young workers, a generation is out planning its escape from the 9-to-5 routine. Travel is always an easy way out, one that comes cloaked in a mantle of respectability: cultural enrichment. In the TIME/CNN poll, 60% of the people surveyed said they plan to travel a lot while they are young. And it's not just rich students who are doing it. "Travel is an obsession for everyone," says Cheryl Wilson, 21, a University of Pennsylvania graduate who has visited Denmark and Hungary. "The idea of going away, being mobile, is very romantic. It fulfills our sense of adventure."

Unlike previous generations of uppercrust Americans who savored a post-graduate European tour as the ultimate finishing school, today's adventurers are picking places far more exotic. They are seeking an escape from Western culture, rather than further refinement to smooth their entry into society. Katmandu, Dar es Salaam, Bangkok: these are the trendy destinations of many young daydreamers. Susan Costello, 23, a recent Harvard graduate, voyaged to Dharmsala, India, to spend time at the headquarters of the Tibetan government-in-exile, headed by the Dalai Lama. Costello decided to explore Tibetan culture "to see if they really had something in their way of life that we seem to be missing in the West."

ACTIVISM: ART OF THE POSSIBLE People in their 20s want to give something back to society, but they don't know how to begin. The really important problems, ranging from the national debt to homelessness, are too large and complex to comprehend. And always the great, intimidating shadow of 1960s-style activism hovers in the background. Twentysomething youths suspect that today's attempts at political and social action pale in comparison with the excitement of draft dodging or freedom riding.

The new generation pines for a romanticized past when the issues were clear and the troops were committed. "The kids of the 1960s had it easy," claims Gavin Orzame, 18, of Berrien Springs, Mich. "Back then they had a war and the civil rights movement. Now there are so many issues that it's hard to get one big rallying point." But because the '60s utopia never came, today's young adults view the era with a combination of reverie and revulsion. "What was so great about growing up then anyway?" says future physician Bruno. "The generation that had Vietnam and Watergate is going to be known for leaving us all their problems. They came out of Camelot and blew it."

Such views are revisionist, since the '60s were not easy, and the revolution did not end in utter failure. The twentysomething generation takes for granted many of the real goals of the '60s: civil rights, the antiwar movement, feminism and gay liberation. But those movements never coalesced into a unified crusade, which is something the twentysomethings hope will come along, break their lethargy and goad them into action. One major cause is the planet; 43% of the young adults in the TIME/CNN poll said they are "environmentally conscious." At the same time, some young people are joining the ranks of radical-action groups, including ACT UP, the AIDS Coalition to Unleash Power, and Trans-Species Unlimited, the animal-rights group. These organizations have appeal because they focus their message, choose specific targets and use high-stakes pressure tactics like civil disobedience to get things accomplished quickly.

For a generation that has witnessed so much failure in the political system, such results-oriented activism seems much more valid and practical. Says Sean McNally, 20, who headed the Earth Day activities at Northwestern University: "A lot of us are afraid to take an intense stance and then leave it all behind like our parents did. We have to protect ourselves from burning out, from losing faith." Like McNally, the rest of the generation is doing what it can. Its members prefer activities that are small in scope: cleaning up a park over a weekend or teaching literacy to underprivileged children.

LEADERS: HEROES ARE HARD TO FIND Young adults need role models and leaders, but the twentysomething generation has almost no one to look up to.

Today's new generation of adults has an innate skepticism about social values that evolved over the past 20–25 years. There is a new assessment of what roles work, marriage, and having children play in their lives.

While 58% of those in the TIME/CNN survey said their group has heroes, they failed to agree on any. Ronald Reagan was most often named, with only 8% of the vote, followed by Mikhail Gorbachev (7%), Jesse Jackson (6%) and George Bush (5%). Today's young generation finds no figures in the present who compare with such '60s-era heroes as John F. Kennedy and Martin Luther King. "It seems there were all these great people in the '60s," says Kasi Davidson, 18, of Cody, Wyo. "Now there is nobody."

Today's potential leaders seem unable to maintain their stature. They have a way of either self-destructing or being decimated in the press, which trumpets their faults and foibles. "The media don't really give young people role models anymore," says Christina Chinn, 21, of Denver. "Now you get role models like Donald Trump and all of the money-makers—no one with real ideals."

SHOPPING: LESS PASSION FOR PRESTIGE Marketers are confounded as they try to reach a generation so rootless and noncommittal. But ad agencies that have explored the values of the twen-

tysomething generation have found that status symbols, from Cuisinarts to BMWs, actually carry a social stigma among many young adults. Their emphasis, according to Dan Fox, marketing planner at Foote, Cone & Belding, will be on affordable quality. Unlike baby boomers, who buy 50% of their cars from Japanese makers, the twentysomething generation is too young to remember Detroit's clunkers of the 1970s. Today's young adult is likely to aspire to a Jeep Cherokee or Chevy Lumina with lots of cup holders. "Don't knock the cup holders," warns Fox. "There's something about them that says, 'It's all right in my world,' That's not a small notion. And Mercedes doesn't have them."

The twentysomething attitude toward consumption in general: get more for less. While yuppies spent money to acquire the best and the rarest toys, young adults believe they can live just as well, and maybe even better, without breaking the bank. They disdain designer anything. "Just point me to the generic aisle," says Jill Mackie, 21, a journalism major at the University of Illinois. Such a no-nonsense outlook has made hay for stores like the Gap, which thrives on young people's

desire for casual clothing at a casual price. Similarly, a twentysomething adult picks a Hershey's bar over Godiva chocolates, and Bass Weejuns (price: $75) instead of Lucchese cowboy boots ($500).

CULTURE: FEW FLAVORS OF THEIR OWN Down deep, what frustrates today's young people—and those who observe them—is their failure to create an original youth culture. The 1920s had jazz and the Lost Generation, the 1950s created the Beats, the 1960s brought everything embodied in the Summer of Love. But the twentysomething generation has yet to make a substantial cultural statement. People in their 20s have been handed down everyone else's music, clothes and styles, leaving little room for their own imaginations. Mini-revivals in platform shoes, ripped jeans and urban-cowboy chic all coincide with J. Crew prep, Gumby haircuts and teased-out suburban perms. What young adults have managed to come up with is either *nuevo* hipster or ultra-nerd, but almost always a bland imitation of the past. "They don't even seem to know how to dress," says sociologist Hirsch, "and they're almost unschooled in how to look in different settings."

Is There Love After Baby?

Why the passage to parenthood rocks even the best of couples today: A cautionary tale.

**Carolyn Pape Cowan, Ph.D.,
and Philip A. Cowan, Ph.D.**

Carolyn Pape Cowan, Ph.D., and Philip A. Cowan, Ph.D., are co-directors of the Becoming a Family Project at the University of California at Berkeley. Carolyn codirects the Schoolchildren and Their Families Project and is the co-editor of Fatherhood Today: Men's Changing Roles in the Family. *Philip is the author of* Piaget: With Feeling, *and co-editor of* Family Transitions: Advances in Family Research, Vol. 2. *They are the parents of three grown children.*

Babies are getting a lot of bad press these days. Newspapers and magazine articles warn that the cost of raising a child from birth to adulthood is now hundreds of thousands of dollars. Television news recounts tragic stories of mothers who have harmed their babies while suffering from severe postpartum depression. Health professionals caution that child abuse has become a problem throughout our nation. Several books on how to "survive" parenthood suggest that parents must struggle to keep their marriage alive once they become parents. In fact, according to recent demographic studies, more than 40 percent of children born to two parents can expect to live in a single-parent family by the time they are 18. The once-happy endings to family beginnings are clouded with strain, violence, disenchantment, and divorce.

What is so difficult about becoming a family today? What does it mean that some couples are choosing to remain "child-free" because they fear that a child might threaten their well-established careers or disturb the intimacy of their marriage? Is keeping a family together harder than it used to be?

Over the last three decades, sociologists, psychologists, and psychiatrists have begun to search for the answers. Results of the most recent studies, including our own, show that partners who become parents describe:

• an ideology of more equal work and family roles than their mothers and fathers had;

•actual role arrangements in which husbands and wives are sharing family work and care of the baby less than either of them expected;

•more conflict and disagreement after the baby is born than they had reported before;

•and increasing disenchantment with their overall relationship as a couple.

To add to these disquieting trends, studies of emotional distress in new parents suggest that women and possibly men are more vulnerable to depression in the early months after having a child. Finally, in the United States close to 50 percent of couples who marry will ultimately divorce.

We believe that children are getting an unfair share of the blame for their parents' distress. Based on 15 years of research that includes a three-year pilot study, a 10-year study following 72 expectant couples and 24 couples without children, and ongoing work with couples in distress, we are convinced that the seeds of new parents' individual and marital problems are sown long before baby arrives. Becoming parents does not so much raise new problems as bring old unresolved issues to the surface.

Our concern about the high incidence of marital distress and divorce among the parents of young children led us to study systematically what happens to partners when they become parents. Rather than simply add to the mounting documentation of family problems, we created and evaluated a new preventive program, the Becoming a Family Project, in which mental-health professionals worked with couples during their transition to parenthood, trying to help them get off to a healthy start. Then we followed the families as the first children progressed from infancy through the first year of elementary school.

What we have learned is more troubling than surprising. The majority of husbands and wives become more disenchanted with their couple relationship as they make the transition to parenthood. Most new mothers struggle with the question whether and when to return to work. For those who do go back, the impact on their families depends both on what mothers do at work and what fathers do at home. The more unhappy parents feel about their marriage, the more anger and competitiveness and the less warmth and responsiveness we observe in the family during the preschool period—between the parents as a couple and between each parent and the child. The children of parents with more tension during the preschool years have a harder time adjusting to the challenges of kindergarten.

For couples who thought having a baby was going to bring them closer together, the first few months are especially confusing and disappointing.

On the positive side, becoming a family provides a challenge that for some men and women leads to growth—as individuals, as couples, as parents. For couples who work to maintain or improve the quality of their marriage, having a baby can lead to a revitalized relationship. Couples with more satisfying marriages work together more effectively with their children in the preschool period, and their children tend to have an easier time adapting to the academic and social demands of elementary school. What is news is that the relationship *between* the parents seems to act as a crucible in which their relationships with their children take place.

The transition to parenthood is stressful even for well-functioning couples. In addition to distinctive inner changes, men's and women's roles change in very different ways when partners become parents. It seems to come as a great surprise to most of them that changes in some of their major roles affect their feelings about their overall

relationship. Both partners have to make major adjustments of time and energy as individuals at a time when they are getting less sleep and fewer opportunities to be together. They have less patience with things that didn't seem annoying before. Their frustration often focuses on each other. For couples who thought that having a baby was going to bring them closer together, this is especially confusing and disappointing.

Why does becoming a parent have such a powerful impact on a marriage? We have learned that one of the most difficult aspects of becoming a family is that so much of what happens is unexpected. Helping couples anticipate how they might handle the potentially stressful aspects of becoming a family can leave them feeling less vulnerable, less likely to blame each other for the hard parts, and more likely to decide that they can work it out before their distress permeates all of the relationships in the family.

But when things start to feel shaky, few husbands and wives know how to tell anyone, especially each other, that they feel disappointed or frightened. "This is supposed to be the best time of our lives; what's the matter with me?" a wife might say through her tears. They can't see that some of their tension may be attributable to the conflicting demands of the very complex stage of life, not simply to a suddenly stubborn, selfish, or unresponsive spouse.

Becoming a family today is more difficult than it used to be. Small nuclear families live more isolated lives in crowded cities, often feeling cut off from extended family and friends. Mothers of young children are entering the work force earlier; they are caught between traditional and modern conceptions of how they should be living their lives. Men and women are having a difficult time regaining their balance after having babies, in part because radical shifts in the circumstances surrounding family life in America demand new arrangements to accommodate the increasing demands on parents of young children. But new social arrangements and roles have simply not kept pace with the changes, leaving couples on their own to manage the demands of work and family.

News media accounts imply that as mothers have taken on more of a role in the world of paid work, fathers have taken on a comparable load of family work. But this has just not happened. It is not simply that men's and women's

roles are unequal that seems to be causing distress for couples, but rather that they are so clearly discrepant from what both spouses expected them to be. Women's work roles have changed, but their family roles have not. Well-intentioned and confused husbands feel guilty while their overburdened wives feel angry. It does not take much imagination to see how these emotions can fuel the fires of marital conflict.

Separate (Time)Tables

As they bring their first baby home from the hospital, new mothers and fathers find themselves crossing the great divide. After months of anticipation, their transition from couple to family becomes a reality. Entering this unfamiliar territory, men and women find themselves on different timetables and different trails of a journey they envisioned completing together.

Let's focus on the view from the inside, as men and women experience the shifting sense of self that comes with first-time parenthood. In order to understand how parents integrate Mother or Father as central components of their identity, we give couples a simple pie chart and ask them to think about the various aspects of their lives (worker, friend, daughter, father, so on) and mark off how large each portion feels, not how much time they spend "being it." The size of each piece of the pie reflects their psychologic involvement or investment in that aspect of themselves.

Almost all show pieces that represent parent, worker or student, and partner or lover. The most vivid identity changes during the transition to parenthood take place between pregnancy and six months postpartum. The part of the self that women call Mother takes up 10 percent of their pictures of themselves in late pregnancy. It then leaps to 34 percent six months after birth, and stays there through the second year of parenthood. For some women, the psychological investment in motherhood is much greater than the average.

Most of the husbands we interviewed took on the identity of parent more slowly than their wives did. During pregnancy, Father takes half as much of men's pie as their wives' Mother sections do, and when their children are 18 months old, husbands identity as parent is still less than one third as large as their wives'. We find that the larger the difference between husbands and wives in the size of their parent piece of the pie when their babies are six months old, the less satisfied both spouses are with the marriage, and the more their satisfaction declines over the next year.

The Big Squeeze

Men's and women's sense of themselves as parents is certainly expected to increase once they have had a baby. What comes as a surprise is that other central aspects of the self are getting short shrift as their parent piece of the pie expands. The greatest surprise—for us and for the couples—is what gets squeezed as new parents' identities shift. Women apportion 34 percent to the Partner or Lover aspect of themselves in pregnancy, 22 percent at six months after the birth, and 21 percent when their children are 18 months. Men's sense of themselves as Partner or Lover also shows a decline—from 35 percent to 30 percent to 25 percent over the two-year transition period.

The size of the Partner piece of the pie is connected to how new parents feel about themselves: A larger psychological investment in their relationship seems to be good for both of them. Six months after the birth of their first child, both men and women with larger Partner/Lover pieces have higher self-esteem and less parenting stress. This could mean that when parents resist the tendency to ignore their relationship as a couple, they feel better about themselves and less stressed as parents. Or that when they feel better about themselves they are more likely to stay moderately involved in their relationship.

At our 18-month follow-up, Stephanie and Art talk about the consequences for their marriage of trying to balance—within them and between them—the pulls among the Parent, Worker, and Partner aspects.

Stephanie: We're managing Linda really well. But with Art's promotion from teacher to principal and my going back to work and feeling guilty about being away from Linda, we don't get much time for *us*. I try to make time for the two of us at home, but there's no point in making time to be with somebody if he doesn't want to be with you. Sometimes when we finally get everything done and Linda is asleep, I want to sit down and talk, but Art says this is a perfect opportunity to get some prepara-

tion done for one of his teachers' meetings. Or he starts to fix one of Linda's toys—things that apparently are more important to him than spending time with me.

Art: That does happen. But Stephanie's wrong when she says that those things are more important to me than she is. The end of the day is just not my best time to start a deep conversation. I keep asking her to get a sitter so we can go out for a quiet dinner, but she always finds a reason not to. It's like being turned down for a date week after week.

Stephanie: Art, you know I'd love to go out with you. I just don't think we can leave Linda so often.

Stephanie and Art are looking at the problem from their separate vantage points. Art is very devoted to fatherhood, but is more psychologically invested in his relationship with Stephanie than with Linda. In his struggle to hold onto himself as Partner, he makes the reasonable request that he and Stephanie spend some time alone so they can nurture their relationship as a couple. Stephanie struggles with other parts of her shifting sense of self. Although Art knows that Stephanie spends a great deal of time with Linda when she gets home from work, he does not understand that juggling her increasing involvement as Mother while trying to maintain her investment as Worker is creating a great deal of internal pressure for her. The Partner/Lover part of Stephanie is getting squeezed not only by time demands but also by the psychological reshuffling that is taking place inside her. Art knows only that Stephanie is not responding to his needs, and to him her behavior seems unreasonable, insensitive, and rejecting.

Stephanie knows that Art's view of himself has changed as he has become a parent, but she is unaware of the fact that it has not changed in the same way or to the same degree as hers. In fact, typical of the men in our study, Art's psychological investment in their relationship as couple has declined slightly since Linda was born, but his Worker identity has not changed much. He is proud and pleased to be a father, but these feelings are not crowding out his sense of himself as a Partner/Lover. All Stephanie knows is that Art is repeatedly asking her to go out to dinner and ignoring her inner turmoil. To her, his behavior seems unreasonable, insensitive, and rejecting.

It might have been tempting to con-

clude that it is natural for psychological involvement in one's identity as Partner or Lover to wane over time—but the patterns of the childless couples refute that. The internal changes in each of the new parents begin to have an impact on their relationship as a couple. When women add Mother to their identity, *both* Worker and Partner/Lover get squeezed. As some parts of identity grow larger, there is less "room" for others. The challenge, then, is how to allow Parent a central place in one's identity without abandoning or neglecting Partner. We find that couples who manage to do this feel better about themselves as individuals and as couples.

Who Does What?

How do new parents' internal shifts in identity, and their separate timetables, play out in their marriage? We find that "who does what?" issues are central not only in how husbands and wives feel about themselves, but in how they feel about their marriage. Second, there are alternations in the emotional fabric of the couple's relationship; how caring and intimacy get expressed and how couples manage their conflict and disagreement have a direct effect on their marital satisfaction.

Husbands and wives, different to begin with, become even more separate and distinct in their years after their first child is born. An increasing specialization of family roles and emotional distance between partners-become-parents combine to affect their satisfaction with the relationship.

Behind today's ideology of the egalitarian couple lies a much more traditional reality. Although more than half of mothers with children under five have entered the labor force and contemporary fathers have been taking a small but significantly greater role in cooking, cleaning, and looking after their children than fathers used to do, women continue to carry the overwhelming responsibility for managing the household and caring for the children. Women have the primary responsibility for family work even when both partners are employed full time.

Couples whose division of household and family tasks was not equitable when they began our study tended to predict that it would be after the baby was born. They never expected to split baby care 50-50 but to work as a team in rearing their children. Once the babies are born, however, the women do more of the housework than before they became mothers, and the men do much less of the care of the baby than they or their wives predicted they would. After children appear, a couple's role arrangements—and how both husband and wife feel about them—become entwined with their intimacy.

Ideology vs Reality

In both expectant and childless couples, spouses divide up the overall burden of family tasks fairly equitably. But new parents begin to divide up these tasks in more gender-stereotyped ways. Instead of both partners performing some of each task, he tends to take on a few specific household responsibilities and she tends to do most of the others. His and her overall responsibility for maintaining the household may not shift significantly after having a baby, but it feels more traditional because each has become more specialized.

In the last trimester of pregnancy, men and women predict that the mothers will be responsible for more of the baby care tasks than the father. Nine months later, when the babies are six months old, a majority describe their arrangements as even more Mother's and less Father's responsibility than either had predicted. Among parents of six-month-old babies, mothers are shouldering more of the baby care than either parent predicted on eight of 12 items on our questionnaire: deciding about meals, managing mealtime, diapering, bathing, taking the baby out, playing with the baby, arranging for baby sitters, and dealing with the pediatrician. On four items, women and men predicted that mothers would do more and their expectations proved to be on the mark: responding to baby's cries, getting up in the middle of the night, doing the child's laundry, and choosing the baby's toys.

From this we contend that the ideology of the new egalitarian couple is way ahead of the reality. The fallout from their unmet expectations seems to convert both spouses' surprise and disappointment into tension between them.

Jackson and Tanya talked a lot about their commitment to raising Kevin together. Three months later, when the baby was six months old, Tanya explained that Jackson had begun to do more housework than ever before but

that he wasn't available for Kevin nearly as much as she would have liked.

Tanya: He wasn't being a chauvinist or anything, expecting me to do everything and him nothing. He just didn't *volunteer* to do things that obviously needed doing, so I had to put down some ground rules. Like if I'm in a bad mood, I may just yell: "I work eight hours just like you. This is half your house and half your child, too. You've got to do your share!" Jackson never changed the kitty litter box once in four years, but he changes it now, so we've made great progress. I just didn't expect it to take so much work. We planned this child together and we went through Lamaze together, and Jackson stayed home for the first two weeks. But then—wham—the partnership was over.

Tanya underscores a theme we hear over and over: The tension between new parents about the father's involvement in the family threatens the intimacy between them.

The fact that mothers are doing most of the primary child care in the first months of parenthood is hardly news. What we are demonstrating is that the couples' arrangements for taking care of their infants are *less equitable* than they expected them to be. They are amazed they became so traditional so fast.

It's not just that couples are startled by how the division of labor falls along gender lines, but they describe the change as if it were a mysterious virus they picked up while in the hospital having their baby. They don't seem to view their arrangements as *choices* they have made.

Husbands' and wives' descriptions of their division of labor are quite similar but they do shade things differently: Each claims to be doing more than the other gives him or her credit for. The feeling of not being appreciated for the endless amount of work each partner actually does undoubtedly increases the tension between them. Compared with the childless couples, new parents' overall satisfaction with their role arrangements (household tasks plus decision making plus child care) declined significantly—most dramatically between pregnancy and six months after baby's birth.

Parents who had been in one of our couples groups maintained their satisfaction with the division of household and family tasks. This trend is particularly true for women. Since the actual role arrangement in the group and non-

group participants were very similar, we can see that men's and women's satisfactions with who does what is, at least in part, a matter of perspective.

Some men and women are happy with traditional arrangements. Most of the men in our study, however, wanted desperately to have a central role in their child's life.

Is There Sex after Parenthood?

Most new parents feel some disenchantment in their marriage. It is tempting to blame this on two related facts reported by every couple. First, after having a baby, *time* becomes their most precious commodity. Second, even if a couple can eke out a little time together, the effort seems to require a major mobilization of forces. They feel none of the spontaneity that kept their relationship alive when they were a twosome.

We asked husbands and wives what they do to show their partners that they care. It soon became clear that different things feel caring to different people: bringing flowers or special surprises,

The division of workload in the family wins hands down as the issue most likely to cause conflict in the first two years.

being a good listener, touching in certain ways, picking up the cleaning without being asked.

New parents describe fewer examples of caring after having a baby compared to before, but as we keep finding in each domain of family life, men's and women's changes occur at different times. Between the babies' six- and 18-month birthdays, wives and husbands report that the women are doing fewer caring things for their husbands than the year before. In the parents' natural preoccupation with caring for baby, they seem less able to care for each other.

Both husbands and wives also report a negative change in their sexual relationship after having a baby. The frequency of lovemaking declines for almost all couples in the early months of parenthood.

There are both physical and psychological deterrents to pleasurable sex for new parents. Probably the greatest interference with what happens in the bedroom comes from what happens between the partners outside the bedroom. Martin and Sandi, for example, tell us that making love has become problematic since Ellen's birth. To give an example of a recent disappointment, Martin explains that he had had an extremely stressful day at work. Sandi greeted him with a "tirade" about Ellen's fussy day, the plumber failing to come, and the baby-sitter's latest illness. Dinnertime was tense, and they spent the rest of the evening in different rooms. When they got into bed they watched TV for a few minutes, and then Martin reached out to touch Sandi. She pulled away, feeling guilty that she was not ready to make love.

Like so many couples, they were disregarding the tensions that had been building up over the previous hours. They had never had a chance to talk in anything like a collaborative or intimate way. This is the first step of the common scenario for one or both partners to feel "not in the mood."

Ninety-two percent of the men and women in our study who became parents described more conflict after having their baby than before they became parents. The division of workload in the family wins hands down as the issue most likely to cause conflict in the first two years. Women

feel the impact of the transition more strongly during the first six months after birth, and their husbands feel it more strongly in the following year.

Why does satisfaction with marriage go down? It begins, we think, with the issue of men's and women's roles. The new ideology of egalitarian relationships between men and women has made some inroads on the work front. Most couples, however, are not prepared for the strain of creating more egalitarian relationships at home, and it is this strain that leads men and women to feel more negatively about their partners and the state of their marriage.

Men's increasing involvement in the preparation for the *day* of the baby's birth leads both spouses to expect that he will be involved in what follows— the ongoing daily care and rearing of the children. How ironic that the recent widespread participation of fathers in the births of their babies has become a source of new parents' disappointment when the men do not stay involved in their babies' early care.

The transition to parenthood heightens the differences between men and women, which leads to more conflict between them. This, in turn, threaten the equilibrium of their marriage.

Needed: Couples Groups

Family making is a joint endeavor, not just during pregnancy, but in the years to come. Men simply have little access to settings in which they can share their experiences about intimate family matters. Given how stressful family life is for so many couples, we feel it is important to help them under-

stand how their increasing differences during this transition may be generating more distance between them. Most couples must rebalance of the relationship.

Our results show that when sensitive group leaders help men and women focus on what is happening to them as individuals and as a couple during their transition to parenthood, it buffers them from turning their strain into dissatisfaction with each other. Why intervene with couples in *groups*? We find that a group setting provides the kind of support that contemporary couples often lack.

Groups of people going through similar life experiences help participants "normalize" some of their strain and adjustment difficulties; they discover that the strain they are experiencing is expectable at this stage of life. This can strengthen the bond between husbands and wives and undercut their tendency to blame each other for their distress.

Group discussions, by encouraging partners to keep a focus on their couple relationship, help the women maintain their identity as Partner/Lover while they are taking on Motherhood and returning to their jobs and careers. Fathers become painfully aware of what it takes to manage a demanding job and the day-to-day care of a household with baby.

The modern journey to parenthood, exciting and fulfilling as it is, is beset with many roadblocks. Most couples experience stress in the early years of family life. Most men and women need to muster all the strength and skills they have to make this journey. Almost all of the parents in our studies say that the joyful parts outweigh the difficult ones. They also say that the lessons they learn along the way are powerful and well worth the effort.

Development During Middle and Late Adulthood and Aging

- Middle Adulthood (Articles 50–52)
- Late Adulthood and Aging (Articles 53–57)

Evidence obtained during the past decade clearly illustrates the fallacy of the stereotypic views of middle and especially later adulthood that are so common in Western cultures. Development during these life phases is not a unitary phenomenon. Individuals adapt in a variety of ways. Moreover, development does not occur in a vacuum. It is very much influenced by the times and the culture in which one lives. Two articles in the first subsection, *Middle Adulthood*, reflect these themes. "The New

Middle Age" considers the ways in which the experience of middle adulthood by the baby boomer generation is likely to differ from the experience of any prior generation.

Perhaps no statistic reflects the changes in the American family across the last generation as effectively as the surge in the number of women who combine family life with careers. Do these dual roles too often prove detrimental to health and happiness? Certainly not, according to "The Myth of the Miserable Working Woman."

The selections comprising the subsection *Late Adulthood and Aging* offer an update on contemporary thinking and research on the last period of life, and they challenge a number of our commonly held misconceptions. Developmentalists hold two extreme points of view about the latter part of the life span. Disengagement theory holds that the physical and intellectual deficits associated with aging are inevitable and should be accepted at face value by the aged. Activity theory acknowledges the decline in abilities associated with aging, but also emphasizes that the aged can maintain satisfying and productive lives. These two approaches to aging are not mutually exclusive. Some individuals adopt an active lifestyle, while others choose a more disengaged approach. Both can lead to satisfying adjustments in the later years.

Some experts even question whether the course of life really progresses through an orderly series of universally experienced stages. Bernice Neugarten in the "The Prime of Our Lives" does not think so and argues strongly against this view.

Although there are common physical changes associated with aging, there are also wide individual differences in the rates of change as well as in the degree to which changes are expressed. Extreme views in any guise risk stereotyping all individuals within a category or class as having the same needs and capabilities. Whether one's reference group is racial, ethnic, cultural, or age-related, stereotyping usually leads to counterproductive, discriminatory social policy that alienates the reference group from mainstream society.

It is common to think of the changes associated with aging as solely physical and generally negative. The popular press devotes considerable space to discussions of the causes and treatment of such debilitating disorders as Alzheimer's disease. However, there are also psychological changes associated with aging, and, as is the case at all age levels, some individuals cope well with change, and others do not. New research on the aging process suggests that physical health and mental health are not highly related. Although a variety of abuses can hasten physical and mental deterioration, proper diet and modest exercise can slow the aging process. In addition, one cannot overstate the importance of love, social interaction, and a sense of self-worth for combating the loneliness, despair, and futility often associated with aging.

Behavioral gerontology remains a specialization within human development that is absent from even most graduate programs in human development. Perhaps this is partly because of the natural tendency of people to avoid confronting the negative aspects of aging, such as loneliness and despair over the loss of one's spouse or over one's own impending death. Nevertheless, contemporary studies do provide fascinating information about the quality of life in the later years and challenge many traditional views about interpersonal relationships and memory processes.

The final article, "Unlocking the Secrets of Aging," profiles a cross section of the burgeoning research on the aging process. New discoveries about the mechanisms that control aging may result in a doubling of the average life expectancy in the not too distant future. This article also considers the enormous social, economic, and political impact of a demographic change of this magnitude and underlines the need for studies on the psychological aspects of aging in pursuit of promotion and enhancement of the quality of life for the elderly.

Looking Ahead: Challenge Questions

What are some of the most positive features for women of combining careers with family responsibilities?

Why are the middle adult years, sometimes called the "prime of life," the forgotten years in inquiries into growth and change, relative to both earlier and later life periods?

Do you think that most individual's lives can be described by a relatively constant sequence of life stages, or are life patterns just too variable for general descriptions to be of use? What are some of the most common stereotypes about aging in our society?

Gerontologists suggest that significantly greater life expectancies are possible even without medical breakthroughs. Control of childhood diseases, better education, better physical fitness, and proper diet are factors that are increasing the average life span. What kind of effects on the individual and on the society will result from such a radical demographic change as a doubling of the average life span?

How would your life differ now if your expected life span were 150 years? How do you think your elderly years will differ from those of your parents?

the new
MIDDLE AGE

MELINDA BECK

A generation verges toward a mass midlife crisis. But wait: it can be a lot better than you think.

The names are culled from driver's license records, credit-card applications, magazine-subscription forms—any place an unsuspecting consumer might have listed his birth date somewhere along the line. They pour into a data-management firm, where they are standardized, merged and purged of duplications. From there, they are assigned one of several different solicitation packets, then bundled and shipped nationwide. It's a point of great pride with the American Association of Retired Persons that on or about their birthdays, roughly 75 percent of the 2.7 million Americans who turned 50 this year received an offer to partake—for just $8!—in all the benefits of membership in the AARP.

Not since the Selective Service Board sent "greetings" to 18-year-old men during the Vietnam War has a birthday salutation been so dreaded by so many. True, the leading edge of the baby boom won't get the official invitations into the quagmire of the 50s for four more years—but these things are always worse in anticipation than in reality. And the icons of the baby boom are already there. Paul McCartney turned 50 this year; so did Aretha Franklin. Bob Dylan is 51, as are Frank Zappa, Paul Simon and Art Garfunkel. Even the heartthrobs have crossed the great divide: Raquel Welch is pinned up at 51, Robert Redford at 55.

Month by month, individually and collectively, the generation that refused to grow up is growing middle aged. The reminders are everywhere—from the gracefully aging Lauren Hutton (49) in the J. Crew catalog to the now ubiquitous prefix *"aging* baby boomers" to the Oval Office itself. Sure, Bill Clinton and Al Gore will breathe new youth into the presidency that has been held for three decades by the PT-109 crowd. But for many in this competitive cohort, their ascension is just one more reminder of time marching on and leaving accomplishment victims in its wake. *See—the president is 46. You're 49. Weren't you supposed to be CEO by now, or at least know what you want to DO with your life?*

To be sure, this is hardly the first generation to hit or anticipate the Big Five-Oh. The baby boomers' group obsession with aging is already sounding, well, old, to everybody else, and, by conventional definitions at least, most boomers have been "middle aged" since they turned 40. But raised with such outsize expectations of life, they may have a tougher time accepting the age of limitations than other generations. "This group was somehow programmed to never get older—that sets us up for a whole series of disappointments," says psychiatrist Harold Bloomfield in Del Mar, Calif. Rice University sociologist Chad Gordon has another take on the angst that is seizing baby boomers. "Let's face it—aging sucks," he says. "It's filled with all those D words—decay, decrepitude, degeneration, dying . . . Then there's balding, paunchiness, losing sex drives and capabilities, back trouble, headaches, cholesterol and high blood pressure—they all go from the far horizon to close up. Then you worry about worrying about those things."

In truth, authorities on aging and ordinary people who've been there say that middle age isn't so bad. "It's the most powerful and glorious segment of a person's life," says Ken Dychtwald, whose company, Age Wave, counsels businesses on how to serve the needs of the aging population. Dychtwald admits, however, that American culture hasn't universally embraced this idea and that most of the soon-to-be-middle-aged themselves haven't gotten into the swing of it yet.

Instead, they are responding with ever more exaggerated forms of foreboding. Bloomfield says he sees an increase in a once rare condition called *dysmorphophobia*—the intense but unfounded fear of looking ugly. In Hollywood, not only do actresses try desperately to disguise their age, but so do agents, scriptwriters and studio executives. "It's hard to age gracefully out here," says Dr. Mel Bircoll, 52, considered the father of the cosmetic pectoral implant, the calf implant and the fat implant (which he layers into face-lifts to add contour and avoid the "overstretched look"). Bircoll says his clients used to start at 55. Now they come to him at about 45.

All of this might have been grist for a great TV series, but when producer Stan Rogow tried it this season, it flopped. Rogow intended "Middle Ages" to be an upbeat portrayal—"pretty hip, pretty life affirming, not angst-ridden. What we tried to do with the show was to say, 'This is OK. It's better than OK'." Critics liked it but viewers never gave it a chance and, in retrospect, Rogow understands why: "The name was a colossal mistake. 'Middle age' is this horrible-sounding thing you've heard throughout your life and hated." As the low ratings piled up, Rogow said to himself: "We have a problem here, and it's called denial."

But the funny thing about denial is that sometimes it works. In the very act of staving off physical aging through exercise, diet and dye, the StairMaster set has actually succeeded in pushing back the boundaries of "middle age." Boomers will look, act and feel younger at 50 than previous generations did. "Fifty will be like 40," says UCLA gerontologist Fernando Torres-Gil, who predicts that this generation won't confront "old age" until well into their 70s. The broad concept of middle age is starting later and lasting longer—and looking better than ever before. "We're seeing that 50 means all kinds of very vibrant, alive, sexy, dynamic people," says June Reinisch, director of the Kinsey Institute for Research in Sex, Gender and Reproduction at Indiana University. "I'm 49 this year. I wear clothes that my mother never would have thought of wearing when she was this age. When skirts went up, my skirts went up." Rogow, 44, says: "I'd really be shocked if I'm wearing plaid golf pants at 60. I suspect I'll be wearing the same ripped jeans I've been wearing for 20 years. They'll be much cooler then."

The new middle age also features more children than ever before, since this generation has delayed marriage and childbearing. Many men are having second families, with even younger children, well into their 50s. Some may be pushing strollers *and* paying college tuition just when psychologists say they should be busting loose and fulfilling themselves. At the same time, today's middle-agers have aging parents who are starting to need care. "For many people, 50 will be just like 20, 30 and 40—tied to providing basic subsistence needs," says University of Texas psychologist David Drum. "They won't see a chance to change, to repattern their lives."

Yet even as they postponed family responsibilities, many people in this fast-track generation reached the peaks of their careers much earlier than their parents did—and are wondering, "Is that all there is?" even in their 30s and 40s. Many of them will top out earlier, too, as record numbers of middle managers chase fewer and fewer promotions. While previous generations worried about sex and marriage, "career crashes are the baby boom's version of midlife crisis," says Barry Glassner, a University of Southern California sociologist. Women, having forged careers of their own in record numbers, may face the same kind of professional crisis traditionally reserved for men—and their incomes will still be needed to make ends meet. "Lose a job—have any piece of the puzzle taken out—and the whole thing falls apart," says Andrea Saveri, a research fellow at the Institute for the Future in Menlo Park, Calif.

The cruel demographic joke is that just as this generation is hitting middle age with unprecedented family responsibilities, corporate America is mustering legions of fiftysomethings out of the work force through early-retirement plans and less compassionate methods. "There is tremendous doubt about the future," says Saveri. "People see their friends getting pink slips. Their M.B.A.s aren't doing them any good now." Retiring earlier—and living longer—will bring a host of financial, emotional and psychological problems in the years ahead. Today's 50-year-olds still have 20 or 30 more years to live. What are they going to do—and how are they going to pay for it? "The 50s are not the beginning of the end—you have an awful long way to go," says University of Chicago gerontologist Bernice Neugarten, now 76. And that may be the most frightening thought of all.

Midway life's journey I was made aware
 That I had strayed into a dark forest,
And the right path appeared not anywhere.

Dante was 35 years old and frustrated in his quest for political position in 1300 when he wrote the first lines of "The Inferno"—describing perhaps the first midlife crisis in Western literature. Shakespeare charted similar midlife muddles in "King Lear," "Macbeth," "Hamlet" and "Othello" in the early 1600s, though he barely used the phrase "middle age." Sigmund Freud and Carl Jung studied midlife transitions around the turn of the 20th century. But then "midlife" came much earlier in time. In 1900, average life expectancy in the United States was 47 and only 3 percent of the population lived past 65. Today average life expectancy is 75—and 12 percent of the U.S. population is older than 65.

The longer life gets, the harder it is to plot the midpoint and define when middle age begins and ends. "We've broken the evolutionary code," says Gail Sheehy, author of "Passages" and "The Silent Passage." "In only a century, we've added 30 years to the life cycle." Statistically, the middle of life is now about 37, but what we think of as middle age comes later—anywhere from 40 to 70. As chronological age has less and less meaning, experts are groping for other definitions. When the American Board of Family Practice asked a random sampling of 1,200 Americans when middle age begins, 41 percent said it was when you worry about having enough money for health-care concerns, 42 percent said it was when your last child moves out and 46 percent said it was when you don't recognize the names of music groups on the radio anymore.

However it is defined, middle age remains one of the least studied phases in life. "It's the last uncharted territory in human development," said MacArthur Foundation president Adele Simmons in 1989, announcing a $10 million grant to fund the largest scholarly look ever at the period. Team leader Gilbert Brim and his colleagues at the Research Network on Successful Midlife Development are now partway through their eight-year effort, trying to answer, among other things, why some people hit their

How do I know if what I achieve in life should be called serenity and not surrender?

—JUDITH VIORST, 61

■ Percentage of baby boomers who say they have been through midlife crisis: 27
■ Average age of men who marry for second time: 39.2
■ Average age of women who marry for second time: 34.8

SOURCE: GALLUP, NATIONAL CENTER FOR HEALTH STATISTICS

strides at midlife and others hit the wall. To date, they have concluded that there are no set stages or transition points—that what happens to people is more the result of accident, personal experiences and the historical period in which they live. "Midlife is full of changes, of twists and turns; the path is not fixed," says Brim. "People move in and out of states of success."

In particular, Brim's group debunks the notion of a "midlife crisis." "It's such a mushy concept—not like a clinical diagnosis in the medical field," he says. But, Brim adds, "what a wonderful idea! You could load everything on that—letting people blame something external for what they're feeling." Other scholars agree that very few people suffer full-blown crackups—and that dumping the spouse for a bimbo is more the stuff of fiction—or fantasy— than reality. So is the Gauguin syndrome: running off to Tahiti at 43. People do have affairs and end up with different mates—but that is often after marriages have failed for reasons other than midlife malaise.

Still, the mythology persists. "You ask people if they've had a midlife crisis and some say they have," says sociologist Ronald Kessler at the University of Michigan's Institute for Social Research. "Then you ask them what it was and they'll say that they didn't get to be vice president. So what did they do—try to kill themselves? Buy a sports car? Well no, people come to terms with getting older in a most gradual way." The idea of a crisis sometimes provides an excuse for wild and outrageous behavior, says psychologist Susan Krauss Whitbourne at the University of Massachusetts at Amherst: "It sounds romantic and fun—certainly better than complete boredom." She also suspects it's a class phenomenon: well-educated people with money "have the luxury to reflect on these things."

What does commonly happen, experts say, is a more subtle acceptance of life's limitations. One key task may be to change your self-image. "A lot of the more tangible rewards come in the first half of life, such as good grades, first jobs, early promotions, marriage, first children," says psychologist Robert E. Simmons in Alexandria, Va. After that, "it's harder and harder to rely on external gratifications because there aren't as many. So one is thrown back more on one's internal self-esteem system." That can mean finding new forms of satisfaction—from coaching Little League to taking up the saxophone to tutoring kids in school.

The sooner you accept the idea that life may not turn out as you planned, the easier the transition will be. "It's the person who has just been driving himself and getting burnt out, who is starting to turn 50 and who feels like, 'My God, my life is over'," says Bloomfield. Gail Sheehy agrees: "For those who deny, postpone, elude or fantasize to escape coming to terms with [reality], it comes up again around 50 with a double whammy." Sheehy can see this now, at 54. She barely mentioned life past 50 in "Passages" because she was only 35 at the time and couldn't visualize herself at an older age. Now she says she knows that "you have to work your way up to saying 'I'm not going to go backward. I'm not going to try to stay in the same place. That way lies self-torture and eventually

foolishness. I'm going to have the courage to go forward'."

Contrary to conventional wisdom, many people find that the 50s is actually a period of reduced stress and anxiety. "In terms of mental health, midlife is the best time," says Ronald Kessler. One tantalizing bit of biomedical research has found that between 40 and 60, people actually lose cells in the locus coeruleus, the part of the brain that registers anxiety, which may help explain the "mellowing" many people feel in middle age. Depression does tend to peak in this period, however, which may also be linked to biochemical changes in the aging brain.

Not all mood shifts are biochemical. There are definite life events that can bring about profound changes of heart and direction. The list includes divorce; illness; losing a job; the kids leaving home (or returning); the death of parents, spouses and friends. Those can happen at any point in life, but they begin to mount up in the 50s. Any kind of change is stressful and simply fearing these things can bring tension. "It also happens when mentors retire," says University of North Carolina sociologist Glen Elder. "You have to think about yourself playing that role. It's a major transition, one that is hard to come to terms with."

Professional disappointments weigh especially heavily on men, and they are inevitable even for the most successful, from George Bush to laid-off steelworkers. Being forced out of a job in midlife can be devastating—or liberating, if it brings about a rethinking of what's most important. Men (and increasingly, women) who sacrificed time with their families for their careers in their younger years may be particularly regretful when success proves as empty as the nest. "Men our age have lived such a macho fake life," says Rogers Brackmann, 61, a former advertising executive in Chicago. "When I was in the agency business, I was up at 5 o'clock, home at 7:30. For the first 15 years I worked every Saturday. I didn't make it to my kid's Little League games. When I left that environment I realized how hard and unproductive the work was." Rogers packed it in five years ago and says, "I was so happy to get out I can't describe it." Since then he has turned to other new businesses, including inventing, and now holds five patents—including one for a golf-ball washer that doesn't get your hands wet.

Can I ask you a question? Why do men chase women? . . . I think it's because they fear death.
—ROSE (Olympia Dukakis) in "Moonstruck"

Typically, men and women cross paths, psychologically, in middle age. Men become more nurturing and family-oriented. Women become more independent and aggressive. Jung described this as the "contrasexual transition." Northwestern University psychologist David Gutmann found the phenomenon not only in American culture, but also in Navajo, Mayan and Middle Eastern Druze societies he studied for his book "Reclaimed Powers: Toward a New Psychology of Men and Women in Later Life"—suggesting that it is more biological than cultural. Much

---

I live like a monk, almost. A monk with red lips, short dresses and big hair.

—TINA TURNER, 53

- Percentage of men aged 40 to 49 who say their lives are exciting: 52.4
- Percentage aged 50 to 59: 43.3
- Percentage of women aged 40 to 49 who find their lives exciting: 45.6
- Percentage aged 50 to 59: 40.7

SOURCE: NATIONAL OPINION RESEARCH CENTER

of it has to do with the demands of child rearing, Gutmann explains, in which men provide for the family's physical needs and women do the emotional work, each suppressing the other parts of their personalities. When the children leave home, those submerged forces tend to reassert themselves, Gutmann says.

Ideally, that crossing should be liberating for both halves of the couple and bring them closer together. But often the transition is rocky. "It can be very threatening for men to see their women soar," says counselor Sirah Vettese, Bloomfield's wife. Some men are so unnerved that they do seek out younger, more compliant women, Gutmann says. He thinks Ernest Hemingway is a prime example: devastated after his third wife left him to pursue her own career, the author became increasingly alcoholic. He took another younger wife and killed himself at 61.

It doesn't help that many men wrestling with self-image adjustments in midlife must also accept declining sexual performance. Testosterone levels gradually drop, which can diminish their libido. Erections are less full, less frequent and require more stimulation to achieve. Researchers once attributed that to psychological factors, but increasingly they find that 75 percent of erection dysfunctions stem from physiological problems. "Smoking, diabetes, hypertension, elevated cholesterol—without a doubt, those are the four erection busters," says University of Chicago urologist Laurence A. Levine. Still, psychology does play a role. "If you think you're going to have a problem, suddenly you're going to begin having a problem," says psychologist Jan Sinnott at Towson State University in Baltimore, Md.

Inevitably, pharmaceutical manufacturers have sensed that there's money to be made in the fear of flaccidity. Gynex Pharmaceuticals is researching a daily under-the-tongue testosterone-replacement product called Androtest-SL and already markets an injectable version that is used every two weeks. But there may be considerable side effects. Excessive use of testosterone may lead to testicular atrophy and infertility and spur the growth of some cancers. Too much testosterone can cause some men to grow small breasts, too.

A better remedy for men who find their potency declining is to change the way they think about sex—to take things slower, more romantically and not mourn the seemingly instant erections of their youth. "The midlife male has to finally get the idea that his primary sex organ is not his penis. It's his heart and his brain," says Bloomfield, author of "Love Secrets for a Lasting Relationship." Talking helps, too, though most men are not accustomed to such openness. "It's really important that men and women sit down and say to each other, 'Our lives are changing'," says Vettese.

In many ways, women have it easier in midlife. For all the new willingness to discuss the hot flashes and mood swings some feel during menopause, many women feel a surge of sexual and psychological freedom once their shifting hormones rebalance and they are no longer concerned about getting pregnant. "With each passing generation, women feel sexier and more desire after menopause," says June Reinisch at the Kinsey Institute. Sheehy says that based on studies she has seen, about one third of women have some noticeable diminution of desire after menopause. That can be rectified with hormone supplements or accepted as it is, if the woman doesn't mind.

What many women *do* mind is finding themselves alone and lost in the discouraging midlife singles scene. Zella Case, co-owner of the Someone Special dating service in Dallas, says, "We have hundreds of women who want in, but so few men." The numbers are right there in the census statistics: there are 14 million single women older than 55, and only 4 million single men. Just ask Victoria Anderson, a Dallas private investigator who turned 50 last month. Divorced 13 years, she's been losing confidence and gaining weight and she frets that she'll never fit into the size 3s in her closet again. She despairs of meeting a new mate on the job—"I deal with criminals and jerks," she says. And as far as the bar scene goes, Anderson says ruefully, the typical question now is not "what's your sign, but what's your cholesterol level?"

Women with stable marriages may find other tensions mounting in midlife. With delayed childbirth, kids may be hitting adolescence just when their mothers are in menopause—a volatile combination. Some women desperately fear losing their faces and their figures—especially if those have been the focus of their self-esteem. But the new burst of postmenopausal independence some feel may help to compensate.

Bobbi Altman literally took flight at midlife. "Turning 50 was the best thing that ever happened to me. I could do anything I wanted to," she says. After suffering through a divorce in her early 40s and raising three children, Altman took up aviation, bought an airplane and, at 59, went to aircraft-mechanic school. Last April she graduated and in June she flew cross-country solo. Now 61, she lives in Laguna Beach, Calif., and is involved with a man who finished law school at 70. Altman flies to work every day at the Santa Monica Museum of Flying, where she is helping to restore a World War II P-39. "Aging is not a loss of youth—it's another stage," she says.

I remember now that the toughest birthday I ever faced was my fortieth. It was a big symbol because it said goodbye, goodbye, goodbye to youth. But I think that when one has passed through that age it's like breaking the sound barrier.
—Writer and director NORMAN CORWIN, 82 quoted in the 1992 book "The Ageless Spirit"

Baby boomers who dread what will happen to them beyond the age of 50 have only to look at what older people are doing with their lives today. The generation preceding them—the first to enjoy the longevity revolution—are going back to school in record numbers, forging new careers and still making great strides in their old ones. Lydia Bronte, a research fellow at the Phelps Stokes Institute in New York, recently com-

---

I feel exactly the same as I've always felt: a lightly reined-in voracious beast.

—JACK NICHOLSON, 55

■ Percentage of married men aged 40 to 49 who admit to infidelity: 28.4
■ Percentage aged 50 to 59: 24.3
■ Percentage of married women aged 40 to 49 who admit to infidelity: 15.21
■ Percentage aged 50 to 59: 3.3

SOURCE: NATIONAL OPINION RESEARCH CENTER

■ **Total face–lifts in U.S., 1990: 48,743 (91% women) percentage aged 35 to 50: 27 percentage aged 51 to 64: 58**
■ **Total tummy tucks in U.S., 1990: 20,213 (93% women) percentage aged 35 to 50: 64 percentage aged 51 to 64: 15**
■ **Total hair transplants in U.S., 1990: 3,188 (100% men) percentage aged 35 to 50: 57 percentage aged 51 to 64: 10**
■ **Median age of an American using hair–color product: women: 43.14, men: 43.02**

SOURCE: AMERICAN SOCIETY OF PLASTIC & RECONSTRUCTIVE SURGEONS, SIMMONS 1992

pleted a five-year study of the work lives of 150 people 65 to 102, and concludes that "many people are as active as they've ever been during those years . . . The single most important thing was that they found work that they loved." Some of Bronte's subjects switched jobs many times over in their lives. Some found their true calling only in their later years. Julia Child, now 80, learned French cooking after her husband took a job in France and started her TV career in her 50s. The late Millicent Fenwick won her first race for Congress at 65.

Still, the image of elderly people as desperate, frail and unproductive prevails, and that brings an unrealistic fear of growing middle aged and older. "People need to profoundly rethink what aging means, not only for themselves as individuals, but for the whole society," says Harry Moody, deputy director of the Brookdale Center on Aging at Hunter College in New York. By 2030, when the oldest boomers are 84 and the youngest have turned 65, thee will be an estimated 65 million Americans 65 and older—more than twice as many as today.

To find more satisfaction and hope in that future, aging baby boomers need to bust out of the rigid "three boxes of life" mentality that has governed the pattern of American lives for so long. Confining education to youth, work and child rearing to the middle years, and retirement to old age makes less and less sense—and it simply won't fly in an economy that is dismissing people from the work world in their 50s, with an ever-longer stretch of life ahead. "We desperately need some real, contributing roles for people in the third third of life," says New York management consultant Bill Stanley. He argues that the whole concept of "retirement" should be retired.

Some change in the image of aging will come about naturally in the decades ahead. Baby boomers, by sheer force of numbers, have always made their stage in life the hip stage to be in. The generation that thought it could change the world overnight has only a few years left before its members become elders themselves. While some of their frantic efforts to stave off aging may constitute denial, some go hand in hand with forging a healthier, more constructive vision of old age that could last even longer than we now suspect. The boomers will go there, riding Stair-Masters to heaven, and that may be their most lasting legacy of all.

With GINNY CARROLL *in Houston,* PATRICIA KING *in San Francisco,* KAREN SPRINGEN *and* TODD BARRETT *in Chicago,* LUCILLE BEACHY *in New York,* JEANNE GORDON *in Los Angeles and* CAROLYN FRIDAY *in Boston*

Far from being the slough of despond it is considered, middle age
may be the very best time of life, researchers say—the "it" we work toward

MIDLIFE MYTHS

WINIFRED GALLAGHER

Winifred Gallagher ("Midlife Myths") is a senior editor of American Health. *Her latest book [is]* The Power of Place: How Our Surroundings Shape Our Thoughts, Emotions, and Actions.

According to the picture of human development drawn by traditional scientific literature, after a busy childhood and adolescence young adults launch their careers and social lives and then stride into a black box, from which they hobble some forty years later to face a darkly eventful senescence. According to popular literature, what takes place inside the box is an anticlimactic, unsatisfying, and even traumatic march over the hill and toward the grave—or, worse, the nursing home. This scenario complements the anecdotes that often figure in conversations about middle age: that friend of a friend whose lifetime investment in career and family went up in the flames of a passion for the au pair, or that second cousin rumored to have gone off the deep end during the "change of life" when the kids left for college.

So entrenched is the idea that middle age is bad or boring or both that the almost 80 million members of the graying Baby Boom generation won't use the term except in referring to Ozzie and Harriet Nelson or Ward and June Cleaver. "We have a problem here, and it's called denial," the television producer Stan Rogow, whose 1992 series *Middle Ages* was a critical success, recently told *Newsweek*. He blames the show's title for its commercial failure: "'Middle age' is this horrible-sounding thing you've heard throughout your life and hated." The denial he describes frustrates the efforts of researchers who are conducting the first comprehensive, multidisciplinary studies of middle age. They are finding that it is not just an aging process but life's peak experience.

The study of development concentrates mostly on life's early stages, when behavioral and physiological growth and change are simultaneous. In the 1960s the new discipline of gerontology revealed that as people lived much further into old age, a reverse synchrony obtained toward life's end. Looking back from studies of the elderly and, to a lesser extent, forward from studies of the young, researchers began to suspect that middle age might be not simply a long interval during which things are worse than they are in youth and better than they are

in old age but a developmental process in its own right—albeit one not particularly tied to changes in the body. Common perceptions of middle age are that it occurs from roughly forty to sixty; in the future, increased longevity and better health may push back the period of middle age even further. The scientists and scholars exploring this part of life, which is probably better described experientially than chronologically—the very concept of middle age itself is something of a cultural artifact, with social and economic components—range from the medically, sociologically, and psychologically oriented John D. and Catherine T. MacArthur Foundation Research Network on Successful Midlife Development (MIDMAC), administered from Vero Beach, Florida, to the psychoanalytically and spiritually grounded C. G. Jung Foundation's Center for Midlife Development in New York City.

Although there are plenty of exceptions, "the data show that middle age is the very best time in life," says Ronald Kessler, a sociologist and MIDMAC fellow who is a program director in the survey research center of the University of Michigan's Institute for Social Research. "When looking at the total U.S. population, the best year is fifty. You don't have to deal with the aches and pains of old age or the anxieties of youth: Is anyone going to love me? Will I ever get my career off the ground? Rates of general distress are low—the incidences of depression and anxiety fall at about thirty-five and don't climb again until the late sixties. You're healthy. You're productive. You have enough money to do some of the things you like to do. You've come to terms with your relationships, and the chance of divorce is very low. Midlife is the 'it' you've been working toward. You can turn your attention toward being rather than becoming."

Whereas Kessler's picture of middle age is drawn from facts and figures, the image in most Americans' minds is based on myths, derived not from the ordinary experiences of most people but from the unusual experiences of a few. Although these make for livelier reading and conversation, they generate an unnecessarily gloomy attitude about the middle years which limits people's horizons, according to Margie Lachman, a psychologist, a MIDMAC fellow, and the director of the Life-span Developmental Psychology Laboratory at Brandeis University. When Lachman asked young adults what it means to be middle-aged, they gave such answers as "You think more

The overwhelming majority of people, surveys show, accomplish the task of coming to terms with the realities of middle age through a long, gentle process—not an acute, painful crisis.

about the past than the future" and "You worry about money for health care." They also assumed that the stress experienced in middle age came from the desire to be young again. Older subjects Lachman surveyed, who knew better, attributed stress to coping with the many demands of the busiest time in life. And whereas the older group saw their lives as generally stable, the younger expected to experience a lot of change—and a crisis—in midlife. "The images and beliefs we have about middle age are the guideposts for our planning, evaluation, and goal-setting," Lachman says. "Are they accurate? Or negative self-fulfilling prophesies?"

Gilbert Brim, a pioneer in the study of social development through the life-span and the director of MIDMAC, agrees. "Passed on from generation to generation," he says, "widely shared cultural beliefs and untested theories about middle age put forward in the media continue to be played out in society. But they're likely to be wrong. There are probably as many myths about midlife now as there were about aging thirty years ago, before the advent of gerontology. The time has come to rid ourselves of these obsolete ideas."

The Inexorable Midlife Crisis?

MOST YOUNGER ADULTS ANTICIPATE THAT BETWEEN their late thirties and their early fifties a day will come when they suddenly realize that they have squandered their lives and betrayed their dreams. They will collapse into a poorly defined state that used to be called a nervous breakdown. Escape from this black hole will mean either embracing an un-American philosophy of eschatological resignation or starting over—jaded stockbrokers off to help Mother Teresa, phlegmatic spouses off to the StairMaster and the singles scene. In short, they will have a midlife crisis.

If youth's theme is potential, midlife's is reality: childhood fantasies are past, the fond remembrances of age are yet to be, and the focus is on coming to terms with the finite resources of the here and now. The overwhelming majority of people, surveys show, accomplish this devel-

opmental task, as psychologists put it, through a long, gentle process—not an acute, painful crisis. Over time the college belle or the high school athlete leans less on physical assets, the middle manager's horizons broaden beyond the corner office, and men and women fortunate enough to have significant others regard the rigors of courtship with indulgent smiles. In relying on brains and skill more than beauty and brawn, diffusing competitive urges to include the tennis court or a community fund-raising project, and valuing long-term friendship and domestic pleasures over iffy ecstasies, these people have not betrayed their youthful goals but traded them in for more practical ones that bring previously unsuspected satisfaction. Ronald Kessler says, "The question to ask the middle-aged person isn't just What has happened to you? but also How has your experience changed your thinking?"

The middle-aged tend to be guided not by blinding revelations associated with emotional crisis but by slowly dawning adaptive insights into the self and others, which Kessler calls "psychological turning points." Early in midlife these usually involve a recognition of limitations: the local politician realizes that she'll never make it to the U.S. Senate, and the high school English teacher accepts that he's not going to be a famous man of letters. In the middle period of middle age the transitions usually concern what Kessler calls a redirection of goals: "You say to yourself, 'I'm killing myself at work, but the thing that really satisfies me is my family. I'm not going to change jobs, but from now on I'm going to focus more on home, and career will mean something different to me.'" In later middle age, turning points, especially for women, often involve a recognition of strength—"just the opposite of what you'd suppose," Kessler says. "The shy violet, for example, finds herself chairing a committee." These soundings taken and adjustments made prompt not dramatic departures from one's life course but gentle twists and curves.

"Mastery experiences," the more robust versions of which figure in Outward Bound–type adventure vacations, can be catalysts for middle-aged people in their ordinary settings as well. One of Kessler's subjects finally got his college diploma at fifty-eight, observing that he

"Mastery experiences," the more robust versions of which figure in Outward Bound–type vacations, can be catalysts for middle-aged people in their ordinary settings as well.

had thereby "resolved a lot of things and completed something important"; in almost the same language, a man of fifty said that he had "done something important" when he became proficient enough in his hobby of electronics to tutor others. Overcoming her lifelong fear of water, one woman learned to swim at the age of forty-five. "One day her family went to the pool, and she just jumped in," Kessler says. "This was a very powerful experience for her, not because she wanted to be a lifeguard but because she had mastered her anxiety as well as a new skill."

Even an apparently negative turning point can have benefits. Quite a few of Kessler's subjects, when asked if they had realized a dream in the past year, said yes, "but quite a few said they had given up on one," he says. "When the folks who have dreamed for years about a big summer house where all the kids would flock finally accept that they don't have the money and the kids have other plans, they release a lot of tension. This kind of surrender is very productive, because dreams that run counter to reality waste a lot of energy."

Although all people make psychological transitions and adjustments in the course of middle age, relatively few experience these as catastrophic. In surveys 10 to 12 percent of respondents report that they have had a midlife crisis, Kessler says. "What they often mean is that the kind of disaster that can happen at other times in life—divorce, or being fired, or a serious illness—happened to them during their middle years." An unusual convergence of such unhappy events can push even a hardy middle-aged person into a state of emotional emergency. "First you notice that your hair is falling out," Gilbert Brim says. "Then you go to the office and learn you didn't get that raise, and when you get home, your wife says she's leaving." But most of those who have a true psychological crisis in middle age—according to MIDMAC, about five percent of the population—have in fact experienced internal upheavals throughout their lives. "They see the world in those terms," says David Featherman, a MIDMAC fellow and the president of the Social Science Research Council, in New York City. "They aren't particularly good at absorbing or rebounding from life's shocks."

People prone to midlife crisis score low on tests of introspection, or reflecting on one's self and on life, and high in denial, or coping with trouble by not thinking about it. "Take the guy who still thinks he's a great athlete," Kessler says. "Somehow he hasn't let reality intrude on his boyhood fantasy. But one day something forces him to wake up. Maybe he's at a family reunion playing ball with his twelve-year-old nephew and he can't make his shots. Suddenly he's an old man, a failure." Heading for the same kind of shock are the people banking on the big promotion that their colleagues know will never happen, along with those who believe that hair transplants and breast implants mean eternal youth. "Such individuals have to work hard to maintain their illusions," Kessler says. "They spend a lot of energy on the cogni-

tive effort of self-delusion, until reality finally intervenes." Because most middle-aged people have grown skilled at monitoring changes in reality—the jump shot isn't what it used to be, the figure has changed for good—they are spared the abrupt, traumatic run-ins with reality that result in a psychic emergency.

Midlife crises are an affliction of the relatively affluent: rosy illusions are easier to maintain when a person is already somewhat shielded from reality. Just as childhood is often constricted among the poor, who early in life face adult realities and burdens, so middle age may be eclipsed by a premature old age brought on by poverty and poor health. Among working-class people, for whom strength and stamina mean earning power, middle age may begin at thirty-five rather than the forty-five often cited in studies by respondents drawn from the sedentary middle class. Because any fanciful notions that poor and blue-collar people might have are rigorously tested by daily life, Kessler says, they rarely dwell in fantasy. "In terms of career, factory workers are likelier to be wherever they're going to be at thirty than executives," he says. "In terms of mental health, being disappointed at what *is* is a better kind of problem to have than being anxious about what will be. Once you know the reality, you can say, 'I can't afford to buy a boat, so I'll rent one for vacations.' Being up in the air is the big problem."

Despite the lurid tales of fifty-year-olds who run off with their twenty-five-year-old secretaries, such events are relatively rare in real-life midlife. Most couples who divorce break up in the first six or eight years of matrimony, and by midlife the majority report being more or less content. "The family-demography side of the midlife crisis just isn't there," says Larry Bumpass, a MIDMAC fellow and a professor of sociology at the University of Wisconsin at Madison, who directs the federally funded National Survey of Families and Households, the largest demographic study of its kind. "After ten or fifteen years together, the probability that a couple will split up is low. I've looked at the data every way possible to see if there's even a blip in the divorce rate when the children leave home, but that's just folklore too."

Even the nature of the difficulties most commonly reported suggests that the majority of the middle-aged operate from a position of strength. "The problems mentioned usually concern not the self but someone else—a child or parent," Kessler says. "Part of the reason for this outward focus is that the middle-aged person has secured his or her own situation and can afford to pay attention to others. Compared with the issues that arise in youth and old age, for most people the management-type problems that crop up in midlife aren't nearly as emotionally devastating."

Carl Jung divided life into halves—the first devoted to forming the ego and getting established in the world, the second to finding a larger meaning for all that effort. He then took the unorthodox step of paying more attention to the second. When shifting from one stage to the other, Jung observed, people experience an external loss of some kind—physical prowess or upward mobility or a relationship. When they treat this loss as a signal that it's time to develop new dimensions, Jung thought, transformation is in store. However, he predicted stagnation or even a breakdown if the loss is met with denial, fear, or a sense of defeat. Aryeh Maidenbaum, the executive director of the C. G. Jung Foundation's Center for Midlife Development, offers the Jungian rule of thumb for midlife crises: "The greater the disparity between the outer and inner person, the greater the chance for trouble. The most important inner need people have is to be seen for who they are. If that's what's happening at midlife, there's no crisis."

The Change for the Worse

IF THERE'S ONE ISSUE REGARDING WHICH MISINFORmation feeds mounting hysteria about middle age, it's menopause. After finishing any of a number of recent books and articles, a reader might conclude that for a few years a middle-aged woman might as well choose between sobbing alone and riding around on a broom. One of the few people who have gleaned their own hard data on the subject is Karen Matthews, a professor of psychiatry, epidemiology, and psychology at the University of Pittsburgh School of Medicine, who has conducted a longitudinal survey of the psychological and physical changes experienced by 500 women passing through menopause. "The fact is that most women do very well in the menopausal transition," she says, refuting the popular image of women who are invariably depressed, extremely unpleasant, or both. "There are some common physical symptoms that aren't fun, notably hot flashes, but only a minority of women—about ten percent—have a tough time psychologically."

Matthews has identified the characteristics of those who experience few problems in menopause and those who experience many. "The women who do well respond to the menopause with action," she says. "That may not be their direct intention, but they end up coping with the stressor by making positive changes. Those who, say, step up their exercise regimen don't even show the biological changes, such as the adverse shifts in lipids implicated in coronary disease, that others do. These 'active copers' say, 'Hey, I look a little different, feel a little less energetic. Why don't I . . .'"

Try hormone-replacement therapy? In evaluating its effects on physical health, women and doctors must juggle evidence suggesting that while HRT cuts the number of hot flashes by about half and reduces vulnerability to osteoporosis and perhaps coronary disease, it may raise the risk of breast cancer and, if estrogen is taken without progestin, uterine cancer. The National Institutes of Health is now conducting a badly needed controlled long-term clinical trial of large numbers of women on HRT which should provide some answers. Meanwhile, some doctors, confronted with incomplete data, tell women that the decision is up to them. Considering the threat of os-

teoporosis and of coronary disease, which is the leading cause of death for women over fifty, many other doctors recommend HRT to those whose risk of breast cancer is low. Still others regard its widespread use with dismay. Their concerns range from the fact that only one in three women is vulnerable to osteoporosis to a flaw in the argument that hormones can prevent heart disease. In part because doctors are cautious about prescribing HRT for women with illnesses such as hypertension and diabetes, the population that takes it is healthier to begin with—a built-in selection bias that skews studies of the therapy's effects. Among HRT's vocal critics are the doctors Sonja and John McKinlay, epidemiologists at the New England Research Institute, in Watertown, Massachusetts. "HRT is inappropriate for the vast majority of women, who shouldn't use it," John McKinlay says. "Yet the pharmaceutical industry's goal is to have every post-menopausal woman on it until death." Having surveyed the literature on menopause and HRT, Alice Rossi, a MIDMAC fellow and an emeritus professor of sociology at the University of Massachusetts at Amherst, says, "I wish we had a better scientific foundation for deciding if it's appropriate for women to take hormones for decades. At this point there's no strong evidence for a pro or anti position."

Although the process of weighing HRT's effects on physical health continues, Matthews has determined that as far as behavioral effects are concerned, HRT is *not* the most important factor in most women's psychological well-being during menopause." For that matter, she says, women who do and don't use HRT may report differing experiences because they are different types of people to begin with. In Matthews's study the typical user was not only better educated and healthier but also likely to be a hard-driving "Type A" person, less content with the status quo. "These women are up on the literature," Matthews says, "more aware of HRT, and more interested in seeking treatment."

If active copers, whether or not they take hormones, fare best during menopause, Matthews says, the women likely to have the worst time have two disparate things in common: HRT and a low regard for themselves. "Women who have poor self-esteem but don't use hormones don't have a hard time," she says. One hypothesis is that reproductive hormones, particularly progesterone, cause some women to become dysphoric, or moody; if a woman who has this adverse reaction to HRT also has a poor self-image, she is likely to be more upset by a stressor such as a menopausal symptom than a woman with a sturdier ego.

"The idea that most women have a hard time psychologically is the major myth our data have dispelled," Matthews says. "Eighty percent of our subjects thought they were going to become depressed and irritable at menopause, but only ten percent did. Those who had a rough time had showed signs long before of being anxious, depressed, or pessimistic. Menopause makes women with that pre-existing set of characteristics, which are not age-related, more emotionally vulnerable."

Much of the dark mythology of menopause derives not from the thing itself but from simultaneous aspects of the aging process. "It's the physical manifestation of aging—and a woman's reaction to it—that's critical in predicting whether the years from forty-five to fifty-five will be difficult or not," Alice Rossi says. "Society's image of an attractive woman is ten years younger than that of an attractive man. Graying at the temples and filling out a bit can be attractive in a man—look at Clinton and Gore. But their wives are still trying to look twenty-eight." Rossi isn't necessarily advocating the grin-and-bear-it attitude toward aging favored by Barbara Bush. Seeming ten years younger than you are can be a good thing, she says, if it means a concern for good health and well-being, rather than an obsession with youth.

Matthews considers a lot of the anxiety expressed by women about menopause to be unnecessary. In response to the often-heard complaint that there has been no good research on the subject, she points to several major long-term investigations—including hers, one by Sonja and John McKinlay, and one conducted in Sweden—that independently show that the majority of women have no serious problems making the transition.

In discussing a recent bestseller on the subject, Gail Sheehy's *The Silent Passage*, she says, "Ms. Sheehy interviewed me at length, but the experience of menopause she describes in her book is not the one that emerges as typical in the three major studies. Some women have a very difficult menopause, and Ms. Sheehy feels there's a message there. We need to figure out why some women do have problems, so that we can help. "There has been no generation of women like this one. They're better educated. They're healthier to the point that they now live half their adult lives after the menopause. For them, the menopausal transition is best characterized as a time of optimism. It's a bridge—an opportunity for women to think about what they want to do next."

Despite persistent rumors, there's probably no such thing as male menopause. Men simply don't experience a midlife biological change equivalent to the one women undergo. Whereas nature is responsible for that inequity, culture is at the bottom of a far more destructive one. For a research project, John McKinlay videotaped visits to doctors' offices made by patients matched for every variable but gender. The films showed that a man and a woman who complained of the same symptoms were often treated very differently: men were twice as likely to be referred to a medical specialist, and women were much likelier to be referred to a psychotherapist; men were urged toward health-enhancing behavior such as dieting and exercise, but women rarely were. ("This is particularly unfortunate where smoking is concerned," McKinlay says, "because the health benefits for women who give it up may be greater than those for men.") He concludes that the gender-related disparities apparent in much medical literature may reflect what doctors see more than actual physiological differences. Accordingly,

Many studies show that satisfaction with the marital relationship climbs again after couples weather the labor-intensive period of launching careers and babies.

he suspects that when middle-aged men complain of bad moods and decreased libido and energy, most doctors see a need for behavioral change. When women report the same symptoms, many doctors attribute them to menopause and prescribe hormones. "Don't forget that most women get their primary health care from a gynecologist," McKinlay says, "which would be like most men getting theirs from a urologist."

Among endocrinologists outside the United States there is more support for the notion of a male climacteric, in which older men's lower testosterone levels cause decreased fertility, increased body fat, bone loss, and skin-tone changes, along with the same behavioral symptoms that are often attributed to female menopause. While allowing that a small percentage of older men suffer from an endocrinological problem and can benefit from hormone-replacement therapy, McKinlay insists that there is no evidence that the majority would benefit. For that matter, he says, testosterone has little effect on the sexuality of those over fifty or fifty-five, and taking it as a supplement may in fact increase the risk of prostate cancer. Having conducted a study of the sex lives of 1,700 men aged forty to seventy which is considered by many to be the best information on the subject, he says, "There's no physiological, endocrinological, psychological, or clinical basis for a male menopause. Whether or not people believe in it has nothing to do with whether it exists, only with whether the pharmaceutical industry can persuade them that it does. In ten years male climacteric clinics will sprout up to treat a condition that may or may not exist—but, of course, they'll make money."

McKinlay's major reservation about most of the existing research on the effects of reproductive hormones is that it has been conducted with "small, atypical" samples of people who are seeking treatment in the health-care system. "What's talked about in the literature—both professional and popular—is the experience of *patients*," he says, "not healthy people, about whom we know very little."

The Best Years of Your Life Are Over

MANY PEOPLE HAVE A MEMORY FROM ADOLES-cence of gazing around a gathering of adults, no longer in the green days of their youth yet dressed to kill and living it up, and thinking the equivalent of "How valiant they are to make an effort at their age." Because Hollywood and Madison Avenue project this same juvenile notion, many of the middle-aged are surprised and relieved to find that their lives aren't nearly so dreary as they expected. After analyzing decades of social research for his 1992 book *Ambition*, Gilbert Brim found that a person's zest for and satisfaction with life don't depend on youth—or on status, sexuality, health, money, or any of the other things one might expect. "What people really want out of life are action and challenge—to be in the ballgame," he says. "To feel satisfied, we must be able to tackle a task that's hard enough to test us, but not so difficult that we'll repeatedly fail. We want to work hard, then succeed."

This maxim has a special resonance for today's middle-aged, career-oriented middle class, often portrayed as beleaguered victims of "role strain" or burnt-out cases operating on automatic pilot. In fact, Brim says, most are instinctively seeking the level of "just manageable difficulty"—an optimum degree of effort that taps about 80 percent of a person's capacity and generates that satisfied, job-well-done feeling. Pushing beyond that level for prolonged periods leaves people stressed and anxious; falling below it leaves them bored. Because what is just manageable at forty might not be at sixty, people rearrange their lives, often unconsciously, to balance capacities and challenges. When one does well at something, one ups the ante; when one fails, one lowers the sights a bit or even switches arenas. Brim draws an illustration from a study of AT&T executives: over time the most successful grew more work-oriented; the others began to turn more to their families and social lives—educating the children or lowering the golf handicap—for feelings of accomplishment. The key point, he says, is that neither group was more satisfied than the other. "This intuitive process by which we constantly reset our goals in response to our gains and losses is one of the most overlooked aspects of adult development."

One way in which the middle-aged are particularly skilled in adjusting their goals is in choosing which Joneses to keep up with. "Our mental health is very much affected by our estimation of how we're doing in terms of the people around us," says Carol Ryff, a psychologist and a MIDMAC fellow who is the associate director of the Institute on Aging and Adult Life, at the University of Wisconsin at Madison. "We all make these important measurements, even though we're often barely conscious of doing so." Whereas the young person launching a career might try to outdo Maurizio Pollini or Donna Karan, the savvy middle-aged one knows that holding to this standard beyond a certain point ensures misery—or a genuine

midlife crisis. Particularly when faced with a difficult situation, the mature person makes a "downward comparison" that puts his own problems in a different perspective and helps him soldier on. Thus the executive who has just been laid off compares his finances not with the Rockefellers' but with those of the couple across the street who are both on unemployment, and reminds himself that at least his wife's position is secure. "The better your mental health, the less often you measure yourself against people who make you feel crummy," Ryff says. "In midlife you begin to say, 'Well, so I'm not in the same category as the Nobelists. That's just not an expectation I'm going to drag around anymore.'"

By middle age most people destined for success have achieved it, which erects some special hurdles in the just-manageable course of life. "Winning is not simply the opposite of losing," Brim says. "It creates its own disruptions." If a person becomes psychologically trapped by the need to do better, go higher, and make more, for example, he can end up operating at 90 to 100 percent of his capacity—a level at which stress makes life very uncomfortable. At this level, too, Brim says, he will begin to lose more than he wins. Burdened with more roles than he can handle, or promoted beyond the level of just-manageable difficulty, he may end up "held together by a thin paste of alcohol, saunas, and antibiotics." Brim says that because our society does not supply many ways to step down gracefully, it "pays the price in burnout and incompetence in high places."

Even those who can sustain Hollywood-style success must do some internal retooling in order to maintain the charge of the just-manageable mode. To keep life interesting, Brim says, the people who handle winning best don't merely raise the challenge in the same area but go into a new one—a sport, a hobby, a community project— where they again find a lot of room for moving up. "Certain professional athletes are good examples," he says. "Because they know that their peak will be short-lived, at a certain point they diversify their aspirations to include family, business interests, and volunteer activities."

So skilled are most people at maintaining a just-manageable life through the years that Brim finds no appreciable differences in the sense of well-being reported by different age groups. Indeed, he says, despite the insistent propaganda to the contrary, "except for concerns about health, most research shows that older people are as happy as younger ones."

Midlife Romance: The Bloom Is Off the Rose

IF MIDDLE AGE IS SEEN AS A DULL BUSINESS, ITS RELA-tionships are imagined to be the dreariest part. In the course of studying beliefs about and images of midlife, Margie Lachman compared the experiences of a group of Boston-area people aged eighteen to eighty-five, and found no evidence that the middle-aged are less loving. In fact, steady levels of intimacy and affection were two of the few constants she tracked. Largely because married people make up the majority of the middle-aged—about 75 percent—most of the data about life relationships concern them. Then too, less is known about other bonds because until the mid-seventies studies of midlife focused on the experience of white middle-class heterosexual men. Although there is still very little information about gay midlife, some data are emerging about how single people in general fare socially during middle age.

It's about time, according to Alice Rossi. "Considering the longer life-span, a person may be without a partner at many points in life," she points out. "We not only marry later today but often have intervals between relationships, and perhaps lengthy spells as widows and widowers." She thinks that the stereotype of the aging spinster who is unfulfilled without a man is heading into the realm of midlife mythology. "There's recent evidence that single women have better mental and physical health and social lives than single men," she says. "Rather than being all alone, they have friends and close family ties, not only with parents but also with young nieces and nephews, with whom they may enjoy special relationships."

As for the married, many studies show that satisfaction with the relationship is lower throughout the child-rearing years that it had been, but climbs again after couples weather the labor-intensive period of launching careers and babies. In Lachman's Boston survey, reports of stress related to marriage decreased steadily from youth through old age. Although divorce and death may account for some of that decline, she says, "people may in fact grow more skilled in handling their relationships." Observing that by midlife couples have fewer fights and more closeness, Ron Kessler says, "Once they get the little kids out of their hair, husbands and wives catch their breath, look at each other, and ask, 'What are we going to talk about now? What was it all about twenty years ago?'"

In his study of sexuality John McKinlay found that only two percent of the 1,700 middle-aged and older men reported having more than one current sexual partner. This figure, vastly lower than the usual guesstimates, challenges the stereotype of the bored middle-aged philanderer. Moreover, although McKinlay recorded steady declines in the men's sexual activity, from lusty thoughts to erections, he found no decrease in their sexual satisfaction—a phenomenon Gilbert Brim calls "a triumph of the adaptation of aspirations to realities." Equivalent data about women have not been gathered, but McKinlay's findings complement other surveys that show that aging has little impact on people's enjoyment of sex.

People and their doctors, McKinlay says, should distinguish between sexual problems caused by aging and those caused by things that often get lumped with it, such as poor health, weight gain, lack of exercise, and the use of nicotine or too much alcohol. Compared with a healthy nonsmoking peer, for example, a smoker who has heart disease has a sevenfold greater risk of impotence.

Psychological fitness, too, plays a vital role. A man may think his primary problem is impotence caused by age when in fact his sexual trouble is a symptom of a very treatable depression. "We must not resort to biological reductionism, which is what women have been struggling against," McKinlay says.

Widely publicized conclusions drawn from the sex lives of the ill—that a vigorous sex life is not a reasonable expectation in middle age, for instance—may cast their pall on the well. "When I hear a healthy fifty-year-old man say, 'That sexy stuff is for kids,' I feel sorry for him," McKinlay says. "Only five percent of the women in our institute's long-term study of menopause reported suffering from vaginal dryness, but women are told it's a very common problem after a certain age." Contrary to the stereotype of the asexual older woman, he says, some women feel liberated by menopause and the end of birth control. If older women have a problem with their sex lives, according to McKinlay, it may be that their husbands aren't in good health. His prescription for a vital midlife: "If I were feeling troubled about aging, I'd look first at the behavioral modifications I could make—diet, exercise, alcohol-monitoring, and so on. If they didn't work, then I'd think about treatments."

Having edited a book about sexuality through the course of life, Alice Rossi observes that although the mature expression of eroticism remains poorly understood by science, let alone by our youth-oriented culture, middle-aged people are likely to expand their definition of sex to include sensual, not just reproductive, acts. "If the message we get from society is that we have to keep on acting as we did at thirty," she says, "a lot of us are going to feel that we have a sexual disorder at some point." After a certain age, for example, men in particular may require physical stimulation to feel aroused. An awareness of this normal tendency, Rossi says, added to modern women's generally greater assertiveness, lays the groundwork for a new kind of relationship for older couples—one in which women have a more active role. "If the middle-aged don't feel pressured to conform to a youthful stereotype," she says, "I think we can predict some good things for their sex lives."

The Empty Nest and the Sandwich Generation

WHEN THE ROLE OF FAMILY IN THE EXPERIence of middle age is mentioned, one of two scenarios usually comes to mind. In the better established, the abandoned mother waves a tearful good-bye to her last chick and dully goes through the motions of life in the "empty nest." According to Larry Bumpass's demographic survey, however, the nest may be anything but empty: expensive housing and a weak economy and job market mean that the young delay their own marriages and are likelier to return home after a brief foray outside.

The more contemporary midlife family myth concerns the plight of the "sandwich generation": in a recent *Doonesbury* cartoon starring a professional couple, the forty-something husband tells his wife, busy juggling the needs of her children and their grandmother, "Don't die. Everyone's counting on you." Women's entry into the job market has focused much attention on a purported host of adults who make the circuit from the day-care center to Gramps's place to the office with nary a moment for themselves. "It's true that there's a lot going on in your life in middle age and you have little time for leisure," Margie Lachman says. "Fortunately, you're also at your peak in terms of competence, control, the ability to handle stress, and sense of responsibility. You're *equipped* for overload." According to Carol Ryff, people busy with both careers and relationships enjoy not only greater financial security and intellectual and social stimulation but also a psychological benefit. The eminent behavioral scientist Bernice Neugarten thinks that the hallmark of healthy middle age is "complexity," or a feeling of being in control of a crowded life and involved in the world at the same time. Ryff found in the course of one of her studies that this quality was most marked among the first generation to combine family and career. "It seems," she says, "that all the role-juggling that middle-aged people complain about actually makes them feel more engaged in life."

Rossi is dubious that the sandwich-generation problem is either new or widespread. "This phenomenon is a lot like the supposed midlife crisis," she says. "There are people who think that spending two hours a week with Mother is a big deal. But the fact is that very few men or women are caring both for little children and for elderly parents." One reason for this is that the "old old" who need considerable care are still a small group, and few of them are a daily drain on their children. Then, too, as Bumpass says, "over the past several decades the elderly have increasingly lived independently. They're economically more able to do so, and both sides prefer things that way." According to research conducted by Glenna Spitze, of the State University of New York at Albany, close involvement by the middle-aged with their parents—usually with a mother who has already cared for and buried her own husband—is likeliest to occur when the middle-aged person's children are older and need less attention. "For that matter," Rossi says, "rather than being a drain, the children are likely to be a comfort and help. It's important to remember that intimacy with children, which bottoms out from ages fifteen to nineteen, climbs steeply through the twenties and thirties. One of the things to look forward to in midlife is the continuity and shared interests that will come as your children in turn become parents."

To the list of underestimated family pleasures Ryff adds the satisfaction that parents take in knowing that grown-up children have turned out all right. She found that adult offspring are a vital if underrecognized element in middle-aged well-being, and that adjusting to how well or poorly they have matured is another of midlife's important developmental tasks. After studying 215 parents, Ryff found that their adult children's level of psychological adjustment was a major predictor for almost all aspects of both fathers' and mothers' mental health—although mothers took more credit for it. "The literature on parenting includes very little on what *parents* get out of it," she says, "or on how it affects their self-image, especially when the kids are older. Parenting never ends."

At Last, the Reward: Wisdom

LONG ON THE PROCESS OF BECOMING, THE LITERATURE of human development remains short on the business of being. That adults don't grow and change in the predictable, simultaneously physiological and behavioral fashion that children do partly explains why. So tidy is early development by comparison that it's even possible to link certain ages to certain behavioral stages, such as the "terrible twos" and the "temperamental teens." Although Gail Sheehy's bestseller *Passages* (described by Gilbert Brim as focused on "selected case studies that illustrate a theory that has no broad empirical support") advanced an adult model of such "age-stage" development, research continues to show that the ways in which adults evolve are not universal, not likely to occur in clear-cut stages, and not tied to particular ages. So poorly do the middle-aged fit into developmental patterns, in fact, that the huge National Survey of Families and Households revealed that of more than forty projected "typical midlife events," none was likely to happen at a certain, predictable age.

Biologically oriented behavioral scientists argue that at the individual level certain basic tendencies evident at birth or shortly after are the immutable building blocks of personality. The aversion to novel stimuli which becomes shyness, denoted by a low score in extroversion, is one such element. Some claim, moreover, that anyone can be defined even in early childhood in terms of how high or low he or she scores in tests that measure the "big five"

Most middle-aged adults benefit from knocking about in the world. When they go down a blind alley, they soon recognize the mistake, and save themselves much time and energy.

traits: neuroticism, extroversion, openness, agreeableness, and conscientiousness. This largely biological programming, trait theorists believe, means that personality is set in concrete around the time that physical development ceases. Afterward one may grow in terms of changing attitudes, skills, interests, and relationships, but only in ways consistent with one's big-five template.

Environment-minded researchers, including the MIDMAC team, take the influence of things like attitudes, interests, and relationships more seriously. They're working on a different, flexible model of adult development, based not on genes but on experience. Brim and his colleagues don't dispute that someone born shy or dutiful may very well stay that way, but they stress that whether he or she is raised in a sociable or a reclusive family, has a happy or an unhappy marriage, gets an exciting or a dull job, and has good or poor health will have considerable impact on identity. Bringing up reports of "aberrant outcomes"—people who early in life seem destined for success or failure yet somehow turn out the other way—Brim observes that adult change is shaped not just by the characteristics a person brings to bear on life but also by what life brings to bear on him or her, from family feuds to fatal attractions, religious experiences to traffic accidents. Accordingly, the MIDMAC group and others interested in tracking adult development focus on the ways in which, as a result of the depth and variety of their experience, their subjects' goals and values alter over time.

To illustrate experiential midlife development, Ron Kessler points to ways in which people are shaped by the influence of the workplace. "During early life you're socially segregated—all your school companions are also eight- or twelve-year-olds from the same neighborhood," he says. "Then comes adulthood, and suddenly you're working alongside different kinds of people of different ages. You can look around and say to yourself, 'In twenty years, if I act like him, I could have a heart attack, or end up divorced.' Or 'Sure, she makes a lot of money, but do I really want to work sixty hours a week?'"

Most middle-aged adults benefit from knocking about in the world, a process that greatly increases their efficiency in managing life. When they go down a blind alley, they soon recognize the mistake, and save themselves much time and energy. "Because they have all this material to plot trajectories with, the middle-aged are equipped to do an enormous amount of internal reshuffling," Kessler says. "Unlike younger people, they don't have to test everything themselves in the real world. Adults who learn from their mistakes change and grow, and those who don't, don't." Kessler describes a bright corporate lawyer who remains developmentally stalled in the "becoming" phase appropriate to youth: "He goes around saying 'This is being a lawyer? I'd rather be a kid wanting to be a lawyer.'"

Perhaps the best refutation of the myths that adults don't develop and that adults do develop but only in rigid stages is a new body of research on the genesis of a psychological and cognitive capacity that scientists can only call wisdom. As is often the case in science, this inquiry began with the investigation of a mistaken premise. Assuming that the formalistic SAT-type process was the human norm in solving problems, those studying the effects of aging concluded that older people suffer a cognitive deficit, because they do worse than the young on such tests. The more researchers explored this apparently biological decline, however, the more they had to consider another possibility: people of different ages may perceive the same problem differently.

Any adult who has debated with a bright adolescent about, say, the likelihood that the world's nations will erase their boundaries and create a passportless global citizenry knows that there are two types of intelligence: the abstract, objective, Platonic-dualism sort that peaks early, and the practical, subjective type, born of shirtsleeves experience, which comes later. When asked the way to Rome, the young trace the most direct route very quickly, while their elders ponder: "Why Rome? Is this trip really a good idea? At what time of year? For business or pleasure? Alone or with others?"

The pre-eminent wisdom researcher is Paul Baltes, a MIDMAC fellow and a co-director of the Max Planck Institute for Human Development and Education, in Berlin. Baltes conducts studies of "whether living long can produce a higher level of mental functioning." The cognitive mechanics of the brain—the speed and accuracy with which we process information—are biological and subject to decline, he finds. But the brain's pragmatics—our knowledge and skill in using information—are not. When Baltes's subjects take the intellectual equivalent of a medical stress test, the young do in two seconds what the older do, with many more mistakes, in eight. But, Baltes says, unlike other species, ours can compensate for biological deficits. "If people have hearing problems, society develops hearing aids, and if I train an older subject in test-taking skills, he'll outperform an untutored younger person. By providing knowledge and strategies for using it, culture outwits biology. In all the areas of functioning in which age means more access to information, older people may be better off than young ones." In short, the middle-aged may be slower but they're smarter.

Beyond the commonsensical savvy acquired through daily experience lies a rarefied ability to deal with the fundamental problems of the human condition: matters ambiguous and existential, complex and conflicted, which call for the wisdom of Solomon. Using literary analysis, Baltes finds evidence in all cultures of people equipped to deal with these difficult issues, and he has devised several ways to test for the presence of this ability. In one type of study, subjects read vignettes of difficult situations—for example, a person pondering how to respond to a friend who has decided to commit suicide—and then "think aloud" through their decision-making process to a resolution of the problem. In another type, people with many contacts in the world of high achievers

AT LAST COUNT

MOTHERS AND JOBS

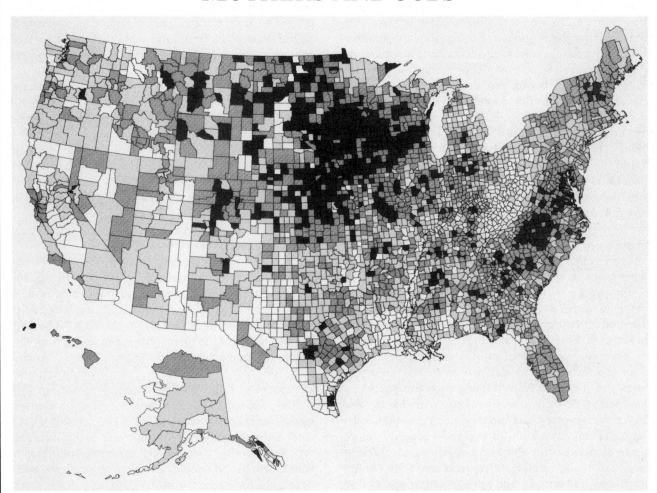

DURING THE PAST generation urban and suburban mothers have been depicted in the media as having made dramatic inroads into the country's work force—and they certainly have done so. But metropolitan areas do not, as a whole, have the highest percentage of working mothers with young children. As the map above illustrates, the two biggest clusters of working mothers are in the rural areas and small towns of the North Central states and the Southeast. There are special historical reasons why.

Economic necessity and personal desire impel mothers toward the workplace in varying degrees in different parts of the country, but the variable that more than any other determines high labor-force participation rates is simply this: the existence of jobs. In the Southeast, jobs for women happen to be relatively plentiful. Over the course of the past century the Southeast has been a magnet for northern industries—textiles, apparel, furniture—seeking lower capital and labor costs. These industries have traditionally employed large numbers of women.

The North Central states, too, have during the past forty years created economic opportunities for women—most recently in retail sales and other service-sector jobs. More important, real wages in the region have been declining significantly since the 1970s, which has encouraged mothers to enter the job market to offset declines in their husbands' incomes. This reaction to falling income—adding a paycheck—is particularly common in the North Central states, some economists say, owing to a heartland work ethic that makes people, including single mothers, more reluctant there than elsewhere to accept public assistance. Another factor contributing to the North Central states' work-force profile is the region's large number of farm wives, who, even though unpaid, are counted as employed by the Census Bureau.
—*Rodger Doyle*

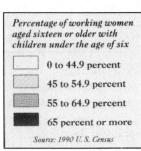

Percentage of working women aged sixteen or older with children under the age of six

0 to 44.9 percent

45 to 54.9 percent

55 to 64.9 percent

65 percent or more

Source: 1990 U. S. Census

are asked to nominate those they consider especially wise; researchers then monitor how these candidates think about difficult problems. Both forms of testing allow Baltes to score subjects on his "wisdom criteria," which include great factual and procedural knowledge, the capacity to cope with uncertainty, and the ability to frame an event in its larger context. "Those who have these attributes are the people we call wise," he says, "and they are easily recognized. People who are said to have this quality do score higher than others."

To sense the difference between the wise and the hoi polloi, one might imagine a successful fifty-year-old urban lawyer who announces that she is going to quit her job, move to the country, and start a mail-order seed and bulb business. Most listeners will think, if not say, something like "What a crazy idea." But there might be someone who says, "Wait. What are the circumstances? Maybe this lawyer feels that her life has grown sterile. Maybe she has some solid plans for this change. Let's talk some more." According to Baltes's statistics, this wise person is probably neither young nor very old but somewhere between the ages of forty and seventy. "The highest grades we record occur somewhere around sixty," he says. "Wisdom peaks in midlife or later."

While intelligence is essential to wisdom, certain personal qualities predict with greater accuracy who will be wise. Thoreau observed, "It is a characteristic of wisdom not to do desperate things," and Baltes agrees. "Modulation and balance are crucial elements," he says, "because wisdom has no extremes. You can't be passionate or dogmatic and wise at the same time." Just as the Lao-tzus and Lincolns among us are likely to be reasonable and open-minded, they are not likely to be motivated by selfish concerns, at least not markedly so: Machiavelli was clever but not wise.

"At some point in middle age," says David Featherman, of the Social Science Research Council, "we're inclined to become more tolerant of the uncertain, the complex, and the impossible, and even to learn to dismiss some problems as unsolvable or not worth our effort. Perhaps most important, we grow more interested in how our solutions affect others. Along with being good at figuring out what to do in real-life situations themselves, the wise are skilled in advising others—in sharing their wisdom. Unfortunately, Americans' Lone Ranger mentality about solving everything on our own means we don't always profit from this resource." The concern for others that is a hallmark of wisdom seems to augur well for those who have it as well as for its beneficiaries. The evolutionary neurobiologist Paul D. MacLean once observed, "We become nicer mammals as we age." Featherman points out that the benignity integral to wisdom seems characteristic of people who enjoy a happy, healthy old age.

In a youth-obsessed culture the suggestion that at least one element of character emerges only in middle age is both appealing and iconoclastic. "Wisdom doesn't happen at the age of six, or eighteen," Featherman says. "It may take a long time for all of its components to be in place. The timing of its emergence means that in maturity we get a new start—a new way of understanding life that's more apt to benefit others. It may turn out that caring about people is the capstone of the process of living."

The Myth of the Miserable Working Woman

She's Tired, She's Stressed Out, She's Unhealthy, She Can't Go Full Speed at Work or Home. Right? Wrong.

Rosalind C. Barnett and Caryl Rivers

Rosalind C. Barnett is a psychologist and a senior research associate at the Wellesley College Center for Research on Women. Caryl Rivers is a professor of journalism at Boston University and the author of More Joy Than Rage: Crossing Generations With the New Feminism.

"You Can't Do Everything," announced a 1989 USA Today *headline on a story suggesting that a slower career track for women might be a good idea. "Mommy Career Track Sets Off a Furor," declaimed the* New York Times *on March 8, 1989, reporting that women cost companies more than men. "Pressed for Success, Women Careerists Are Cheating Themselves," sighed a 1989 headline in the* Washington Post, *going on to cite a book about the "unhappy personal lives" of women graduates of the Harvard Business School. "Women Discovering They're at Risk for Heart Attacks," Gannett News Service reported with alarm in 1991. "Can Your Career Hurt Your Kids? Yes, Say Many Experts," blared a* Fortune *cover just last May, adding in a chirpy yet soothing fashion, "But smart parents—and flexible companies—won't let it happen."*

If you believe what you read, working women are in big trouble—stressed out, depressed, sick, risking an early death from heart attacks, and so overcome with problems at home that they make inefficient employees at work.

In fact, just the opposite is true. As a research psychologist whose career has focused on women and a journalist-critic who has studied the behavior of the media, we have extensively surveyed the latest data and research and concluded that the public is being engulfed by a tidal wave of disinformation that has serious consequences for the life and health of every American woman. Since large numbers of women began moving into the work force in the 1970s, scores of studies on their emotional and physical health have painted a very clear picture: Paid employment provides substantial health *benefits* for women. These benefits cut across income and class lines; even women who are working because they have to—not because they want to—share in them.

There is a curious gap, however, between what these studies say and what is generally reported on television, radio, and in newspapers and magazines. The more the research shows work is good for women, the bleaker the media reports seem to become. Whether this bizarre state of affairs is the result of a backlash against women, as *Wall Street Journal* reporter Susan Faludi contends in her new book, *Backlash: The Undeclared War Against American Women,* or of well-meaning ignorance, the effect is the same: Both the shape of national policy and the lives of women are at risk.

Too often, legislation is written and policies are drafted not on the basis of the facts but on the basis of what those in power believe to be the facts. Even the much discussed *Workforce 2000* report, issued by the Department of Labor under the Reagan administration—hardly a hotbed of feminism—admitted that "most current policies were designed for a society in which men worked and women stayed home." If policies are skewed toward solutions that are aimed at reducing women's commitment to work, they will do more than harm women—they will damage companies, managers and the productivity of the American economy.

THE CORONARY THAT WASN'T

One reason the "bad news" about working women jumps to page one is that we're all too willing to believe it. Many adults today grew up at a time when soldiers were returning home from World War II and a way had to be found to get the women who replaced them in industry back into the kitchen. The result was a barrage of propaganda that turned at-home moms into saints and backyard barbecues and station wagons into cultural icons. Many of us still have that outdated postwar map inside our heads, and it leaves us more willing to believe the horror stories than the good news that paid employment is an emotional and medical plus.

In the 19th century it was accepted medical dogma that women should not be educated because the brain and the ovaries could not develop at the same time. Today it's PMS, the wrong math genes or rampaging hormones. Hardly anyone points out the dire predictions that didn't come true.

You may remember the prediction that career women would start having more heart attacks, just like men. But the Framingham Heart Study—a federally funded cardiac project that has been studying 10,000 men and women since 1948—reveals that working women are not having more heart attacks. They're not dying any earlier, either. Not only are women not losing their health advantages; the lifespan gap is actually widening. Only one group of working women suffers more heart attacks than other women: those in low-paying clerical jobs with many demands on them and little control over their work pace, who also have several children and little or no support at home.

As for the recent publicity about women having more problems with heart disease, much of it skims over the important underlying reasons for the increase: namely, that by the time they have a heart attack, women tend to be a good deal older (an average of 67, six years older than the average age for men), and thus frailer, than males who have one. Also, statistics from the National Institutes of Health show that coronary symptoms are treated less aggressively in women—fewer coronary bypasses, for example. In addition, most heart research is done on men, so doctors do not know as much about the causes—and treatment—of heart disease in women. None of these factors have anything to do with work.

But doesn't working put women at greater risk for stress-related illnesses? No. Paid work is actually associated with *reduced* anxiety and depression. In the early 1980s we reported in our book, *Lifeprints* (based on a National Science Foundation–funded study of 300 women), that working women were significantly higher in psychological well-being than those not employed. Working gave them a sense of mastery and control that homemaking didn't provide. More recent studies echo our findings. For example:
• A 1989 report by psychologist Ingrid Waldron and sociologist Jerry Jacobs of Temple University on nationwide surveys of 2,392 white and 892 black women,

conducted from 1977 to 1982, found that women who held both work and family roles reported better physical and mental health than homemakers.
• According to sociologists Elaine Wethington of Cornell University and Ronald Kessler of the University of Michigan, data from three years (1985 to 1988) of a continuing federally funded study of 745 married women in Detroit "clearly suggests that employment benefits women emotionally." Women who increase their participation in the labor force report lower levels of psychological distress; those who lessen their commitment to work suffer from higher distress.
• A University of California at Berkeley study published in 1990 followed 140 women for 22 years. At age 43, those who were homemakers had more chronic conditions than the working women and seemed more disillusioned and frustrated. The working mothers were in good health and seemed to be juggling their roles with success.

In sum, paid work offers women heightened self-esteem and enhanced mental and physical health. It's unemployment that's a major risk factor for depression in women.

DOING IT ALL—AND DOING FINE

This isn't true only for affluent women in good jobs; working-class women share the benefits of work, according to psychologists Sandra Scarr and Deborah Phillips of the University of Virginia and Kathleen McCartney of the University of New Hampshire. In reviewing 80 studies on this subject, they reported that working-class women with children say they would not leave work even if they didn't need the money. Work offers not only income but adult companionship, social contact and a connection with the wider world that they cannot get at home.

Doing it all may be tough, but it doesn't wipe out the health benefits of working.

Looking at survey data from around the world, Scarr and Phillips wrote that the lives of mothers who work are not more stressful than the lives of those who are at home. So what about the second shift we've heard so much about? It certainly exists: In industrialized countries, researchers found, fathers work an average of 50 hours a week on the job and doing household chores; mothers work an average of 80 hours. Wethington and Kessler found that in daily "stress diaries" kept by husbands and wives, the women report more stress than the men do. But they also handle it better. In short, doing it all may be tough, but it doesn't wipe out the health benefits of working.

THE ADVANTAGES FOR FAMILIES

What about the kids? Many working parents feel they want more time with their kids, and they say so. But does maternal employment harm children? In 1989 University of Michigan psychologist Lois Hoffman reviewed 50 years of research and found that the expected negative effects never materialized. Most often, children of employed and unemployed mothers didn't differ on measures of child development. But children of both sexes with working mothers have a less sex-stereotyped view of the world because fathers in two-income families tend to do more child care.

However, when mothers work, the quality of non-parental child care is a legitimate worry. Scarr, Phillips and McCartney say there is "near consensus among developmental psychologists and early-childhood experts that child care per se does not constitute a risk factor in children's lives." What causes problems, they report, is poor-quality care and a troubled family life. The need for good child care in this country has been obvious for some time.

What's more, children in two-job families generally don't lose out on one-to-one time with their parents. New studies, such as S. L. Nock and P. W. Kingston's *Time with Children: The Impact of Couples' Work-Time Commitments,* show that when both parents of preschoolers are working, they spend as much time in direct interaction with their children as families in which only the fathers work. The difference is that working parents spend more time with their kids on weekends. When only the husband works, parents spend more leisure time with each other. There is a cost to two-income families—the couples lose personal time—but the kids don't seem to pay it.

One question we never used to ask is whether having a working mother could be *good* for children. Hoffman, reflecting on the finding that employed women—both blue-collar and professional—register higher life-satisfaction scores than housewives, thinks it can be. She cites studies involving infants and older children, showing that a mother's satisfaction with her employment status relates positively both to "the quality of the mother-child interaction and to various indexes of the child's adjustment and abilities." For example, psychologists J. Guidubaldi and B. K. Nastasi of Kent State University reported in a 1987 paper that a mother's satisfaction with her job was a good predictor of her child's positive adjustment in school.

Again, this isn't true only for women in high-status jobs. In a 1982 study of sources of stress for children in low-income families, psychologists Cynthia Longfellow and Deborah Belle of the Harvard University School of Education found that employed women were generally less depressed than unemployed women. What's more, their children had fewer behavioral problems.

But the real point about working women and children is that work *isn't* the point at all. There are good mothers and not-so-good mothers, and some work and some don't. When a National Academy of Sciences panel reviewed the previous 50 years of research and dozens of studies in 1982, it found no consistent effects on children from a mother's working. Work is only one of many variables, the panel concluded in *Families That Work,* and not the definitive one.

What is the effect of women's working on their marriages? Having a working wife can increase psychological stress for men, especially older men, who grew up in a world where it was not normal for a wife to work. But men's expectations that they will—and must—be the only provider may be changing. Wethington and Kessler found that a wife's employment could be a significant buffer *against* depression for men born after 1945. Still, the picture of men's psychological well-being is very mixed, and class and expectations clearly play a role. Faludi cites polls showing that young blue-collar men are especially angry at women for invading what they see as their turf as breadwinners, even though a woman with such a job could help protect her husband from economic hardship. But in highly educated, dual-career couples, both partners say the wife's career has enhanced the marriage.

THE FIRST SHIFT: WOMEN AT WORK

While women's own health and the well-being of their families aren't harmed by their working, what effect does this dual role have on their job performance? It's assumed that men can compartmentalize work and home lives but women will bring their home worries with them to work, making them distracted and inefficient employees.

Perhaps the most dangerous myth is that the solution is for women to drop back—or drop out.

The only spillover went in the other direction: The women brought their good feelings about their work home with them and left a bad day at home behind when they came to work. In fact, Wethington and Kessler found that it was the *men* who brought the family stresses with them to work. "Women are able to avoid bringing the contagion of home stress into the workplace," the researchers write, "whereas the inability of men to prevent this kind of contagion is pervasive." The researchers speculate that perhaps women get the message early on that they can handle the home front, while men are taking on chores they aren't trained for and didn't expect.

THE PERILS OF PART-TIME

Perhaps the most dangerous myth is that the solution to most problems women suffer is for them to drop back—or drop out. What studies actually show is a significant connection between a reduced commitment to work and increased psychological stress. In their Detroit study, Wethington and Kessler noted that women who went from being full-time employees to full-time housewives reported increased symptoms of distress, such as depression and anxiety attacks; the longer a woman worked and the more committed she was to the job, the greater her risk for psychological distress when she stopped.

What about part-time work, that oft-touted solution for weary women? Women who work fewer than 20 hours per week, it turns out, do not get the mental-health work benefit, probably because they "operate under the fiction that they can retain full responsibility for child care and home maintenance," wrote Wethington and Kessler. The result: Some part-timers wind up more stressed-out than women working full-time. Part-time employment also provides less money, fewer or no benefits and, often, less interesting work and a more arduous road to promotion.

That doesn't mean that a woman shouldn't cut down on her work hours or arrange a more flexible schedule. But it does mean she should be careful about jumping on a poorly designed mommy track that may make her a second-class citizen at work.

Many women think that when they have a baby, the best thing for their mental health would be to stay home. Wrong once more. According to Wethington and Kessler, having a baby does not increase psychological distress for working women—*unless* the birth results in their dropping out of the labor force. This doesn't mean that any woman who stays home to care for a child is going to be a wreck. But leaving the work force means opting out of the benefits of being in it, and women should be aware of that.

As soon as a woman has any kind of difficulty—emotional, family, medical—the knee-jerk reaction is to get her off the job. No such solution is offered to men, despite the very real correlation for men between job stress and heart attacks.

What the myth of the miserable working woman obscures is the need to focus on how the *quality* of a woman's job affects her health. Media stories warn of the alleged dangers of fast-track jobs. But our *Life-prints* study found that married women in high-prestige jobs were highest in mental well-being; another study of life stress in women reported that married career women with children suffered the least from stress. Meanwhile, few media tears are shed for the women most at risk: those in the word-processing room who have no control at work, low pay and little support at home.

Women don't need help getting out of the work force; they need help staying in it. As long as much of the media continues to capitalize on national ignorance, that help will have to come from somewhere else. (Not that an occasional letter to the editor isn't useful.) Men need to recognize that they are not just occasional helpers but vital to the success of the family unit. The corporate culture has to be reshaped so that it doesn't run totally according to patterns set by the white male workaholic. This will be good for men *and* women. The government can guarantee parental leave and affordable, available child care. (It did so in the '40s, when women were needed in the factories.) Given that Congress couldn't even get a bill guaranteeing *unpaid* family leave passed last year, this may take some doing. But hey, this is an election year.

ON GROWING OLD

Not Every Creature Ages, But Most Do. The Question Is Why

ROBERT M. SAPOLSKY *and*
CALEB E. FINCH

ROBERT M. SAPOLSKY *is an assistant professor of biology and neuroscience at Stanford University.* CALEB E. FINCH *is professor of gerontology at the University of Southern California in Los Angeles. His book* LONGEVITY, SENESCENCE, AND THE GENOME *was recently published by University of Chicago Press.*

> *I can do anything now at age ninety that I could when I was eighteen. Which shows you how pathetic I was at eighteen.*
> —George Burns

IT HAS BEEN OBSERVED more than once that human beings are the only creatures on earth haunted by an awareness of their own mortality. People know that life is desperately fragile and that any of myriad intrusions can kill them instantly: an aneurysm, a cerebral hemorrhage or a heart attack; a fire, an earthquake, a traffic accident or a mugger's bullet. And they know that even should they escape sudden disaster, the end remains inevitable. If nothing else, the years themselves take a fatal toll. Muscles weaken, eyesight dims, memories fade, and people become ever more conscious of the discrepancy between what they were and what they have become. In short, they senesce: they age.

To the gerontologist seeking to understand the aging process, the phenomenon of senescence is defined in terms of vulnerability: a "pathetic" eighteen-year-old college student is more likely to survive a certain challenge or insult than is a ninety-year-old curmudgeon. Each one may slip and fall on ice or play host to a single cancerous cell or contract a dangerous fever. Yet the older person is more likely to suffer a broken pelvis from the fall, to develop a malignant tumor from the cancerous cell, to perish from the fever. The risk that an illness or an injury will prove fatal increases with age.

Given such dark prospects, one is tempted to fantasize about living in a sort of never-never land where there is no such thing as senescence, no increase in vulnerability with each passing year. There would be no more crow's feet, sagging jowls or thinning hair and, more to the point, no degenerative heart disease, hardened arteries or Alzheimer's disease. We would all look great and feel wonderful. And we would live forever. Or would we?

The overall risk of mortality in the population at large is lowest at around age eleven. Suppose, magically, that the entire population, with every succeeding year, were somehow able to retain the adolescent's physiological near-invulnerability—in other words, suppose no one ever aged. Then half the people would still be alive by their 600th birthday, but by the same token half would be gone. Certainly that is an improvement, but immortality it is not. The point is that physiological invulnerability goes only so far. Even in a world populated solely with nonsenescing creatures there would be some constant mortality rate, one dependent entirely on the rate of external insults or ecological danger. Such a hypothetical population of Dorian Grays (or Dick Clarks, perhaps) would slowly but steadily decline in size with the passage of time because of airplane crashes, earthquakes or substance abuse. In some unit of time (600 years, for instance) half the population would die from extrinsic causes, in the next unit half the survivors would die, and so on.

For a real aging population the mortality rate increases with time because of an interaction between the rate of extrinsic insults and the extent of internal senescence. As the anatomy deteriorates with age, the person becomes increasingly vulnerable to intrusions by the outside world. Organs, bones and muscles wear out with time, and at age sixty, seventy or eighty, one cannot withstand the same kinds of stresses one sloughed off at eleven. It is all depressingly tragic but certainly not surprising. Things fall apart. How could life be otherwise?

STARTLINGLY ENOUGH, for many species things *are* otherwise. Bristlecone pine trees and rockfish, certain parameciums and some social insect queens, to name just a few, do not senesce. Populations of such plants and animals suffer constant attrition from extrinsic threats. In some insect species a queen dies at the proverbial hands of her minions: when her nuptial sperm supply runs out after many years, she is killed by the workers. But even at an advanced age those organisms do not show any of the usual signs of internal deterioration associated with other representatives of their phyla. For example, unlike most other trees, a bristlecone pine shows no increased sensitivity to insect infestations with age. Although it is unclear how many species are nonsenescers, it is known that there are a great many of them, particularly in groups such as bony fishes, sea anemones and bivalve mollusks.

One might very well wonder what stroke of evolutionary good fortune, what extraordinary biological innovation, has allowed those species to evade decrepitude. What feature have they evolved that humans and most other animals have not? On closer examination, however, it becomes clear that rockfish, parameciums, mollusks and the like are not the real innovators. Quite to the contrary, such perennially youthful species are typically among the most ancient, primitive organisms. Indeed it appears that nonsenescence was the original state of living things on earth. The mammalian line, one of the latest and certainly the most sophisticated of the chordate classes, can be considered an island of senescence among most of its evolutionary relatives. If, then, aging is a relatively recent development, another question arises: What possible evolutionary advantages are conferred by such a dismal characteristic?

THE ATTEMPT to understand the adaptive benefits of senescence is almost as old as the idea of evolution itself. One of the first to explore the issue was the English naturalist Alfred Russel Wallace, who shares with Darwin the credit for having founded the theory of evolution by natural selection. Darwin and Wallace established that the driving force of evolution is the quest for optimizing reproductive success, a goal best realized by leaving the maximum number of copies of one's own genes for future generations. (As the sociobiologists say, "A chicken is an egg's way of making another egg.")

There are two fundamental strategies for ensuring the proliferation of one's genes: either reproducing a lot or, failing that, doing whatever is possible to increase the reproduction of one's relatives—a kind of genetic altruism known as kin selection. Wallace speculated that aging is a kin-selection strategy; in other words, at some stage in its life the best way for an organism to pass on its genes is for it to senesce and get out of the way, leaving the resources it would otherwise consume behind for its descendants to share as they multiply the genetic line.

Since Wallace's day many other theories of adaptive senescence have been advanced, based on studies of aging patterns in a range of living things. To illustrate one popular recent theory, compare the extremely long lived, nonsenescing rockfish with the short-lived, senescing guppy. As one might expect, the guppy population, subject to both external insult and internal deterioration, dies off at a much faster rate than the rockfish population does. Still, guppies enjoy one crucial advantage over rockfish: earlier in life they fare substantially better at reproduction. In general, species that age follow the same pattern: they die off sooner, but they reproduce earlier in life and more successfully than their nonsenescing counterparts.

For a number of years many biologists have recognized that in senescing species the enhanced fecundity earlier in life and the increased mortality rate later on might express an evolutionary trade-off. The essence of the idea, which has acquired the forbidding label "negative pleiotropy," is that genes have evolved that confer marked advantages on an organism at certain stages in its life, only to extract a cost at certain other stages. Unlike Wallace's notion of altruistic kin selection, negative pleiotropy is a genetically "selfish" mechanism: it would operate solely to maximize the reproductive potential of individual organisms, without regard for the greater good of subsequent generations of the species.

When genes are viewed as negatively pleiotropic, they are double-edged swords. Perhaps the best-known example of this kind of duality—though one not related to aging—is the gene for sickle-cell anemia. The sickle-cell gene can bring about a dreadful, life-threatening disease, in which insufficient oxygen is delivered to the cells of the body. Yet the same gene confers resistance to malaria, a disease that takes a horrendous toll in Africa, where sickle-cell anemia evolved. Whereas senescence may be an instance of negative pleiotropy over time, sickle-cell anemia can be thought of as negative pleiotropy over space: thus the sickle-cell gene offers advantages only in those environments in which malaria is rampant. In the evolution of such trade-offs the critical issue becomes how often the advantage is conferred compared with how often the deleterious bill arrives. Apparently, with sickle-cell anemia the payoffs have led to widespread selection for the trait. That is small comfort to sickle-cell victims who live in, say, urban America, where shored-up resistance to malaria is of little use. Betrayed by geography, American carriers of the sickle-cell gene are forced to pay its price without enjoying any of its benefits.

ALTHOUGH THE IDEA of negative pleiotropy as a driving force in aging looks good on paper, specific examples of the phenomenon have been surprisingly hard to track down. One instance may be Huntington's disease, best known for having afflicted the folksinger Woody Guthrie. People stricken with Huntington's disease generally begin sometime during their forties to suffer from a variety neurological symptoms: flailing and spasms of the limbs, paralysis, rigidity and dementia. Death usually comes after about fifteen years.

A subtle, intriguing feature of Huntington's disease usually manifests itself early on. The illness initially appears to be a psychiatric disorder: the victim's behavior and personality begin to change dramatically before the neurological symptoms emerge. In a few years a quiet and uncontentious person might begin to lose self-control, becoming loud, uninhibited and more aggressive. Clinical lore also holds that a behavioral feature of early Huntington's is hypersexuality; in fact, one recent study indicates that Huntington's patients outreproduce their unaffected siblings. No one has a clue to just how the disease works —especially to why some of the behavioral traits and the neurological symptoms should emerge from the same disorder. Nevertheless, one can speculate that if the gene that accelerates mortality at age sixty also confers increased reproduction by age forty, the gene would work to the overall advantage of the organism in the evolutionary sense. Such a mechanism for the disease would constitute a neat illustration of negative pleiotropy at work in the aging process.

One can imagine any number of other negatively pleiotropic scenarios that give rise to senescence. There could be many genes that confer early advantages in exchange for later costs, each affecting discrete organ systems. One feature of human aging, for instance, is that older men have a much greater chance than younger men of developing prostate cancer. What if such a tendency toward uncontrolled carcinogenic growth were a side effect of a gene that, earlier in life, increased the rate of prostate metabolism and cell division? One result might be that the younger man could produce more seminal fluid, having greater sperm mobility, and thus be a more fertile individual. If the reproductive advantages of better sperm at age thirty outweigh the reproductive disadvantages of dying from prostate cancer at sixty-five, the gene will be selected. Some investigators already consider senescent increases in the frequency of prostate cancer to be a valid example of negative pleiotropy.

Another, more hypothetical example is the potentially adaptive effect of fat stored on the body early in life. In periods of drought or famine fat might act as a buffer, thereby keeping the individual alive through the reproductive years. As a person grows older, however, the advantages of that storage tendency begin to be counterbalanced by the accompanying risk of heart disease and diabetes. In physiology, as in so many other spheres, there are no free lunches; ultimately, the check arrives.

IF NEGATIVE PLEIOTROPY is to account for the emergence of senescence in humans, one would expect to find that certain advantageous traits of youth are genetically linked to whatever turn out to be the mechanisms of decline. Understanding those mechanisms, of course, is one of the central aims of gerontological research. Gerontologists have searched for a single cause of aging—a critical gene, hormone or organ that goes awry. But in the light of the rather sparse evidence in support of that idea, many investigators have adopted another hypothesis: that senescence results from the gradual but steady deterioration of cells, which over time become less proficient at maintenance and self-repair. After all, there is no question that the lives of cells are finite; a cell divides a fixed number of times and then dies. What causes that abrupt cessation? What changes take place in a cell as it approaches the end of its line? These questions are of central concern to gerontologists. And it is becoming increasingly clear that there are no easy answers and that if the key to aging is cellular deterioration, aging is a complex, multifaceted process, perhaps involving not one but a host of regulatory genes.

In the past decade or so a number of theories have been put forward that try to explain what causes cells to wear down. According to one such theory, as it ages a lineage of cells accumulates harmful metabolic "garbage," which can damage nucleic acids, proteins and other vital cellular building blocks. One class of physiological debris may be the oxygen-free radicals: such molecules can lodge in the cell membrane, disrupt and destroy fats and protein by linking them inappropriately, and perhaps impair the functioning of DNA.

Another line of investigation implicates glucose in a process that is severely destructive to animal cells. Glucose can attach itself to proteins via a process called nonenzymatic glycosylation, which binds the proteins together into a nonfunctional yellowish brown mess. (The biochemist Anthony Cerami of Rockefeller University in New York has named such accumulations of disabled proteins "advanced glycosylation endproducts," allowing the acronym AGE.) As animals age, AGE proteins appear to damage vital organs and connective tissue. There is also speculation that, like the oxygen-free radicals, AGE proteins may somehow interact with DNA, causing mutations and obstructing the cell's ability both to repair damage and to replicate. The role of AGE proteins in aging is an intriguing subject for future research. At this point, however, they have been studied only in people and in laboratory rodents. Whether and to what degree other animals accumulate these protein masses may say a great deal about aging patterns across the various species.

TO THE AVERAGE, reluctantly senescing person, aging connotes a gradual, albeit inexorable, slide from summer into autumn and, with any luck, on to winter. But not all the earth's aging creatures necessarily decline and fall in the same way people do. Even in some relatively long-lived species senescence and death can come in a flash, sometimes in a matter of weeks or days. Well-known victims of such sudden death are the five species of Pacific salmon. In the mating season the adult fish heroically fight their way upstream to the pools where they were born in order to spawn—only to die off, en masse, a few days later. Fish captured during the dying-off period typically display enlarged adrenal glands, ulcers and kidney lesions; their immune systems have collapsed and they are teeming with parasites and opportunistic infections.

A similar pattern occurs in about a dozen species of marsupial mice in Australia. Those animals have an annual, synchronized mating season after which, in the course of a few weeks, all the males die. Remarkably the mice exhibit symptoms nearly identical with the symptoms of the salmon. People seemingly age by going to pieces idiosyncratically over decades; one person gets arthritis, another gets diabetes, a third gets cancer. Here instead, an identical pathological switch is thrown in each individual of the species, causing a kind of pansenescence: the population ages almost overnight.

Studies over the past thirty years have traced the sudden-death switch to the adrenal glands, which in times of physical or psychological stress secrete hormones belonging to a class known as the glucocorticoids. Such hormones come in many varieties; in humans they take the form of hydrocortisone, also known as cortisol. Glucocorticoids can be extremely handy in a physical emergency: a lot of energy must be released suddenly when one is, say, sprinting away from an onrushing predator. The hormones work by mobilizing glucose, freeing it from storage sites in the body and sending it into the blood. At the same time they increase the heart rate and raise blood pressure to speed the delivery of the glucose to the muscles. Glucocorticoids also turn off all kinds of long-term, energy consumptive building projects that can be put on hold until the emergency has passed: digestion, growth, reproduction, tissue repair and the maintenance of the immune system, among others.

All these effects are wonderful when you are running for your life, but they are disastrous at other times. In long periods of chronic psychological stress, for instance, the constant mobilization of energy at the cost of storage can waste the muscles away. An increase in cardiovascular tone for a long enough period brings about hypertension. By repeatedly deferring long-term building projects, the body eventually deteriorates: stomach walls ulcerate; growth, reproduction and immunity are irreparably impaired. To a large extent the illnesses that accompany chronic stress are consequences of an overexposure to glucocorticoids.

Pacific salmon and marsupial mice meet sudden death when their bodies loose a veritable flood of glucocorticoids. The phenomenon has been most thoroughly observed in marsupials. Around the mating period three changes take place that guarantee catastrophe. First, far more glucocorticoids than normal are secreted. Second, the concentration of proteins in circulation that can bind glucocorticoids—in effect sponging them up and buffering organs from the effects of the hormones—falls sharply, allowing the glucocorticoids unrestrained access to target tissues. Finally, parts of the brain, as yet unknown, that normally curtail glucocorticoid secretion before too much damage is done, fail to function. How all these steps work is poorly understood, but the result is that massive, pathological levels of glucocorticoids pummel the body. The Pacific salmon and the marsupial mice die from the effects of half the stress-related illnesses on earth, packed into a few miserable weeks.

The most dramatic proof of this account is that if, just after the salmon or the mice have mated, one blocks the secretion of glucocorticoids by removing the adrenal glands, the animals will live on for a year or more instead of the usual few weeks. The procedure demonstrates how drastically the aging process can be accelerated in otherwise diverse creatures that happen to have evolved the same hormonal death switch.

THE EVOLUTIONARY PURPOSE served by such abrupt pansenescence remains unclear. From one point of view Pacific salmon and marsupial mice can be regarded as classic examples of negative pleiotropy: they reproduce in abundance and then pay for their fecundity with their lives. But whether or not there is a pure trade-off of enhanced reproduction for greater mortality later on has not been established. There has been some speculation—and it is no more than that—that ties the Pacific salmon to Wallace's theory of kin selection. Some investigators have suggested that by quickly dying and decomposing in the water, the salmon are contributing nutrients to the ecosystem and hence improving the lot of future generations. The hypothesis is certainly intriguing, but it is still unsubstantiated by experimental evidence.

Are there any examples of greatly accelerated senescence in people? No doubt, devotees of the lurid tabloids ever present at supermarket checkout counters will immediately recall one possibility. Publications of that stripe have a morbid fascination with progeria, a supremely rare hereditary disease that afflicts children. Progerics appear to age incredibly prematurely. By the age of twelve, shortly before their deaths, they may have gray hair or be completely bald, and they manifest the bony chins, beaked noses and dry, scratchy voices common to elderly people. Children stricken with progeria can also

suffer from hearing loss, arteriosclerosis or heart disease. When an attempt is made to grow certain cells from their bodies in a laboratory dish, the cells act like the well-worn tissue of a seventy-year-old—that is, they divide very infrequently. The implication seems to be that for a progeric the body's rate of aging has run amuck.

Progeric children, however, are not aged in every respect. For example, they do not show increased tendencies toward dementia or cancer, two major diseases strongly linked to aging. Thus even in progerics there is no single aging clock gone mad, and by the same token, there is no one such timepiece ticking at a normal pace in the rest of us. Instead the development of progeria suggests a mosaic of aging mechanisms, a variety of clocks of which only some are out of joint. Although the macabre disease gives rise to certain features associated with senescence, it is not, by itself, accelerated aging. Almost certainly, many nonprogerics also suffer dire but less spectacular consequences that have been brought on because some, but not all, of their aging clocks have sped out of control: witness the early onset of certain types of cancer in some people. But on the whole there remains sparse evidence of accelerated aging in humans, and even that is not at all like the affliction that befalls Pacific salmon and Australian marsupial mice.

SALMON, MICE AND PROGERICS notwithstanding, there are some species in nature that display determinedly more upbeat patterns of senescence, creatures for which the aging process is greatly slowed down. In spite of our own species' chronic despair about the ephemerality of life, a typical human being comes off next to immortal compared with an average laboratory rat. After only two years the rat is plagued by cataracts, reproductive problems and memory loss. Indeed the maximum human life span of 120 years or so is impressive in almost any context. (Notice that the occasional claims for the existence of substantially older populations such as one in Soviet Georgia usually prove attributable to some blend of bemused exaggeration and the inhabitants' lack of rigor about personal chronology.) There are other species in the range of human longevity —notably apes, elephants, sturgeons, clams and Galápagos tortoises. And there are some that far outstrip us, particularly certain trees such as conifers that can live for more than a millennium. The point is not that such species do not senesce; they do, but they also happen to be long-lived. The decline of a given population comes about quite slowly, over a great many years.

In a few cases species can temporarily arrest the encroachments of age and physical decline and, in effect, achieve suspended animation. One familiar example is hibernation, a dormant state during which the mortality rate of an entire population of animals is essentially frozen. Hibernation has been thoroughly studied in Turkish hamsters. The investigators manipulated the length of hibernation in the laboratory by adjusting the environmental temperature and found, remarkably, that for every day the hamsters hibernated, the animals' life spans were extended by about a day. The hamsters had managed to stop their aging clocks.

Hibernation is only one of several ways senescence can

be temporarily slowed or halted by dormancy. A somewhat more exotic example is the diapause, a holding stage in the development of certain organisms—particularly some insects such as worker bees—which can last for more than a year. If an insect enters diapause, its life span is extended by an equal amount of time. Various African and South American fishes can enter diapause even before they have hatched. As it turns out, the fishes' behavior is opportunistic: They live in ponds that disappear during dry seasons. Rather than start off life just as their homes have been turned into mud flats, unhatched eggs go into diapause amid the dried mud and await the return of the waters—perhaps for a year or more.

People, of course, are desperate for news of any intervention that might forestall decline. Newspapers have recently been filled with reports that the administration of growth hormone apparently reverses some aspects of human aging, in particular the loss of muscle mass and diminution of organ size that typically occur in the elderly. Despite this good news, growth hormone treatment has not been shown to increase the life span. Is there anything in the works, then, that can actually help us live longer?

At the moment, unfortunately, the answer is no. That fact notwithstanding, there are a number of entrepreneurial biologists who—for a handsome price—will contract to freeze you after you die, in the optimistic hope that future scientists will be able to effect your resurrection. Some of these so-called cryobiologists are even lobbying to freeze live but terminally ill patients on the assumption that some later generation of physicians might be able to revive them when a cure is available. (That approach is currently illegal, though a California man with terminal cancer recently initiated a court challenge.) Nevertheless, there is precious little experimental evidence to support any attempt to induce suspended animation in mammals. And there are many reasons such an effort would fail in any organism as large as a human being; for one, the cells could not be frozen quickly enough to avoid severe tissue damage. Even if suspended life were possible, it might not be all that desirable, especially if the hibernation worked as it does in hamsters. It is a safe bet that few of us would care to live on for centuries if all but seventy-two of those years were spent packed in ice. What we presumably want is a full, decidedly nondormant life that lasts beyond the present limits.

REMARKABLY there is one technique that for the past half-century has been known to extend mammalian life. It is not, however, what one would call an inviting alternative. In the 1930s it was discovered that if rats are deprived of nourishment (in this case, 30 percent of calories) indefinitely, beginning just after weaning, they live as much as one-third longer than rats given unrestricted access to food—the equivalent of extending human life expectancy from seventy-five years to a century. Before long a number of investigators had replicated the finding in other rodents, and today an entire branch of gerontology is devoted to studying the benefits of what is variously called dietary restriction or diet optimization.

It is now known that most of what tends to fall apart in

an unmolested aging rat does so more slowly in a diet-restricted rat: organs such as the liver, the immune and reproductive systems and possibly parts of the brain such as the hippocampus. Dietary restriction also protects the rat from tumor growth, to which the animal normally becomes progressively susceptible as it grows older. One relatively recent discovery is that dietary restriction need not be as severe as it was in the initial studies in order to prolong an animal's life. Other strategies can be just as effective: cutting back calorie consumption by as little as 30 percent; beginning restriction in adulthood instead of after weaning; or restricting only some dietary constituents such as protein intake instead of the total number of calories consumed.

Gerontologists in this subfield spend most of their time trying to figure out precisely why cutting back on food leads to longevity. One of many attractive answers is that decreasing the diet may slow the accumulation of AGE proteins, the dysfunctional mess slung together over time by glucose. If AGE accumulation is, in fact, one of the basic cellular pacemakers of aging, a delay in its generation might well account for the deceleration of the aging process that dietary restriction seems to effect in so many organ systems.

A number of investigators, however, have raised a somewhat more deflating explanation for the effect. In their view the average laboratory rat, confined to a cage and given unrestricted access to food, eats far more than a normal wild rat does, simply for lack of anything better to do. In the process the animal drives itself into an early grave by contracting some of the diseases that kill millions of Americans. It may well be that dietary restriction is merely a means of getting a bored and gluttonous rat to adopt wild eating habits and thereby live a normal life span. In that circumstance dietary restriction would not change the basic nature of aging, but it would reduce the impact of diet-associated diseases on the aging process. Clarification will come once investigators know more about the eating habits of wild rodents. Only then can one know whether the normal laboratory rat gorges itself on an unrestricted diet.

Assuming, for the moment, that dietary restriction does extend the maximal life span of rodents, should we all start limiting our diets? How general is the phenomenon? Clearly such questions are hard to resolve. For rats or mice that live just a few years it is tedious (not to mention expensive) to manipulate diet over the lifetime of a population. To do the same for creatures that live for decades is far more difficult, and it makes the optimistic assumption that the investigator will live long enough to complete the project. Thus no one knows whether food restriction will work for our pets, our livestock or ourselves.

One observation offers little hope. Actuarial tables show that people with extreme body weights—the thinnest as well as the stoutest—tend to live shorter lives than people who stand somewhere in between. On the other hand, one can retort that some people are thin not because of a lifetime of restricted eating but because of genetics, chronic diseases or any number of other confounding characteristics. At bottom no one yet knows whether eating less means living longer. Nevertheless, the rodent data are sufficiently convincing to have motivated at least one respected gerontologist, Roy L. Walford of the University of California at Los Angeles, to keep himself on a restricted diet for years. Walford's colleagues eagerly—but not too eagerly, of course—await the results of his self-experimentation.

Any review of aging research is necessarily somewhat disjointed, an account of what is currently a rather disparate patchwork of unconnected studies. The hope is that a unified theory of senescence will one day emerge. Perhaps there is some thread that draws together AGE production in people, pansenescence in salmon, negative pleiotropy and other anecdotal and hypothetical aspects of aging into the wider context of evolution. On the other hand, senescence may turn out to be resolutely untidy, as complex and varied in its mechanisms as the aging species themselves. Further-more, all the many lines of inquiry into senescence, even if they converge on a fundamental understanding of the phenomenon, may not add a day to human life expectancy. Perhaps we will have to content ourselves with curing the prevalent diseases of aging, such as Alzheimer's or atherosclerosis, rather than aging itself. That alone would obviously be of incalculable benefit.

But if bristlecone pines, marsupial mice and fishes tell us nothing about our aging problems, why study them? One could as easily ask why anatomists pass their lifetimes documenting the ways the primate pelvis can be constructed, why ethologists catalogue dialects of bird songs or why geneticists devote study to the hereditary patterns of worms. If we are to understand our place in the scheme of nature, it is perhaps important for us to realize that ours is not the only way to evolve, appear or behave. Or even to grow old.

The Prime of Our Lives

*WHAT SEEMS TO MARK OUR ADULT YEARS
MOST IS OUR SHIFTING PERSPECTIVE
ON OURSELVES AND OUR WORLD. IS THERE A
COMMON PATTERN TO OUR LIVES?*

Anne Rosenfeld
and Elizabeth Stark

*Anne Rosenfeld and Elizabeth Stark, both
members of* Psychology Today*'s editorial staff,
collaborated across cohorts to write this article.*

"My parents had given me everything they could possibly owe a child and more. Now it was my turn to decide and nobody ... could help me very far...." That's how Graham Greene described his feelings upon graduation from Oxford. And he was right. Starting on your own down the long road of adulthood can be scary.

But the journey can also be exciting, with dreams and hopes to guide us. Maybe they're conventional dreams: getting a decent job, settling down and starting to raise a family before we've left our 20s. Or maybe they're more grandiose: making a million dollars by age 30, becoming a movie star, discovering a cure for cancer, becoming President, starting a social revolution.

Our youthful dreams reflect our unique personalities, but are shaped by the values and expectations of those around us—and they shift as we and our times change. Twenty years ago, college graduates entered adulthood with expectations that in many cases had been radically altered by the major upheavals transforming American society. The times were "a-changin'," and almost no one was untouched. Within a few years many of the scrubbed, obedient,

wholesome teenagers of the early '60s had turned into scruffy, alienated campus rebels, experimenting with drugs and sex and deeply dissatisfied with their materialistic middle-class heritage.

Instead of moving right on to the career track, marrying and beginning families, as their fathers had done, many men dropped out, postponing the obligations of adult life. Others traveled a middle road, combining "straight" jobs with public service rather than pursuing conventional careers. And for the first time in recent memory, large numbers of young men refused to serve their country in the military. In the early 1940s, entire fraternities went together to enlist in World War II. In the Age of Aquarius, many college men sought refuge from war in Canada, graduate school, premature marriages or newly discovered medical ailments.

Women were even more dramatically affected by the social changes of the 1960s. Many left college in 1967 with a traditional agenda—work for a few years, then get married and settle down to the real business of raising a family and being a good wife—but ended up following a different and largely unexpected path. The women's movement and changing economics created a whole new set of opportunities. For example, between 1967 and 1980, women's share of medical degrees in the United States rocketed from 5 percent to 26 percent, and their share of law degrees leaped from 4 percent to 22 percent.

A group of women from the University of Michigan class of 1967 who were interviewed before graduation and again in 1981 described lives very different from their original plans. Psychologists Sandra Tangri of Howard University and Sharon Jenkins of the University of California found that far more of these women were working in 1981 than had expected to, and far more had gotten advanced degrees and were in "male" professions. Their home lives, too, were different from their collegiate fantasies: Fewer married, and those who did had much smaller families.

Liberation brought problems as well as opportunities. By 1981, about 15 percent of the women were divorced (although some had remarried), and many of the women who "had it all" told Tangri and Jenkins that they felt torn between their careers and their families.

Living out our dreams in a rapidly changing society demands extreme flexibility in adjusting to shifting social realities. Our hopes and plans, combined with the traditional rhythms of the life course, give some structure, impetus and predictability to our lives. But each of us must also cope repeatedly with the unplanned and unexpected. And in the process, we are gradually transformed.

For centuries, philosophers have been trying to capture the essence of how people change over the life course by focusing on universally experienced stages of life, often linked to specific ages. Research on child development, begun earlier in this century, had shown that children generally pass through an orderly succession of stages that correspond to fairly specific ages. But recent studies have challenged some of the apparent orderliness of child development, and the pattern of development among adults seems to be even less clear-cut.

When we think about what happens as we grow older, physical changes leap to mind—the lessening of physical prowess, the arrival of sags, spreads and lines. But these take a back seat to psychological changes, according to psychologist Bernice Neugarten of Northwestern University, a pioneer in the field of human development. She points out that although biological maturation heavily influences childhood development, people in young and middle adulthood are most affected by their own experiences and the timing of those experiences, not by biological factors. Even menopause, that quintessentially biological event, she says, is of relatively little psychological importance in the lives of most adult women.

In other words, chronological age is an increasingly unreliable indicator of what people will be like at various points. A group of newborns, or even 5-year-olds, shows less variation than a group of 35-year-olds, or 50-year-olds.

What seems to mark our adult years most is our shifting perspective on ourselves and our

STAGE THEORIES ARE A LITTLE LIKE HOROSCOPES— VAGUE ENOUGH TO LET EVERYONE SEE SOMETHING OF THEMSELVES IN THEM. THAT'S WHY THEY'RE SO POPULAR.

world—who we think we are, what we expect to get done, our timetable for doing it and our satisfactions with what we have accomplished. The scenarios and schedules of our lives are so varied that some researchers believe it is virtually impossible to talk about a single timetable for adult development. However, many people probably believe there is one, and are likely to cite Gail Sheehy's 1976 best-seller *Passages* to back them up.

Sheehy's book, which helped make "midlife crisis" a household word, was based on a body of research suggesting that adults go through progressive, predictable, age-linked stages, each offering challenges that must be met before moving on to the next stage. The most traumatic of these transitions, Sheehy claimed, is the one between young and middle adulthood—the midlife crisis.

Sheehy's ideas were based, in part, on the work of researchers Daniel Levinson, George Vaillant and Roger Gould, whose separate studies supported the stages of adult development Erik Erikson had earlier proposed in his highly influential model (see "Erikson's Eight Stages," next page).

Levinson, a psychologist, had started his study in 1969, when he was 49 and intrigued with his own recent midlife strains. He and his Yale colleagues intensively interviewed 40 men between the ages of 35 and 45 from four occupational groups. Using these interviews, bolstered by the biographies of great men and the development of memorable characters in literature, they described how men develop from 17 to 65 years of age (see "Levinson's Ladder," this article).

At the threshold of each major period of adulthood, they found, men pass through predictably unstable transitional periods, including a particularly wrenching time very close to age 40. At each transition a man must confront issues that may involve his career, his marriage, his family and the realization of his dreams if he is to progress successfully to the next period. Seventy percent to 80 percent of the men Levinson interviewed found the midlife transition (ages 40 to 45) tumultuous and psychologically painful, as most aspects of their lives came into question. The presumably universal timetable Levinson offered was very rigid, allowing no more than four years' leeway for each transition.

Vaillant's study, although less age-bound than Levinson's, also revealed that at midlife men go through a period of pain and preparation—"a time for reassessing and reordering the truth about adolescence and young adulthood." Vaillant, a psychiatrist, when he conducted his study at Harvard interviewed a group of men who were part of the Grant Study of Adult Development. The study had tracked almost 270 unusually accomplished, self-reliant and healthy Harvard freshmen (drawn mostly from the classes of 1942 to 1944) from their college days until their late 40s. In 1967 and 1977 Vaillant and his team interviewed and evaluated 94 members of this select group.

They found that, despite inner turmoil, the men judged to have the best outcomes in their late 40s "regarded the period from 35 to 49 as the happiest in their lives, and the seemingly calmer period from 21 to 35 as the unhappiest." But the men least well adapted at midlife "longed for the relative calm of their young adulthood and regarded the storms of later life as too painful."

While Levinson and Vaillant were completing their studies, psychiatrist Roger Gould and his colleagues at the University of California, Los Angeles, were looking at how the lives of both men and women change during young and middle adulthood. Unlike the Yale and Harvard studies, Gould's was a one-time examination of more than 500 white, middle-class people from ages 16 to 60. Gould's study, like those of Levinson and Vaillant, found that the time around age 40 was a tough one for many people, both personally and maritally. He stressed that people need to change their early expectations as they develop. "Childhood delivers most people into adulthood with a view of adults that few could ever live up to," he wrote. Adults must

confront this impossible image, he said, or be frustrated and dissatisfied.

The runaway success of *Passages* indicated the broad appeal of the stage theorists' message with its emphasis on orderly and clearly defined transitions. According to Cornell historian Michael Kammen, "We want predictability, and we desperately want definitions of 'normality.'" And almost everyone could find some relationship to their own lives in the stages Sheehy described. Stage theories, explains sociologist Orville Brim Jr., former president of the Russell Sage Foundation, are "a little like horoscopes. They are vague enough so that everyone can see something of themselves in them. That's why they're so popular."

But popularity does not always mean validity. Even at the time there were studies contradicting the stage theorists' findings. When sociologist Michael Farrell of the State University of New York at Buffalo and social psychologist Stanley Rosenberg of Dartmouth Medical School looked for a crisis among middle-aged men in 1971 it proved elusive. Instead of finding a "universal midlife crisis," they discovered several different developmental paths. "Some men do appear to reach a state of crisis," they found, "but others seem to thrive. More typical than either of these responses is the tendency for men to bury their heads and deny and avoid all the pressures closing in on them."

Another decade of research has made the picture of adult development even more complex. Many observations and theories accepted earlier as fact, especially by the general public, are now being debated. Researchers have espe-

Erikson's Eight Stages

According to Erik Erikson, people must grapple with the conflicts of one stage before they can move on to a higher one.

BONNIE SCHIFFMAN

Old Age	Integrity vs. Despair, Disgust
Maturity	Generativity vs. Self-absorption
Young Adulthood	Intimacy vs. Isolation
Adolescence	Identity vs. Identity Confusion
School Age	Industry vs. Inferiority
Play Age	Initiative vs. Guilt
Early Childhood	Autonomy vs. Shame, Doubt
Infancy	Trust vs. Mistrust

1 2 3 4 5 6 7 8

SOURCE: ADAPTED FROM "REFLECTION ON DR. BORG'S LIFE CYCLE"; ERIK H. ERIKSON, DAEDALUS, SPRING 1976.

Oh, God, I'm only twenty and I'll have to go on living and living and living.
—Jean Rhys, *Diary*

At thirty a man should know himself like the palm of his hand, know the exact number of his defects and qualities, know how far he can go, foretell his failures—be what he is. And above all accept these things.
—Albert Camus
Carnets.

cially challenged Levinson's assertion that stages are predictable, tightly linked to specific ages and built upon one another.

In fact, Gould, described as a stage theorist in most textbooks, has since changed his tune, based upon his clinical observations. He now disagrees that people go through "formal" developmental stages in adulthood, although he says that people "do change their ways of looking at and experiencing the world over time." But the idea that one must resolve one stage before going on to the next, he says, is "hogwash."

Levinson, however, has stuck by his conceptual guns over the years, claiming that no one has evidence to refute his results. "The only way for my theory to be tested is to study life structure as it develops over adulthood," he says. "And by and large psychologists and sociologists don't study lives, they study variables."

Many researchers have found that changing times and different social expectations affect how various "cohorts"—groups of people born in the same year or time period—move through the life course. Neugarten has been emphasizing the importance of this age-group, or cohort, effect since the early 1960s. Our values and expectations are shaped by the period in which we live. People born during the trying times of the Depression have a different outlook on life from those born during the optimistic 1950s, according to Neugarten.

The social environment of a particular age group, Neugarten argues, can influence its so-

WHAT WAS TRUE FOR PEOPLE BORN IN THE DEPRESSION ERA MAY NOT HOLD FOR TODAY'S 40-YEAR-OLDS, BORN IN THE UPBEAT POSTWAR YEARS.

cial clock—the timetable for when people expect and are expected to accomplish some of the major tasks of adult life, such as getting married, having children or establishing themselves in a work role. Social clocks guide our lives, and people who are "out of sync" with them are likely to find life more stressful than those who are on schedule, she says.

Since the 1960s, when Neugarten first measured what people consider to be the "right" time for major life events, social clocks have changed (see "What's the Right Time?" this article), further altering the lives of those now approaching middle age, and possibly upsetting the timetable Levinson found in an earlier generation.

As sociologist Alice Rossi of the University of Massachusetts observes, researchers trying to tease out universal truths and patterns from

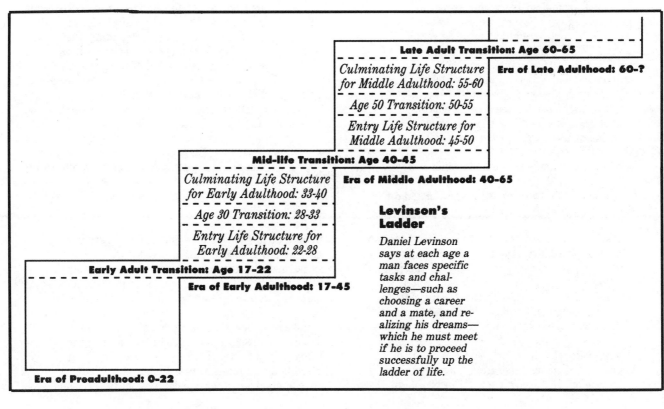

Late Adult Transition: Age 60-65

Culminating Life Structure for Middle Adulthood: 55-60

Era of Late Adulthood: 60-?

Age 50 Transition: 50-55

Entry Life Structure for Middle Adulthood: 45-50

Mid-life Transition: Age 40-45

Culminating Life Structure for Early Adulthood: 33-40

Era of Middle Adulthood: 40-65

Age 30 Transition: 28-33

Entry Life Structure for Early Adulthood: 22-28

Levinson's Ladder

Daniel Levinson says at each age a man faces specific tasks and challenges—such as choosing a career and a mate, and realizing his dreams—which he must meet if he is to proceed successfully up the ladder of life.

Early Adult Transition: Age 17-22

Era of Early Adulthood: 17-45

Era of Preadulthood: 0-22

SUDDENLY I'M THE ADULT?

BY RICHARD COHEN

Several years ago, my family gathered on Cape Cod for a weekend. My parents were there, my sister and her daughter, too, two cousins and, of course, my wife, my son and me. We ate at one of those restaurants where the menu is scrawled on a blackboard held by a chummy waiter and had a wonderful time. With dinner concluded, the waiter set the check down in the middle of the table. That's when it happened. My father did not reach for the check.

In fact, my father did nothing. Conversation continued. Finally, it dawned on me. Me! I was supposed to pick up the check. After all these years, after hundreds of restaurant meals with my parents, after a lifetime of thinking of my father as the one with the bucks, it had all changed. I reached for the check and whipped out my American Express card. My view of myself was suddenly altered. With a stroke of the pen, I was suddenly an adult.

Some people mark off their life in years, others in events. I am one of the latter, and I think of some events as rites of passage. I did not become a young man at a particular year, like 13, but when a kid strolled into the store where I worked and called me "mister." I turned around to see whom he was calling. He repeated it several times—"Mister, mister"—looking straight at me. The realization hit like a punch: Me! He was talking to me. I was suddenly a mister.

There have been other milestones. The cops of my youth always seemed to be big, even huge, and of course they were older than I was. Then one day they were neither. In fact, some of them were kids—short kids at that. Another milestone.

The day comes when you suddenly realize that all the football players in the game you're watching are younger than you. In-

Richard Cohen is a syndicated columnist for The Washington Post.

stead of being big men, they are merely big kids. With that milestone goes the fantasy that someday, maybe, you too could be a player—maybe not a football player but certainly a baseball player. I had a good eye as a kid—not much power, but a keen eye—and I always thought I could play the game. One day I realized that I couldn't. Without having ever reached the hill, I was over it.

For some people, the most momentous milestone is the death of a parent. This happened recently to a friend of mine. With the burial of his father came the realization that he had moved up a notch. Of course, he had known all along that this would happen, but until the funeral, the knowledge seemed theoretical at best. As long as one of your parents is alive, you stay in some way a kid. At the very least, there remains at least one person whose love is unconditional.

For women, a milestone is reached when they can no longer have children. The loss of a life, the inability to create one—they are variations on the same theme. For a childless woman who could control everything in life but the clock, this milestone is a cruel one indeed.

I count other, less serious milestones—like being audited by the Internal Revenue Service. As the auditor caught mistake after mistake, I sat there pretending that really knowing about taxes was for adults. I, of course, was still a kid. The auditor was buying none of it. I was a taxpayer, an adult. She all but said, Go to jail.

There have been others. I remember the day when I had a ferocious argument with my son and realized that I could no longer bully him. He was too big and the days when I could just pick him up and take him to his room/isolation cell were over. I needed to persuade, reason. He was suddenly, rapidly,

the lives of one birth cohort must consider the vexing possibility that their findings may not apply to any other group. Most of the people studied by Levinson, Vaillant and Gould were born before and during the Depression (and were predominantly male, white and upper middle class). What was true for these people may not hold for today's 40-year-olds, born in the optimistic aftermath of World War II, or the post baby-boom generation just approaching adulthood. In Rossi's view, "The profile of the

midlife men in Levinson's and Vaillant's studies may strike a future developmental researcher as burned out at a premature age, rather than reflecting a normal developmental process all men go through so early in life."

Based on her studies of women at midlife, Nancy Schlossberg, a counselor educator at the University of Maryland, also disagrees that there is a single, universal timetable for adult development—or that one can predict the crises

older. The conclusion was inescapable: So was I.

One day you go to your friends' weddings. One day you celebrate the birth of their kids. One day you see one of their kids driving, and one day those kids have kids of their own. One day you meet at parties and then at weddings and then at funerals. It all happens in one day. Take my word for it.

I never thought I would fall asleep in front of the television set as my father did, and as my friends' fathers did, too. I remember my parents and their friends talking about insomnia and they sounded like members of a different species. Not able to sleep? How ridiculous. Once it was all I did. Once it was what I did best.

I never thought that I would eat a food that did not agree with me. Now I meet them all the time. I thought I would never go to the beach and not swim. I spent all of August at the beach and never once went into the ocean. I never thought I would appreciate opera, but now the pathos, the schmaltz and, especially, the combination of voice and music appeal to me. The deaths of Mimi and Tosca move me, and they die in my home as often as I can manage it.

I never thought I would prefer to stay home instead of going to a party, but now I find myself passing parties up. I used to think that people who watched birds were weird, but this summer I found myself watching them, and maybe I'll get a book on the subject. I yearn for a religious conviction I never thought I'd want, exult in my heritage anyway, feel close to ancestors long gone and echo my father in arguments with my son. I still lose.

One day I made a good toast. One day I handled a headwaiter. One day I bought a house. One day—what a day!—I became a father, and not too long after that I picked up the check for my own. I thought then and there it was a rite of passage for me. Not until I got older did I realize that it was one for him, too. Another milestone.

in people's lives by knowing their age. "Give me a roomful of 40-year-old women and you have told me nothing. Give me a case story about what each has experienced and then I can tell if one is going to have a crisis and another a tranquil period." Says Schlossberg: "What matters is what transitions she has experienced. Has she been 'dumped' by a husband, fired from her job, had a breast removed, gone back to school, remarried, had her first book published. It is what has happened or not happened

to her, not how old she is, that counts. . . . There are as many patterns as people."

Psychologist Albert Bandura of Stanford University adds more fuel to the anti-stage fire by pointing out that chance events play a big role in shaping our adult lives. Careers and marriages are often made from the happenstance of meeting the right—or wrong—person at the right—or wrong—time. But, says Bandura, while the events may be random, their effects are not. They depend on what people do with the chance opportunities fate deals them.

The ages-and-stages approach to adult development has been further criticized because it does not appear to apply to women. Levinson claims to have confirmed that women do follow the same age-transition timetable that men do. But his recent study of women has yet to be published, and there is little other evidence that might settle the case one way or the other.

Psychologists Rosalind Barnett and Grace Baruch of the Wellesley Center for Research on Women say, "It is hard to know how to think of women within this [stage] theory—a woman may not enter the world of work until her late 30s, she seldom has a mentor, and even women with lifelong career commitments rarely are in a position to reassess their commitment pattern by age 40."

But University of Wisconsin-Madison psychologist Carol Ryff, who has directly compared the views of men and women from different age groups, has found that the big psychological issues of adulthood follow a similar developmental pattern for both sexes.

Recently she studied two characteristics highlighted as hallmarks of middle age: Erikson's "generativity" and Neugarten's "complexity." Those who have achieved generativity, according to Ryff, see themselves as leaders and decision makers and are interested in helping and guiding younger people. The men and women Ryff studied agreed that generativity is at its peak in middle age.

Complexity, which describes people's feeling that they are in control of their lives and are actively involved in the world, followed a somewhat different pattern. It was high in young adulthood and stayed prominent as people matured. But it was most obvious in those who are now middle-aged—the first generation of middle-class people to combine family and work in dual-career families. This juggling of roles, although stressful, may make some men and women feel actively involved in life.

Psychologist Ravenna Helson and her colleagues Valory Mitchell and Geraldine Moane at the University of California, Berkeley, have recently completed a long-term study of the lives of 132 women that hints at some of the forces propelling people to change psychologically during adulthood. The women were studied as seniors at Mills College in California in

> *The first forty years of life furnish the text, while the remaining thirty supply the commentary.*
> —Schopenhauer, *Parerga and Paralipomena.*

the late 1950s, five years later and again in 1981, when they were between the ages of 42 and 45.

Helson and her colleagues distinguished three main groups among the Mills women: family-oriented, career-oriented (whether or not they also wanted families) and those who followed neither path (women with no children who pursued only low-level work). Despite their different profiles in college, and their diverging life paths, the women in all three groups underwent similar broad psychological changes over time, although those in the third group changed less than those committed to career or family.

Personality tests given through the years revealed that from age 21 to their mid-40s, the Mills women became more self-disciplined and committed to duties, as well as more independent and confident. And between age 27 and the early 40s, there was a shift toward less traditionally "feminine" attitudes, including greater dominance, higher achievement motivation, greater interest in events outside the family and more emotional stability.

To the Berkeley researchers, familiar with the work of psychologist David Gutmann of Northwestern University, these changes were not surprising in women whose children were mostly grown. Gutmann, after working with Neugarten and conducting his own research, had theorized that women and men, largely locked into traditional sex roles by parenthood, become less rigidly bound by these roles once the major duties of parenting decline; both are then freer to become more like the opposite sex—and do. Men, for example, often become more willing to share their feelings. These changes in both men and women can help older couples communicate and get along better.

During their early 40s, many of the women Helson and Moane studied shared the same midlife concerns the stage theorists had found in men: "concern for young and old, introspectiveness, interest in roots and awareness of limitation and death." But the Berkeley team described the period as one of midlife "consciousness," not "crisis."

In summing up their findings, Helson and Moane stress that commitment to the tasks of young adulthood—whether to a career or family (or both)—helped women learn to control impulses, develop skills with people, become independent and work hard to achieve goals.

According to Helson and Moane, those women who did not commit themselves to one of the main life-style patterns faced fewer challenges and therefore did not develop as fully as the other women did.

The dizzying tug and pull of data and theories about how adults change over time may frustrate people looking for universal principles or certainty in their lives. But it leaves room for many scenarios for people now in young and middle adulthood and those to come.

People now between 20 and 60 are the best-educated and among the healthiest and most fit of all who have passed through the adult years. No one knows for sure what their lives will be like in the years to come, but the experts have some fascinating speculations.

For example, Rossi suspects that the quality of midlife for baby boomers will contrast sharply with that of the Depression-born generation the stage theorists studied. Baby boomers, she notes, have different dreams, values and opportunities than the preceding generation. And they are much more numerous.

Many crucial aspects of their past and future lives may best be seen in an economic rather than a strictly psychological light, Rossi says. From their days in overcrowded grade schools, through their struggles to gain entry into college, to their fight for the most desirable jobs, the baby boomers have had to compete with one another. And, she predicts, their competitive struggles are far from over. She foresees that many may find themselves squeezed out of the workplace as they enter their 50s—experiencing a crisis at a time when it will be difficult to redirect their careers.

But other factors may help to make life easier for those now approaching midlife. People are on a looser, less compressed timetable, and no longer feel obliged to marry, establish their careers and start their families almost simultaneously. Thus, major life events may not pile up in quite the same way they did for the older generation.

Today's 20-year-olds—the first wave of what some have labeled "the baby busters"—have a more optimistic future than the baby boomers who preceded them, according to economist Richard Easterlin of the University of Southern California. Easterlin has been studying the life patterns of various cohorts, beginning with the low-birthrate group born in the 1930s—roughly a decade before the birthrate exploded.

The size of a birth cohort, Easterlin argues, affects that group's quality of life. In its simplest terms, his theory says that the smaller the cohort the less competition among its members and the more fortunate they are; the larger the cohort the more competition and the less fortunate.

Compared with the baby boomers, the smaller cohort just approaching adulthood "will have much more favorable experiences as they grow

WHAT'S THE RIGHT TIME?

Two surveys asking the same questions 20 years apart (late 1950s and late 1970s) have shown a dramatic decline in the consensus among middle-class, middle-aged people about what's the right age for various major events and achievements of adult life.

Activity/Event	Appropriate Age Range	Late '50s Study % Who Agree Men	Women	Late '70s Study % Who Agree Men	Women
Best age for a man to marry	20-25	80%	90%	42%	42%
Best age for a woman to marry	19-24	85	90	44	36
When most people should become grandparents	45-50	84	79	64	57
Best age for most people to finish school and go to work	20-22	86	82	36	38
When most men should be settled on a career	24-26	74	64	24	26
When most men hold their top jobs	45-50	71	58	38	31
When most people should be ready to retire	60-65	83	86	66	41
When a man has the most responsibilities	35-50	79	75	49	50
When a man accomplishes most	40-50	82	71	46	41
The prime of life for a man	35-50	86	80	59	66
When a woman has the most responsibilities	25-40	93	91	59	53
When a woman accomplishes most	30-45	94	92	57	48

SOURCE: ADAPTED FROM "AGE NORMS AND AGE CONSTRAINTS TWENTY YEARS LATER." P. PASSUTH, D. MAINES AND B.L. NEUGARTEN. PAPER PRESENTED AT THE MIDWEST SOCIOLOGICAL SOCIETY MEETING, CHICAGO, APRIL 1984.

up—in their families, in school and finally in the labor market," he says. As a result, they will "develop a more positive psychological outlook."

The baby busters' optimism will encourage them to marry young and have large families—producing another baby boom. During this period there will be less stress in the family and therefore, Easterlin predicts, divorce and suicide rates will stabilize.

Psychologist Elizabeth Douvan of the University of Michigan's Institute for Social Research shares Easterlin's optimistic view about the future of these young adults. Surprisingly, she sees as one of their strengths the fact that, due to divorce and remarriage, many grew up in reconstituted families. Douvan believes that the experience of growing up close to people who are not blood relatives can help to blur the distinction between kinship and friendship, making people more open in their relationships with others.

Like many groups before them, they are likely to yearn for a sense of community and ritual, which they will strive to fulfill in many ways, Douvan says. For some this may mean a turn toward involvement in politics, neighborhood or religion, although not necessarily the religion of their parents.

In summing up the future quality of life for today's young adults and those following them, Douvan says: "Life is more open for people now. They are judging things internally and therefore are more willing to make changes in the external aspects. That's pretty exciting. It opens up a tremendous number of possibilities for people who can look at life as an adventure."

How OLD Is OLD

~~~~~ ....

Abe Brown

Don't look now, but you're aging. Surprised? You didn't think it would happen to you? And so soon! Well, it can and it is. In fact, it started the moment you were born. It's inevitable. Benjamin Franklin said that nothing is certain "except death and taxes." He should have added, "and growing older." And it happens to everyone, regardless of sex, race, or whether you are rich or poor.

But what *happens* to you as you age—as you grow older—is another matter. It can be a great experience, full of energy, enthusiasm, good health. Or it can be a bummer. It all depends on you. You are in charge.

Being young, and feeling young, are great. We all hope the feeling will last indefinitely. We have the idea, while we're young, that we are biologically invulnerable—we feel that nothing bad can happen to us, that we're going to live forever no matter how much we abuse our health and our bodies. As supermen and superwomen, we believe we can conquer any illness or injury. We think that existing on junk food, smoking, abusing alcohol or drugs, missing meals, losing sleep, or too much activity cannot harm us, because we are young.

Kidding Yourself

Maybe so. Probably not. It's a great dream, but you're kidding yourself if you think good health and good aging happen automatically. They don't. You are going to have to make them happen. If you want to have a long life full of good health and vitality, being physically and mentally sharp, and being able to enjoy all the good things that go with good health, you'll have to work at it—all the time.

As a young person today, more so than the youth in earlier generations, you have the best chances to stay "young" for a long time. You've

got a great head start. You don't have to worry about the so-called childhood diseases that were threats to your parents. Vaccines and public health campaigns have gone a long way to protect you against such diseases as polio, tuberculosis, mumps, diphtheria, tetanus, pertussis (whooping cough), chicken pox, measles, rubella (German measles). Smallpox, once a highly feared contagious disease, no longer exists anywhere in the world.

You won't have control over everything that happens to you as time goes by; there are some physical changes that take place in your body regardless of what you do. Some of them are due to heredity, some are due to your environment, temperament, or family history.

Your Biological Age

But much of the change that occurs as you grow older can be controlled. You can slow down your aging. Your important "age," as you grow older, will not be your age in birthdays—your "calendar age." It will be your biological or "vital" age.

It all depends on you. Some people are "old" at 40, others are "young" at 70. There can be as much as a 30-year difference between your biological age and your actual age in years. You can choose to age poorly or to age well. It's up to you, not to the medical profession.

Why give any thought to all this now? Do you have to worry, now, at your age, what your life is going to be like way down the road? You bet you do. If you want to avoid the serious consequences of smoking, the time to quit is *now*. (Better yet, decide you'll never start smoking in the first place.) If you want to avoid the hazards of alcohol, the time to decide about drinking is *now*. If you fool around with drugs, the time to stop is *now*. If you want to retain your energy, vitality, stamina, healthy heart

Know Any "Opals" or "Grumpies"?

What do older people want to be called?

Seniors? Old-timers? Golden-agers? Elderly? Mature people? Or what?

Some have suggested "opals" (older people with active lifestyles) or "grumpies" (grown-up mature people). None has caught on. The problem is that any term associated with "old" is considered derogatory.

Some older people dislike the term "senior" so much that they forego senior discounts at restaurants, lodgings, and elsewhere.

Not Page Smith, a historian. In a newspaper column, he wrote: "I will not condescend to use that foul phrase, 'senior citizen,' or its shorter version, 'senior.' They are hardly more than mealy-mouthed euphemisms as is 'golden-ager.' "

But then he told the story about the first time he was asked if he was a senior (he was in a theater ticket line). "I responded with an ill-natured tirade against the word and the category." The ticket-taker viewed him wearily, and said: "Mister, the regular price is $5. Seniors are $2.75."

Smith did not hesitate: "I am a senior," Page replied.

and circulation, the time to acquire good exercise and nutrition habits is *now*. There is no magic formula. You must be concerned with the problems of the future when you are young.

Many of today's adult illnesses are often related to factors within your control: such ailments as heart disease, stroke, various types of cancer. These are affected by factors such as good nutrition, exercise, stress, and smoking.

Natural Changes

Nevertheless, as people grow older, more or less predictable changes occur, in spite of what they do. Aging is not a disease, and these age changes are natural reductions in some of the body's functions. What are some of these changes?

• *The body's immune system slowly grows less efficient.* The immune system loses some of its ability to protect against the invasion of bacteria and viruses. It may fail to protect against abnormal cell growth, as in cancers. In some cases, the immune system may go haywire and attack the body's own normal cells, thus creating such autoimmune diseases as rheumatoid arthritis and some other forms of arthritis, myasthenia gravis (a muscle disease), some allergies, juvenile diabetes, and rheumatic fever.

• *The skin may start to wrinkle as it becomes thinner.* This age-related

Gray Myths

There are many persistent myths about aging. These myths stereotype and stigmatize people on the basis of age. Here are some of the more common myths—and the facts.

Myth: Most older people are in poor health.
Fact: Not so. There are neither biological nor physiological reasons to connect poor health with growing older. Older people are more likely to be affected with illness and physical disabilities than you are, but old age itself is not a disease. It is possible to remain physically fit throughout your life.

Myth: When you get old, you become senile.
Fact: Older minds can be as bright as young minds. Senility is a sign of disease; it is not part of the normal aging process. In a 1985 study of men ages 20, 40, 60, and 80 years, no evidence was found to indicate that aging was associated with an inevitable decline in intellectual performance, in generally healthy people.

Myth: Old age is sexless.
Fact: This myth dies hard because romance is associated with youth. Men and women continue to feel sexy and sensual in later life. Healthy seniors can have a satisfying romantic life—often into their 80s and longer. How about that?

Myth: Older people are rigid, unable to change.
Fact: Older people are as diverse in their lifestyles and flexibility as are young and middle-aged people. Despite the enormous stresses they deal with—death of loved ones or job, financial, and domestic problems—they cope miraculously well. Older people give up smoking and break other bad habits just as successfully as younger people.

Who Says Older People Are Not Productive?

How about these:

• Actress Jessica Tandy (who starred in "Driving Miss Daisy") is winning acting awards in her 80s.

• Former CBS News anchorman Walter Cronkite is still broadcasting at 75.

• Comedian George Burns still packs them in at 95. At 87, he wrote *How to Live to Be 100—or More*. He'll make it.

• General Dwight D. Eisenhower became president of the United States at 62; Harry Truman at 60; Ronald Reagan at 69; George Bush at 64.

• Violinist Isaac Stern, 71, draws standing-room-only audiences wherever he performs; jazz pianist and composer Dave Brubeck, also 71, keeps recording hit albums and gaining new young fans.

• Cab Calloway is still "scat" singing in his 80s.

And there are thousands of others you may not have heard about. At 71, Virginia is an avid surfer. At 103, Jane is a pilot and author. At 78, Morris plays in a softball league. At 90, Daddy Bruce still runs his BBQ restaurant. At 79, college student Etta gets straight A's. Wilfred, at 81, competes in 80-meter hurdles.

You can join these ranks someday, too.

change may vary by as much as 20 years in the time it appears. This depends on heredity, exposure to the sun, and some other factors. You can protect your skin from aging ef-

fects, and from the most common type of skin cancer, by avoiding excessive exposure to the sun's ultraviolet rays.

• *The hair turns gray (or may fall out).* This change is pretty much determined by heredity.

• *There is a reduction in sharpness of vision and hearing.*

• *Reflexes slow down, normally.* The gait will be a little slower. You may have less stamina. All these are more or less inevitable changes to which a person can accommodate easily and smoothly.

Changes That Need Not Happen

But many other age changes that can happen to people need not happen. Physical fitness can be maintained. Intelligence and memory can stay sharp. Good nutrition and exercise can protect the heart, the bones, the efficiency of the joints, as well as flexibility. We can postpone the biological signs of aging for a long time.

Getting old doesn't mean getting sick, or getting senile, or getting useless, or losing your good looks. Getting old is not an inevitable slide into illness or immobility.

Getting old means more knowledge, more freedom, more experiences. There are medical experts who maintain that the mind is still young at 50, that the brain does not reach its full capacity until about 60. Mental efficiency may decline slowly from 60 on, which simply means that people can be mentally productive well into their 70s and 80s. Brain cells are stimulated by use. A challenged brain doesn't quit learning. Intellectual changes are more often the result of disuse rather than aging.

Many abilities can stay with you until late in life: knowledge, experience, intelligence, the desire to be active and involved, the ability to find pleasure in everything, and the drive to be useful.

Each of us changes differently as we grow up and grow older. You are aging differently from young people

in previous generations, because of the social changes that have taken place.

Like snowflakes, there have never been two human beings exactly alike, among the billions of people who have ever lived. People grow at different speeds: Some are tall, some short, some fat, some thin, some smart, some not so smart, some coordinated, some clumsy. In short, each person is a unique individual, unlike anyone else. And, the older people get, the more they differ biologically. They age in a variety of different ways.

How Old *Is* "Old"?

The answer has changed over the years. More than 200 years ago, at the birth of our Republic, you were old at 35. That was the average life expectancy then. At the turn of this century, as medical knowledge advanced, the average life span increased to 45. In 1950, 70-year-olds were really old. Today, a healthy 70-year-old is looking forward to many more active years. Barring accident or unavoidable illness, the prospects of your being old for many, many years look very good.

So, how old is old? The answer is one you've heard many times, from all sorts of people. "You are as old (or young) as you feel." The calendar simply tells you how many years you have lived. Your body tells you how well you've lived.

"Youth," wrote an anonymous author, "is not a time of life—it is a state of mind. Nobody grows old by merely living a number of years; people grow old by deserting their ideals."

Old is a point of view. Alice Brophy, when she was with the New York City Commission for the Aging, said, "It annoys me when people say, 'Gee, you look young for your age.' What does that mean? Is there some model in the Smithsonian that you're supposed to look a certain way at 65 and 75 and 85? You know you can die old at 30 and live young at 80."

A Raw Deal

Older people, for a long time, have been getting a raw deal. You've been exposed to negative images of aging men and women. They have been portrayed as feeble, slow, foolish, crabby, irascible, opinionated, helpless, boring, stingy, needing to be patronized. All old people are portrayed to be about the same. (Some old people are, of course, crabby and unpleasant. So are some young people.)

These negative images suggest that later years are not times of intimacy, wisdom, pleasure, awareness, joy, and love.

Older people have often been unkindly treated in the media—in movies, television, in the comics, even on radio. They were portrayed as senile, bumbling, empty-headed, helpless characters who always got in the way, causing problems for their offspring and for society in general.

For the most part, however, that picture of older people is now history. Older people are getting their rightful place in the entertainment media. They are now shown more often as they are: useful, intelligent, active, alert, compassionate, humorous, productive, romantic, loving, attractive. With an occasional exception, you no longer see sitcoms that demean older people as ones who drool, are dopey, and are there only to get laughs at their actual or implied infirmities.

Millions of Busy Older People

The stereotype of the shuffling, bent-over old person is on the way out. Millions of older people are busy working, exercising, painting, writing, entertaining, creating, helping, living fully, and helping society regardless of their chronological age. Older people are skydiving, spelunking, mountain climbing, cross-country skiing, learning new languages, starting new careers and businesses, volunteering, leading community activities.

These older people you see around you are your parents, grandparents, aunts, uncles, neighbors.

Your attitudes toward older people, and your images of them, can develop most accurately through your experiences with them. The opportunities to interact with parents, relatives, and neighbors can give you an awareness of their alertness, their involvement with life. They can be a resource and an inspiration. You can learn from them, and they can learn from you.

Let's give George Burns, a great comedian and nonagenarian, the last words on this subject:

"It's good to mix with younger people (and vice versa)," he wrote in his book *How to Live to Be 100—or More.* "I love being around young people. I figure maybe some of that youth will rub off on me.... And maybe some of what I've got might rub off on them."

For More Information
American Academy of Dermatology
Communications Department
P.O. Box 1661
Evanston, IL 60204-1661
Pamphlet: "The Sun and Your Skin," single copy free with self-addressed, stamped envelope.

American Dietetic Association
c/o Lee Enterprises
Dept. 22 (if ordering "Food for Young Men")
Dept. 23 (if ordering "Food for Young Women")
P.O. Box 1068
South Holland, IL 60473
Pamphlets: "Food for Young Men" and "Food for Young Women," $1 each with a self-addressed, stamped envelope.

President's Council on Physical Fitness and Sports
Dept. 157
450 Fifth St. N.W.
Washington, DC 20001
Pamphlet: "Exercise and Weight Control," single copy free.

American Council on Alcoholism, Inc.
The Health Information Center
White Marsh Business Center
5024 Campbell Blvd., Ste. H
Baltimore, MD 21236
or call 1-800-527-5344
Pamphlet: "The Most Frequently Asked Questions about Teenage Drinking," single copy free.

How Do You Get to Be Good and Old?

Plan ahead. You can't hold back the calendar (darn!) but you can *feel* young for a long time. Good health habits, now, will pay off later. If you take care of yourself now, most probably someone else won't have to later on.

Here's what health experts advise:
- Don't smoke.
- Practice good nutrition. Eat food low in fats and cholesterol and high in nutrients and fiber.
- Exercise regularly and moderately. The "no pain, no gain" refrain is nonsense.
- Stay away from alcohol; or, when you are legal age, drink in moderation if you drink at all.
- Don't experiment with drugs.
- Develop a network of good friends who have the same positive goals you have.
- Be upbeat.

The Return of Wonder in Old Age

Allan B. Chinen

Allan B. Chinen, M.D., is a psychiatrist in San Francisco, Calif.

Creativity and a sense of wonder are two of the most endearing traits in children. With school and later with career and family, however, the child's native delight in the world soon becomes the adult's pragmatism and responsibility. For most adults, wonder and fascination recede into distant memory, particularly by retirement age. Yet it is in later life that men and women have a second chance at mystery and wonder. That, at least, is the message of "elder tales"—fairy tales specifically about "old" people. Handed down over generations, elder tales contain accumulated folk wisdom about aging (Chinen, 1989), and one of their recurrent themes is the return of wonder in old age. A charming story from Japan, typical of elder tales from around the world, illustrates the motif (Mayer, 1985; Ohta, 1955).

THE SIX STATUES

Once upon a time, there lived an old man and woman who were very poor. One New Year's Eve, they found they had no money to buy rice cakes, a traditional delicacy for the holiday. Then they remembered several straw hats the old man had made earlier. So he took them to the village to sell. Try as he might, though, no one bought any hats. Late in the afternoon, he trudged up the snowy trail back to his house, wrapped in misery. On the way, the old man noticed six statues, standing in the snow. They were the guardian deities of children, and they looked cold and lonely. The old man

paused. "I cannot leave you to shiver here!" he exclaimed. So the old man tied a straw hat on each of the gods, to keep the snow off their bald heads. Then the old man returned home. That evening, he and his wife ate a meager meal and went quietly to bed.

The message of 'elder tales' is that despite inevitable declines, the possibility of psychological and spiritual renewal remains.

At midnight, the old couple were awakened by strange noises outside their house. "Who could that be?" the old man exclaimed. They listened and made out the sound of people singing. At that moment, the door flew open, and a bag landed in the middle of their hut, full of the prettiest rice cakes the old man and his wife had ever seen. And when they looked through their door, they saw six gods, each wearing a straw hat, wishing them a happy New Year!

LOSS AND RETURN OF WONDER

Although apparently simple, this story is deeply perceptive and instructive—like elder tales in general. The drama begins with an impoverished old man and woman, and their dismal lot aptly symbolizes the many losses of later life. Yet in this situation magic unexpectedly returns. This is a central message in elder tales: Despite the inevitable declines of old age, the possibility of psychological and spiritual renewal remains. The pre-

sent story emphasizes the optimistic theme with a subtle detail. The drama takes place on New Year's Eve, the last day of the old year and the first of the new. The old man and his wife thus have a choice of looking backward to the old or forward to the new. Psychologically, they can dwell on losses and deprivation or on growth and development.

Lacking money to celebrate the holiday, the old man and his wife do not complain, give up, or become bitter. The old man simply goes to the village to sell his hats. His actions contrast sharply with those of young protagonists in fairly tales like "Cinderella" or "Snow White." Young heroes and heroines typically wait helplessly until a fairy godmother aids them. The old man is far more practical, resourceful, and realistic, as are the protagonists of other elder tales.

Unable to sell his hats, the old man returns home. On the way, he stops beside six stone statues and then does something extraordinary. He talks to the statues, sympathizes with their plight, and gives them all straw hats to protect their bald heads from the snow. The old man's action is unexpected and seemingly irrational. After all, he could keep the hats and try to sell them later. And what would people think if they saw him talking to the statues? Here we come to another vital theme in elder tales, from "The Simple Grasscutter" in Arabia (Lang, 1914) to "The Shining Fish" from Italy (Calvino, 1978). Elder tales consistently portray older adults doing something apparently outrageous or foolish, after years of being practical and predictable. As the present story quickly indicates, breaking away from conventional reason leads to the return of wonder, magic, and creativity.

According to the tale, the six statues come to life on New Year's Eve and

From *Generations*, Vol. 15, No. 2, Spring 1991, pp. 45-48. © 1991 by The American Society on Aging. Reprinted with permission from *Generations*, 833 Market Street, Suite 511, San Francisco, CA 94103.

bring the old man and his wife rice cakes and good wishes. The old man treats them like living beings, and they obligingly come alive. The same theme, I might add, appears in other elder tales like the Cossack story of "The Straw Ox" (Bain, 1895). On one level, the symbolism is fairly direct: Inanimate objects come alive, reiterating the theme that no matter how dreary things seem in old age, the chance for renewal remains. There is a deeper meaning here, though. Treating stone statues as if they were living people is *animism*. A good example comes from children, who regard their teddy bears not simply as stuffed animals but as real personalities. Animism is also the attitude that enlivens the mythic consciousness of aboriginal cultures (Berman, 1981; Campbell, 1959). The ancient hunter apologized to his prey before killing it, because he believed the animal was conscious and had a spirit, just as he did. And the aboriginal woodcutter placated the tree he felled, speaking to it and making offerings, respecting it as a person. What the present tale suggests is that animism and mythic awareness reappear in later life.

Researchers early on noted such an increase in animism and magical thinking in old age.

Researchers early on noted such an increase in animism and magical thinking in old age (e.g., Papalia and Bielby, 1974; Gutmann, 1964; Sheehan, et al., 1981). This was initially interpreted as regression—the intellectual deterioration that was thought to be inevitable with old age. However, a growing body of research reveals the reverse. Complex, subtle forms of reasoning, which are missed by traditional psychological tests, develop in maturity. This wisdom of aging has only recently become the subject of systematic research (e.g., Kramer, 1989; Labouvie-Vief, 1980; Labouvie-Vief et al., 1989; Sinnott, 1984; Sternberg, 1990). And wisdom appears to involve the return of wonder and mythic delight in the world (Labouvie-Vief, 1990). "The Six Statues" illustrates this development, and the tale adds a mischievous detail to underscore the motif. The six statues in the story are not

likenesses of the Goddess of Mercy or the Buddha, to whom adults were more likely to pray in Japan. The story specifically—and playfully—says that the six statues are those of the guardian deities of *children!* The story thus suggests—and other elder tales repeat the theme—that reclaiming the wonder and creativity of childhood is a task of later life.

If "The Six Statues" is charming and heartwarming, the crucial question is whether the sentiment of wonder returns in real life. Statements from older individuals provide the clearest answer. Flora Arnstein, for example, a retired teacher, wrote the following poem in her 90s:

That it can never be known
Makes it all the more alluring,
Enticing, too, so that one goes on trying.
Every morning is an invitation,
The sun friendly as an unafraid child,
Each trifle enjoyable: the shoe-horn
Emerging from the shoe-heel,
The tooth-brush rinsed of paste;
All small delectables: the brewing coffee,
Even the charred toast,
And the thrust of cool air
As one reaches the street.
This is no euphoria, just an aura
Of good feeling.

In her verse a spirit of mythic delight emerges. Arnstein celebrates the present, very ordinary moment. The sense of wonder returns—the marvel a child might feel when first encountering toothpaste or coffee. And the greatest magic is that this delight reappears on the ten-thousandth time around.

Central to the attitude of wonder is an affirmation of life just as it is in the present.

The return of wonder often emerges as delight in nature. One woman in her 60s, for instance, came to therapy for depression after her husband was diagnosed as having Alzheimer's disease. She learned cope with the stresses of attending to her disabled husband by returning to an old delight in nature. As she described her experience: "I take walks every morning, rain or shine, and I love it. The world seems so fresh. Everything is alive—the trees, the birds,

the water on the lake!" For other men and women, wonder returns with grandparenthood. One woman described her reaction upon seeing her grandchild for the first time: "It was a wonder, a mystery, and there was something else, too— a wonder at nature. It was a spiritual or religious experience. You know, just as if you would sit there and look at a flower for a long time—that kind of feeling, a religious feeling" (Kornhaber and Woodward, 1981, p. 54).

Along with wonder in later life comes an enjoyment of the present moment. Romano Guardini (1957), a philosopher, described his experience, writing when he was 70.

Existence now takes on the character, we might say, of a still-life in a Cezanne. There is a table. Upon the table, a plate. Upon the plate, some apples. Nothing else. Everything is there, clear and evident. Nothing left to ask or to answer. And yet mystery everywhere. There is more in these things than meets the eye, more than the simple individuality of each thing. . . . It might even be that mystery is the very stuff of being: things, events, everything that happens and which we call life" (pp. 78–79).

Central to the attitude of wonder is an affirmation of life just as it is in the present. The individual neither hankers after a lost past nor a future yet to be. Here we come to a close connection between the return of wonder and Erikson's (1959, 1983) notion of ego-integrity. The latter is an affirmation of one's life just as one lived it, for better or worse. Ego-integrity is thus an affirmation of one's *past*. The return of wonder involves a similar affirmation of the *present*, down to its small, ordinary events. The return of wonder is thus an extension and deepening of ego-integrity. The reclamation of childhood delight is actually the fruit of maturity.

The connection between ego-integrity and wonder can be seen in a comment by the psychoanalyst Martin Grotjahn (1982) writing in the last years of his life:

I don't work anymore, I don't walk anymore. Peculiarly enough, I feel well about it. . . .
I sit in the sun watching the falling leaves slowly sail across the waters of the swimming pool. I think, I dream, I draw, I sit—I feel free of worry— almost free of this world of reality.
If anyone had told me that I would be quietly happy just sitting here, reading a little, writing a little, and enjoy-

ing life in a quiet and modest way, I, of course, would not have believed. That a walk across the street to the corner of the park satisfies me when I always thought a four-hour walk was just not good enough: that surprises me" (p. 234)

A quiet, delightful magic animates Grotjahn's experience. The world comes to life in a tranquil way, and even small events become filled with magic and wonder. The ambitions of youth—four-hour walks!—are replaced by delight in the present.

If the reclamation of magic and mystery in everyday life is an ideal goal of the later years, elder tales help achieve it. Stories like "The Six Statues" are ideal for grandparents telling tales to grandchildren. While awakening magic in young children, elder tales reawaken old enchantments for the mature adult. The medium is truly the message. The magic of elder tales is their goal—to bring back the wonder of the first years in the last.

REFERENCES

Bain, R. N., 1895. *Cossack Fairy Tales and Folk Tales*. New York: Stokes.

Berman, M., 1981. *The Re-enchantment of the World*. Ithaca, N.Y.: Cornell University Press.

Calvino, I., 1978. *Italian Folktales*. Translated by G. Martin. New York: Pantheon.

Campbell, J., 1959. *The Masks of God: Primitive Mythology*. New York: Penguin.

Chinen, A., 1989. *In the Ever After: Fairy Tales and the Second Half of Life*. Wilmette, Ill.: Chiron.

Erikson, E., 1959. *Identity and the Life Cycle*. New York: International Universities Press.

Erikson, E., 1983. *The Life Cycle Completed*. New York: Norton.

Grotjahn, M., 1982. "The Day I Got Old." *Psychiatric Clinics of North America* 5: 233–37.

Guardini, R., 1957. "The Stages of Life and Philosophy." *Philosophy Today* 1: 75–80.

Gutmann, D., 1964. "An Exploration of Ego Configurations in Middle and Later Life." In B. L. Neugarten, ed., *Personality in Middle and Late Life*. New York: Atherton.

Kornhaber, A. and Woodward, K., 1981. *Grandparents/Grandchildren: The Vital Connection*. Garden City, N.Y.: Doubleday.

Kramer, D., 1989. "Development of an Awareness of Contradiction Across the Lifespan and the Question of Post-formal Operations." In M. L. Commons et al., eds., *Beyond Formal Operations II: Comparison and Applications of Adolescent and Adult Developmental Models*. New York: Prager, pp. 133, 159.

Labouvie-Vief, G., 1980. "Beyond Formal Operations: Uses and Limits of Pure Logic in Lifespan Development." *Human Development* 23: 141–61.

Labouvie-Vief, G., DeVoe, M. and Bulka, B., 1989. "Speaking About Feelings: Conceptions of Emotion Across the Life Span." *Psychology & Aging* 4: 425–37.

Labouvie-Vief, G., 1990. "Wisdom as Integrated Thought: Historical and Developmental Perspectives." In R. Sternberg, ed., *Wisdom: Its Nature, Origins and Development*. Cambridge: Cambridge University Press, pp. 52–83.

Lang, A., 1914. *The Brown Fairy Book*. London: Longmans, Green.

Mayer, F. H., 1985. *Ancient Tales in Modern Japan*. Bloomington, Ind.: Indiana University Press.

Ohta, M., 1955. *Japanese Folklore in English*. Tokyo: Miraishi.

Papalia, D. E. and Bielby, D. D., 1974. "Cognitive Functioning in Middle and Old Age Adults: A Review of Research Based on Piaget's Theory." *Human Development* 17: 424–43.

Sheehan, N. W., Papalia-Finlay, D. E. and Hooper, F. H., 1981. "The Nature of the Life Concept Across the Life-Span." *International Journal of Aging & Human Development* 12: 1–13.

Sinnott, J., 1984. "Postformal Reasoning: The Relativistic Stage." In M. Commons, F. A. Richards and C. Armon, eds., *Beyond Formal Operations: Late Adolescent and Adult Cognitive Development*. New York: Praeger, pp. 298–325.

Sternberg, R. J., 1990. "Wisdom and Its Relations to Intelligence and Creativity." In R. Sternberg, ed., *Wisdom: Its Nature, Origins and Development*. Cambridge: Cambridge University Press, pp. 142–59.

Unlocking the Secrets of Aging

Scientists are deciphering genetic codes they say will lead to keeping people alive much longer. But the social and ethical implications of sharing the Fountain of Youth are impossible to ignore.

Sheryl Stolberg

Times Medical Writer

In his laboratory at the University of Colorado, molecular biologist Thomas Johnson is studying a translucent worm no bigger than a printed comma. In this simple animal, composed of just 959 cells, Johnson believes he may find the answers to complex questions that have eluded scientists for centuries:

What makes us grow old? Can we stop aging, or at least slow it down?

By breeding tens of thousands of these nematodes, Johnson has created a strain that can live for about five weeks—about 70% longer than the worm's average three-week life span. It appears that the difference between the elderly worms and their shorter-lived counterparts lies in a single gene. Now, Johnson is trying to isolate that gene, and he says he is close.

And if genes can be manipulated to extend the lives of worms, the 48-year-old researcher asks, might not the same be true of people?

"Maybe there are major genes in humans that, if we alter [them], we could project a longer human life span," Johnson said. "This would be an absolutely tremendous sociological finding. It would affect . . . every aspect of the way we live our lives if we all of a sudden had average life spans of 120 years instead of 70 years."

Tremendous indeed. Johnson's work is on the cutting edge of a fascinating scientific sojourn, a modern-day quest for the legendary Fountain of Youth. He is among a growing corps of 2,000 molecular biologists, geneticists, immunologists and other researchers across the United States who are trying to unlock the secrets of aging.

They are tinkering with genes, human growth hormones and new drugs, and with strategies of diet, nutrition and exercise. They are studying patterns of survival in worms, fruit flies, mice and people. They are examining the links between aging and illness—cancer, Alzheimer's, Parkinson's, osteoporosis, heart disease, stroke—as well as the effect of environment on aging.

Their strides in recent years have been so significant that a startling new body of thought has emerged, one that says humans may one day live much longer than anyone dreamed possible. Some go so far as to say that the maximum life span, now at 120 years, and average life expectancy, about 75 years in the United States, could double or triple.

"The ideal of all our work is that sometime in the future, we would take pills that would slow or postpone our aging," said UC Irvine biologist Michael Rose, who is breeding fruit flies that can live up to three times as long as the average fly. "That's the ultimate goal, the man on the moon for all this research. We're not going to have that in five years. But someday it will happen."

Michal Jazwinski, a Louisiana State University biologist who has isolated "longevity assurance genes" in yeast, said: "In the next 30 to 50 years, we will in fact have in hand many of the major genes that determine longevity in humans. What we have been able to see with our yeast is a doubling of the life span. So that could be something that we might aim for in the future."

Scientists are pondering the social and ethical implications of their work. They raise a litany of questions: If the research is successful, what would happen to the nation's overburdened health care and Social Security systems? Would the work force be so crowded with elderly people who have postponed retirement that young people will not be able to find jobs? Would a population boom cause a housing crunch? What would be the effect on our fragile environment?

And, perhaps most important, will living longer also mean living healthier?

"If we are able to produce 150-year-old people but those 150-year-old people spend the last 40 years of their life in a nursing home, we would have created a disaster," said Dr. Richard Sprott, a top official at the National Institute on Aging. "The big public worry is that by increasing the number of people who make it [to advanced ages] we will produce this huge increase in the amount of disease."

In some respects, that is occurring. As the population has grown older, the incidence of age-related diseases such as Alzheimer's and osteoporosis has skyrocketed. The Alliance for Aging Research estimates that it costs the nation $90-billion a year to treat people with Alzheimer's, which affects at least 2 million and possibly 4 million Americans. As these costs continue to rise, experts say, society has a vested interest in finding ways to keep older people healthier.

What we have to do as a society is come to the realization of how much money is going into the medical care of the elderly," said Raymond Daynes, a cellular immunologist at the University of Utah. "We are becoming incredibly sophisticated in preventing individuals who have some acute, devastating illnesses from dying. But we are way behind in providing preventive measures so that [illness] doesn't happen in the first place."

Life expectancy in the United States has increased dramatically since 1900, from 47.3 years to 75.4 years. The greatest gains occurred during the first half of this century, largely because of dramatic reductions in infant mortality and infectious diseases. More recently, as

Daynes notes, smaller gains have resulted from progress against major fatal illnesses, such as heart disease, cancer and stroke.

Improvements in sanitation and living conditions have also made a big difference, and are likely to continue to do so, said James R. Carey, a medical demographer at UC Davis whose recent work with fruit flies has been cited as evidence that there is no arbitrary cap on human life span.

"The people that are 100 years old today were born in 1892," Carey said. "Think about all the things they went through, in terms of lack of medicine and nutrition. They were working hard to make it to 100. Now think about a newborn of today, with the emphasis on nutrition and exercise and medical advances. I would bet that we are going to find 125-, 130-year-olds by the 22nd Century just because of these changes in conditions."

Whether the pace proceeds more quickly than Carey suggests will depend on the outcome of the research being conducted in laboratories today—particularly in the area of genetics, scientists say. Few researchers, however, are willing to make predictions about how soon a breakthrough might come.

Yet as demographic shifts create an older society, and as scientific advances continue, the study of gerontology is enjoying an unprecedented boom. Once suspiciously regarded as the province of charlatans and snake-oil salesmen, longevity research is gaining attention and respect. Now, top-flight scientists are flocking to a field that, as little as five years ago, failed to draw the best and the brightest.

"Aging," said Daynes, "is finally coming of age."

This trend is reflected in funding: The federal government's National Institute on Aging is among the fastest-growing branches of the National Institutes of Health, with a budget that has nearly doubled in the past three years—from $222 million in 1989 to $402 million this year.

However, the budget is still small compared to that of some other arms of NIH—the National Cancer Institute has an annual budget of nearly $2 billion.

Much of the growth in aging research has been fueled by intense interest in Alzheimer's and other age-related diseases. The media have lavished much attention on the subject, particularly since a highly publicized 1990 study in which doses of a synthetic form of human growth hormone were reported to restore youthful vigor to elderly people.

Within the past decade new technologies—such as the ability to conduct transgenic experiments, in which a gene can be transferred from one organism into another—have become available to biologists, making possible certain types of gene research that used to be unthinkable.

"For the last 20 years, a lot of the research has been simply trying to characterize aging in a descriptive way," said Huber Warner, deputy associate director of the NIA's Biology of Aging program. "Now people are beginning to find out what the mechanisms of the aging process are so that they can then try to develop interventions that will slow the process down or prevent it altogether."

Judith Campisi is among those whose work is funded by the National Institute on Aging. At UC's Lawrence Berkeley Laboratory she is studying cellular senescence, the process by which cells keep dividing until they grow old and die. When she entered the field five years ago, she said, science had barely begun to examine the basic mechanisms that control aging.

"Before," she said, "nobody quite knew how to ask critical questions about aging. That has changed dramatically in the past five years. The field has now reached a level of maturity where . . . we are beginning to see a path to at least dream about approaching some answers. Until recently, that dream was not a very viable one."

The answers remain elusive. Aging is an extraordinarily complex puzzle—affected by genetics and the environment and individual habits, such as cigarette smoking and diet and exercise—and Campisi said she and her compatriots each hold only one small piece of it. "We all need each other terribly," she said.

R esearch is proceeding on many different—albeit interwoven—fronts:

At Bemidji State University in Minnesota, biochemist Gary W. Evans recently reported that dietary supplements of the metal chromium can extend the life span of rats by one-third, and may do the same for humans. At USC, noted gerontologist Caleb Finch is exploring new terrain with his studies on how aging affects the brain.

In Irvine, biologist Rose is breeding red-eyed fruit flies that can live 80 days—double the life span of an average fly—by mating selected flies that are able to reproduce late in life. Rose theorizes that these elderly flies, some of which live six months, are passing longevity genes to their offspring. But a key question remains: Which genes are responsible?

At the University of Colorado, Johnson, the biochemist who is breeding round worms, is taking a slightly different tack. He is mating long-lived nematodes with short-lived ones in an effort to follow the worms' DNA trails. Through a process by which he marks the DNA of the elderly worms, Johnson can see which genetic patterns reappear in the offspring. He has narrowed his search for a "longevity assurance gene" down to a 50-gene region of a single, 3,000-gene chromosome.

In Kentucky, pharmacologist John Carney has learned that when a synthetic compound known as PBN—phenyl butyl nitrone—is injected into gerbils, certain proteins in the brain that deteriorate with age are restored, resulting in improved short-term memory for the animals.

PBN works by combatting the effects of "free radicals"—damaging oxygen byproducts that occur natu-

rally in the body, destroying fats and proteins that are crucial to the way cells function. In certain diseases such as Alzheimer's and Parkinson's, researchers believe, these free radicals run amok.

In addition, scientists at the National Institute on Aging say they have evidence that free radicals speed the aging process. The theory is that if free radicals can be controlled, so too can aging. Researchers are also exploring the effects of "dietary antioxidants"—foods and vitamins including Vitamins C and E, and beta-carotene, a compound that turns into Vitamin A in the body—that may help combat free radicals.

Soon, Carney hopes, PBN will be tried in humans. He and his partner, a biochemist at the University of Oklahoma, have set up a pharmaceutical company to manufacture the drug and are hoping to gain government approval for testing within the next two years.

While Carney studies how a synthetic drug might slow the aging of the brain, Dr. Daniel Rudman of the Veterans Administration Medical Center in Milwaukee has spent the past five years examining how human growth hormones, which occur naturally in the body but decline in secretions as people grow older, affect aging.

Rudman has administered a synthetic form of the hormones to 42 men, ages 60 to 90, and the results have been nothing short of dramatic. Some signs of old age—the shrinking of certain organs, such as the spleen and liver, and the increase of fatty tissue in the body—were reversed by the hormones. After a few months of therapy, Rudman said, 70-year-old men looked as though they were 55.

But a growth hormone is not a cure-all. Given in doses that are too large, it can cause carpal tunnel syndrome, a repetitive stress disorder that commonly affects the wrists of computer users, breast enlargement and a rise in blood sugar. Moreover, it failed to curb other factors associated with aging, such as memory loss and softening of bones. "This,"

Rudman said, "is by no means a total reversal of the aging process."

Another promising hormone is DHEA, a steroid whose natural secretions decline with age. At the University of Utah, immunologist Daynes has discovered that when laboratory mice are given small amounts of DHEA-Sulfate—a water-soluble form of the hormone that had been thought to be irrelevant to the functioning of the body—their immune systems work better and their skin looks more youthful.

Over the long term, Daynes hopes that the hormone might be used as a sort of vitamin for the elderly. "I believe that over the next few years, we are going to prove beyond a shadow of a doubt that some of the physiological changes which are used to define old age are totally preventable," he said. "They don't have to happen."

In the Arizona desert, meanwhile, UCLA Prof. Roy Walford is trying to delay the onset of old age through his diet.

W alford and seven other scientists who are living in a glass-enclosed three-acre greenhouse known as Biosphere II are engaged in the first human version of a well-known study in which Walford found that a severely restricted, low-calorie diet could double the life expectancy of rats and mice.

Now, Walford and the other biospherians are subsisting on 1,800 calories per day, compared to the usual 2,500. According to Walford, the group eats only what is grown in the dome—grains, vegetables, fruit and one serving of meat per week.

According to the 68-year-old Walford, who has been following the diet for more than five years, the group is exhibiting the same changes as the rodents. Each has dropped an average of 14% in body weight since the experiment began 13 months ago. Their cholesterol is lower—an average of 130, down from 200—and their blood sugar has declined.

"This is the first well-monitored human application of the idea," Walford said, "and it indicates that humans respond the same as animals."

But be it gene manipulation, hormones, drugs or nutrition, researchers agree that if their work proves anything, it is that there is no Fountain of Youth, no single elixir that has the power to stop or even slow the aging process.

Instead, they say, advances that come in disparate arenas will over time be put together to create a greater understanding of the aging process. And only when the age-old mystery of aging is unraveled will scientists figure out ways to stop it, or slow it down.

"There is no silver bullet," said Edward Schneider, dean of USC's Andrus Center of Gerontology. Instead, Schneider likens the state of aging research to the decades-old search for a cure for cancer.

"Picture cancer research 30 years ago," he said. "People thought it's simple, we'll give one drug and it will cure all cancer. Well, it didn't work. In the next 10 or 20 years we'll have specific therapies for specific cancers, because cancer is a complex process.

"Imagine cancer being a 1,000-piece puzzle and we have a third of the pieces. Aging is a 100,000-piece puzzle, and we maybe have a tenth of the pieces."

Credits/ Acknowledgments

Cover design by Charles Vitelli

1. Genetic and Prenatal Influences on Development
Facing overview—Who photo. 41—Photo by Bob Sacha. 44—Photo by E. Fuller Torrey, National Institute of Mental Health. 45—Photo by Nick Kelsh. 46—Photo by The American Philosophical Society.

2. Development During Infancy and Early Childhood
Facing overview—United Nations photo by John Isaac.

3. Development During Childhood
Facing overview—EPA Documerica.

4. Family, School and Cultural Influences on Development
Facing overview—United Nations photo by John Isaac. 148—Photo by Subjects & Predicates. 182—Illustration by Andrea Eberbach. 190—Photo by Harold W. Stevenson. 190-194—Charts by Laurie Grace.

5. Development During Adolescence and Early Adulthood
Facing overview—United Nations photo. 220—United Nations photo by L. Barnes.

6. Development During Middle and Late Adulthood and Aging
Facing overview—Colonial Penn Group, Inc.

ANNUAL EDITIONS ARTICLE REVIEW FORM

■ NAME: _____ DATE: _____

■ TITLE AND NUMBER OF ARTICLE: _____

■ BRIEFLY STATE THE MAIN IDEA OF THIS ARTICLE: _____

_____

_____

_____

_____

■ LIST THREE IMPORTANT FACTS THAT THE AUTHOR USES TO SUPPORT THE MAIN IDEA:

_____

_____

_____

_____

_____

_____

■ WHAT INFORMATION OR IDEAS DISCUSSED IN THIS ARTICLE ARE ALSO DISCUSSED IN YOUR
TEXTBOOK OR OTHER READING YOU HAVE DONE? LIST THE TEXTBOOK CHAPTERS AND PAGE
NUMBERS:

_____

_____

_____

_____

_____

_____

■ LIST ANY EXAMPLES OF BIAS OR FAULTY REASONING THAT YOU FOUND IN THE ARTICLE:

_____

_____

_____

_____

_____

■ LIST ANY NEW TERMS/CONCEPTS THAT WERE DISCUSSED IN THE ARTICLE AND WRITE A
SHORT DEFINITION:

_____

_____

_____

_____

_____

*Your instructor may require you to use this Annual Editions Article Review Form in any number of ways:
for articles that are assigned, for extra credit, as a tool to assist in developing assigned papers, or simply
for your own reference. Even if it is not required, we encourage you to photocopy and use this page;
you'll find that reflecting on the articles will greatly enhance the information from your text.

ANNUAL EDITIONS:
HUMAN DEVELOPMENT 94/95
Article Rating Form

Here is an opportunity for you to have direct input into the next revision of this volume. We would like you to rate each of the 57 articles listed below, using the following scale:

1. **Excellent: should definitely be retained**
2. **Above average: should probably be retained**
3. **Below average: should probably be deleted**
4. **Poor: should definitely be deleted**

Your ratings will play a vital part in the next revision. So please mail this prepaid form to us just as soon as you complete it.
Thanks for your help!

We Want Your Advice

Annual Editions revisions depend on two major opinion sources: one is our Advisory Board, listed in the front of this volume, which works with us in scanning the thousands of articles published in the public press each year; the other is you—the person actually using the book. Please help us and the users of the next edition by completing the prepaid article rating form on this page and returning it to us. Thank you.

Rating	Article	Rating	Article
	1. The Gene Dream		28. Of a Different Mind
	2. A New Genetic Code		29. Putting Children First
	3. Clone Hype		30. Same Family, Different Lives
	4. Reproductive Revolution Is Jolting Old Views		31. Can Your Career Hurt Your Kids?
	5. The Human Mind: Touching the Intangible		32. Bringing Up Father
	6. Choosing a Perfect Child		33. The Lasting Effects of Child Maltreatment
	7. What Crack Does to Babies		34. Helping Children Cope with Violence
	8. Sperm Under Siege		35. Children of Violence
	9. War Babies		36. Children after Divorce
	10. Nature or Nurture? Old Chestnut, New Thoughts		37. Why Kids Have a Lot to Cry About
	11. Eugenics Revisited		38. Alienation and the Four Worlds of Childhood
	12. A New Perspective on Cognitive Development in Infancy		39. Culture, Race Too Often Ignored in Child Studies
	13. The Amazing Minds of Infants		40. Tracked to Fail
	14. A Child's Theory of Mind		41. Creating Creative Minds
	15. "I Forget"		42. Learning from Asian Schools
	16. Sizing Up the Sexes		43. The Thunder Years
	17. The Day Care Generation		44. A Much Riskier Passage
	18. The Good, the Bad, and the Difference		45. The Gender Machine
	19. TV Violence—What Influence on Young Minds?		46. Teenagers and AIDS
	20. A Push for PG-Rated Playthings		47. Reaching the Child within Us
	21. Your Loving Touch		48. Proceeding with Caution
	22. Places Everyone		49. Is There Love after Baby?
	23. The Miracle of Resiliency		50. The New Middle Age
	24. Toddler Talk		51. Midlife Myths
	25. Young Children's Moral Understanding: Learning About Right and Wrong		52. The Myth of the Miserable Working Woman
	26. Understanding Bilingual/Bicultural Young Children		53. On Growing Old
	27. Clipped Wings		54. The Prime of Our Lives
			55. How Old Is Old?
			56. The Return of Wonder in Old Age
			57. Unlocking the Secrets of Aging

(Continued on next page)

ABOUT YOU

Name_____ Date_____
Are you a teacher? ☐ Or student? ☐
Your School Name _____
Department _____
Address _____
City _____ State _____ Zip _____
School Telephone # _____

YOUR COMMENTS ARE IMPORTANT TO US!

Please fill in the following information:

For which course did you use this book? _____
Did you use a text with this Annual Edition? ☐ yes ☐ no
The title of the text? _____
What are your general reactions to the Annual Editions concept?

Have you read any particular articles recently that you think should be included in the next edition?

Are there any articles you feel should be replaced in the next edition? Why?

Are there other areas that you feel would utilize an Annual Edition?

May we contact you for editorial input?

May we quote you from above?

ANNUAL EDITIONS: HUMAN DEVELOPMENT 94/95